D0301636

Role Theory:

Concepts and Research

Role Theory:
Concepts and Research

Edited by

Bruce J. Biddle

Departments of Psychology
and Sociology, The University of Missouri

and

Edwin J. Thomas

School of Social Work and
Department of Psychology
The University of Michigan

JOHN WILEY & SONS, INC. New York London Sydney

Library of Congress Catalog Card Number: 66-11520
Printed in the United States of America

Foreword

Some years ago I prepared a short paper for a conference on role theory at the University of Missouri, in which the editors of this volume also participated. Entitled "Concept in search of variables," it began by noting that some concepts are useful because they mark off a rough area of discourse; their use carries the message: "I want you to know that I am thinking of this sector of the universe rather than other sectors." They are connotative and inclusive. Others are denotative, being distinguished from neighboring concepts in terms of specified attributes. There is room for both in any discipline, but many of us, I ventured to suspect, have admitted the connotative *role* into our theoretical domiciles only to entertain it as a denotative member of the conceptual family. We have, moreover, assigned to it so many kinds of work that it cannot become expert at any of them. I went on to confess that for at least two decades I had continued to consider the role concept "a promising one" for empirically oriented social scientists. And, finally, I warned that any concept that failed to attract unto itself a set of properties and variables that were both distinctive and operationable could not long maintain its appeal.

I had the wit not to publish the paper. This was not necessarily because its complaints were unjustified; a perusal of the literature on the common theme up to very recent years should document my complaint rather well. Rather, I came to the conclusion that what was needed was not a dirge but a prescription for the patient's recovery, and I was far from satisfied with my own rather lame efforts in that direction.

Readers of the chapters that follow—especially the first four of them—will agree, I believe, that my Jeremiads were not needed. While most of the work that I had called for still remains to be done, a groundwork for it has now been laid down by Professors Biddle and Thomas. We have in Chapter 2 a comprehensive analysis of "partitioning concepts," clearly distinguished as applicable to persons, to behavior, and to persons-and-their-behaviors, together with analyses of relationships and combinations among them. We have in Chapters 3 and 4 a sophisticated attack upon problems of role properties and role variables, respectively. I could not have asked for more, or better, at this level.

The editor-authors have—wisely, in my judgment—meticulously adhered to a policy of stating definitions in classificatory rather than in descriptive terms. One consequence of this policy is that matters of "content" that many readers are accustomed to look for in definitions are to be found, distributed rather than concentrated, under the headings of the several properties and variables. The occasional result, it seems to me, is a lack of emphasis on certain properties that are probably more pervasive than others. For example, I would have liked more stress upon a pervasively important feature of social positions, namely, the influence brought to bear upon their occupants, by reason of collective recognition (perhaps on the part of no more than two interacting persons). A position is, among other ways of looking at it, a locus of influence, the nature of which varies with the nature of the position. The latter can, as the editor-authors demonstrate, be described in terms of position variables, and thus it can be assigned a location in some sort of multi-dimensional space, preferably relative to that of other positions in the same space. Such an approach forces one to search for spacial dimensions, with the ensuing possibility that different positions can be assigned different loci in terms of specified dimensions, rather than merely in phenotypic categories (cf. Newcomb, Turner, and Converse, 1965, Chapter 11).*

Of definitions of role, as the following chapters amply reveal, there seems to be no end. Thomas and Biddle have, I think, found the best possible way out of this maze in suggesting (p. 29) that the term "by itself" be used only to denote the generic idea, i.e., "the entire person-behavior matrix," more specific terms being used for specified segments of the matrix. For better or for worse, the day has passed when the single term, by itself, dependably conveys to the reader exactly and only what its user had intended. If I may

* T. M. Newcomb, R. H. Turner, and P. E. Converse, *Social psychology: the study of human interaction*. New York: Holt, Rinehart and Winston, 1965.

cite an instructive parallel, the term *behavior*, which for most psychologists is one of daily usage, is now hardly more than a primitive. As English and English put it in their dictionary* (p. 61), "Since, for most psychologists, behavior is the central concept for their science, its limitation is important; it is also difficult." They then devote one-half column to the difficulties, followed by nearly five columns of more specific, compound phrases that include the troublesome term. For social psychologists and sociologists, *role* is beset by analogous problems, and Thomas and Biddle's first four chapters have gone far toward resolving them.

If I may intrude a predilection of my own, I see the central problem, toward the solution of which a family of role concepts is needed, as that of *regularities in interpersonal relationships*—including both overt behavior and psychological states (relationships of persons' attitudes and expectations, for example). From this point of view the concept of role relationship, between two or more persons characterized by some regularity of interaction, is primary to concepts referring to the contribution of any one of them to that relationship (such a contribution being the equivalent, by some definitions—Linton's, for example—of a single role). I find some support for this position in the fact that Thomas and Biddle have taken pains (Chapter 2, pp. 32–41) to list several criteria for "relationship concepts," but to me the phenomena of relationship are more than one among many families of concept; they provide the distinctive, integrative concept.

Of empirical studies of role phenomena, the following pages show that we have at least a strong beginning; nearly half of the selections included in Parts III through X are devoted, in part at least, to reports of research pointed at role-related questions. These twenty-odd papers, along with as many others that wrestle mainly with theoretical and analytic problems, in my judgment represent the very best of their respective genres, as of now. When—perhaps within the next decade—a successor to the present volume has been issued, we may expect that a significant increase in sophisticated research, dealing with specifically role-relevant concepts and variables, will have emerged. If so, the present work will have contributed to that end.

Meanwhile, I find a distinct satisfaction in not having published a lugubrious paper that, as the following chapters show, was quite unnecessary.

THEODORE M. NEWCOMB

* H. B. English and Ava C. English, *A comprehensive dictionary of psychological and psychoanalytic terms.* New York: Longmans, Green, 1958.

Preface

In the field of role there are a recognizable community of thought, a voluminous and growing literature, a vigorous research endeavor, and an application of the knowledge in practical affairs. These developments indicate that the study of role may well be on the threshold of becoming an area of specialized inquiry in the behavioral sciences. But the methods, knowledge, and theory in role have not yet evolved into an articulate, defined, and well-integrated discipline of study. Despite the existence of a rich and wide-ranging literature, the field has no text, no collection of readings, and no comprehensive statement of its concepts, theory, and knowledge. One of the principal tasks facing the role field is that of achieving some coalescence of its efforts so as to crystallize its identity as a prospective specialization in the behavioral sciences. This book was prepared to help the field move toward this objective.

We could have approached this task in many ways. A text or a systematic review of the research and theory might have been written. Such an effort would probably have been premature. Or a collection of readings might have been edited to illustrate the range of present-day research and theory. This, in contrast, would have been insufficient. We decided, instead, that a realistic objective would be to prepare a book that would provide readers with at least some of the integration of a text combined with the scope and depth of a compilation of readings. Thus, in the essays prepared for this book, an effort was made to articulate the domain of role theory through an analysis of the component activities of the field, their history, and current status; and to present the basic role concepts, along with some features of their underlying structure. In the readings, we sought to bring together theory and research on central but limited topics in the field of role.

These commitments and the inevitable limitations of space meant that certain types of selection could not be included. We had to forego the reprinting of significant writings on role playing and those on techniques and practical applications in general. Many excellent writings on role in various institutional contexts could not be included and still achieve adequate coverage of the more general contributions. We excluded all papers that attempted to review the concepts of the field or to define the field itself because these papers, however excellent otherwise, were not sufficiently comprehensive. The writings of significant figures in the history of role theory had to be omitted as well. Although some scholars of role may miss these early seminal writings, they may be consoled by the fact that, with few exceptions, recent research and theory have made these writings less timely and informing.

The first four chapters of the book are essays that serve as text. The first chapter of Part I, in presenting the nature and history of role theory, is an introduction to this field of study. The next three chapters of Part II are devoted to a presentation of the conceptual structure of role theory, with each of the chapters covering a class of basic concepts. Chapter II is devoted to concepts for classifying the phenomena of role. Chapter III deals with concepts for the properties of role phenomena, and Chapter IV with concepts for the variables of role phenomena.

The selections of the book are organized into eight parts, each part being preceded by a brief introduction. We have attempted to arrange parts so that the topics covered progress from the simpler to the more complex and from the more fundamental to the more specialized. Thus Parts III through VI deal with positions, prescriptions, descriptions, and performance and interdependence, respectively; whereas the remaining parts cover differentiation, specialization, and division of labor (Part VII), consensus and conflict (Part VIII), sanctioning and conformity (Part IX), and learning and socialization (Part X). A bibliography and name and subject indexes are included as well.

This book was written for a wide audience, and it may be used for diverse purposes. Instructors of the numerous courses that include social role and role theory may employ the book as the main text, as a supplementary text, or as a reference for outside reading. Outside the classroom, scholars, researchers, and students may find the book a useful and readily accessible reference for theory, research, and bibliography on the many subjects of role theory. And practitioners and men of affairs in general may find the research and theory covered in the book to be helpful in understanding role problems and to be a guide to action concerning the amelioration of these problems.

Speaking more personally, the publication of this book represents a fulfillment of long-standing professional interests of the editors. For many years now both of us have worked on selected theoretical and empirical problems in role theory, and we have sorely missed a book such as this. The preparation of the four chapters authored by us afforded an opportunity to combine our theoretical interests and to achieve better understanding of the nature of the field and of its conceptual structure. The editing of the selections gave us a chance to make visible and put together, in a single source, some of the worthwhile writings on role that were buried in so many different journals and books.

In many ways this book is a "spin-off" product from research on specific problems of role engaged in by both of us. Supporters of the research from which this book derived in part are thus due much credit. Specifically, Biddle has had research supported at the University of Missouri by the Office of Naval Research (Group Psychology Branch) and by the Office of Education, Department of Health, Education, and Welfare; and Thomas has had support from funds of The Russell Sage Foundation, granted to him through the University of Michigan.

Specific thanks are owed to a number of persons. To George Barker, William S. Bennett, Jr., Nancy Barron, Howard R. Delaney, Sandie Eveloff, Graeme Fraser, Paul F. Green, Daniel Hays, Gerald Jellison, Roger Miller, Sue Titus, Edward Tomich, Jean Hoffman Tomich, J. Paschal Twyman, and Diana Warshay go thanks for help with preparation of the bibliography. Rosemary Cogan, Audrey Corcoran, Judith Brown, and Beverly Ingraham have had primary responsibility for preparation of the manuscript at the University of Missouri; and Neva Mastin and Marian Iglesias provided valuable secretarial assistance at the University of Michigan. We owe special gratitude to Luigi Petrullo for his encouragement and support; and to Ted Newcomb for inspiring our initial appreciation of the importance of role theory when we were his students at the University of Michigan. Sincere thanks are due to many colleagues, both at Michigan, Missouri, and elsewhere, who have graciously read and commented on portions of drafts of the original essays; our debts to Raymond Adams, Michael Banton, David Birch, Harumi Befu, Clinton Fink, Robert W. Habenstein, Merrill Jackson, Fred Katz, George Levinger, Henry Meyer, Paul C. Rosenblatt, Jack Rothman, Richard Videbeck, and H. Clyde Wilson are deeply felt.

We owe special gratitude to the authors and publishers of the selections reprinted here, the specific permissions for which are acknowledged in the places where the selections appear in the book. The following credits are also acknowledged: to The University of Chicago Press, for permission to quote excerpts from pages 154–156 of *Mind, Self and Society*, by G. H. Mead (R. T. Morris, Ed.), The University of Chicago Press, Chicago, 1934; to The Macmillan Company, New York, for permission to quote from pages 80 and 81 by J. L. Moreno of *The Sociometry Reader*, J. L. Moreno et al. (Editors), published by The Free Press, 1960, and for permission to quote excerpts from pages 70–71 from *The Theory of Social Structure*, by S. F. Nadel, The Free Press, 1957; to Appleton-Century-Crofts for permission to quote excerpts from pages 113–115 of *The Study of Man*, by R. Linton, Appleton-Century Company, New York, 1936; to Presses Universitaires de France for permission to reproduce portions of the table on pages 38 and 39 of *La Notion de Role en Psychologie Sociale*, by Anne-Marie Rocheblave-Spenlé, Presses Universitaires de France, Paris, 1962; to Doubleday and Company, for permission to quote from page xi of *The Presentation of Self in Everyday Life*, by Erving Goffman, Doubleday and Company, Garden City, N.Y., 1959; to Scientific American for permission to use Figure 1, page 256, which originally appeared in R. F. Bales, "How People Interact in Conferences," *Scientific American*, **192**, March 1955; and to The University of Chicago Press for permission to use Figure 3, page 261, which originally appeared in L. D. White (Ed.), *The State of the Social Sciences*, The University of Chicago Press, Chicago, 1956.

B.J.B.
E.J.T.

December, 1965

Contents

part I Background and Present Status

WHAT IS ROLE THEORY, what are its historical beginnings, and what is it attempting to do? These are among the first questions likely to be asked about role theory. Information pertinent to these questions, surprisingly, is difficult to cull from the literature, and the few statements to be found on these topics tend to be fragmentary and incomplete. The fact is that the domain called "role theory" has not been distinguished. Few persons have traced its historical roots and its current status has been inadequately analyzed and described. These are the problems addressed in Chapter I.

chapter I The Nature and History of Role Theory

EDWIN J. THOMAS AND BRUCE J. BIDDLE

"All the world's a stage,
And all the men and women merely players:
They have their exits and their entrances;
And one man in his time plays many parts,
His acts being seven ages. At first the infant,
Mewling and puking in the nurse's arms.
And then . . ." (W. Shakespeare, *As You Like It*, Act II, Scene 7)

INTRODUCTION

It is perhaps difficult to believe that these oft-quoted lines of Shakespeare would have any bearing whatever on the modern field of behavioral science called "role theory." Aside from the poetry, however, there are noteworthy parallels between Shakespeare's characterization of men and role theory. Both express a particular perspective of human behavior, which for Shakespeare was that social life was similar to acting on the stage of a theater, with all its scenes, masks, and airs, and both employ a special language, the terms of which for Shakespeare were those of drama and the theater.

But even though role theory owes much to the theater, its perspective and language allow for more than a metaphorical characterization of human behavior. Furthermore, the field of role consists of a body of knowledge, theory, characteristic research endeavor, and a domain of study, in addition to a particular perspective and language. In these respects role theory is not unlike its sister specializations in behavioral science, and like any scientific endeavor role theory aspires to understand, predict and control the particular phenomena included in its domain of study.

Role theory is a new field of inquiry and this fact perhaps more than any other accounts for the differences between it and the more mature scientific fields. Role theory is not presently a universally recognized specialization, even in the behavioral sciences closest to it.[1] Indeed, with the exception of fragmented commentary, the scholars of role have not identified, articulated, and analyzed the component aspects of role theory; namely, its domain of study, perspective, language, body of knowledge, theory, and method of inquiry.

The objective of this first chapter is to indicate the nature of these components of role theory, and to provide an historical perspective and current picture of the field. Basic concepts will be referred to only briefly because the objectives of the chapters following this one are to identify and analyze them in detail.

DOMAIN OF STUDY

The role analyst is concerned with describing and understanding many of the same complex aspects of human behavior about which dramatists, novelists, journalists, and historians write. A woman's behavior as wife and mother, a child's behavior as pupil and son, or a man's behavior as employee and husband generally fall within the role analyst's domain of interest, but such minute behaviors as the knee-jerk, the stomach contraction, or the memory of a nonsense syllable generally do not interest him. Sometimes the role analyst focuses on the behavior of a given individual, sometimes on a specific aggregate of individuals, and sometimes he studies particular groupings of individuals who display given behaviors. Many facets of real-life behavior may be studied: the individual's appraisal of himself or others, the adequacy of the person's performance or how his performance affects others, how people learn to perform, how performances of some groups are related to those of other groups, and much more. Role analysts examine patterned forms of such complex real-life behavior, which includes the types and varieties of differentiated aggregates, social positions, specializations, and divisions of labor. And communication, learning and socialization, sanctioning and conformity, and interdependence are among the processes examined for individuals and aggregates. There are numerous particular classes of behavioral and personal phenomena of concern in role theory, the elaboration of which we defer to Chapters II, III, and IV.

[1] A category of role analysis appeared for the first time as a specialization in the 1964 periodic inventory of scientific manpower conducted by the National Science Foundation.

THE ROLE PERSPECTIVE

The Viewpoint

The role perspective consists of a particular viewpoint regarding those factors presumed to be influential in governing human behavior, and it may best be introduced by resorting again to a theatrical analogy.

When actors portray a character in a play, their performance is determined by the script, the director's instructions, the performances of fellow actors, and reactions of the audience as well as by the acting talents of the players. Apart from differences between actors in the interpretation of their parts, the performance of each actor is programmed by all of these external factors; consequently, there are significant similarities in the performances of actors taking the same part, no matter who the actors are.

Now let us take this analogy into real life, using some of the terms of role theory. Individuals in society occupy positions, and their role performance in these positions is determined by social norms, demands, and rules; by the role performances of others in their respective positions; by those who observe and react to the performance; and by the individual's particular capabilities and personality. The social "script" may be as constraining as that of a play, but it frequently allows more options; the "director" is often present in real life as a supervisor, parent, teacher, or coach; the "audience" in life consists of all those who observe the position member's behavior; the position member's "performance" in life, as in the play, is attributable to his familiarity with the "part," his personality and personal history in general, and more significantly, to the "script" which others define in so many ways. In essence, the role perspective assumes, as does the theater, that performance results from the social prescriptions and behavior of others, and that individual variations in performance, to the extent that they do occur, are expressed within the framework created by these factors.

This emphasis on the controlling power of one's immediate social environment—past and present—reflects a doctrine of limited social determinism. The behavior of the individual is examined in terms of how it is shaped by the demands and rules of others, by their sanctions for his conforming and nonconforming behavior, and by the individual's own understanding and conceptions of what his behavior should be. Determining factors such as these are studied in the contexts of families, informal and work groups, therapy groups, school groups, organizations, communities, and societies. Natural developmental phases of these behaviors are charted from infancy to old age; the fit between individual and social mold is studied; and personal factors which influence the individual's behavior in the face of these determining factors are also examined. This perspective does not deny the facts of individual differences, but it does highlight the social determinants that may have entered into creating such differences, and it does focus the role analyst's attention upon the conditions under which the social determinants will be more rather than less influential.

Contributors to the Perspective

Although many seminal thinkers in Western thought have expressed views of human behavior which were consistent with, or fostered, what we have called the "role perspective," there was a group of influential social philosophers and early behavioral scientists whose ideas could be traced to the present. We have called these writers the "precursors" of role theory because their contribution was mainly to the role perspective at a time just prior to the emergence, during the 1930's and later, of a discriminable role language and of specialized inquiry into problems of role.

Table 1 presents a decade-by-decade listing of these precursors and the dates when their major books or articles appeared. As the table indicates, some precursors were European, some American; some were philosophers, psychologists, sociologists, and anthropologists. The reader will recognize many of these precursors as being among the important early writers in the disciplines of behavioral science. Indeed, some of the differences between contemporary psychological, sociological, and anthropological approaches to role theory in Europe and the United States may be traced to these early writers.

Although the precursors mainly contributed a perspective to role theory, as was observed, virtually all also had substantive interests that would fall into the domain of role theory. Thus Durkheim (1893)[2] wrote a classic work on the division of labor; Sumner (1906) proposed the well-known distinction between folkways and mores and offered a taxonomy of prescriptive phenomena that has not been greatly improved upon to this day; James (1890), Baldwin (1897),

[2] References cited in this chapter may be found in the role bibliography at the end of the volume.

TABLE 1 MAJOR PRECURSORS OF ROLE THEORY

Period	Origins and Disciplinary Tradition			
	American Psychologists and Social Philosophers	American Sociologists and Anthropologists	European Psychologists	European Sociologists, Anthropologists, and Social Philosophers
Prior to 1900	James (1890) Hall (1891, 1898) Baldwin (1891, 1897, 1899) Dewey (1899) Royce (1900)		Binet (1900)	Maine (1861) Bergson (1889, 1900) Durkheim (1893, 1894, 1897)
1901–1910		Cooley (1902, 1909) Sumner (1906) Ross (1908)		
1911–1920		Thomas and Znaniecki (1918)	Blondel (1914)	Scheler (1913, 1915) Moreno (1919) Simmel (1920)
1921–1930	Dewey (1922)	Park and Burgess (1924) Morgan (1929)	Guillaume (1925) Blondel (1927) Janet (1928, 1929)	Müller-Freienfels (1923, 1925) Moreno (1923) Von Wiese (1924) Scheler (1926) Löwith (1928)
1931–1940		Mayo (1933) Roethlisberger and Dickson (1939) Park (1939)	Janet (1932, 1936, 1937) Piaget (1932) Blondel (1932)	Müller-Freienfels (1933) Eggert (1937)

Note: Adopted, with revision, from Rocheblave-Spenlé, 1962b.

and Cooley (1902) made important contributions to the theory of the self; and Piaget (1932) did an early study of rules and of rule-complying behavior. And many of these precursors, especially those just named, employed concepts which survive today or which have their modern counterparts in present-day role theory. We shall discuss these in more detail shortly.

There is no evidence in the current writings on role to indicate that the role perspective today is basically different from the viewpoint that we have attributed to the precursors. But present role analysts in sociology and anthropology are often likely to emphasize the social determinants of behavior more strongly than their counterparts in social psychology and psychology.

THE LANGUAGE OF ROLE

The language of role theory, like all vocabularies, consists of concepts and their designating terms. The concepts make it possible properly to identify and analyze the objects of study, and the terms for these concepts make communication possible. The idea of role is only one of the concepts of role theory, but because it is central in the language, we will discuss it here in more detail than related ideas.

Evolution of "Role" as Term and Concept

An examination of the writings of the precursors of role theory and others of that era reveals that they employed concepts similar to modern conceptions of role. James, Baldwin, and Cooley wrote about the self; Dewey analyzed habit and conduct; Sumner developed conceptions of mores and folkways; Maine introduced the idea of status; Simmel discussed interaction; and Durkheim and Ross wrote about social forces. The concepts of person, social type, personality, and function were also among those in the thoughtways of that time. It would be an easy but unnecessary exercise to identify modern counterparts for these ideas in role theory.

There is every evidence, however, that during these same decades the term "role" was part of the common languages in which these authors wrote. The term has an interesting history of usages, which Moreno has summarized.

> "Role" originally a French word which penetrated into English is derived from the Latin *rotula* (the little wheel, or round log, the diminutive of rota-wheel). In antiquity it was used, originally, only to designate a round (wooden) roll on which sheets of parchment were fastened so as to smoothly roll ("wheel") them around it since otherwise the sheets would break or crumble. From this came the word for an assemblage of such leaves into a scroll or book-like composite. This was used, subsequently, to mean any official volume of papers pertaining to law courts, as in France, or to government, as for instance in England: rolls of Parliament—the minutes or proceedings. Whereas in Greece and also in ancient Rome the parts in the theater were written on the abovementioned "rolls" and read by the prompters to the actors (who tried to memorize their part), this fixation of the word appears to have been lost in the more illiterate periods of the early and middle centuries of the Dark Ages, for their public presentation of church plays by laymen. Only towards the sixteenth and seventeenth centuries, with the emergence of the modern stage, the parts of the theatrical characters are read from "roles," paper fascicles. Whence each scenic "part" becomes a role. (Moreno, 1960, p. 80.)

Because the word "role" was a part of English and various European languages for many years, the question arises as to when it was used to refer to a technical concept. Although we know that Simmel (1920) made reference to "Spielen einer Rolle" in one paper and that Park and Burgess (1921) used the title "The Self as the Individual's Conception of His Role" to introduce a paper by Binet they reproduced in their influential *Introduction to the Science of Sociology*, the term "role" was not commonly employed by the precursors of role theory to designate a technical concept.[3] To our knowledge it was not until the decade of the 1930's in this country that the term was employed technically in writings on role problems. Mead, Moreno, and Linton are three significant theorists whose writings deserve comment in this context.

George Herbert Mead's most influential work, *Mind, Self and Society*, was published posthumously in 1934 and was based upon his unpublished writings and the class notes of his students. Two of Mead's preoccupations were directly relevant to role theory. In the words of Anselm Strauss, these were a concern with "the rise and function of socially reflexive behavior," and with "the problem of maintaining order in a continuously changing social organization—that is, the problem of intelligent social control" (1956, p. ix). While examining problems of interaction, the self, and socialization, Mead employed the concept of "role taking," along with such related ideas as the "generalized other," the "self," the "I" and "me," and "audience." Mead's influence on his associates and students was great during the years 1911 through 1925 at the University of Chicago, and from this influence grew the school of symbolic interactionism in sociology. A not insignificant portion of current research on problems of role is being carried out in the tradition established by Mead.

During much the same period that Mead was inspiring students at the University of Chicago, Jacob Moreno was experimenting with groups of role players in the theater of spontaneity in Vienna (see the review by Nehnevajsa, 1960). Although Moreno had published earlier in German, his work did not become well known in this country until after his arrival here in the 1930's and the publication in 1934 of his classic work *Who Shall Survive?* Moreno pioneered in the use of role playing in psychodrama and sociodrama and was the creative inspiration for the cluster of specializations we now associate with sociometry. Moreno founded the *Sociometric Review* in 1936, followed by *Sociometry* in 1937, and he was a prolific writer and a persuasive spokesman, as were many of his students—some of whom are prominent behavioral scientists of this era.

Although the terms "role" and "role playing" appeared in the 1934 edition of Moreno's *Who Shall Survive?* we find these concepts articulated better in some of his later writings. With regard to the concept of role itself, Moreno distinguished three categories: "(a) psychosomatic roles, as the sleeper, the eater, the walker; (b) psychodramatic roles as *a* mother, *a* teacher, *a* Negro, *a* Christian, etc.; and (c) social roles, *the* mother, *the* son, *the* daughter, *the* teacher, *the* Negro, *the* Christian, etc. The genesis of roles goes through two stages, role-perception and role enactment." (Moreno, 1960, p. 81, reprinted from *Who Shall Survive?* 2nd ed., 1953.)

[3] The word "role" did not appear in the index of the volume by Park and Burgess, and it was not referred to in Binet's paper.

Moreno made important contributions to the understanding of behavior, but he is best known perhaps for his innovations in the technology of change. Moreno's interest in changing behavior is represented well in his conception of role playing. In his terms: "*Role-playing may be considered as an experimental procedure, a method of learning to perform roles more adequately*" (Moreno, 1960, p. 84). Moreno apposed this notion to Mead's idea of taking the role of the other: "*In contrast with role-playing, role-taking is an attitude already frozen in the behavior of the person.* Role-playing is an act, a spontaneous playing; role-taking is a finished product, a role conserve" (Moreno, 1960, p. 84).

In 1936 the eminent anthropologist Ralph Linton proposed a classic distinction between status (position) and role.

> A status, as distinct from the individual who may occupy it, is simply a collection of rights and duties.... A *role* represents the dynamic aspect of a status. The individual is socially assigned to a status and occupies it with relation to other statuses. When he puts the rights and duties which constitute the status into effect, he is performing a role. Role and status are quite inseparable, and the distinction between them is of only academic interest. There are no roles without statuses or statuses without roles. Just as in the case of *status*, the term *role* is used with a double significance. Every individual has a series of roles deriving from the various patterns in which he participates and at the same time *a role*, general, which represents the sum total of these roles and determines what he does for his society and what he can expect from it. (Linton, 1936, pp. 113–114.)

Linton's ideas were also influential: his insistence upon a close relationship between role and position has been followed by most modern writers on role; the implication that positions and the attending roles were elements of societies suggested new possibilities for analyzing social structure; and the idea that an individual's behavior could be construed as role performance implied that role was one linkage between individual behavior and social structure.

The writings and teachings of Mead, Moreno, and Linton did much to establish role—both as term and concept—and related ideas, too, in the thoughtways of social science during and after the 1930's. These writers were shortly joined by others in articulating the vocabulary of the role language (we are thinking here of such persons as Cottrell, 1933; Sherif, 1936; Hughes, 1937, 1938; Parsons, 1937, 1942, 1945; Newcomb, 1942; Sarbin, 1943). Thus, the 1930's marks the beginning of contemporary role study inasmuch as it was during these years that a technical role language was first apparent and that systematic study of role phenomena was begun. It is not difficult to understand these developments when one recalls that the prior period of precursors was characterized by a community of thought which included what we have called a "role perspective" as well as many concepts closely related to the idea of role, and that "role" was already a popular word in the common languages of these writers.

It was not until after World War II, however, that extensive use of role-related terms appeared in the titles of empirical studies. Evidence for this may be found by examining the major index categories of *Psychological Abstracts.* Although this journal first appeared in 1927, it was not until 1944 that "role playing" appeared as a major index category; "role" itself did not appear as such a category until 1945, and "sex role" not until 1959.

One of the significant features of the contemporary study of role is the progressive elaboration and refinement of its language. There are many among the modern writers on role who have made contributions to the role language. (A list of selected modern contributors is given in Table 2, with contributors assembled by period of publication.) The reader is referred particularly to such contributors listed in Table 2 as Lindesmith and Strauss (1949), Davis (1949), Merton (1949, 1957), Newcomb (1950), Parsons (1951), Parsons and Shils (1951), Toby (1952), Argyle (1952), Rommetveit (1954), Lang (1956), Turner (1956), F. L. Bates (1956, 1957), Morris (1956), Spiegel (1957), Levinson (1959), Pellegrin and F. L. Bates (1959), and Gouldner (1960). These writers and others have used role as an adjective to modify such concepts as performance, enactment, conception, behavior, discontinuity, relationship, set, network, conflict, strain, conflict resolution, distance, reciprocity, complementarity, and many more. And whereas at one time there was little more than the single notion of position, writers now refer to position sets, position systems, relational positions, focal and counter positions, intraposition and interposition role conflict, and many others.

Since the introduction of role into behavorial science, there has been a diffusion of role concepts. Many texts today in social psychology, socioloyg, and anthropology employ a role

TABLE 2 SELECTED, CONTEMPORARY CONTRIBUTORS TO ROLE THEORY, BY PERIOD OF PUBLISHED WORKS

Period of Publication of Contribution	Authors of Contributions	
1931–1935	F. H. Allport (1934) Cottrell (1933)	Lumpkin (1933) Mead (1934) Moreno (1934)
1936–1940	Benedict (1938) Hughes (1937, 1938) Linton (1936)	Parsons (1937) Sherif (1936) Sullivan (1939, 1940)
1941–1945	Benoit-Smullyan (1944) Cottrell (1942a) Hughes (1945) Jennings (1943)	Linton (1945) Newcomb (1942) Parsons (1942, 1945) Sarbin (1943)
1946–1950	Benne and Sheats (1948) Cameron (1947) Davis (1949) Festinger, Schachter and Back (1950) Festinger, et al. (1950) Homans (1950) Komarovsky (1946) Lindesmith and Strauss (1949) Merton (1949)	Moreno (1946) Murdock (1949) Murphy (1947) Newcomb (1947, 1950) Reissman (1949) Sarbin (1950) Sherif (1948) Stouffer (1949) Sullivan (1947)

terminology (see, for example, Sherif, 1948; Lindesmith and Strauss, 1949; Davis, 1949; Newcomb, 1950; Homans, 1950; Faris, 1952; Hartley and Hartley, 1952; Shibutani, 1961; and Spindler, 1963); and an increasing number of integrative theories in these fields employ role terms (see, for example, Parsons, 1951; Parsons and Shils, 1951; Levy, 1952; and Nadel, 1957). Increasingly, too, one finds role concepts in articles and books in fields dealing with the professional concerns of personal and social change, and many workers in education, industry, and interpersonal helping have adopted selected terms from the vocabulary. Role concepts are not the *lingua franca* of the behavioral sciences, but perhaps they presently come closer to this universal language than any other vocabulary of behavioral science.

Selected Common Terms of Role Theory

There are scores of words and ideas in the vocabulary of role today, but there are only a dozen or so terms that appear again and again. We have assembled in Table 3 the words and ideas that occur most frequently. For each term the common-language definition and selected meanings from current technical usage are presented, along with the pages of Part II, where the concepts are discussed. The reader will hasten his orientation to role by learning the distinctions in the table, and he is therefore urged to become familiar with it. As the table is perused the reader should remember that this is but a small sample of the entire vocabulary; also he should know that the definitions given for current usage are not meant to be exhaustive, authoritative, or "correct." The terms and usages favored by the authors are to be found on the pages indicated in the right-hand column of the table. More intimate familiarity with the concepts of role theory may be gained by reading the chapters of Part II and the selections that follow.

Current Status of the Language

During its relatively brief history, the language of role has grown from a few to many concepts, from vague to more precise ideas, and from concept to operational indicator. The role analyst

TABLE 2—*continued*

Period of Publication of Contribution	Authors of Contributions	
1951–1955	Argyle (1952)	Neiman and Hughes (1951)
	Asch (1952)	Newcomb (1954)
	Bales and Slater (1955)	Parsons (1951)
	Coutu (1951)	Parsons and Shils (1951)
	Getzels and Guba (1954)	Rommetveit (1954)
	Hall (1955)	Sarbin (1952, 1954)
	Herbst (1952)	Sarbin and Jones (1955)
	Janis and King (1954)	Sargent (1951)
	Jaques (1952)	Stouffer and Toby (1951)
	Killian (1952)	Toby (1952, 1953)
	Levy (1952)	Wilson, Trist, and Curle (1952)
	Moreno (1953b)	Yablonsky (1953)
		Zelditch (1955)
1956–1960	Anderson and Moore (1957)	Jackson (1960)
	Angell (1958)	Lang (1956)
	Bales (1958)	Levinson (1959)
	Bates, F. L. (1956, 1957)	Lieberman (1956)
	Blood and Wolfe (1960)	Mann (1956)
	Borgatta (1960b)	Mann and Mann (1959)
	Bott (1957)	Merton (1957)
	Brim (1958)	Morris (1956)
	Cattell (1957)	Pellegrin and Bates (1959)
	Eisenstadt (1956)	Pierce (1956)
	Foa (1958)	Sayres (1956)
	Galtung (1959b)	Spiegel (1957)
	Gerard (1957)	Thibaut and Kelley (1959)
	Goffman (1959)	Thomas (1957)
	Goode (1960 a, b)	Turner (1956)
	Gouldner (1957 a, b; 1960)	Videbeck and Bates (1959)
	Gross, Mason, and McEachern (1957)	Zander, Cohen, and Stotland (1957)
	Grusky (1959)	Zetterberg (1957)
	Guetzkow (1960)	

may now describe most complex real-life phenomena using role terms and concepts, with an exactness that probably surpasses that which is provided by any other single conceptual vocabulary in behavioral science. The reason for this, we believe, derives more from the shortcomings of alternative vocabularies than it does from the maturity of the role language itself. The fact is that there is no complete, molar language for depicting real-life behavior; there are only part vocabularies, such as those for personality, for "group" and "social" behavior, for making decisions, or for economic or political activity, and so on.

But despite this presumed superiority, there are identifiable shortcomings of the role language which must be overcome if the language is to realize its ultimate promise. We shall discuss two basic difficulties: the lack of denotative clarity and the incompleteness of the language.

Lack of Denotative Clarity. Careful examination of Table 3 reveals problems that characterize the language of role in general as well as the selected set of common terms and concepts assembled

TABLE 3 SELECTED COMMON TERMS IN ROLE THEORY AND THEIR COMMON-LANGUAGE AND ROLE MEANINGS

Classes of Terms	Definitions: Common-language Meanings	Definitions: Selected Meanings in Role Theory	Definitions: Pages Where Discussed in Part II
Terms for Partitioning Persons			
Actor	1. A doer. 2. A theatrical performer.	1. A person engaged in interactions with others. 2. A person who is an object of study.	24 24
Alter [*Ego*]	1. A second. 2. A second self. 3. A friend.	A person related to someone under discussion.	24
Ego	1. The entire person. 2. The phenomenal experiencer. 3. The self.	A person under discussion (usually contrasted with *alter*).	24
Other	1. One (or more) as distinct from those previously mentioned. 2. Additional. 3. Alternate.	An individual whose behavior is not the main object of inquiry but one in relationship to whom that person behaves.	24
Person	[*L*, *persona*, a mask used by actors] 1. A character or part in a play (archaic). 2. A human being; an individual. 3. Bodily presence. 4. The real self.	The individual upon whom attention is focused; an actor, target, ego, alter, subject, or object, depending on context.	24
Self	1. The individual; a being regarded as having a personality; a being in its relations to its own identity. 2. Identity considered abstractly.	1. The sense of personal identity. 2. The set of all standards, descriptions, and concepts held by an actor for himself.	27 26, 27
Terms for Partitioning Behaviors			
Expectation	1. A state of affairs looked for in the future; an anticipation. 2. A tentative or theoretical description or model of existing events. 3. A hoped-for state of affairs. 4. An idea concerning what ought to occur.	1. A concept held about a behavior likely to be exhibited by a person. 2. A standard held for the behavior of a person. 3. An anticipation. 4. A norm. 5. An attitude.	27 26 27 26 26, 27

TABLE 3—*continued*

Classes of Terms	Definitions: Common-language Meanings	Definitions: Selected Meanings in Role Theory	Pages Where Discussed in Part II
Terms for Partitioning Behaviors			
Norm	[*L*, *norma*, a rule, pattern, or carpenter's square] 1. A rule or authoritative standard; a model, type, or pattern. 2. A standard of development of achievement; the mode or median.	1. A standard held for the behavior of a person or group.	26
		2. A description of, or concept held about, a behavior pattern likely to be exhibited by a person or group.	27
		3. Behavioral uniformity of actors.	34
		4. Role.	29–31
Performance	[*F*, *parfornir*, to finish or complete] 1. The execution of required functions. 2. A deed or feat, hence a presentation.	Overt activity; role behavior; goal-directed behavior.	26
Sanction	[*L*, *sanctio*, to render sacred or inviolable] 1. Solemn or ceremonious ratification. 2. That which induces observance of law or custom such as reward, loss, or coercive intervention.	1. Behavior by an actor which rewards or punishes another contingent upon conformity by the other to norms or rules.	27
		2. Descriptions, concepts, or anticipations of contingent rewards or punishments.	27
Terms for Partitioning Sets of Persons and Behaviors			
Position (*or Social Position*)	1. A positioning or placing; the manner in which anything is placed. 2. An office, rank, status, or employment. 3. A spot, place, or condition giving one an advantage over another.	1. A designated location in the structure of a social system.	28, 29
		2. A set of persons sharing common attributes or treated similarly by others.	28–31
		3. A role.	29–31
Role	[*F*, the *roll* on which an actor's part is written] 1. A part or character performed by an actor in a drama.	1. A behavioral repertoire characteristic of a person or a position.	28–31
		2. A set of standards, descriptions, norms, or	

TABLE 3—*continued*

Classes of Terms	Definitions: Common-language Meanings	Definitions: Selected Meanings in Role Theory	Pages Where Discussed in Part II
Terms for Relating Sets of Persons and Behaviors			
Role	2. A part or function taken or assumed by any person or structure.	concepts held (by anyone) for the behaviors of a person or a position.	26–28
		3. A position.	
Status	1. A state or condition of a person. 2. One's rank, particularly high rank. 3. Social class.	1. A position. 2. Power, prestige, or wealth associated with a social position.	28, 29
Accuracy	1. Conformity to truth or some standard. 2. Exactness.	Agreement between an event and a description of it.	40
Conformity	Agreement, harmony, congruity.	1. Correspondence between behavior and prescriptions for it.	38–40
		2. Correspondence between individual behavior and behavior patterns evidenced by a group.	38–40
Consensus (*or Sharing*)	1. Agreement in opinion or testimony. 2. Convergent trends in opinion.	1. Sameness of commonly held norms, conceptions.	33, 35
		2. Sameness of behavior in general.	32–36
Role Conflict	[Not in the common language]	1. Inconsistent prescriptions (or other standards) held for a person by himself or by one or more others.	33
		2. The attribution of inconsistent prescriptions (or standards) to others, applicable to one's self.	27, 33
		3. Feelings of unease resulting from the existence or assumption of inconsistent prescriptions (or standards).	
Specialization	1. Particularization. 2. To restrict to a particular use or end. 3. Structural adaptation. 4. Concentration of effort.	The fact that persons display behaviors differentiated from those of others.	33–35, 40

there. Thus we observe that the terms have popular as well as technical meanings and that the two are not always identical, that the terms frequently pertain to more than one concept and that even the technical meanings are not always exact. In these ways the terms of the language are not denotatively specific.

Many of the denotative difficulties may be illustrated by examining role metaphors, the use and extension of which have greatly increased the articulateness of the role language. Consider the dramaturgical metaphor, a particularly popular source of inspiration and one that has been studiously cultivated by some writers. In his preface to *The Presentation of Self in Everyday Life*, Erving Goffman has remarked as follows:

> The perspective employed in this report is that of the theatrical performance; the principles derived are dramaturgical ones. I shall consider the way in which the individual in ordinary work situations presents himself and his activity to others, the ways in which he guides and controls the impression they form of him, and the kinds of things he may and may not do while sustaining his performance before them. In using this model I will attempt not to make light of its obvious inadequacies. The stage presents things that are make-believe; presumably life presents things that are real and sometimes not well rehearsed. More important, perhaps, on the stage one player presents himself in the guise of a character to characters projected by other players; the audience constitutes a third party to the interaction—one that is essential and yet, if the stage performance were real, one that would not be there. In real life, the three parties are compressed into two; the part one individual plays is tailored to the parts played by the others present, and yet these others also constitute the audience. (Goffman, 1959, p. xi.)

Role enactment, role playing, role-playing ability, role taking, coaching, altercasting, front, realization, performance, actor, mask, persona, psychodrama, sociodrama, part, presentation of self, identity, as-if behavior—these are some of the metaphorical concepts inspired mainly by a dramaturgical model of human behavior. (Although the metaphor of drama has been most pervasive, there are also other types of metaphor in role theory. Concepts such as "self," "ego," "alter," "I," and "me" appear to be mentalistically inspired, whereas "position," "network," and "relationship" imply a structural model.)

Masserman's characterization of the early writings of psychoanalytic theory as "more scenaristic than scientific, and more literary than literal" (Masserman, 1946, p. 94) applies with equal force to the metaphors of role theory. Indeed, metaphorical concepts may be criticized on numerous grounds. Nash (1963) has summarized five such criticisms: (a) irrelevance to scientific theory, (b) lack of parsimony, (c) unbelievability, (d) imprecision of comparison, (e) and conducibility to error. All of these criticisms may be leveled against the metaphors of the role vocabulary, especially the last point—this being the most general and telling. The error which attends a thoroughgoing metaphorical conceptual scheme is that of a distorted view of human behavior. The dramaturgical model, for instance, may easily go beyond the plausible implication that some behavior is intentionally engaged in to foster given impressions and to achieve instrumental objectives, generally, to the extreme view that all human encounter is fraught with self-interest, calculation, manipulation, deception, guile, deceit, and suspicion.

The metaphorical concept has great heuristic value, however, especially in the early stages of scientific effort. Metaphors suggest new antecedents and effects of behavior which more neutral terms might not; and metaphors, by their very nature as imprecise similes, enable one to force out the real from the spurious. The impressive growth and development of the specialization called "sociometry" illustrates how a field can live with and begin to outgrow the metaphors of its origin.

But the ideal of one concept, clearly defined, with one verbal label has still to be attained in role theory. At present the language of role is a partially articulate vocabulary that stands midway in precision between the concepts of the man in the street, who uses what the common language just happens to offer as a terminology, and the fully articulate, consensually agreed-upon set of concepts of the mature scientific discipline.

Incompleteness of Language. Despite the conceptual richness of the language, there are phenomena logically belonging to role theory that have yet to be identified and conceptualized. We often apply the term "conformity" to prescribed behavior that corresponds to that which is prescribed, but sometimes the prescriptions themselves correspond to, and are controlled by, the prescribed behavior itself. What is the latter process and what are we to call it? Some prescriptions appear only in writing, some as expressed verbal demands, and others as subvocal directives for oneself or others. In what ways are these prescriptions similar and different, and do they merit separate concepts and terms? A sizable proportion of the continuous outpouring of publications on role is devoted to the identification and conceptualization of previously unrecognized phenomena of role.

THE BODY OF KNOWLEDGE

The field of role is also a body of knowledge based upon many hundreds of studies. Even a casual perusal of the selections included in this volume will suggest the variety and scope of inquiry in this field.

Much is known, for instance, about occupational groups. There have been many studies made of educational roles such as those of the teacher, school administrator, school-board member, school counselor, and pupil. Studies of medical roles have included the physician, medical student, nurse, psychiatrist, and chiropractor; such helpers as the clinical psychologist and social worker have received attention as well. The minister has come under scrutiny, as has his wife; so has the business executive and his wife. College professors have been studied as teachers, researchers, men of knowledge, and Fulbright-fellowship recipients. The officer-leader, the field sergeant, the aircraft commander, and the military chaplain are among the military positions that have been scrutinized.

Another subject of considerable interest has been that of deviancy. Role studies have been completed of the juvenile delinquent, prisoner, drug addict, alcoholic, handicapped, the dying, and even the fool. The role perspective has also been employed in the study of various corrective agencies, such as the prison and the police department; the social-work agency and the half-way house have also been scrutinized.

A major institution which has been extensively studied with the role perspective is the family. Studies have been made of the roles of father, mother, and children, with emphasis upon specializations, role conflict, and socialization. Efforts have also been made to study role phenomena in the discussion group, the classroom, the jury room, the large-scale organization, and the political arena. Although there have as yet been few studies made of roles in the community and in social movements, there have been some inquiries into role phenomena for small societies.

There is an impressive literature on role playing as a technique used for training and therapy, and numerous investigations of therapeutic processes themselves have been conducted under the guidance of a role perspective.

Still another group of investigations has been addressed to such processes as learning and socialization and to developmental sequences; to conformity, sanctioning, and behavioral control; and to role conflict and the attending resolutions and mechanisms of adjustment.

But despite these many inquiries one cannot presently point to, display, or describe the body of knowledge in the field of role. There are only a few reviews of the literature, and these pertain to relatively specialized topics. Thus Brown (1956) has surveyed the studies of sex-role development, Goldstein (1962) has appraised studies of role anticipations in psychotherapy, Mann (1959) has reviewed inquiries into the relationship between personality and leader behavior in groups, and Sarbin (1954) has reported on many of the studies of the self in relationship to role. The existing knowledge of role in general, however, has yet to be organized, codified, reviewed, and evaluated.

THEORY OF ROLE

The field of role has unfortunately come to be known as "role theory." This implies that there is actually more theory than in fact is the case. The role field exhibits much speculation, and there are certainly hypotheses and theories about particular aspects of the subject, but there is no one grand "theory."

A close examination of that which is regarded as "role theory" indicates that its statements appear in essentially three forms: (a) as single hypotheses, (b) as sets of logically unrelated hypotheses on the same topic, and (c) as sets of logically, as well as topically, related hypotheses. Zelditch's (1955) proposition that adult males tend to specialize in instrumental tasks more than female adults and that the females, in turn, tend to engage in the maintenance tasks more than the males, illustrates the first form. Cottrell's (1942 a, b) hypotheses about the factors of role (such as conflict and lack of clarity) that relate to marital difficulty exemplify the second form. And Eisenstadt's (1956) provocative propositions concerning some of the conditions that affect age grading in societies and the effects of the various types of grading are, in many cases, logically interrelated—this being an example of the third form of theory. Furthermore, the three forms of theory appear either as verbal propositions, as in Zelditch (1955), or as more formal assertions, cast in mathematics or logic.

Some of the differences between early and contemporary theory in the field of role may be expressed in the above terms. Although instances of all forms for the precursive and modern period could be cited, there would appear to be more theories today that (a) consist of but one or a few hypotheses, (b) concern a delimited, as opposed to a broad, area of inquiry, (c) articulate causal relations self-consciously and with attempted exactness, and (d) assert hypotheses formally. Also, many of the role-related hypotheses of yesterday, like those of the "armchair" theorists in general, were difficult to test empirically. For this reason, and because hypothesis testing then was uncommon, early hypotheses were rarely subjected to empirical corroboration. The hypotheses of today, in contrast, are generally tied closely to factual information (see, for instance, studies by Stouffer, 1949; Wilson, Trist, and Curle, 1952; Getzels and Guba, 1954; Zelditch, 1955; Bales and Slater, 1955; Hall, 1955; Lieberman, 1956; Gerard, 1957; Bott, 1957; Zander, Cohen, and Stotland, 1957; Gross, Mason, and McEachern, 1958; Videbeck and A. P. Bates, 1959; Blood and Wolfe, 1960; Guetzkow, 1960; Borgatta, 1960).

These are encouraging trends and eventually portions of the field of role may merit the presumptuous appellation by which it has come to be known—namely, role *theory*. Eventually, too, it may be apparent how such theories of role differ from, and are similar to, theories in the related disciplines of psychology, social psychology, sociology, and anthropology. As part of the task of determining the genuine uniqueness of theories of role it will be necessary also to specify the theoretical variables of the field, as opposed to those that are merely descriptive. As one surveys the numerous concepts in the field it is not presently apparent which are theoretical variables, characterizations of complex states of real-world behavior, or both.

RESEARCH ENDEAVOR

From the late nineteenth century to the present most specializations in behavioral science can claim an increase in total scholarly output as well as in empirical inquiry, a broadened scope of inquiry combined with more penetrating study of delimited areas, and greater use of more sophisticated research methods and techniques. All of these trends characterize research endeavor in the field of role as well. We discuss below the particular details of these trends in the study of role.

Research and Scholarly Output

Even casual observation suggests that the volume of research in role is large and has been increasing over the years since the 1930's and 1940's. This observation is confirmed by results of two small inquiries conducted by the authors.

The first inquiry reveals trends in empirical research clearly identified as relating to role. The frequencies of titles under the categories of "role," "role playing," and "sex role" in *Psychological Abstracts* were tallied in three-year intervals for the period 1927, when this journal first appeared, to 1963. Figure 1 presents the trends. As reported previously, these categories did not appear in the journal until 1944 and thereafter; thus for the years 1927–1942 there were no entries. From 1943 on there has been an increasing number of role entries, reaching 145 entries for 1958–1960 and 141 in 1961–1963. The decade of the 1950's marks the period when a sizable and increasing empirical literature was apparent.

In contrast to the first, the second inquiry reveals trends in all research endeavor in the field of role, including both empirical and scholarly writings. The frequencies are based upon the bibliography of references to writings on role found at the end of this volume.[4] The frequencies are also charted in Figure 1 by three-year intervals. It is not surprising to learn that the research output, both scholarly and empirical, as indexed by the frequencies from the Role Bibliography, appreciably exceeds that indicated by the data from the *Psychological Abstracts*. We learn, too, that this more general research output appears a decade earlier—during the 1940's—than the strictly empirical literature. Aside from these differences, however, there are noteworthy parallels between the two sets of frequencies; both show a discernible beginning after World War II, with the major surge and peaking of output occurring during the decade of the 1950's. (It is interesting to note the similarities between these trends and those revealed by Table 2, where selected contributors to modern role theory have been referenced.)

[4] This bibliography is derived from an annual review of more than 250 sources. References were included in the bibliography even if the term "role" was not used in the title. Hortative and impressionistic studies were not included, thus eliminating much early writing on role playing and role taking. The Role Bibliography is more inclusive than the frequencies tallied for the *Psychological Abstracts*, and of course the latter frequencies are contained in the former.

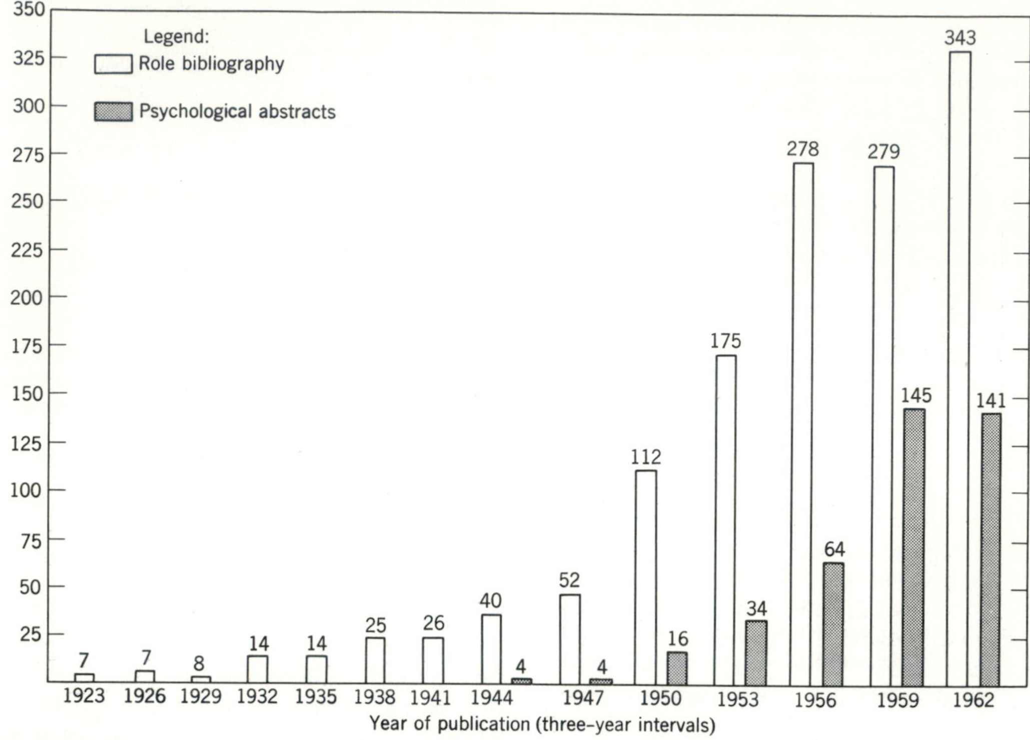

Figure 1. Frequencies of articles and books relating to role theory tabulated from the role bibliography (1922–1963) and *Psychological Abstracts* (1927–1963).

Breadth and Scope of Research

An increasing variety of topics have been examined in the role mode through the years. Such subjects as conflict, differentiation, expectancy, prejudice, reversal of role, adjustment, learning, socialization, and assignment have recently been studied, and more and more positions have been examined, among them positions representing nearly every major institution in modern society. Recent role studies have also scrutinized problems much more searchingly. Whereas Stouffer's (1949) paper on role conflict was perhaps the first empirical study of this problem, we now find over 100 titles pertaining to this subject.

Methods of Inquiry

There is no evidence that studies of role have required techniques and methods of research which differ significantly from those commonly employed in the behavioral sciences in general. The variables of role may be operationalized in many ways, and authors have commonly chosen those most appropriate to their interests and training. But, in general, researchers in role have favored some methods and techniques more than others.

Laboratory experiments and intensive studies of role are common, whereas extensive surveys and experiments in real-life settings are much less frequent. Comparative studies of role phenomena across cultures, nations, communities, organizations, and small groups are still difficult to locate. There is heavy reliance upon the respondent's verbal report as the source of data, and questionnaires are perhaps the most frequently used technique. But even where interviews and sociometric techniques are employed, there is still a bias toward subjective report as opposed to observations of behavior or to other more "objective" methods. Role playing is commonly found, of course. The use of role playing to assess behavior and to produce behavior change was probably indigenous to the field of role, after its having been adopted from psychodrama and sociodrama, but role playing is now among the accepted techniques of research in behavioral science (for more details, see Mann, 1956).

There is no single shortcoming that characterizes methods of inquiries on role, and it is presumptuous to prescribe remedies for an aggregate of researches as disparate and as complex as those in the field of role. But, nonetheless, the correction of some of the biases suggested in the above paragraph would probably produce a more balanced and valid body of information upon which to build a scientific specialization.

WHITHER ROLE THEORY?

What is to be the fate of role theory in the market place of specializations? In order to consider the plausibility of various possibilities it is necessary first to appraise the extent to which the field of role is unique in the behavioral sciences. Our conclusions here are based upon the earlier discussions of this chapter.

The only aspect of role theory that is unique is its language—its terms and concepts—for the domain of study and perspective of role are shared with various disciplines of behavioral science. The theories and hypotheses of role are not always discernibly different from theoretical statements in related disciplines; the methods of inquiry in role studies mirror selected broader practices and trends characteristic of the behavioral sciences in general; and the uncollated knowledge of role is buried in numerous articles and books in many fields. But despite these many commonalities between role theory and the interests and practices of other fields, it is only in the field of role that we find this unique *combination* of domain of study, perspective, language, knowledge, theory, and research endeavor. It is in these ways, then, that role theory is a unique field of study.

Granting the validity of this characterization, it follows that various extreme prognostications for the future can be readily discounted. One of these is the view that role theory is a passing fancy destined soon to be forgotten. This is untenable because the problems with which the field is concerned are too basic, the approach of role theory too well established, and the modest contributions of the field too useful for the entire effort to be dropped. A different extreme view is that role theory is a new specialization soon to supplant or dominate some of the existing behavioral sciences. This, also, is implausible if only because the field is not sufficiently mature and independent of the related behavioral sciences to validate such vaulting ambition.

Our appraisal of the current state of the field indicates that it would be realistic for role analysts to work toward establishing role theory as a distinct specialization in behavioral science, one which maintains close ties with the particular disciplines that in the past have contributed so greatly to it and with the practical endeavors that consume and apply its knowledge. In order for the field to pursue this objective, future effort will involve consolidation of present gains as well as much innovation. At least three general tasks deserve high priority. First, the large and complex domain that is role theory will have to be analyzed and more clearly defined. Second, the now partially articulate vocabulary of role will have to be made more precise denotatively, more comprehensive of all the relevant phenomena requiring particular designation, and more firmly established as a single, agreed-upon technical language. And third, the theoretical and empirical knowledge in the field will need to be reviewed, collated, organized, appraised, and formulated into general statements.

SUMMARY

Role theory is a new field of study; and although it has not yet been widely recognized, it shares with more mature fields of behavioral science the fact that it possesses an identifiable domain of study, perspective, and language; and that it has a body of knowledge, some rudiments of theory, and characteristic methods of inquiry.

The field apparently has chosen as its domain of study nothing more nor less than complex, real-life behavior as it is displayed in genuine on-going social situations. Role analysts examine such problems as the processes and phases of socialization, interdependences among individuals, the characteristics and organization of social positions, processes of conformity and sanctioning, specialization of performance and the division of labor, and many others.

Another identifiable characteristic of the field is its perspective, i.e., its particular viewpoint regarding the determinants of complex, real-life behavior. This perspective, in brief, is a limited, social determinism that ascribes much, but rarely all, of the variance of real-life behavior to the operation of immediate or past external influences. Such influences include the prescriptive framework of demands and rules, the behavior of others as it facilitates or hinders and rewards or punishes the person, the positions of which the person is a member, and the individual's own understanding of, and reactions to, these factors.

Although the perspective of role was part of the thoughtways of many precursors of role theory in the decades immediately prior to the 1930's, our analysis indicates that the technical vocabulary we now associate with role theory did not appear until the 1930's and later. But there were two important conditions necessary for the development of a technical role language that existed even prior to the 1930's. The first was the currency of many concepts similar to contemporary notions of role, and the second was the fact that the term "role" had long been a part of English and of the European languages in which the precursors of modern role theory wrote. During the 1930's and later, early role concepts were joined with role terms, resulting in a quasi-technical language of role. Many behavioral scientists made contributions to this language, but the writings and teachings of Mead, Moreno, and Linton were particularly influential. Each of these men articulated ideas, terminology, and problems of study that survive today in the thoughtways of the traditions these men established.

The diffusion of the role language was not abundantly evident in scholarly publications until the decade of the 1940's. Since that time, however, the language of role has appeared increasingly in studies, in texts in behavioral science, in integrative theories, and in the writings of professional fields concerned with action and change.

Despite the impressive growth of this language and the fact that it probably serves to articulate complex real-behavior as well as, or better than, any other single, analogous vocabulary, the language is only partially articulate. The battery of concepts necessary to describe and study complex real-life behavior is incomplete, and too many of the existing concepts are denotatively imprecise.

The body of knowledge in the field of role is large, and it ranges over many subjects. But because this knowledge resides in many hundreds of publications in diverse fields, it is difficult to do more than illustrate its scope and depth. The fact is that the knowledge that comprises role theory, with but minor exceptions, has yet to be reviewed, collated, organized, and evaluated.

The field of role consists of many hypotheses and theories concerning particular aspects of its domain, but these propositions, like the knowledge to which they relate, have yet to be reviewed and integrated. And even if the propositions were brought together in some organized form, they would undoubtedly not constitute a single, monolithic theory of the sort that the appellation "role theory" implies, nor would they always be distinguishable from other theoretical statements in such disciplines as psychology, sociology, and anthropology.

When the research endeavors in the role field are analyzed it is not surprising to discover that they tend to mirror selected general trends characteristic of the behavioral sciences during the last half-century. Whereas the output of all behavioral science increased markedly after World War II, we find in the field of role that the volume of empirical studies increased greatly during the 1950's and is apparently still increasing. These trends for empirical studies were parallel to all research and scholarly output in role, although nonempirical studies began a discernible increase about a decade earlier than empirical studies. Inquiries in role have also increased in breadth and scope through these years. And like the methods of inquiry in behavioral science in general, we find that those in role theory have become more diverse and sophisticated. Role analysts use techniques and methods of research which are a particular set of all those available in the behavioral sciences. Although the problems of role have apparently not generally necessitated the development of unique approaches, researchers on role have tended to favor selected available techniques and methods over others, with a consequent biasing of some results.

The field of role is unique by virtue of its commitment to this particular combination of domain of study, perspective, language, knowledge, theory, and research endeavor. But of these single aspects of the field only the language qualifies as distinctive, for all of the other features are to varying degrees shared also with other fields and disciplines. In view of its newness as a field and its as yet undetermined place in the spectrum of behavioral-science specializations, the question of what the future will hold for the field comes naturally to mind. Our analysis compels us to reject the pessimistic view that role theory will disappear like a passing fancy and, similarly, to discount the optimistic notion that role theory is destined soon to reign supreme over some existing disciplines. It is realistic, we believe, to prognosticate that the field will aspire actively to become a coherent specialization in behavioral science rather than merely to remain the community of individuals with similar interests and practices which it presently is. Role theory is probably on the threshold of recognition as a specialized field, but its claim to such accord should be validated by further specifications of its domain of inquiry, by clarification and extension of its language, and by organization, review, and integration of its knowledge and theory.

REFERENCES

Masserman, J. H., 1946. *Principles of dynamic psychiatry*. Philadelphia. W. B. Saunders.

Nash, H., 1963. The role of metaphor in psychological theory. *Behavioral Science*, **8**, 336–347.

For all references in this chapter not listed here, see bibliography at the end of the volume.

part II The Conceptual Structure

THE TERMS AND CONCEPTS comprising the language of role are generally unique to role theory. But when attempting to become conversant with the language, one encounters a bewildering profusion of labels and ideas and a disconcerting absence of agreement among experts concerning the definitions of terms. When the ideas are examined closely, as was observed in Chapter I, they will not be found to comprise a complete inventory, nor will all be denotatively precise. These problems of language usually become problems of thought. Imprecise terms lead to fuzzy thinking, and a limited battery of concepts means that an arbitrarily selected portion of the world will be set apart for analysis, with the remainder being ignored. Theory, research, and application alike are adversely affected by these problems of language.

A sizable portion of the writings on role have been addressed precisely to this question of language. The terminological difficulties have been amply documented, and there is no dearth of appeal for terminological and conceptual clarification. More important, perhaps, are the articles devoted to refinement of existing concepts and to the elaboration of new ideas. But despite the excellence of many of the contributions, the problems of language remain. This is understandable, however, when one realizes the magnitude and complexity of the difficulties.

The three chapters in this part are provisional statements directed toward clarifying role terminology and concepts. The concepts presented are the products of a conceptual analysis of the ideas of role theory based upon an examination of the works of others and upon our own independent thought. The numerous concepts employed by others served, in effect, as the data from which we inferred basic role concepts, and our thinking was necessarily required as we augmented, interrelated, generalized, and integrated those ideas. To the extent that the concepts discussed in these chapters are truly general, independent, and comprehensive, the concepts of others are either exemplars, instances, or special cases of them. It is in this sense that the concepts proposed here are "basic."

Three types of basic concept are discussed: those for classifications, for properties, and for variables. These basic concepts and the criteria entering into their formulation constitute an integrated and interrelated set of ideas. This is what is meant when we refer to a "conceptual structure" of role ideas. Although we do not hold any brief for the names given to concepts—this being a matter fundamentally of arbitrary designation—we do believe that this inventory is generally comprehensive of most specific notions current in role theory and that the complex ideas of role that are not exemplars of these basic concepts may be reconstructed from various combinations of the basic concepts.

chapter I... ifying the

EDWIN J. TH...

In connectio... history of role... chapter that t... domain of stu... the language... precise deno... concepts of r... from the the... those to fol... general pro... here describ... life behavic... field of rol... not final o... general, indep... prehensive. And third, by treating classificatory concepts in this chapter and the concepts for properties and variables later, and by distinguishing the use of concepts from their nature, we have endeavored to help the reader identify better that which is descriptive, theoretical, or both.

THE CLASSIFICATORY CONCEPT

Because the concepts given in this chapter are classificatory, we should indicate some of the reasoning behind this distinction. Stated most simply, a classificatory concept categorizes something upon some basis.

Classificatory concepts in role theory deal with a limited set of *phenomenal referents*; mainly, these referents are behaviors, persons, or persons and their behaviors. For example, "individual" is a term whose phenomenal referent is a person, "norm" references a behavior, while "position" references both persons and their behaviors.

Role concepts are generally classified using two bases: a conceptual operation and a criterion for subclass formation. We discovered three *conceptual operations* involved in the formulation of role concepts: (a) the analytic partitioning of phenomenal referents, (b) the relating of analytic partitions, and (c) the combining of analytic partitions. "Individual," for example, is a concept

...n analytic partitioning of the ...rent, person; "consensus" is a ...ntails the relating of analytic ... "division of labor" requires a ... analytic partitions.

...*ulation criteria* have been used for ...asses of phenomenal referents, ...ing similarity, determination, and ...lustrating but one of these, an ... may be distinguished from an ...of persons by the criterion of

...ry classificatory concept has *cate-...nts*, these being units of a phenom-... formed into a subclass. In the ... labor," for example, the elements ...e specializations.

Now, every classificatory concept has (a) a phenomenal referent, (b) a conceptual operation involved in the formation of a subclass of the phenomenal referent, (c) elements partitioned, related, or combined, and (d) a formulation criterion by which the subclass is formed. Thus, the concept of "differentiation" refers to behaviors (the phenomenal referent) that are related (the conceptual operation), and to the comparison of two or more previously identified behavioral partitions (the elements related), by the criterion of similarity (the formulation criterion).

A concept is classificatory by its very nature, as indicated above, but that which is categorized by the concept may or may not have theoretical significance.[1] Because of this and because it only

[1] Properly speaking, classification and division are different but allied processes. In division a genus is differentiated into various subclasses, or species, whereas in classification individuals are grouped into classes, and these classes into more general ones (Cohen and Nagel, 1934). Our definitions are formed more from an examination of individual definitions which were then grouped into classes rather from a purely logical, deductive division of a genus into classes. It was for this reason that the resulting concepts were termed "classificatory" rather than "divisionary."

As in Chapter I, citations for writings on role in this and subsequent chapters of Part II may be found in the Role Bibliography at the end of the volume.

identifies and pigeon-holes aspects of complex behavior, the classificatory concept lends itself more to description than to the theoretical purposes of prediction and explanation. Concepts for variables, to be discussed in Chapter IV, we believe are more suitable than the classificatory concepts for prediction and explanation. The reasoning behind this judgment should become more apparent as the reader progresses through these chapters.

The basic classificatory concepts of this chapter are presented in groupings, organized mainly on the basis of the conceptual operation involved. Basic concepts entailing partitioning are for persons, for behavior, and then for persons and their behavior; those requiring relating are offered second, and finally those involving combining are given.

PARTITIONING CONCEPTS FOR PERSONS

The reader of role theory will encounter many terms applying to persons. "Ego," "alter," "self," "other," "reference group," "actor," and "group" are some of these. The concepts found in the literature on role refer to one or more of four basic analytic partitionings: namely, to the persons studied, to the behaving persons, to the number of persons, or to particularized persons.

Persons Studied

Perhaps the most elementary distinction for person concepts is between the persons studied and those not studied, i.e., between *subjects* and *nonsubjects*. A special category of persons who are nonsubjects is researchers conducting the study, the *investigators*. Although these distinctions serve a limited function, many role analysts have ignored them, and in so doing they have confused other concepts with them.

Behaving Persons

The terms "actor" and "performer" are commonly used to designate persons who behave in given ways. At least four categories deserve identification. The first is that of *behaver*, the person who emits behavior. It is important to differentiate the behaver from the *target*, the latter being one who may be affected by the behavior of the behaver.

Concepts for behaving persons in role have not regularly been distinguished from those for subjects, with some resulting ambiguity. The fact is that the subjects of inquiry may be behavers or targets. This distinction is particularly important in situations of rapid interaction where persons may alternately be behaver, then target, and then behaver again.

Numbers of Persons

The feature of persons denoted by some concepts in role is simply the number of persons. Thus the individual is distinguished from the group or some other aggregate. When such denotation is required, it is convenient to use the familiar term *individual* for the single person, *aggregate* for more than one person, and *every person* for all persons. Persons studied and behaving persons may be individuals, aggregates or, hypothetically, every person.

Particularized Persons

Concepts of numerosity apply to any individual, aggregate, or universe of persons, and the functional identification of persons either as objects of study or as behaving persons similarly does not particularize the persons. Concepts for persons are said to be particularized when a generic or specific classification is employed that sets given individuals apart from others. "Mrs. Jones," "self," "other," "teachers," and "leaders" are examples.

Generic particularization takes at least three forms. In the first, a person or aggregate is particularized by his behavior (e.g., "the rapist," "the fish eater," "the baby sitter"). In the second, positional designation serves to particularize ("the student," "the teacher," "the mother"). And in the third, the one person and the other are distinguished as *self* and *other* (or ego and alter), a difference that amounts generally to no more than a difference between designating a first person and a second. Sometimes there is the necessity also to name a third, fourth, and so on, in order to keep the participants straight.

Specific particularization is the unique categorization of an individual or aggregate. "Mary Jones" is illustrative, when naming a specific person; the New York Yankees, United States citizens, the Elmsville Drinking and Poker Club are other names for particular aggregates of persons.

Persons as Referents: An Aside

"Reference group" and "reference person" are names for aggregates or individuals who are referred to in some way or another. As we shall see, reference to persons is quite common in certain forms of behavior. Because such behaviors exhibit references to persons, the reader might think that referent persons constituted a legitimate partitioning of the phenomenal category of persons. Actually, referent persons are not behaving persons at all; rather, they are human objects to which behavers refer in various ways. This does not preclude, of course, the possibility that a behaving person is in fact referenced. However, nonbehaviors are often referenced along with other types of phenomena. (Referents, along with other behavioral properties, are treated in Chapter III.)

PARTITIONING CONCEPTS FOR BEHAVIOR

Many concepts in role theory expressly pertain to behavior, or may be so construed. In selecting concepts pertinent to the complex behavior of interest in role theory, the role analyst has virtually infinite freedom, in principle, for nothing constrains him to adopt the current conceptions of related behavioral-science disciplines. It is therefore of interest to consider just what particular classifications of behavior the role analysts have chosen to reject or adopt.

The rejected categories are perhaps the easiest to identify. The general concept of behavior favored by the behaviorally oriented psychologist has apparently been too generic for most role analysts, for aside from occasional references to "role behavior," the concept of behavior *qua* behavior and the word "behavior" itself are rarely encountered. Similarly, the division of behavior into voluntary *versus* nonvoluntary, and the differentiations made between motives, feeling, perception, motor activity, cognition, belief, attitude, habit, and reflex are not particularly common. This reluctance to employ many behavioral conceptions from psychology proper is ironic in view of the fact that the psychologists have been among the most prolific producers of empirical inquiries in the field of role and that more than any other behavioral science, psychology claims behavior as its subject of inquiry.

Psychology has made some contributions to the behavioral distinctions of role theory, however, as have sociology and anthropology. But it has probably been social psychology that has enriched the behavioral conceptions of role theory more than any of the other behavioral sciences. This mixture of borrowed distinctions is one important feature of the classificatory concepts for behavior in role theory, and it may account for the impression of disorder and lack of systematization that one gains when first surveying role ideas. Careful examination of the behavioral concepts indicates, however, that some occur much more commonly than others and, more importantly, that they may be grouped into more general categories. The set of basic concepts that emerges, taken as a whole, bears little resemblance to other existing sets.

Behavioral Partitions

When a role analyst employs a specific concept of behavior, such as norm, performance, conception, or sanction, he implies that the particular behavior singled out for conceptualization is somehow different from behavior in its most inclusive sense and that he has some criterion for partitioning behavior as he did. When examining concepts of behavior we discovered that most role analysts did not justify their particular concepts, i.e., they did not indicate the criteria they employed in partitioning behavior in certain ways and not in others. Those analysts might have asserted that the particular behavior discussed was worthy of consideration because it was a significant determinant of other behavior, because it was a singular consequence worthy of special attention, or because the particular behavior had other fundamental properties. To be sure, many role analysts often implied some of these criteria, but rarely did they assert them, let alone demonstrate the validity of the specific partitioning used. One is therefore left with the task of inferring the criteria that role analysts may have employed.

We found that the basic concepts for behavior used by most role analysts could be classified as action, description, evaluation, prescription, or sanction. As we shall indicate below, for each of these partitions there is descriptive similarity among the behaviors falling within a classification, and this is apparently what distinguishes basic behavioral concepts from one another. Descriptive similarity is to be distinguished from functional similarity in which a behavior operates reliably either as an antecedent or consequence in relationship to other behavior. Behaviors partitioned as action, prescription, evaluation, description, and sanction have indeed been indicated in many studies to be an antecedent or consequent of other behavior, as numerous selections in this volume amply demonstrate. But there is also evidence to indicate that such behavior does not always reliably function in these ways; and, as Chapter IV will show, there are significant variables that must also be considered in order to determine how specific partitioned behavior operates. We conclude, therefore, that although the behavioral partitions presented below may be shown eventually to be functionally unitary, they can only be regarded confidently at present as classes of descriptively similar behavior.

Action

Action is behavior distinguished on the basis of its having been learned previously, its goal-directedness, and its apparent voluntariness. The concepts of "performance" and "role performance" are the most common terms used for this partitioning of behavior, but "role enactment," "role behavior," and "behavior pattern" are also employed in this sense. Most of these terms pertain to overt action. But behavior viewed as action may be covertly represented as well, as a motive to achieve, a desire, an intention. We shall use the term *performance* for overt behavior classified as action and the term *motive*[2] for covert tendencies to engage in behavior that, if made overt, would be designated as action. (Parsons, 1951; Parsons and Shils, 1951; Eisenstadt, 1956; and Zetterberg, 1957 are among the writers who have classified behavior by the criterion of action.)

There are no basic varieties of performance, fixed and unalterable; there are only performances classified plausibly on the basis of common features of the behavioral repertoires. "Work performance," "school performance," "sex-role behavior," and "athletic performance" are examples of designations of performance repertoires. The term "role performance" generally refers to the performances of a particular category of persons, where the common features of the performances are left undesignated or assume meaning by virtue of the context in which the expression is employed. Various criteria are found for determining the basis upon which performances are classified. References to "work performance" and "school performance" derive from a classification in terms of institutional context. Classifications of performances by designations of "leader" versus "follower" or "task performance" versus "socioemotional performance" illustrate the operation of functional criteria. Occupational and kinship criteria are among others that are called to mind. All of these are plausible but arbitrary designations of the content of performance.

More progress has been made in isolating varieties of motives than in demarking varieties of performance. Thus there are motives to achieve, to affiliate, to command with power, to understand—examples of action tendencies classified on the basis of their goals. Although research has been devoted to the isolation and dynamics of these and other motives, we know of no agreed upon inventory of motives, only of lists of motives defined plausibly but arbitrarily (see Murray, 1936).

Prescription[3]

There are many terms used in role theory that apply to prescriptive behavior. The term "role" itself is often used prescriptively, as referring to behaviors that somehow "ought to" or "should" be performed; and "expectations," "role expectations," "standards," "norms," and "rules" are others. Most writers have failed to distinguish the covert from the overt prescription, using one concept for both. We have again made this distinction, using the term *norm* for a covertly held prescription and *demand* for the overt expression of a prescription.

It is evident that much of social behavior is affected by prescriptions, and many social situations are dominated by the expression of overt demands. Many parental communications to children, for instance, are in the form of demands for their behavior. Demands also appear in politics, work, education, and in small-group situations. By the time we are adults, however, many of the more important prescriptions that govern our behavior are learned and, when interiorized, they govern our behavior without further need for the pressure of external demands. We are all familiar with the moral precepts of the Judeo-Christian ethic, with customs and etiquette, and with many of the laws of our society. These frequently affect our behavior regardless of whether we are in the presence of, or at a distance from, others who would constrain us to conform to them. Prescriptions are also apt to develop idiosyncratically; thus the family, the work group, the recreational club, the local community are all likely to develop standards for behavior

[2] The terms "attitude" or "need disposition" also might easily have been used for this concept.

[3] We owe to Zetterberg (1957) a debt of gratitude for suggesting, in another context, the utility of the concepts of prescription, evaluation, and description for the problem of partitioning behavior that we faced.

that are distinct from others. It is apparent that there is no sphere of social life that is totally free from prescriptions.

Considering the pervasiveness of prescriptions in social life it is not surprising to discover that scholars have tried to identify their varieties. Thus folkways have been distinguished from mores, customary from enacted law, fad from fashion, custom from convention, informal from formal norms. These ideas generally involve more than purely behavioral distinctions, and thus they are not pursued here (the reader is referred for additional details to Selections 7 and 8, where these matters are discussed). More germane to the present focus are classifications of prescriptive behavior *per se*. Thus prescriptive behaviors may be designated as moral, religious, aesthetic, scientific, legal, and economic, or as associated with home, school, church, recreation, factory, farm, or other institutional realms. Prescriptions may be designated as "negative" if they forbid behavior, or as "positive" if they permit behavior. But like performance, prescriptive behavior cannot now be said to consist of fixed, nonarbitrary subclasses. There are only plausible and convenient distinctions to be made for subvarieties of norms and demands.

Evaluation

Behavior is partitioned as evaluative when it relates primarily to approval or disapproval. "Preference," "value," "affect," and "esteem" are terms which generally pertain to evaluative behavior, and sometimes the terms "reward," "punishment," and "sanction" do as well. The term we shall employ for covert behavior involving evaluation is *value*, with *assessment* reserved for overt behavior that is evaluative.

Like prescriptions, evaluations are pervasive in social life. The friend who frowns, the teacher who grades a paper, the audience member who claps or boos, the mother who rejoices over her child's performance—all are expressing overt assessments of the performance of others. Values, too, are often influential in governing behavior, particularly in such institutional contexts as religion, politics, and the family.

Unlike prescriptions, evaluations have received little analytic discussion in the role literature. Evaluative behaviors are often said to be "positive" or "negative," depending upon whether they indicate approval or disapproval, respectively, and they are sometimes classified by the objects to which they pertain, such as the self or others. These distinctions are among those that may be useful analytically.

Description

Behavior in which persons represent events, processes, and phenomena, without evaluative or affective accompaniments, is designated as descriptive. We shall call covertly held description a *conception*, the essence of which is well conveyed by the ordinary English word "idea"; overtly expressed descriptions shall be termed *statements*, these simply being verbal descriptions.

Descriptions and descriptive processes are nearly ubiquitous in human activity. Overt statements about the nature of the situation are sought and regularly appear when persons enter new situations, and statements constitute a large proportion of educational and recreational interactions. On the covert side, it is difficult to see how anyone would be able to plan effective activity if he did not have an adequate cognitive picture of his environment and the anticipated reactions of others.

The majority of concepts for descriptions in the role literature refer to conceptions, not to statements, and furthermore, those conceptions discussed make reference mainly to the past, present, or future. "Role descriptions," "role perceptions," or simply "memories" refer generally to the past; "role conceptions," "cognitions," and "subjective role" are concepts not bounded by time, whereas "anticipations," "expectancies," and "subjective probability" are terms many role analysts use to refer to conceptions of future events.

Sanction

Behavior is considered a sanction when it is engaged in with intention to achieve change in some other behavior, the direction of desired change generally (although not necessarily) being toward increased conformity with prevailing prescriptions. The term "sanctions" is itself the commonly encountered term in the role literature, but the words "punishment," "reward," "incentive," and "motivation" are also sometimes used in this context. We shall speak of *covert sanction* when referring to the covertly represented sanction and to *overt sanction* for its overtly displayed counterpart. Sanctions may be classified further as "positive" or "negative," the former generally involving reinforcement for engaging in the desired behavior and the latter typically implying punishment for failure to display the desired behavior.[4]

Independence of Partitions

The partitioning of behavior into action, prescription, evaluation, description, and sanction is meant to capture the basic classes of behavior to which concepts of behavior in role refer. It turns out that the partitions are not fully independent. Only three—prescription, evaluation, and description—are logically exclusive among themselves; provided that it is unambiguous, a behavior classified into one cannot be classified also into any of the others. But a behavior classified in any one of the categories may also be classified as action, and a behavior classified as action may also be classified as a prescription, description, or evaluation. Sanctions may, of course, be composed of any other behavioral partition, provided that we know that the intent of the behaver is to influence the other. (The reason for these assertions will become apparent to the reader as he reads the section on transitor referents in Chapter III.)

Symbolic Records of Behavior: An Aside

In literate societies much of the recorded information consists of records of behavior. Consider written prescriptions. In addition to the theatrical script, we find, in other areas of art, choreography for the dance and arrangements in music. In business there are sales agreements and contracts; in organizations there are job prescriptions, organization charts, and organizational roles; in legal affairs there are court decisions, constitutions, and statutes enacted at local, state, and federal levels. Games such as bridge, old maid, pinochle, and poker have written prescriptions; in sports there are rules governing bowling, football, baseball, tennis, and squash; in construction and manufacturing there are blueprints; in health and medicine there are hospital regulations, doctors' written orders, drug prescriptions.

Evaluations, descriptions, sanctions, and actions are also represented in the symbolic records of the society. Among evaluations we encounter book, motion-picture, and dramatic reviews. Descriptions include official reports of all kinds, newspaper accounts, and scientific records. Sanctions have their counterparts in the specifications of punishments to be meted out to those convicted of criminal offenses. Action is recorded in case records and quality control data, among others.

Despite their importance, few role analysts have given much attention to symbolic records of behavior. For this reason we did not include such records as a class of phenomenal referents along with persons, behavior, and persons and their behavior. (When it is necessary to distinguish symbolic records of behavior from behavior proper we speak of *rules* for recorded prescriptions, of *appraisal* for recorded evaluations, of *representation* for recorded descriptions, and of *recorded sanction* and *recorded action* for recorded sanctions and actions, respectively.)

PARTITIONING CONCEPTS FOR PERSONS AND THEIR BEHAVIORS

Because the role analyst is concerned with complex, real-life behavior, many of his concepts pertain both to persons and behavior. Some of these concepts refer to combinations of particular aspects of behavior and partitions for persons already discussed. Thus when the role analyst speaks of a "group norm" we can see readily that this concept is based upon a combination of "norm" as a behavioral partition and upon "aggregate" as a partition of persons. It is perhaps not surprising to realize, however, that there are still other concepts employed by the role analyst that refer to different and more complex person-behavior combinations (e.g., "specialization" and "division of labor"). In this section we present basic concepts inclusive of both types mentioned above.

Position

The notion of position is among the most widely used concepts in role theory, and most writers in the field have followed the example set by Linton (1936) of defining role in relationship to a position. In addition to the word "position," one also encounters the terms "niche," "status," and "office." A "unit of social structure" is the most frequent denotation for position (cf., Gross, Mason, and McEachern, 1957; Newcomb, 1950), but some writers, notably Sarbin (1954), have defined it as a cognitive organization, i.e., as a set of cognitions. Some authors imply that at a minimum a position is a category of individuals, and there is widespread reference to occupational designations to illustrate the concept (policemen,

[4] Some role theorists use the term "sanction" to refer to the anticipations of behavior by the other that reinforces or punishes performance. This latter concept is useful and may be incorporated in our conceptual scheme. It is not intended, here, however.

physicians, teachers, mothers, and children are cited as examples). Furthermore, few writers have employed the concept to denote behavior alone, although many authors have had particular behavior in mind. This is roughly the extent of agreement on the concept's meaning.

The key to understanding the idea of position is that it virtually always refers to a collectively recognized *category* of persons. The category must be distinct in the minds of most persons. Names (e.g., those named "MacGregor"), awareness of entry conditions (e.g., apprenticeship, educational requirements), and salience of the behavior of the persons in the category (e.g., those who teach) are among the ways by which a category comes to be recognized. But given that a category of persons is recognized collectively, there is usually more than one basis upon which the members of the position are differentiated from others, and this may be one reason for definitional disagreements.

Attributes such as age, sex, or skin color may be the main basis for category differentiation. Thus the positions of children, adults, and the aged derive from age grades; male and female from biological sex; and Negro, Caucasian, and Mongolian from such factors as skin color. Behavioral similarities may be the basis for category differentiation, and not attributes as described above. Thus when such positions as homosexual-heterosexual and leader-follower are distinguished, particular common behaviors of the persons in question serve as the basis for category differentiation. Still another basis for differentiation is that of the behavior of others toward the persons in question; the word "scapegoat" refers to a category of persons differentiated mainly by how persons are treated, not necessarily by the commonalities of their own behavior. The main points above may be summarized with the following definition: *Position* is a collectively recognized category of persons for whom the basis for such differentiation is their common attribute, their common behavior, or the common reactions of others toward them.

Role

The concept of role is the central idea in the language of most role analysts but, ironically, there is probably more disagreement concerning this concept than there is for any other in role theory. Reviews of role definitions have indicated a striking diversity of definition (cf., Neiman and Hughes, 1951; Rommetveit, 1954; and Gross, Mason, and McEachern, 1957). The idea of role has been used to denote prescription, description, evaluation, and action; it has referred to covert and overt processes, to the behavior of the self and others, to the behavior an individual initiates versus that which is directed to him. Perhaps the most common definition is that role is the set of prescriptions defining what the behavior of a position member should be. But this much agreement is at best but an oasis in a desert of diverging opinion. A careful review of the definitions reveals, however, that there is one nearly universal common denominator, namely, that the concept pertains to the behaviors of particular persons.

As originally suggested by Linton, it is possible to confine the definition of role to those behaviors associated with a position and that of position to those persons who exhibit a role. Such a set of definitions suggests the interrelationships between aggregates of persons whom we choose to differentiate and their characteristic behavior. But the definitions are too restrictive. As we have just seen, positions may be differentiated upon behavioral or nonbehavioral criteria, and significant portions of role analysis treat positions based upon physical characteristics, or accidents of birth. Similarly, the role concept has also been applied to behaviors not associated with positions. In addition, the definitions suggested by Linton commit us to considering only those roles that are collectively recognized. If we confine the concepts in these ways, the compass of role theory becomes too limited.

The preference of the authors is to define role in broader terms and thereby encompass the numerous and subtle ways in which persons may be associated with behaviors. To handle systematically these relationships, we shall define and discuss a person-behavior matrix that deals with the interface between persons and behavior.

The Person-Behavior Matrix. The general idea of the person-behavior matrix merits elaboration, for it is basic to this discussion. A simple, abstract, version of the matrix is presented in Figure 1, and with its aid, we shall explain the important elements.

The matrix is comprised of a set of behaviors ordered by a set of subjects and a set of behavioral classes. The *subject set* consists either of individuals or of aggregates of subjects falling into two or more of the categories for persons previously discussed. Thus the units of the subject set (indicated by P_1, P_2, etc., in Figure 1) may be individuals or aggregates, behavers or targets,

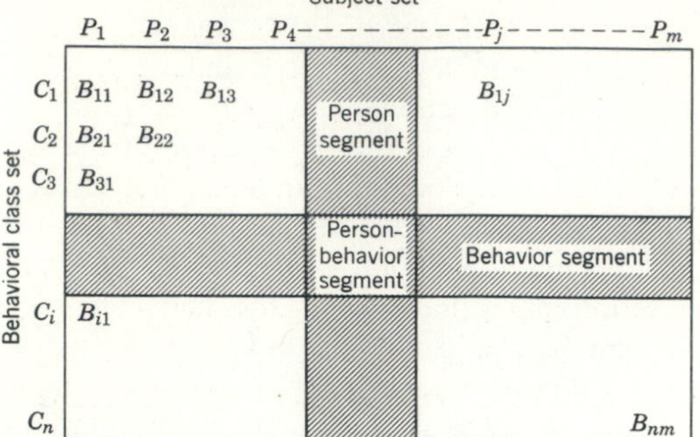

Figure 1. The person-behavior matrix and its segments.

males or females, employees or employers, and so on, or any combination of such categories of persons. In the general case, the subject set consists of all possible, relevant units of person partitions. But in any particular analysis, the subject set is generally limited to units of a particular partition, e.g., to family members or to workers in a factory.

The *behavioral class set* consists of a group of content units that corresponds to some partitioning of behavior. Each behavioral class is a category that brings together specific individual behaviors. Thus the behavioral classes (indicated by C_1, C_2, etc., in Figure 1) might be specific content areas of prescriptions, descriptions, evaluations, actions, or sanctions, in either covert or overt form, and other categories may be formed as well. The important consideration is that each of the behaviors placed in a behavioral class must be entered by some clear criterion. In the general case, the behavioral class set also consists of all possible relevant units, and again, the set of classes is limited when particular behavioral domains are analyzed. (For additional comments on the behavioral class concept see Chapter III.)

Entered into the matrix are the behaviors of the individual units of the subject set. These are ordered by the chosen behavioral classes (B_{11}, B_{12}, etc., through B_{nm} in Figure 1). Any or all of the behavior units of Figure 1 may be of interest to the role analyst. But three segments of the total matrix are of interest because of their generic properties. The *person segment* is a vertical slice through the matrix consisting of all behaviors of a set of subjects. Analogously, the *behavior segment* is a horizontal slice consisting of behaviors of all subjects for a chosen set of behavior classes. Finally, the *person-behavior segment* is a set of behaviors of a selected group of subjects for a chosen set of behavior classes. The diversity and complexity of the phenomena included in a person-behavior matrix can be made more manageable by thinking in terms of these three segments of the matrix.

The three segments of the person-behavior matrix correspond to three types of concept for role. The person segment lists behaviors for particular persons, irrespective of the behavior in question; the behavior segment given behaviors of a given class, irrespective of particular persons; and the person-behavior segment consists of specific behaviors of specific subjects.

What is needed now to make a person-behavior matrix for the referents of various concepts of role is the stipulation of a subject set and behavioral class set. The partitions for persons and behavior given earlier offer a provisional guide to these sets, none other being available. By indicating the specific units of the subject set (i.e., individuals, aggregates, behavers, targets, etc.), the units for the behavior set (norms and demands as prescriptions, conceptions and assertions as descriptions, etc.), an exceedingly large matrix could have been prepared. This exercise was foregone in deference to reader interest, for the table would have been difficult to read and it would have implied, falsely, a high degree of order and finality. We have chosen instead to describe in words various portions of this matrix that merit attention.

Concepts for Person Segments. Along with the definitions below are given some of the labels from the role literature that sometimes have been used to designate the same concept. The concepts used in these definitions were given in earlier sections.

1. *Individual role*—all behavior of an individual. (Related terms: "subjective role," "personal role," "total individual role.")
2. *Aggregate role*—all behavior of an aggregate. (Related terms: "group role," "cultural role," "total aggregate role.")
3. *Behaver role*—all behavior of a behaver. (Related terms: "sent role," "active role.")
4. *Target role*—all behavior of a target person. (Related terms: "received role," "passive role.")

Person segments may refer to some or all behavior of particularized persons as well, in which case one may refer to a "self role" or an "other role," to a "male role" or a "female role," to a "supervisor role" or "employee role," to a "children's role" or "adult role," to a "mother role," "father," "leader role," "teacher role," "doctor role," "patient role," and so on. The generic behavior identified by particular person segments might be called *particularized roles*.

Concepts for Behavior Segments. Behavior segments are not associated with particular persons; rather, they are person-general and behavioral-class specific.

1. *Overt role*—overt behaviors of all persons. (Related terms: "public role," "objective role," "role behavior," "role performance.")
2. *Covert role*—covert behaviors of all persons. (Related terms: "private role," "subjective role," "implicit behavior," "nonobservable behavior.")
3. *Prescriptive role*—the prescriptions of all persons. (Related terms: "normative role," "norm," "rules," "standards.")
4. *Descriptive role*—the descriptions of all persons. (Related terms: "role conceptions," "subjective role.")
5. *Evaluative role*—the evaluations of all persons. (Related term: "norms.")
6. *Active role*—the actions of all persons. (Related terms: "social action," "role performance," "motivation," "goal-directed behavior.")
7. *Sanctioning role*—the sanctions of all persons. (Related terms: "the norm system," "the sanctioning system," "sanctions," "norm enforcer.")

Concepts for Person-Behavior Segments. Concepts within the person-behavior segment combine particularizations from both the person set and the behavioral region set. For instance, we may easily distinguish the *overt-behaver role* from the *overt-target role*, and both of these from the *covert-prescriptive role*, and so forth. Other, more specialized person-behavior roles also appear in the literature. One of these centers on the term "characteristic." Roles are sometimes defined as those patterns of behavior characteristic of certain persons. The idea of "characteristic" is that the behaviors referenced *are* performed by the persons designated—and often. Thus, it is characteristic for policemen to stand on corners and direct traffic. In order to isolate a *characteristic role*, one would have to sort through the person segment for those individuals designated to find out which behaviors were frequently emitted. (See Chapter IV for an additional discussion of this concept under *behavioral commonality*.) A *unique role* would be a characteristic role found only for the persons designated.

Among the most useful role concepts are those that enable the role analyst to refer to the specific behavior of an individual or aggregate. For example, the role analyst may wish to designate a covert prescription held by an individual. The requisite concepts for this have already been discussed, namely, covert versus overt behavior, prescription and related partitions of behavior, and the notions of individual and aggregate. What is now needed, therefore, is a term for the concept which specifies these factors. The label "individual norm" might be suitable. If norms are shared among an aggregate of persons, we may refer to "aggregate norm."

Table 1 contains suggested terms for the concepts that pertain to the overt or covert varieties of particular behavior as evidenced either by an individual or aggregate. A large proportion of the concepts in the literature of role that pertain to the person-behavior segment of the person-behavior matrix are instances of one or another of these concepts, and many of the concepts that are not such exemplars are those that are even more specific in that they specify particular individuals or aggregates.

Postscript. It is impossible to capture the diversity and complexity of the person-behavior matrix with a single concept such as role. The specific referents for the segments relating to persons, to behavior, and to persons and behavior call for scores of concepts and identifying terms, as the prior discussion demonstrates. Because the single idea of role is inarticulate in the face of such complexity, the question naturally arises as to whether the word "role" should be abandoned altogether. We think not, provided that the word is employed only by itself to denote the generic idea of the particular behavior of given persons, i.e., to refer to the entire person-behavior matrix, and provided that more specific concepts are used when speaking of given segments of the matrix.

The task of conceptualizing the relevant features of the person-behavior matrix has barely begun. We have no illusions that the analysis of the matrix presented here is in any way final. It is an illustration that hopefully captures at least some of the general and specific categories of person and behavior referents currently found in role theory. If our analysis provides some order and system for current efforts, so much the better. But it is important to acknowledge that the

TABLE 1 TERMS FOR PARTITIONING CONCEPTS OF BEHAVIOR FOR AN INDIVIDUAL OR AN AGGREGATE

Behavioral Partitions	Person Distinction			
	Individual		Aggregate	
	Observability of Behavior		Observability of Behavior	
	Covert	Overt	Covert	Overt
Action	Individual Motive	Individual Performance	Aggregate Motive	Aggregate Performance
Prescription	Individual Norm	Individual Demand	Aggregate Norm	Aggregate Demand
Evaluation	Individual Value	Individual Assessment	Aggregate Value	Aggregate Assessment
Description	Individual Conception	Individual Statement	Aggregate Conception	Aggregate Statement
Sanction	Individual Covert Sanction	Individual Overt Sanction	Aggregate Covert Sanction	Aggregate Overt Sanction

semblance of order and system achieved here was derived from particular partitions for persons and behavior, put together so as to highlight particular combinations and not others. Other partitions of persons and behavior could have been adopted as the bases for stipulating the sets of persons and behavior in the person-behavior matrix, and other concepts for referents in the segments of the matrix could have been evolved. Although there may never be a final, complete person-behavior matrix, there will assuredly be more mature and comprehensive matrices than the one presented here.

RELATIONSHIP CONCEPTS

We turn now to the discussion of relationship concepts in role theory. The discussion will be organized around various formulating criteria for relating partitioned elements to one another. As a rule, we shall attempt to present first those relationship concepts that may be defined for partitioned behaviors. (The authors were unable to find any major role concepts that pertained only to the relating of person partitions.) However, many relationship concepts pertain to persons and their behaviors, as will be evident from the discussion.

The Criterion of Similarity

Behavioral partitions may be related to one another in terms of their similarity, or lack thereof. Two children who are both eating their ice cream are performing similarly. A person who conforms to a social norm is evidencing behavior that is similar to a prescription for it. We review here various role concepts in which the formulating criterion is similarity.

Differentiation. Two or more behavioral partitions are said to be differentiated if they are discernibly different. An individual may hold different norms for himself as compared with those he holds for others, or differences may relate to his conceptions, evaluations, action tendencies, or covert sanctions; or a group may hold different demands for its members as compared with those it holds for others, and so on.

As used here the concept of differentiation is restricted to a comparison of the relationship of behavioral partitions for a subject who may be an individual, aggregate, or for every person; thus in the comparison, the persons are held constant, as it were, so that only the similarity or difference between behavioral elements may be determined. This restriction has been adopted so that the concept of differentiation is kept

TABLE 2 VARIETIES OF CONSENSUS AND DISSENSUS

Selected Behavioral Partitions	Forms of Consensual Relationships					
	Consensus		Nonpolarized Dissenus		Polarized Dissensus	
	Observability of Behavior		Observability of Behavior		Observability of Behavior	
	Covert	Overt	Covert	Overt	Covert	Overt
Prescription	Norm Consensus	Demand Consensus	Norm Dissensus	Demand Dissensus	Norm Conflict	Demand Conflict
Evaluation	Value Consensus	Assessment Consensus	Value Dissensus	Assessment Dissensus	Value Conflict	Assessment Conflict
Description	Conception Consensus	Statement Consensus	Conception Dissensus	Statement Dissensus	Conception Conflict	Statement Conflict
Sanction	Covert Sanction Consensus	Overt Sanction Consensus	Covert Sanction Dissensus	Overt Sanction Dissensus	Covert Sanction Conflict	Overt Sanction Conflict

distinct from those of specialization and the division of labor, concepts involving both persons and their behaviors.

Consensus. Writers on role have commonly used the term "consensus," and less frequently, one encounters references to terms such as "consensual validation" and "social reality." "Norm conflict," "role conflict," "expectation conflict," "conflict" and simply "dissensus" have been employed to depict disagreement of individuals. *Consensus* is defined here as the degree of agreement of individuals on a given topic.

Writers on role have generally restricted the concept of consensus to behaviors partitioned as prescription, evaluation, description, or sanction, and we have also adopted this restriction. The reason is that consensus implies that one must "agree" or "disagree" *about something*, i.e., there is some object of agreement or disagreement implicated in the individual's behavior. Only behavior classified as prescription, description, evaluation, or sanction is. "about something," i.e., takes objects. When one prescribes, he prescribes "something"; when one describes, he describes "something"; when one evaluates, he evaluates "something"; and so on. And in all cases the agreement or disagreement is reckoned in terms of the degree of similarity of the "somethings" prescribed, described, evaluated, or sanctioned.

There are varieties of consensus, depending upon which of these is analyzed. Thus there may be consensus of prescription, evaluation, description, or sanction. And further, such agreements may be covert or overt. The designations for these varieties of consensus are presented in Table 2. By distinguishing consensus in these ways the role analyst has a more articulate descriptive vocabulary than is provided by the broad word "consensus" alone.

Whereas there is only one way for everyone to agree, there are at least two distinct ways for persons to disagree. In the first, everyone may disagree such that all possible disagreements are about equally represented. This near maximal disagreement is *nonpolarized dissensus.* In the second type of disagreement the majority of persons fall into but a few of the categories of possible agreement; they gravitate to opposing camps, as it were, and hence the appropriateness of the term *polarized dissensus.*[5]

Most writers on role have attended to the polarized case, for which terms such as "role conflict" and "norm conflict" have been employed. But few role analysts have focused upon the nonpolarized case and, consequently, there is essentially no terminology. The two types of

[5] We are indebted to George Levinger for suggesting these terms for the phenomena discussed here.

dissensus must be differentiated terminologically. In Table 2 the polarized cases are labeled as "conflict," and the nonpolarized varieties as "dissensus." The table also considers terms for disagreement of prescription, description, evaluation, and sanctions, both overt and covert.

Uniformity. The above discussion of "consensus" did not apply to action, for it makes little sense to speak of commonalities of such behaviors as consensus. When referring to commonalities and differences between and among persons for the same area of action, we speak instead of uniformity. In the literature on role, "behavior pattern," "performance uniformity," and sometimes "norm" have been employed to refer to uniformity, and the terms "deviance" and "atypicality" have sometimes been applied to nonuniformities.

Uniformity of action may be manifested overtly as *performance uniformity* or covertly as *motive uniformity.* The nonuniformities that may be found in any of these areas are, again, the two types: the polarized and the nonpolarized.

Specialization. An analysis of the phenomena referred to when the term "specialization" is employed discloses that two different things appear to govern its use: first, the amount of behavior engaged in by an individual, relative to others; and second, the number of differentiated behaviors engaged in for a given domain of behavior. The difference between the part-time and full-time teacher involves the amount of teaching, whereas the differences between the neurosurgeon and the general practitioner involves the amount *and* the number of differentiated behaviors, called "medical practice," customarily performed by each. We might refer to both the full-time teacher and neurosurgeon as "specialists," but for different reasons.

Specialization is thus a term that refers to the amount and numbers of types of particular, differentiated behaviors engaged in by a person. Stated differently, specialization is a relationship involving the distribution over persons of behavior as to its amount and differentiated type, for a given behavioral area. A definition of specialization must be restricted to some particular behavioral domain—occupational, institutional, or other "content" area—for if it pertained to all possible behaviors, everyone would be a nonspecialist, at least to some extent.

The two components of specialization—"amount" and "type"—deserve elaboration, for the varieties of specialization derive from consideration of both. The amount of behavior engaged in, for a given domain, varies from all to none—relative to the participation of others. And the number of differentiated behaviors ranges from many (or all for a domain) to essentially none. Although these are but gross distinctions, when they are considered together they generate seven basic varieties of person specialization for a domain of behavior. Table 3 presents these varieties and provisional designations for each.

To illustrate these specializations let us select

TABLE 3 DESIGNATIONS FOR VARIETIES OF SPECIALIZATIONS, BY AMOUNT OF BEHAVIOR ENGAGED IN AND THE NUMBER OF DIFFERENTIATED BEHAVIORS, FOR A GIVEN DOMAIN OF BEHAVIOR

	Differentiation in a Given Domain of Behavior		
Amount of Behavior Engaged in	Many Differentiated Behaviors	A Few Differentiated Behaviors	Mainly Undifferentiated Behavior
All	I Exclusive Generalist	II Exclusive Multispecialist	III Exclusive Specialist
Some	IV Nonexclusive Generalist	V Nonexclusive Multispecialist	VI Nonexclusive Specialist
None		VII "Nonparticipant"	

the domain of behaviors involved in running an institution of higher learning and let us further suppose that the behaviors may be plausibly differentiated into teaching, research, community service, administration, and maintenance activities for the institution. The student in such an institution would typically be a "nonparticipant" (Type VII) in these particular behaviors. A professor whose activities consisted of teaching alone would be a specialist, but because there are other professors who also teach he would be a nonexclusive specialist (Type VI). A professor who did nothing but research would be a specialist also, but if he were the only professor engaged in research, he would be an exclusive specialist (Type III). The professor who engaged in some combination of teaching and research, teaching and service, teaching and administration, or some other limited combination, whose colleagues also engaged in some of the same behaviors, would be nonexclusive multispecialist (Type V). The exclusive multispecialist (Type II), in contrast, would in effect monopolize a few differentiated behaviors, such as research and administration, or teaching and administration—an unlikely specialization today in most universities. The exclusive generalist (Type I) would be another improbable specialization, a kind of one-man university, as it were, who engaged in most or all differentiated behaviors essentially all by himself. Much more common in today's university is the nonexclusive generalist (Type IV), as illustrated by the part-time teacher, researcher, administrator, and provider of community services.

A judgment concerning which of these seven specializations obtains depends upon a prior stipulation of some domain of behavior, or set of "tasks," with respect to which given persons may specialize, and upon some analysis of the possible differentiated subdivisions of the behavioral area. The "tasks," "jobs," or "content" differentiated for the area of behavior derive from the analytic objectives of the role analyst, for there are no fixed, agreed-upon divisions of domains or repertoires of behavior.

One of the commonest divisions of specialization, however, is that generated by the basic partitioning concepts for behavior. Thus, role theorists often speak of *prescribers*, *evaluators*, *describers*, *actors*, or *sanctioners* rather than the more generic classification, behavers. Similarly, a person may be described as a performer or as one who is motivated, a norm-holder (or "norm sender") or demander, if it is desired to make distinctions between covert and overt specializations. Specializations for target persons include those of *prescribee*, *evaluatee*, *describee*, *actee*, and *sanctionee*.

Specialization, uniformity, and consensus are similar concepts in that they all pertain to commonalities of particular behavior of particular persons. Thus, when one speaks of nonspecialization, uniformity, or consensus, some set of behavior is common for some group of persons. But each of the concepts differentiates a distinct aspect of commonality. Consensus and uniformity typically involve a limited domain of behavior with respect to which many persons are compared, whereas specialization generally involves a much broader domain of behavior with respect to which a few or many persons are compared. Consensus and uniformity are thus similar, but as indicated earlier, consensus applies to prescription, description, evaluation, and sanctioning, whereas uniformity pertains to action. Specialization presupposes lack of consensus or uniformity for the behavior in question, but the existence of dissensus or nonuniformity does not determine the extent or types of specialization.

Consistency. The next concept to be taken up—consistency—is also involved with the criterion of similarity. Two behaviors are said to be inconsistent if the existence of one of them implies the converse or nonexistence of the other. The commandment "Thou shalt not kill" is inconsistent with prescriptions necessitating the killing of enemies during wartime. An assertion that a man is a physician is inconsistent with an assertion that this man is also an undertaker. A child's positive evaluation of a parent may be accompanied by disapproval of that parent's disciplinary activities, an example of evaluative inconsistency.

These examples illustrate two different bases for inconsistency. In the first, prescriptions to kill and not to kill exemplify *logical inconsistency*. Logical inconsistency is actually a form of nonsimilarity. It may occur when two nonsimilar behavioral partitions are exhibited by, or held for, the same person. Since it is based on logic, logical consistency may be dealt with using the tools of logic.

The second example involving the man who is described as both a physician and as an undertaker illustrates another basis of inconsistency—*cognitive inconsistency*. Two behavioral partitions are defined as cognitively inconsistent if one of them implies an event that is denied by the other. Although it is logically consistent that a man be both an undertaker and physician, and further this is possible behaviorally, social forces common in our society conspire against this combination of callings—these two behavioral partitions are cognitively inconsistent.

Although consistency may be defined so that the inconsistent elements are exhibited by two persons, its significance is usually assumed to lie in problems created for the individual. Thus, "cognitive dissonance" is presumed to occur when the person discovers inconsistent elements. Inconsistency has been studied as "cognitive imbalance," "ambivalence," and "conflict," depending partly upon the behaviors that are inconsistent.

The Criterion of Determination

In this section we discuss concepts in which the relationship between partitioned elements involves the criterion of determination.

Problem of Interdependence. Interdependences between and among individuals take many guises. The existence of crime and criminals provides gainful employment for policemen, and others too; the employee on an assembly line behaves so as to make possible the performance of a co-worker; the salesman's high sales are obtained at the expense of fellow salesmen sharing the same territory; and the members of a football team all benefit from the touchdown score of the halfback. Some analysts would describe the phenomena of the first example as a "functional" relationship; the behavior on the assembly line might simply be called "interdependence"; the salesmen might be called competitors in "competition"; the shared fate of the members of the football team might be described as a situation of "cooperation." There are many terms for the complex phenomena of interdependence.

When these phenomena are examined closely, there emerges one common element: all instances of *interdependence* appear to involve a *determining*, or causal, relationship between the behavior of the persons involved. And furthermore, there appear to be two different determining relationships; the first involves behavioral facilitation or hindrance, whereas the second entails the rewards and costs accruing to the persons.

Facilitation and hindrance. A linkage of facilitation and hindrance exists between one behavior and another when the first facilitates, hinders, or does not affect the likelihood of occurrence for the second. It is convenient for present purposes to regard any designated unit of behavior as an "act." With this idea, facilitation and hindrance may be defined more precisely. Specifically, act 1 "facilitates" act 2 if the performance of act 1 makes the performance of act 2 more likely than had act 1 not been performed; analogously, act 1 "hinders" act 2 if the performance of act 1 makes the performance of act 2 less likely than had act 1 not been performed; and act 1 is "independent" of act 2 if the performance of act 1 does not alter the likelihood of the performance of act 2. Now consider the simplest case of facilitation between two individuals, *A* and *B* (a self and an other, for instance). *A* is behaver for *B* as target person,

TABLE 4 VARIETIES OF FACILITATION AND HINDRANCE BETWEEN PERSONS A AND B, WITH DESIGNATIONS

Effects of *B*'s Performance on *A*'s Performance	Effects of *A*'s Performance on *B*'s Performance		
	Facilitates	No Effects	Hinders
Facilitates	I Mutual Facilitation	II Facilitation of *A*	III Asymmetrical Facilitation
No Effects	IV Facilitation of *B*	V Independence	VI Hindrance of *B*
Hinders	VII Asymmetrical Facilitation	VIII Hindrance of *A*	IX Mutual Hindrance

and *B* is behaver for *A* as target person; and both may facilitate, hinder or be independent of the other. Table 4 presents the resulting possibilities, with tentative designations. Because some of these are generically identical, only six varieties need to be discussed.

When *A* and *B* both facilitate one another, there is "mutual facilitation" (Type I). Groups ordinarily called "cooperative," in which the members actually facilitate the performance of one another, would of course be illustrative. So would F. J. Allport's (1924) "co-acting" groups in which the members performed relatively simple, individual tasks while sitting in one another's presence. The performance of individuals under these conditions was found to be faster than the performance of individuals working alone on identical tasks. This "social facilitation," as it was called, was presumed to occur partly because of the stimulation of the sights and sounds of others doing the same thing.

"Mutual hindrance" (Type IX) occurs when *A* and *B* both hinder the performance of the other. No word in English is reasonably synonymous with this condition, but everyone will recognize the case; faulty "cooperation," in which each person acts so as to hinder the others, is well known. A less obvious illustration is provided by another finding from the early research of F. H. Allport (1924). When individuals performed complex tasks individually in the presence of others, their qualitative performance was often inferior to that of individuals who performed the same tasks while working alone. The quality of performance was "subvaluent," due in part to an "attitude of social conformity" aroused by the sights and sounds of others working on the same tasks.

Two instances of "facilitative dependence" are noted in the table; one is facilitation of *B* by *A* (Type IV), the other is facilitation of *A* by *B* (Type II). One office mate, for example, may facilitate the performance of the other and not himself be affected by what the other does. Parallel to facilitative dependence is "hindering dependence," of which there are again two exemplars: hindrance of *B* by *A* (Type VI), and of *A* by *B* (Type VIII). Consider two typists sharing an office: Miss O is unaffected by Miss X's typing but Miss O's typing decreases the speed of Miss X's.

Dependencies should be distinguished from the so-called asymmetries. Asymmetrical facilitation (Types III and VII), in which one unit is facilitated and the other hindered, is common and examples perhaps are unnecessary.

"Independence" is a special case in which the probability of *A*'s acts are unaffected by *B*'s, and vice versa.

Reward and cost. The second aspect of interdependent relationships involves considerations of reward and cost. Reward may be construed generally as any gain, reinforcement or "benefit" accruing to a person, and cost may be considered as loss (material or psychological) or an aversive condition. (A more detailed exposition of these concepts is presented in the early sections of Selection 25 by Thibaut and Kelley.) Rewards and costs in behavioral encounters with others are hypothetically independent of the facilitation and hindrance attending such contacts. And for purposes of analysis we treat only rewards-costs, reserving for later the many combinations of rewards and costs and facilitation and hindrance that may obtain in actual interdependencies.

Now consider two persons (or aggregates if

TABLE 5 VARIETIES OF REWARD AND COST IN BEHAVIOR OF *A* AND *B*, WITH DESIGNATIONS

Effects of *B*'s Behavior on *A*	Effects of *A*'s Behavior on *B*		
	Reward	No Reward-Cost	Costs
Rewards	A Mutual Reward	B One-Party Reward (*A*)	C Exploitation (of *B*)
No Reward-Cost	D One-Party Reward (*B*)	E Benefit Independence	F One-Party Cost (*B*)
Costs	G Exploitation (of *A*)	H One-Party Cost (*A*)	I Mutual Cost

preferred), *A* and *B*. *A* is behaver for *B* as target person, and *B* is behaver for *A* as target person, and both may reward the other, incur costs for the other, or not affect the rewards and costs for the other. Nine varieties of reward or cost are generated when all possible combinations are considered, as Table 5 indicates. Because some of these are basically identical, only six need to be discussed.

"Mutual reward" (Type A) occurs when both parties reward the other. The successful completion of a sexual encounter for a man and woman is illustrative. "Cooperative" reward structures in which all share alike and members are actually successful in achieving the objectives that produce the rewards are also illustrative.

When both parties incur costs for the other, there is "mutual cost" (Type I). Two marital partners may experience mutual cost if both obtain sexual gratification outside of the marriage, to the detriment of both, or if both squander funds, thereby depriving the other.

There are two asymmetries of reward or cost. First, there is one-party reward (Types B and D) in which the behavior of one party rewards the other, but the behavior of the other neither rewards the other nor incurs costs for him. Altruistic acts and nonreciprocated gift giving are among many examples called to mind. Second, there is one-party cost (Types F and H) in which the behavior of one party incurs costs for the other, and the behavior of the other neither achieves rewards nor incurs costs for him. Numerous illustrations could be drawn from games, business transactions, and interpersonal relations.

The exploitative relationship (Types C and G) is defined by reward for one party and cost for the other. Although these relationships are extreme and potentially unstable, they do occur. Thus a husband may incur costs for a wife while she acts mainly to reward him, or a merchant may sell overpriced, defective, or misrepresented goods which incur costs for customers and profits for him.

"Benefit independence" (Type E) is the special case of reward and cost in which neither party incurs costs for, or rewards, the other.

Varieties of interdependence. The two components of interdependence analyzed here relate directly to outcomes of practical and theoretical concern. Facilitation and hindrance are generally coordinate to work accomplishment and matters of productivity. Thus, if the behaviors with respect to which productivity are measured are hindered, productivity will be low, but if such behaviors are facilitated, then productivity will be high. The other aspect of interdependence—rewards and costs—relates to the "goodness" of outcome, to satisfaction with the relationship, and these, in turn, are related to the cohesion and stability of the relationship. Thus, if marital partners encounter more mutual cost than reward, or if the rewards and costs are one-sided or exploitative, one or both of the partners may not derive enough satisfaction to continue in the relationship. Because of the importance of such outcomes it is important to consider the varieties of interdependence that may actually be found in interaction.

As was observed, hypothetically, there may be all combinations of facilitation-hindrance and reward-cost between performers. Any one of the nine varieties of facilitation and hindrance may combine with any one of the nine varieties of reward and cost, yielding eighty-one possible types of interdependence among two, interacting persons. Needless to say, the number of possible interdependence types is very great in larger groups. We spare the reader an explication of these types because most of the needed observations may be made about them without this effort. And, of course, it is entirely sufficient for purposes of the analysis of interdependence in actual interpersonal relationships to examine first the type of facilitation and hindrance and then the variety of reward and cost for that relationship.

For many real-world interdependences the two components of interdependence will be tied, i.e., facilitation of the behavior of an individual will also reward that person and hindrance of his behavior will incur costs for him. Such linked interdependencies are common in work situations, especially when there is means control as the main basis for the facilitation or hindrance. Thus, if Mr. Jones does his job well Mr. Smith can perform his work as well (a means-controlling relationship), and the facilitation of Mr. Smith by Mr. Jones also rewards Mr. Smith, whereas the hindrance of Mr. Smith by Mr. Jones incurs costs for Mr. Smith. (See Selection 25 by Thibaut and Kelley for an elaboration of additional linked interdependencies.)

Some actual interdependencies involve a separation of facilitation and hindrance from rewards and costs. Consider an instance of mutual facilitation combined with mutual loss. Thomas (1957) found in an experimental situation involving high means-controlling interdependence in which each member facilitated, and was facilitated by, the performance of the other that the high ensuing productivity of members was associated with "emotional tension" generated by the speed of work, but participants in this study who had less means-controlling work relationships, and less facilitation, also experienced less emotional tension. Or consider an instance of mutual hindrance combined with mutual gain. Many intended work stoppages or slowdowns in factory assembly work, where the employees seek to press claims and advantages for purposes of gaining improvements in work benefits, would be illustrative.

Concepts related to interdependence. This discussion of varieties of interdependence would not be complete without a postscript on some related concepts. At the beginning of this section on interdependence reference was made to the terms "function," "competition," and "cooperation" as concepts that some writers have employed in the context of interdependence. Sometimes these ideas are used to refer to one or another variety of interdependence, as here conceived. Thus a "functional" relationship may turn out, upon close examination, to be one in which a given behavior of a person or group serves to facilitate the behavior of another party or to reward the person or group, and analogously, a "nonfunctional" relationship may turn out to denote hindrance, or the incurring of costs. When this is the case, the more specific terms for the varieties of interdependence might better be used instead of the global term "function."

"Function" has other connotations, too. Merton (1957) distinguishes between manifest and latent functions in terms of the awareness of social participants that a relationship of interdependence between performances obtains. Levy (1952) broadens the concept of function to include interdependence relationships between any set of performances (structure) and the effects they produce over time (function), be the latter performances, or any other type of outcome. Our position is that the term "function" might fruitfully be abandoned in the context of behavioral interdependence. It is at once too broad in its many connotations and lacks specificity as to the source of the interdependence to which it refers.

The terms "competition" and "cooperation" also may sometimes be found, when the user's denotation is analyzed, to refer to one or another variety of interdependence. But generally these terms have been employed to refer to something other than the outcomes of facilitation or hindrance or of gains or losses. In more popular parlance, the words generally pertain to rivalrous intentions, in the case of competition, or to intentions to be helpful, in the case of cooperation. In the social psychological literature they refer generally to the nature of the reward structure. Competition refers to a structure such that if one party obtains the reward (or goal), then the other units cannot; cooperation has denoted a structure such that if one obtains a reward (or goal), then all others can do so (cf., Deutsch, 1949).

These structures do not define actual outcomes but rather refer to the potentiality for sharing or not sharing a reward. A competitive or cooperative structure of potential rewards may result in a variety of actual gain-loss outcomes for members, depending upon such factors as the magnitude of reward, frequency of reward and probability of reward, in the case of competition, and upon whether or not members are "successful" and whether the payoff is large or small, in the case of cooperation. And also, the research on the results of competition and cooperation does not sustain firm generalizations concerning the likely effects of these situations on the facilitation or hindering of performance. Consider competition: although this situation results in higher performance rates when all subjects are grouped together, not all participants are stimulated positively (Hare, 1962); some perform more rapidly with competitors, some more rapidly without competitors. Similar results could be cited for cooperative situations.

Criteria of Similarity and Determination

The criteria of similarity and determination both enter into the formulation of selected concepts. Here we discuss conformity, adjustment, and accuracy.

Conformity. When an individual's action corresponds with that which is prescribed by a norm or demand, it is commonly referred to as "conforming performance." The term "conformity" is widely used in role theory to describe this relationship, and it is difficult to read on the subject of prescription without encountering a discussion of conformity as well. When most authors use the concept of conformity, they intend it to mean that the conforming performance occurs because of the prescription; the idea is that the norm or demand determines the complying action. Conformity may be to prescriptions held by the performer himself, or to prescriptions held by someone else. These are the senses in which we wish to speak of conformity.[6]

A special case of prescriptive conformity is often what many role analysts have referred to as "role-conflict resolution." This phrase has generally been applied to the actions of individuals exposed to conflicting prescriptions, with distinctions made concerning which mode of resolution is employed. Thus, "preferential selection" of alternatives refers to action consistent with one or the other set of opposing prescriptions, "compromise" pertains to action which is partly but not fully consistent with both sets of opposing prescriptions, and "avoidance" applies to action which is inconsistent with both sets of conflicting prescriptions. These "modes of resolving role conflict" are instances of prescriptive conformity, under the special condition of conflicting prescriptions, to the extent that the prescriptions in fact govern the ensuing action.

Adjustment. A different case of similarity between prescription and action is that which derives from the effects of the action, not the prescription. Often prescriptions are shaped by the behavior prescribed, as in the case of the parent of a mentally defective child who sets demands for the child commensurate with its performance level. When it is possible to assert that action determines the prescription consequent to it, either fully or partly, then the concept of *adjustment* is appropriate. (Adjustment may also be applied to the relationship of a behavior and an evaluation that is determined by it.)

Accuracy. When descriptions are compared with the actual events described, are judged to be similar and are determined by the events, then *accuracy* may be said to exist. The concept of accuracy is a familiar one in behavioral science. Thus memories and cognitions are described as "accurate" or "inaccurate," perceptions are called "veridical" or "selective," and clinicians analyze thoughts as being "reality-oriented," "autistic," or "distorted."

[6] It should be noted parenthetically that it is possible for actions to conform to descriptions or evaluations in just the same way that actions conform to prescriptions. This latter use is not often discussed in the literature, however, and its occurrence is probably rare without also the appearance of a prescription that corresponds to the description or evaluation displayed. Consequently, we will restrict our observations to compliance and noncompliance achieved by prescriptions.

COMBINING CONCEPTS

We now turn to the last of three, major groupings of basic concepts, those formed by the combining of analytic partitions.

Division of Labor

The *division of labor* refers to the particular complement of specializations for a given domain of behavior and for a specific set of persons. For example, a typical division of labor would involve the listing of all specializations for a profession, an industry, a community, a family. The division of labor may be determined only after some domain of behavior has been selected for analysis, after a judgment about the differentiation of such behavior has been made, and after the set of persons of interest has been demarked.

In addition to the entire complement of specializations there are at least three components of the complement that merit attention in an analysis of the division of labor. First, there is the basic question of the ratio of participants to nonparticipants. Thus the analyst of agriculture, as a domain of occupational behavior, may report the percentage of farmers for a given population. Second, there is the ratio of exclusive to nonexclusive specializations. The researcher on agriculture may thus report the percentage of full-time farmers, and also possibly a finer breakdown of the proportions of time devoted to farming. Third, there is the ratio of specialists to generalists. Our agricultural researcher might report the proportion of general farmers, the proportion of beet growers, corn growers, dairy farmers, beef raisers, and so on.

In the paragraph above the examples were drawn from one occupational area. The division of labor may be analyzed also of course for other occupational areas, and for large-scale organizations, families, primary groups, and for entire communities and societies as well.

Role Set

Once specializations have been established for an aggregate and the division of labor has been established, we may be interested in the *role set* for each participating person. This concept refers to the complement of specializations characteristic of each behaver. In some types of social situations, specializations will be diffused among a number of persons. In other situations a large number of specializations will accrue to one or two individuals. The concepts of role set and division of labor are related, for a listing of all role sets for each person in the system would add up to the division of labor for these persons.

Individual Position Set

"Position set," "status set," and sometimes the words "role set" have been employed to refer to the particular complex of positions in which an individual holds simultaneous membership. Male, father, husband, lodge member, Caucasian, businessman, son, Catholic, uncle, and Democrat are designations for a partial set of such positions in which a given man may hold membership. Every individual has his own particular set of such positions to which he belongs, referred to here as the *individual position set*. This concept and that of role set are probably closely related, although they are independent concepts.

Aggregate Position Complement

A family has various positions associated with it—male, female; father, mother, children; aunts, uncles, cousins; grandparents and grandchildren; and so on. This complement of positions associated with a given aggregate is the *aggregate position complement*. The concepts of individual position set and aggregate position complement are related, for the set of positions of an individual must be drawn from those in the complement of positions in the aggregates of which a person is a member.

SUMMARY

The basic concepts for classifying the phenomena of role were presented in this chapter. These concepts were derived from an analysis of the numerous, specific concepts of this type found in the literature of role theory. An effort was made to evolve general and independent concepts that were comprehensive of the phenomena to which the specific classificatory concepts in the literature pertained. The concepts presented here are "basic" in this sense.

A classificatory concept classifies something upon some basis, and in the field of role, it is a categorization of a subclass of a phenomenal referent in which the subclass devolves from a specific conceptual operation and a criterion. The

TABLE 6 GLOSSARY TABLE OF THE NAMES FOR BASIC CLASSIFICATORY CONCEPTS OF ROLE THEORY

Factors Entering into the Formation of Concepts				Names for Basic Concepts
Conceptual Operation	Phenomenal Referent	Elements Involved in Operation	Formulation Criterion	
Partitioning	Persons	(Persons)	Function in Inquiry	*Subjects, Nonsubjects, Investigators*
↓	↓	↓	Function in Behaving	*Behavers, Targets*
↓	↓	↓	Numerosity	*Individual, Aggregate, Every Person*
↓	↓	↓	Particularization	*Self, Other* (see text for additional terms)
↓	Behaviors	(Behaviors)	Evidences Prior Acquisition, Goal-directedness and Apparent Volition	*Action*
↓	↓	↓	Criteria for Action and Covert	*Motive*
↓	↓	↓	Criteria for Action and Overt	*Performance*

TABLE 6—*continued*

Factors Entering into the Formation of Concepts				Names for Basic Concepts
Conceptual Operation	Phenomenal Referent	Elements Involved in Operation	Formulation Criterion	
Partitioning ↓	Behaviors ↓	(Behaviors) ↓	Indicates Oughtness or Shouldness	*Prescription*
			Criteria for Prescription and Covert	*Norm*
			Criteria for Prescription and Overt	*Demand*
			Displays Approval or Disapproval	*Evaluation*
			Criteria for Evaluation and Covert	*Value*
			Criteria for Evaluation and Overt	*Assessment*
			Represents Events, Processes, or Phenomena	*Description*
			Criteria for Description and Covert	*Conception*
			Criteria for Description and Overt	*Statement*
			Displays Intention to Change Behavior in the Other	*Sanction*
	Persons and their Behaviors ↓	Categories of Persons ↓	Collective Recognition of Common Attributes, Behaviors, or Reactions of Others	*Position*
		Sub-set of the Person-Behavior Matrix (see text) ↓	All Behavior of an Individual	*Individual Role*
			All Behavior of an Aggregate	*Aggregate Role*
			All Behavior of Behavers	*Behaver Role*
↓	↓	↓	All Behavior of Targets	*Target Role*

TABLE 6—*continued*

Factors Entering into the Formation of Concepts				
Conceptual Operation	Phenomenal Referent	Elements Involved in Operation	Formulation Criterion	Names for Basic Concepts
Partitioning	Persons and their Behaviors	Sub-set of the Person-Behavior Matrix (see text)	All Behavior of Particularized Persons	*Particularized Role*
↓	↓	↓	Behaviors Frequently Emitted by Designated Persons	*Characteristic Role* (Also see Specialization)
↓	↓	↓	All Behavior of Subjects within a Specified Behavioral Partition	*Overt* (*Covert*) *Role*, *Active* (*Motivational*, *Performing*) *Role*, *Prescriptive* (*Normative*, *Demanding*) *Role*, *Evaluative* (*Value*, *Assessing*) *Role*, *Descriptive* (*Conceptual*, *Stating*) *Role*, *Sanctioning Role* (see text for details)
Relating	Behaviors	Two or More Behavioral Partitions	Similarity	*Differentiation*
↓	Persons and Their Behaviors	Specific Prescriptions, Descriptions, or Evaluations held by Two or More Distinct Persons	Similarity	*Consensus* (see text for specific types)
↓	↓	↓	Distributed Dissimilarity	*Nonpolarized Dissensus* (see text for specific types)
↓	↓	↓	Polarized or Modalized Dissimilarity	*Polarized Dissensus*, *Conflict* (see text for specific types)
↓	↓	Specific Actions of Two or More Distinct Persons	Similarity	*Uniformity* (see text for specific types)
↓	↓	↓	Distributed Dissimilarity	*Nonpolarized Non-uniformity* (see text for specific types)
↓	↓	↓	Polarized or Modalized Dissimilarity	*Polarized Nonuniformity*

TABLE 6—*continued*

Factors Entering into the Formation of Concepts				Names for Basic Concepts
Conceptual Operation	Phenomenal Referent	Elements Involved in Operation	Formulation Criterion	
Relating	Persons and their Behaviors	Amount and Types of Differentiated Behavior	Similarity	*Specialization* (see text for specific types)
		Two or More Specific Behaviors	Similarity of Implication	*Consistency*
		Specific Actions of Two or More Distinct Persons	Determination	*Interdependence* (see facilitation-hindrance, reward-cost)
		Specific Actions of Two or More Distinct Persons	Determination by Increase or Decrease in Probability of Other's Behavior	*Facilitation, Hindrance* (see text for specific types)
			Determination by Gain or Loss to Persons	*Reward, Cost* (see text for specific types)
		Action and a Prescription that Corresponds to it	Similarity and Determination (by the Prescription)	*Conformity*
		Description and the Events Represented	Similarity and Determination (by the Event)	*Accuracy*
		Prescription and the Behavior Prescribed	Similarity and Determination (by the Behavior)	*Adjustment*
Combining	Persons and their Behaviors	Specializations of Two or More Persons for Some Behavioral Domain	Interest in a Particular Complement of Specializations	*Division of Labor*
		Specializations of One Person Across Behavioral Domains	Interest in a Particular Complement of Specializations	*Role Set*
		Positions Associated with a Person	Interest in a Particular Complement of Positions	*Individual Position Set*
		Positions Associated with an Aggregate	Interest in a Particular Complement of Positions	*Aggregate Position Complement*

phenomenal referents in the field of role are mainly either persons, behaviors, or persons and their behaviors. Three conceptual operations form basic role concepts, the operations of partitioning, relating, or combining. There are many criteria for differentiating subclasses of role concepts, among them being numerosity, similarity, and determination of the analytic elements.

More specifically, every basic classificatory concept has (a) a phenomenal referent, (b) a conceptual operation involved in the formation of a subclass of the phenomenal referent, (c) elements which are partitioned, related, or combined, and (d) a criterion by which such a subclass is formed. If there is an underlying structure for the classificatory concepts of role, these, or something very much akin to them, are the components of such a structure. By specifying every component one defines a basic classificatory concept. Thus the concept *individual* is a partitioning of a subset of persons by the criterion of their numerosity. That is, the phenomenal referent is persons, the conceptual operation is partitioning, the elements thus partitioned are a subset of persons, and the criterion for forming the subclass is that of the numbers of persons.

Because these components enter into every classificatory concept, it is possible to summarize the many basic concepts presented in this chapter by specifying their components. Table 6 is a glossary table containing the specifications for most of the classificatory concepts discussed earlier in this chapter. The way to "read" the table may be illustrated with the term *action*; the label *action* is a term for a concept which refers to a partitioning of a subset of the phenomenal referent of behavior in terms of the criteria that the behavior evidences prior acquisition, goal directedness, and apparent volition. The table is not a substitute for studying the text (not all concepts defined in this chapter are in it), but it serves as a summary of the discussion and as a glossary of terms.

One of the most useful ideas for role theory is that of the person-behavior matrix. This matrix, and its component person, behavior, and person-behavior segments, may be used not only to illustrate various definitions of the role concept but also to generate a number of other ideas. Consequently, the reader will find these analytic ideas throughout Table 6.

By its very nature the classificatory concept serves to categorize or pigeon-hole aspects of behaviors, persons, or persons and their behaviors, but that which is thus classified may or may not have theoretical significance. The classificatory concept therefore is well suited to description. Although it may be employed also for purposes of prediction and explanation, there are other types of concepts—namely, concepts for properties and variables—that are better suited to these more theoretical purposes.

REFERENCES

Cohen, M. R., and Nagel, E., 1934. *An introduction to logic and scientific method.* New York: Harcourt, Brace, pp. 241–244.

Deutsch, M., 1949. A theory of cooperation and competition. *Human Relations*, **2**, 129–152.

Hare, A. P., 1962. *Handbook of small group research.* New York: The Free Press of Glencoe, pp. 344–346.

Murray, H. A., 1938. *Explorations in personality.* New York: Oxford University Press.

For all references in this chapter not listed here, see bibliography at the end of the volume.

chapter III Basic Concepts for the Properties of Role Phenomena

EDWIN J. THOMAS AND BRUCE J. BIDDLE

INTRODUCTION

This chapter reports basic concepts for the properties of role phenomena. It begins with a discussion of the concept of property and then develops concepts for behavior, for positions, and for the properties of behavior having referents. The coverage of concepts in this chapter might appear to be less comprehensive than that presented for the classificatory concepts in the last chapter. But when one realizes that much more conceptual effort has been devoted to classificatory concepts than to other types and that the classificatory concepts are in some respects logically prior to others—and perhaps simpler as well—then the relatively restricted coverage is understandable.

THE PROPERTY

A property is a characteristic that pertains to all cases of a phenomenon, event, or process but which is not the "essence," or defining condition, for that phenomenon, event, or process. In the field of role a property is some characteristic presumed to hold for all of the phenomena to which one or more classificatory concepts pertain but which is not the defining condition for the classification. Consider, for example, the membership condition, a concept for a property of position to be discussed more fully later. All positions may be presumed to have conditions for the acquisition, maintenance, and relinquishment of membership, but membership condition is not the defining condition of position, as the reader will recall from the earlier discussion. The classificatory concept, in brief, classifies something upon some basis, while the concept for a property identifies some characteristic presumed to hold for all cases thus classified. Although all the properties discussed here are characteristics of the phenomena to which classificatory concepts refer, the properties are not necessarily unique to these alone. The condition of membership mentioned above as a property of positions, for instance, applies to all groups as well as to positions.

Concepts for properties of role phenomena, like classificatory concepts, may be employed for descriptive or theoretical purposes; but unlike concepts for variables, to be discussed in the next chapter, concepts for properties appear to be better suited to description than to the more theoretical objectives of explanation and prediction.

THE PROPERTY OF BEHAVIORAL SCALABILITY

All behavior is scalable; indeed, it is impossible to study any behaviors without having a scale of behavioral alternatives in mind into which those behaviors observed may be mapped. (In Chapter II we referred to such a scale of behavioral alternatives as a "behavioral class.") Often the scale consists of but two behavioral alternatives, "presence" and "absence" of the behavioral quality in mind. Sometimes a scale consists of a number of nominal categories. For instance, "walking," "skipping," "hopping," "crawling," and "running" constitute a nonordered set of alternatives for mapping forms of locomotor activity. And finally, some scales are formed from ranked or interval-scaled behavioral alternatives. For example, a scale of "number of cigarettes smoked per day" allows one at least to rank the behaviors of individual smokers.

The fact that any observed behavior may be mapped into a behavioral scale implies that an aggregate set of behaviors forms a distribution over the set of behavioral alternatives. That is, for any observed aggregate of behaviors, we are able to establish their frequencies of occurrence for each of the behavioral alternatives of the scale. (So many children are "walking," so many are "skipping," and so on.)

Behavioral scalability also has implications for those behavioral forms that reference other behaviors. Prescriptions, evaluations, and descriptions all make statements about behaviors, thus all may refer to one or more of the behavioral alternatives of a scale. As we shall see in Chapter IV, these three forms may be ordered by variables. Prescriptions exhibit some degree of *permission*, evaluations may be ordered for their *approval*, descriptions exhibit some degree of *declaration*. Each of these variables may also be said to form distributions with respect to the behavioral alternatives of the scale. Technically, all concepts involving similarity comparisons (such as consensus, accuracy, and conformity) are definable as relationships between the observed, permitted, approved, and declared distributions.

PROPERTIES OF BEHAVIOR HAVING REFERENTS

Behavior classified as prescription, description, evaluation, and sanction implies objects, whereas behavior classified as action does not. Thus when a person engages in prescription, it may be said that there is someone for whom behavior is prescribed; similarly, descriptions imply objects of description; evaluations imply objects of evaluation; and sanctions imply objects of sanction. But to engage in behavior called action does not necessarily imply an object. These objects implied or asserted when behavior is classified as prescription, evaluation, description, or sanction are termed *referents*. To distinguish behavior having referents from that which cannot be said to have this property, we speak of *transitor behavior*. Prescription, description, evaluation, and sanction are transitor behaviors, as suggested above.

Classes of Referents

In the section of the last chapter on concepts for persons it was observed that reference persons and groups were not concepts for actual persons but pertained, rather, to persons referred to, i.e., were referents. Such persons are object persons, one among various classes of referent to be discussed here. The *referent system* is this set of classes of referents for transitor behaviors.

Object Persons

Consider the following examples: (1) Joe demanded that Mary not set fire to the building; (2) Joe described Mary's effort to set fire to the building; (3) Joe disapproved of Mary's attempt to set the building on fire; and (4) Joe punished Mary in order to keep her from setting fire to the building. These are four statements for behavior classified as prescription, description, evaluation, and sanction, respectively. In all four Mary is the *object person*, i.e., the person to whom the behavior in question applies. Object persons are generally particularized, and hence there is no general set of categories applicable to them. By virtue of the fact that object persons are persons referred to in given statements about behavior, or are implied by the behavior so classified, the persons referred to may or may not actually exist as behavers or as targets.

Object Behavior

Behavior as well as persons may be the referent of a statement. Thus in example 1 above, the object is "not set fire"; in 2 it is "effort to set fire"; in 3 it is "attempt to set . . . fire"; and in 4 it is "setting fire." Although all transitor statements imply object behavior, they need not always actually stipulate it, and analogously, the object persons may be omitted with or without the object behavior being omitted as well. This latter is illustrated by the following statement: Joe described athletic performance. In general, statements of description and prescription are likely to stipulate both persons and behavior as objects, whereas statements of evaluation may omit either the person or his behavior, and sanctions are frequently unclear as to the behavior referenced.

Extended transitor sequences. The fact that transitors reference object behavior means that the object behavior may itself be a transitor. Consider the following statement: Mary asserts that her mother disapproves of her friends' norms for "how far a girl should go" when dating a boy. Mary is the behaver, and her behavior of asserting is an overt description, a transitor behavior. This is the only behavior actually engaged in; the rest concerns the several referents of the assertion. Mary's mother is the object person of the description, and evaluation is the object behavior assigned Mary's mother. But unlike the examples given previously, in this one the object behavior is itself a transitor, and as such it too may have an object person and object behavior. If the latter, in turn, should again be a transitor, the sequence will, again, be extended. Thus, in this example, the evaluation assigned to Mary's mother applies to the norms (object behavior) of Mary's friends (object persons), and the friends' norms, in turn, pertain to the object behavior of "how far a girl should go," a performance. The sequence of transitors terminates here because performance, and behavior categorized as action in general, is not transitor behavior. We see, therefore, that unless the last object behavior is action or the statement is incomplete, the sequence of object behaviors, with the attending object persons, may be extended interminably. Transitor sequences may be complex and highly varied.

Types of transitor sequence. We now turn to the important question of types of transitor sequence. In the literature on role one frequently encounters terms such as reciprocity, reflexivity, interpersonal norms, ego-oriented behavior, and others. The concepts implied by many of these terms involve particular relationships between and among the classes of referents in a statement involving an extended sequence of transitors.

Consider, first, the relationship between behavers and object persons, of which there are two main types. If the behavers are the same as the object persons, then the statement is *reflexive* (e.g., norms held for policemen by policemen). But if the behavers are not the same as the object persons, then the statement is *interpersonal* (e.g., norms held for criminals by policemen). Additional types are generated by considering whether the object behavior referenced in a transitor is assigned to the self or another. Where the object person is the "self," the assignment is *self assigned* (e.g., policemen's descriptions of the norms of policemen), and this assignment, in turn, may be reflexive or interpersonal. Where the object person is the "other," the assignment is *other assigned* (e.g., policemen's descriptions of the norms of criminals), and again, this assignment may also be reflexive or interpersonal.

Now, consider types of statement on which the relationship between the behavior class and object behavior is the axis for generating a typology. If the initial transitor and all reference transitors are prescriptive, one may speak of a *prescriptive sequence*. Analogous definitions may be offered for *sequences that are descriptive*, *evaluative*, or *sanctioning*. These are "pure sequences" in that the behavior class is the same as the class of object behavior. These two are often different, however, and when this is the case it is convenient to label them "mixed sequences."

The above discussion lists but a few of the subclasses that may be formed on the basis of a relationship between referent classes in the referent system of transitor behaviors. The reader may have noted that these subclasses are not properties, strictly speaking, but also they are not classificatory concepts for the phenomenal referents of behavior; rather, they pertain to classes of object for particular partitions of behavior. The subclasses are simply types of statements that derive from a recognition of the particular properties of the referent system.

Utility of transitor analysis: An aside. Statements involving transitor sequences are ubiquitous: they appear frequently in common parlance (and presumably in the thought processes of speakers and of those referred to) and in some of the oldest and most favored concepts in role theory. We may illustrate the usefulness of transitor sequences by analyzing two of these concepts.

The notion of the "generalized other" and the related process of role taking is best understood by first examining G. H. Mead's conceptualization of what is involved in playing a game.

> The organized community or social group which gives to the individual his unit of self may be called "the generalized other." The attitude of the generalized other is the attitude of the whole community. Thus, for example, in the case of such a social group as a ball team, the team is the generalized other in so far as it enters—as an organized process or social activity—into the experience of any one of the individual members of it. . . .
>
> It is in the form of the generalized other that the social process influences the behavior of the individuals involved in it . . . . In abstract thought the individual takes the attitude of the generalized other toward himself, without reference to its expression in any particular other individual . . . . Only through the taking by individuals of the attitude or attitudes of the generalized other toward themselves is the existence of a universe of discourse, as that system of common or social meanings which thinking presupposes as its context, rendered possible. (Mead, 1934, pp. 154–156.)

Such complex ideas must be analyzed in some detail if they are to be specified with the concepts used here. The behaver is the individual. His behavior is of two types, we must presume, and for each we may make statements. First, he conceives of the attitude of the community toward him, and second, he "takes the attitude of the generalized other toward" himself. Now, consider what the referent behaviors are. There is the "attitude" of the community. Then there are the object persons, of which there are two. The first is "the community," which is a set of referent persons called "the generalized other," and the second is the individual himself, when behaving toward himself in terms of the generalized other. Now, let us put these all together. First, Mead speaks of the individual's conception of the attitude of the community toward him. Secondly, the individual is said to take the attitude of the generalized other toward himself. In this rendition of Mead the notion of attitude was accepted at face value. But if one were to presume that there were components of attitude, such as prescription, evaluation, description, and sanction, then the explication would become correspondingly more elaborate.

Cooley's well-known concept of the "looking-glass self" also involves extended transitor sequences.

> Each to each a looking glass
> Reflects the other that doth pass.
> (Cooley, 1902, p. 152.)

Cooley also suggested, less poetically, that the principal elements of the looking-glass self were "the imagination of our appearance to the other person, the imagination of his judgment of that appearance, and some sort of self-feeling, such as pride or mortification" (Cooley, 1902, p. 152).

In our terms, the first of these elements is a conception about himself assigned by the person to another. The second element is also assigned by the person to the other, only this time the other is conceived as holding a value about the person. The third element is the individual's evaluation of himself, probably covert.

These analyses help make salient certain interesting parallels between these seminal ideas of Mead and Cooley. For both, the basic behavior, in contrast to its referents, is an individual's conception. And for both, self-assigned, reflexive behavior is the final outcome of the conceiving process. Furthermore, if we assume that "attitude" for Mead was inclusive of the descriptive and evaluative processes suggested by Cooley, then it follows that the processes referred to in Cooley are but a special case of the processes referred to in Mead. It should be pointed out, however, that the "generalized other" refers to those referent persons who are presumed to reflect while "the looking-glass self" refers to that which is reflected.

Object-Behavior Conditions

Statements about object behavior may stipulate the "conditions" for engaging in such behavior. The *object-behavior conditions* involve such factors as the *time* (i.e., when to engage in behavior), *place* (i.e., where to engage in behavior), or *means* (i.e., how to engage in behavior). In the four examples given earlier, these conditions are all implicit, but they need not have been. Thus, to take only the description (example 2), it could have read as follows: Joe described Mary's effort to set a fire with gasoline rags and matches (means) to the home at 711 S. Street, West Wooly (place) at 11:00 A.M. on September 3, 1935 (time).

Object-Behavior Targets

Object behavior may also involve actual or intended targets. Thus, "the building" is the target of the object behavior of "set fire" in the first example (Joe demanded that Mary not set fire to the building). In this example the target was nonhuman. But the target may be human, too, as in the Biblical injunction "Thou shalt not kill," where by implication the targets of killing are fellow humans.

PROPERTIES OF POSITIONS

As a collectively recognized category of persons differentiated on the basis of common attributes, common behavior, or the common reactions of others, a position has noteworthy properties. Two of these are discussed here: symbols of identification and conditions of membership.

Symbols of Identification

Symbols of identification are a property of all positions. Identifying symbols should be distinguished from the collective recognition of the position in that symbols are the concrete manifestations upon which recognition is based. Identifying symbols may be names for the position (e.g., "mother," "physician," "policeman"), dress and artifact (e.g., uniforms, badges, robes, rings, jewelry), speech, manner or gesture (e.g., salutes, bows, grammar), or physical location (e.g., home, playground, schoolroom, office, factory). By means of such symbols the members of one position may generally be distinguished from others.

Conditions of Membership

The problems that relate to conditions of membership may be introduced by citing Linton's well-known distinction between achieved and ascribed statuses (positions).

> *Ascribed* statuses are those which are assigned to individuals without reference to their innate differences or abilities. They can be predicted and trained for from the moment of birth. The *achieved* statuses are, as a minimum, those requiring special qualities, although they are not necessarily limited to these.

They are not assigned to individuals from birth, but are left open to be filled through competition and individual effort (Linton, 1936, p. 115).

Most writers have construed Linton's apposition of ascribed and achieved statuses as one which distinguishes two basic types of position. It is more accurate, however, to regard the apposition as pertaining to two different criteria for acquiring membership in a position. Thus in the case of the ascribed position, entry is nonvolitional for the individual in question, whereas for the achieved position it is entered volitionally, by choice, and through one's own effort. (The fact that conditions of entrance differ in the degree of individual achievement required of members is another implication of Linton's distinction, and this is discussed in Chapter IV.)

To recognize that positions have conditions of membership leads readily to the idea that they also have conditions for maintaining membership and that these two conditions are not always the same (cf., Nadel, 1957, pp. 22–41). And given these points, it is difficult to avoid the thought that positions also have conditions of departure and that these conditions are also generally different from the conditions of entrance and of maintenance. Thus, the conditions of position membership involve requirements which govern an individual's entrance into, maintenance in, and departure from, a position.

Consider these conditions as they relate to membership in a professional association. To acquire membership the applicant must generally demonstrate appropriate educational achievement, experience, and often personal qualifications as well. To maintain membership, however, it is frequently necessary only to pay one's dues and to avoid violating the ethics and prescriptions of the association. To relinquish membership one may stop paying dues, be judged to have violated an ethical precept concerning the proper behavior of members, or resign, among others.

In the above example the conditions of entrance, maintenance, and departure were different. But all of these conditions may be the same. Thus the conditions for entering the position called "Negro"—possessing various physical attributes—are generally identical to those which govern the maintenance and the relinquishing of membership. The fact that the conditions for these different aspects of membership do coincide in some cases, and the practice of grossly labeling these as either "achieved" or "ascribed" may have kept many writers from recognizing the analytic difference between requirements for entrance, maintenance, and departure.

SUMMARY

Concepts for selected properties of role were presented in this chapter. Although it is not a defining condition, a property is a characteristic that pertains nonetheless to all instances of a phenomenon, event, or process. In the field of role a property is some characteristic presumed to hold for all cases of the phenomena to which one or more classificatory concepts pertain but which is not the defining condition for the phenomena in question. While the classificatory concept serves to categorize something upon some basis, the concept for a property identifies some characteristic presumed to be present for all cases thus classified.

Behavior partitioned as prescription, description, evaluation, and sanction asserts or implies referents, and behavioral partitions having referent properties were called "transitor behavior." Four classes of referents were identified and discussed, these four comprising the referent system for transitor behavior. The first class was called "object persons," defined as the person(s) to whom the behavior in question pertains. In the statement "Joe demanded that Mary not set fire to the building," "Mary" is an object person of the prescription. The second class of referent was termed "object behavior," defined as the behavior to which the transitor behavior pertains. In the above example the object behavior is indexed by "not set fire." The third class of referent was called "object-behavior conditions," specified by such factors as the time and place to engage in behavior or the means of engaging in such behavior. In the above example the object-behavior conditions were not specified (i.e., no time, place, or means was stipulated). The fourth referent class is called "object-behavior targets," i.e., the human and nonhuman targets of the object behavior. In the above example the object behavior is "not set fire" and its target is "the building"—a nonhuman target.

When the object behavior is transitor behavior which in turn has its own referent system, extended and complex sequences of transitors may ensue. These extended transitor sequences and their various types were discussed. Then, concepts for referents were applied to two complex and seminal ideas of role theory, namely, to Mead's "generalized other" and Cooley's "looking-glass self." The application helped make apparent important parallels between the ideas of these two writers.

The chapter concludes with a presentation of two properties of positions: the symbols by which positions are identified and the conditions of membership.

Concepts for properties may be employed for descriptive or theoretical purposes, but like the classificatory concepts, they appear to be better suited to description than to explanation and prediction.

chapter IV Basic Concepts for the Variables of Role Phenomena

EDWIN J. THOMAS AND BRUCE J. BIDDLE

INTRODUCTION

This chapter continues the exposition of basic concepts that derived from our study of the ideas used in role theory and from our analysis of those concepts. Basic concepts for the variables of role have been brought together in this chapter. First we present a discussion of the concept of variable, and then the concepts that pertain to behaviors, to positions and roles, and to interdependence and personal adaptation.

As the reader progresses through this chapter he should be aware that role analysts have given less thought to variables than to classificatory concepts, and consequently, the coverage of this chapter is less comprehensive than that presented in the chapter on classificatory concepts. The concepts for variables are important, however, because they give the key notions in many of the hypotheses and theories found in role theory.

THE VARIABLE

A variable is some quantity the values of which may be employed to order some phenomenon, event, or process. In the field of role the variable is some quantity with respect to which the phenomenal referents or properties of role may be differentially ordered. A variable for ordering positions, for example, is that of aggregate differentiation, to be discussed more fully later. All positions may be compared and arrayed in terms of the degree to which the aggregate of behavers in question displays common behavior; some positions will thus be highly differentiated, some moderately differentiated, and still others relatively undifferentiated.

We shall talk about many types of variables. Some are formal, as is illustrated by permission, to be discussed in connection with prescriptive behavior (such variables are sometimes also called "dimensions"), and some are empirical, such as reinforcement and punishment. Some variables are independent in that their variation is treated as an antecedent condition, whereas other variables are dependent in that their variation is construed as a putative effect—as a consequent. Some variables are at best only quasi-quantitative in that they are really orderings of more than one thing, while other variables are much more pure quantitatively, and some variables allow only a crude ranking, while others permit a finely graded, precise scaling. Many of the variables are general, and some are significant ideas in the theories of one or another of the behavioral sciences. Although many of these differences among the types of variables do have implications for research and theory, the factor that we wish to highlight in this discussion is what they have in common, namely, that they are variables, and as such, they differ from properties and phenomenal classifications. As the field matures, however, role analysts will probably find it necessary to make distinctions between varieties of variables.

The concepts for role variables are understandably used more frequently to interpret, explain, and predict than to describe, although they may be employed descriptively as well.

As we have said, concepts for variables are generally better suited to explanation and prediction than are those for classifications and properties, whereas the latter are generally more appropriate for description.

VARIABLES FOR BEHAVIOR

Some variables for behavior apply only to particular behavioral partitions, while others pertain to any behavioral partition. The discussion below treats the more specific variables first and then progresses to the more general ones.

Permissiveness of Prescription

The commandment "Thou shalt not kill" asserts that the taking of human life is forbidden behavior, the factory regulation that says that work commences on the second shift at 8.10 A.M. indicates obligatory behavior, and the sign that says "smoking permitted" indicates that smoking is indifferent behavior. All prescriptions define given behavior as forbidden, obligatory, or indifferent, and basic to each of these is the idea of permission. If behavior is permitted, it is "allowed"; it "may" or "may not" be performed, it is "optional." Now, "forbidden" behavior is behavior which is not permitted; "obligatory" behavior is behavior with respect to which it is not permitted not to perform it; and "indifferent" behavior is behavior in respect to which it is permitted to perform it and it is also permitted not to perform it. (For a more rigorous treatment of the logic of prescriptions see Selection 10 by Anderson and Moore.)

We may now consider the variable of permission. Obligatory and forbidden behavior are alike in that, for each, certain behavior is not permitted and consequently, neither is "indifferent," as this term was defined above, whereas, for behavior defined as indifferent, it is permitted to engage or not to engage in it. A *unipolar scale of permission* may be formed that ranges from indifferent behavior, at one extreme, to obligatory *or* forbidden behavior, at the other extreme (see Figure 1). The variable of permission may be employed also to construct a *bipolar scale of permission* in which indifference is a midpoint between obligatory or forbidden behavior (again see Figure 1). Each scale has its merits, depending upon whether or not it is necessary for the role analyst to distinguish obligating from forbidding prescriptions. In general, if these may be ignored then the unipolar scale is suitable. If not, then the bipolar scale is appropriate.

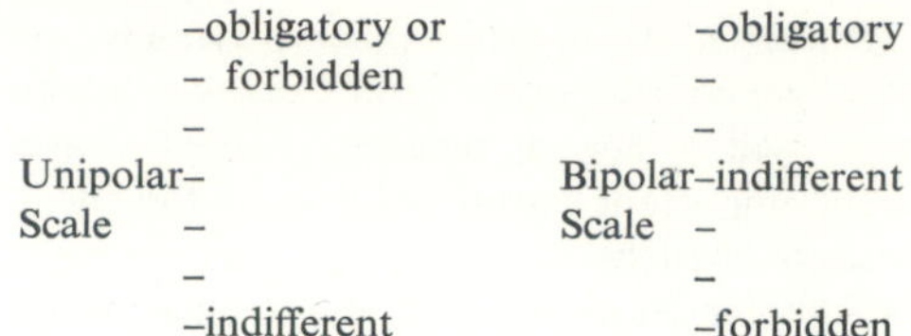

Figure 1. Two scales of permission for ordering prescriptions.

Approval of Evaluation

Evaluations may be characterized as involving some degree of approval. Thus mothers approve (or disapprove) of the behavior of their children, employers approve (or disapprove) of the performances of their employees, critics approve (or disapprove) of the artistic performances they are called upon to judge.

Approval may either be positive or negative, and this dimension may range from indifference to high degrees of approval or disapproval. A scale of approving behavior may be unipolar or bipolar, and if figures were made for these scales, they would be analogous to the two scales for permission presented in Figure 1. A unipolar scale of approval is suitable if the investigator wishes to ignore the sign of approval and he is concerned only with departures from neutrality. If sign is important, the bipolar scale is to be preferred.

Adequacy of Performance

When performance is compared against some standard of excellence, it is being ordered in terms of its adequacy. The world of work provides numerous examples. The quality of performance is often the basis for reckoning its adequacy, as is illustrated in an appraisal of the soundness of the decisions that an administrator makes. The quantity of performance is another basis for determining adequacy. Thus the amount of a product that is made is calibrated, or the frequency or rate of production is worked out against some production criterion. Quality, amount, frequency, or rate are but alternative means by which performance may be ordered against a standard, and generally both quality and quantity are combined. The variable of performance adequacy ranges from some point defined as adequate through successive departures from this point.

Complexity of Performance

Performances are behavioral repertoires, and as such the repertoires may be composed in an almost infinite variety of patterns. Complexity is a significant characteristic of any repertory pattern. Consider the difference between the performance repertoire of the employee who repetitively fits part X on part Y in an assembly operation and does nothing else as contrasted with the repertoire of the company's vice president in charge of production. The vice president's repertoire, if he is typical, is more complex than that of the line worker in at least three important respects. First, it is more extensive by virtue of the more numerous and diverse performance elements contained in it; second, the repertoire contains many more performance alternatives, the contingencies for which must be determined; and third, the number of linked performances, or the performance sequence, is lengthy. In this example the "extensiveness," "contingentness," and "sequence length" of performances were all high, and repertoires thus characterized are indeed *complex*. Repertoires, of course, need not be complex in all of these ways, for all combinations of extensiveness, contingentness, and sequence length may be found in actual repertoires. It is in these ways that performance repertoires may vary in complexity.

Declaration of Description

It is characteristic of all descriptions that they are declarative statements. The historian's claim that the Norman invasion of England occurred in 1066 is a declaration, and so is the testimony given by a witness at a trial, an opinion poll, or a weather forecast. In each there is a declaration about what has happened, is happening, or is likely to happen.

Declaration is a dimension, and any given declarative statement may stipulate the occurrence or nonoccurrence for discrete events (e.g., the statement that the Norman invasion occurred in 1066, or it did not), or a declarative statement may stipulate the degree or amount of that which is described (e.g., "most policemen are honest men," or "Beethoven wrote but one opera"). Unlike the former scale, the latter may range from "zero" through positive values; the former, in contrast, takes only two, either "zero" in nonoccurrence or "one" for occurrence. The distribution for an aggregate of declarations may be formed for either of these scales, and where the actual events or phenomena about which the descriptions make declarations are known, judgments about the accuracy of the declarations may be made.

Distortion of Description

Descriptions may be inaccurate because they distort some aspect of the object ostensibly represented. This form of inaccuracy is an error of commission rather than an error of omission. Thus a description of a prescription may exaggerate its permissiveness (a "benevolent" distortion) or its forbiddenness (a "malevolent" distortion); a description of an evaluation may represent more approval or disapproval than is actually the case; or a description of performance may depict it as more or less adequate than it truly is. All descriptions may be ordered in terms of their distortion, with descriptions judged as possessing too much distortion being termed "inaccurate." (Descriptions may reveal no distortion, however, and still be construed as inaccurate by virtue of their incompleteness, to be discussed below.)

Completeness of Transitors

The partitions of behavior that involve objects, namely the transitors, may or may not specify the referents. Thus a description of a prescription may not represent the persons to whom the prescription applies (the object persons), the persons affected by the behavior of the object persons (the object-target persons). Prescriptions, evaluations, and sanctions may also be incomplete. Because transitor behaviors may be ordered in terms of the degree to which they are complete, we speak of the variable of *completeness*.

It is interesting to note some of the special cases of transitor incompleteness. When terms such as "role ambiguity," "norm ambiguity," "norm unclarity," and "expectation vagueness" are carefully analyzed, they are frequently found to be nothing other than words for incomplete prescriptions or, less commonly, for incomplete descriptions, evaluations, or sanctions.

Transitor Complexity

The statement that Mary asserts that her mother disapproves of her friends' norms for "how far a girl should go" when dating a boy, is a description of an evaluation of a prescription for performance—an extended sequence of transitors. To be more specific, it is a sequence of three transitors—description, evaluation, prescription. The *complexity* of a transitor sequence is defined as the number of transitors referred to in all instances of behavior appearing in the statement. A statement with one transitor has first-order transitor complexity; the statement of Mary, above, is one having a third-order complexity. The variable of transitor complexity ranges from one to any positive integer.

Although in principle there is no limit to how complex transitor sequences may be, one finds in reality that statements rarely reach the order of four or more. There are at least three reasons for this. The first and most important perhaps derives from the limited capacity of most humans to conceive of such complex webs of relationships. Beyond a certain point of complexity most persons simply find themselves unable to retain the details. Second, the requirements of communication do not often require the specification of the complex transitor sequences potentially denotable. Conventions, shorthand references to complex phenomena, and elliptical allusions often suffice. And third, the actual webs of transitor behaviors themselves probably do not often become complex. How often, for example, are there prescriptions of *A* for *B* for *C* for *D* that one may wish to describe, evaluate, or sanction?

Transitor Universality

Consider the difference between a detour sign and the Biblical commandment "do unto others as you would they should do unto you." The sign refers to a temporary route rather than to a permanent one; it pertains to the specific place on the road where the sign is located; it pertains only to persons driving along that route; and it is restricted to the behavior of driving on that road. The commandment, in contrast, is relatively timeless, pertains to most if not all places, all persons, and to all behaviors having to do with others. Four dimensions of universality are contained in these contrasts. The first is that of *time universality*, which of course ranges from but a moment to all eternity; the second is *place universality*, and it ranges from a circumscribed place to all of space; the third is *person universality*, which may be one, more than one or every person; and the fourth is *behavior universality*, and this ranges from a most narrow aspect to all of human activity. Any statement containing a transitor may be given a place on one or more of these dimensions of universality, as was illustrated in the examples above. Universality is thus not a variable itself so much as it is a point (or set of points) on the various dimensions of time, place, person, and behavior universality.[1]

Codification

Codification is complex, for it too involves various factors. One is the extent to which behavior is represented in writing as contrasted with being unwritten, and others are the extent to which the statements of the behavior are brought together, organized, and explicated. All of these may vary in degree, and again, statements about behavior may be ordered on one or more of these dimensions. Laws and manuals of procedure in organizations are illustrative of codified prescriptions; histories and newspaper accounts are instances of codified description and, sometimes, of codified evaluation as well. The codes of morals and beauty, and the ideologies of religion, economics, and politics are largely codified evaluation, and quality-control data on the speed and quality of production in a factory exemplify codified performance. In a nonliterate society codification is generally achieved through ritual and ceremony.

Organismic Involvement

Behavior may be engaged in with differing degrees of organismic involvement, according to Sarbin (see Selection 20). This variable of the intensity of behavioral participation is directly related to the number of organic systems involved. Sarbin has contrasted seven levels of involvement: at the low end of the scale is behavior in which the person is but minimally involved, few organic systems are engaged, and there is little effort (e.g., shopping in a supermarket); at the high end of the scale there is maximal involvement, the entire organism is engaged, and there is much effort (e.g., assuming the role of the moribund person). The reader is referred to the selection by Sarbin for additional details.

Presentation Bias

The concert pianist doesn't merely play the piano uncommonly well, for he typically embellishes his performance with an impressive entrance on the stage; his mannerisms, body movements, and posture are generally calculated to foster an image of excellence and inspiration, and his exit from the stage and returning and bowing to acknowledge applause are more than perfunctory. These aspects of behavior may be said to be a "dramatic realization" of performance, to use Goffman's colorful phrase (see Selection 21).

[1] Indeed, these "dimensions" may be analytically subdivided. For instance, transitors not universal with respect to time may be stated about past, present, or future events. Most evaluative transitors, for instance, are "reactive" to past events.

Dramatic realization is but one way in which performance and behavior in general may be idealized. The idealization of behavior is a presentation bias, one in which the behavior is altered or augmented so as to foster the impression that it is exemplary. Behavior need not necessarily be biased toward idealization, of course, but when it is visible and public, as Goffman has observed, it tends characteristically toward idealization. The behavioral repertoire of individuals has both a visible, public component and an unseen underworld, as it were, and the public segment is likely to be more idealized than its more private counterpart. Contrast the performance of the waitress while waiting on customers, with her other actions while she is in the kitchen, out of the scrutiny of customers, or the performance of a funeral director when commiserating with the bereaved, as compared with the more mundane tasks of directing the funeral and embalming the body. Presentation bias is a variable that ranges from none to a very high degree, with dramatic realization, idealization, lying, fraud, and deceit being among the varieties of misrepresentation. The reader is referred to Goffman's discussion in Selection 21 for his discussion of idealization, front, misrepresentation, and other biases of performance.

Environmental Constraint

The physical environment, including its human and nonhuman components, may exercise immense control over behavior. A man in a jail cell is obviously restricted in his behavior, but environment constraints are imposed as well by the layout of rooms and corridors in buildings, by the placement of buildings and streets in cities, by the numbers and contiguity of other humans, by the rivers, mountains, lakes, oceans, and forests, and by the ecological context in general.

There are essentially three ways in which an environment may affect whether or not a given behavior is engaged in; the environment may simply preclude engaging in the behavior at all; it may permit but not fully determine engaging in the behavior; or in extreme cases it may literally force the behavior into being. The concept of means control is applicable to the "precluding" and "permitting" effects, these being the most common. An element of the environment may be said to exercise *means control* when its presence permits, but does not fully determine, given behavior and when its absence precludes the possibility of engaging in particular behavior. There are many examples: the behavior of others may exercise means control over individuals, as in work on an assembly line or in the division of labor more generally; the very presence of others exercises means control over a host of interpersonal behaviors; and the natural resources of an area exercise means control over a people's sustenance, industry, occupational structure, and much of the entire division of labor.

Reinforcement

A smile, a knowing look or casual comment may express approval just as may the more unambiguous behaviors of providing outright approval, money, or valued goods. The problem is that any of these behaviors may also serve to convey disapproval for certain persons under given conditions. Any behavior evidenced in response to the behaviors of another person may function differently from what an observer might suppose when judging it only on the basis of its apparent features. Thus the descriptive classification of behaviors as being expressions of approval or disapproval of the acts of others is sometimes misleading, and it is inadequate for determining the true function of the behavior. The same comments apply to classifications of behavior as sanctions, prescriptions, or descriptions.

The concept of reinforcement expresses a functional relationship between a response and the stimuli which follow it. The use of such a concept therefore removes some of the uncertainty and arbitrariness inherent in a purely descriptive classification. A behavior is said to be a reinforcement if it increases the probability of the response which it follows (Skinner, 1953). Some reinforcers are primary; they work naturally without the necessity of prior learning. Examples would be food, water, pain, and sex. Reinforcers are also secondary; they are stimuli which were previously neutral that have acquired a capacity to reinforce on the basis of having been paired earlier with one or more primary reinforcer. Approval, money, and attention are common examples. These are examples of generalized reinforcers as well, for approval, money, and attention have been associated with more than one primary reinforcer in the past histories of most individuals, and the reinforcing capacity of each is independent of the momentary states of deprivation relating to specific primary reinforcers.

There are two types of reinforcement, the positive and the negative. In a positive reinforcement the presentation of a positive reinforcer serves to increase the probability of the response which it follows. The increase in the tendency of a child to pronounce a word correctly after occurrences of correct pronunciations, which in turn were followed by the parent's comment "correct," would be illustrative. In negative reinforcement the withdrawal of a negative reinforcer serves to increase the probability of the response which it follows. The increased tendency to close open windows on cold days when this serves to remove the aversiveness of the cold air is an example. Negative reinforcement is a particular form of reinforcement and should not be confused, as it often is, with punishment.

Reinforcement is one variable that may aid in understanding the function of behavior classified as evaluation, sanction, prescription, or description. Expressions of approval or disapproval may or may not be reinforcing for the behavior which they follow; sanctions, whether positive or negative, may or may not be reinforcing when behavior is emitted consistent with the intention of the sanction; and so on. When employed in this way, reinforcement is a variable in terms of which any behavioral partition may be ordered to determine its function.

When behavior A reinforces behavior B, behavior B increases in strength, by definition, and this increase is one form of facilitation, as this concept was defined earlier in the context of interdependence. Thus the variable of reinforcement may be employed by the role analyst to help explain facilitation and hindrance of persons in relationships of interdependence. When behavior is prescribed, and the performance of others serves to reinforce it, then reinforcement may be evoked to help explain the resulting conformity of the behavior to the prescription. When two persons share the labor on a job, the behavior of each could be reinforcing for the other in such a way that we could say that each rewarded the other, even if there were no facilitation in their interdependence; in this instance, again, reinforcement could be evoked to help account for the reward-cost factors incurred by those in interdependence.

Punishment

Any behavioral partition may also be punishment for oneself or others. There are two forms of punishment. The one closest to common understanding occurs when an aversive stimulus is *presented* following a response. A severe spanking of a child following his theft of a wallet would probably be illustrative. Note that if the spanking were a positive reinforcer for the child and not purely an aversive stimulus, then the spanking would serve to increase thefts, and the example would illustrate positive reinforcement, not punishment. The other form of punishment is defined by the *withdrawal* of a positive reinforcer following a response. Taking away a child's allowance following a misdeed would be an example, providing that the allowance was a positive reinforcer. If it were not, there would be no punishment. (For additional details see Holland and Skinner, 1961; and Skinner, 1953.)

Now, the application of punishment to the understanding of the functions of behavior is analogous to the use of the concept of reinforcement discussed above. The behavior of person A may serve to punish the behavior of person B and thus decrease, at least for a time, the probability of its occurrence. This decrease in B's behavior is nothing other than hindrance, as this concept was conceived earlier in the context of interdependence. The applicability of the concept of punishment to the phenomena of reward and cost in interdependence and to problems of the conformity of action to prescription and of prescription to action should be apparent as well.

As an addendum to the above discussion, it is useful to highlight the relationship of three related sets of concepts that have been discussed in these chapters. Positive and negative sanctioning deal with the intent of the behaver; reward and cost with benefits to the person; and reinforcement and punishment with the functional relationships between stimuli and responses. Sanctions do not necessarily imply rewards and costs, nor do either of these two sets of concepts necessarily imply reinforcement or punishment.

Postscript

When one considers the entire theoretical literature of behavioral science as a pool from which possibly relevant variables may be drawn for purposes of ordering the behavioral phenomena of role, many other variables than those presented here could have been treated. Concepts of imitation, identification, need, drive, incentive, cognitive dissonance, respondent conditioning, perception, discrimination, generalization are among others that are here called to mind. While the variables presented in this section were chosen because of their particular pertinence to problems of role, the complement is neither definitive nor complete; and theories of role in the future will undoubtedly make more use of the broader spectrum of variables available in behavioral science than is presently the case.

VARIABLES FOR POSITIONS

Selected variables pertaining to positions have been brought together in this section.

Membership Achievement

No individual achievement is required to be born with white skin, for the conditions that determine the actual color of one's skin are not ordinarily controlled by the individual, but individual achievement generally is involved in affiliating with a church, or with an occupational or professional association. "Achievement" is the term given to the degree to which the individual himself, through his own effort, controls whether or not he meets the condition for position membership. As a variable, achievement ranges from zero to a very high degree.

The concept of membership achievement derives from Linton's idea of the achieved status, but the notion that achievement is a variable for ordering the conditions of position membership differs from Linton's in at least two respects. First, Linton's apposition of the achieved and ascribed statuses implies that positions are either entirely achieved or nonachieved, whereas actual positions vary over a wide range of required achievement, with many positions falling into an intermediate range. By viewing achievement as a variable it becomes possible to order positions on a finer-grained scale. Second, Linton's apposition appears to be restricted to conditions of position entrance. As we have seen in Chapter III this is unfortunate because positions may be seen as having conditions of maintenance and departure in addition to those of entrance. The variable of membership achievement, when applied separately to each of these conditions of membership, forces the conclusion that the degree of achievement required for entrance may be more or less than that needed to remain in a position, and analogously, that departure from the position may also vary greatly in achievement. Indeed, every position may be characterized in terms of the degree of achievement which attends the conditions of entrance, maintenance, and departure.

The limitations of the oversimple apposition between achieved and ascribed statuses immediately becomes apparent when one tries to characterize certain real positions. Consider the inherited position of "king." Although entrance into the position involves no achievement for the incumbent, if the kingship is inherited, considerable achievement may be required to remain as king through meeting many performance requirements, quelling insurrections, and even in fighting pretenders to the throne, and if the kingship may be abdicated, then there is some achievement involved in departure. Similar complexities are encountered when one endeavors to characterize the positions designated by "mother," "father," "uncle," "Jew," or "mental patient," to name but a few. Only when the conditions of entrance, maintenance, and departure all involve either a very high or a low degree of achievement is the global distinction between "achieved" and "ascribed" serviceable (e.g., contrast "physicians" versus "imbeciles").

Characteristic Discriminability

The attributes and behaviors of individuals by which position membership may be determined vary over a wide range of discriminability. A light-skinned Negro, for instance, may be difficult to classify as either "Negro" or "Caucasian"; or an eccentric person may be difficult to order into categories of "normal," "mentally ill," "neurotic," "psychotic," or what have you. The discriminability of a characteristic generally reduces itself to the clarity of the stimuli in question and is a variable with respect to which all three conditions of position membership may be ordered—namely, conditions of entrance, maintenance, and departure.

Position Continuity

Ruth Benedict (1938) introduced the concept of role discontinuity to characterize the lack of order and smooth sequence in the cultural role training of the life cycle. She documented how various primitive cultures provided for more continuity in their training for responsibility, dominance, and sexuality than was characteristic in the United States. The "storm and stress" of adolescence so often attributed only to physiological changes, she concluded, was in fact due to the particular discontinuities resulting from prior role training.

Although Benedict used the term in connection with age-graded transitions universal for all mankind, it is but a simple step to realize that discontinuities may occur also for specific groups and individuals whenever there is a transition from one position to another. Thus the death of a spouse or parent may occasion the necessity for others to assume new responsibilities for which their prior training was inadequate, or an individual may abruptly find himself disabled, unemployed, or arbitrarily retired.

The "continuity" of any two positions between which a person may move is defined as the degree of similarity of the requirements for achievement associated with the membership conditions of the two positions. Although the variable of continuity ranges from complete continuity to maximal discontinuity, there are three noteworthy points on the scale. The first is "continuity," this being characterized by two positions having virtually identical achievement requirements; the second is "graded discontinuity," this being met when two positions differ in achievement requirements but the more difficult of these is readily attainable (e.g., going from first to second grade in public school, for most students); and the third is "nongraded discontinuity," a transition in which the achievement requirements are different and those more difficult to achieve are not readily attainable (e.g., going from high school to college, for some youths). Benedict's "role discontinuity" corresponds to our nongraded discontinuity, and her "role continuity" to our graded discontinuity. Although Benedict's "role continuity" also implies our complete continuity, she did not appear to have this in mind and consequently, we believe, she overlooked the dysfunctional aspects of an insufficiently graded sequence of positions through which persons may be constrained to move.

Joint Membership

Positions may be linked together in many ways, depending upon the basis for determining such relationships. Many formal and descriptive standards come to mind. But if one is concerned with linkages having behavioral consequences, as we are, then there are basically only two ways in which positions may be linked, to our knowledge.

The first derives from an individual's joint membership in both positions. This is an intrapersonal linkage, as it were, for one and the same individual is common to both, is affected by both, and in turn, may affect the behavior displayed for both. "Male" and "husband," "female" and "wife," "male" and "son," "female" and "secretary" are names for pairs of positions of which, for each pair, one person may hold simultaneous membership. We may think of the linkage of joint membership as a variable and define it as the extent to which the members of any two positions are members of both positions. The variable may be expressed quantitatively as the ratio of members having membership in both positions to the total number of members of the two positions, a variable ranging from zero to one. The pairs of positions named above would undoubtedly have relatively high joint-membership ratios, if these were calculated; we could thus say that the pairs of positions were "mutually related." In contrast, pairs of positions such as male—female, sister—brother, or wife—husband have joint-membership ratios of zero; in a word, these are "mutually exclusive" positions. There are still other pairs of positions having joint membership ratios above zero but much less than one. Mother—employee, male—dancer, son—employee are examples.

Nadel (1957) has succinctly summarized the importance of joint membership between positions.

> As regards the disadvantages . . . it is that of imposing upon individuals roles and relationships which are incompatible, and hence creating strains and tensions both in the personality and in the society itself. [Consider] . . . the example of the conflict of loyalties facing a woman who is a "wife," "sister," and "daughter" at the same time . . . . It has its corollary in the strained relations between a man and his wife's kin. . . .
>
> The advantages of role summation [joint membership] lie in the strengthening of social integration and of social control. For the more roles an individual combines in his person, the more he is linked by relationships with persons in other roles and in diverse areas of social life. Equally, any additional role assumed by an individual ties him more firmly to the norms of society (Nadel, 1957, pp. 70–71).

Interpersonal Contact

The second linkage between positions consists of contact between the members of the positions. Such contact is generally face-to-face, as is illustrated by a meeting between a mother and her child's teacher, but nonface-to-face communication qualifies as well. Husbands and wives, mothers and daughters, and teachers and pupils are examples of pairs of positions involving such interpersonal contacts, as are males and musicians, teachers and physicians, and friends and enemies. But the first set of examples involves considerably more frequent contact of members than is ordinarily the case for the latter set. The variable of interpersonal contact ranges from some value representing no contact between the members of the two positions to some value indicating maximal contact of some or all members of one position with some or all members of other positions.

VARIABLES FOR ROLE

The variables for role reported here derive in large part from the person-behavior matrix presented in Chapter II.

Behavioral Commonality

The literature of role contains numerous references to role as some particular common behavior of persons; "shared" and "patterned" are other terms that often have the same meaning, while "unique" and "deviant" have the opposite connotation. A definition of role in terms of behavioral commonality is misleading because the commonality of behavior is a variable (or dimension) in terms of which behavioral units may be ordered for all persons. (See also the concept of *characteristic role* in Chapter II.) The variable of behavioral commonality ranges hypothetically from a minimal value of zero, indicating that no persons display that behavior, to a maximal value representing the fact that all persons display that behavior. When actual behaviors are ordered by their commonality, they typically range from relative uniqueness to relative commonness, with many revealing moderate degrees of commonness.

Repertoire Extensiveness

The variable of repertoire extensiveness, in contrast to that of behavioral commonality, derives from a comparison of persons over behaviors in the person-behavior matrix, rather than vice versa. A repertoire consists of the particular classes of the behavior actually emitted by a person; and it ranges in extensiveness from a minimum of zero, indicating that the person exhibited none of the behaviors mapped by the behavioral classes chosen, to a maximum of the entire set of behavioral classes. Persons having relatively extensive repertoires are sometimes spoken of colloquially as "jacks of all trades," "versatile," "flexible," "talented," "generalists," whereas those having limited repertoires are sometimes said to have but "one string on the bow," to be "specialists," "incompetent," "deviant."

Aggregate Differentiation

A fundamental variable of the person-behavior matrix is that of aggregate differentiation. An aggregate is differentiated to the extent its members have behaviors in common that differ from those behaviors of members of other aggregates. Table 1 presents an example of a person-behavior matrix in which various possibilities for differentiated aggregates are laid out. Symbolized are the behaviors of fifteen women, ordered by six behavioral classes dealing with sex-related activities. The entries in Table 1 are the behaviors displayed by the individuals indicated. For instance, individuals P_1, P_2, and P_3 all evidence behaviors of class C_2 (wears female dress), C_4 (has male sex partners), and C_6 (has female mannerisms). As may be seen, the fifteen persons fall into five differentiated aggregates in terms of the sex-related behaviors given (indicated by I, II, III, IV, and V).

TABLE 1 AN ILLUSTRATION OF AGGREGATES DIFFERENTIATED BY THE SIMILARITY OF BEHAVIORS IN THEIR BEHAVIORAL REPERTOIRES

	Subject Set (All Females)				
Behavioral Set	P_1 P_2 P_3	P_4 P_5 P_6	P_7 P_8 P_9	P_{10} P_{11} P_{12}	P_{13} P_{14} P_{15}
C_1 (Wears Male Dress)			X X X		X X X
C_2 (Wears Female Dress)	X X X	X X X		X X X	X X X
C_3 (Has Female Sex Partners)		X X X	X X X		X X X
C_4 (Has Male Sex Partners)	X X X		X X X	X X X	X X X
C_5 (Has Male Mannerisms)		X X X	X X X	X X X	X X X
C_6 (Has Female Mannerisms)	X X X				X X X
	I	II	III	IV	V
	Differentiated Aggregates				

Now let us discuss the relationship of the concept of differentiated aggregate to relevant concepts presented earlier. First, a differentiated aggregate of persons sometimes is distinguished as a position. This occurs when at least one (but usually more) of the behavioral classes involved serves as a basis for collective recognition of the aggregate. For instance, in Table 1, Aggregate I would usually be recognized (on the evidence presented) as a group of "heterosexual females," Aggregate II would probably be designated as "homosexual females," and although positional recognition would be less clear in this case, Aggregate III would probably be called "transvestite females." This should not imply, however, that all aggregates differentiated in terms of sex-related behaviors are positions. Aggregate IV is a case in point, for it represents no commonly recognized category except by the slang terms "abnormal" or "queer," when they refer to deviations from heterosexuality.

It is clear, then, that while many differentiated aggregates may be recognized as positions, other aggregates may be viewed rather as representatives of a more general category containing various differentiated aggregates, or not be recognized at all. In the extreme case when an aggregate is not collectively recognized, it is a "nameless aggregate," but one that is nonetheless differentiated. Its opposite is the position collectively recognized, but which lacks behavioral aggregate differentiation—a "fictional aggregate." An example might be the position designated by "wild teenager," the members of which are assumed by some adults to behave in diverse immoral, and illicit ways, little of which may actually be represented in the behaviors of the aggregate of teenagers.

Other characteristics of the differentiated aggregate concept should also be stressed. The behaviors common among members of a differentiated aggregate may themselves be ordered in terms of behavioral commonality. For instance, among "heterosexual females," having male mannerisms may be more common than having a female sex partner. The extensiveness of the behavioral repertoires of a differentiated aggregate may also be characterized. Brief inspection reveals that Aggregate V of Table 1 (which might be characterized as "ambisexual") has the most extended repertoire.

If there is a basic unit in role theory to which most other phenomena relate—particularly those of position and role—the differentiated aggregate is a leading contender. Without differentiated aggregates there would be no real human aggregations having behaviors held in common; positions would mainly be behavioral stereotypes or collectivities having only common attributes; and social structure would be largely a cognitive system.

This conception of aggregate differentiation—and that of the person-behavior matrix upon which it is based—is general and inclusive. Above we indicated the relationship of aggregate differentiation to position. Now, castes, classes, associations, and primary groups of various types are also differentiated aggregates, although these aggregates have other distinguishing features. One key to the proper linkage of role phenomena to these various social groupings, we believe, is through further analysis of these groupings, as particular differentiated aggregates.

Social Structure: An Aside

The topic of social structure goes beyond the bounds of role theory, but there is an interface of the two upon which we should comment briefly. Any analysis of social structure requires at least two general tasks: (a) the isolation of structural parts or elements and (b) the determination of the relationships between and among these parts. This analysis of the phenomena and concepts of role suggests that role theory may contribute something to both tasks.

First, with respect to the elements of a social structure, role theory offers both analytic and concrete concepts. Among the former are the differentiated aggregate and the role concepts of the person-behavior matrix. Among the latter are the concepts of position and characteristic role, units that often appear in the culture of a group. Second, positions may be analyzed in terms of their continuity, their linkages of joint membership and of interpersonal contact.

VARIABLES FOR INTERDEPENDENCE

The two components of interdependence—facilitation-hindrance and reward-cost—may be considered also as variables.

Facilitation and Hindrance

Any act may hinder, facilitate or not affect the performance of another act and, consequently, one may view facilitation-hindrance as a bipolar variable. At one extreme is high facilitation, at the other high hindrance, with the midpoint being neither facilitation nor hindrance—namely, independence. This is illustrated in Figure 2. Acts may thus be ordered on this scale in terms of the various degrees that they facilitate or

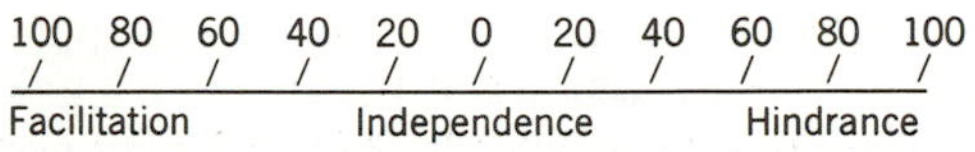

100	80	60	40	20	0	20	40	60	80	100
Facilitation					Independence					Hindrance

Figure 2. A bipolar scale of facilitation-hindrance.

hinder performance of another act. The distribution of a series of such acts on the facilitation-hindrance scale would enable the investigator to depict their central tendencies and dispersion.

Reward and Cost

Acts may affect the rewards and costs for the behaver and his targets independently of their relationship to facilitation and hindrance. Reward-cost is also a bipolar variable and ranges, as Figure 3 indicates, from a high degree of reward

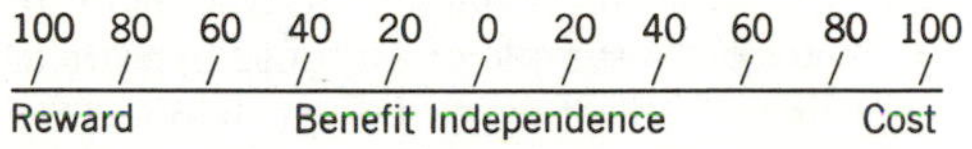

100	80	60	40	20	0	20	40	60	80	100
Reward					Benefit Independence					Cost

Figure 3. A bipolar scale of reward-cost.

through lesser degrees to benefit independence and then, by increasing degrees, to high cost. If the proper information is available, any act may be placed on such a scale in terms of its reward or cost for the person himself or for others. Again, a series of acts may be represented as a distribution on this scale, allowing the calculation of such measures as central tendency and dispersion.

VARIABLES FOR PERSONAL ADAPTATION

Among the most important yet most complex of role phenomena is the adaptation of the person to his position and role. Variables of person-role fit and pressure and strain, although global, are relevant in this context.

Person-Role Fit

When we speak colloquially of the individual who is a "misfit" or "a square peg in a round hole," we are referring generally to the lack of fit between the person and the social and cultural mold to which he is constrained to adjust. The young lady who proposes to pursue a career in nursing will find a more accommodating academic and occupational world than she who aspires to be a builder of bridges, a theoretical physicist, or surgeon, and so will the young man who desires to become a businessman instead of a ballet dancer, a lawyer instead of an interior decorator, a doctor instead of a nurse. The general problem is that the range and variety of individual differences exceed those provided by the societies' mold of alternatives, with the consequence that some persons simply do not fit well into the given system of positions.

Individuals differ remarkably in intelligence, temperament, physique, and in the learning that they have acquired. All of these differences may be reflected in the individual's particular total behavioral repertoire. But the person faces a relatively fixed social mold. The society and its component groups offer but a limited set of positions into which the individual is entered (e.g., sex, age, ethnic, and race categories) and the remainder are hypothetically open for membership. But not all of these open positions are really viable alternatives, for some are culturally disapproved, some too difficult to enter or demand relatively high achievement; and many involve the undesirable consequences of high membership costs or behavioral hindrances.

Furthermore, for any given set of positions the individual will face a particular environment of others who will make demands upon him, describe his behavior in given ways, react to him with approval and disapproval, and act so as to facilitate or hinder him and to provide various gains and losses for him. The individual cannot alter this entire complex at will, and his choices are confined to a relatively limited set of alternatives. It is in this sense that the metaphor "social mold" is indeed apt.

It is probably correct to say that few persons find this social mold fully suitable in every respect, and for many the mold is more appropriately likened to a strait jacket. Clearly, the degree of person-role fit is variable; some individuals are out-of-joint, as it were, with most of the system, while others experience only occasional petty annoyances with it. Most individuals, at least in the United States, are likely to encounter malfitting at some periods as they progress from infancy to old age.

The malfit between person and role may take a multitude of forms. Nonconformity is of course most probable, as is the conflict of one's norms with the demands of others, the conflict of one's conceptions with the statements of others, the conflict of one's action tendencies with the performances of others, and the conflict of one's own values with the assessments of others. The offended individual may derive excessive hindrances or incur high costs at the hands of others, and the transitions occasioned by life's circumstances may be uncommonly discontinuous. Any or all of these may function as pressure for the person, and role strain is certainly a most patent outcome.

Pressure and Strain

The metaphors "pressure" and "strain" are terms for two sides of an important coin in role theory. Pressure pertains to all those factors relating to role which singly or in combination are sources of potential difficulty for the individual. Strain, in contrast, has been defined by Goode as "the felt difficulty in fulfilling role obligations" (1960a, p. 483). If pressure is strong and enduring it of course results in strain.

This is a familiar apposition: the externally imposed versus the internal reaction, the stressor versus the stress, the aversive stimulus versus the response of anxiety. But there is one important difference: both the pressure and the strain are role related. The pressure may derive from conflicts of demands and norms, from opposing evaluations of the actor by others, from differences between the actor's conceptions of himself and the statements about him by others, from interdependencies excessive in hindrance or cost, from a problematic complement of positions, from a discontinuous transition between positions—and many others. And role strain differs from threat, anxiety, and stress in general by virtue of its being generated by role phenomena.

SUMMARY

A variable is some quantity the values of which may be employed to order some phenomenon, event, or process. In the field of role the variable is some quantity with respect to which the phenomenal referents or properties of role may be differentially ordered. The ordering concepts brought together in this chapter differ in specificity, function, and in precision, but these differences, although relevant in other contexts, were not pursued here in order that the discussion highlight the substance of each ordering idea.

The ordering concepts of role have generally received less attention than the classificatory concepts, but the ordering concepts are significant because they are among some of the central ideas in the hypotheses and theories of role. Concepts for variables, like those for classifications and properties, may be used for descriptive or theoretical purposes, but unlike these other types of concepts, the ordering ideas are particularly well suited to interpretation, explanation, and prediction.

Variables for behavior range from those applicable to specific behavioral partitions to those having more general applicability. Prescriptions may be ordered in terms of a unipolar or bipolar scale of permission; evaluations may be similarly ordered in terms of approval; performance may be ordered in terms of its adequacy and complexity; descriptions may be arrayed in terms of declaration and distortion; any transitor may be considered in terms of its completeness, complexity, universality and degree of codification; and any aspect of behavior may be ordered in respect to the organismic involvement it displays, the bias it presents, the constraint imposed upon it by the environment, and its possible function as reinforcement or punishment. Although these are among the variables most relevant for ordering behavior in the field of role, they are but a sample of all those hypothetically pertinent. Role theory will probably draw more heavily in the future on the entire reservoir of variables available in the behavioral sciences.

This chapter also presented variables for ordering aspects of positions. Achievement is a variable applicable to the conditions of entrance, maintenance, and departure associated with positions; characteristic discriminability is a variable that pertains to the clarity of the attributes or behavior that determine position membership for persons; continuity refers to the degree of similarity between the achievement requirements of any two positions; and joint membership and interpersonal contact have reference to two different linkages that may obtain between and among positions.

Variables were presented also that were relevant to problems of ordering aspects of role. The behaviors of roles may be arrayed in terms of their commonality; entire behavioral repertoires may be ordered by the extensiveness of the behavioral elements included in them; and aggregates may be scaled in terms of their differentiation from others. The variable of aggregate differentiation relates significantly to many key aspects of role theory, and it was therefore discussed at some length.

With regard to interdependence, the associated behaviors may be ordered in terms of a bipolar scale of facilitation-hindrance, and the benefits and losses for the persons involved may be arrayed by a bipolar scale of reward-cost.

The most complex and global variables presented were those relating to personal adaptation. In this context, the variables of person-role fit were described as were those of role pressure and strain.

REFERENCES

Holland, J. G., and Skinner, B. F., 1961. *The analysis of behavior*. New York: McGraw-Hill.
Skinner, B. F., 1953. *Science and human behavior*. New York: Macmillan.

For all references in this chapter not listed here, see bibliography at the end of the volume.

part III Positions

IN NO SOCIETY, however homogeneous, are the members entirely alike or are the individual differences among members random and unordered. In all human groups, entire categories of persons behave more or less alike in selected areas of life and are treated alike in some respects and not others. When such categories of individuals are collectively recognized in the society, we call them positions. Father, son, mother, daughter, leader, follower, dwarf, Negro, teacher, and mechanic are among a legion of positions in our society.

The individuals in such collectively recognized categories may obtain recognition in at least three separate ways. First, the members may all behave similarly in selected ways; this is illustrated in part by the persons referenced by the terms "postman," "athlete," and "leader." Second, the reactions of others may be a significant basis for collective recognition; consider, for example, the persons referred to by the terms "scapegoats," "oppressed peoples," and "outcasts." And third, common attributes may be the basis for collective accord. These attributes are apparent for the positions called "Negro," "redhead," and "dwarf." It is important to observe, however, that the members of positions are often differentiated in more than one of these ways. Thus individuals who behave similarly are likely to be reacted to by others in similar ways (consider "leaders"), and common attributes, when they serve as a basis of collective recognition, are likely to be associated with common behavior of the individuals possessing such attributes and also the common reactions of others (consider the attribute of skin color and its relationship to the behavior of persons called "Negroes" and of the reactions of others toward individuals having dark skin and other Negroid features).

All of us are members of numerous positions. Thus a person may be a male, husband, father, son, uncle, employee, college-educated person, Protestant, Caucasian, club member, among many others. This complement of positions is the individual position set. Some positions require no achievement on the person's part and are thus ascribed (e.g., male and Caucasian), others are achieved (e.g., employee, college-educated person); some positions involve life-long tenure (e.g., male, son), while others may be briefly held, (e.g., club member). Positions vary as well in the ease with which the individual may make a transition from one to another, in the degree to which the position is collectively recognized, in the discriminability of the characteristics entering into the differentiation of the aggregate, and in many other ways as well.

Positions are important for both individuals and groups. The very complement of positions in a group serves as a system of niches in which all members must somehow find a place. The very fact that one complement exists and not others and that the members of such positions may behave alike implies the constraints by which individuals come to manifest such patterns of regularity. The symbols by which most positions become collectively recognized enable persons to predict the behavior of others and to respond appropriately. The complement of positions is relatively fixed, or is at least finite and discernible, for families, organizations, communities, and society. The division of labor and the structure of such groups is indexed in part by these complements of positions, and sociologists and anthropologists often relate the functioning and accomplishments of the groups to the specific positions involved.

In the first and most general of the selections presented here, Davis defines the position concept and relates it to other structural features of groups in a social system. (Davis uses the term "status" to refer to the concept of position, and this usage should not be confused with the idea that "status" is the person's rank in some hierarchical system.) Davis defines "status" as the person's "identity" in a social situation. He distinguishes this more general concept from the specific idea of "office," the latter being a specific position in an organization. He also suggests the term "station" for a cluster of statuses that cohere in a single individual and "stratum" for a group of persons having similar stations, as for instance, in a social class. Achieved and ascribed statuses are distinguished as types, and defining criteria and examples are provided for both.

Two particular problems of position are treated in detail by Merton: namely, the complex of distinct positions assigned to individuals (the status set) and the succession of positions through which an individual moves (the status sequence). The author elaborates various functions of simultaneous or sequential membership in positions, with emphasis upon problems for the individual as well as the social systems involved.

One important implication of the fact that individuals occupy particular sets of positions is pursued in the selection by Benoit. The author notes that the positions of which a person may be a member may not necessarily be ranked at identical levels. Benoit uses the term "status" to refer to the relative rank of an individual according to some criterion. The three common criteria by which positions are normally ranked in human societies are the economic, the political, and the accorded prestige. These three criteria are sources of power for the individual in that if he has high rank on them, he may exert pressure against others, sanction others, and set norms for them. Benoit indicates also that there is a tendency toward status equilibration in most societies such that a man's rank on all three criteria will become equivalent. Various means are discussed by which individuals whose statuses are not equilibrated achieve greater similarity in the relative rankings. When the relative rankings are similar for most persons in the society, this writer says that it is reasonable to speak of the existence of social classes.

Two papers deal with positions and the terms by which they are identified in families. In his analysis of the nuclear and extended family, Murdock points out that the biological facts of reproduction and the social fact that in all societies primary socialization takes place in the nuclear family, place restrictions on the possible forms of kinship that will occur and be recognized. Murdock accounts for known kinship distinctions in terms of six major criteria (generation, sex, affinity, colaterality, bifurcation, polarity) and three minor criteria (relative age, speaker's sex, and decedence).

In a related selection, Service links kinship terminology and other position designations with various evolutionary stages of societal development. Thus, in the early stages of societal development, terminology of positions is familistic, first being egocentric and then progressing to sociocentric, and in the later stages of development, position terms are more nonfamilistic, again the egocentric terms preceding the sociocentric.

In the final selection, Oeser and Harary present a description of the structure of formal organizations in terms of graph theory. The authors' discusssion may be characterized in nonformal terms as dealing with sets of people, positions, and tasks, and the various relationships among these elements—such as power and precedence. The authors are able to provide graph theoretical depictions of personnel assignments, task allocations, the formal role of a position, the job of a person, and many other useful concepts. The paper concludes with some of the more general implications of their analysis.

selection 1 Status and Related Concepts

KINGSLEY DAVIS

IDENTITY WITHIN THE SITUATION

Essential in the interacting situation is the identity of each participant, for not everybody is supposed to expect the same thing. A husband expects sexual response from his wife, but not every man has the right to expect such a response from her. A president expects certain advice and help from his cabinet ministers, but nobody else may expect these things from them. A person therefore enters a social situation with an identity already established. His identity refers to his *position*, or *status*, within the social structure applicable to the given situation, and establishes his rights and obligations with reference to others holding positions within the same structure. His position and consequently his identity in the particular situation result from all the other positions he holds in other major social structures, especially in the other structures most closely related to the one he is acting in at the moment.

In the course of an individual's life very broad positions are first acquired. He begins with a general identity—such as that of class, sex, and family—which will later govern his position in many particular situations. As he goes through life he acquires more specific positions, and his actual behavior in the various situations to which these positions apply serves to refine and modify the initially assigned identity. Thus as time goes by he has for each new situation a more complete and more unique identity. Such progressive refinement gives a dynamic, developmental character to his positional history. For instance, a male acquires certain broad rights and obligations simply because of his quality of maleness, and these enter to some degree into nearly every situation in which he participates. But his subsequent personal history in day-to-day interaction contributes further to his social identity and differentiates him in many respects from other males.

The normative system lays down the formal rights and obligations in connection with a position. Though it permits a certain amount of legitimate variation within the limits imposed, it also lays down rules to be followed in case the individual oversteps the limits. A right is a legitimate expectation entertained by a person in one position with respect to the behavior of a person in another position. From the point of view of the other person this claim represents an obligation. "Right" and "obligation," therefore, are simply different definitions of the same relationship.

Although many norms are expressed independently of particular positions and situations—like the simple exhortation to be honest—they must, when applied in behavior, vary according to the status of the actor and the situation he is in. Absolute honesty in the sense of speaking the truth on all occasions is an impossible ideal; there are many occasions when persons do not wish to hear the truth, particularly about themselves, and will penalize the person who tells it to them. The same is true of other absolute or abstract norms. All norms, no matter how expressed, are relative to the particular situation. Which norm applies in a given case depends upon the relations between the statuses of the interacting persons.

THE ORGANIZATION OF STATUSES

Each person occupies many different statuses. We sometimes speak of *the* status or *the* social position of a given individual, meaning the sum total of his specific statuses and roles, especially in so far as they bear upon his general "social standing." More often, however, we qualify our statement by giving at the same time the context to which our statement applies. Thus we may say that Dr. Jones has a high standing *in his profession*, or that Mrs. Jones is well known *as a clubwoman*. In other words we rate the person's behavior according to the norms applying to a specific status. We implicitly recognize that he has many statuses and that we are singling one out for particular mention.

Abridged from Chapter 4 of a book by the same author entitled *Human Society*, 1949, New York: Macmillan. Reprinted by permission of the author and Macmillan.

All the positions occupied by a single individual constitute when taken together an important element in his personality. Since each person has but so much time, energy, and ability, and since his activity must achieve results and satisfy needs, his system of statuses must be to some degree integrated. His personal efficiency, his mental stability and contentment depend to a large extent on the integration of his various social positions.

Similarly, the total system of positions in the entire society or group must be reasonably well integrated. Otherwise the society or group could not carry on its existence. Ordinarily the various statuses—occupational, familial, political, religious—are so bound together in terms of interlocking rights and obligations that their manifestation in behavior gets things accomplished and the collectivity is perpetuated. One of the things that is perpetuated, of course, is the system of positions itself. Basically the positions tend to remain the same; it is mainly the occupants of the positions who change.

Status and Office

For clarity one should recognize that some social positions are, so to speak, in the folkways and mores whereas others are merely in the by-laws and rules of specific organizations. Some are generalized and known to everybody; others are limited and known only to a few. Perhaps it will aid understanding if we give a name to each half of this continuum, calling the one *status* and the other *office*. The term status would then designate a position in the general institutional system, recognized and supported by the entire society, spontaneously evolved rather than deliberately created, rooted in the folkways and mores. Office, on the other hand, would designate a position in a deliberately created organization, governed by specific and limited rules in a limited group, more generally achieved than ascribed. An example of a status in our society would be "skilled laborer"; of an office, "head carpenter of the Blank Construction Company." Another example of status would be "professor"; and of a corresponding office, "professor of government at the University of Arizona."

Station and Stratum

Since any single individual occupies not one but many statuses and offices, and since for his personal and social efficiency he must find some coherence in the several positions he fills, we could expect that in any society certain positions will tend to adhere together in different individuals. Such is actually the case and so we may speak of a *station*, meaning by this term a cluster of statuses and offices that tend to be combined in one person as a locus and are publicly recognized as so combined in a great many cases. Whereas a single status or office defines one's position with reference to a limited sector of social interaction, a station embodies one's generalized status (the sum total of one's major positions) in the over-all social structure. A station is therefore a recurrent combination of statuses having a certain degree of fixity.

The name that is given to a particular station often comes from one of the major statuses constituting it. For instance, we sometimes speak of the "landowning class" by which we mean more than simply landownership. We mean a whole group of rights and privileges which happen to be associated with landowning but are not necessarily a part of it. A man may own no land and still be a member of the landowning class, because he has all the other positions that landowners in the given society generally have; and contrariwise a man may own land without being a member of the landowning class. Furthermore, the particular position that gives a name to the whole station may not itself be uniform; it may be really a name for a class of positions which are roughly similar and which tend to have the same associated positions. Thus doctor, lawyer, and professor are each different occupational positions, but are on about the same level of evaluation and accompanied by similar allied positions. A common name, "professionals," designating a station is therefore given the incumbents.

For a mass of persons in a given society who enjoy roughly the same station, we can use the word *stratum*. Any population is commonly divided into strata. In fact, specifying the strata is one of the most convenient and frequently used ways of giving a shorthand description of a social structure. Such a procedure implies the existence of relative rank. Different stations are felt to be unequal in the public estimation and hence a hierarchy of strata is recognized. It is also known that individuals occupying the same station and hence falling in the same stratum tend to look at the world from the same point of view. They have like interests and common problems. Sometimes though not always they stick together, manifesting a solid front towards persons in other strata. We may speak of this collective front, when it occurs, as stratum solidarity.

Several types of stratified organization may be distinguished according to the kinds of positions constituting the station, the degree of stratum solidarity, the methods by which persons reach and leave the station, etc. The best known types are the caste system at one extreme and the open class system at the other.

HOW POSITIONS ARE FILLED: ASCRIPTION AND ACHIEVEMENT

The process by which the statuses in a society are constantly being filled by the infiltration of new personnel to take the place of the old is sometimes called, by organic analogy, social metabolism. Such metabolism is fully as important to a society as digestion is to an organism. In both cases raw materials are being absorbed and made to furnish the energy that gives life to the whole structure. In the case of the organism it is food substances that are taken in, whereas in the case of society it is new individuals.

Faced with a constant stream of raw material in the form of new babies, which it must so process and so distribute that the variegated system of interlocking adult statuses will be filled and the business of group living accomplished, every society is caught on what Linton (1936, p. 115) regards as the horns of a dilemma. On the one hand, as we know, the formation of the individual's habits and attitudes begins at birth; consequently the earlier his training for specific statuses can begin, the more complete will be his eventual adjustment. For this reason there arises a tendency to ascribe the individual's status at birth and to begin fitting him at once for the duties that will subsequently be his. On the other hand, we know that no two individuals (not even identical twins) are inherently the same at birth. Their capacities differ from one to another and there is as yet no way of telling, short of subsequent experience, what their peculiar capacities are. For this reason there arises a tendency to postpone the determination of adult statuses until each individual has shown which statuses he is peculiarly fitted for.

Here, then, are two opposite possibilities—the ascription of status independently of individual qualities or the achievement of status according to individual accomplishment—each with societal advantages and disadvantages on its side. Every society is confronted with the necessity of making an unconscious but difficult choice between the two. It is possible to imagine one type of society in which status is exclusively ascribed and to deduce the qualities that such a society would have. In fact, there are some societies that go far in this direction. It is equally possible to imagine another type of society in which status is exclusively achieved and to deduce the qualities that it would have. But the truth is that no human society seizes either horn of the dilemma completely. Every known society makes some use of both principles. The question really boils down, then, to what is the degree of ascription and achievement in any given case, and also what types of statuses lend themselves to one or the other kind of recruitment.

ASCRIBED STATUS[1]

The fabrication of the infant for future positions must begin as soon as possible. Socialization is at best a long and tedious process, one that is never perfectly achieved. It pays to begin the training as soon as possible when the child is in its most plastic stage.

Paradoxically, however, the fabrication of the child for future statuses cannot begin until he already has a status. This is due to the fact that the work of socialization, if it is to be accomplished, must be assigned to particular persons whose responsibilities and rights with respect to the infant are clearly defined and who are motivated by various social mechanisms to perform the appropriate tasks. Such assignment, such arbitrary connection of the child with persons who already have a status in the social structure, immediately gives the infant membership in the society and a specific place in the system of statuses. The statuses he receives at this time, some temporary and some permanent, are clearly ascribed statuses because the infant has certainly not achieved them.

However blind and arbitrary the ascription of statuses may be from the point of view of innate capacity, it is nonetheless done according to a certain unconscious order—an order varying from one society to another and yet everywhere having an underlying uniformity. The rationale of the process can be seen by raising this question: What is there about the infant that a society *can* use as a basis for the arbitrary assignment of status? The newborn baby is so undifferentiated, so inscrutable as to its future capabilities, that one wonders what a society does or *can* seize

[1] Parts of this section are taken almost verbatim from Kingsley Davis (1940).

upon as a basis for immediate status ascription. The answer is that there is little indeed to serve such a purpose. What little there is can be reduced to four categories, viz. sex, age, age relationship, and kinship. Let us discuss each of these.

Sex

The infant's sex is a definite, highly visible physiological fact which appears at birth and remains fixed for life. It provides a universally applicable dichotomy for dividing all individuals into two permanent classes, male and female. It also denotes on the part of each class a differential but complementary system of biological traits and processes which during a long period of the person's life will be associated with reproductive functions. The biological system, furthermore, is characterized by the peculiar primate reproductive physiology leading to continuous sexual interest and elaborate sexual conditioning and harboring a libidinous urge tremendously significant in human motivation. Sex difference is consequently a very convenient, not wholly fortuitous basis for the ascription of lifetime statuses. This is why in every society it is utilized not only for assigning definite statuses but also for giving monopolies on achieved statuses—which means in effect that many otherwise achieved positions are at the same time sex-ascribed.

Given this functional ascription on the basis of sex it seems inevitable that an evaluative ascription should also be made, one sex receiving more prestige than the other. Social position, as we have seen, is seldom merely a matter of prescribed activities. It is usually also a matter of invidious judgment as well.

The great error in interpreting the ascription of status on the basis of sex (as in other cases of ascription) is to assume that the ascribed behavior springs from the biological qualities of the groups concerned. In many societies the male-female division of statuses is rationalized in terms of the alleged inherent traits of men and women. In Western culture, for instance, women were long pictured as naturally more stupid, delicate, emotional, intuitive, religious, and monogamous than men. This notion justified women's exclusion from higher education and better occupations, their disbarment from certain property rights, their submission to the double standard of morality, and their subordination to men generally.

The secret both of woman's physical weakness and of her usual assignment of status is her child-bearing function. Forced to carry the parasitic embryo in her body for an extended time and to nurse the helpless young for a period thereafter, she is limited as to what she can do. As in most mammalian species her whole body is specialized to some extent for reproduction whereas the male, with his readier strength but shorter life-span, is specialized for fighting. It is not surprising, then, that the tasks usually associated with womanhood are those most compatible with reproduction. Keeping house, cooking, gardening, sewing, making pots, etc., all fit with bearing and rearing children. Hunting, fishing, fighting, herding cattle—particularly if they require long trips and great physical exertion—are not so compatible and tend to be allocated to men.

Age

Among the various bases for the ascription of status, age holds a peculiar place. Like sex, it is a definite, highly visible physiological fact apparent at birth. The baby's zero age does not distinguish him from other infants but it does separate him from older persons. Unlike sex, however, age is a steadily changing condition and therefore cannot give rise to permanent lifetime statuses. Each individual, if he lives, must eventually abandon any given category. The only way age can give a permanent status is in terms of an *age relationship* between given persons (e.g., between parent and child, elder brother and younger brother, senior member and junior member) in which case it is the time interval between the parties and not age itself that remains fixed. The feature of variability makes age totally impractical as a basis of caste and, in contrast to race or sex differentiation, minimizes the development of a characteristic personality for each rung in the scale.

Furthermore, except in terms of an age relationship, age is not a dichotomy but a continuum which can provide a basis for several rather than two general statuses. It is a continuum with infinitely small gradations, yet if too many distinctions are made within this continuum age loses its character of high visibility (small differences of chronological age being hard to detect) and its character of intrinsic social relevance (for only in terms of broad age grades can there be an intrinsic connection between the physical condition and the social condition associated with age). Hence there are usually only a few age statuses—fixed in the culture but not permanently for the person—through which, if he lives, every individual passes. These stages must usually be characterized by definite manifestations such as those of infancy, childhood, puberty, maturity, and old age. No matter how broadly they are conceived, however, the grades overlap and the classification becomes arbitrary. Most age statuses that purport to be based on physiology are in reality dependent to an equal degree on social events and attitudes that have at best only a rough correlation with actual age.

All societies recognize age as a basis of status, but some of them emphasize it more than others do. It is well known, for example, that in the old culture of China and Japan a great deal depended on the person's age, whereas in modern Western society much less depends on it.

Age status would be exhibited in its purest form if it were not limited by any other basis of status. As a matter of fact, however, it is always limited by sex status since in all known cultures men and women of the same age are treated differently. It tends also to be limited by kinship status. In the Chinese and Japanese cases it was clearly tied to kinship, for the stress was upon filial piety and in particular upon the father-son relationship. In some primitive tribes, however, everybody of roughly the same age and sex is regarded as belonging to a certain organized social group, a phenomenon called *age-grading* by the social anthropologists.

Generally a society recognizes at least four age periods: infancy, childhood, maturity, and old age. Many societies have in addition two other peculiar age periods to which they attach importance—namely, the unborn and the dead. The unborn may be believed to be the spirits of departed ancestors. The primitive Australians, for example, thought these spirits dwelt in the clan's totemic water hole and that one entering the womb of a woman was later born as a member of the clan. The Hindus think of the unborn in a vague way as the spirits of persons or animals who lived in former incarnations. Sometimes unborn children are betrothed to other unborn children according to some pattern of arranging marriages.

Kinship

In addition to sex and age another characteristic of the raw infant which can be utilized in giving him an initial status is kinship, his relation to his parents and siblings. The simplest form of ascription on this basis is the identification of the infant's status in the community with that of his parents. Even more than in the previous cases mentioned, such ascription is highly arbitrary. There is no necessary relation between the capacities of the parents and those of the offspring. Brilliant parents may have stupid children and vice versa. The socially ascribed identity between parent and child is therefore more complete than the genetics of inheritance would warrant. Consequently the universal tendency to ascribe status on the basis of this identity cannot be explained in terms of biological fact, as the apologists of class rigidity have sometimes attempted to do. It must be explained in terms of sociological principles, and the first of these is that it is socially convenient. The family appears as a universal social institution, and in it the child is closely associated with the parents and is initially socialized by them. In view of this close association and the fact that the parents are given responsibility for the child, it is a matter of pure economy to identify the child's status with them rather than with someone else. This is what was meant when it was said earlier that the rearing of the child requires that he be given a status at the very start; somebody must be made responsible for him and hence must be given a status with reference to him. The first responsibility and hence the first status connection, accordingly rests with the parents.

The child may take the parents' status immediately as in a caste system, or he may acquire it later but begin training for it at once (as in succession or inheritance). In the latter case we may speak of the process as "delayed ascription." Finally, the child may seek achieved positions that are different from those of the parents but with a competitive advantage or disadvantage provided by his parents (as in open-class occupational placement). This we may speak of as "fluid ascription," understanding that in this the element of achievement has reached a rather large proportion but has not entirely displaced the element of ascription. In any case, through identification with the parents the child becomes automatically related to the rest of the society and is trained accordingly. So important, indeed, is this *jus sanguinis* principle that a wide number of important statuses depend upon it. The ascription of citizenship, religious affiliation, and community membership, for instance, is in most cases a matter of identification with parents who are already citizens, communicants, and members. From an ethical point of view the most controversial type of status transmitted from parent to child is that of class position. The child inevitably derives an advantage or disadvantage according to his parents' rank in the social scale, and in some societies his position is fixed for life.

The child at birth not only acquires some elements of the parents' status in the larger society but he acquires a position in the family itself. He acquires an individual status as son or daughter. Since his parents are kin to other individuals his relation to his parents defines his relation to these more distant kinsmen. Thus he is not only a son but also a grandson, a nephew, a brother, a cousin, etc. Human societies universally recognize rights and obligations in accordance with these kinship connections. In some cases much of social life is governed by them. In other cases, as in our own society, the extended kinship ties have dropped into the background but the immediate family ties remain socially important. Although there is great variation in the precise kinds of rights and obligations associated with kinship statuses, the fact of such association is universal.

Other Bases of Ascription

Sex, age, and kinship do not exhaust all the bases for the ascription of status. The newborn infant, for example, manifests the physical stigmata of his race. It is therefore possible to assign him a status on the basis of his racial traits and thus create in the society a system of racial castes. Since racial features are inherited, however, this basis of ascription is very similar to ascription on the basis of the parents' status. In fact, even when a racial basis is assumed there is a tendency to assign the child's position on the basis of his parents' position. In the United States a child of "Negro" parentage tends to be defined as "Negro" regardless of the fact that he may be almost totally white in a physical sense. Some of the Southern states define as a Negro any person who has a drop of Negro blood in his veins. Such a definition is obviously more sociological than racial.

There are still other circumstances affecting the child's status. Illegitimacy, for example, prevents full identification with the parents. Plural birth in some societies gives the children so born a peculiar status, occasionally resulting in death for them. The total number of children born in the family, the fact of adoption, the fact of the death of a parent, the occurrence of divorce—all these can affect the infant's status independently of his will. One can see that the so-called "accident of birth" is ubiquitous and extremely important in society.

THE ACHIEVEMENT OF STATUS

In any society, no matter how rigid, there is knowledge of individual accomplishment and individual failure. The give and take of everyday life, the intimate play of personalities in the interacting situation, provide a setting for the irrepressible expression of natural differences. People assess one another with shrewd and practiced eyes and give their private allegiance to those who are kindly, capable, talented, and original. The role and the role personality are never governed solely by the status and the status personality but are determined by individual differences of many kinds. It follows that esteem and prestige are not necessarily synonymous, that an ascribed status system is never able to hold all individuals in complete fixity. There are always men who are so cunning, so gifted, so energetic, and so drivingly ambitious that they become leaders despite every known obstacle. The history of all lands and all times is studded with their names, for they are the men who make history. They are the men who can use the institutional machinery whatever its form to control other people and can subtly change the system in order to give themselves a place in it.

Our present interest, however, lies not in the exceptional individual but in the institutional order itself. Though we know that personal accomplishment always plays a part in interaction we still must ask to what extent the social system institutionalizes the recognition of achievement. To what extent does it provide for an orderly and legitimate change of status according to the individual's manifestation of talent and effort? If the social system encourages its members in this way it will not drive the exceptional person into illicit channels but will make use of his capacities for common social ends. It will also make use of people who would not have the genius to overcome great obstacles but who, with encouragement, can put into effect very useful capacities that would otherwise be suppressed. Finally, by providing for an orderly change of status the social system can prevent the filling of high positions by incompetents who would become simply tools in the hands of sharp-witted but unscrupulous and irresponsible men.

It is not easy to say why some societies institutionalize achieved status and others do not, but it is possible to cite some interesting correlations between these factors and other societal traits. In primitive society an emphasis on achieved status apparently goes with warfare and dangerous occupations such as hunting, raiding, and deep sea fishing. In civilized society a tendency toward commerce, an extreme division of labor, urban conditions of life, and rapid social change seem to be correlated with an emphasis on achieved status. Whether such social characteristics are the result or the cause of the prominence of achieved status is virtually impossible and perhaps not important to decide; but the functional relations are easy to see. Commercial activity implies that economic behavior has won some independence from noneconomic controls; and since it deals with scarce commodities purely as means to greater gain, it offers the individual a prime opportunity to advance by the use of his native capacities. An extreme division of labor gives a competitive advantage to the person who is talented in his work; but it is possible to overemphasize this point, because a person trained from childhood to perform the duties of an ascribed status may develop a high skill despite a merely average talent. By concentrating a large population in small territory and supporting itself by varied enterprises, the city enables individuals to be readily selected for particular positions according to their manifest achievements. Finally, rapid social change provides continually new statuses which, precisely because they are new, cannot be filled by ascription.

It is interesting to ask not only what kinds of societies emphasize achieved status but also what kinds of statuses are likely to be thrown open to achievement. Obviously one would expect that those statuses requiring the possession of unusual talent would be the first to be thrown open. All the education in the world will not make of a mediocre person a great violinist or a great mathematician, a great actor or a great writer, a great prize fighter or a great track star. Next, one would expect that those statuses depending on the informal and spontaneous approval of the populace would be predominantly achieved. For this reason the theatre and the sports arena, the rostrum and the printed page have long been avenues by which persons of humble birth could advance themselves socially. Finally, one would guess that those statuses requiring such long and costly education that private resources cannot supply it and hence necessitating public provision of training, would be thrown open to achievement. The training of the doctor or lawyer in modern society cannot be accomplished within the family. It requires large schools with elaborate resources and professional faculties. Anyone who can get himself into these schools and show enough effort and ability to pass through them is in a fair way to becoming a doctor or a lawyer. The schools are therefore channels of vertical mobility.

THE RELATION OF ASCRIBED TO ACHIEVED STATUS

Both ascription and achievement are found in every culture. Each, though opposite in principle, is complementary in function and therefore essential to society. In order that the infant be fabricated for specialized statuses his socialization must start at the earliest possible moment. For this he must be initially placed in the social structure. Yet it is precisely at this point that least is known about him. The initial placement, therefore, despite its tremendous subsequent importance is a matter of arbitrary social rule based on the few available external characteristics. Later the individual's achievements must also be recognized, and not long after birth each child's accomplishments begin to set him off from others. These accomplishments, however, are already partial products of statuses ascribed at birth, so that differences of achievement can never be interpreted purely as differences of inherent capacity. Ascribed statuses, coming first in life, lay the framework within which the transmission of the cultural heritage is to take place. They determine the general goals (e.g., the adult statuses) toward which training shall aim and the initial persons who shall carry it out. When, accordingly, we know the child's sex, age, age relations, and the class, religion, region, community, and nation of his parents, we know fairly well what his socialization—indeed, his life—will be.

Ascribed statuses also give a feeling of security that purely achieved positions can never give. All of life cannot be thrown open to competition. One cannot feel that every person is a competitor for whatever status one holds. Above all one cannot feel that there is no limit to the sheer manipulation of means, no rules and principles that are fixed beyond the power of the ambitious to change. Hence laborers, bureaucrats, and professionals each band together to lessen competition among themselves. Businesses enter collusive agreements to hold up prices. Producers advocate tariffs to protect themselves from foreign competition. The community frowns on easy divorce, on repeated changes of religious belief, on rapid change of citizenship, on outright and open opportunism in all things.

On the other hand, within the framework of authority and security laid down by the system of ascribed statuses there must necessarily be some achievement. The value of achieved status is not only that it places the right persons in the right place but that it stimulates effort. The duties connected with statuses are often onerous and exacting and cannot be accomplished without hard training. Without competition there would be an inevitable tendency to demand the rewards of the status without adequately fulfilling its duties. The lassitude of monopoly and the stimulation of competition are too well known to require documentation.

The usual condition in society, then, is that broad outlines of status are laid down by ascription while many specific statuses are open to achievement. Even an ascribed status requires, unless it is purely passive, some degree of training. A king who rules by divine right must nevertheless know something about the behavior required of a king. Even an achieved status is usually limited in one way or another by ascription. The usual mode of limitation of achieved status is through limitation of the number of competitors. In a sense the presidency of the United States is an achieved office, since no one can get there without going through the competitive process of winning an election. But the Constitution forbids anyone to compete for this office who is not a native born citizen, not thirty-five years of age or over, and not at least fourteen years a resident within the country. Furthermore, we know that there are certain customary limitations that are as effective as if they were written into the constitution. No woman, no Negro, no Oriental, no Jew has ever been president. It is conceivable that one of these might someday get the office, but it will be only by overcoming a great handicap. Thus [a large proportion] in the United States are effectively excluded from becoming president of the United States. Nearly always there are such limitations on achieved status, so that any concrete social position can generally be said to be partly ascribed, partly achieved. In this sense ascription and achievement are abstractions, but they are nonetheless real.

REFERENCES

Davis, K., 1940. The child and the social structure. *Journal of Educational Sociology*, **14**, 217–229.
Linton, R., 1936. *The study of man.* New York: Appleton-Century.

selection 2 The Social Dynamics of Status-Sets and Status-Sequences

ROBERT K. MERTON

The status-set refers to the complex of distinct positions assigned to individuals both within and among social systems. Just as there are problems of articulating the role-set [see Selection 34], so there are problems of articulating the status-set. In some measure, these problems are similar, though not identical, in structure.

Status-sets plainly provide one basic form of interdependence between the institutions and subsystems of a society. This stems from the familiar fact that the same persons are engaged in

Abridged from pp. 381–384 of a book by the same author entitled *Social Theory and Social Structure* (Rev. ed.) 1957, New York: The Free Press. Reprinted by permission of the author and The Free Press.

distinct social systems. It should be noted, furthermore, that, just as groups and societies differ in the number and complexity of social statuses comprising part of their structure, so individual people differ in the number and complexity of statuses comprising their status-sets. Not everyone in a "complex social structure" has the same complexity of status-sets. As a parochial example of one extreme, consider the actually enumerable though seemingly endless statuses occupied at the same time by Nicholas Murray Butler, and as an hypothetical example of the other extreme, the relatively few statuses occupied by a rentier-scholar who has actually succeeded in withdrawing himself from most social systems —busy at his work though formally "unemployed," unmarried and unmated, unconcerned with political, religious, civic, educational, military and other organizations. The problems of articulating the role-requirements of the complex status-set in the one instance and of the simple status-set in the second are presumably of quite differing order.

Complex status-sets not only make for some form of liaison between subsystems in a society; they confront the occupants of these statuses with distinctly different degrees of difficulty in organizing their role-activities. Furthermore, primary socialization in certain statuses, with their characteristic value-orientations, may so affect the formation of personality as to make it sometimes more, sometimes less, difficult to act out the requirements of other statuses.

Counteracting such difficulties which are potentially involved in complex status-sets are several types of social process. For one thing, people are not perceived by others as occupying only one status, even though this may be the controlling status in a particular social relationship. Employers often recognize that employees also have families, and on patterned occasions, temper their expectations of employee-behavior to the exigencies of this fact. The employee who is known to have experienced a death in his immediate family is, as a matter of course, held, for the time being, to less demanding occupational requirements. This social perception of competing obligations entailed in status-sets serves to cushion and to modify the demands and expectations by members of the role-sets associated with some of these statuses.

This kind of continuing adaptation is in turn related to the values of the society. To the extent that there is a *prior* consensus on the relative "importance" of conflicting status-obligations, this reduces the internal conflict of decision by those occupying these statuses and eases the accommodation on the part of those involved in their role-sets.

There are, of course, forces militating against such ready adaptations. Those involved in the role set of the individual in one of his statuses have their own patterned activities disturbed when he does not live up to his role-obligations. To some extent, they become motivated to hold him to performance of his role. If self-interested motivation were in fact all-compelling, this would make for even more stress in status-systems than actually occurs. Members of each role-set would in effect be pulling and hauling against those in other role-sets, with the occupant of the several statuses continuously in the middle. But self-interested motivation is not all, and this provides patterned leeway in accommodating to conflicting demands.

In psychological terms, empathy—the sympathetic understanding of the lot of the other—serves to reduce the pressures exerted upon people caught up in conflicts of status-obligations. To call it "psychological," however, is not to suggest that empathy is nothing but an individual trait of personality which people happen to have in varying degree; the extent to which empathy obtains among the members of a society is in part a function of the underlying social structure. For those who are in the role-sets of the individual subjected to conflicting status-obligations are in turn occupants of multiple statuses, formerly or presently, actually or potentially, subject to similar stresses. This structural circumstance at least facilitates the development of empathy. ("There, but for the grace of God, go I.")

Social structures are not without powers of learned adaptations, successively transmitted through changed cultural mandates. This helps mitigate the frequency and intensity of conflict in the status-set. For the greater the frequency with which patterned conflict between the obligations of multiple statuses occurs, the more likely that new norms will evolve to govern those situations by assigning priorities of obligation. This means that each individual caught up in these stressful situations need not improvise new adjustments. It means, further, that members of his role-sets will in effect make it easier for him to settle the difficulty, by accepting his "decision" if it is in accord with these functionally evolved standards of priority.

Social mechanisms for reducing such conflict can also be considered in terms of status-sequences —that is, the succession of statuses through which an appreciable proportion of people move. Consider sequences of what Linton called *achieved* (or, more generally, what may be called *acquired) statuses*: statuses into which individuals move by virtue of their own achievements rather than having been placed in them by virtue of fortunate or unfortunate birth, (which would be *ascribed* statuses). The principal idea here holds that the components of status-sets are not combined at random. A process of self-selection —both social and psychological—operates to reduce the prospects of random assortments of statuses. Values internalized by people in prior dominant statuses are such as to make it less likely (than would be the case in the absence of these values) that they will be motivated to enter statuses with values incompatible with their own. (It is not being implied that this process invariably operates with full and automatic efficiency, but it does operate.)

As a result of this process of self-selection of successive statuses, the status-set at any one time is more nearly integrated than it would otherwise be. In terms of the value-orientations already developed, people reject certain statuses which they could achieve, because they find them repugnant, and select other prospective statuses, because they find them congenial. An extreme case will illuminate the general theoretical point: those reared as Christian Scientists and committed to this faith do not ordinarily become physicians. To say that this is self-evident is of course precisely the point. These two successive statuses —Christian Science and medicine—do not occur with any frequency as a result of the process of self-selection. But what holds for this conspicuous and extreme case may be supposed to hold, with much less visibility and regularity, for other successions of statuses. It is this same theoretical idea, after all, which was employed by Max Weber in his analysis of the Protestant Ethic in relation to business enterprise. He was saying, in effect, that owing to the process of self-selection, along the lines we have sketched, a statistically frequent status-set included both affiliation with ascetic Protestant sects and capitalistic business. In due course, moreover, these two statuses developed increasingly compatible definitions of social roles. In short, they operated to reduce the actual conflict between statuses in a statistically frequent status-set below the level which would have obtained, were it not for the operation of these mechanisms of self-selection and of progressive re-definition of status-obligations.

By the same mechanism, it becomes possible for statuses which are "neutral" to one another to turn up with considerable frequency in the same status-sets. By "neutral" is meant only that the values and obligations of the respective statuses are such that they are *not likely* to enter into conflict. (Concretely, of course, almost any pair of statuses may, under certain conditions, have conflicting requirements; some pairs, however, are more clearly subject to such conflict than others. Other pairs may be mutually reinforcing, as we have seen, and still others may simply be neutral.) For example, it is concretely possible that a locomotive engineer will be more subject to conflicting status-demands if he is of Italian rather than of Irish extraction, but the social system being what it is, this combination of statuses would seem to have high neutrality. The pattern of mutually indifferent statuses provides for some measure of variability in status-sets without entailing conflict among statuses. It helps account for the demonstrable fact that, although the statuses in a status-set are not randomly assorted, they are also not fully and tightly integrated.

selection 3 Status, Status Types, and Status Interrelations

EMILE BENOIT

THE VARIETIES OF SOCIAL STATUS

Status has been defined as relative position within a hierarchy. There are, of course, an indefinitely large number of respects in which individuals are compared and adjudged superior or inferior, and it would be theoretically possible to set up a comparably large number of distinct hierarchies and types of status. There are three types of status, however, that appear to be especially fundamental and to provide especially important and objective indices of the individual's hierarchical location in most societies. They are economic status, political status, and prestige status. The individual's standing with respect to wealth, power, or prestige will of course depend to a large degree on his relative rank in the particular concrete hierarchies which the society thinks important. The seniority principle, for example, is extremely important in many societies. It is our view, however, that the high social status of the aged in such societies derives not from the biological fact of age itself but from the wealth, power, or prestige that society accords, or makes available, to its older members. Each society is apt to take for granted the "naturalness," inevitability, and intrinsic rightness of its own customary manner of awarding status. If we would avoid ethnocentrism, however, and achieve theories which will apply to all societies, including those of the future, we must attempt to catch the basic abstract elements which any possible social structure would exhibit. It is in this sense that we consider economic, political, and prestige statuses to be fundamental types, although we concede that other types of status of a comparable degree of abstractness and comprehensiveness exist, and might, in particular societies, even become very important.

Abridged from *American Sociological Review*, 1944, **9**, 151–161. Reprinted by permission of the author and the American Sociological Association.

Political and Economic Status

Power is the capacity to make (or participate in) decisions which require other individuals to act in ways in which they would not act in the absence of such decisions. Wealth or income is the possession of goods or services (or claims to goods or services) which yield satisfaction directly or facilitate the production of more goods and services. In normal economic relationships in a competitive market economy, wealth is always offered as part of an exchange in which both parties alike stand to gain. The ratio in which the different forms of wealth exchange are, moreover, approximately established by the competitive bidding of many buyers and many sellers, so that neither the buyer nor the seller confers any particular favor on the other. When confined to such uses wealth is not identical with power, and its chief value to those who hold it is its capacity to provide creature comforts, and not any delight of domination. Power on the other hand enables the individual to act "arbitrarily," and to "punish" or "reward" others. It is true, of course, that the use of wealth outside of market relationships, where there is no objectively determined normal price for a particular commodity or service, conveys power since the price paid can either convey a favor or impose a punishment. To the extent that the relationship diverges from the pole of pure competition and approaches that of monopoly it loses its economic, and takes on a political, character.

The right to transfer wealth by gift or bequest (i.e. in the absence of a *quid pro quo*) necessarily endows the property holder with arbitrary power, but such a right is not an intrinsic and essential part of the right to private property, and it has already been substantially limited by inheritance and gift taxation. In sum, wealth in our society frequently confers political as well as economic status but not insofar as it is used within the confines of a purely economic (market competitive) situation.

The fact that political and economic status are distinct in essence, is further evidenced by the fact that a perfect correlation between the two types of status does not always obtain. Thus, under the Russian Soviet system, particularly in the early phase of strong communist idealism, a high political status did not guarantee a high economic status. The party leaders who wielded immense power possessed virtually no wealth and enjoyed incomes which were much lower than the incomes of many private traders, artists, engineers, and others of much lower political status. Moreover, in modern capitalist democracies, there are at least a few rich men who, because of lack of political ambition or because of democratic scruples, have not used their wealth to buy power, and have a far lower political status than some men of comparatively low economic status (as, e.g., government officials and trade union leaders).

Prestige Status

The chief criteria of prestige are five in number. The person of high prestige is: (a) an object of admiration, (b) an object of deference, (c) an object of imitation, (d) a source of suggestion, and (e) a center of attraction. The admiration may or may not be based on objective characteristics or personal achievements. Deference is the symbolic expression of another's priority: it is manifested in the presumptive right of another to take the initiative in many social relations, to enter first or to occupy a special "place of honor" in certain assemblies and ceremonies, to be addressed in certain distinctive ways, and, other factors being equal, to be given specially favored treatment in many social situations. With regard to imitation we may say that the behavior of the person of high prestige becomes a model and is deliberately or unconsciously reproduced by others. Deliberate imitation may be intended to create a favorable impression upon the one imitated, but in many cases some psychological mechanism like identification will probably be required to account for the imitative behavior. Those having high prestige status are sources of suggestion, in that the ideas they express are accepted more readily than the same ideas expressed by others.

The fact that the man of high prestige is also a center of attraction has particular sociological interest. This attraction results from the fact that prestige is *contagious*. Those who associate with people of high prestige, participate in that prestige; even fleeting contact confers some prestige. ("Shake hands with the man who shook hands with the President.") Prestige contagion is a common-place phenomenon, though its psychological origin, like that of prestige suggestion, remains obscure. It shows an undoubted resemblance to other psychological contagion phenomena, as, e.g., contagious magic. Those who regularly associate with a person of high prestige status, come, in some mysterious fashion, to "participate" in the prestige, at least to the extent of raising their own. For this reason even menial offices rendered to a king tend to ennoble, and the servants of the great assume a supercilious demeanor. *Per contra*, close association with those of markedly lower prestige status tends to degrade. These facts explain in large part the ceaseless struggle of those of low prestige to lessen the physical, and *a fortiori* the social distance separating them from those of high prestige; and the no less determined efforts of those of high prestige to avoid physical and *a fortiori social* propinquity with those of lower prestige. Prestige contagion and prestige participation explain the various manifestations of the nearly universal phenomena of social climbing and snobbery.

Since the members of a family are in a relationship of peculiar intimacy, they will in most societies participate to some degree in one another's prestige status, and particularly in the prestige status of the "head" of the family (however defined). (The degree of participation may of course be limited by sex or other considerations.) Marrying into a family of high prestige is therefore a major method of prestige participation. In some societies the normal explanation of A's high prestige lies in his (socially defined) biological or in-law relationship to B.

Data on the importance of participation techniques in our own society may be found in the society columns of the daily newspaper. In the particular social stratum popularly known as "society," the acquisition, maintenance, and improvement of prestige status is a dominant preoccupation. It is remarkable how nearly exclusively the news about this stratum is concerned with the topic of social distance. Almost without exception the reports tell who entertained or was entertained by whom, who was married, or was promised in marriage to whom, who appeared (and in what company) at some public gathering, and who has become a member of a charitable or other group (of which the previously existing membership is known). Even where the ostensible concern of the narrative is the artistic or charitable activities of certain individuals, it requires no very practiced eye to perceive that the real interest resides in the question of who thereby associates with whom. Moreover, any description of the principals involved (especially when the news is concerned with engagements, marriages, births, or deaths) places heavy emphasis on genealogical data, revealing the major role of prestige participation in social location within this social stratum.

It may be well to remark at this point that the above described criteria of prestige should not be confused with the sources or occasions of prestige. Skill, beauty, strength, old age, wisdom, luck, holiness, insanity, and many other attributes may in particular societies be sources of prestige, depending upon the society's value system. In our society, for example, beauty is a major source of prestige for women, but an insignificant source for men. The *criteria* of prestige, as distinguished from the *sources* of prestige, are not characteristics of persons as such, but of the social interactions surrounding persons.

Interrelation of Forms of Status

That prestige status is not identical with economic and political status is suggested by the following observations. First, in some societies high prestige status is sometimes possessed by learned or holy men whose economic and political status are both low. Second, there have been many examples of dispossessed aristocracies, which maintained a high prestige status for some time after losing both their money and their power. Third, there is the significant prejudice against *nouveaux arrivés*, which results in their being accorded a lower prestige status than others of the same economic or political status who have inherited their possessions. The millionaire who has just made his money does not rank as high in the "social elite" as the somewhat less wealthy millionaire who inherited the money from his great-grandfather. "The 400," "the social registerites," "the best people," "the smart set,"—these groups are not completely identical with the richest or the most powerful members of a community.[1]

On the other hand, there is no denying that prestige status is to a very large degree dependent on the other types. It is significant that the dispossessed aristocrat does not indefinitely retain his prestige unless he is sooner or later able to win back his power. Similarly, the *nouveaux riches*, though snubbed persistently, do sooner or later gain in prestige status providing they retain their money. We have to do here with one phase of an interesting social process which we may name "status conversion." Wealth is frequently "converted" into power by direct or indirect bribery, by purchasing posts of command or weapons of coercion, by hiring the services of guards or soldiers or propagandists. Power, on the other hand, may be converted into wealth by direct forceful appropriation and enslavement, by levying tribute and taxes, and by securing strategic economic positions shielded against the impact of competition (franchises, tariffs, or other forms of monopolistic advantage). The conversion of economic or political status into prestige status possesses certain special features which are worthy of attention. One technique frequently utilized is buying or forcibly appropriating the external manifestations of prestige (titles, badges, offices, etc.). Another and a more subtle method is buying or forcibly winning a favorable reduction in social distance through imposed intimacy or familial alliances and thereby participating in the high prestige status of others.

It would appear, moreover, that certain psychological tendencies facilitate prestige conversion in a more direct fashion. A variety of suggestion, comparable perhaps to the "halo effect" which psychologists have discovered in other fields, leads the uncritical or unsophisticated observer to assume a prestige status corresponding to the political or economic status displayed. Status is perceived "globally" by the unsophisticated as a homogeneous unit. Evidence of much wealth or of high political status creates an undifferentiated total impression of "greatness" and produces a sort of awe in the ordinary beholder. Shakespeare's audience felt strongly that "there's such divinity doth hedge a king, that treason can but peep to what it would"; and many persons today cannot help being "impressed"

[1] Professor Warner (1941, p. 788) found in his field investigations a lack of exact correlation between economic status and what we should call prestige status. "Some of the men," he writes, "who were consistently placed at the top of the social heap, had less money than those at the bottom."

when first introduced into the presence of a multimillionaire or a dictator, no matter how the wealth or power in question has been acquired. A term which might well be utilized to designate this psychological aspect of status conversion is "status displacement."

Status Equilibration

As a result of status conversion processes which are normally at work in every society, there exists a real tendency for the different types of status to reach a common level, i.e., for a man's position in the economic hierarchy to match his position in the political hierarchy and for the latter to accord with his position in the hierarchy of prestige, etc. This tendency may conveniently be called "status equilibration," and a social situation in which a high degree of correlation obtains between the different forms of status, an "equilibrium status structure." There are historical grounds for supposing that when legal, customary, or other barriers seriously hamper the equilibrating tendency, social tensions of revolutionary magnitude may be generated.

The idea of status equilibrium enables us to achieve a more exact conception of the nature of *social* status. Existing usage with reference to this term is almost anarchical. The terms "status," "social status," "socio-economic status," and "economic status" are all used more or less interchangeably and without specific denotation. We, on our part, have defined status as relative position in a hierarchy and have distinguished carefully between the three chief hierarchies and the corresponding three types of status. There remains the question whether the term "social status" is to be assigned a meaning distinct from any of the special status types. Sociologists as well as laymen apparently find occasions when they wish to refer to an undifferentiated type of status which is not specifically economic, or specifically political, but generically "social." Within the framework of the "equilibration" theory this concept can be given meaning. "Social status" is the limiting term of the status equilibrating process: it is the status which would exist if the equilibrating process were to be completed and if a perfect equilibrium status structure were present. A first approximation to it would be obtained by taking an average of the separate economic, political, and prestige statuses of the individual or group in question. Closer approximations would be achieved by introducing corrections based on existing conversion tendencies properly weighted according to their relative potency.

While there are many situations in which an unsophisticated use of the term will be adequate, we would certainly favor the use of specific status categories wherever possible, and an avoidance of the term *social* status unless the undifferentiated form is specifically meant. In the latter case, two general considerations at least should be borne in mind. In the first place, the concept will be more easily and realistically applied in a social situation in which a high degree of status equilibrium already exists. It seems a reasonable hypothesis that the degree of status equilibrium varies directly with the simplicity of the social structure. Thus in the societies of preliterates there is a good probability that the political chief is the richest man and has the highest prestige. In our highly differentiated society, particularly in urban areas, the high degree of dissociation between economic, political, and prestige hierarchies makes difficult the ready ascription of a single social status to any individual. In the second place, it will be desirable to remember that, while a simple average (of the three specific statuses) may yield an approximation adequate for certain purposes, a more exact estimate will require a judgment as to the strength of the various currents of conversion, and the relative importance of each status type in a given society and a given period. In fact, the data suggest that economic status has been the dominating element in our own recent history, and that the priority may possibly be shifting to political status at this time.

REFERENCES

Warner, W. L., 1941. Social anthropology and the modern community. *American Journal of Sociology*, **46**, 785–796.

selection 4 Analysis of Kinship

GEORGE P. MURDOCK

A kinship system differs in one important respect from [other] types of social organization. In the various forms of the family, sib, clan, and community, interpersonal relationships are structured in such a manner as to aggregate individuals into social groups. A kinship system, however, is not a social group, nor does it ever correspond to an organized aggregation of individuals. It is merely a structured system of relationships in which individuals are bound one to another by complex interlocking and ramifying ties. Particular kinship bonds, isolated from others, may and often do serve to unite individuals into social groups, such as a nuclear family or a lineage, but kinship systems as wholes are not, and do not produce, social aggregates.

Within the nuclear family are found eight characteristic relationships. Though functionally differentiated, all tend to be characterized, as compared with extra-family relationships, by a high degree of reciprocal cooperation, loyalty, solidarity, and affection. Despite cultural differences, each of the eight primary relationships reveals a markedly similar fundamental character in all societies, in consequence of the universality of the family's basic functions. These relationships, with their most typical features, are as follows:

Husband and wife: economic specialization and cooperation; sexual cohabitation; joint responsibility for support, care, and upbringing of children; well defined reciprocal rights with respect to property, divorce, spheres of authority, etc.

Father and son: economic cooperation in masculine activities under leadership of the father; obligation of material support, vested in father during childhood of son, in son during old age of father; responsibility of father for instruction and discipline of son; duty of obedience and respect on part of son, tempered by some measure of comradeship.

Mother and daughter: relationship parallel to that between father and son, but with more emphasis on child care and economic cooperation and less on authority and material support.

Mother and son: dependence of son during infancy; imposition of early disciplines by the mother; moderate economic cooperation during childhood of son; early development of a lifelong incest taboo; material support by son during old age of mother.

Father and daughter: responsibility of father for protection and material support prior to marriage of daughter; economic cooperation, instruction, and discipline appreciably less prominent than in father-son relationship; playfulness common in infancy of daughter, but normally yields to a measure of reserve with the development of a strong incest taboo.

Elder and younger brother: relationship of playmates, developing into that of comrades; economic cooperation under leadership of elder; moderate responsibility of elder for instruction and discipline of younger.

Elder and younger sister: relationship parallel to that between elder and younger brother but with more emphasis upon physical care of the younger sister.

Brother and sister: early relationship of playmates, varying with relative age; gradual development of an incest taboo, commonly coupled with some measure of reserve; moderate economic cooperation; partial assumption of parental role, especially by the elder.

All of the above relationships, naturally with local elaborations, are found in any complete family with at least two children of each sex. A typical male in every society, at some time in his life, plays the roles of husband, father, son, and brother in some nuclear family, and a female, those of wife, mother, daughter, and sister. Incest taboos, however, prevent a man from being husband and father in the same family in which

---

Abridged from Chapter 6 of a book by the same author entitled *Social Structure*, 1949, New York: Macmillan. Reprinted by permission of the author and Macmillan.

he is son and brother, and a woman from being wife and mother in the family where she is daughter and sister. Both, on marrying, become members of a nuclear family other than that into which they were born. Hence, as we have seen, every normal adult individual in any society belongs to two nuclear families, the family of orientation in which he was born and reared and the family of procreation which he establishes by marriage. He is a son or daughter and a brother or sister in the former, a husband or wife and a father or mother in the latter.

It is this universal fact of individual membership in two nuclear families that gives rise to kinship systems. If marriages normally took place within the nuclear family, there would be only family organization; kinship would be confined to the limits of the family. But by virtue of the fact that individuals regularly belong to two families, every person forms a link between the members of his family of orientation and those of his family of procreation, and ramifying series of such links bind numbers of individuals to one another through kinship ties.

The term *primary relatives* is applied to those who belong to the same nuclear family as a particular person—his father, mother, sisters, and brothers in his family of orientation, and his husband or wife, his sons, and his daughters in his family of procreation. Each of these relatives will have his own primary relatives, most of whom will not be included among the primary relatives of Ego. From the point of view of the latter these may be called *secondary relatives.* Potentially, a person can have 33 distinct kinds of secondary relatives, namely: FaFa (paternal grandfather), FaMo (paternal grandmother), FaBr (paternal uncle), FaSi (paternal aunt), FaWi (stepmother), FaSo (half brother), FaDa (half sister), MoFa, MoMo, MoBr, MoSi, MoHu, MoSo, MoDa, BrWi, BrSo, BrDa, SiHu, SiSo, SiDa, WiFa (or HuFa), WiMo (or HuMo), WiBr (or HuBr), WiSi (or HuSi), WiHu (or HuWi, i.e., co-spouse), WiSo (or HuSo), WiDa (or HuDa), SoWi, SoSo, SoDa, DaHu, DaSo, and DaDa. Each secondary relative, in turn, has primary relatives who are neither primary nor secondary relatives of Ego, and who may thus be termed *tertiary relatives.* Among these there are 151 possibilities, including eight great-grandparents, eight first cousins, the spouses of all uncles, aunts, nephews, and nieces, and many others. It would be possible in similar fashion to distinguish quaternary relatives (like first cousins once removed), quinary relatives (like second cousins), etc., but for our purposes it will be sufficient to class all who are more remote than tertiary relatives as *distant relatives.*

Primary relatives are linked by bonds of blood or biological kinship, with one exception, namely, husband and wife, who, because of incest taboos, are linked only by a marital bond. This gives rise to a fundamental dichotomy in relatives at all levels. Whenever the connection between two relatives, whether primary, secondary, tertiary, or distant, includes one or more marital links, the two have no necessary biological relationship and are classed as *affinal* relatives. WiMo, DaHu, and MoBrWi are examples. Relatives between whom every connecting link is one of blood or common ancestry, on the other hand, are known as *consanguineal relatives.*

Kinship systems constitute one of the universals of human culture. The author is not aware of any society, however primitive or decadent, that does not recognize a system of culturally patterned relationships between kinsmen. Remembrance of kinship ties naturally tends to disappear with time and with remoteness of actual relationship, but social groupings, like those based on common residence or descent, often help to preserve the memory of tradition of certain kinship bonds for surprising periods. Indeed, the author knows of no society which does not reckon kinship well beyond tertiary relatives, at least in some directions.

Even if we ignore for the moment some of the finer distinctions between relatives made by some societies, any individual in any society has potentially seven different kinds of primary relatives, 33 of secondary relatives, 151 of tertiary relatives, and geometrically increasing numbers of distant relatives of various degrees. To associate a distinctive pattern of behavior with each potentially distinguishable category of relationship would be impracticable and intolerably burdensome, and no society attempts to do so. The problem is solved in all societies by reducing the number of culturally distinguished categories to a manageable number through grouping or coalescence. The varying methods by which such coalescence is accomplished give rise to many of the principal differences in kinship structure. Before they are considered, however, it is necessary to introduce the subject of kinship terminology.

Part of the reciprocal behavior characterizing every relationship between kinsmen consists of a verbal element, the terms by which each addresses the other. Although some peoples commonly employ personal names even among relatives, all societies make at least some use of special kinship terms and the great majority use them predominantly or exclusively in intercourse between relatives. An interesting and fairly common usage intermediate between personal names and kinship terms is called *teknonymy* (Tylor, 1889, p. 248). In its most typical form it consists in calling a person who has had a child "father (or mother) of So-and-so," combining the parental term with the child's name, instead of using a personal name or a kinship term.

Kinship terms are technically classified in three different ways—by their mode of use, by their linguistic structure, and by their range of application (Lowie, 1928, p. 264). As regards their use, kinship terms may be employed either in direct address or in indirect reference. A *term of address* is one used in speaking to a relative; it is part of the linguistic behavior characteristic of the particular interpersonal relationship. A *term of reference* is one used to designate a relative in speaking about him to a third person; it is thus not part of the relationship itself but a word denoting a person who occupies a particular kinship status. In English, most terms for consanguineal relatives are employed in both ways, though "nephew" and "niece" are seldom used in direct address. Terms for affinal relatives are rarely used in address by English speakers, consanguineal terms or personal names being substituted. Thus a man normally addresses his mother-in-law as "mother," his stepfather as "father," and his brother-in-law by the latter's given name or a nickname. The special terms of address in English are mainly diminutive or colloquial, e.g., "grandpa," "granny," "auntie," "dad," "papa," "ma," "mummy," "hubby," "sis," and "sonny." Some peoples have completely distinct sets of terms for address and reference, others make only grammatical distinctions or none at all, and still others have varying combinations.

Terms of reference are normally more specific in their application than terms of address. Thus, in English, "mother" as a term of reference ordinarily denotes only the actual mother, but as a term of address it is commonly applied also to a stepmother, a mother-in-law, or even an unrelated elderly woman. Moreover, terms of reference are usually more complete than terms of address. It may be customary to use only personal names in addressing certain relatives, or a taboo may prevent all conversation with them, with the result that terms of address for such kinsmen may be completely lacking. Furthermore, terms of address tend to reveal more duplication and overlapping than do terms of reference. For these reasons, terms of reference are much more useful in kinship analysis, and are consequently used exclusively in the present work.

When classified according to linguistic structure kinship terms are distinguished as elementary, derivative, and descriptive (Lowie, 1932, p. 568; Davis and Warner, 1937, p. 303). An *elementary term* is an irreducible word, like English "father" or "nephew," which cannot be analyzed into component lexical elements with kinship meanings. A *derivative term* is one which, like English "grandfather," "sister-in-law," or "stepson," is compounded from an elementary term and some other lexical element which does not have primarily a kinship meaning. A *descriptive term* is one which, like Swedish *farbror* (father's brother), combines two or more elementary terms to denote a specific relative. In actual use, the qualifying lexical element in derivative terms is quite commonly dropped unless there is need to be precise. Thus, in English, a man is as likely to say "my son" as "my stepson" in referring to his wife's son by a previous marriage, and in many societies a mother's sister is optionally referred to as "mother" or designated by a derivative term translatable as "little mother." In all languages it is apparently possible to resort to a descriptive term if the reference of any other term is ambiguous. Thus in English, if I mention "my sister-in-law" and am asked to specify which one, I can refer to either "my brother's wife" or "my wife's sister," or even to "my elder brother's second wife," etc. Except for such supplementary clarrifying use, descriptive terms appear only sporadically in kinship terminologies.

As regards range of application, kinship terms are differentiated as denotative and classificatory. A *denotative term* is one which applies only to relatives in a single kinship category as defined by generation, sex, and genealogical connection. Sometimes such a term, for a particular speaker, can denote only one person, as in the case of English "father," "mother," "husband," "wife," "father-in-law," and "mother-in-law" (see Davis and Warner, 1937). Often, however, a denotative term applies to several persons of identical kinship connection, as do the English words "brother," "sister," "son," "daughter," "son-in-law," and "daughter-in-law." A *classificatory term* is one that applies to persons of two or more kinship categories, as these are defined by generation, sex, and genealogical connection. Thus, in English, "grandfather" includes both the father's father and the mother's father; "aunt" denotes a sister of either parent or a wife of either a maternal or a paternal uncle; "brother-in-law" applies equally to a wife's or a husband's brother or a sister's husband; and "cousin" embraces all collateral relatives of one's own generation, and some of adjacent generations, irrespective of their sex, their line of genealogical connection, or even their degree of remoteness. It is primarily through the liberal use of classificatory terms that all societies reduce the number of kinship categories from the thousands that are theoretically distinguishable to the very modest number, perhaps 25 as an approximate average (Kroeber, 1909, p. 79), which it has everywhere been found practicable to recognize in actual usage.

The several categories of primary relatives (Fa, Mo, Br, Si, Hu, Wi, So, Da) are denoted by as many different terms in the great majority of societies. These terms are nearly always elementary, though in seven societies in our sample siblings are called by descriptive terms, e.g., "father's daughter" or "mother's daughter" instead of a special term for sister. Terms for primary relatives may be either denotative or classificatory, but if they are the latter they usually include one primary and one or more secondary relatives rather than two categories of primary relatives. Exceptions occur, though they are rare. Occasionally, for example, a term meaning "spouse" is employed for both husband and wife, or a term meaning "child" for both son and daughter, or a sibling term is used by both sexes but denotes "brother" to one and "sister" to the other. In general, however, all primary relatives are terminologically differentiated from each other. In addition, the majority of societies distinguish elder from younger brothers and sisters by separate terms, thus fully reflecting all functional differences in relationships within the nuclear family.

In the designation of secondary, tertiary, and distant relatives, though new elementary terms are applied to distinctive relatives, derivative and descriptive terms appear with increasing frequency. Denotative terms become rare with secondary relatives and practically disappear with tertiary kinsmen, giving way to classificatory terminology. This results in large measure, of course, from the increasing number of potentially distinguishable categories—33 for secondary and 151 for tertiary relatives—and from the correspondingly increased practical necessity of reducing the recognized number by grouping or coalescence. This can be achieved either by extending a term originally denoting some primary relative to one or more categories of secondary or remoter kinsmen, or by applying a distinctive term to several categories of secondary, tertiary, or distant relatives. Our own kinship system follows the latter method exclusively, reflecting the isolated character of our nuclear family, but in cross-cultural perspective the former method is rather more common.

A classificatory term can arise only by ignoring one or more fundamental distinctions between relatives which, if given full linguistic recognition, would result in designating them by different denotative terms. The pioneer researches of Kroeber (1909) and Lowie (1929; see also Davis and Warner, 1937) have led to the recognition of six major criteria which, when linguistically recognized as a basis of terminological differentiation, yield denotative terms but the ignoring of any of which produces classificatory terms. These criteria are generation, sex, affinity, collaterality, bifurcation, and polarity. They are the criteria employed above in calculating the number of potential categories of primary, secondary, and tertiary relatives. In addition, the same authors have isolated three subsidiary criteria—relative age, speaker's sex, and decedence—the linguistic recognition of which makes a classificatory term less inclusive or a denotative term more specific. These nine criteria have an empirical as well as a logical basis; severally and in combination they appear to include all the principles actually employed by human societies in the linguistic classification and differentiation of kinsmen. Each will now be considered individually.

The *criterion of generation* rests on a biological foundation. The facts of reproduction automatically align people in different generations: Ego's own generation, which includes brothers, sisters, and cousins; a first ascending generation, which embraces parents and their siblings and cousins; a first descending generation, which includes sons, daughters, nephews, and nieces; a second ascending or grandparental generation; a second descending or grandchildren's generation; and so on. Since marriages in most societies normally occur between persons of the same generation, affinal relatives tend to be aligned by generation in the same manner as consanguineal relatives.

Most kinship systems give extensive recognition to generation differences. Our own, for example, ignores them in only a single unimportant instance, namely, when the term "cousin" is applied to a "cousin once (or twice) removed," i.e., one or two generations above or below Ego.

The *criterion of sex* derives from another biological difference, that between males and females, and is also widely taken into account in kinship terminology. Our own system, for example, ignores sex in respect to only one basic term, namely, "cousin." Some societies employ a single classificatory term for both a son and a daughter, or for a parent-in-law of either sex. The commonest instances of the ignoring of sex in kinship terminology are found, however, in the second descending and second ascending generations, where many societies have terms approximately equivalent to "grandchild" or "grandparent." It is, of course, in precisely these generations that an individual is most likely to find relatives who are mainly too young to be significantly differentiated sexually or too old to be sexually active.

The *criterion of affinity* arises from the universal social phenomena of marriage and incest taboos. In consequence of the latter, marital partners cannot normally be close consanguineal relatives. Among relatives of like degree, therefore, whether they be primary, secondary, tertiary, or distant, there will always be one group of consanguineal kinsmen, all equally related biologically to Ego, and a second group of affinal relatives whose connection to Ego is traced through at least one marital link and who are biologically unrelated or only remotely related to him. This difference is widely recognized in kinship terminology. In our own system, for example, it is completely ignored only in the term "uncle," which includes the husbands of aunts as well as the brothers of parents, and in the word "aunt," which similarly includes the wives of uncles as well as the sisters of parents. Elsewhere we recognize affinity only partially, through the use of derivative terms with the prefix "step-" or the suffix "-in-law," in which respect we differ from most societies, who ordinarily apply elementary terms to affinal relatives. Classificatory terms resulting from the ignoring of this criterion are particularly common in societies with preferential rules of marriage. For example, under a rule of preferential cross-cousin marriage with the FaSiDa, the latter may be called by the same term as wife, and a single term may suffice for FaSi and WiMo.

The *criterion of collaterality* rests on the biological fact that among consanguineal relatives of the same generation and sex, some will be more closely akin to Ego than others. A direct ancestor, for example, will be more nearly related than his sibling or cousin, and a lineal descendant than the descendant of a sibling or cousin. Our own kinship system consistently recognizes the criterion of collaterality and, with the sole exception of "cousin," never employs the same term for consanguineal kinsmen related to Ego in different degrees. The majority of societies, however, ignore collaterality with greater frequency, and in this way arrive at various classificatory terms. The phenomenon of grouping lineal and collateral kinsmen, or relatives of different degrees, under a single classificatory term is technically known as *merging* (see Lowie, 1917, p. 109). Among the relatives most commonly merged are a parent and his sibling of the same sex, a sibling and a parallel cousin (child of a FaBr or MoSi), a wife and her sister, and a son or daughter and a nephew or niece.

The *criterion of bifurcation* (forking) applies only to secondary and more remote relatives, and rests on the biological fact that they may be linked to Ego through either a male of a female connecting relative. Recognition of this criterion involves applying one term to a kinsman if the relative linking him to Ego is male and quite another term if the connecting relative is female. Our own kinship system ignores the criterion of bifurcation throughout, and derives many of its classificatory terms from this fact. Thus we call a person "grandfather" or "grandmother" irrespective of whether he is the father's or the mother's parent. The majority of societies, however, make terminological distinctions between some or most of these relatives.

The *criterion of polarity*,[1] the last of the six major criteria for differentiating kinship terminology, arises from the sociological fact that it requires two persons to constitute a social relationship. Linguistic recognition of this criterion produces two terms for each kin relationship, one by which each participant can denote the other. When polarity is ignored, the relationship is treated as a unit and both participants apply the same classificatory term to each other. In our own kinship system polarity is recognized

[1] In the literature this criterion is commonly called "reciprocity." See, for example, A. L. Kroeber (1909), R. H. Lowie (1917, pp. 165-166), and B. Malinowski (1926, pp. 24-27).

throughout, with the sole exception of the term "cousin." The fact that two brothers, two sisters, two brothers-in-law, or two sisters-in-law also apply the same term to one another is really an incidental result of the recognition of other criteria, as becomes clear when we observe that the same term can be used for the same relative by a relative of opposite sex, in which case the reciprocal term is different. Polarity is occasionally ignored in sibling relationships, as where a brother calls his sister by the same term that she uses for him, and in avuncular relationships, as where a maternal uncle and his sisters' children refer to one another by the same term. It is most commonly ignored, however, in the terms used by relatives two generations removed; grandparents and grandchildren in many societies refer to one another by identical terms.

The *criterion of relative age* reflects the biological fact that relatives of the same generation are rarely identical in age. Of any pair, one must almost inevitably be older than the other. While ignored completely in our own kinship system, and not treated as one of the six basic criteria in our theoretical analysis, relative age is widely taken into account in kinship terminologies. A significant majority of all systems differentiate terminologically between elder and younger siblings of the same sex, and 100 out of 245 in our sample do likewise for siblings of opposite sex.

The *criterion of speaker's sex* rests on the biological fact that the user of a kinship term, as well as the relative denoted by it, is necessarily either a male or a female. Kinship systems which recognize this criterion will have two terms for the same relative, one used by a male speaker and the other by a female. Among the Haida (see Murdock, 1934, pp. 360–362), for example, there are two denotative terms for father, one employed by sons and one by daughters.

The *criterion of decedence*, the last and least important of the nine, is based on the biological fact of death. Like the creation of bifurcation, it applies particularly to secondary relatives and depends upon the person through whom kinship is traced. But whereas the crucial fact in bifurcation is whether the connecting relative is male or female, in the criterion of decedence it is whether that relative is dead or alive. A very few societies, especially in California and adjacent areas (see Kroeber, 1909, p. 79), have two kinship terms for certain relatives, one used during the lifetime of the connecting relative, the other after his death. The distinction occurs almost exclusively in terms for relatives who are potential spouses under preferential levirate or sororate marriage. While not itself of great consequence, decedence completes the roster of criteria which, through linguistic recognition or nonrecognition, yield most if not all of the known variations in kinship nomenclature.

Though of fundamental importance for analysis, the foregoing criteria do not of themselves explain differences in kinship terminology. The crucial scientific problem is that of discovering the factors which have led different peoples to select or reject particular criteria as a basis for differentiating kinsmen of some categories, and equating others, in arriving at a practicable number of culturally recognized categories out of the hundreds or thousands of potentially distinguishable ones. Before a solution to this problem is sought, consideration must be given to the question of the interrelations between kinship terminology and kinship behavior.

As has already been indicated, terms of address form an integral part of the culturally patterned relationships between kinsmen, even though they are an aspect of habitual verbal rather than gross muscular behavior. Terms of reference, on the other hand, are linguistic symbols denoting one of the two statuses involved in each such relationship (or both statuses where their polarity is ignored). However, since any status is defined in terms of the culturally expected behavior in the relationship in which it is embedded, there are *a priori* reasons for assuming a close functional congruity between terms of reference and the relationships in which the denoted kinsmen interact. The data analyzed for the present study provide abundant empirical support for this assumption, and most students of kinship have arrived at the same conclusion. The congruity between kinship terms and behavior patterns, though firmly established as an empirical generalization, is nevertheless not absolute.

Although there are substantial grounds for assuming an essential congruity between kinship terms and the culturally patterned behavior toward the relatives they denote, this by no means implies either (a) that the behavior patterns in particular societies are as sharply differentiated from one another as the associated terms, or (b) that the associated behavior patterns in different societies show an approximately equal degree of differentiation. With the exception of derivative and descriptive terms, which constitute a distinct minority, all kinship terms are independent words, and as such are completely and thus equally differentiated from one another. Patterns of kinship behavior, on the other hand, run the gamut between practical identity and extreme dissimilarity, with countless intermediate gradations. The application of completely differentiated terms to incompletely and variably differentiated phenomena results inevitably in a lack of strict comparability.

That kinship nomenclature is closely correlated with culturally patterned norms of behavior toward relatives must be assumed. This assumption accords with *a priori* reasoning, with the overwhelming testimony of the data surveyed for the present study, and with the experience and the declared or admitted views of nearly all competent anthropological authorities. Further exploration of the subject would become primarily an exercise in semantics, a study of the relation between words and the things they denote. Moreover, it would be irrelevant, for the real scientific problem is not to derive terminology from patterned behavior, or *vice versa*, but to explain both phenomena on the basis of causal factors lying outside of the kinship complex.

In both cases the determinants must be independent variables, i.e., causal factors arising outside the realm of kinship phenomena. Such factors can be expected to exert an influence on both behavior patterns and nomenclature. In some cases they may affect both at the same time and in like degree. In others they may change initially only the patterns of kinship behavior, setting in motion an adaptive process which with the passage of time produces congruent modifications in terminology. Sometimes, perhaps, they may even alter first the kinship terms, with behavior undergoing subsequent adjustment, but this is probably relatively rare since new words and new meanings of old words do not ordinarily precede the things they designate. In any event, the ultimate effect of an outside causative factor is to alter both relationships and terminology, which always maintain their essential integration.

REFERENCES

Davis, K., and Warner, W. L., 1937. Structural analysis of kinship. *American Anthropologist*, **39**, 291–313.

Kroeber, A. L., 1909. Classificatory systems of relationship. *Journal of the Royal Anthropological Institute*, **39**, 77–84.

Lowie, R. H., 1917. *Culture and ethnology*. New York: McMurtrie.

Lowie, R. H., 1928. A note on relationship terminologies. *American Anthropologist*, **30**, 263–267.

Lowie, R. H., 1929. Relationship terms. *Encyclopaedia Britannica*, 14th ed. London: Encyclopaedia Britannica, Inc., Vol. 19, pp. 84–89.

Lowie, R. H., 1932. Kinship. *Encyclopaedia of the Social Sciences*, **8**, 568.

Malinowski, B., 1926. *Crime and custom in savage society*. London: Harcourt.

Murdock, G. P., 1934. Kinship and social behavior among the Haida. *American Anthropologist*, **36**, 355–385.

Tylor, E. B., 1889. On a method of investigating the development of institutions. *Journal of the Royal Anthropological Institute*, **18**, 245–272.

selection 5 Kinship Terminology and Evolution

ELMAN R. SERVICE

Kinship terms are aspects of social life and in some important measure their patterns must be determined by characteristics of the society itself.

FOUR KINDS OF STATUS TERMS

Status terms can be divided into two basic subdivisions, *familistic* and *nonfamilistic*. Familistic terms include any named social positions which are found in a group of kindred or which have as their prototypes or derivations such positions—that is, any familial or "family-like" terms. Families are internally differentiated by certain genealogical or quasi-genealogical and affinal social relationships and by sex and age distinctions. Some of these criteria of social differentiation may be extended beyond the actual kin group. Intermarrying moieties (as generalized affinal groups), age-grades, and the Australian classes are groups defined in family-like terms with family-like relations among them. All of these I shall call familistic and when they are named as status positions relating to interpersonal conduct the names are familistic status terms.

Examples of status positions that are nonfamilistic are such things as occupational specializations, political offices, social classes, and the like. When the names or titles related to such positions are used and affect interpersonal conduct then they are nonfamilistic status terms.

There is another useful way of discriminating status terms into two kinds. A term which specifies a social position relative to another particular person—an "ego"—could be called *egocentric*. One which specifies a social position relative to the structure of the society itself could be called *sociocentric*. A few examples should make this distinction clear.

"(My) son," "(his) uncle," "(your) wife," "(Absolom's) father," "The (Dean's) Secretary," are egocentric status terms in their normal use. They may be either terms of address or reference or both (sometimes the same term is used either way), but the status exists always with respect to a relationship *to* somebody. The egos are placed in parentheses in the above examples because they do not always need to be specified. But when they are not actually specified, the context must always reveal who they are, for the egocentrically defined social position depends on two things: the kind of relationship to ego and who the ego is—the grandfather relationship is one thing, but *my* grandfather might not be your grandfather. In short, the "kinship terminology" that anthropology professors diagram on blackboards is usually an egocentric system.

Sociocentric terms refer to social positions in the society itself, not to a relationship with another person. Names of moieties and clans, occupational specialties and guilds, socioeconomic classes, titles of office, names of family lines, place of birth, and so on, all may in certain social contexts, in some society or another, function as status terms. All refer to a person's position in the society at large and thus are sociocentric. A person is *in* this status no matter who is addressing or referring to him.

One cannot tell whether a given word is egocentric or sociocentric, or even whether it is in fact a status term, just by looking at it. For example, is the word "father" egocentric or sociocentric? Answer: it all depends . . . You say to your own father: "Yes, Father, I shall heed your advice." Father is here an egocentric status term. You reply to a Catholic priest: "Yes, Father, I shall heed your advice." In this case the term is sociocentric, a title used for a category of persons in the society—the priest is not the father *of* anybody. Many other terms have been borrowed, so to speak, or derived from egocentric usage to label whole groups sociocentrically. "Grandfather" or sometimes "uncle" are terms used in many societies to label not only those relatives of particular persons but also for any person of the class "old men" or "respected men." Take the statement: "Why don't you help

Abridged from the *American Anthropologist*, 1960, **62**, 747–763. Reprinted by permission of the author and the American Anthropological Association.

that old lady? She may be somebody's mother." She may be *a* mother, a person of an age, sex, and familial position that merits a kind of general respect no matter whose mother she is. Similarly, to be *a* wife—a member of the general class "married women"—is sociocentric and a very different usage from specifying the *President's* wife, *your* wife, or the *prisoner's* wife. Members of unions such as the Brotherhood of Railway Engineers address each other as "brother," a sociocentric term in this case, but they are not confused by the fact that the word also has an egocentric usage with a quite different meaning. All of this should be no more confusing than any discussion of the meaning of words; some are more ambiguous than others, but in all cases the present meaning is related to the present context.

It is apparent that the two kinds of subdivisions, familistic-nonfamilistic and egocentric-sociocentric, cut across each other. Any status term, therefore, can be assigned to one of four categories. They are illustrated above.

EGOCENTRIC-FAMILISTIC

Terms of address: "Son," "Mom," "Auntie," "Dad."
Terms of reference: "John's son," "Your old man," "My kid," "She's my sister-in-law."

SOCIOCENTRIC-FAMILISTIC

Terms of address: "Brother can you spare a dime" ("Brother" is used here to suggest equality and mutual dependence); "Sonny," "Gramps" (when age or generational status is the criterion); "Sister" (among nuns); "Axe" (child of my father's clan).
Terms of reference: "He's a father" (of children); "All those men are Blackmouths" (Clan brothers); "She's a Hatfield, in-law to the Coys."

EGOCENTRIC-NONFAMILISTIC

Terms of address: "M'Lord," "Dear old friend," "Your faithful, obedient servant," "Meet my boss," "Adios, Amigo."
Terms of reference: "John's slave," "Your barber," "That is my captain," "(you'll love) my friends."

SOCIOCENTRIC-NONFAMILISTIC

Terms of address: "George" (to a Pullman porter), "Your Honor," "Sir," "Doctor," "Tex," "Soldier."
Terms of reference: "She's a proper Bostonian," "He's a Comrade" (member of a political party), "He (she) is a Scout, a Sophomore, a member of UAW, G.A.R., G.O.P., A.A., Y.M.C.A."

STATUS TERMS IN GENERAL EVOLUTIONARY PERSPECTIVE

Each of the above criteria of subdivision bears an obvious functional connection to social levels in cultural evolution.

Egocentric terms are personal, in a sense, and are used typically within small face-to-face groups. On the other hand, sociocentric terms have impersonal referents and have their greatest utility in a larger society where people meet who do not know much about each other's multitude of egocentrically defined social positions. Egocentric terms are prevalent, therefore, in the most primitive societies and within the small family units of larger societies. Sociocentric terms proliferate as society grows larger and more subdivided into corporate groups, ranks, and classes. And later, of course, in urban-industrial societies great numbers of sociocentric terms for occupational specializations which are relevant to social status appear.

The relation of the familistic-nonfamilistic distinction to the evolution of society is even more obvious. The most primitive societies are composed of kindred alone. As these societies grow larger and more complex familistic terms are extended egocentrically and then sociocentrically until a certain point is reached. This point, of course, is the great cultural revolution based on intensive agriculture which transformed tribal

STAGE I

SOCIETY

A small, isolated kindred.

TERMINOLOGY

Egocentric-familistic terminology alone.

This is merely the usual egocentered "kinship system."

Remarks: This stage is hypothetical and idealized. No known society is completely isolated, but relative isolation is a significant factor and to place a hypothetical familial group in a social vacuum helps make clear the significance of complexity. Only in isolation would a family be altogether without sociocentric terms. If one group of "other" people was present, there would undoubtedly be names for both "we" and "they," and these names, of course, would be sociocentric. They would be used as status terms to the extent that social relations would occur between the two groups. The society is "small" enough that the internal social relations would be predominantly face-to-face, consistent (hence patterned), and therefore the terms of status relationship would be familistic only and egocentric only. There would be no need for sociocentric terms, all classes of people in such a small society (males-females, young-old, married-unmarried) would be known individually and thus sufficiently identifiable by the egocentric kinship terminology.

STAGE II

SOCIETY

This stage may be thought of as including societies like the average primitive "tribe." It has in it not only domestic families but greater families in some number. They are tied together by broad familistic bonds conceived in terms of individual relationships and also in terms of the relationships of groups, segments, and categories of the society. Corporate groups such as sodalities have appeared in addition to kinships segments of societies (moieties, clans, etc.), and classes of persons (those who share some particular characteristic, such as married men, generations, etc.) are now larger and more objectively and impersonally defined.

TERMINOLOGY

Sociocentric-Familistic Terminology

Gross familistic categories such as in-law groups, generations, marital statuses, clans, moieties, lineages and various combinations of these are named and added to the previous system of egocentric-familistic terminology.

Remarks: The status terminology is still predominantly familistic because the whole tribe is still conceived of as a great extension of the family. Some of the sociocentric-familistic terms are derived from the egocentric, which is to say that terms like "grandfather" and "brother" may have acquired their original significance, etymologically speaking, from the egocentric usage, but come to be applied in a different context with a different meaning to such classes of persons as various age-grades, male members of a clan, and the like. Other terms, particularly those referring to corporate groups and segments, may not "sound like" familistic terms (The "Blackmouth clan," for example) because they are not derived from kinship usage, but the group itself nevertheless is defined in familistic terms—it has certain familistic relationships to the whole society and to its various other parts; one clan may be "father" to another, "in-law" to another, etc. At higher levels of tribal society, groups may come into being which are not necessarily nor always familistic—captives ("slaves"), craft specialists, "brave men," dog soldiers, ceremonial clowns, and so on. The transition from egocentric-familistic to sociocentric-familistic and on to the next stage is gradual and cumulative just as is the increasing complexity of society. The concepts used here are watertight compartments, but actual societies occupy transitional positions between the stages.

society into a much larger, more complex supra-tribal society. This change from a kinbased society to nonkin society has been widely recognized as defining two basic evolutionary stages of society; status terms, both egocentric and sociocentric, are largely familistic in "tribal" (or "gentile") society, but with great numbers of nonfamilistic terms added in "civil" society.

Putting the two different criteria together to make four categories results in a doubly more specific connection between the evolution of society and kinds of status terms. For succinctness I have arranged below the four kinds of terms as stages in one column, matched in the parallel column by the related levels of society. Note that while each stage is given a single characterizing name, this is only for the sake of simplicity; the new terminology is actually *added to* the preceding terms rather than replacing them.

STAGE III

SOCIETY

Society is the non-industrialized civil type, standing between tribal society and urban-industrial nations. "Feudal" society could be included (but see below). All, or many, of the elements making up the societies of the first two stages may be present, but the society is now larger and more complex and has certain new elements such as socio-economic classes, political or bureaucratic offices, clearly delineated rich and poor, and other new kinds of criteria of social position.

TERMINOLOGY

Egocentric-Nonfamilistic Terminology.

This stage has terminology which is egocentric, but for the first time, nonfamilistic. "My (his, so-and-so's) Lord, vassal, page, maid, cook," and so on are examples. Titles which refer to hereditary bureaucratic positions and/or positions in relation to other persons are frequent. In reference, titles are often sociocentric, but in address are more frequently egocentric ("My," "your," etc. being understood if not actually stated).

Remarks: Society is now of a supra-kinship order and therefore terms which refer to nonfamilistic statuses become more prevalent. Many of these, however, depend on the character of the relationship to other persons, hence egocentric terms are common even when they are nonfamilistic. This is not to say that familistic terms, both egocentric and sociocentric, do not continue in use. And as any particular society may contain a greater or lesser number of corporate groupings, occupational specializations, clubs, and so on, so it may have many or few sociocentric-nonfamilistic terms. This stage is not named because of the *predominance in use* of one or another kind of terminology, but because the new appearance of this particular kind of terminology may be fairly taken to characterize it. The fact that nonfamilistic positions have arisen in this society, but that many of them continue to take their significance from personal relationships, is a point that has been remarked often, particularly with respect to feudalism—it is a society "impersonal in content but personal in phrasing."

But a difficulty has arisen at this point that must be faced. As culture evolves it creates more and more heterogeneous societies; specific evolutionary lines ramify and adapt to more diverse kinds of situations. To take as one stage all societies which are supra-tribal but infra-industrial is to include a tremendous variety of kinds of socio-cultural systems. I do not know, in fact, precisely what I should list as the average social characteristics of society at this stage in the evolution of culture.

To solve the problem posed by all of the heterogeneity included in the present category would not be impossible. Each society would show peculiarities in its status terminologies equal to and understandable in terms of the peculiarities of its social system, as well as a commensurate heterogeneity. Feudal society could be shown to have more terms based on relationship to land and to personal hierarchies, but few based on occupational specialization or wealth. As commercialism supervenes, as in the maritime cities of Northern Italy, the egocentric-nonfamilistic terms would recede in significance and sociocentric-nonfamilistic terms relating to wealth, political office, and professional specialization would arise.

STAGE IV

SOCIETY

With modern industrialism, society expanded rapidly—exploded—with the increased size and density accompanied by much greater complexity. The number of social positions based on economic specialization and membership in corporate groups increased commensurately and is the most noticeable aspect of the new stage.

TERMINOLOGY

Sociocentric-Nonfamilistic Terminology.

The number of possible status terms of this sort in modern industrial society is tremendous. There are titles ("Doctor," "Mister," "Professor") now which do not refer to personal ties; names of economic, social, and political categories of people, as well as specific gradations within them; named professional specialties; and great numbers of corporate groups having special purposes like clubs, labor unions, and organizations in general. None of these terms are familistic and obviously they are all sociocentric.

Remarks: Although the anterior kinds of terminologies are retained in each successive stage, they may also undergo certain changes related to the general social changes. Egocentric-familistic terms from the first stage are still in use, but the system has altered in the direction of specifying individual descent lines (the "descriptive" system) as the domestic family becomes nucleated, isolated, neolocal, smaller, and as individual inheritance of property becomes more significant. Also, these terms are less used as family ties decline in importance and others gain. Certain sociocentric-familistic terms disappear as clans, moieties, corporate descent groups, and the like disappear from the society. Egocentric-nonfamilistic terms are less prominent also, as society becomes depersonalized. (A servant, for example, is less a personal dependent nowadays and more a member of a profession, perhaps even a member of a labor union.) It seems possible, in the light of these trends, that the Brave New World of the future might come to have sociocentric-nonfamilistic terms only. Even now in many modern families children address their parents by name rather than as father and mother.

selection 6 Role Structures: A Description in Terms of Graph Theory

OSCAR A. OESER AND FRANK HARARY

The purpose of this paper is to set forth a mathematical system of terms and concepts for discussing role structure. The discussion throughout makes consistent use of the concepts and terminology of graph theory, which has recently been applied to a variety of problems in behavioral science (see Harary and Norman, 1953; and Harary, Norman and Cartwright, 1965). A sequel to this paper may be found in Oeser and Harary (1964) which develops axioms for structural problems concerning roles.

Abridged from an article entitled "A Mathematical Model for Structural Role Theory, I"; *Human Relations*, 1962, **15**, 89–109. Reprinted by permission of the authors and *Human Relations*.

DEVELOPMENT OF TERMINOLOGY

Rationale for Choosing the Elements of a Role Structure

The most pervasive fact about a society or a group is that it comes into existence and continues to exist because there must be a division of labor. A group without a goal, without some set of tasks which it is actively striving to complete, is a mere haphazard collection of people.

The Task

The phrase "division of labour" implies that not everyone does identically the same job. Even in so simple a task as placing one heavy tree-trunk across a stream, different people will be active at different portions of the trunk or points of the terrain. In other words, specific precedence relationships of time and place are inherent in the task and thus are generated between or imposed upon the members of the group.

The "labour," the completed *job*, is a task system, that is, it consists of several interrelated tasks. This task system may be said to be the *goal* of the group. The concepts of task, job, or goal are quite general. They refer to any co-ordinated or directed activity of a person. Building a house will include non-physical (symbolic) tasks such as dreaming up the ideal plan, selecting a site, and estimating costs, in addition to the obviously physical tasks. Some jobs or goals may even be almost wholly symbolic, such as conducting a religious ceremony. Nevertheless, any job will be extended in time, will be continuous or iterative, and will demand that the people concerned with it be organized so that there will be a correspondence between the set of task elements and the set of people.

The total job will, in general, be split into tasks or *task elements*. How many elements there will be depends partly on the nature of the task itself, partly on the number of people available to do it. The time-and-motion expert may split some elements into many smaller ones, the work-study or organization expert collapse several into larger units.

The Concept of Position

Two quite general observations can be made about all groups that maintain a division of labour: first, the people who deal with the task elements are given generic names, such as teacher and students; labourers, carpenters, electricians, plumbers, and bricklayers; batsmen, fielder, and umpire; and many more. Second, once these names or titles have been assigned, people are exchangeable, but with certain significant restrictions. If, during the building of a house, carpenter John Smith dies, the builder will advertise for another carpenter. He will not advertise for another John Smith or even for Bill Jones; anyone who satisfies the worker specifications for the *position* or *office* of "carpenter" will do, but a plumber will not. The restrictions are thus rules or specifications for the kind of abilities (not personalities) required for the task. In other words, the *titles* such as "teacher," "carpenter," are labels for what certain kinds of people must or may do; the *position* of "teacher" or "carpenter," however, is defined in terms of sociological characteristics such as age, sex, and education; in terms of psychological characteristics or traits such as skills, intelligence, capacity for leadership, temperament; in terms of relationships to other people or positions; and in terms of ability to perform certain tasks. Thus the definition of the position. "secretary" enables us to identify (i) certain types of person; (ii) their duties towards others in other positions; and (iii) their sections of the task system. Empire-building bureaucrats have a tendency to multiply positions (Parkinson, 1957).

To sum up: tasks and people are real entities, but "position" is a concept connoting several sets of relationships between tasks and the persons who carry out the tasks.

The Concept of Person

People are real entities, but persons are not. By "person" we shall mean a set of attributes.

Suppose that the position of carpenter, or high-school teacher of Latin, is to be filled. This position, then, is said to be "occupied by a person," which means that someone is assigned to, selected for, promoted to, the position, Consequently, in so far as we are concerned with the general invariant structural system of the division of labour, the idea that the position will be occupied by a specific, unique individual personality is inappropriate. Personality has no place in the theory as yet, though it will be introduced later, when process, change, or development of the system is to be studied.

A "person" who fills or is assigned to a certain position clearly has no attributes other than those which are laid down in the "worker specification" that is, in the definition of the set of rules which enables a foreman or a school principal to select from a population certain persons to fill given positions. A "person" is simply a human being who is related to task elements through a co-ordinating set of relationships called a position.

The Concept of Role

Let us sum up and illustrate the discussion to this point by inspecting a complex organization, the family, which confronts both physical and symbolic task elements. The task or goal of the family can be described in idealistic or realistic terms or both. We are not concerned with the metaphysics or semantics of the situation, but only with what people do. We notice, then, that the father and the mother carry out some similar, some identical, and some different tasks. These may be differently prescribed by the rules of different cultures or subcultures but are remarkably constant within any given culture or subculture. Some tasks have physical goals, such as farming or some other way of "earning a living" for the father, and tasks inside the household such as repairing the roof; some have symbolic goals such as maintaining family solidarity or prestige and safeguarding the morals of daughters. Similarly, the mother has tasks, and so have the children.[1] Every culture has a minimal set of specifications for the behaviour of father, mother, and children, so that it is possible to say of someone, he is a "stepfather," or she is a "foster-mother," or that he is an "adopted child," meaning that the person in question is (or should be) carrying out the prescribed duties of the biological father, mother, or child.

We notice again that what a society calls "the role of father" can be carried out by any male person who satisfies the cultural selection criteria or "norms," and who thereupon interacts according to specified rules with the mother and the children in the general task of maintaining household and family. What are the precise specifications, the rules of action and interaction, is a purely empirical question. But in their totality they constitute *the structure of the family relation* and regulate the recurrent interpersonal behaviour sequences (RIBS) for each person.

We speak of the *relationship* between two elements (two individuals, two positions, or two tasks) and of the *relation* which defines the whole set of related elements. Thus if h_1 likes h_2 and h_2 likes h_3, there is a relationship (of liking) from h_1 to h_2 and from h_2 to h_3. The relation is "liking." Similarly, the relationships between father, mother, and children together constitute "the family relation."

The concept of role, then, applies neither to unique individual personalities nor to persons, but to positions within a structural system that includes persons, positions, and tasks. That "personality" shows itself in the way in which an individual carries out his tasks and RIBS is irrelevant to the notion of structure. That the personality of an individual may change as a result of his being promoted to a more responsible position is a problem for theories of personality or learning. We are concerned here not with process or change, but solely with the invariant aspects of *structure*, the invariant relationships set up by the rules of recruitment or positional interaction, and task requirements. If a position such as "soldier" requires the "personality trait" or attribute of physical aggressiveness, this is specified in the selection rules; an infantryman who is not or cannot be trained to be aggressive is removed to some other position in the army system. But the physical aggressiveness of a teacher is deliberately kept within very narrow limits by the rules of an educational system; and if he refuses to be confined within those limits, he is regarded as having been wrongly selected for the position of teacher. In other words, the rules are specified by what are often called "social norms." The latitude which is permitted to any individual while acting according to these norms varies widely between different positions and between similar positions in different cultures. Concepts like latitude and efficiency of role performance belong to later papers, in which role systems in action may be discussed.

This discussion was foreshadowed, and may be summed up, by the following quotation from Znaniecki (1939): "The group is not an association of concrete individuals, but a synthesis of members' roles. Members' roles and groups are cultural products, systems of values, and activities regulated in accordance with definite historical patterns."

We now have the elements required to begin outlining a structural model for a role system. The elements are persons, positions, and tasks. The relationships between the elements are specified in three sets of rules, variously called "institutional or consensus imperatives" (Newcomb, 1950) and "social norms" (many authors): those that specify the selection of persons for positions; those that specify the admissible relationships between positions; and those that allocate task elements to position elements. We shall call these the *formal* sets of relationships.

That there also exist informal relationships is

[1] For a descriptive analysis of formal role patterns in one culture see Oeser and Emery (1954, Part III) and Oeser and Hammond (1954, Parts III and IV).

intuitively obvious. Thus carpenter and foreman or husband and wife establish relationships among themselves that are not specified by the formal sets of rules, the "consensus imperatives." How these informal sets of relationships operate to alter the formal structure is beyond the scope of this paper. We attempt here to define rigorously only those elements and relationships prescribed by the rules which persist over considerable stretches of time. *In this structural system, the rules laid down by the group, the "norms," take absolute precedence over the individual's values, perceptions, or other idiosyncratic modes of behaving.*

ORGANIZING A STRUCTURAL ROLE SYSTEM

Formal Categories

Let us suppose a company wants to set up a new branch. It has (a) a new building, various machines for making a certain product, and *job specifications* of the product and how the machines are to be used for seven tasks; (b) an *organization chart* for five personnel; (c) a recruitment policy, or *worker specification*, which says what sort of people are to be recruited for the various positions in the organization chart. The positions are advertised. Fifty people apply and the personnel officer, after interviewing them all, hires five of them.

At this stage, the new organization consists of five people, h_1, h_2, h_3, h_4, h_5, who form the *set of people H*. There are five positions, p_1, p_2, p_3, p_4, p_5, which form the *set of positions P*. There are seven tasks, $t_1, \ldots, t_7$, which form the *set of tasks T*. We assume that no one knew anyone else before joining. That, to begin with, there are no relations (such as "likes") between the persons may be depicted as in Figure 1.

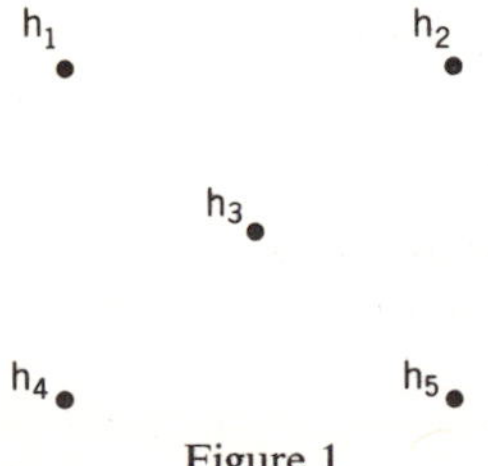

Figure 1

A figure like *Figure* 1 is called "a totally disconnected digraph."[2] The only kind of measurement applicable to it is the kind of "measurement" known as a nominal scale (see Thrall, Coombs, and Davis, 1954).

[2] [Editors' note: The original article from which this abridgement was made contains a Glossary on the terms and definitions of graph theory applied to role structure.]

Suppose next that the organization chart was originally defined as a *power* relation on the set P of positions, as in *Figure* 2.

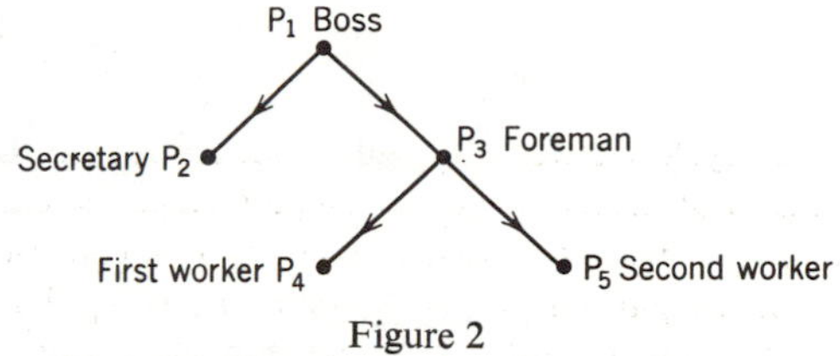

Figure 2

By the *P-graph* of an organization we mean the official organization chart of the institution. Note that this graph, the points of which are positions and the directed lines of which stand for power relationships, has a position p_1, to which all others are subordinate.

A *relationship* is a single link or directed line between two points; a *relation* is the whole graph, which may contain several relationships.

The five persons who have been hired are assigned to these five positions. Schematically we have:

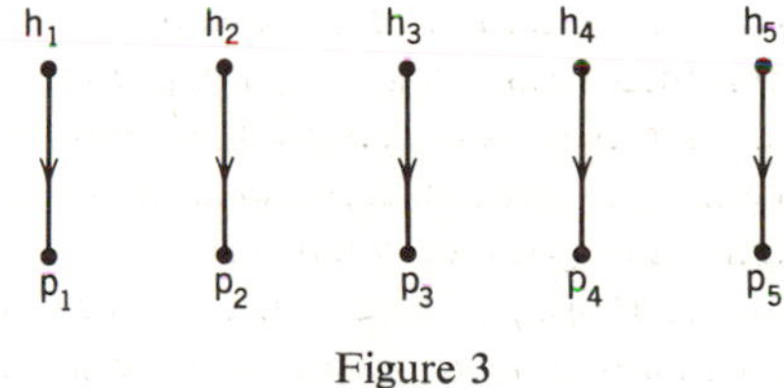

Figure 3

The tasks to be done we suppose to be related as in *Figure* 4:

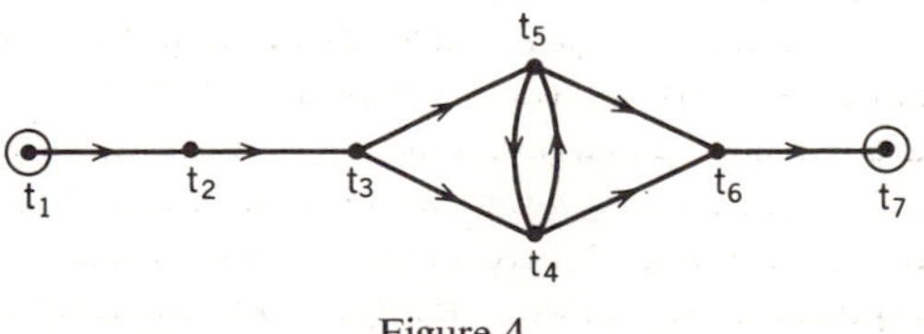

Figure 4

By the *T-graph* we mean the official work layout, the points of which are tasks and the directed lines of which stand for precedence relationships, that is, the order in which the tasks are to be done.

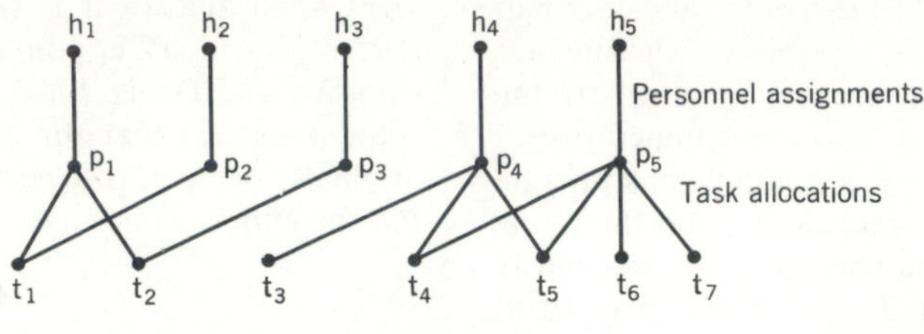

Figure 5

The cycle between t_4 and t_5 means that it is immaterial which of these is performed before the other. Thus to reach t_6 from t_3, one can use one of the paths t_3, t_5, t_4, t_6, or t_3, t_4, t_5, t_6. The circles round t_1 and t_7 indicate that these points are marked out in some way. We need to note that the job (i.e., the whole set of tasks) has a beginning and an end, and that a continuous transition through all the tasks is possible. In digraph terms, a complete path exists from t_1 to t_7.

Thus far we have the following relations:

(a) The original nominal scale on H, or H-graph;
(b) The power relation on P, or P-graph;
(c) The precedence relation on T, or T-graph.

These relations interact with each other so that the job can be done. In the following diagram, *Figure* 5, we do not repeat all the directed lines of *Figures* 2, 3, and 4, for reasons of visual clarity, but understand that they are present.

Notice that two new sets of lines have been introduced. There is the set of *personnel assignments* which tell who goes to what position; this is called the *H-P graph*. The other is the set of *task allocations*—which position is responsible for carrying out which tasks; this is the *P-T graph*. We are now ready to define *the formal role of a position.*

We observe that the personnel officer of this company, when he hired the five persons, did three things: he gave each position a title or name of an office (boss, secretary, worker); he said in the advertisement what qualifications were required for each position; and he said what the persons would have to do and who would be responsible to whom. Being a knowledgeable man, he drew some graphs:

Figure 6(*a*), in which different relations are symbolized by different kinds of lines (or colours), gives the following kinds of information:

(a) Person h_1 is selected for and assigned to position p_1;
(b) Position p_1 has immediate subordinate positions, p_2 and p_3;
(c) Tasks t_1 and t_2 are allocated to position p_1.

The digraph of *Figure* 6(*a*) constitutes the descriptive definition of the formal role of

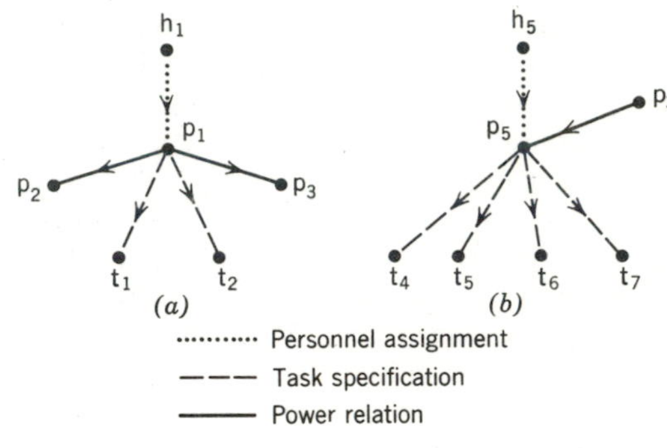

Figure 6

position p_1, the office of "boss." That is, *the formal role of position* p *is defined by the digraph which contains* p *and all elements of the* H, P, *and* T *graphs reachable from* p *in one step. Figure* 6(*b*) tells us that:

(a) Person h_5 is selected for position p_5;
(b) Position p_5 is immediately subordinate to position p_3;
(c) Tasks t_4, t_5, t_6, t_7 are allocated to position p_5.

This constitutes the descriptive definition of the formal role of position p_5, the office of "second worker."

Many students of a social system such as this hypothetical factory will be most interested in finding out who does what. In that case, the simpler diagram of *Figure* 7 suffices.

Figure 7 omits the rules which assign certain types of people to positions, as well as the rules of task allocation and responsibility.

For the ensuing conceptualization of a structural role system, it is of crucial importance to remember that people are not allocated to tasks directly, but only through a mediating set of

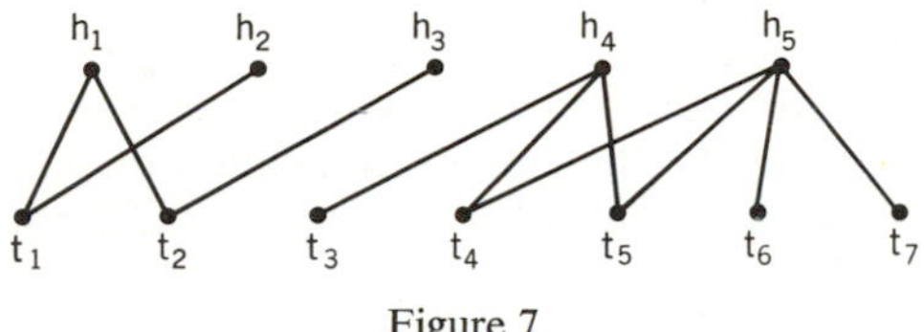

Figure 7

positions or offices. *Figure* 7 can be made meaningful for a system only by carrying out certain computations, which take into account the effects of the power relation and the position specifications. How these computations are carried out may be described in a later paper.

It remains to define "*the job of a person.*" Clearly, the job of person h_1, in the position of "boss" is wider than that which has here been defined as the formal role of his position p_1. He has power over the whole organization digraph or chart, in which he is a "source." His formal responsibilities extend over the whole department of which he is in charge, that is, over all positions and the tasks allocated to those positions. We therefore define the job of a person, h, as *all elements in the structural role digraph* D *that are reachable from* h.

This, of course, is the purely formal definition. After an axiom system has been developed, it will have to be related to empirical propositions. How responsibilities are to be weighted (this boss has less responsibility for the work of the second worker than for that of the foreman) and what the effect of such weighting is, will have to be defined by additional empirical postulates.

The Intrusion of Informal Relationships

From common experience we know that as soon as persons are brought together they inevitably establish "informal" relationships with each other, that is, relationships which are not laid down in the formal worker (position) or task specifications. In other words, they will manifest certain personality traits and activities such as "talking to others," "liking," "valuing." Thus they will not only respond to the physical stimuli of tasks or the symbolic stimuli of required communication patterns among positions, but will also behave in terms of habits incurred during their life-history and of symbolic value judgements about the tasks themselves, the people with whom they interact, and the processes of interaction.

The notion of the set of relationships on H, the persons, must therefore be extended. There is not one set; there are many sets. Each, when introduced into our new factory organization, must be taken into account, since it will interact with all the other relationships and so modify them. We suppose that, in the course of time, several kinds of informal relationships develop and stabilize, two of which are illustrated in Figures 8(a) and 8(b).

(a) The five people develop a pattern of liking (valuing) each other;
(b) They develop a preferred mode of communication with each other.

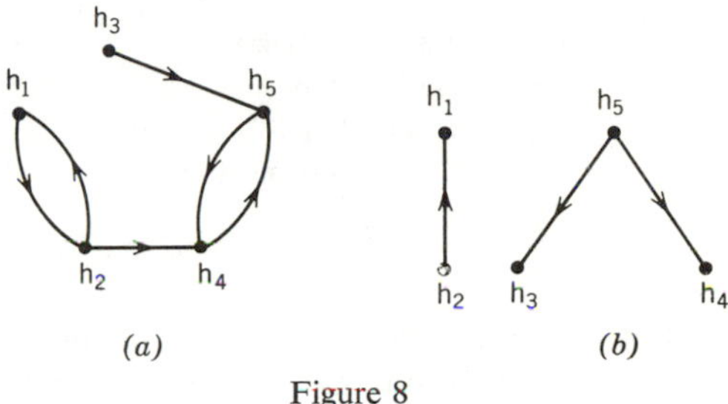

Figure 8

Superimposed on *Figures* 1, 2, 5, and 6, therefore, we can now imagine additional patterns of lines, laid out in different hatchings (or colours) to represent the informal relations of liking (valuing) and preferred mode of communicating.

Let us take as an illustration only one digraph, that of the formal role of position p_5, "second worker," illustrated in *Figure* 6(*b*). If we add the informal relations "liking" and "prefers to communicate with," using two new kinds of broken line, we see from *Figure* 9 that the role of p_5 has now expanded. Because of the preferred communication relation, h_5 is also directly connected to h_3 and h_4, having originally had no link to other persons; and he is additionally connected to h_4 by the relationships "h_5 likes h_4" and "h_4 likes h_5."

The *informal interpersonal role of person* h_5 is depicted by the top part of the figure; the *actual role of position* p_5 is the total digraph of *Figure* 9.

Moreover, in the communication chart for the whole organization (which is sometimes the same as the power relation chart), h_5 is now only two steps removed from h_1 who occupies the office of boss, because h_5 prefers to communicate with h_3. The personnel officer, being not only knowledgeable about graphs, is also experienced enough to be able to warn h_3, the foreman in position p_3, that there is a possibility of h_4 and h_5 forming a coalition against him, since each likes the other and likes no one else.

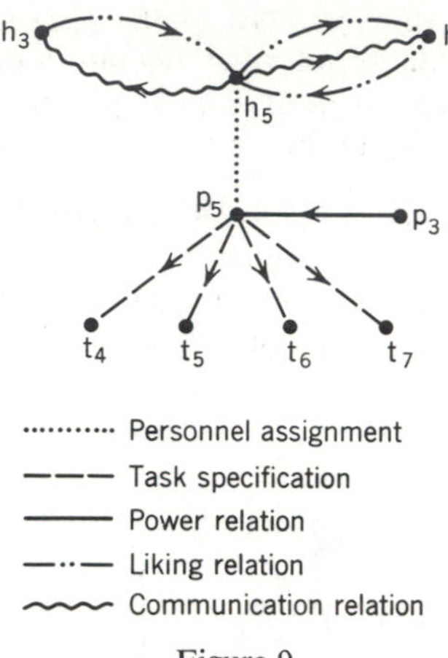

Figure 9

These observations on the effect of informal interpersonal relations can be taken one step further, though the rigorous analysis of what happens must be postponed. The fact that h_5 can now reach (i.e., communicate with) h_3 and h_4 implies that the positions p_3, p_4, and p_5 may become involved. Surely these three people would talk about their jobs. The informal liking and communication relationships may well affect how they operate the formal rules of their positions. For instance, the rules for relating position p_2 to its tasks (those of secretary) may include one which says h_2 must not tell others lower than the foreman on the organization power chart what is the content of policy documents. If she does, she is changing the h_2-p_2 personnel allocation rules ("not talking out of turn," "not breaking security regulations"). Thus if changes are made in the *H*-graph, they will induce changes in the *P*-graph and these in turn will induce changes in the *T*-graph. The empirical axioms required to interpret from digraphs to reality will be worked out later.

The relations listed on page 96, therefore, can now be more fully enumerated:

0. (a) Formal: Nominal scale on *H*, denoted R_0.
   (b) Informal: Relations R_{01}, R_{02}, . . . all on *H*. (Examples: likes, prefers to work with, taller than, older than, communicates with, teases, assumes responsibility for, helps, advises, fights with, brother of.)
1. Formal: The prescribed power relation on *P* or who controls whom, denoted R_1.
2. Formal: The precedence relation on *T*, the admissible order of doing the tasks, denoted R_2.
3. Formal: The assignment relation of persons to positions, denoted R_3.
4. Formal: The allocation relation of tasks to positions, denoted R_4.
5. (a) Formal: The induced relation from *H* onto *T* (*Figure* 7), or who does what, denoted R_5.
   (b) Informal: Relations of the kind "h_1 likes task t_k better than his other tasks."

One more new term must be introduced, "*the universal set*," U, of all people in a given social system from whom the workers in our miniature factory system are drawn. (Recall that from the total population which read the advertisement, 50 applied and $h_1 \ldots h_5$ were hired.) This term is introduced now, to indicate that we shall later be concerned with the meaning of terms like "role overlap," "role conflict," and "social structure." Originally $h_1 \ldots h_5$ of *Figure* 1 had no interpersonal relationships in the new organization. All they had was interpositional relationships laid down by the organization chart (*Figure* 2). However, they may have relationships in other role systems outside the factory. Thus h_1 may be a father, a trade union secretary, and president of a bowling club; and some of his duties or activities in these role systems may assist or interfere with his duties or activities in the factory role system.

SYNTHESIS AND ANALYSIS OF STRUCTURAL ROLE SYSTEMS

Up to here, we have described the concept of a structural role in terms of a rather complex digraph containing several persons, positions, and tasks. The formal role of a position p_j was defined as the subgraph containing that position and all elements linked to it by one step in the *H*, *P*, and *T* graphs. That definition thus yields a "unit of a role system"; and we note that to isolate invariant social units had been one of our aims. Let us now, without prejudice to that definition, examine the singular case of one man who has one task to do. Suppose the task is to repair a chair. Clearly, the total resources of his personality, social status, and a host of other attributes are not going to be employed on this task. To do it, he has to think of himself (or we simply label him) as a "carpenter, temporary, unpaid."

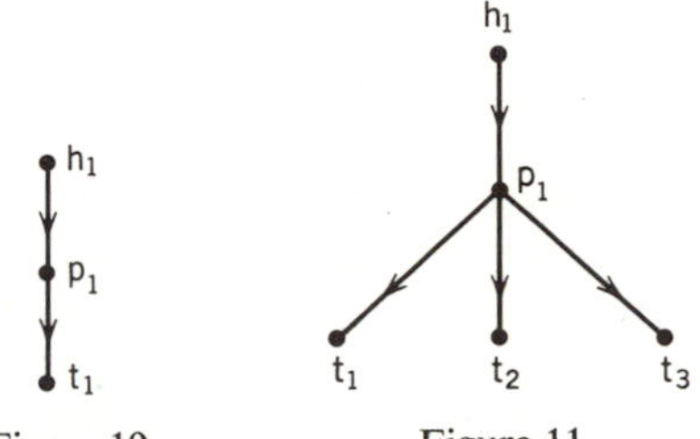

Figure 10 Figure 11

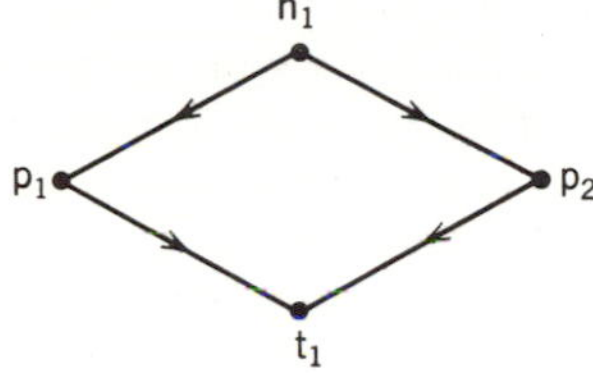

Figure 12

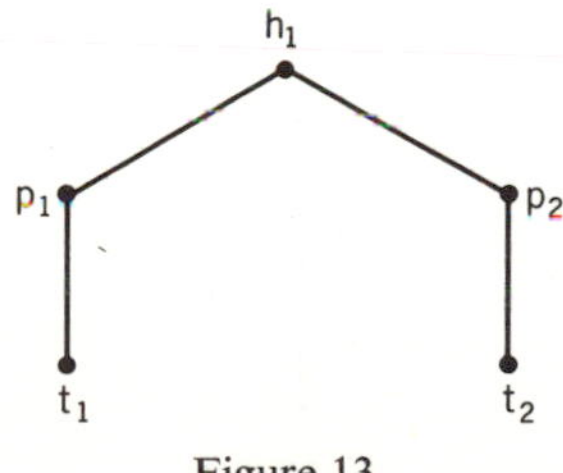

Figure 13

Thus this man h_1, is in the single position, p_1, of having to accomplish his task t_1. In accordance with the description of a role system in previous sections, we may represent this situation by the digraph of *Figure* 10.

But everyone knows that life is much more complicated than this. The same man might have to do two tasks in this position, or even three tasks, as shown in *Figure* 11.

Sometimes a situation develops in which he needs to occupy two different positions in order to accomplish his original single task, as shown in *Figure* 12. (For instance, to repair the chair properly, he must occupy positions of carpenter and painter.)

A common situation is that of one man with two different appointments, say in teaching and research at the same university. He has separate offices in different buildings for these appointments and separate duties. The two offices may be designated by positions p_1 and p_2 and all his teaching duties may be lumped together, or *coalesced*, and called task t_1, while all his research duties, when coalesced, are called task t_2. This situation is shown in *Figure* 13.

If we set out each teaching duty and each research duty separately, and if we assume for simplicity that there are only three such individual tasks for each of these two positions, then we have a diagram as shown in *Figure* 14.

The *multiplicity* of a position is the number of tasks allocated to it. In particular, a *simple position* is one which has a unique task, and a *trivial position* is a sinecure, one which has no task at all. Thus in *Figure* 14 each position has multiplicity 3.

If a man has two positions, each of which has two allotted tasks and these two tasks are the same for both of these positions, then we have the situation in *Figure* 15.

Figure 15 may seem to imply inefficiency, but it certainly happens. Any experienced bureaucrat can recall examples of a person who, in one capacity, writes a letter to himself in another capacity, to get something done.

Now consider *Figure* 14 as representing this

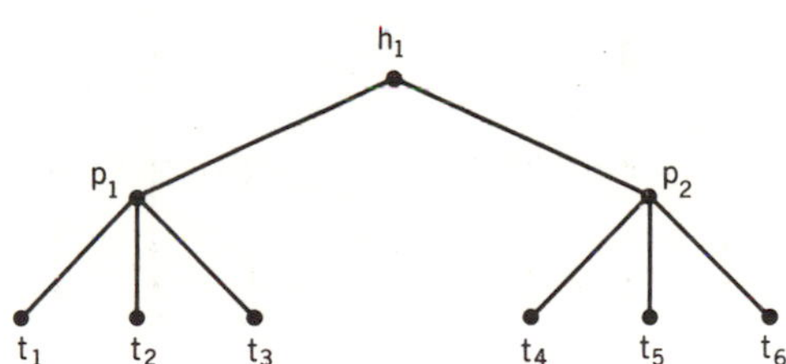

Figure 14

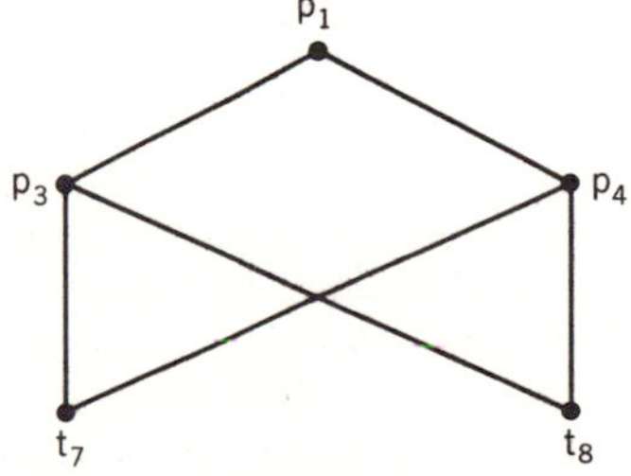

Figure 15

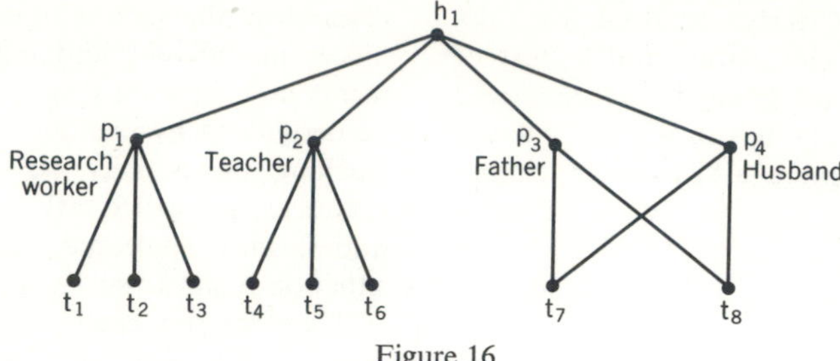

Figure 16

man and his two university positions and *Figure* 15 as part of his life at home. The fact that this is the same man can be indicated by *coalescing* the preceding two digraphs with respect to the point h_1. The resulting digraph is shown in *Figure* 16.

The complexity of one man in various positions doing assorted tasks can obviously be multiplied at will.

Now let us graduate to the two-person situation. We may illustrate this with man and wife in a family situation, each of whom has certain positions to occupy (say three each, to preserve equality of the sexes), and for simplicity let us say that each position is *simple*, one to which a unique task is allotted. Then the diagram of *Figure* 17 summarizes this role system.

Note that each of the connected pieces of the digraph of *Figure* 17 tells of the activities of the two persons separately, just as each of *Figures* 10–16 tells of one or more activities in a single individual.

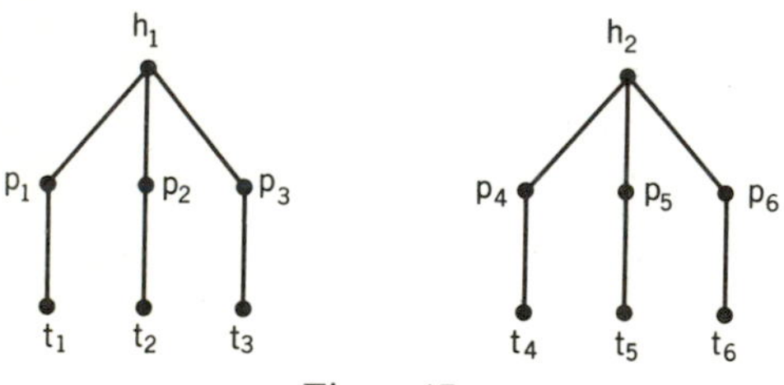

Figure 17

The completion of *Figure* 17 to make it approximate a real-life situation would necessitate drawing the various informal relationships between the two persons, the organization chart (power relation) between the two sets of positions (here a matter for anthropologists or social workers), and the precedence relation on the tasks. The building up or *synthesis* of a role system with any number n_0 of people, n_1 of positions, and n_2 of tasks is straightforward. If we denote as previously the *sets* of all people, positions, and tasks by *H*, *P*, and *T* respectively, then we can summarize any role system whatsoever by the digraph of *Figure* 18.

Thus the reader is once again confronted by a diagram identical with that of *Figure* 10, except that h_1, p_1, and t_1 have been metamorphosed to *H*, *P*, and *T*. Clearly, thinking about role systems and carrying out mathematical (that is, logical) operations on them can, and do, imply many levels of complexity, from the simplest of *Figure* 10 to a level which might strain the resources of an electronic computer. The encouraging aspect of this synthesizing, coalescing, and analyzing by means of diagrams is that it is not merely a visual aid to the reader and the student of social structure: the theory of digraphs may lead to conceptual and predictive advances. The diagrams are more than visual allegories.

Figure 18

At this stage, however, we merely note that two kinds of units have been isolated for use in thinking about role structures as defined in this paper: a collection of sets of relations on sets of persons, positions, and tasks respectively. The first unit is the most elementary building block, consisting of one isolated person in one position doing one task.

The second kind of unit comprises several persons, positions, and tasks. If the man mending a chair (*Figure* 10) had been ordered to do so by his wife, while one of his children kept running away with the hammer, we would at once be able to report the structural role of his carpenter position *in this context* as being closely akin to that of p_5, the second worker of *Figure* 9, in the *quite different context* of the factory. *The structural (formal) role of a position, then, can be regarded as one of the important invariants of social structure.* Even the actual role has invariant properties, though these may not remain constant for long periods, as do the properties of the formal role.

This second kind obviously comprises an indefinitely large number of "units," one for each conceivable formal structural role system. Consequently the most economical building blocks are h_i, p_j, t_k, one person in one position doing one task, and *HPT*, a set of persons in a set of positions doing a set of tasks. Clearly, an important further step is to create a *taxonomy* (Oeser, 1960) of such *HPT* systems. It seems odd that not even anthropologists and sociologists have as yet created a role taxonomy.

We note in passing that the notion of "the context of role behavior" has become more precise. "*Context*" *means the total set of relations embodied in a structural role digraph.*

True, we have abstracted virtually everything that makes the study of man interesting to social scientists, especially to anthropologists and clinical psychologists. However, after abstract analysis comes synthesis. Bit by bit we hope to add other attributes, until something approximating to the infinite complexity and variety of human life and labour has been captured in a more comprehensive theory. But for the time being we shall continue to study structure in the abstract.

SOME IMPLICATIONS FOR THEORY AND RESEARCH

Figure 19 displays in a highly schematic form the general digraph of any structural role system.

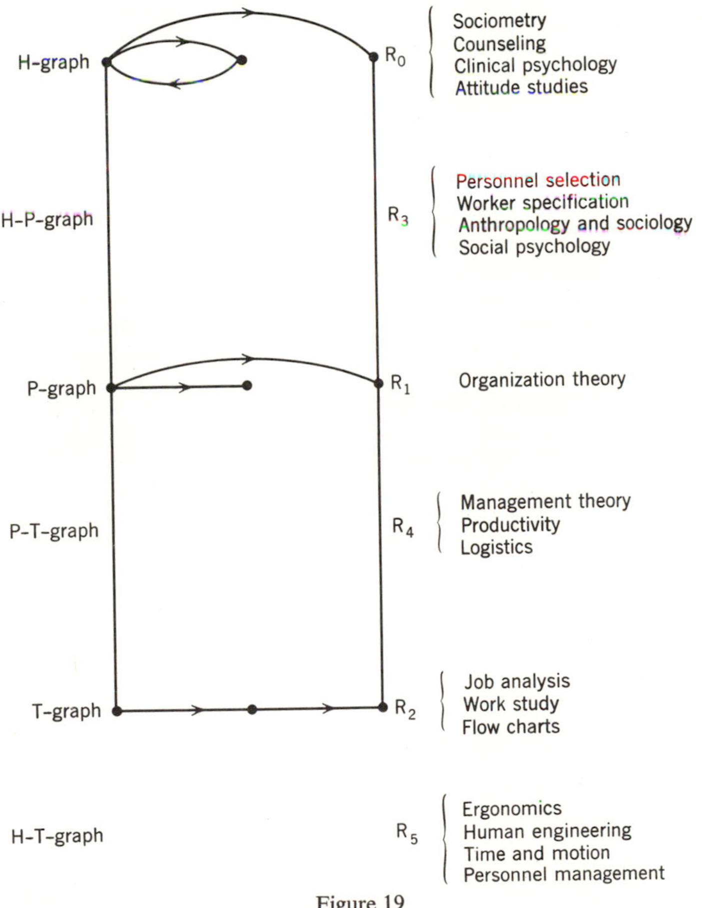

Figure 19

In addition to summarizing in one schema the various logical relations and definitions discussed in this paper, it sets out our view of the relationship of the theory of structural roles to other fields of social psychology and sociology. Studies of sociometry and attitudes (the set of R_0 relations) or of human engineering and personnel management (the induced *H–T* relation, R_5) or of any of the other fields briefly noted on the chart of *Figure* 19, proceed as if these relations were the only ones that are relevant to their particular subject-matter. To study parts in isolation is certainly a legitimate analytic practice in science. But ultimately the parts must be fitted together; and unless the whole is also studied on its own right there will be unexplained gaps and distortions in the synthesis, because of the interaction of the parts.

One example may suffice to illustrate the assertion that a structural role theory is one necessary tool for unifying as well as clarifying the diverse fields of the social sciences.

Sociometric studies of the classroom produce many puzzling and even conflicting results. The reason is not far to seek. They all omit to consider that, both in and out of the classroom, pupils are embedded in a matrix of relations not only to other pupils and the teacher but also to the positions they occupy in their various formal and informal groups, and to the task systems which are the *raisons d'être* of any group whatsoever. As the position relationships, or the task relationships, or the informal relationships between persons change, so the total pattern of relations will change. It is not sufficient, therefore, to ask questions such as "next to whom would you like to sit?" or "with whom would you choose to work?" The answer must depend on context, and we have defined context as the totality of relations of the structural role digraph. What is true of sociometry is also true of other branches of psychology noted on *Figure* 19.

Finally, this brief (and possibly somewhat dogmatic) section highlights again the importance of constructing a formal taxonomy of structural roles and role systems.

REFERENCES

Harary, F., and Norman, R. Z., 1953. *Graph theory as a mathematical model in social science.* Ann Arbor, Mich.: Institute for Social Research.

Harary, F., Norman, R. Z., and Cartwright, D., 1965. *Structural models: an introduction to the theory of directed graphs.* New York: Wiley.

Newcomb, T. M., 1950. *Social psychology.* New York: Dryden.

Oeser, O. A., 1960. Prolegomena to a theory of roles and the measurement of role behavior. *Proceedings of XVIth International Congress of Psychology.* Bonn. August, 1960 (abstract).

Oeser, O. A., and Emery, F. E., 1954. *Social structure and personality in a rural community.* New York: Macmillan.

Oeser, O. A., and Hammond, S. B. (Eds.), 1954. *Social structure and personality in a city.* New York: Macmillan.

Oeser, O. A., and Harary, F., 1964. A mathematical model for structural role theory, II. *Human Relations*, **17**, 3–17.

Parkinson, C. N., 1957. *Parkinson's law.* London: John Murray; New York: Houghton Mifflin.

Thrall, R. M., Coombs, C. H., and Davis, R. L., 1954. *Decision processes.* New York: Wiley.

Znaniecki, F., 1939. Social groups as products of participating individuals. *American Journal of Sociology*, **44**, 799–812.

part IV Prescriptions

THE CONCEPT OF PRESCRIPTION is a central idea in role theory, and it has appeared under the guise of diverse labels—as "norm," "role expectation," and "rule," among many. Prescriptions are behaviors that indicate that other behaviors should (or ought to) be engaged in. Prescriptions may be specified further as demands or norms, depending upon whether they are overt or covert, respectively.

Because prescriptions are ubiquitous and salient in their various forms, they appear to be among the most significant guides and standards by which men live. Indeed, by defining the rights and obligations of individuals, prescriptions appear to be among the most potent factors in the control of human behavior, either by directly triggering conformity behavior, or through a system of positive and negative sanctions that accompany them. Prescriptions are important also because they emerge from the interaction of individuals and groups and thus, to some extent, are themselves controlled by some of the same behavior which they are presumed to govern. There are numerous and subtle inter-relationships between prescriptions and the behaviors to which they presumably relate.

Among the reasons for the diversity of relationship between prescription and the behavior prescribed is that prescriptions themselves differ in important ways. Prescriptions are formal and informal, expressed and implicit, individual and shared; and whatever their form, prescriptions may vary in permissiveness, completeness, complexity, and in the degree to which they are codified and universal. The selections presented in this part specify these considerations more fully by elaborating some of the antecedents and consequences of prescriptive behavior as well as the diverse forms in which prescriptions may be found.

In the first selection, by Davis, significant types of prescriptions (here called norms) are elaborated. Thus Davis distinguishes folkways from mores, and customary from enacted law. He also distinguishes among custom, morality, religion, convention and etiquette, fashion and fad, and treats institutions and the relationships between society and the normative order.

The selection by Morris is also addressed to the problem of types of norms, but unlike Davis' classification, Morris develops a typology of dimensions by which prescriptions may be ordered. Thus, norms may be contrasted in terms of the extent of the subject's knowledge of the norm, the extent of acceptance of the norm, and the extent of the application of the norm to objects.· The examples given pertain to various dimensions for ordering prescriptive phenomena, all of these being classified as aspects of the distribution of the norm. Morris also deals with dimensions relating to the mode of enforcement of the norm, transmission of the norm, and conformity to the norm.

Jackson's major concern, in the third selection, is with the variables associated with norms and with the effects of norms on the behavior of individuals. (Although Jackson also uses the term norm, his analysis is pertinent to all forms of prescription.) The author points out that norms have two basic dimensions—behavior and evaluation—and that norms may be graphed as a distributional form in terms of these dimensions. He designates the normative distribution as a return-potential curve, pointing out that norms prescribe the performance of the individual and provide information to him about the probable approval or disapproval associated with his performance. The author then presents various other properties of norms implied by his basic model, among them being intensity, approval-disapproval ratio, point of maximum return, crystallization, and ambiguity. Jackson also points out how such inter-individual concepts as scope, integration, congruence, correspondence, and accuracy may be derived from the scheme. Finally, the implications of his model for conformity and self-esteem are discussed.

The selection by Anderson and Moore examines still another aspect of prescriptions, namely, their logical properties. These authors point out that the vague concepts of "consistency" and "balance" in many social theories have no simple applicability when one considers the complex relationships that obtain among prescriptive elements. They then turn to a formalism known as Deontic Logic and demonstrate its applicability to the problems of normative relationships. Principles are defined and then applied to normative examples.

The selection by Homans treats the important problem of the relationship between norms (again, in our terms, prescriptions) and behavior. In providing a somewhat broader view of norms than we have previously encountered, Homans points out that a norm is not only an "idea in the minds of the members of a group . . . specifying what the members or other men should do," but also that "a statement of the kind described is a norm only if any departure of real behavior from the norm is followed by some punishment." Homans notes that norms not only affect the behavior prescribed by them, but he acknowledges also that the opposite may obtain, i.e., behaviors may significally shape the norms. Homans also proposes the interesting idea that "members of the group are often more nearly alike in the norms they hold than in their overt behavior."

A number of important problems are discussed in Gouldner's selection on the norm of reciprocity. He indicates that the concept of reciprocity is inherent in the functionalist explanation of society and that the norm of reciprocity is probably a cultural universal. But he notes that societies differ in the degree to which reciprocity is institutionalized and appears to govern social relationships. The author also distinguishes among various forms of reciprocity and between reciprocity and complementarity.

In the last selection, by Cloward and Ohlin, the specific norms of delinquent sub-cultures are discussed. These authors indicate that criminals and delinquents are generally not isolated individuals who simply did not learn the prescriptions of the society, but rather that delinquent subcultures have normative systems of their own that run counter to the general norms of society. Various processes of delinquent sub-cultures are discussed, and the authors distinguish three types of deviant sub-cultures found in contemporary society: the criminal, conflict, and retreatist.

selection 7 Social Norms

KINGSLEY DAVIS

CLASSIFICATION OF NORMS

One cannot discuss for long the general subject of norms without making some distinction between the different types. Yet there are so many distinctions which cross one another that a systematic classification is difficult. One way is to differentiate norms on the basis of the kind of sanctions applied. Some rules are supported merely by mild disapproval of the violator, while others are supported by physical force. This distinction is correlated to some extent with another one—namely, the degree of importance attached to the rule in the society—and with still another, the manner by which the rule comes into being (whether by deliberate legislation or by unconscious growth). Finally there is apparently a slight correlation between these criteria and the degree of spontaneity with which the rule is followed as well as the rapidity with which the rule changes. These correlations, however, are very rough. What sociologists have done is simply to group norms into several broad classes, admitting that the various criteria of distinction overlap considerably and that the classification is therefore crude. In this way they usually distinguish what are called folkways, mores, and law, and sometimes differentiate fashion, fad, convention, etiquette, and honor. We shall follow this same procedure.

FOLKWAYS

Most of the patterns applied in everyday behavior consist of folkways. These are relatively durable, standardized practices regarded as obligatory in the proper situation but not absolutely obligatory, enforced by informal social controls (gossip, ridicule, ostracism) rather than by formal complaint or coercion, and originating in an unplanned and obscure manner rather than by deliberate inauguration. The grammar and vocabulary of a language, for example, form a system of verbal folkways, of most of which we are entirely unaware. Likewise such things as the number of meals per day, less the modes of preparing food, the kinds of food chosen, the regular brushing of the teeth, the use of tables, chairs, beds, etc., are all folkways. It is through the folkways that the business of living in a socio-cultural environment is made possible, and their unreflecting character makes for efficiency and frees our minds for the more problematic events of life. Those folkways that are repeated often enough become habits—habits of thought as well as of action—and they come to form the unstated premises in our mental life. They provide a high degree of predictability both of our own and of others' behavior, so that we feel some security and some order in life. To violate some of the folkways is usually possible, but it is impossible to violate all of them, for then the individual would find himself virtually excluded from social contact. Survival in such a circumstance would be extremely difficult, not merely from an external or physical point of view, but also from an internal or mental point of view. The very reasons for nonconformity in one particular situation are apt to be, for the individual in question, the folkways prevailing in most other situations. If the alpha and omega of human existence are to be found anywhere it is in the folkways, for we begin with them and always come back to them.

MORES

Whereas each folkway is not considered tremendously important and is not supported by an extremely strong sanction, each *mos* is believed to be essential for social welfare and is consequently more strongly sanctioned. There is a greater feeling of horror about violating a *mos*, a greater unwillingness to see it violated. Presumably, therefore the mores relate to the fundamental needs of society more directly than do the folkways—or it would be better to say that the emphasis put upon a given *mos* is proportional, first, to the importance of the need which the behavior serves and, second, to the obstacles (either in the

---

Abridged from Chapter 3 of a book by the same author entitled *Human Society*, 1949, New York: Macmillan. Reprinted by permission of the author and Macmillan.

organism or in the environment) to meeting that need.

Folkways and mores are similar, however, in being of remote and obscure origin, unplanned, unquestioned, and relatively unchanging. They are also similar in that the sanctions are informal and communal in nature, depending on the spontaneous reactions of the group rather than on the reactions of officials acting in some special capacity. The mores represent the hardest core of the normative system. The folkways are, so to speak, the protoplasm of the cell, the bulky part, while the mores are the nucleus, the essential part. It is only when the mores are called into question that people reflect upon them. Ordinarily the mores are taken for granted as being a highly important part of the nature of things. Belief rationalizes them in the form of myth, ritual expresses them in the form of symbols, and action embodies them in the form of right conduct. The mores are morally right, their violation morally wrong. Hence the profoundest measuring rod of right and wrong is found precisely in the mores, which fact has given rise to the expression that the mores can make anything right or anything wrong (Sumner, 1906, Ch. 15). In public opinion there is no higher court than that of the mores themselves, and in many simple societies no further type of norm is needed for the proper regulation of the membership. The mores have no need of justification, because they exist of their own right. They are not subject to deliberate change or to analysis, and criticism of them draws down strong punishment upon the head of the critic. The members of society, in short, share sentiments highly favorable to the mores. There is a sense of unreflecting solidarity among people who share the same mores because their sentiments are alike; and there is a sense of resistance and antagonism towards anyone with different mores. Whereas foreign folkways are merely disconcerting because they upset old habits and familiar grooves, foreign mores are deeply disturbing because, in addition, they offend profound sentiments.

Taboos are mores expressed in negative form. The rules against incest, for example, are in the mores, but they tell us not so much what relationship should prevail between parent and child, brother and sister, as what relationship should *not* prevail. On the other hand the rule regarding the wife's sexual relations with men other than her husband is stated both positively (a wife must be sexually faithful to her husband) and negatively (she must not commit adultery); it thus involves both an exhortation and a taboo.

CUSTOMARY LAW

There are not many societies which entirely lack special organization for the enforcement of the social rules. Most societies, including many primitive bands and all peasant communities, have some elements that are associated with what is generally called law. Usually the first such element to appear is a judicial body which renders judgment when cases of infraction or conflict arise. Thus the Hottentots, an African people closely related to the Bushmen, have or did have a tribal council. Among the offenses tried before this council were murder, manslaughter, treason, theft, incest, adultery, and sodomy.

> As soon as a man was known or suspected of having committed such an offence, every member of the kraal considered it a duty to arrest him at the first opportunity, unless he succeeded in making his escape. Once captured he was safely held until the council assembled, which was always as soon as possible. The councillors sat in a circle, and the accused was placed in the centre, where he could hear all that was said and himself be heard by everybody around. The accuser then stated his case, and produced all his proofs, supported by witnesses. The prisoner, in return, offered all means of defence the case would suggest, advancing any contradictory evidence at his command, and his answer was listened to with undivided attention. The matter was then thoroughly discussed by the councillors, the verdict being arrived at by the decision of the majority. If the accused was acquitted, a few head of cattle from the herds of his accusers were adjudged to him as compensation. But if he was found guilty, and the headman, in whose hands the final sentence lay, pronounced in favour of death, the sentence was immediately executed. The headman, as chief executioner, rushed towards the criminal and felled him to the ground with a heavy blow of the kirri; all the other men then violently attacked him until he was beaten to death (Schapera, 1930, pp. 339–340).

It is clear that the Hottentots did not have specialized policemen. Every man in the community was supposed to exercise police functions. It is also clear that they did not have a legislative body or a constitution. They had only an informal judicial body, a council of elders. This judicial body enforced certain of the communal rules—rules that, were it not for such specific enforcement, would be simply mores. In short, the first step in the emergence of law is generally the emergence of some kind of organization for judging guilt and pronouncing punishment. The community as a whole can do the rest. The norms are not enacted but are simply part of the immemorial tradition of the community.

When the mores thus come to have some special organization for their enforcement, we may call them laws. Seldom are all the mores thus enforced, but only the more important ones. Since, however, there is no legislative body for the enactment of new rules not previously part of the cultural heritage, the law in this case should be called "customary law." This category then includes everything between sheer folkways and fully developed law. Insofar as human societies have had any law at all, this is what they have generally had. Only with the development of large-scale political organization, extensive specialization, and writing has complete or genuine law come into existence.

ENACTED LAW

In complex societies mere public opinion, informal force, and moral conscience cannot ensure order. Some form of special political organization becomes necessary. At first it may be nothing more than a headman assisted by the clan or tribal elders, but it helps to mobilize the group for war and to settle disputes that threaten internal unity. The greater its role, the more such government must command, interpret, and enforce a system of rules governing social relations. At first it utilizes the rules already there (the mores) and simply undertakes to interpret and apply them in the name of the community at large. It must decide what the mores are, which ones apply in a given case, and what the penalty should be. In the face of growing social complexity and increasing group size, however, this judicial function ceases to be sufficient. The community at large can no longer be expected to apprehend the criminals and carry out the penalties, for the people may be too scattered and too preoccupied with other matters. There must be created some enforcement agency—persons authorized to use force if necessary—which will assume police duties. Also, with conditions changing rapidly and life becoming more complicated the old mores no longer suffice to give complete guidance. Here one of two paths may be adopted: (a) There may arise no concept of enacting new rules and hence no legislating agency, but the courts may rely on past decisions embodying new applications of the old mores. Here precedent is supposedly king, but through legal fiction and new interpretations the law actually changes. Laws that are not formally enacted but are formally decided and enforced are sometimes called customary law, and in the case of Anglo-American countries, "common law." (b) On the other hand the chief, king, or other governing official may frankly make new rules; or a special body—a legislative council, parliament, or what not—may be created for this purpose. In this case the old mores are not necessarily overthrown. They may be embodied in an unwritten constitution, a written constitution, or a continuing body of "common law." They supposedly remain effective unless definitely overruled by the new enacted laws, and usually the enacted laws are conceived as somehow carrying out the spirit of the ancient mores.

The manner of deciding what the law is depends on how it is made. If it is enacted law the exact wording of the statute must be examined and interpreted in the light of a given case. If it is not enacted law its exact nature is determined by precedent, the decision of prior tribunals being taken as final. In either case a written language is almost indispensable, in the one case to preserve the exact wording of the statute and in the other to store the prior decisions of the courts. For this reason what we regard as fully developed law is hardly to be found apart from the use of writing.

It can be seen that law is a more deliberate, more clearly stated thing than folkways or mores. It is a product of conscious thought and planning, of deliberate formulation and voluntary application. It is not only necessitated by a complex society but it also makes such a society possible. Like most of the conscious and rational aspects of social life law is in one sense superficial. It does not determine the fundamental sentiments but is rather a product of them. For instance, the things that are first enacted into law usually begin as mores; so that law is sometimes defined as mores given the specific sanction of governmental enforcement. And laws which are not supported by the folkways and mores usually have little chance of being enforced. Yet superficial as they are from this point of view, laws perform a genuine function in giving precision, scope, and a means of formal enforcement to the mores in societies where multiplicity of groups and interests, accumulation of culture, and improved means of communication have broken down the solidarity of the small community and substituted for it a larger, more dynamic, and more secularized society.

INSTITUTIONS

It is now necessary to point out that the totality of folkways, mores, and laws in a society are related in a systematic fashion and that consequently a fruitful approach to understanding social structure is in terms of the normative system.

An institution can be defined as a *set* of interwoven folkways, mores, and laws built around one or more functions. It is a part of the social structure, set off by the closeness of its organization and by the distinctness of its functions. It is therefore inclusive rather than exclusive of the concepts previously defined; for without folkways and mores there could be no institutions. Marriage, for example, embraces the complex of folkways surrounding the approved mating of men and women, including in our culture engagement and wedding rings, rice throwing, the honeymoon, lifting the bride over the threshold, showers, etc. It also embraces certain mores—premarital chastity, postmarital fidelity, taking of the vows, obligation of support, etc. Finally, it embraces certain laws—license, record, right of divorce for cause, protection against fraud, proper age, absence of prohibitive kinship bonds, etc. All of these norms taken together form a definite structure—the institution of marriage—which has meaning as a whole and which, when operative in behavior, results in the performance of certain social and individual functions such as reproduction and child rearing on the social side, sexual gratification and affection on the individual side. Similarly it can be said that economic, political, religious, and recreational institutions each represent a distinguishable set of interrelated folkways, mores, and laws coherently organized and capable of performing distinct functions.

CUSTOM, MORALITY, AND RELIGION

In any language there are words vaguely designating different kinds of norms. English has many such words, including "custom," "convention," "etiquette," "morality," "usage," "fashion," and "fad." The meanings overlap but they are sufficiently distinct to indicate that there are many kinds of folkways and mores.

"Custom" is a broad term embracing all of the norms classified as folkways and mores. It connotes long established usage and is therefore frequently contrasted with what is new, as when we speak of "the customary way of doing things," or say that a given innovation is "contrary to custom." Custom refers primarily to practices that have been oft-repeated by a multitude of generations, practices that tend to be followed simply because they have been followed in the past. The term is therefore closer to folkways than to mores, but it tends to convey the traditional, automatic, mass character of both of them.

"Morality" on the other hand lays stress upon the inner sense of obligation, the feeling of right and wrong. It implies real sentiment behind the observance of the rule and a certain amount of principle and firmness of character in one's conduct. The norm is observed not simply because it is traditional, not simply because others around one observe it, but because it conforms to an abstract principle of justice, purity, fairness, truth, etc. It is more self-conscious, abstract, and consistent than sheer custom. It is therefore closer to the mores, although it stresses the sentiment, rationalization, and consistency behind the mores. On an extremely intellectual or philosophical level morality becomes an "ethic." The latter is often related to the norms of special groups (as when we speak of "medical ethics") or is reserved for the speculative systems of outstanding thinkers (as when we speak of the ethics of Aristotle).

Every major religion stands in intimate relation to the morality of the people who profess the religion. Certain of the moral tenets are explained as having a supernatural origin; the powers of the other world are conceived as supporting and cherishing these principles, being ready to punish their violation and to reward their observance; and salvation and blessedness are interpreted in terms of the individual's relation to the moral ideals. Religion therefore adds something to morality and strengthens it by connecting it with the world lying beyond the senses. It often happens that not all the moral rules are embodied in religion. Some of the lesser rules may be conceived in purely secular terms. Nevertheless, there is usually a feeling that the supernatural world somehow is connected with the whole of group morality as a system. In other words the sense of guilt at having violated a moral principle is very close to the sense of sin even when the specific norm is not religiously sanctioned. When, therefore, we speak of Christian morality we mean something much broader than merely the Ten Commandments.

CONVENTION AND ETIQUETTE

Convention and etiquette are both special kinds of folkways, distinguished by a certain awareness that they have no deeper meaning but are merely matters of convenience in social relations. In this sense they stand at an opposite pole from morality, though they share with the latter an element of traditionalism. Because of their intrinsic meaninglessness both convention and etiquette often acquire an invidious symbolism that plays a part in class relations.

Convention is more a matter of principle and less a matter of adornment than etiquette. It prescribes rather rigid forms which social relations in given situations must follow. It thus eliminates trial and error and hence confusion in human interaction. The rule that motorists must drive on the right side of the road is a convention. Nobody considers this a sacred rule or one involving some mystic principle. It is merely an agreed-upon procedure, and when one is in England one adjusts quite readily to driving on the left instead of the right. Everybody recognizes that without some such rule the highway would be a much more dangerous place than it is. The essential thing is not the particular rule but some standardized procedure by which mutual activities are regulated and prevented from interfering with each other. People are constantly forced to adjust to the presence of others in going about their daily business. They must go through the same doorways, get on and off the same public conveyances, patronize the same shops, seek the same goods. The conventions afford a *modus vivendi* in all these situations. The fact that the relationships go as smoothly and automatically as they do, with a minimum of confusion and friction, suggests that the conventions are generally satisfactory. The mental subtleties as well as the physical conveniences of social interaction are subject to convention. In conversation, for example, certain topics are ignored by tacit agreement because they might create tension if openly expressed. Certain forms of speech and behavior are used to keep a relationship on a superficially friendly basis, when underneath there is a real antipathy or conflict of interest. One does not say to a man's face what one says to his friends, and one does not say to his friends what one says to his enemies. A humane conspiracy prevails by which, except in extraordinary circumstances, a man is permitted to cherish his own illusions about himself. In make-believe, in humor perhaps, a person may tell the truth, but only because it is assumed not to be true. Without these conventions human intercourse would indeed be uncouth and unbearable.

Etiquette, or "good manners," is concerned with the choice of the proper form for doing something. It implies that a choice is possible and that there is a hierarchy of the possible alternatives. For this reason it serves as a ready if superficial device, an external symbol by which a person's class status may be identified. From the point of view of social efficiency and convenience it makes little difference how one disposes of one's knife, fork, and napkin, introduces two strangers, or dresses for the evening meal. But from the point of view of punctilio it makes a great deal of difference, because it is by a proper or improper choice in these little matters that one's standing in the social hierarchy is often judged. Etiquette is thus mainly a discriminating device, although it also serves as an external manifestation of good intentions toward others, as in greeting, well-wishing, and other behavior classified under the heading of politeness.

FASHION AND FAD

When we speak of folkways and mores, customs and morals, convention and etiquette, we think of them as relatively fixed. We know that they do change, but the change comes so slowly that it is hardly perceptible. There was no precise moment, for example, when the pronunciation of English in the United States became suddenly different from the pronunciation in England. The divergence evolved gradually and unconsciously, yet it has now reached such a stage that the two peoples have difficulty in understanding each other. When philologists look back over the history of language, they find that such changes occur persistently and regularly; but within a single lifetime they are hardly discernible. Thus the bulk of the folkways and mores remain relatively permanent, and any attempted change in them tends to arouse emotional resistance in the public at large. People feel insecure, confused, and angry when established custom is "flouted" or "outraged."

Man does not live, however, by security alone. He yearns for something new, for variety and novelty. At first it might seem that this desire could not be satisfied through social norms because the norms emphasize obligation and conformity. Yet curiously, the human animal manages to be a conformist even when he is seeking change. He achieves this strange anomaly by a set of norms that demand an intense conformity while they last but which endure only a short time. These norms go by such names as "fashion," "fad," and "craze."

Time is the very essence of fashion. The same style of dress that was in vogue three years ago may appear ridiculous today, and the style that seems so beautiful, so exquisitely appropriate today will inevitably appear ludicrous a few years hence. A set of old photographs arouses our laughter. We wonder how we could have worn such foolish hats, such peculiar trousers, such ugly dresses, and we congratulate ourselves on showing much better taste now. Since we cannot visualize what changes the future will bring, the standard of today seems somehow perfect and ultimate, and so we do not hesitate to stand once more before the camera.

Fashion is necessarily more prevalent in modern civilized society than in primitive tribes or peasant communities. Modern society has gone farther than any other in its positive evaluation of change, in its tolerance of differences, and in its cultivation of individual taste. It therefore places few shackles on the cycle of fashion. At the same time its mobile class structure with numerous ill-defined strata gives individuals a powerful incentive to be "in the swim." Urban life with its fleeting and specialized contacts makes the individual's rating depend on readily observable externalities and thus magnifies the importance of fashion as a status device.

What we have said about fashion is true *a fortiori* of fads and crazes. The latter are merely special cases of fashion distinguished by the quickness with which they alternate, the utter superficiality of their content, and the irrationality and intensity of the temporary fascination with them. The famous dancing mania of the Middle Ages was a craze; the late and unlamented dance step called the "Lindy Hop" was a fad. By virtue of their extremity fads and crazes are generally limited to a smaller proportion of the population than is fashion. Correspondingly, the societal importance of fads and crazes is less than that of fashion in general. We hardly think of them as norms at all but rather as examples of crowd behavior.

SOCIETY AND THE NORMATIVE ORDER

It should now be clear that social norms are extremely varied and extremely pervasive, that they are a peculiar feature of human society, and that they are an essential part of what we call social order. They have arisen as a feature of cultural adaptation. The individual acquires them through a process of indoctrination. Some of them he internalizes and these become part of his personality. Some of them he respects because of their consequences. Regardless of whether or not he obeys the norms completely, they influence his behavior and his thinking. It is largely through them that his conduct is regulated and integrated with the conduct of his fellows. It is through them that a society acquires a coherent structure and manages to get the business of group life tended to.

REFERENCES

Schapera, I., 1930. *The Khoisan peoples of South Africa.* London: Routledge.
Sumner, W. G., 1906. *Folkways.* Boston: Ginn.

selection 8 A Typology of Norms

RICHARD T. MORRIS

Almost fifty years have passed since Professor Sumner (1906) proposed his famous classification of norms into folkways and mores. Since that time there have been few efforts to elaborate or criticize this basic classification, even though there has been a tremendous increase in interest in the empirical investigation of norms during this period. Sorokin vigorously attacked Sumner's typology, calling it "a kind of grocery basket into which are dumped together [all sorts of norms]" (1947, p. 87), and has replaced it with his classification of law-norms, technical norms, norms of etiquette and fashion, and a final category of norms of "something else" (1947, p. 85), in which the grocery basket is still evident. Linton (1936, Ch. 16) has contributed the well-known

Abridged from the *American Sociological Review*, 1956, **21**, 610–613. Reprinted by permission of the author and the American Sociological Association.

categories: universals, specialties, and alternatives. Most recently, Robin Williams (1951, Ch. 3) has revised and elaborated Sorokin's classification in his proposal of technical, conventional, aesthetic, and moral norms, and has further suggested a classification in terms of the major dimensions of norms, together with a sketch of the characteristics of a type called "institutional norms."

The typology of norms presented here, while based in part upon these prior efforts, attempts a classification employing additional dimensions (or criteria), directed toward the establishment of the *salience* of particular norms in any given hierarchical, normative system.

The development of the typology arose partially from the realization that other schemes of classification dealt only with certain aspects of norms. Sumner's classification is based largely upon the degree of conformity required and the kinds of sanction applied. Linton's classification is based upon the mixed criteria of extent of acceptance (universals and alternatives) and extent of application (specialties). Sorokin's classification utilizes the mixed criteria of content, i.e., what areas of behavior or belief the norms regulate, in his distinction between the technical norms and norms of etiquette and fashion, and the criterion of degree of conformity required (obligatory vs. free norms), in his distinction between law norms and moral norms. He also uses the criterion of reciprocity or "two-sidedness" in the latter distinction. Williams uses content criteria, i.e., what areas of behavior are regulated, in his classification of technical, conventional, aesthetic, etc., norms, and suggests the use of such characteristics as extent of agreement, modes of enforcement, explicitness, and specificity as criteria, although he never proceeds to a systematic classification on these bases. He does suggest a single type, institutional norm, which has several of the characteristics.

The various classifications based upon these selected criteria, or characteristics of norms, are useful for the particular problems which these writers had in mind, e.g., the developmental problems of Sumner, the cultural homogeneity problems of Linton, and so on. The present classification is based upon the somewhat different problem of establishing and predicting the salience of norms. It is but a first step, prior to the development of empirical measures of the variables outlined below.

The characteristics of norms selected for the classification are presented as grouped continua. These are arranged so that types or profiles can be constructed by a vertical reading of the characteristics of a given norm on all continua.

I. Distribution of Norm

Extent of knowledge of norm

(1) By subjects (those who set the norm)
very few . . . . almost everyone

(2) By objects (those to whom the norm applies)
very few . . . . almost everyone

Extent of acceptance, agreement with norm

(3) By subjects
very few . . . . almost everyone

(4) By objects
very few . . . . almost everyone

Extent of application of norm to objects

(5) To groups or categories
very few . . . . almost everyone

(6) To conditions
in specified few . . in almost all

II. Mode of Enforcement of Norm

(7) Reward—punishment
more reward than punishment . . . . . . more punishment than reward

(8) Severity of sanction
light, unimportant . . heavy, important

(9) Enforcing agency
specialized, designated responsibility . . . general, universal responsibility

(10) Extent of enforcement
lax, intermittent . . rigorous, uniform

(11) Source of authority
rational, expedient, instrumental . . divine, inherent, absolute, autonomous

(12) Degree of internalization by objects
little, external enforcement required . . . . . . great, self-enforcement sufficient

III. Transmission of the Norm

(13) Socialization process
late learning, from secondary relations . . early learning, from primary relations

(14) Degree of reinforcement by subjects
very little . . . high, persistent

IV. Conformity to the Norm

(15) Amount of conformity attempted by objects
attempted by very few . . . attempted by almost everyone

(16) Amount of deviance by objects
very great . . . . . very little

(17) Kind of deviance
formation of sub-norms . patterned evasion . . idiosyncratic deviation

It should be noted at once that the above selection of characteristics of norms *is* a selection: it does not intend to represent all of the features of norms which may be useful in analysis. For example, the following characteristics were considered as candidates for inclusion in the typology: specificity and explicitness in the statement of the norms, formal vs. informal sanctions, repressive vs. restitutive sanctions, degree and kind of conflict with other norms, locus of conflict (intra-group vs. inter-group), perceived consequences of deviance by subjects and objects. These characteristics were excluded from the typology, either because they seemed not to vary consistently in possible polar types with the other criteria used, or because they were subsumed under the criteria listed in the typology. Probably the most striking omission is the content of the norms.[1]

The classification here is not based upon content criteria, e.g., between technical and aesthetic norms, norms referring to behavior vs. norms referring to beliefs, feelings, or cognition. The position taken here is that these various norms, classified according to content, may all have the characteristics selected for the typology just outlined. In other words, constructed types based upon the characteristics listed above apply equally well to norms in any of the content areas. A further step in the application of the type is to investigate the relations between the types of norms and the content areas to which they apply.

The two types which appear most obviously are the polar ones. Reading down the extreme right-hand end of each of the continua, one may construct a polar type of norm which may be called an *absolute norm*: a norm which is known and supported by everyone, which applies to everybody under all conditions, which is rigorously enforced by heavy sanctions. Reading down the left-hand end of each continua, the opposite polar type may be constructed which may be designated a *conditional norm*, suggesting its limited application and sporadic enforcement.

The arrangement of the continua above points up at once the similarity between the present typology of norms and the familiar folk-urban, sacred-secular typology of Tönnies, Redfield, Becker, and others. This is not surprising since it has long been hypothesized, sometimes in other terms, that a folk society has a high ratio of absolute norms, and an urban society a high ratio of conditional norms. There is also some resemblance between the absolute norm and Williams' (1951, pp. 28–29) concept of institutional norm.

The placement of existing norms, group, organizational or societal, along the various continua in the typology should result in the formulation of additional mixed types which will be useful in the analysis and prediction of changes in single norms or in the normative structure.

[1] "Content" is used here in two senses: classification of norms according to the area of behavior regulated, e.g., technical and aesthetic, as in Sorokin or Williams; or classification of norms according to the nature of action called for by the norms, e.g., norms regulating behavior, belief, or feeling, as in Parsons (1953, Ch. 1).

REFERENCES

Linton, R. A., 1936. *The study of man.* New York: Appleton-Century.

Parsons, T., 1953. The superego and the theory of social systems. In T. Parsons, R. F. Bales, and E. A. Shils, *Working papers in the theory of action.* New York: The Free Press, pp. 13–29.

Sorokin, P. A., 1947. *Society, culture and personality.* New York: Harper and Row.

Sumner, W. G., 1906. *Folkways.* Boston: Ginn.

Williams, R. M., Jr., 1951. *American Society.* New York: Knopf.

selection 9 Structural Characteristics of Norms

JAY M. JACKSON

The idea *norm* is now such a familiar one that its meaning in ordinary discourse is generally assumed. Yet, as with many abstractions that fall readily into general use, this concept refers to highly complex phenomena within which many component processes can be recognized and a large number of meaningful characteristics distinguished. For example, norms may be described as ambiguous, highly restrictive, poorly crystallized, or very potent, although it is not clear how these characteristics are related to one another or precisely what they mean.

In the absence of some scheme for representing the structure of a norm, much of its potential as a tool for analysis of groups fails to be realized. In this paper a model is introduced which tries to incorporate the essential properties of the idea. A large number of characteristics of this model will then be examined, and each will be related to observable phenomena.

A MODEL FOR ANALYSIS AND MEASUREMENT OF NORMS

A Dimension of Behavior

A norm is always about something; it has an object. Ordinarily its object is some behavior on the part of a person that is considered to be appropriate or inappropriate. A student is expected to wear certain articles of clothing and not others in the classroom. There are norms about coming to class on time, about being absent, about disagreeing with the instructor—in fact, about most aspects of behavior in an instructional situation. One essential element of a model for describing norms is, therefore, a *behavior dimension.* Norms also exist for attitudes, or tendencies to behave. There may be a norm regarding the appropriate attitude to have toward the Soviet Union or the school superintendent. Some norms have as their object an activity of the group itself, for example, one defining the appropriateness of discussing a particular topic. Ultimately, however, norms about attitudes or group activities concern the behavior of individual members, since attitudes are inferred from behavior and activities consist of patterned behavior of group members.

Characteristic of a norm is the specification of the amount or degree of behavior that is expected of a person. The instructor may be expected to control the activities of the group. How much control is appropriate? Either too much or too little may be disapproved. A student may be frowned upon by others for over- or underparticipation. Some behaviors, such as overt sexual behavior, are so taboo in an instructional group that most persons may consider it unnecessary to think of them as varying in degree. A qualitative dimension might still be useful, however, for describing a norm in this area. For example, behavior could be located on a dimension from "highly overt" to "completely covert." Thus, it is desirable to think of any behavior as varying in degree along a dimension of quantity or quality.

A Dimension of Evaluation

Implicit in almost every conception of the norm is the idea of evaluation. Even when we refer to a person's individual norms for perceiving or judging the objects in his environment, we clearly imply that he has expectations about what he will consider to be appropriate or inappropriate. A norm that exists in a group involves shared tendencies to approve or disapprove a particular dimension of behavior. If, for example, a student relates to an instructor in too obsequious a manner, he may arouse strong feelings of disapproval among the other students. In some instructional situations the identical behavior might be considered quite acceptable, and in others might even

Abridged from Chapter 7 in The Dynamics of Instructional Groups: Socio-Psychological Aspects of Teaching and Learning. *Yearbook of the National Society for the Study of Education*, 1960, **59**, Chicago: University of Chicago Press, edited by M. B. Henry. Reprinted by permission of the author and the University of Chicago Press.

be highly approved. In medical school, according to Merton and his colleagues, "If he acts presumptuous about his knowledge, a student will be reproached by his classmates, whereas an admission of ignorance on his part may evoke their approval" (1957). The evaluation of an act of behavior can vary from strong approval to strong disapproval through some middle point of indifference. An *evaluation dimension* is thus an essential element of any scheme for describing norms.

The behavior dimension and the evaluation dimension are the two main components of the model presented in Figure 1. The following section describes how they are put together to derive a number of structural characteristics of norms.

Distribution of Approval-Disapproval

For any particular behavior dimension, the amount of approval or disapproval felt by members of a group toward a particular act may in principle fall anywhere along the evaluation dimension. It is possible, therefore, in any concrete situation, to plot a curve to describe the feelings of the members of a group. Figure 1 shows what the distribution of approval-disapproval might be in a group over a behavior dimension.

Suppose that the behavior dimension represents the number of times a member speaks in an hour's session of a discussion group. The scale varies from zero participation to speaking eight times, an arbitrary maximum. Instead of referring to approval-disapproval we have adopted the neutral term, *return*, for the evaluation dimension. It is also convenient to apply a numerical scale to this *return dimension.* If a person behaves in an approved manner he potentially could receive some positive return; if he behaves in a disapproved manner he potentially could receive some negative return. If group members are indifferent to his behavior, the person could receive a neutral or indifferent return.

The curve itself is referred to as a *return potential curve* and is plotted by taking the mean of group members' feelings about each scale position on the behavior dimension. In the example in Figure 1,

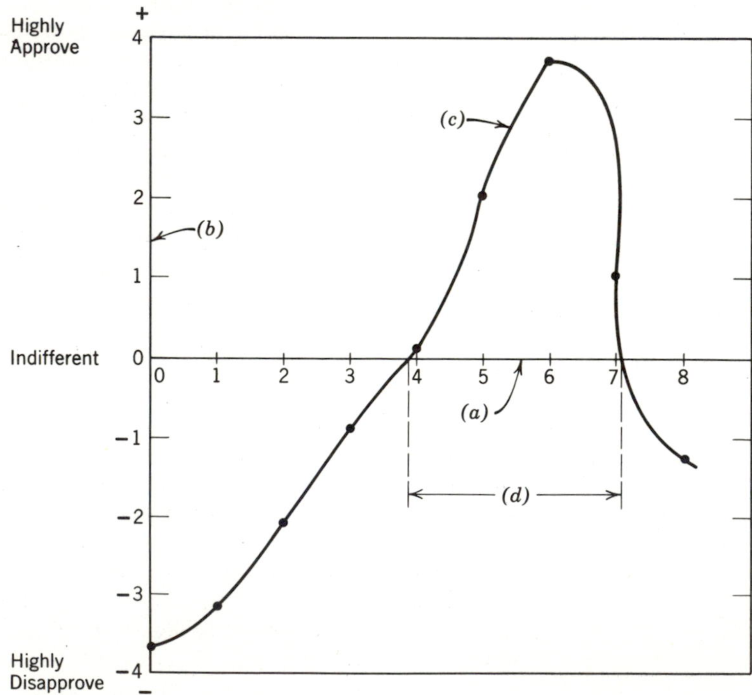

Figure 1. Schematic diagram showing the *Return Potential Model* for representing norms. (*a*) A *behavior dimension;* (*b*) an *evaluation dimension;* (*c*) a *return potential curve*, showing the distribution of approval-disapproval among the members of a group over the whole range of behavior; (*d*) the range of tolerable or approved behavior.

group members highly disapprove a member who does not participate in any of the discussion. In fact, unless a member participates at least four times his behavior is disapproved. At the other end of the scale, there is a tendency to decrease approval of a person's participation when it exceeds six times, but disapproval is not felt unless a member participates more than seven times. The curve does not specify how much return the actor will receive but how much he potentially could receive if all members of the group were to express their feelings toward his behavior.

The return potential curve describes the distribution of feelings of approval and disapproval by a particular group of persons for a given dimension of behavior. It incorporates the essential elements of the idea *norm*. Yet, clearly, the curve tells us nothing about the actual behavior that occurs in the group, only about the feelings held in abeyance, waiting to be triggered off if certain acts of behavior occur. Sometimes the term *norm* is used in describing the standard behavior in a group, i.e., for what is "normal." A more appropriate word for this idea is *mode*, since in many cases behavior "piles up" at a certain point on the behavior dimension even when no feelings of approval or disapproval exist. It would be possible, for example, to count the number of times each member of a group crossed and uncrossed his legs and establish the modal frequency of this behavior. Only under rare circumstances, however, would a norm as defined in this paper exist for this activity. It is important to distinguish between common behavior which represents parallel responses to the same environmental conditions and behavior which is normatively regulated by shared feelings of approval and disapproval.

CHARACTERISTICS OF A NORM

In the situation illustrated by Figure 1, the norm for participation is very restrictive for members of the group; it places a premium upon active participation; strong feelings exist about conformity and deviation; and over the entire behavior dimension there is a greater probability of a member being disapproved than approved. Each of these statements about the return potential curve describes a property of the norm. In some groups, the shape of the curve would be entirely different. Perhaps failure to participate would be quite acceptable behavior or even highly approved. In principle, a return potential curve can take any form. In studies now under way, it appears that in our culture a small number of forms predominate.

In the analysis and measurement of norms, it is desirable to distinguish among their various properties and to describe each as rigorously as possible. This will facilitate the study of problems such as how norms differ from group to group; how norms of a group change, or how changes in norms affect the members of a group. A precise description of the properties of a norm will also clarify the meaning of certain expressions in common usage, such as "norm conflict" or "internalization of norms."

Range of Tolerable Behavior

If one were asked to describe the norm represented in Figure 1, a number of different answers might be given. Is the norm to be defined as the particular point on the behavior dimension which is most approved by the members, as in this case about 6.5? A different definition of norm might be the *range of tolerable behavior*, to use a term introduced by Sherif (1956). Behavior between 3.8 and 7.4 on the scale would constitute the norm by this definition. In one sense, however, the entire return potential curve defines the norm, since it describes how behavior is regarded over the entire range.

The *range of tolerable behavior*, (d) in Figure 1, is that part of a behavior dimension which members of a group approve. The range might be relatively narrow or broad, depending upon whether a norm imposes high or low restrictions upon behavior. It has been suggested (Sherif and Sherif, 1956) that the greater the consequence behavior has for a group and its central concerns, the narrower will be the range of tolerable behavior. The norms about behavior of members with different status in the group might also vary with respect to this characteristic. In important matters, Sherif states, the range of tolerable behavior for a leader is narrower than for other members. Others have pointed to the lack of adequate studies in this area but have suggested that a certain degree of deviation from particular norms may be permitted leaders (Riecken and Homans, 1954). The issue is especially pertinent as it relates to instructional groups. Is the range of tolerable behavior narrower for the instructor than for the students? If so, is this true for all behavior or only for certain types of behavior? These are questions that can be answered empirically, providing the range of tolerable behavior can be measured with adequate precision.

Intensity of a Norm

In certain areas of behavior, a transgression is punished severely; in others there seems to be little concern by members of a group regardless of how individuals behave. There are some behavior dimensions where ideal behavior is accorded tremendous approval and reward; for example, in instances involving acts of heroism or self-sacrifice. Norms differ greatly with respect to the intensity of approval or disapproval evoked by appropriate or inappropriate behavior.

The *intensity* of a norm can be described in terms of the return potential curve. An index can be developed by summing the ordinates or height of the curve at each scale position on the behavior dimension, and represents the total area encompassed by the curve. This measure describes the over-all intensity of feeling in the group, whether of approval or disapproval, regarding the particular behavior. The steeper the curve in either direction, the greater is the intensity of the norm. In areas where behavior is not strictly regulated or controlled, members of a group are relatively indifferent to a person's behavior regardless of where it falls on the continuum. The curve for such a norm is relatively flat, and the intensity is quite low. Norms about matters of personal taste, such as style of speaking, walking, or dress, usually have lower intensity than those about behavior of vital concern to a group, such as the instructor's behavior in relating to individual members.

One of the areas where there is both concern and disagreement about norms for instructional groups is that of discipline. Our analysis of norms suggests the question, "What properties of norms are involved in this problem?" For example, does a "strict" discipline imply a narrow range of tolerable behavior, high intensity of both approval and disapproval, or just the latter? Does it perhaps refer to the proportion of behavior dimensions in the situation which are regulated by norms, defined in a later section as the *scope* of the norms? Answers to such questions would make more meaningful findings like the one recently reported by Kent and Davis (1957), that the children of more "demanding" parents develop intellectually more rapidly than do those whose parents are somewhat "unconcerned."

Approval-Disapproval Ratio

When the range of tolerable behavior is narrow for a particular norm, one would expect a noticeable effect upon the learning atmosphere of an instructional group. This property of a norm expresses the proportion of the possible range of behavior that would be approved; and its complement signifies the proportion that would be disapproved. Thus, a narrow range of tolerable behavior implies a greater likelihood that a person's behavior will elicit disapproval rather than approval, unless he perceives accurately the structural properties of the norm. If many behavior dimensions in a group were characterized by similar narrow tolerances, life in the group would be essentially threatening rather than promising. One might predict a low level of initiative and creativity among members, high concern for the opinions of others, especially of those possessing high status, and a relatively high level of anxiety.

Thus, in terms of its implications for the feelings and behavior of members, a ratio of approval to disapproval appears to be a meaningful property of a norm. A better method of expressing this property is to compute a *potential return ratio*, the mean intensity of positive potential return divided by the mean intensity of negative potential return over the entire behavior dimension. Where feelings of approval for appropriate behavior are just as strong as feelings of disapproval for inappropriate behavior, the potential ratio would be 1. When the ratio is below unity, the atmosphere for the behavioral area in question is threatening; to the degree that the ratio exceeds unity, the atmosphere is correspondingly supportive. In recent work we have found it preferable, for technical reasons, to substitute the *potential return difference*. *PRD* is calculated by taking the difference between the sum of the positive ordinates and the sum of the negative ordinates of the return potential curve (see Jackson, 1962a, b, c).

An experiment by Schachter and Hall (1952) illustrates the importance of threatening and non-threatening atmospheres for members' behavior. They found that more students were willing to volunteer to participate in an experiment when the "group restraints" were reduced. But when the atmosphere was more threatening, a higher proportion of those who had volunteered to participate actually appeared for their appointments. Thus, depending upon whether an instructor wants to encourage spontaneity and initiative, or "good" behavior, he should strive to increase or decrease the potential return ratio of behavioral norms in the group.

Expressions of feeling concerning the role of the psychiatric aide in the mental hospital were obtained by the author from psychiatric nurses in a workshop setting. When the return potential curves were drawn, it was discovered that on certain behavior dimensions on aide could not elicit any positive return but only disapproval or indifference. It is likely that norms of this type, having very low potential return ratios, are often shared by higher status members of an organization with respect to the behavior of lower status members, such as service personnel. Since it is impossible for these people to obtain approval, it is likely that they will not be motivated to meet expectations and that much of their energy will be devoted to nonwork problems. Similar consequences might be expected in instructional groups where the potential return ratios for behavioral norms are too low.

Point of Maximum Return

Another interesting characteristic of a norm is the point on the behavior dimension which would be maximally approved. This *point of maximum return* represents ideal behavior in the eyes of group members, assuming that they are the "norm-setters." It is probable that this point varies for different members of a group according to their status. On certain behavior dimensions it would be located differently for male and female members. Discovering the point of maximum return would be another way of determining whether, as Sherif (Sherif and Sherif, 1956) suggests, norms are more exacting for leaders than for ordinary members. This property of a norm also lends itself to comparisons of a group's norms over a period of time or of the norms of different groups for the same behavior dimension.

Crystallization of a Norm

In most instructional groups that have a history, a high proportion of the behavior of the members and the instructors will be regulated by norms, either those brought into the group from previous situations or those generated by interaction of the participants of the group. The instructor, leader, or trainer, as he is variously called, is the most influential norm-setter. Yet there will be many aspects of behavior for which norms are not available, especially in a new group, since it takes time for them to develop or to become crystallized.

One of the important questions in regard to any instructional group is whether a norm exists for a particular dimension of behavior. The question is quite ambiguous in this simple form and needs to be formulated in terms of the return potential model. The query could be in terms of the intensity of return. Where the over-all intensity of the norm is very low, it could be said that a norm does not exist for that type of behavior. There are a number of other conditions, however, which might also imply the nonexistence of a norm. Suppose, for example, that there is little agreement among the members of a group in regard to a given area of behavior. Feelings of approval or disapproval might be widely scattered for any given position on the behavior dimension. The return potential curve in this situation would typically be quite flat, indicating a low over-all intensity. But since the points on the curve are plotted by taking the average return potential for all members of the group, the flatness of the curve might be concealing very intense feelings of approval-disapproval by members who are in disagreement.

A measure called the *crystallization* of a norm can be derived from the return potential model by summing the total variance or dispersion of the return potential for all scale positions on the behavior dimension. When the amount of dispersion is large, indicating that members' ideas of appropriate or inappropriate behavior do not coincide, the degree of crystallization is low. In recent studies Cronbach's, 1953, distance function, D^2, has been used as a measure of crystallization. This provides an index which can then be employed in analyses of variance or other statistical analysis (see Jackson, 1962b; Glick, 1962).

Although both low intensity and low crystallization of a norm could signify that a norm does not exist, they represent different conditions in the group's culture. Gibb (1963) maintains, for example, that the experiences in a T-group can be understood in terms of the development of a number of norms critical for effective group functioning. Initially these norms do not exist, and members typically suffer confusion and strain before the requisite norms emerge from the interaction. In the early stages of such a group, the crystallization of norms would be low, in spite of high intensity of individual feelings. Even in its final hour, however, there would be norms for certain areas of behavior whose intensity would be low in spite of high crystallization. The statement that no norm exists in a group for a particular behavior dimension might, thus, have different implications for predicting interaction among members, depending upon whether it meant low crystallization of the norm with high intensity or low intensity in spite of high crystallization.

When crystallization is high and intensity low, it might mean that the behavior dimension is not considered to be important by most group members or that they are apathetic. When crystallization is low, it may permit a number of interpretations, depending upon other conditions of the group. As Gibb (1963) has pointed out, this condition might simply point to the relative "immaturity" of the group. If the group is well established, some writers would take low crystallization of norms to be a sign of disintegration (Sherif and Sherif, 1956). A study by Georgopoulos (1956) of an industrial organization found that agreement concerning norms, or high crystallization, was positively related to organizational effectiveness. He selected behavior dimensions that were judged to be of central importance. There will be many areas of behavior in a group or organization, however, in which the degree of crystallization may not be so significant. In Merton's (1957) study of medical education, for example, a faculty member points to low crystallization without exhibiting great concern, saying that "there just aren't many 'ground rules' in this area."

One might also devise a measure, *crystallization of an individual's norm*, by obtaining repeated spaced measures of an individual's approval-disapproval tendencies and calculating the average variation for all positions on the behavior dimension. This would be, in effect, a measure of reliability of his norm but would indicate to what degree he had stabilized tendencies to approve or disapprove the behavior. Comparisons between the degree to which a norm had crystallized for a group and for individual members would also yield information about the latter's membership position.

Ambiguity of a Norm

A special case of low crystallization of a norm is found when the total consensus among a group's members is low for some behavior dimension but consensus within cliques or subgroups is high. The return potential curve would be quite flat for this norm, as in Figure 2(c). For the total group

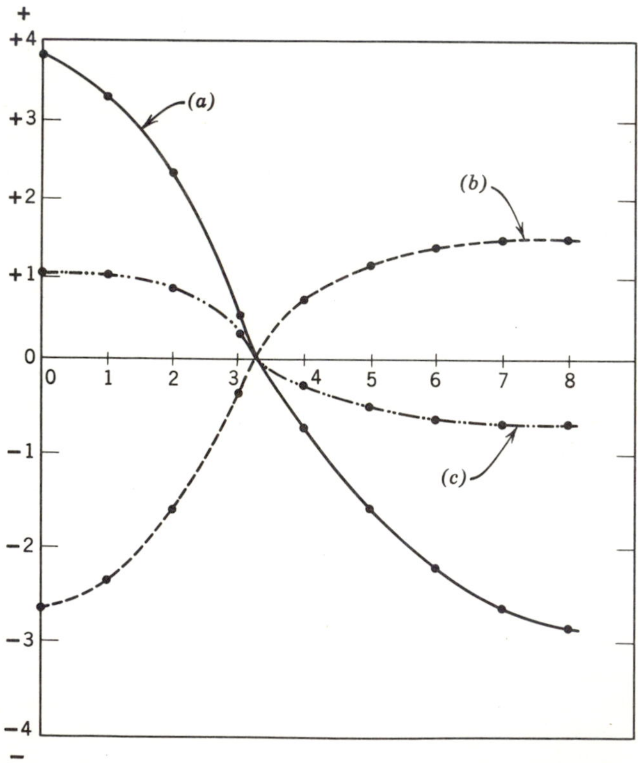

Figure 2. Schematic diagram for representing the *ambiguity* of a norm. In this situation there are two distinct return potential curves: (*a*) curve representing feelings of one subgroup; (*b*) curve representing feelings of a different subgroup; (*c*) return potential curve for total group where norm has high ambiguity.

it would be appropriate, in one sense, to say that there is no norm, since there is both low crystallization and low intensity. To stop at this point in the analysis, however, would be to ignore a crucial property of the group's normative structure, which might be responsible for much of the subsequent behavior of group members.

In the situation depicted in Figure 2, two distinct norms exist in the group for the same behavior dimension. Each has high intensity and may be highly crystallized. These norms might serve to identify the persons who have opposite feelings as belonging to different subgroups; in this sense there is not one group but two. For example, the two return potential curves might represent the feelings (a) of the faculty and (b) of the students or training participants. A newcomer to this group would be confronted with a highly ambiguous situation, as would any member who was trying to identify with the group as a whole. Thus the *ambiguity* of a norm may be a useful concept for describing conditions in some instructional groups. It can be defined in terms of the bimodality of distribution of return; that is, by the presence of two highly crystallized but different curves for the same behavior dimension.

PROPERTIES OF A GROUP'S NORMATIVE STRUCTURE

Many educators have welcomed such "atmospheric" concepts as *democratic*, *autocratic*, *group-centered*, *teacher-centered*, *permissive*, and *supportive*, since they were badly in need of terms to describe the instructional group's internal social environment. Yet, such concepts have serious limitations. They are often used in an evaluative rather than a descriptive sense to express the speaker's agreement or disagreement with the values that he thinks are represented in the group's atmosphere. Another difficulty is that precise meanings of these labels are not widely shared; how many instructors agree on exactly what behaviors are involved in being "democratic"? In the absence of clear and common conceptualization, it is impossible to develop adequate methods of measuring these attributes of a group's internal social environment.

In the preceding sections, each of the concepts introduced was a property of a single norm which could vary from one time to another or from one group to another. The study of the development, change, and consequences of norms in the instructional group should be facilitated by the use of concepts such as these. It is desirable, however, to develop similar concepts for describing the *normative structure* of a group, that is, the characteristics of its total pattern of norms for regulating members' behavior on many different dimensions. An adequate description of a group's normative structure may offer a more differentiated, systematic, and operational approach to the study of social environment. A number of properties that appear to be useful for this purpose can be derived from the return potential model.

Scope of Norms

One way in which groups differ that is significant for their internal social environment is in the *scope* of behavior regulated by norms. In families, for example, there are norms with high crystallization and intensity for most behaviors that a member engages in, including motor activities, language, manners, dress, sexual activity, and work. The behavior dimensions for which norms exist are numerous and cover a broad scope of activity. In contrast with this extensive regulation of a member's behavior, some groups have norms for only limited areas of behavior. A curriculum committee, for example, might have well-developed norms defining the responsibilities of members' behavior by and toward authority, and activities deemed essential to the achievement of the group's objectives. The scope of its norms is narrow, however, compared to that of the family.

The scope of norms probably varies greatly among instructional groups. In some classes, for example, the only norms that affect members' behavior are those set by the instructor, since interaction among members is highly restricted. Such norms may regulate work activities only or may also include "disciplinary" matters. There has been an increasing tendency in American education, however, to conceive of the school or classroom group as a "second family" that accepts major responsibility for socialization of the child. The degree to which this is the appropriate function of an instructional group is a controversial question and is much discussed in the current re-evaluation of our educational system. One aspect of this important issue can be described in terms of the scope of norms of an instructional group, that is, the number of different behavior dimensions for which there is high intensity and crystallization of approval-disapproval tendencies.

In his discussion of the emotional dimensions of group life, Cartwright (1952) suggests that if members of a group have little freedom to pursue their personal goals they are likely to suffer frustration. If the scope of norms is broad, there will remain few areas of privacy for the individual in which he is free to behave "as he likes" without being concerned about his effect upon the group or the consequences of his behavior for his membership position. A similar theme is elaborated by both Riesman (1950) and Whyte (1956) in their provocative discussions of the society's and organization's effects upon individual members. They deplore the overregulation of individual behavior, the "other-directedness," with its feared consequences of mass-produced personalities and the attenuation of the courageous and creative strains in our citizenry. Neither of these seductively convincing works, unfortunately, rests upon the systematic evidence that is required to provide definitive answers to the questions it raises.

There is evidence against the position that a broad scope of norms in a group (including an organization, community, or society, to use the term loosely) is necessarily harmful to the individual. To return to an earlier example, the family, most students seem to agree that membership in this primary group provides security, support, and orientation to the degree that it embraces many areas of an individual's life. Action research in England directed toward readjusting returned prisoners of war has demonstrated the effectiveness of transitional communities which provided a normative structure of broad scope for the members' behavior (Curle and Trist, 1947). Many of the newer techniques of adult education, including the re-education of the socially maladjusted, involve the creation of an all-encompassing social environment—a "cultural island" (Bradford, *et al.*, 1953), a "therapeutic community" (Jones, 1953)—to achieve changes in individual members. It would appear that the problem of determining the optimal scope of norms in an instructional group is far from resolved and that research might lead to some specification of the conditions under which a broad or narrow scope will produce particular consequences in members of the group.

Integration of Norms

Another important characteristic of a group's normative structure is the degree of *integration* among its norms. Although for purposes of analysis it is useful to distinguish single behavior dimensions, people behave in meaningful sequences of activities that are multidimensional. If it is possible for a member of a group to engage in behavior that is considered to be appropriate according to the several norms involved, these norms are integrated into a system. But, if a member is always in danger of violating some norms in order to adhere to others, there is a low degree of integration among the norms. In many groups and institutions with long traditions, new norms are continually being developed without the older norms being modified or discarded. Unless considerable care be given to the integration of norms, a normative structure can evolve in which it becomes increasingly difficult for members to avoid disapproval and which places them periodically in a state of conflict.

A common conflict in educational institutions is found between norms about scholarship and those about participation in social activities. Some students make a practice of staying up all night to study once or twice a week in an attempt to resolve the conflicting demands of their social responsibilities and their course work. But this makes it difficult for them to adhere to the norm about staying awake in class. Instructors often find themselves in conflict, too, arising from poor integration of norms about productivity, on the one hand, and about behavior by and toward authority, on the other. High output of work may be demanded by an instructor, perhaps because this is the norm for the larger educational system of which the instructional group is a part. If he then helps to establish a norm that approves initiative and self-direction on the part of group members, the students may find themselves in a normative structure in which it is impossible for them to behave appropriately.

The lack of integration of norms regulating behavior in the areas of authority, achievement, and membership account for much of the conflict and anxiety found in many training groups. As Gibb (1963) points out, however, human relations training groups have as an objective the sensitizing of members to interpersonal and group processes involved in the development of norms, both crystallization and integration of norms. In his discussion of the sociology of medical education, Merton (1957) lists a number of incompatible norms in the practice of medicine and concludes that "medical education can be conceived as facing the task of enabling students to learn *how to blend* incompatible or potentially incompatible norms into a functionally consistent whole." In its broader sense, all education is confronted with essentially the same problem.

Derived Properties of Normative Structure

There are undoubtedly many other properties of a group's normative structure that warrant precise conceptualization, measurement, and study. A number of these, each a *group* measure of one of the individual characteristics described previously, will be listed. The major problem involved in arriving at the following indices is the selection of the behavior dimensions to be included. For example, if a group property is the average of a number of individual properties of norms, it will be necessary to establish some criterion of crystallization and/or intensity and to include in the group measure all those behavior dimensions that meet the criteria.

The *mean range of tolerable behavior* is one such property. It may be useful in describing the degree to which behavior is regulated in a group and for comparing the atmospheres of different groups.

The *mean intensity of norms* in a group describes the strength of feelings in the group about members' behavior. Thus, it appears to be another index of the extent to which behavior is regulated and should be positively related to the mean range.

The *mean return ratio* was utilized in one study to describe the degree to which norms of a group are "punitive" or "supportive" (Jackson and Butman, 1956). This seems to be an important characteristic of a group's internal social environment.

The *mean crystallization* of norms in a group may be indicative of its "maturity" or degree of development. A longitudinal study of groups utilizing such an index might yield much-needed data about the growth, development, and change of groups under various conditions. (This measure has been employed successfully in a longitudinal study of the changes in behavioral norms of students in a church-related liberal arts college; see Glick, 1963).

The list might be expanded by utilizing other parameters, but those presented serve to illustrate the possibilities of the approach.

Comparative Analysis of Norms

Much of the empirical research in the area of group norms has been concerned with questions of comparison rather than description of single norms or normative structures. Investigators have focused on problems of conflicting norms, role conflict, and accuracy of perceptions of norms (comparison between perceived and objective norms). The return potential model provides a framework for more precise conceptualization of such phenomena.

Congruence of Norms among Groups

An individual belongs to many different but overlapping groups. Groups may be said to overlap in a number of ways. The fact that even a single person belongs to two different groups makes them overlap with respect to membership. More important for the person who is a member of both groups, it is inevitable that some dimensions of his behavior will be regulated by norms in each group. If it happens that the norms of one group are the same as those of another, persons having membership in both groups will have a consistent environment and feel little conflict between the demands of dual membership. *Congruence* of norms of different groups may result when norms are determined by some central authority in a larger organization; although it is likely that such official rules and regulations are reinterpreted and modified within each group in the system. Congruence may also develop by parallel experience of groups in similar situations or by conscious cooperation guided by shared values or goals.

Since norms can vary in so many different ways, it is difficult to define a unitary measure of congruence of norms among groups. One can compare the ranges of tolerable behavior and discover that some groups are more permissive or restrictive than others. In his analysis of conflicting norms, Stouffer (1949) says that an individual's behavior in one group can be understood only by an examination of how the ranges of tolerable behavior overlap in all the groups to which he belongs. Groups can also be compared with respect to the crystallization of norms for a given dimension of behavior, or a group may be compared with itself at different periods in its history (Glick, 1963). For some purposes it may be instructive to examine these properties of norms across different dimensions of behavior, asking questions like: "Is the norm for attendance more crystallized than that for lateness?" or "Are members of the group more tolerant of deviation with respect to completing individual assignments than completing group assignments?" Ordinarily, however, a comparison of norms will be most productive when a single dimension of behavior is involved, simply because the scales on both behavior and return dimensions vary in their interpretation from one item of behavior to another. For example, is tolerating three absences a month more or less tolerant than tolerating three latenesses a month? Such comparison is obviously meaningless.

One measure of *congruence* between norms that has proved to be useful can be defined in terms of the relative intensities of two norms. Reexamining the return potential curves of the two sub-groups in Figure 2, it may be noted that they are clearly discrepant. By subtracting from the value of the more positive ordinate the value of the less positive ordinate, and by summing the differences for each position on the behavior dimension, a measure of congruence is obtained. This measure is, of course, the sum of the differences between means. Similarly, if one desired, a measure of congruence of crystallization could be developed by utilizing the differences between standard deviations or variances at each position on the behavior dimension.

There is some evidence that congruence between the norms of different groups is an important determinant of the behavior of those who have multiple memberships, although the studies that have been made have not conceptualized and measured this property rigorously. One investigation of the effect of conflicting authority upon the child reported that unconstructive activity and oscillating behavior resulted from adults' commands that provided children with contradictory directions (Meyers, 1944). The study was conducted in an experimental playground but probably has implications for situations in which the norms of the family and the classroom lack congruence. Sherif (Sherif and Sherif, 1956), has stated that the degree to which members adhere to norms in one group will depend upon the congruence of the norms of all the groups to which they belong. Georgopoulos (1956) has reported that "normative consistency" or the degree to which the norms of management agree with those of employees is related to a measure of organizational effectiveness.

It seems likely that the ability to make exact comparisons between the norms of instructional groups depends upon some measure such as the congruence of norms. Very low congruence, i.e., a high index, could be interpreted as conflict between norms and should have implications for understanding the behavior of individuals caught between conflicting demands.

Norm Correspondence or Noncorrespondence

Just as it is possible to make comparisons between the norms of different groups and describe them in terms of congruence, it is also possible and, at times, desirable to make comparisons between the norms of individuals or between those of a person and a group. Theories about the socialization of children, for example, commonly describe the process of "internalizing" norms. Similarly, the stages by which a person becomes a full-fledged member of a group can be described in terms of the gradual assimilation of the group's norms. At any point in the process, a measure of *correspondence* would be useful to describe the degree of similarity between the person's norm on a particular behavior dimension and that of the group. Such a measure can be developed from the return potential curves, using the same procedure employed for defining congruence between the norms of different groups.

An illustration of correspondence of norms is seen in Figure 3, in which the return potential curves are presented for three psychiatric nurses about patients' "eating behavior." There is high correspondence between the norms held by Nurse A and Nurse B, but low correspondence between their norms and that of Nurse C. One could predict that if all three nurses were coming into contact with the same patient at different times, it would be difficult for the latter to understand why his behavior sometimes evoked approval and sometimes disapproval. When there is low correspondence among the internalized norms of key authority figures, such as different teachers in a school or teachers and parents, the children concerned suffer the anxieties implicit in such inconsistent social environments. Their resolution of such conflict may be to conform publicly but to maintain their own private standards and behavior, cut off, as Newcomb (1950) has pointed out, from the possibility of modification because they cannot be communicated.

One of the areas of behavior where high correspondence between norms appears to be critical for group functioning is the amount of direction and control asserted by its leader. In the Georgopoulos (1956) study it was found that, when supervisors and subordinates did not share norms regarding the amount of pressure it was appropriate for the former to apply to the latter, the effectiveness of the organization was judged to be low. In a different organization that was studied (Jackson, Butman, and Schlesinger, 1958), utilizing the present framework, the norms approved a high degree of control by chairmen of executive committees over members, and there was very high correspondence between the leaders

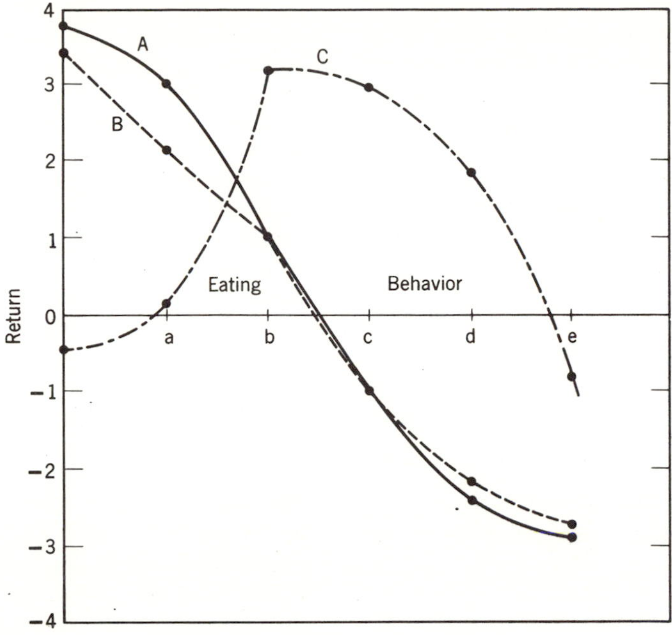

Figure 3. Return potential curves for three psychiatric nurses on a dimension, patients' "eating behavior," illustrating correspondence or noncorrespondence among norms. The *return* dimension was phrased in terms of whether a patient was judged healthy enough to live in the community without specialized assistance or sick enough to require further hospitalization. (From an unpublished study by the author.)

and the led. It should not be assumed that an authority figure can always set the norms for the group; it will depend upon the degree to which a norm has previously become crystallized in the group. For example, in his study of nursery-school children, Merei (1949) found that once a group had established norms about its activities, dominant members who had formerly been its leaders were often unable to change the norms and could only reassert their "leadership" by accepting the norms of the group.

Accuracy of Perceiving Norms

One of the determinants of an individual's ability to behave appropriately in a social situation is the accuracy with which he perceives the existing norms. When, for one reason or another, the person is prevented from perceiving or understanding the approved and disapproved regions of behavior, it is likely that his needs will be deprived rather than gratified, regardless of how much he is motivated to conform, especially where the range of tolerable behavior is narrow. Thus, in the most important areas of behavior, those in which norms are most crystallized, most intensive, and deviation least tolerated, the individual with inaccurate perception of norms is most likely to receive negative return in his interaction with others. Once this process has begun, it is extremely difficult to reverse, because, as Newcomb (1950) has pointed out, the individual cannot communicate successfully to others and will cut himself off from communication if he is receiving too much negative return. Cartwright (1952) observes that the power of a group either reinforces or reduces the individual's security, depending upon whether or not he accepts the group's norms. "It would appear from experience with groups," he says, "that a particularly disturbing situation is one where the member cannot anticipate with certainty which forms of his behavior will produce group support and which group hostility."

Accuracy of perceiving norms is a special case of correspondence. Instead of describing the amount of discrepancy between a norm of a group and of an individual, or between norms of two individuals, it describes the discrepancy between the norm and an individual's perception of it. Thus, for every member of a group, it is possible to obtain a *perceived* return potential curve, namely, the curve attributed by him to the other group members, collectively, and to compare this curve with the members' actual return potential curve. The resultant measure, derived like any measure of congruence or correspondence, is an index of the person's accuracy in perceiving the group norm for the behavior dimension in question. It would be possible, similarly, to obtain a more general measure of the person's perceptual accuracy by averaging accuracy indices across many different behavior dimensions. This was done in one study of the accuracy with which informal leaders perceived norms in an office situation (Jackson and Butman, 1956). It was found that their accuracy depended upon the area of behavior and also upon the characteristics of the social environment.

THE CONSEQUENCES OF NORMS FOR INDIVIDUALS

Conformity and Deviation

It will be apparent that any discussion of a person's *conformity* or *deviation* must take into consideration a number of the issues discussed in preceding sections. When a person's behavior is judged to be inappropriate, who is doing the judging? What degree of correspondence is there between the norms of actor and judge? Does the person perceive the norm in question with relative accuracy, or does he fail to do so and believe that he is behaving appropriately in terms of his perception of the norm? Would he like to conform, but finds the range of tolerable behavior defined too narrowly for his abilities or skills? Are the norms ambiguous or poorly crystallized in the group, making it difficult for members to perceive them accurately? Or is the person behaving in a manner calculated to obtain most gratification, since the potential return for deviation has less intensity in this group than for that conformity in some other group to which he belongs? These and other questions suggested by the return potential model indicate that the problem of conformity is somewhat more complex than it is generally represented to be.

Gratification-Deprivation and Self-Esteem

An analysis of norms in instructional groups appears to be of considerable importance for understanding the attitudes, feelings, and behavior of individual members. There are several ways in which individual behavior can be influenced by group norms. One process of gaining conformity to norms involves the transmission of cues of approval or disapproval by group members to one another, rewarding appropriate and punishing inappropriate behavior. Thus, behavior is brought within the tolerated range; or, if it remains outside, the deviant risks criticism, snubs, or various forms of rejection including outright exclusion. However, instructional group managers customarily attempt to solve the problem of social control by increasing sources of gratification within the group rather than by adding to the deprivations for deviation.

Much more common and effective for socialization in any society or group is the creation of an environment which perpetuates and reinforces a particular culture. The norms of this subculture are "internalized" by individual members, just as a child grows up with the prejudices of its family. The individual thus becomes his own judge, approving or disapproving his behavior in terms of internal standards. This is essentially the idea of Freud's concept of super-ego. Without discussing here the various theoretical explanations for the individual's learning the norms of his society, community, or group, the process clearly occurs in varying degrees for different individuals.

We have already discussed concepts and measures that can be used to describe the correspondence or noncorrespondence between a person's own standards or norms and those of some person or group. It is possible thus to determine whose norms the individual has internalized. This knowledge is important for an understanding of his personality structure, since his self-system develops by a continuous process of interacting with others and developing attitudes toward himself which are influenced by others' attitudes and evaluations. A person's self-evaluation or self-esteem, and his attendant level of confidence or anxiety, is highly susceptible to the acceptance and evaluations of other group members, especially members with high status and power such as parents or instructors. Evidence for this generalization can be found in many studies. Bennis and Burke (1958) found, for example, that after the intensive give-and-take of a human-relations training group, members' self-concepts had changed in the direction of a more realistic self-image.

One measure of the amount of gratification a member of a group is receiving, relative to his deprivation, can be called *total potential return*. By determining where his habitual behavior falls on a behavior dimension and drawing the ordinate to the group's return potential curve, his potential return for that behavior is indicated. The algebraic sum of his potential gratifications minus his potential deprivations would constitute his total potential return. If it be assumed that, during the course of interaction among the members of an instructional group, feelings of approval and disapproval will be communicated, the potential return becomes the actual: members will be rewarded or punished interpersonally in accordance with where their behavior falls on the behavior dimension. Thus, a measure of *total return* should indicate whether a person is receiving gratification or deprivation of his needs from his interaction with other members of the group. In his analysis of educational problems, Jensen (1957) points out the importance for the personality of achieving an optimum "gratification-deprivation balance."

If a member's accuracy of perceiving the group's norms is low, the discrepancy between his perceived return and his actual return from the group may be substantial and may lead to frustration and anxiety. Studies of the behavior of persons in frustrating situations indicate that, if highly motivated behavior does not lead to gratification, the result is withdrawal, aggression, or rigidity. Increasing the accuracy with which norms are perceived is one approach to decreasing frustration and its unfortunate consequences for the individual.

If the norms of the group are internalized by an individual member, that is, if high correspondence exists between his own return potential curve and that of the group, he not only receives gratification in his interaction with others but he receives high return from himself. He approves his own behavior. But under the same circumstances, when the person accepts the norms of the group but is deficient in ability, skill, or control, so that his behavior falls outside the tolerated range, he will receive negative return, not only from the group but also from himself. He will disapprove of his own behavior. Such a state of the self-system could lead to increased striving, or it could lead to defensive changes in perception to avoid anxiety. It is important to our understanding of the individual member of an instructional group to determine just what return he is receiving from himself.

The concept *return self* may be useful as an index of self-evaluation or self-esteem, By obtaining measures of the individual's own return potential curve on relevant behavior dimensions, and then determining where his actual behavior falls on these dimensions, his *return self* can be determined. There are many questions related to the development of the self-system of persons in instructional situations that require systematic investigation. One such question is: "Do individuals have the same return potential curve for their own behavior that they have for others?" Do they judge themselves by the same standards they use in judging others? The ideas and methods developed in this selection have proved useful in the preliminary exploration of such questions.

REFERENCES

Bennis, W. G., and Burke, R., 1958. Changes in self-concept and perception—congruity as a result of a training group experience. Paper read at the annual meeting of the American Psychological Association, Washington.

Bradford, L., *et al.*, 1953. *Explorations in human relations training.* Washington: National Training Laboratories.

Cartwright, D., 1952. Emotional dimensions of group life. In M. L. Reymert (Ed.), *Feelings and emotions.* New York: McGraw-Hill, pp. 439–447.

Cronbach, L. J., and Gleser, Goldine C., 1953. Assessing similarity between profiles. *Psychological Bulletin,* **50**, 456–473.

Curle, A., and Trist, E. L., 1947. Transitional communities and social reconnection. *Human Relations,* **1**, 45–68, 240–288.

Georgopoulos, B. S., 1956. The normative structure of social systems: a study of organizational effectiveness. Unpublished doctoral dissertation, University of Michigan.

Gibb, J. R., 1963. A norm-centered view of T-Group training. In L. Bradford (Ed.), *Theories of T-Group training.* Washington: National Training Laboratories.

Glick, O. W., 1962. The effects of behavioral norms on the selection of associates. Unpublished master's thesis, University of Kansas.

Glick, O. W., 1963. An investigation of the change in behavioral norms of the students in a liberal arts college. Unpublished doctoral dissertation, University of Kansas.

Jackson, J. M., 1956. A comparative study of the social systems of two commercial offices. Unpublished manuscript.

Jackson, J. M., 1962a. A conceptual and measurement model for norms and roles. Lawrence, Kansas: Comparative Studies of Mental Hospital Organization.

Jackson, J. M., 1962b. Authoritative behavior norms in a state system of mental hospitals. Unpublished manuscript, University of Kansas.

Jackson, J. M., 1962c. The normative regulations of authoritative behavior. In W. J. Gore (Ed.), *Administrative decision making*. New York: The Free Press, 1964.

Jackson, J. M., and Butman, Jean W., 1956. The effect of organizational factors on the social sensitivity of affective and effective leaders. Paper read at American Sociological Society, Washington.

Jackson, J. M., Butman, Jean W., and Schlesinger, L., 1958. An investigation of norms about the allocation of power in a formal organization. Unpublished manuscript.

Jensen, G. E., 1957. The gratification-deprivation balance of personality systems. In G. E. Jensen (Ed.), *Socio-psychological analysis of educational problems*. Ann Arbor, Mich.: Ann Arbor Publishers.

Jones, M., 1953. *The therapeutic community*. New York: Basic Books.

Kent, H., and Davis, D. R., 1957. Discipline in the home and intellectual development. *British Journal of Medical Psychology*, **30**, 27–33.

Merei, F., 1949. Group leadership and institutionalization. *Human Relations*, **2**, 23–39.

Merton, R. K., Reader, G. G. and Kendall, Patricia L. (Eds.), 1957. *The student-physician*. Cambridge, Mass.: Harvard University Press.

Meyers, C. E., 1944. The effect of conflicting authority on the child. *University of Iowa Studies in Child Welfare*, **20**, 31–98.

Newcomb, T. M., 1950. *Social psychology*. New York: Dryden.

Riecken, H. W., and Homans, G. C., 1954. Psychological aspects of social structure. In G. Lindsey (Ed.), *Handbook of social psychology*, Vol. II. Cambridge, Mass.: Addison-Wesley.

Riesman, D., 1950. *The lonely crowd*. New Haven, Conn.: Yale University Press.

Schachter, S., and Hall, R. L., 1952. Group-derived restraints and audience persuasion. *Human Relations*, **5**, 397–406.

Sherif, M., and Sherif, Carolyn W., 1956. *An outline of social psychology*. New York: Harper and Row.

Stouffer, S. A., 1949. An analysis of conflicting social norms. *American Sociological Review*, **14**, 707–717.

Whyte, W. H., Jr., 1956. *The organization man*. New York: Simon and Schuster.

selection 10 The Formal Analysis of Normative Concepts

ALAN R. ANDERSON AND OMAR K. MOORE

Although mathematical logic has been applied in several empirical disciplines, logicians have only recently begun to develop formal systems that are likely to be of special interest to sociologists. From the point of view of modern logic, indefinitely many systems can be constructed; but whether such tools are to be of use to sociologists depends in part on the amount of interchange across disciplinary boundaries. This article is written in the hope of enlisting the support and interest of investigators treating problems to which such notions as *rule*, *norm*, *obligation*, etc. are central.

Concepts of this kind are of obvious importance for sociological theory; almost all sociologists

From the *American Sociological Review*, 1957, **22**, 9–17. Reprinted by permission of the authors and the American Sociological Association. This paper reports one aspect of a more general research program supported by the Office of Naval Research, Group Psychology Branch.

make use, in one way or another, of such notions. But in spite of the widespread use of normative concepts, very little is known of their logic. For the most part logicians have restricted their attention to descriptive discourse (variously called "informative," "factual," "cognitive," etc.), as opposed to prescriptive discourse (or "emotive," "normative," "expressive," etc.). Powerful technical tools have been developed for the analysis of the former, but there have been only a few attempts to provide analogous machinery for the latter. Whatever the reasons for the neglect of the prescriptive may be, this situation seems unfortunate. We all do, as a matter of fact, draw conclusions from a variety of statements that may, broadly speaking, be called "normative." We reason from moral precepts, from imperatives, from commands, from statements of legal responsibility and obligation, and from sets of rules for games like chess, bridge, and football.

These facts suggest that there are grounds for optimism concerning the possibility of developing a formal logic for norms. There have been many informal discussions of normative discourse, centering usually around imperatives; but there have been very few attempts to give a rigorous and formal characterization of the logical structure of the family of related notions consisting of legal or moral obligations, prescriptions, sets of directions, recipes, fiats, technological commands, and the like. Among these are Mally (1926), Menger (1939), Hofstadter and McKinsey (1939), von Wright (1951), Feys (1955), and Prior (1956). Space does not permit a general review of these systems, though each of them merits consideration. We have selected for initial discussion a system which is particularly relevant to sociology, namely von Wright's *Deontic Logic*.[1] But before discussing this formalism, it may be helpful to outline informally a problem typical of those on which the logical analysis might be expected to throw light.

Some sociological theorists have maintained that under certain circumstances there is a "strain of consistency," and under other circumstances a tendency toward inconsistency, among the norms of a given social order. An empirical test of such a thesis presupposes a reasonable explication of the concept of "consistency" as used in such analyses. In many instances it is difficult to see precisely what is meant by "consistency" as applied to sets of norms.[2] Despite the vagueness and ambiguity of the term "consistency," however, we would expect to find some uniformity in its application by sociologists. Consider as illustrations the following three cases.

I. If a set of norms both obligates and forbids an agent to execute a given act under the same circumstances, the set of norms would no doubt be regarded as inconsistent.

II. If a set of norms (a) makes it obligatory to do act B if act A is done, (b) permits act A, but (c) forbids act B, then again the set would no doubt be held to be inconsistent. It might be maintained, that is, that doing the permitted never commits an agent to doing the forbidden within a consistent set of norms.

III. Consider a set of norms which (a) makes act B or act C obligatory if act A is done, (b) permits act A, but (c) forbids both act B and act C. To say that such a set of norms is inconsistent amounts to saying that an act which commits an agent to forbidden alternatives would itself be forbidden by a consistent set of norms.

For such simple cases, it seems that common sense suffices to decide whether normative systems are consistent (though of course we are all familiar, from recent developments in science, with the fact that common sense may well be inadequate even for problems which appear to be easily resolved). But in any event it is clear that common sense does not take us very far. The following case, although undoubtedly much simpler than many situations which actually arise, will provide an illustration.

IV. Consider a set of norms from which it follows that (a) it is obligatory that if act D be done then act B not be done, (b) it is forbidden that if act A is done then act C is done, (c) it is obligatory that if act A is done then either act B or else both act C and act D be done, and (d) it is permitted that act D be done. Should (a)–(d) be taken as evidence that the set of norms is inconsistent or not? Even if it is clear to the reader how this question should be answered, it is obvious that realistic cases of much greater complexity might arise. Moreover, it would be valuable to have a clear statement of principles in accordance with which any case, simple or complex, could be decided.

But complexity is not the only problem. Some apparently simple questions may be puzzling and difficult to resolve, in part, because they are rarely raised. For example, suppose that a set of norms obligated an agent to perform some act

[1] "Deontic Logic" is the logic of the modes of obligation. Expositions of von Wright's system may be found in von Wright (1951a); von Wright (1951b); or Prior (1955).

[2] It should be emphasized that "consistency," in such contexts, frequently has only a vague analogical resemblance to "consistency" in the various logical senses. For the latter see A. Church (1955), especially pp. 108-109.

which is impossible for causal or perhaps even logical reasons. Should such a set of norms be regarded as consistent? If not, then what should be said about logically impossible acts? Are they to be forbidden? Or should we treat them as permitted? Or should they perhaps be regarded as indifferent? Or should we say that, inasmuch as contradictory acts are vacuous in the sense that they cannot be performed in any case,[3] none of the terms "obligatory," "permitted," "forbidden," are applicable to them?

Evidently what is required is a system of concepts that will handle not only the easier problems, but will also enable us to deal effectively with complex and/or unfamiliar cases. The system of deontic logic proposed by von Wright provides, among other things, a tool for treating just such questions as have been outlined above.

FORMAL DEONTIC LOGIC

Von Wright's system assumes a universe of discourse consisting of "acts," or perhaps better, "act-types." The word "embezzlement," for example, refers to a *kind* of incident, or a class of incidents, rather than to any particular occasion on which something is embezzled. As variables for "act-types" (for brevity, now, simply "acts") he uses "A," "B," "C," . . . In addition to the atomic acts over which the variables range, there are various combinations of acts:

Corresponding to any act A there is a *negation-act* of A, symbolized ~A. ~A is that act which is performed by an agent if and only if he does not perform A; to use von Wright's example, "The negation of the act of repaying a loan is not repaying it."

The *conjunction-act*, symbolized (A & B), is that act which is performed by an agent if and only if he performs both act A and act B.

The *disjunction-act* (A ∨ B) is that act which is performed by an agent if and only if he performs either act A or act B (or both).

The *implication-act* (A → B) is that act which is performed by an agent if and only if it is not the case that A is performed and B is not.

The *equivalence-act* (A ↔ B) is that act which is performed by an agent if and only if he performs both A and B, or neither A nor B.

The only primitive deontic concept is "permission"; the others (i.e., obligatory, indifferent, forbidden) are defined in terms of this primitive concept. "Permission" is symbolized by "P," and the result of applying "P" to the name of an act is a formula of the system. That is, "PA" is to be interpreted as expressing the proposition that acts of kind A are permitted. (The notion of permission is, of course, always to be understood as relative to some set of norms.) Similarly, "P ~ A" is to be understood as saying that it is permitted not to do A, etc.

"P" together with the act-types thus provide a collection of deontic propositions. As was remarked previously, there is available adequate technical machinery for manipulating propositions, and von Wright brings to bear on the deontic propositions the classical two-valued propositional calculus. This calculus contains analogues of the operations just described for the calculus of acts.[4] The other deontic concepts may then be defined in terms of the concept of permission as follows:

Definition 1. OA = df ~ P ~ A
Definition 2. FA = df ~ PA
Definition 3. IA = df(PA) & (P ~ A).

Definition 1 says that an act A is obligatory ("O") if and only if it is not permitted not to do A; definition 2 says that an act A is forbidden ("F") if and only if A is not permitted; and definition 3 says that an act A is indifferent ("I")[5] if and only if it is permitted to do A and also permitted to do ~A (i.e., not to do A). As von Wright remarks, indifference is a narrower concept than permission. Everything indifferent is permitted, but not conversely; obligatory acts, e.g., are permitted but not indifferent.

The definitions above make use of connectives drawn from the propositional calculus as well as

[3] An example of a contradictory act, one that cannot be performed, is smoking-and-not-smoking (at the same time by the same person). This sort of contradictory act is not to be confused with, e.g., smoking in defiance of a "No Smoking" sign, or with sometimes smoking and sometimes not smoking.

[4] That is, corresponding to any proposition p there is a denial $\sim p$ which is true if and only if p is false, and for any two propositions p and q there is a conjunction $(p \,\&\, q)$ (which is true if and only if both p and q are true), a disjunction $(p \vee q)$ (which is true if and only if at least one of p and q is true), an implication $(p \rightarrow q)$ (which is true if and only if it is not the case that p is true and q is false), and an equivalence $(p \leftrightarrow q)$ (which is true if and only if p and q are both true or both false). Expositions of this calculus may be found in any standard textbook in symbolic logic. Of course the symbols "~," "&," etc., are here used in a different sense, but no ambiguity need arise since, for example, "~" applied to an act-name always yields an act-name, whereas negation (symbolized the same way) applied to a proposition always yields a proposition.

[5] Von Wright discusses this concept, but does not specify notation for it; we introduce a special symbol for "indifference." For expository purposes, trivial changes and occasional departures from extreme rigor will be found here and elsewhere.

from the calculus of acts. And the application of the propositional calculus to the deontic propositions yields many formulae which are theorems in virtue of their propositional structure alone. For example $(PA \rightarrow PA)$, i.e., if A is permitted then A is permitted. However, the interesting theorems from the sociological point of view are those that depend for their status as theorems on the deontic concepts, and on the two principles governing them, which we quote from von Wright:

> I. The Principle of Deontic Distribution. If an act is the disjunction of two other acts, then the proposition that the disjunction is permitted is the disjunction of the proposition that the first act is permitted or the proposition that the second act is permitted (von Wright, 1951, p. 7).
>
> II. The Principle of Permission. Any given act is either itself permitted or its negation is permitted (von Wright, 1951, p. 9).

The formal analogue of Principle I is

$$P(A \vee B) \leftrightarrow [(PA) \vee (PB)];$$

that is, if it is permitted to do A or B and if it is permitted to execute the disjunction act (A or B), either it is permitted to do A or it is permitted to do B and conversely. The formal analogue of Principle II is

$$(PA) \vee (P \sim A);$$

that is, either it is permitted to do A or it is permitted to do $\sim A$.

With the aid of the three definitions and the two principles, von Wright developed a decision procedure[6] as a method of determining which formulae are theorems. The system therefore shares with axiomatic formulations the property of providing a rigorous (and in this case effective) method of testing expressions for "logical truth." The illustrative examples mentioned earlier can easily be tested by von Wright's method, and it develops that in each of the cases, (I), (II), and (III), the formal results accord with the presumed common sense solution. In case (IV) von Wright's decision procedure shows that the set of norms is inconsistent.[7]

As regards the puzzling questions concerning the deontic status of impossible acts, it appears that several alternatives are available. Von Wright (1951, p. 11) discusses this question, and proposes a principle of deontic contingency: "A tautologous act is not necessarily obligatory, and a contradictory act is not necessarily forbidden." This principle is consistent with the other two principles mentioned above, but it is not the only way to resolve the problem. In a system to be mentioned below, for example, application of the deontic categories is limited to contingent states of affairs (i.e., those which are neither necessary nor impossible).

It is not feasible to discuss the alternatives available in detail without giving a complete and rigorous formulation of the systems. Since it lies beyond the scope of this paper to present these systems *qua* formal systems, we will content ourselves with mentioning two more general considerations relevant to von Wright's logic.

In the first place, leaving aside for the moment the fact that certain expressions are provable as theorems, the formalism provides a clear explication of a number of normative concepts. In this respect it may be compared with the Hohfeldian analysis of such notions as duty, demand-right, power, immunity, etc. (1923). That analysis at this level is not without value may be seen from Hoebel's (1954) application of the Hohfeldian concepts to primitive law (1923).

In the second place, the deontic concepts of von Wright's system have close formal connections with other logical concepts, a fact first pointed out in recent literature by von Wright himself. In fact it was the observation of formal similarities between the notions "obligatory," "permitted," "indifferent," "forbidden," and the extensively studied concepts "necessary," "possible," "contingent," "impossible," which led von Wright to formalize a deontic logic. The formal similarities extend to other concepts as well, as summarized in the table of modal categories. (See Table 1.)

The *alethic* modes are predicated of propositions, in such contexts as "It is necessary that *p*,"

[6] There are in general two ways of specifying the set of theorems of formal systems, either by means of an axiomatization, or a decision procedure. An axiomatization consists of a list of axioms together with one or more principles of inference that lead to theorems. A decision procedure is an effective method for determining whether or not an arbitrarily given expression of the system is a theorem. Although for some systems there are both axiomatizations and decision procedures, the two techniques are in general independent; some systems have axiomatizations and no decision procedures, others have decision procedures and no axiomatizations. The decision procedure for von Wright's system consists roughly of a truth-table analysis of expressions in disjunctive normal form. There is as yet no axiomatization of the system in print, though it would be a simple exercise to produce one.

[7] A complete truth-table analysis of example (IV), carried out in the manner proposed by von Wright, would involve initially a two-valued truth-table with 2^{16} rows (some of which would be deleted). The amount of labor involved in testing such expressions can be vastly reduced by adapting methods of Alan Ross Anderson (1954, pp. 201-214).

TABLE 1 MODAL CATEGORIES*

Alethic	Existential	Epistemic	Deontic
a. necessary	universal	verified	obligatory
b. possible	existing	unfalsified	permitted
c. contingent	partial	undecided	indifferent
d. impossible	empty	falsified	forbidden

* This classification appears in G. H. von Wright, (1951, p. 2). We have again made slight changes for expository reasons. In particular, von Wright did not supply terms to designate two of the modes, on the grounds that no suitable English words were available. We have inserted "partial" and "unfalsified," by fiat. So far as we know, this use of "partial" is new.

and "It is impossible that *p*,"—*p* being any proposition. These modes have been treated in the systems of Strict Implication due originally to Lewis (1918), and further studied by McKinsey (1941), von Wright (1951), and others. The *existential* modes are regarded in many important contexts, as properties of classes. For example, the statement that there are no rich professors can be construed as saying that the class of rich professors is empty. The existential modes are handled in the theory of quantification, for which one *locus classicus* is *Principia Mathematica* (Whitehead and Russell, 1913). The *epistemic* and *deontic* modes were first investigated formally by von Wright. It is clear that the epistemic modes, like the alethic, apply to propositions. Von Wright, as previously noted, takes the deontic modes as applying to acts, though other alternatives are available, one of which will be discussed in the next section.

Among the formal similarities noted by von Wright are the following (where the letters refer to entries in the table): whatever is *a* is *b*, whatever is *b* is not *d*, and whatever is *c* is neither *a* nor *d*. To put the last relation more concretely: a *contingent* proposition is neither *necessary* nor *impossible*; a *partial* class is neither *universal* nor *empty*; an *undecided* proposition is neither *verified* nor *falsified*; and an *indifferent* act is neither *obligatory* nor *forbidden*. Of course these examples by no means exhaust the relations among modes in a given category. Moreover, there are systems of logic, some of which von Wright discusses, which combine concepts from two or more categories. In our opinion, a more adequate conceptual scheme for the analysis of normative concepts would involve a combination of the modal categories listed above.

FURTHER DEVELOPMENTS

Given a social group with an empirically specified normative structure, von Wright's logic would clearly facilitate the analysis of relations among the norms. However, these relations by no means exhaust the interesting and important aspects of normative systems. Two crucial aspects of such systems are the following. (1) There is a need for a method of relating norms to the system of social sanctions or penalties that support them. (2) It is important to relate both norms and sanctions to possibilities for action.

1. It is, of course, customary to couch discussion of norms in terms of the consequences of conforming to, and deviating from, their demands. The lack of such consideration is not to be regarded as a defect in von Wright's approach; it is in fact common in logical studies to isolate concepts and consider only some of their formal properties. Von Wright's system simply exhibits the methodological principle of dividing difficulties in order to conquer them individually, a practice characteristic of twentieth century studies in mathematics and logic. But this lacuna does point to the need for an expansion or elaboration of von Wright's system so as to take adequate account of sanctions.

Although it is clear that the notions of sanction must somehow be got into relation with the deontic logic, methods of effecting this rapprochement have not yet been extensively explored. However, some work has been done toward analyzing the relation between commands (rather than norms) and sanctions.

In an article primarily concerned with commands and imperatives, Bohnert (1945) suggested a formal analysis of the role of "penalties" in imperative discourse. In brief, he recommends that commands be treated as ellipses for disjunctive propositions, one part of which is ordinarily unverbalized, but nevertheless understood in the context of utterance of the command. The locution "Do A," for example, is to be understood as elliptical for the declarative proposition "Either you will do A, or else S," where "S" is understood as referring to a penalty or sanction that the recipient of the command will presumably attempt to avoid. Alternatively "Do A" might, depending on the context, be understood as an ellipsis for "Either you will not do A, or else R," where now "R" refers to a reward which the recipient of the command will presumably attempt to attain.

Bohnert's suggestions have not been axiomatized, but they show at least one way in which commands can be related to penalties so as to yield propositions. This feature of Bohnert's analysis is a distinct advantage, since it makes possible the application of the usual logic of propositions to commands.[8] Other ways of relating commands to propositions have been proposed (see Hare, 1952), but Bohnert seems to have been the first to formulate such a relation in a way that brings in penalties and rewards explicitly.

It would not be difficult to treat Bohnert's suggestion axiomatically, and the resulting "logic of sanctions," as we might call it, would constitute a rigorous formal theory on a par with von Wright's *deontic logic*. The obvious next step would be to construct a formal theory that encompasses both these systems so as to bring out the relations between obligations, the imperative sentences which express these obligations, and the sanctions associated with them.

2. It is clear that the possibilities of human action can be studied without regard either to particular realizations of these possibilities, or to the consequences of acting in any particular way. As an illustration of this point we may take the theory of games (von Neumann and Morgenstern, 1947). The analysis of any game begins with a complete characterization of all possible ways of playing, these possibilities being circumscribed only by the (non-normative) rules of the game, and not by their chances of success or failure. From among these possibilities, certain strategies are selected as, roughly speaking, most likely to win.

The case seems to us to be similar in analyzing normative systems. If we think of possibilities for action as being bounded by non-normative "rules" consisting of "laws of nature," then the social norms stipulate that certain of these possibilities will, if actualized, lead to rewards or penalties.

There are extensively studied formal systems suitable for the analysis of possibilities (and the other alethic modes). Pioneer work on this subject was done by Lewis in 1918, and since then the systems S1 to S5 (Lewis and Langford, 1932), S6 (Alban, 1943), S7 and S8 (Halldén, 1950), M (von Wright, 1951), and T (Feys, 1938), to mention only a few, have been constructed and discussed extensively. These modal systems provide alternative explications of the concepts of possibility, necessity, contingency, etc., and this kind of analysis is required for the clarification of the vague notion of "possibilities for human action."

Just as deontic logic makes a contribution to the analysis of normative systems, and the "logic of sanctions" could also contribute to this end, so the logic of "possibility," taken together with the foregoing, may shed light on the problem. What is wanted is a formal frame of reference rich enough to incorporate at least these three facets of normative systems.[9] From the formal point of view, (1) and (2) above motivated the construction of systems more comprehensive than von Wright's upon which we will comment briefly.

The system O′M*[10] has the following features. In addition to the usual primitive notions of alethic modal logic,[11] O′M* takes only the notion "sanction" symbolized "S," as primitive. The basic deontic modes are defined with the help of this notion in such a way that von Wright's system (with appropriate qualifications) emerges as a sub-system of O′M*. The only axiom mentioning the sanction states that the sanction is contingent; i.e., it is possible to behave in such a way that the penalty or sanction will occur, and also in such a way that it will not occur. The deontic modes are construed as applying only to contingent propositions; that is, (a) propositions *p*, *q*, *r*, . . . rather than acts, are the elements of the universe of discourse,[12] and (b) the question of what to do with contradictory and tautologous propositions is answered by limiting the range of deontic modes to propositions that are contingent.

[8] Traditionally, commands have not been regarded as propositions, primarily on the grounds that we are not inclined to ask of a command such as "Mail this letter" whether it is true or false. Certain writers have evinced an extreme reluctance, for philosophical and grammatical reasons, to admit any very close relation between propositions and commands. In our opinion this is an open question, to be decided by constructing logical systems whose utility can be tested in scientific practice.

[9] Of course there are other important aspects of normative systems; there are, for example subtle problems concerning the relations between possibilities for action, and beliefs about these possibilities. There are a number of ways in which the systems we are discussing might be extended so as to cover such questions. Epistemic modal operators may prove of value in this connection, and one obvious and important way in which these systems should be extended is by adding quantification theory (a generalization of the existential modes).

[10] This system is closely related to a group of new systems described and elaborated in Alan Ross Anderson (1956).

[11] The underlying alethic system of O′M* is in fact von Wright's system M (shown to be equivalent to Fey's system T by Boleslaw Sobocinski, 1953, pp. 171–178). Choice of alternative alethic logics yields systems somewhat different from O′M*. The exposition here of O′M* does not reflect various "reductions" effected for the family of systems OM of Anderson (1956).

[12] The letter "*p*," for example, is a variable ranging over propositions. In this context, the propositions may be about "acts," in von Wright's sense.

This point should not be construed as meaning that "acts" are unimportant, or have somehow been done away with; taking propositions as elements of the universe of discourse is simply *an* alternative interpretation worth investigating. There may well be others, e.g., propositional functions.

It is beyond the scope of this paper to present O′M* in detail, but it may be of interest to mention the way in which the deontic modes are defined. We use the letter "M" to represent "possibility"; that is, "Mp" is read "it is possible that *p*."

Definition 4.[13] O′p = df [(M*p*) & (M ~ *p*)] & ~M (~*p* & ~S).

In this definition of obligation "O′," the first clause, [(M*p*) & (M ~ *p*)], says that *p* is contingent, i.e., possibly true and possibly false. That is, it is possible to act in such a way as to make *p* true, and also in such a way as to make it false. The last clause ~M(~*p* & ~S) says that it is impossible that *p* and the sanction should *both* be false; thus, if *p* is false, then the sanction S is true. This amounts to saying that *p* is obligatory if and only if it is contingent, and failure to do what is required to make *p* true would lead to the sanction.

Similarly, we define:

Definition 5. F′*p* = df [(M*p*) & (M ~ *p*)] & ~M(*p* & S).

That is, *p* is forbidden if (as before) *p* is contingent, and moreover it is impossible that *p* should be true and S false. In other words, it is impossible to act to make *p* true without incurring the sanction.

Definition 6. I′*p* = dfM(*p* & ~S) & M(~*p* & ~S).

That is, *p* is indifferent if it is possible that *p* should be true and S false, and it is also possible that *p* should be false and S false, i.e., it is possible to act so as to make *p* true, without incurring the sanction and also possible to act so as to make *p* false, without incurring the sanction. (The contingency of an indifferent *p* is a logical consequence of the definition of indifference, and hence need not be explicitly stated.)

With these definitions the relations expressed in Def. 1–3 all become provable as theorems of O′M*; moreover, the two principles enunciated by von Wright are also theorems of O′M*.[14] This means that von Wright's system is a subsystem of O′M*; and that some account is also taken of Bohnert's suggestions. It would be pointless to try to characterize O′M* further in such a brief compass; formal systems always require intensive study if their explanatory power is to be fully appreciated.

If the "explanatory power" of such constructs seems highly abstract or remote, the situation should be compared with contemporary physical theories, where mathematical theories much more recondite than those presented here have a direct and immediate bearing on empirical research. And just as many mathematical developments were initiated by empirical problems, so the development of O′M* was motivated by the hope of throwing light on some empirical problems in small-group research. More specifically, in experiments currently being conducted in the Yale Interaction Laboratory, opportunities are available for studying under well-controlled conditions, small groups in the process of developing normative structures. A clear and accurate account of these interactional processes calls for a precise and rigorous conceptual framework within which to characterize the behavior of the group.

Small-groups research is of course only one, and not necessarily the most important, area of application of such formal systems. It is hoped that the foregoing discussion will have suggestive value for workers in other sociological fields and will stimulate interest in current research in mathematical logic, especially modal logic. This research is not remote from the daily affairs of sociologists. For instance, whenever instructions are given for filling out a questionnaire, commands expressing obligations are involved. More generally, any adequate sociological theory must encompass, in our opinion, the concepts *norm*, *obligation*, etc. It is therefore a matter of importance to develop sound techniques for analyzing norms and systems of norms.

SUMMARY

The development of an adequate theoretical structure for sociology will in all likelihood require interdisciplinary cooperation between sociologists and those working in the formal sciences if it is to proceed in a maximally fruitful way. The purpose of this article is to bring to the attention of sociologists recent work in mathematical logic which has direct relevance for their research. Von Wright's deontic logic offers promising leads for the analysis of normative structures; the family of systems of which O′M* is a member provides a more comprehensive framework, taking account of the role of penalties and possibilities for action *vis-à-vis* norms.

[13] Definitions 4–6 are arranged to facilitate comparison with definitions 1–3. We here use "O′" instead of "O," etc., to distinguish these notions from those of von Wright. An analogue of von Wright's primitive notion of permission is defined in O′M* as follows:

P′*p* = df M ~ *p* & M (*p* & ~ S)

[14] As applied to contingent propositions, that is; this qualification applies elsewhere as well.

REFERENCES

Alban, M. J., 1943. Independence of the primitive symbols of Lewis's calculi of propositions. *The Journal of Symbolic Logic*, **8**, 25–26.

Anderson, A. R., 1954. Improved decision procedures for Lewis's calculus S4 and von Wright's calculus M. *The Journal of Symbolic Logic*, **19**, 201–214.

Anderson, A. R., 1956. The formal analysis of normative systems. Technical Report 2, Contract No. SAR/Nonr-609(16), Office of Naval Research, Group Psychology Branch.

Bohnert, H. G., 1945. The semiotic status of commands. *Philosophy of Science*, **12**, 302–315.

Church, A., 1955. *Introduction to mathematical logic*, Vol. I. Princeton, N.J.: Princeton University Press.

Feys, R., 1938. Les logiques nouvelles des modalités. *Revue Neoscholastique de Philosophie*, **41**, 217–252.

Feys, R., 1955. Expression modale du "devoirêtre." *The Journal of Symbolic Logic*, **20**, 91–92.

Halldén, Sören, 1950. Results concerning the decision problem of Lewis's calculi S3 and S6. *The Journal of Symbolic Logic*, **14**, 230–236.

Hare, R. M., 1952. *The language of morals*. Oxford: Clarendon.

Hoebel, E. A., 1954. *The law of primitive man*. Cambridge: Harvard University Press.

Hofstadter, A., and McKinsey, J. C. C., 1939. On the logic of imperatives. *Philosophy of Science*, **6**, 446–457.

Hohfeld, W. N., 1923. *Fundamental legal conceptions as applied in judicial reasoning and other essays*. New Haven: Yale University Press.

Lewis, C. I., 1918. *A survey of symbolic logic*. Berkeley, Calif.: University of California Press.

Lewis, C. I., and Langford, C. H., 1932. *Symbolic logic*. New York: Century.

McKinsey, J. C. C., 1941. A solution of the decision problem for the Lewis systems S2 and S4, with an application to topology. *The Journal of Symbolic Logic*, **6**, 117–134.

Mally, E., 1926. *Grundgesetze des Sollens*. Graz: Leuschner and Lubensky.

Menger, K., 1939. *A logic of the doubtful*. On optative and imperative logic. Reports of a mathematical colloquium, 2nd series. Notre Dame, Ind.: Notre Dame University Press, pp. 53–64.

Prior, A. N., 1955. *Formal logic*. Oxford: Clarendon.

Prior, A. N., 1956. *Time and modality*. Oxford: Clarendon.

Sobocinski, B., 1953. Note on a modal system of Feys-von Wright. *The Journal of Computing Systems*, **1**, 171–178.

von Neumann, J., and Morgenstern, O., 1947. *Theory of games and economic behavior*. Princeton, N.J.: Princeton University Press.

von Wright, G. H., 1951a. Deontic Logic. *Mind*, **60**, 1–15.

von Wright, G. H., 1951b. *An essay in modal logic*. Amsterdam: North-Holland.

Whitehead, A. N., and Russell, B., 1910, 1912, 1913. *Principia mathematica*. Cambridge: Cambridge University Press.

selection 11 Norms and Behavior

GEORGE C. HOMANS

NORMS

What do we mean by norms? Sociologists and anthropologists are always saying that such and such behavior is, in a particular group, "expected" under such and such circumstances. How do they know what is expected? Sometimes the members of a group will state quite clearly what the expected behavior is, but sometimes it is a matter of inference. The process of construction by which social scientists determine the expectations of a group—and the process must be complex—seems to be taken for granted by the less sophisticated among them in their textbooks and popular works. Here we never take such things for granted, though we may not spend much time on them. Suppose, for example, three men are in a room. One goes out, and one of the two that remain says to the other, "I don't believe we've met. My name is Smith." Or, in another variation of the same scene, a man comes into a room where two others are already standing. There is a silence, and then one of the two says, "I'm sorry. I should have introduced you two, but I thought you had met. Mr. Jones, this is Mr. Smith." From observing several events of this kind, the sociologist infers that, in this particular group, when two men are in the presence of one another and have not met before, the third man, if he has met both, is expected to tell each the other's name, but that, should he fail to do so, each is expected to act on his own account and tell the other his name. The sociologist's inference may be confirmed when he reads in a book of etiquette current in this group, "When two persons have not met before, their host must introduce them to one another." Inferences of this kind we shall call *norms*. Note that most norms are not as easily discovered as this rather trivial one, and confirmation by a book of etiquette or its equivalent is not always possible. The student should turn to *Management and the Worker* (Roethlisberger and Dickson, 1939) and run over the material from which the inference was reached that about 6,600 or, according to the type of equipment being wired, 6,000 completed connections were considered in the Bank Wiring Observation Room the proper day's work of a wireman. For example, Mueller (W2) said in an interview:

> Right now I'm turning out over 7,000 a day, around 7,040. The rest of the fellows kick because I do that. They want me to come down. They want me to come down to around 6,600, but I don't see why I should (p. 417).

In few works of social science are the norms, whose existence the sociologist often appears to assume so lightly, traced back to their referents in word and deed as carefully as they are in the Roethlisberger and Dickson book.

A norm, then, is an idea in the minds of the members of a group, an idea that can be put in the form of a statement specifying what the members or other men should do, ought to do, are expected to do, under given circumstances. Just what group, what circumstances, and what action are meant can be much more easily determined for some norms than for others. But even this definition is too broad and must be limited further. A statement of the kind described is a norm only if any departure of real behavior from the norm is followed by some punishment. The rule of the Bank Wiremen that no one should wire much more or much less than two equipments a day was a true norm, because, as we shall see, the social standing of a member of the group declined as he departed in one way or another from the norm. Nonconformity was punished and conformity rewarded. A norm in this sense is what some sociologists call a sanction pattern. But there are many other statements about what behavior ought to be that are not norms and are often called ideals. "Do as you would be done by," is an example. In an imperfect world, departure from the golden rule is not followed by specific punishment,

---

Abridged from pages 121–127 of a book by the same author entitled *The Human Group*, 1950, New York: Harcourt, Brace. Reprinted by permission of the author and Harcourt, Brace.

and this is precisely what gives the rule its high ethical standing. If a man lives by it, he does so for its own sake and not because he will be socially rewarded. Virtue is its own reward.

We have defined norms as the expected behavior of a number of men. This is justified: each of the Bank Wiremen was expected to wire about 6,000 connections a day. But some norms, though they may be held by all the members of a group, apply to only one of them: they define what a single member in a particular position is supposed to do. A father is expected to treat his children, a host, his guests, a foreman, his men in certain special ways. A norm of this kind, a norm that states the expected relationship of a person in a certain position to others he comes into contact with is often called the *role* of this person. The word comes, of course, from the language of the stage: it is the part a man is given to play, and he may play it well or ill. A man's behavior may depart more or less from the role, and if the real behavior of enough persons in enough such positions over a long enough time departs far enough from the role, the role itself will change. For instance, our notion of the way a father ought to behave toward his children has changed greatly in the last century, as circumstances have made the patriarchal role of fathers on small, subsistence farms no longer appropriate for many fathers today.

One point must be made very clear: our norms are ideas. They are not behavior itself, but what people think behavior ought to be. Nothing is more childishly obvious than that the ideal and the real do not always, or do not fully, coincide, but nothing is more easily forgotten, perhaps because men want to forget it. A possible objection to the word *norm* itself is that we may easily confuse two different things: norm A, a statement of what people ought to do in a particular situation, and norm B, a statistical, or quasi-statistical, average of what they actually do in that situation. Sometimes the two coincide, but more often they do not. In the same way, the word *standard* suggests, on the one hand, a moral yardstick by which real behavior is judged and, on the other hand, in the phrase *standard of living*, a certain level of real behavior in the field of consumption.

THE RELATION OF NORMS TO BEHAVIOR

We must not mix norms and actual behavior together in a shapeless mass if we are to examine the relations between the two, and the relations do confront us and demand analysis. It is clear, for instance, that norms do not materialize out of nothing, but emerge from ongoing activities. If the Bank Wiremen had not been doing the wiring job, and if their output had not reached the neighborhood of 6,000 connections per man per day (or about two equipments), it is hard to believe that this particular norm would ever have got itself established. If we think of a norm as a goal that a group wishes to reach, we can see that the goal is not set up, like the finish line of a race, before the race starts, but rather that the group decides, after it starts running, what the finish line shall be. Once the norm is established it exerts a back effect on the group. It may act as an incentive in the sense that a man may try to bring his behavior closer to the norm. But the norm can be a mark to shoot for only if it is not too far away from what can be achieved in everyday life. If it gets impossibly remote—and just how far that is no one can say—it will be abandoned in favor of some more nearly attainable norm. Society's preaching and its practice are elastically linked. Each pulls the other, and they can never separate altogether.

The really interesting question is not "Does behavior coincide with a norm?" but "*How far* does the behavior of an individual or a subgroup measure up to the norms of the group as a whole?"

We have made an assumption without proof. Earlier in dealing with a single social unit, the Bank Wiring group, rather than the subgroups within this unit, we have talked about "the norms of a group as a whole." What do we mean? We mean that, the more frequently men interact with one another, the more nearly alike they become in the norms they hold, as they do in their sentiments and activities. But we mean still more than this. No doubt the norms accepted in a group vary somewhat from one person to another, and from one subgroup to another, and yet *the members of the group are often more nearly alike in the norms they hold than in their overt behavior*. To put the matter crudely, they are more alike in what they say they ought to do than in what they do in fact. Thus the Bank Wiremen were more nearly, though perhaps not wholly, alike in what they said output ought to be than in what they actually turned out. Perhaps the explanation of this rule, if it is one, lies in the fact that a person's subjective recognition of a norm, although under influence from other aspects of the social system, is under less immediate influence than his social activity itself, and thus varies less than his social activity. Being an idea, the norm comes closer to having an independent life of its own.

Norms do not materialize out of nothing; they emerge from ongoing activities. This remark is true but needs to be amplified. The norms alive in a particular group do not all arise out of the activities of *that* group. Thus in the Bank Wiring Observation Room, the rule that about 6,000 connections should be wired in a day must have grown up in the main department from which the men came. The more general idea of restriction of output or, as labor sees it, "a fair day's work for a fair day's pay," is a part of the American, or Western, industrial tradition. That is, it is common to a large number of groups whose members have had some communication with one another. Again, the feeling that no man should act as if he had authority over someone else is an article in the democratic creed—and note that the creed is realized to some degree in American society and would not survive unless it were. Men bring their norms to a group; they work out new norms through their experience in the group; they take the old norms, confirmed or weakened, and the new ones, as developed, to the other groups they are members of. If the norms take hold there, a general tradition, the same in many groups, may grow up. The freight most easily exported is the kind carried in the head. In fact the environment determines the character of a group in two chief ways: through its influence on the external system, and through widely held norms.

REFERENCES

Roethlisberger, F. J., and Dickson, W. J., 1939. *Management and the worker*. Cambridge, Mass.: Harvard University Press.

selection 12 The Norm of Reciprocity: A Preliminary Statement

ALVIN W. GOULDNER

The aims of this paper are: (a) to indicate the manner in which the concept of reciprocity is tacitly involved in but formally neglected by modern functional theory; (b) to clarify the concept and display some of its diverse intellectual contents, thus facilitating its theoretical employment and research utility; and (c) to suggest concretely ways in which the clarified concept provides new leverage for analysis of the central problems of sociological theory, namely, accounting for stability and instability in social systems.

RECIPROCITY AND FUNCTIONAL THEORY

My concern with reciprocity developed initially from a critical reexamination of current functional theory, especially the work of Robert Merton and Talcott Parsons. The fullest ramifications of what follows can best be seen in this theoretical context. Merton's familiar paradigm of functionalism stresses that analysis must begin with the identification of some problematic pattern of human behavior, some institution, role, or shared pattern of belief. Merton (1957) stipulates clearly the basic functionalist assumption, the way in which the problematic pattern is to be understood: he holds that the "central orientation of functionalism" is "expressed in the practice of interpreting data by establishing their consequences for larger structures in which they are implicated" (pp. 46–47). The functionalist's emphasis upon studying the *existent* consequences, the on-going functions or dysfunctions, of a social pattern may be better appreciated if it is remembered that this concern developed in a polemic against the earlier anthropological notion of a "survival." The survival, of course, was regarded

Abridged from the *American Sociological Review*, 1960, **25**, 161–178. Reprinted by permission of the author and the American Sociological Association.

as a custom held to be unexplainable in terms of its existent consequences or utility and which, therefore, had to be understood with reference to its consequences for social arrangements no longer present.

Functionalism, to repeat, explains the persistence of social patterns in terms of their ongoing consequences for existent social systems. If social survivals, which by definition have no such consequences, are conceded to exist or to be possible, then it would seem that functionalism is by its own admission incapable of explaining them. To suggest that survivals do not help us to understand other patterns of social behavior is beside the mark. The decisive issue is whether existent versions of functional theory can explain social survivals, not whether specific social survivals can explain other social patterns.

It would seem that functionalists have but one of two choices: either they must dogmatically deny the existence or possibility of functionless patterns (survivals), and assert that all social behavior is explainable parsimoniously on the basis of the same fundamental functionalist assumption, that is, in terms of its consequences for surrounding social structures; or, more reasonably, they must concede that some social patterns are or may be survivals, admitting that existent functional theory fails to account for such instances. In the latter case, functionalists must develop further their basic assumptions on the generalized level required. I believe that one of the strategic ways in which such basic assumptions can be developed is by recognizing the manner in which the concept of *reciprocity* is tacitly involved in them, and by explicating the concept's implications for functional theory.

The tacit implication of the concept of reciprocity in functional theory can be illustrated in Merton's analysis of the latent functions of the political machine in the United States. Merton inquires how political machines continue to operate, despite the fact that they frequently run counter to both the mores and the law. The *general* form of his explanation is to identify the consequences of the machine for surrounding structures and to demonstrate that the machine performs "positive functions which are at the same time not adequately fulfilled by other existing patterns and structures" (1957, p. 73). It seems evident, however, that simply to establish its consequences for other social structures provides no answer to the question of the persistence of the political machine (cf. Gouldner, 1959). The explanation miscarries because no explicit analysis is made of the feedback through which the social structures or groups, whose needs are satisfied by the political machine, in turn "reciprocate" and repay the machine for the services received from it. In this case, the patterns of reciprocity, implied in the notion of the "corruption" of the machine, are well known and fully documented.

To state the issue generally: the demonstration that A is functional for B can help to account for A's persistence only if the functional theorist tacitly assumes some principle of reciprocity. It is in this sense that some concept of reciprocity apparently has been smuggled into the basic but unstated postulates of functional analysis. The demonstration that A is functional for B helps to account for A's own persistence and stability only on two related assumptions: (a) that B *reciprocates* A's services, and (b) that B's service to A is *contingent* upon A's performance of positive functions for B. The second assumption, indeed, is one implication of the definition of reciprocity as a transaction. Unless B's services to A are contingent upon the services provided by A, it is pointless to examine the latter if one wishes to account for the persistence of A.

It may be assumed, as a first approximation, that a social unit or group is more likely to contribute to another which provides it with benefits than to one which does not; nonetheless, there are certain general conditions under which one pattern may provide benefits for the other despite a *lack* of reciprocity. An important case of this situation is where power arrangements constrain the continuance of services. If B is considerably more powerful than A, B may force A to benefit it with little or no reciprocity. This social arrangement, to be sure, is less stable than one in which B's reciprocity *motivates* A to continue performing services for B, but it is hardly for this reason sociologically unimportant.

The problem can also be approached in terms of the functional autonomy (see Gouldner, 1959) of two units relative to each other. For example, B may have many alternative sources for supplying the services that it normally receives from A. A, however, may be dependent upon B's services and have no, or comparatively few, alternatives. Consequently, the continued provision of benefits by one pattern, A, for another, B, depends not only upon (a) the benefits which A in turn receives from B, but also on (b) the power which B possesses relative to A, and (c) the alternative sources of services accessible to each, beyond those provided by the other. In short, an explanation of the stability of a pattern, or of the relationship between A and B, requires investigation of mutually contingent benefits rendered and of the manner in which this mutual contingency is sustained. The latter, in turn, requires utilization of two different theoretical traditions and general orientations, one stressing the significance of power differences and the other emphasizing the degree of mutual dependence of the patterns or parties involved.

Functional theory, then, requires some assumption concerning reciprocity. It must, however, avoid the "Pollyanna Fallacy" which optimistically assumes the structures securing "satisfactions" from others will invariably be "grateful" and will always reciprocate. Therefore it cannot be merely hypostatized that reciprocity will operate in every case; its occurrence must, instead, be documented empirically. Although reciprocal relations stabilize patterns, it need not follow that a lack of reciprocity is socially impossible or invariably disruptive of the patterns involved. Relations with little or no reciprocity may, for example, occur when power disparities allow one party to coerce the other. There may also be special mechanisms which compensate for or control the tensions which arise in the event of a breakdown in reciprocity. Among such compensatory mechanisms there may be culturally shared prescriptions of one-sided or unconditional generosity, such as the Christian notion of "turning the other cheek" or "walking the second mile," the feudal notion of "*noblesse oblige*," or the Roman notion of "clemency." There may also be cultural prohibitions banning the examination of certain interchanges from the standpoint of their concrete reciprocity, as expressed by the cliché, "It's not the gift but the sentiment that counts." The major point here is that if empirical analysis fails to detect the existence of functional reciprocity, or finds that it has been disrupted, it becomes necessary to search out and analyze the compensatory arrangements that may provide means of controlling the resultant tensions, thereby enabling the problematic pattern to remain stable.

THE "EXPLOITATION" PROBLEM

It was not only the functionalist polemic against the concept of survivals that obscured the significance and inhibited the study of unequal exchanges. A similar result is also produced by the suspicion with which many modern sociologists understandably regard the concept of "exploitation." This concept of course is central to the traditional socialist critique of modern capitalism. In the now nearly-forgotten language of political economy, "exploitation" refers to a relationship in which unearned income results from certain kinds of unequal exchange.

The continued use of the concept of exploitation in sociological analyses of sexual relations stems largely from the brilliant work of Willard Waller on the dynamics of courtship. Waller's ambivalent comments about the concept suggest why it has fallen into sociological disrepute. "The word exploitation is by no means a desirable one," explains Waller, "but we have not been able to find another which will do as well. The dictionary definition of exploitation as an 'unfair or unjust utilization of another' contains a value judgment, and this value judgment is really a part of the ordinary sociological meaning of the term" (1951, p. 163). In short, the concept of exploitation may have become disreputable because its value implications conflict with modern sociology's effort to place itself on a value-free basis, as well as because it is a concept commonly and correctly associated with the critique of modern society emphasized by the political left. But the concept *need* not be used in such an ideological manner; it can be employed simply to refer to certain transactions involving an exchange of things of unequal value. It is important to guarantee that the ordinary value implications of a term do not intrude upon its scientific use. It is also important, however, to prevent our distaste for the ideological implications of exploitation from inducing a compulsive and equally ideological neglect of its cognitive substance.

The unsavory implications of the concept of exploitation have *not* excluded it from studies of sexual relations, although almost all other specializations in sociology eschew it. Why this is so remains a tempting problem for the sociology of knowledge, but cannot be explored here. In the present context, the important implications are the following: If the possible sexual exploitation of daughters by fathers gives rise, as Davis (1949) suggests, to mechanisms that serve to prevent this, then it would seem that *other* types of exploitation may also be controlled by *other* kinds of mechanisms. These may be no less important and universal than the incest taboo. If the exploitation of women by men (or men by women) is worthy of sociological attention, then also worth studying is the exploitation of students by teachers, of workers by management or union leaders, of patients by doctors, and so on. If the notion of exploitation, in a value-free sense, is useful for the analysis of sexual relations, then it can be of similar aid in analyzing many other kinds of social relations.

Doubtless "exploitation" is by now so heavily charged with misleading ideological resonance that the term itself can scarcely be salvaged for purely scientific purposes and will, quite properly, be resisted by most American sociologists. This is unimportant. Perhaps a less emotionally freighted —if infelicitous—term such as "reciprocity imbalance" will suffice to direct attention once again to the crucial question of unequal exchanges.

COMPLEMENTARITY AND RECIPROCITY

The question of the meaning of the concept of reciprocity should be reexamined. Consideration of some of the ways in which the reciprocity problem is treated by Parsons helps to distinguish reciprocity from other cognate concepts. "It is inherent in the nature of social interaction," writes Parsons, "that the gratification of ego's need-dispositions is contingent on alter's reaction and vice versa" (1951, p. 21). Presumably, therefore, if the gratification of either party's needs is not contingent upon the other's reactions, the stability of their relation is undermined. This, in turn, implies that if a social system is to be stable there must always be some "mutuality of gratification" (Parsons and Shils, 1951, p. 107). Social system stability, then, presumably depends in part on the mutually contingent exchange of gratifications, that is, on reciprocity as exchange.

This, however, remains an insight the implications of which are never systematically explored. For example, the implications of differences in the *degree* of mutuality or in the symmetry of reciprocity are neglected. Again, while the concept of "exploitation" assumes *central* importance in Parsons' commentary on the patient-doctor relation, it is never precisely defined, examined, and located in his *general* theory.

One reason for Parsons' neglect of reciprocity is that he, like some other sociologists, does not distinguish it from the concept of complementarity. Parsons uses the two concepts as if they are synonymous and, for the most part, centers his analysis on complementarity to the systematic neglect of reciprocity rigorously construed. The term complementarity, however, is itself an ambiguous one and is not, in all of its meanings, synonymous with reciprocity. Complementarity has at least four distinct meanings:

Complementarity$_1$ may mean that a right (x) of Ego against Alter implies a duty $(-x)$ of Alter to Ego. Given the often vague use of the term "right," it is quite possible that this proposition, in one aspect, is only an expansion of some definition of the concept "right." To that degree, of course, this is simply an analytic proposition. The interesting sociological questions, however, arise only when issues of empirical substance rather than logical implication are raised. For example, where a group shares a belief that some status occupant has a certain right, say the right of a wife to receive support from her husband, does the group in fact also share a belief that the husband has an obligation to support the wife? Furthermore, even though rights may logically or empirically imply duties, it need not follow that the reverse is true. In other words, it does not follow that rights and duties are always transitive. This can be seen in a second meaning of complementarity.

Complementarity$_2$ may mean that what is a duty (−x) of Alter to Ego implies a right (x) of Ego against Alter. On the *empirical* level, while this is often true, of course, it is also sometimes false. For example, what may be regarded as a duty of charity or forebearance, say a duty to "turn the other cheek," need not be *socially* defined as the *right* of the recipient. While a man may be regarded as having an unconditional obligation to tell the truth to everyone, even to a confirmed liar, people in his group might not claim that the liar has a *right* to have the truth told him.

The other two meanings of complementarity differ substantially. Complementarity$_3$ may mean that a right (x) of Alter against Ego implies a duty $(-y)$ of Alter to Ego. Similarly, complementarity$_4$ may mean that a duty (−x) of Ego to Alter implies a right (y) of Ego against Alter.

In these four implications of complementarity—sometimes called reciprocal rights and obligations—there are two distinctive types of cases. Properly speaking, *complementarity* refers only to the first two meanings sketched above, where what is a right of Ego implies an obligation of Alter, or where a duty of Alter to Ego implies a right of Ego against Alter. Only the other two meanings, however, involve true instances of *reciprocity*, for only in these does what one party receives from the other require some return, so that giving and receiving are mutually contingent.

In short, complementarity connotes that one's rights are another's obligations, and vice versa. Reciprocity, however, connotes that *each* party has rights *and* duties. This is more than an analytic distinction: it is an *empirical* generalization concerning role systems the importance of which as a datum is so elemental that it is commonly neglected and rarely made problematic. The English philosopher MacBeath suggests that this empirical generalization may be accounted for by the principle of reciprocity (1952). This would seem possible in several senses, one of which is that, were there only rights on the one side and duties on the other, there need be no exchange whatsoever. Stated differently, it would seem that there can be stable patterns of reciprocity *qua* exchange only insofar as *each* party has both rights and duties. In effect, then, reciprocity has its significance for *role systems* in that it tends to structure *each* role so as to include both rights and duties. It is now clear, at any rate, that reciprocity is by no means identical with complementarity and that the two are confused only at theoretical peril.

THE NORM OF RECIPROCITY

Contrary to some cultural relativists, it can be hypothesized that a norm of reciprocity is universal. As Westermarck stated, "To requite a benefit, or to be grateful to him who bestows it, is probably everywhere, at least under certain circumstances, regarded as a duty" (Westermarck, 1908, p. 154). A norm of reciprocity is, I suspect, no less universal and important an element of culture than the incest taboo, although, similarly, its concrete formulations may vary with time and place.

Specifically, I suggest that a norm of reciprocity, in its universal form, makes two interrelated, minimal demands: (a) people should help those who have helped them, and (b) people should not injure those who have helped them. Generically, the norm of reciprocity may be conceived of as a dimension to be found in all value systems and, in particular, as one among a *number* of "Principal Components" universally present in moral codes.

To suggest that a norm of reciprocity is universal is not, of course, to assert that it is unconditional. Unconditionality would, indeed, be at variance with the basic character of the reciprocity norm which imposes obligations only contingently, that is, in response to the benefits conferred by others. Moreover, such obligations of repayment are contingent upon the imputed *value* of the benefit received. The value of the benefit and hence the debt is in proportion to and varies with —among other things—the intensity of the recipient's need at the time the benefit was bestowed ("a friend in need . . ."), the resources of the donor ("he gave although he could ill afford it"), the motives imputed to the donor ("without thought of gain"), and the nature of the constraints which are perceived to exist or to be absent ("he gave of his own free will . . ."). Thus the obligations imposed by the norm of reciprocity may vary with the *status* of the participants within a society.

Similarly, this norm functions differently in some degree in different *cultures*. In the Philippines, for example, the *compadre* system cuts across and pervades the political, economic, and other institutional spheres. *Compadres* are bound by a norm of reciprocity. If one man pays his *compadre's* doctor's bill in time of need, for example, the latter may be obligated to help the former's son to get a government job. Here the tendency to govern all relations by the norm of reciprocity, thereby undermining bureaucratic impersonality, is relatively legitimate, hence overt and powerful. In the United States, however, such tendencies are weaker, in part because friendship relations are less institutionalized. Nonetheless, even in bureaucracies in this country such tendencies are endemic, albeit less legitimate and overt. Except in friendship, kinship, and neighborly relations, a norm of reciprocity is not imposed on Americans by the "dominant cultural profile," although it is commonly found in the latent or "substitute" culture structure in all institutional sectors, even the most rationalized, in the United States.

In otherwise contrasting discussions of the norm of reciprocity one emphasis is notable. Some scholars, especially Homans, Thurnwald, Simmel, and Malinowski, assert or imply that the reciprocity norm stipulates that the amount of the return to be made is "roughly equivalent" to what had been received. The problem of equivalence is a difficult but important one. Whether in fact there is a reciprocity norm specifically requiring that returns for benefits received be *equivalent* is an empirical question. So, too, is the problem of whether such a norm is part of or distinct from a more general norm which simply requires that one return some (unspecified) benefits to benefactors. Logically prior to such empirical problems, however, is the question of what the meaning of equivalence would be in the former norm of equivalent reciprocity.

Equivalence may have at least two forms, the sociological and psychodynamic significance of which are apt to be quite distinct. In the first case, heteromorphic reciprocity, equivalence may mean that the things exchanged may be concretely different but should be equal in *value*, as defined by the actors in the situation. In the second case, homeomorphic reciprocity, equivalence may mean that exchanges should be concretely alike, or identical in form, either with respect to the things exchanged or to the circumstances under which they are exchanged. In the former, equivalence calls for "tit for tat"; in the latter, equivalence calls for "tat for tat." Historically, the most important expression of homeomorphic reciprocity is found in the *negative* norms of reciprocity, that is, in sentiments of retaliation where the emphasis is placed not on the return of benefits but on the return of injuries, and is best exemplified by the *lex talionis.*

Finally, it should be stressed that equivalence in the above cases refers to a definition of the exchangeables made by actors in the situation. This differs of course, from holding that the things exchanged by people, will, in the long run, be *objectively* equal in value, as measured by economists or other social scientists. Here, again, the adequacy of these conceptual distinctions will be determined ultimately by empirical test. For example, can we find reciprocity norms which, in fact, require that returns be equivalent in value and are these empirically distinguishable from norms requiring that returns be concretely alike? Are these uni-dimensional or multi-dimensional? Similarly, only research can resolve such questions as whether a norm of retaliation exists in any given group, is the polar side of the norm of reciprocity, or is a distinctive norm which may vary independently of the reciprocity norm. These conceptual distinctions only suggest a set of research possibilities and have value primarily as guides to investigation.

RECIPROCITY AND SOCIAL SYSTEMS

As mentioned above, sociologists have sometimes confused the notion of complementarity with that of reciprocity and have recently tended to focus on the former. Presumably, the reason for this is because of the importance of complementarity in maintaining the stability of social systems. Clearly, if what one party deems his right is accepted by the other as his obligation, their relation will be more stable than if the latter fails to so define it. But if the group stabilizing consequences of complementarity are the basis of its theoretical significance, then the same consideration underwrites with equal potency the significance of reciprocity. For reciprocity has no less a role in maintaining the stability of social systems.

Note that there are at least two ways, not merely one, in which complementarity as such can break down. In the one case, Alter can refuse to acknowledge Ego's rights as his own duties. In the other case, however, Ego may not regard as rights that which Alter acknowledges as duties. The former is commonly viewed as the empirically more frequent and as the theoretically more significant case. That this often seems to be taken as a matter of course suggests the presence of certain tacit assumptions about basic human dispositions. It seems to assume, as Aristotle put it, that people are more ready to receive than to give benefits. In short, it premises a common tendency toward what used to be called "egoism," a salient (but not exclusive) concern with the satisfaction of one's own needs.

This or some cognate assumption appears to be eminently reasonable and empirically justified. There can be no adequate systematic sociological theory which boggles at the issue; indeed, it is one of the many virtues of Parsons' work that it confronts the egoism problem. His solution seems to be sidetracked, however, because his overwhelming focus on the problem of complementarity leads to the neglect of reciprocity. If assumptions about egoistic dispositions are valid, however, a complementarity of rights and obligations should be exposed to a persistent strain, in which each party is somewhat more actively concerned to defend or extend his own rights than those of others. There is nothing in complementarity as such which would seem able to control egoism.

One way out may be obtained by premising that socialization internalizes complementary rights and obligations in persons, before they fully assume responsible participation in a social system. Even if socialization were to work perfectly and so internalize such rights and obligations, there still remains the question as to what mechanism can sustain and reinforce these during full participation in the social system. The concept of complementarity takes mutually compatible expectations as given; it does not and cannot explain how they are maintained once established. For this we need to turn to the reciprocities processes because these, unlike pure complementarity, actually mobilize egoistic motivations and channel them into the maintenance of the social system. Benthamite utilitarianism has long understood that egoism can motivate one party to satisfy the expectations of the other, since by doing so he induces the latter to reciprocate and to satisfy his own. As Max Gluckman might put it with his penchant for Hegelian paradox, there is an altruism in egoism, made possible through reciprocity.

Furthermore, the *existential belief* in reciprocity says something like this, "People will usually help those who help them." Similarly, the *norm* of reciprocity holds that people should help those who help them and, therefore, those whom you have helped have an obligation to help you. The conclusion is clear: if you want to be helped by others you must help them; hence it is not only proper but also expedient to conform with the specific status rights of others and with the general norm. Both the existential belief in and the norm of reciprocity enlist egoistic motivations in the service of social system stability.

A full analysis of the ways in which the whole reciprocities complex is involved in the maintenance of social systems would require consideration of the linkages between each of its various elements, and their relation to other general properties of social systems. There is no space for such consideration here. Instead, I examine only one part of the complex, namely, the generalized *norm* of reciprocity, and suggest some of the ways in which it contributes to social system stability.

If, following Parsons, we suppose that social systems are stable to the extent that Ego and Alter conform with one another's expectations, we are confronted with the problem of why men *reciprocate* gratifications. Parsons holds that once a stable relation of mutual gratification has been established the system is self-perpetuating; presumably, no special mechanisms are necessary to maintain it. Insofar as this is not simply postulated in analogy with the principle of inertia in physics, apparently reciprocity is accounted for by Parsons, and also by Homans, as a result of the development of a beneficent cycle of mutual reinforcement. That is, Ego's conformity with Alter's expectations reinforces Alter's conformity with Ego's expectations, and so on.

This explanation of reciprocity *qua* transaction is particularly strange in Parsons' case since he often stresses, but here neglects, the significance of shared values as a source of stability in social systems. So far as the question here is not simply the general one of why men conform with the expectations of others but, rather, the more specific problem of why they *reciprocate* benefits, part of the answer would seem to be that they have commonly internalized some general *moral norm*. In short, the suggestion is that the motivation for reciprocity stems not only from the sheer gratification which Alter receives from Ego but also from Alter's internalization of a specific norm of reciprocity which morally obliges him to give benefits to those from whom he has received them. In this respect, the *norm* of reciprocity is a concrete and special mechanism involved in the maintenance of any stable social system.

Why should such a norm be necessary? Why is it that expedient considerations do not suffice to mobilize motivations to comply with other's expectations, thereby inducing them to provide reciprocal compliances? One major line of analysis here would certainly indicate the disruptive potentialities of power differences. Given significant power differences, egoistic motivations may seek to get benefits without returning them. (It is notable that Parsons fails to define the power situation in his basic model of Ego-Alter equilibrium.) The situation is then ripe for the breakdown of reciprocity and for the development of system-disrupting exploitation. The norm of reciprocity, however, engenders motives for returning benefits even when power differences might invite exploitation. The norm thus safeguards powerful people against the temptations of their own status; it motivates and regulates reciprocity as an exchange pattern, serving to inhibit the emergence of exploitative relations that would undermine the social system and the very power arrangements which had made exploitation possible.

As we have seen, Parsons stresses that the stability of social systems largely derives from the *conformity* of role partners to one another's expectations, particularly when what they do is a duty. This formulation induces a focus on conformity and deviance, and the degrees and types of each. Presumably, the more that people pay their social debts the more stable the social system. But much more than conformity and deviance are involved here.

The idea of the reciprocities complex leads us to focus on the historical or genetic dimension of social interaction. For example, Malinowski, in his discussion of the Kula Ring, carefully notes that the gifts given are not immediately returned and repayment may take as long as a year. What is the significance of this intervening time period? It is a period governed by the norm of reciprocity in a double sense. First, the actor is accumulating, mobilizing, liquidating, or earmarking resources so that he can make a suitable repayment. Second, it is a period governed by the rule that you should not do harm to those who have done you a benefit. This is a time, then, when men are morally constrained to manifest their gratitude toward, or at least to maintain peace with, their benefactors.

Insofar as men live under such a rule of reciprocity, when one party benefits another, an obligation is generated. The recipient is now *indebted* to the donor, and he remains so until he repays. Once interaction is seen as taking place over time, we may note that the norm of reciprocity so structures social relations that, between the time of Ego's provision of a gratification and the time of Alter's repayment, falls the shadow of indebtedness. An adequate analysis of the dynamics of social interaction requires us to go beyond the question of deviance from or conformity with the parties' obligations to one another. A second basic dimension needs to be examined systematically, namely, the time period when there is an obligation still to be performed, when commitments which have been made are yet to be fulfilled.

These outstanding obligations, no less than those already given compliance, contribute substantially to the stability of social systems. It is obviously inexpedient for creditors to break off relationships with those who have outstanding obligations to them. It may also be inexpedient for *debtors* to do so because their creditors may not again allow them to run up a bill of social indebtedness. In addition, it is *morally* improper, under the norm of reciprocity, to break off relations or to launch hostilities against those to whom you are still indebted.

If this conclusion is correct, then we should not only look for mechanisms which constrain or motivate men to do their duty and to pay off their debts; we should also expect to find mechanisms which induce people to *remain* socially indebted to each other and which *inhibit* their complete repayment. This suggests another function performed by the requirement of only *rough* equivalence of repayment that may be involved in one of the norms of reciprocity. For it induces a certain amount of ambiguity as to whether indebtedness has been repaid and, over time, generates uncertainty about who is in whose debt. This all hinges, however, on a shared conception of the moral propriety of repayment, engendered by the norm of reciprocity.

Still another way in which the general norm of reciprocity is implicated in the maintenance of social system stability is related to an important attribute of the norm, namely, its comparative indeterminacy. Unlike specific status duties and like other general norms, this norm does not require highly specific and uniform performances from people whose behavior it regulates. For example, unlike the status duties of American wives, it does not call upon them to cook and to take care of the children. Instead, the concrete demands it makes change substantially from situation to situation and vary with the benefits which one party receives from another.

This indeterminacy enables the norm of reciprocity to perform some of its most important system-stabilizing functions. Being indeterminate, the norm can be applied to countless *ad hoc* transactions, thus providing a flexible moral sanction for transactions which might not otherwise be regulated by specific status obligations. The norm, in this respect, is a kind of plastic filler, capable of being poured into the shifting crevices of social structures, and serving as a kind of all-purpose moral cement.

Not only does the norm of reciprocity play a stabilizing role in human relations in the *absence* of a well developed system of specific status duties, but it contributes to social stability even when these are *present* and well established. Status duties shape behavior because the status occupant believes them binding in their own right; they possess a kind of *prima facie* legitimacy for properly socialized group members. The general norm of reciprocity, however, is a second-order defense of stability; it provides a further source of motivation and an additional moral sanction for conforming with specific status obligations. For example, an employer may pay his workers not merely because he has contracted to do so; he may also feel that the workman has earned his wages. The housewife may take pains with her husband's meals not merely because cooking may be incumbent on her as a wife; she may also have a particularly considerate husband. In each case, the specific status duties are complied with not only because they are inherent in the status and are believed to be right in themselves, but also because each is further defined as a "*repayment*." In sum, the norm of reciprocity requires that if others have been fulfilling their status duties to you, you in turn have an additional or second-order obligation (repayment) to fulfill your status duties to them. In this manner, the sentiment of gratitude joins forces with the sentiment of rectitude and adds a safety-margin in the motivation to conformity.

The matter can be put differently from the standpoint of potential deviance or nonconformity. All status obligations are vulnerable to challenge and, at times, may have to be justified. If, for any reason, people refuse to do their duty, those demanding compliance may be required to justify their claims. Obviously, there are many standardized ways in which this might be done. Invoking the general norm of reciprocity is one way of justifying the more concrete demands of status obligations. Forced to the wall, the man demanding his "rights," may say, in effect, "Very well, if you won't do this simply because it is your duty, then remember all that I have done for you in the past and do it to repay your debt to me." The norm of reciprocity thus provides a second-order defense of the stability of social systems in that it can be used to overcome incipient deviance and to mobilize auxiliary motivations for conformity with existent status demands.

REFERENCES

Davis, K., 1949. *Human society*. New York: Macmillan.

Gouldner, A. W., 1959. Reciprocity and autonomy in functional theory. In L. Gross (Ed.), *Symposium on sociological theory*. Evanston, Ill.: Row, Peterson, pp. 241–270.

MacBeath, A., 1952. *Experiments in living*. London: Macmillan.

Merton, R. K., 1957. *Social theory and social structure* (Rev. ed.). New York: The Free Press.

Parsons, T., 1951. *The social system*. New York: The Free Press.

Parsons, T., and Shils, E. A. (Eds.), 1951. *Toward a general theory of action*. Cambridge, Mass.: Harvard University Press.

Waller, W., 1951. *The family: a dynamic interpretation*. New York: Dryden.

Westermarck, E., 1908. *The origin and development of the moral ideas*, Vol. 2. London: Macmillan.

selection 13 Norms of Delinquent Subcultures

RICHARD CLOWARD AND LLOYD E. OHLIN

DELINQUENT NORMS

Every culture provides its members with appropriate beliefs, values, and norms to carry out required activities. This is equally true of the subculture, which is distinguished by the prefix "sub" only to focus attention on its connection with a larger environing culture from which it has become partially differentiated. While he is being inducted into the subculture, the new member encounters and learns ways of describing the world about him which equip him to engage in these prescribed activities, enabling him to understand, discriminate, predict, and interpret the actions of others in relation to himself as a member of the subculture. These characteristic descriptions acquire the force of beliefs which are passed on as part of the subcultural tradition. The new member is also encouraged to adopt a set of evaluations which guide his judgments, comparisons, and preferential choices. These values are integrated with the beliefs that he has acquired. The beliefs and values that the subculture provides are in turn mobilized to support its prescriptions, which become elaborated as a set of norms for directing and controlling the behavior of its members. Descriptions, evaluations, and prescriptions, then, are provided by the subculture and shared as common property by its members.

Abridged from Chapter 1 of a book by the same authors entitled *Delinquency and Opportunity—A Theory of Delinquent Gangs*, 1960, New York: The Free Press. Reprinted by permission of the authors and The Free Press. This investigation was supported by funds from the Ford Foundation.

The most crucial elements of the delinquent subculture are the prescriptions, norms, or rules of conduct that define the activities required of a full-fledged member. Every delinquent subculture is based upon a set of dominant roles which involve the performance of delinquent acts. Members of the subculture share a knowledge of what is required for the competent performance of these roles, which give the subculture its distinctiveness. What we have called the criminal subculture prescribes disciplined and utilitarian forms of theft; the conflict subculture prescribes the instrumental use of violence; the retreatist subculture prescribes participation in illicit consummatory experiences, such as drug use. Thus the delinquent norms that govern these activities are the primary identifying and organizing elements of delinquent subcultures.

The prescriptions of delinquent subcultures are supported, ordered, and closely integrated with appropriate values and beliefs, which serve to buttress, validate, and rationalize the different types of prescription in the various delinquent subcultures. Members of the criminal subculture, for example, believe that the world is populated by "smart guys" and "suckers"; members of the conflict gang see their "turf" as surrounded by enemies; retreatists regard the world about them as populated by "squares." Similarly, each subculture is characterized by distinctive evaluations: criminals value stealth, dexterity, wit, "front," and the capacity to evade detection; street-warriors value "heart"; retreatists place a premium on esoteric "kicks." The integration of beliefs and values with norms provides stability for the essential activities of the subculture.

THE LEGITIMACY OF NORMS

A person attributes legitimacy to a system of rules and corresponding models of behavior when he accepts them as binding on his conduct. If a system of rules is defined as legitimate, this means that the rules are accepted as an authoritative set of directives for action. Conversely, any pattern of social action may be regarded as illegitimate if participants in a group feel that no member should accept it as an authoritative model of behavior. The acceptance or rejection of a system of rules gives the system an imperative quality so that the group member perceives it as a set of rules that he *must* or *must not* follow.

It is our view that members of delinquent subcultures have withdrawn their attribution of legitimacy to certain of the norms maintained by law-abiding groups of the larger society and have given it, instead, to new patterns of conduct which are defined as illegitimate by representatives of official agencies. Most of the behavior of delinquents conforms to conventional expectations; their violations of official norms are selective, confined to certain areas of activity and interest. However, those norms of delinquent subcultures which require the practice of theft, street warfare, and drug use are in direct opposition to official norms. Delinquents have withdrawn their support from established norms and invested officially forbidden forms of conduct with a claim to legitimacy in the light of their special situation. They recognize that law-abiding persons regard their behavior as illegitimate and they accept the necessity of secrecy and circumspection.

It should be noted that the attitude toward official norms, the imputation of legitimacy to officially prohibited conduct, and the rationalizations that make this conduct acceptable to the delinquent are best exemplified by the fully indoctrinated member of the subculture. Members may waver from time to time in the relative degree of legitimacy they attribute to official and delinquent norms. Nevertheless, the delinquent subculture calls for the withdrawal of sentiments supporting official norms and the tendering of allegiance to competing norms. To the extent that members waver in their allegiance to delinquent norms, the subculture comes to lack stability and validity as a style of life.

VARIETIES OF DELINQUENT SUBCULTURE

As we have noted, there appear to be three major types of delinquent subculture typically encountered among adolescent males in lower-class areas of large urban centers. One is based principally upon criminal values; its members are organized primarily for the pursuit of material gain by such illegal means as extortion, fraud, and theft. In the second, violence is the keynote; its members pursue status ("rep") through the manipulation of force or threat of force. These are the "warrior" groups that attract so much attention in the press. Finally, there are subcultures which emphasize the consumption of drugs. The participants in these drug subcultures have become alienated from conventional roles, such as those required in the family or the occupational world. They have withdrawn into a restricted world in which the ultimate value consists in the "kick." We call these three subcultural forms "criminal," "conflict," and "retreatist," respectively.[1]

The Criminal Pattern

The most extensive documentation in the sociological literature of delinquent behavior patterns in lower-class culture describes a tradition which integrates youthful delinquency with adult criminality. In the central value orientation of youths participating in this tradition, delinquent and criminal behavior is accepted as a means of achieving success-goals. The dominant criteria of in-group evaluation stress achievement, the use of skill and knowledge to get results. In this culture, prestige is allocated to those who achieve material gain and power through avenues defined as illegitimate by the larger society. From the very young to the very old, the successful "haul"—which quickly transforms the penniless into a man of means—is an ever-present vision of the possible and desirable. Although one may also achieve material success through the routine practice of theft or fraud, the "big score" remains the symbolic image of quick success.

The means by which a member of a criminal subculture achieves success are clearly defined for the aspirant. At a young age, he learns to admire and respect older criminals and to adopt the "right guy" as his role-model. Delinquent episodes help him to acquire mastery of the techniques and orientation of the criminal world and to learn how to cooperate successfully with others in criminal enterprises. He exhibits hostility and distrust toward representatives of the larger society. He regards members of the conventional world as "suckers," his natural victims, to be exploited when possible. He sees successful people in the conventional world as having a "racket"—e.g., big businessmen have huge expense accounts, politicians get graft, etc. This attitude successfully neutralizes the controlling effect of conventional norms. Toward the in-group the "right guy" maintains relationships of loyalty, honesty, and trustworthiness. He must prove himself reliable and dependable in his contacts with his criminal associates although he has no such obligations toward the outgroup of noncriminals.

One of the best ways of assuring success in the criminal world is to cultivate appropriate "connections." As a youngster, this means running with a clique composed of other "right guys" and promoting an apprenticeship or some other favored relationship with older and successful offenders. Close and dependable ties with income-producing outlets for stolen goods, such as the wagon peddler, the junkman, and the fence, are especially useful. Furthermore, these intermediaries encourage and protect the young delinquent in a criminal way of life by giving him a jaundiced perspective on the private morality of many functionaries in conventional society. As he matures, the young delinquent becomes acquainted with a new world made up of predatory bondsmen, shady lawyers, crooked policemen, grafting politicians, dishonest businessmen, and corrupt jailers. Through "connections" with occupants of these half-legitimate, half-illegitimate roles and with "big shots" in the underworld, the aspiring criminal validates and assures his freedom of movement in a world made safe for crime.

The Conflict Pattern

The role-model in the conflict pattern of lower-class culture is the "bopper" who swaggers with his gang, fights with weapons to win a wary respect from other gangs, and compels a fearful deference from the conventional adult world by his unpredictable and destructive assaults on persons and property. To other gang members, however, the key qualities of the bopper are those of the successful warrior. His performance must reveal a willingness to defend his personal integrity and the honor of the gang. He must do this with great courage and displays of fearlessness in the face of personal danger.

The immediate aim in the world of fighting gangs is to acquire a reputation for toughness and destructive violence. A "rep" assures not only respectful behavior from peers and threatened adults but also admiration for the physical strength and masculinity which it symbolizes. It represents a way of securing access to the scarce resources for adolescent pleasure and opportunity in underprivileged areas.

Above all things, the bopper is valued for his "heart." He does not "chicken out," even when confronted by superior force. He never defaults in the face of a personal insult or a challenge to the integrity of his gang. The code of the bopper is that of the warrior who places great stress on

[1] It should be understood that these terms characterize these delinquent modes of adaptation from the reference position of conventional society; they do not necessarily reflect the attitudes of members of the subcultures. Thus the term "retreatist" does not necessarily reflect the attitude of the "cat." Far from thinking of himself as being in retreat, he defines himself as among the elect.

courage, the defense of his group, and the maintenance of honor.

Relationships between bopping gang members and the adult world are severely attenuated. The term that the bopper uses most frequently to characterize his relationships with adults is "weak." He is unable to find appropriate role-models that can designate for him a structure of opportunities leading to adult success. He views himself as isolated and the adult world as indifferent. The commitments of adults are to their own interests and not to his. Their explanations of why he should behave differently are "weak," as are their efforts to help him.

Confronted by the apparent indifference and insincerity of the adult world, the ideal bopper seeks to win by coercion the attention and opportunities he lacks and cannot otherwise attract. In recent years the street-gang worker who deals with the fighting gang on its own "turf" has come to symbolize not only a recognition by conventional adult society of the gang's toughness but also a concession of opportunities formerly denied. Through the alchemy of competition between gangs, this gesture of attention by the adult world to the "worst" gangs is transformed into a mark of prestige. Thus does the manipulation of violence convert indifference into accommodation and attention into status.

The Retreatist Pattern

Retreatism may include a variety of expressive, sensual, or consummatory experiences, alone or in a group. In this analysis, we are interested only in those experiences that involve the use of drugs and that are supported by a subculture. We have adopted these limitations in order to maintain our focus on subcultural formations which are clearly recognized as delinquent, as drug use by adolescents is. The retreatist preoccupation with expressive experiences creates many varieties of "hipster" cult among lower-class adolescents which foster patterns of deviant but not necessarily delinquent conduct.

Subcultural drug-users in lower-class areas perceive themselves as culturally and socially detached from the life-style and everyday preoccupations of members of the conventional world. The following characterization of the "cat" culture, observed by Finestone (1957) in a lower-class Negro area in Chicago, describes drug use in the more general context of "hipsterism." Thus it should not be assumed that this description in every respect fits drug cultures found elsewhere. We have drawn heavily on Finestone's observations, however, because they provide the best descriptions available of the social world in which lower-class adolescent drug cultures typically arise.

The dominant feature of the retreatist subculture of the "cat" lies in the continuous pursuit of the "kick." Every cat has a kick—alcohol, marijuana, addicting drugs, unusual sexual experiences, hot jazz, cool jazz, or any combination of these. Whatever its content, the kick is a search for ecstatic experiences. The retreatist strives for an intense awareness of living and a sense of pleasure that is "out of this world." In extreme form, he seeks an almost spiritual and mystical knowledge that is experienced when one comes to know "it" at the height of one's kick. The past and the future recede in the time perspective of the cat, since complete awareness in present experience is the essence of the kick.

The successful cat has a lucrative "hustle" which contrasts sharply with the routine and discipline required in the ordinary occupational tasks of conventional society. The many varieties of the hustle are characterized by a rejection of violence or force and a preference for manipulating, persuading, outwitting, or "conning" others to obtain resources for experiencing the kick. The cat begs, borrows, steals, or engages in some petty con-game. He caters to the illegitimate cravings of others by peddling drugs or working as a pimp. A highly exploitative attitude toward women permits the cat to view pimping as a prestigeful source of income. Through the labor of "chicks" engaged in prostitution or shoplifting, he can live in idleness and concentrate his entire attention on organizing, scheduling, and experiencing the esthetic pleasure of the kick. The hustle of the cat is secondary to his interest in the kick. In this respect the cat differs from his fellow delinquents in the criminal subculture, for whom income-producing activity is a primary concern.

The ideal cat's appearance, demeanor, and taste can best be characterized as "cool." The cat seeks to exhibit a highly developed and sophisticated taste for clothes. In his demeanor, he struggles to reveal a self-assured and unruffled manner, thereby emphasizing his aloofness and "superiority" to the "squares." He develops a colorful, discriminating vocabulary and ritualized gestures which express his sense of difference from the conventional world and his solidarity with the retreatist subculture.

The word "cool" also best describes the sense of apartness and detachment which the retreatist experiences in his relationships with the conventional world. His reference group is the "society of cats," and "elite" group in which he becomes isolated from conventional society. Within this group, a new order of goals and criteria of achievement are created. The cat does not seek to impose this system of values on the world of the squares. Instead, he strives for status and deference within the society of cats by cultivating the kick and the hustle. Thus the retreatist subculture provides avenues to success-goals, to the social admiration and the sense of well-being or oneness with the world which the members feel are otherwise beyond their reach.

REFERENCES

Finestone, H., 1957. Cats, kicks, and color. *Social Problems*, **5**, 3–13.

part V Descriptions

IN THE LITERATURE on role one encounters many different terms that refer to descriptions. "Concept," "anticipation," "expectation," "schema," "cognition," and "attribution" are among the most frequently encountered, but one also finds "attitude" and "perception" employed as well. Some descriptions purport to represent some aspect of the past, while others pertain to the present, and still others have reference to the future. Furthermore, a description may be overt or covert, distorted or nondistorted; it may vary also in the extent to which it is complete, codified, universal, and complex. Descriptions are the individual's representation of aspects of the real world, and, as such, there are complex relationships between these descriptions and the events they describe. Thus we find that descriptions are significantly shaped by the individual's experience —by the positions to which he belongs, by the role behavior engaged in while a member of positions, by the number of ways in which he is interdependent with others—and that the individual's cognitive representations, in turn, affect his behavior in many ways.

In Turner's general discussion of role taking and reference groups, various descriptive processes are assumed. The author focuses on the various forms of empathy and role taking, and he points out that the individual may either: (1) adopt the other's standpoint, (2) understand the other's standpoint in a depersonalized sense as the other interacts with a third party, or (3) understand the other's standpoint by way of anticipating interaction with the other. The validating and implementing functions of role taking are discussed as well as the relationships between role taking, autonomy, and empathy. Finally, the author discusses the many possible meanings of the reference-group concept, including those of identification, interaction, valuation, and audience group.

The selection by Beatrice Wright examines the effects of conformity and nonconformity to expectations held for the disabled. The author points out that disabled persons are often faced with the problem of adjusting to expectations held for their behavior, either by themselves or by others. If their performances exceed those expectations, they are likely to provoke incredulity; if they fail, anguish and despair. Since expectations for the disabled are not anchored in common experiences, and since the performance of the disabled is usually governed less by desires of the disabled person than by physical limitations, the problem of conformity is acute. Wright suggests that a number of factors relate to this problem, among them being cognitive spread, the position of the subject who holds the expectations, the requirement of mourning, wish for improvement, and cognitive blurring due to anxiety. She also discusses various strategies for meeting the problem of nonconformity, these being cognitive revision, perceptual distortion, and the anormalizing of the disabled person.

Thomas takes up the relationships between role conceptions and the size of the organization. Presenting data from social welfare agencies of three different sizes, the author is able to show that consensus of role conceptions, breadth of role conceptions, ethical commitment, and quality of role performance are all greater in the smallest organization. Further analysis revealed, however, that most of these results could be attributed to characteristics of the communities in which the welfare bureaus were located, for the size of the communities—and other factors as well—was directly associated with the size of the welfare bureaus. This study suggests that the linkage between structural characteristics of organizations and aspects of organizational role behavior may be indirect and complicated when factors such as the community are also part of the organization's natural context.

The selection by Jones, Davis, and Gergen is a

report of an experiment on the relationship between role performance and the perceptions others have of this performance. The hypothesis was that individuals who conform in their behaviors to stated norms are perceived to reveal little of themselves, whereas persons who do not conform to all prescriptions of a role are perceived by others to be reflecting the needs of their own personalities—to be revealing more of themselves. This hypothesis was tested in an experiment in which subjects were presented with stimulus persons who either conformed or did not conform to prescriptions given by the experimenter. Those who did not conform were perceived to be revealing their true personalities, and persons who conformed were recalled more accurately.

The last two selections relate to different aspects of role and psychotherapy. In the first of these, Lennard and Bernstein present the results of a study on role expectations in the therapeutic situation. The authors observe that therapy, as a social system, may be thought of as involving two subsystems, those of role expectations and communication. Their study attempts to document the hypothesis that asymmetry in the system of role expectations is reflected in asymmetry in the system of communication. If the therapist and patient differ from one another in the expectations each holds for behavior in the therapeutic situation, strains will appear, and the participants will adopt certain strategies to resolve the strains. The authors offer a discussion of this problem and data bearing on the strategies of resolution.

In the other selection concerning therapeutic situations, Overall and Aronson propose that when patients of lower socioeconomic class hold expectations for psychotherapy at variance with the actual behaviors of the therapist they encounter during the initial treatment session, there will be a higher drop-out rate following the initial treatment session than when the patients hold more accurate expectations. An instrument for measuring expectations of therapy was developed for administration to patients prior to entering therapy, and the authors found support for their hypothesis.

selection 14 Role-Taking, Role Standpoint, and Reference-Group Behavior

RALPH H. TURNER

Role-taking in its most general form is a process of looking at or anticipating another's behavior by viewing it in the context of a role imputed to that other. It is thus always more than simply a reaction to another's behavior in terms of an arbitrarily understood symbol or gesture.

With only unimportant qualifications, we shall accept the delimited meaning of role-taking proposed by Walter Coutu (1951), which distinguishes the imaginative construction of the other's role (role-taking) from the overt enactment of what one conceives to be one's own appropriate role in a given situation (role-playing) and from the overt enactment of a role as a form of pretense ("playing-at" a role). Role-taking may proceed from identifying a position to inferring its role and in this manner anticipating the behavior of an individual. Or it may proceed from observing a segment of behavior to identifying the feelings or motives behind the behavior or to anticipating subsequent behavior. In either case certain actions are interpreted or anticipated upon the basis of the entire role of which they are assumed to be a part.

In the present discussion the manner in which an individual conceives the role of another will not be examined as an isolated form of behavior. The self-other relationship will be viewed as an aspect of a total social act.[1] The actor takes the role of another in carrying out some behavior of his own; role-taking is an adjunct to the determination or application of one's own role in a given situation. Accordingly, for present purposes we shall disregard the usage of role-taking as the enactment of roles in the sociodramatic setting when the usage detaches the roles from their specific implications for the way in which the actor will define his own role (e.g., see Sarbin, 1943). Furthermore, our purpose in understanding how the role-taking process shapes the actor's own behavior will determine the basis on which we shall distinguish types of role-taking activity. The critical differentiae for types of role-taking will revolve about the manner in which the self-other relationship affords a directive to the individual in the formulation of what his own behavior shall be.

STANDPOINT IN ROLE-TAKING

Taking the role of another may or may not include adopting the standpoint of the other as one's own. The role of the other may remain an object to the actor, so that he understands and interprets it without allowing its point of view to become his own, or the actor may allow the inferred attitudes of the other to become his own and to direct his behavior. Another way of stating the distinction is to note that an individual who is taking the role of another may identify with the role of that other, or else he may retain a clear separation of identity between the self-attitudes and the attitudes of the other. When role-taking includes adoption of the standpoint of the other, the role-taking process is an automatic determiner of behavior. One simply acts from the standpoint of the role. When the standpoint of the other is not adopted, some other factor must intervene to determine the kind of influence which the role imputed to the other will have on the actor.

An occasional confusion between taking the role of another and adopting the standpoint of another is partly responsible for the view that facility in role-taking necessarily results in altruistic or sympathetic behavior or eliminates divergence of purpose between opposing factions. Certain types of exploitation, for example, require elaborate role-taking behavior on the part of the exploiter. The "confidence man" frequently

[1] "Social act" is used in the sense indicated by Ellsworth Faris and George Herbert Mead. For a brief statement of this conception see Ellsworth Faris (1937).

Abridged from the *American Journal of Sociology*, 1956, **61**, 316–328. Reprinted by permission of the author and the University of Chicago Press.

succeeds because of his ability to identify accurately the feelings and attitudes of the person with whom he is dealing while completely avoiding any involvement or identification with these feelings.

The standpoint is not, of course, something apart from the role. It is the core of the role. The difference to which we are referring concerns the ability to engage in an imaginative construction of the role of another while maintaining the separation of personal identities.

The early role-taking activity of the child does not make such a separation. To the degree to which he thinks or feels himself into a situation of another, he adopts as his own the attitudes appropriate to that situation. The more complex behavior in which the actor is able to see the other's role while maintaining a separation of identities appears to develop through two processes. First, the individual becomes concerned simultaneously with *multiple others*. As he takes the roles of two others simultaneously, he cannot simultaneously adopt the standpoints of each. Thus, in simultaneously taking the roles of his mother and his playmate, he cannot orient himself from each standpoint at the same time. Hence he may take the role of a playmate, but, in reacting to the imputed role, he may adopt the standpoint of his mother. The existence of conflicting standpoints in the varied roles which the individual has learned to take forces upon him a separation between taking the role and adopting its standpoint.

On the other hand, the presence of *stable purposes or needs* gradually leads the individual to engage in role-taking in an adaptive context. Such rudimentary understandings of the roles of others as the child may achieve are quite early put to use in the attempted pursuit of his own objectives. Role-taking makes possible both the manipulation of others and adjustment to them, becoming a means to a pre-existing end of some sort. The attitude and skill of role-taking which were learned in a relationship of identification become divorced from that relationship as it is discovered to be useful in promoting the individual's own purposes.

These two ways in which role-taking is divested of identification remain as two somewhat different kinds of standpoint which can be adopted toward the imputed role of the other. (a) In the former instance the standpoint adopted is that of a third party. The third-party standpoint indicates what behavior is expected of the actor, depending upon the inferences made concerning the role of the other. The point of view of the mother, for example, may be that her child should be friends with a neighbor only if that neighbor conceives his role as being a decent and respectable child. The role of the other, when divorced from adoption of its standpoint, becomes a datum in carrying out the standpoint of the third party.

The third-party standpoint may be recognized as that of a specific person or group, or it may be depersonalized into a norm. Such a norm provides the individual with a directive to action which is contingent upon his placing some construction on the role of the relevant other. In a study (Turner, 1952) of college students' reactions toward a friend who had committed a hypothetical breach of the mores, for example, the majority volunteered some estimate of the role context in which the friend had committed the disapproved act. Some respondents found it appropriate not to report their friend's theft to the authorities when it could be assumed that the general role of the friend was still that of an honest, law-abiding person whose inconsistent behavior reflected unusual stress. For these respondents the norms defining their own responsibility were more dependent upon the role of the other than on any specific behavior in which he had engaged. Whether the third-party standpoint is personalized or not, the actor engages in role-taking in order to determine how he *ought* to act toward the other.

(b) When role-taking is in the adaptive context, however, the standpoint consists of a purpose or objective rather than a specific directive. The actor must examine the probable interaction between the self-role and the other-role in terms of the promotion of a purpose. He lacks a specific or detailed directive supplied by the standpoint of a third party and consequently must shape his own role behavior according to what he judges to be the probable *effect of interaction* between his own role and the inferred role of the other.

This latter kind of role-taking behavior may be clarified with George Herbert Mead's classic distinction between "play" and the "game," as illustrated in baseball (1934). The skilful player in a game such as baseball cannot act solely according to a set of rules. The first baseman can learn in general when he is to field the ball, when to run to first base, etc. But, in order to play intelligently and to be prepared for less clearly defined incidents in the game, he must adjust his role performance to the roles of all the other players. This adjustment is in terms of the effect of interaction among roles toward the end of minimizing the score of the opposing team. Whether the first baseman fields the ball, runs to first, throws to home, etc., will depend upon what he thinks each of the other players will do and how his action will combine most effectively with theirs to keep the score down.

Mead has pointed out that in the "game" the actor must have in mind the roles of all the other players. However, there is more which is distinctive about this kind of role-taking than merely the simultaneous attention to multiple other-roles. The manner in which the actor relates his own role to the others is in terms of their *interactive effect* rather than simply in terms of accepting their direction. It is not so much what the pitcher wants him to do that determines the first baseman's action as what the first baseman judges will be the consequences if each acts in a particular way.

This type of role-taking can be even more clearly illustrated in the case of exploitation or of salesmanship directed toward a reluctant buyer, in which cases the actor's purpose is not shared by the relevant other. In these instances the actor holds constantly in mind his imaginative construction of the role of the other and adjusts his own behavior so as to elicit and take advantage of behavior in the other which will enhance his own objectives. He sensitizes himself to the attitudes of the other while divesting himself of any identification with these attitudes. And these attitudes enter into determination of his own behavior through the criterion of effect in interaction with potential self-behavior.

Recapitulating this section, we have observed that an individual who in some sense puts himself in the position of another and imaginatively constructs that other's role may do so from one of three general standpoints. First, he may adopt the other's standpoint as his own, in which case he is identifying with the other-role and allowing it to become an automatic guide to his own behavior. Second, the role of the other may remain an object viewed from the standpoint of some personalized third party or depersonalized norm, in which case the role of the relevant other becomes a datum necessary in implementing the third-party directive. Third, the role of the relevant other may be viewed from the standpoint of its effect in interaction with potential self-behavior, as contributing toward some individual or shared purpose. The standpoint of the actor in role-taking may change in the course of a single act, or he may be plagued by alternative standpoints. But the manner in which the imagined other-role affects the actor's behavior will be different with each standpoint.

REFLEXIVENESS IN ROLE-TAKING

Borrowing a term from George Herbert Mead (1934), we shall suggest that a second major distinction be made between reflexive and nonreflexive role-taking. Mead uses the term "reflexive" in referring to the "characteristic of the self as an object to itself." When the role of the other is employed as a mirror, reflecting the expectations or evaluations of the self as seen in the other-role (see Cooley, 1922), we may speak of *reflexive role-taking*.

While role-taking is a process of placing specific behaviors of the other in the context of his total role, the attention of the actor is never equally focused upon all the attitudes implied by that role. Rather, one's orientation determines that only certain attitudes of the other-role will be especially relevant to the determination of his own behavior. Role-taking in abstraction is importantly different from role-taking in a situation which calls for a determination of how the actor's role should be played, for the demands of the actor's role determine the selection of aspects of the other-role for emphasis. In one context one particular set of attitudes may be relevant to the determination of the actor's behavior; in another context the same set of attitudes may be irrelevant.

One of the most important distinctions which can be made among the kinds of other-attitudes is between those which are expectations or evaluations or images directed toward the self and those which are not. When the attention of the role-taker is focused upon the way in which he appears to the other, the role-taking is reflexive.

Reflexiveness is connected with what we popularly call "self-consciousness." When role-taking is reflexive, the individual is led not merely to consider the effects of his action or their compatibility with some standard or code but to picture himself specifically as an object of evaluation by someone else. An additional perspective is added to his conception of his own behavior.

The criteria of reflexiveness and standpoint placed in combination serve to delineate more sharply the different ways in which the self-other relationship can determine behavior. We shall examine role-taking from each of the three standpoints in order in its nonreflexive and reflexive forms.

1. When the standpoint of the other-role is adopted, the other may serve as a model or standard which is accepted without self-consciousness either in the absence of alternative models or because of prestige or dependence in the relationship. Role-taking which is nonreflexive and identifying is probably the simplest and earliest form. The child's "playing-at" various roles shifts fairly imperceptibly into such role-taking in real-life situations. When confronted with situations like those in which he has seen a parent or older sibling enact a role, the child adopts as his own the attitudes of the role as he understands them. For example, a child of three or four who has been taught in a firm but kindly manner not to touch various objects will suddenly adopt as his own the entire role and standpoint of the parent when he finds himself in company with a younger and less responsible child. The behavior of the younger child calls up in the older the role which adults have taken toward him. Accordingly, he naïvely acts toward the younger child as he has learned to understand the role of the parent toward himself.

The same pattern of role-taking continues to be a major source of the values and attitudes of the individual. Whenever there is close attachment of one person to another, there is a tendency for the standpoint of the other to be adopted. Probably the attachment need not be positive in character. An attachment loaded with negative affect giving rise to intense rivalry leads each person to take the role of his rival and unwittingly adopt that rival's standpoint in many respects. Whenever prestige is accorded to someone, there is a tendency to take the role of the prestigeful person without disentangling that other's standpoint.

2. In contrast to this nonreflexive relationship a desire to conform to the other's expectations or to appear favorably in the other's eyes may shape the self-behavior into conformity with the other.

When role-taking involves identification and is reflexive, the self becomes specifically an object evaluated from the standpoint of the other. The attitudes of the other which are adopted as one's own are the attitudes toward one's self rather than toward external objects and values in the environment. At this stage a self-image is beginning to be formed, though it is not yet independent of the particular other whose role is being taken. From reflexive identifying role-taking the individual begins to develop an estimate of his own adequacy and worth. His own self-esteem is the adoption of the estimate of himself which he infers from the standpoint of the role of the other. The bonds of intimacy and prestige or the absence of alternative standpoints determine that the evaluations of relevant others will become the self-evaluations of the individual.

3. The distinction in self-consciousness is also important when the standpoint of a third party or norm is being adopted. Nonreflexive role-taking of this sort directs attention to attitudes in the role of the other whose recognition makes it possible to act according to a pre-existing directive. This pre-existing directive (incorporated in the third-party standpoint) may be of two sorts. It may, as already illustrated, make the appropriate self-behavior conditional upon the role of the other. Or it may direct the actor to employ the roles of certain others as standards or models to compare with his own behavior. The third-party standpoint enables the actor to react discriminatingly toward the aspirations and attitudes of others in determining which shall be used as standards for his own aspirations and attitudes.

4. When role-taking from a third-party standpoint is reflexive, the standpoint enables the actor to react selectively to his audiences. His concern is not merely how he compares with the other but how he appears to the other. But his appearance to the other does not direct his own behavior in an automatic manner as in the case of identification. Instead, he can accept the evaluations of certain others as legitimate and reject the evaluations and expectations of different others as lacking legitimacy (see Turner, 1954).

As the third-party standpoint becomes stabilized and generalized so as to become a fairly consistent standpoint in the individual, it operates in reflexive role-taking as a fully evolved self-conception or self-image. Such a self-conception permits the actor to react selectively on two bases. First, it may tell the subject whose approval is worth seeking and whose is not. The parent tries to teach his child, for example, to seek the respect of his teachers and the children from "good" homes, while disregarding the opinions that children "without breeding" have of him. Second, it may designate the type of image one wishes to see reflected in the other's conception of one's self. The individual may wish to appear to all as an honest man, as an independent person, or as a good fellow. The self-conception directs the individual to behave in a manner which will evoke such an image of himself in the role of his audience.

The two bases of selection may also operate together. Thus, the self-image (or third-party standpoint) may tell the actor that he should appear strong and distant to others in subordinate relations with himself, easy to get along with to others who are his peers and intimates, liked by others who are loyal citizens, and hated by others who are not loyal citizens.

5, 6. When role-taking occurs from the standpoint of interactive effect, it becomes reflexive when the reflected self-image is manipulated by the actor as a means of achieving his ends. The salesman who tries to create the impression that he would rather lose the sale than sell a person what he does not want, the propagandist attempting to appear "folksy," and the counselor responding nonevaluatively to his client are all trying to manipulate the image of themselves held by the other so as to foster their purposes. On the other hand, in baseball the role-taking is more concerned with the attitudes of the others toward the game than toward each other and is therefore nonreflexive. The difference between reflexive and nonreflexive role-taking of this sort appears in two levels of playing a game such as poker. Each player will attempt to judge what other players are likely to do. But the superior player will also attempt by such techniques as bluffing, conspicuous misplay, randomized strategies, or the "poker face" to establish a false image of himself which will modify the play of others in anticipated directions.

SIGNIFICANCE OF THE TYPES

The types we have suggested are important because each finds the actor in a somewhat different relationship to the relevant other whose role he is attempting to infer. The types also differ in the complexity of the process and in the kind of discretion they permit the actor in shaping his own behavior. Though they are analytically distinguishable, however, the types are not characteristically found in complete empirical separation. They are importantly interrelated in the behavior of any individual in two ways: (a) hierarchically and (b) as alternative orientations to the other.

(a) The fundamental source of social values appears to be the *standpoint of the other*. Accordingly, we may speak of role-taking which involves identification as being *derivative* with respect to the values of the individual. The person derives his values through adopting others' standpoints. In contrast, the other types of role-taking are implementive or validative with respect to values. They serve as means through which the values already acquired may be validated by reference to some standard or implemented in practice. Hence, these types are dependent upon role-taking with identification in two ways. They are dependent upon some prior role-taking as the source of values they express. And they are dependent upon prior learning of the skills of role-taking before the role-taking can be detached from adoption of the role standpoint.

Validation has to do with determining the personal relevance of values which one already accepts. One may adopt a value without making it a demand upon one's self. Or one may adopt a value with varying levels of aspiration regarding its achievement. Such validation—setting degrees of personal relevance and levels of aspiration—takes place in part through the simple laws of effect in learning theory and in part through role-taking. To the extent that it occurs through role-taking, it does so either via the reflexive attention to what others expect of the individual or through the comparison of the self with designated standards.

Part of the particular significance of reflexive role-taking lies in its validative function. When one adopts the other's standpoint in reflexive role-taking, he does more than simply adopt certain values; he adopts a definition of what is expected of him regarding that value. The child, for example, who identifies with the parent and adopts his attitudes toward others often does not see the personal relevance of these attitudes except in limited situations. The child is typically "hypocritical" and is distressed when the parent directs attention to his own behavior. At other times the child attempts to make every value a directive to his own behavior and must learn that what he admires in others is not necessarily required of himself.

The values derived in identification role-taking also point to certain groups or persons who serve as standards of comparison in performing the validation function. The individual takes the role of those to whom his attention is thus directed in order to judge what their attitudes are toward the values they profess, what their aspirations are, what effort they put forth, so that he may use these estimates comparatively in setting his own levels.

The *implementive function* of role-taking is carried out, as we have already described, either as demanded by a norm which makes the actor's behavior conditional upon the role of the relevant other or through the consideration of probable effects of the interaction of roles in promoting a given objective. Such implementation is dependent upon both the derivative and the validative functions. The individual must have both adopted values and formed some conception of their personal relevance before he proceeds to carry them out.

(b) The hierarchical relationship among types of role-taking is important from the point of view of socialization or the genetic backgrounds of current attitudes. But, from the point of view of the act in process, the important relationship among types of role-taking lies in the fact that they are *alternative relationships* which the individual can establish to the role of the other which will make the effect of that other's attitudes quite different. In order to predict the behavior of a person, it is not sufficient to know that he will take the role of another or to know how accurately he will take that role. A small cue may change his relationship toward the perceived other-role. The high-pressure salesman who is exploiting the attitudes in the other-role to the full may suddenly begin to identify with the attitudes of that other and be rendered incapable of continuing his sales talk. Or an individual identifying with the role of another who is in misfortune may suddenly remember a social norm which leads him to detach himself and treat the other-role as an object.

The alternative relationships to the other-role may exist as recognized conflicts to the individual. The most frequently noted conflict between standpoints is between adopting the standpoint of the other and subjecting the role of the other to the scrutiny indicated by some norm. For example, a subject who inferred a set of attitudes in a friend which would account for his having committed a theft concluded that his obligation was to report the friend to the authorities. By adding that "he will probably hate me for it," he gave explicit recognition to the conflict. Important also is the conflict between derivative and validative orientations, when the values adopted as part of a standpoint are not adequately supported in the indicated validating relationships. Conflicts also frequently exist between role-taking from the standpoint of interactive effect and the other types.

From the distinction among types of role-taking emerges a major theoretical problem for the study of role behavior. The problem is to isolate the variables which determine what kind of role-taking relationship the individual will assume with respect to any specific relevant other. We have already suggested that strong affect directed toward the other makes the more complex forms less likely to take place and that according prestige to the other has a similar effect. Another determinant is the degree to which the roles of different statuses receive normative sanction from the standpoint of a generalized other. For example, the tendency for a parent to identify with the role of his child when the latter has been hurt is reinforced by the fact that this is in keeping with the generalized standpoint in the society. Thus there is a more generalized imperative operating on the parent than the spontaneous identification arising out of affective involvement. There are also differences in the situational focus of attention which affect role-taking relationships.

BOUNDARIES TO ROLE-TAKING

The coexistence of different relationships in role-taking leads us to the further question of whether the concept has been so broadened in application as to lose its analytic utility. If we say, as some writers have, that, whenever an individual experiences an attitude toward some object, he is taking the role of some relevant other toward that object, then every action has been made into role-taking. On the other hand, if we limit role-taking to instances in which the subject recognizes and can conceptualize what he is doing, we make a dividing line which is indefensible in light of modern psychological understanding. The criterion of consciousness, then, is too narrow and the criterion of attitude source is too broad.

The key to a useful delimitation of the term becomes clear when we distinguish between a genetic or socialization framework in which we look into past experiences for the explanation of present behavior and an action framework in which we examine the dynamic interrelations among the elements contemporarily operating to determine action. The concept of role-taking belongs in the latter framework, designating a kind of relationship which may be contemporarily assumed toward a relevant other in the context of an act in process. Within the action framework we may say that a person is engaged in role-taking whenever the individual's conception or performance of his own role is altered by modifying his construction of the other-role.

Even though we may suppose that all attitudes

originate in some role-taking, the self-role can become autonomous; that is, it can become independent of the role-taking relationship which originally gave rise to it. Under the latter circumstance the self-role becomes stabilized so that the role-taking process is omitted or role-taking ceases to modify the self-role. One form of this autonomy is indicated when a person is said to have interiorized a social norm, meaning that an earlier process of role-taking has become truncated. The self-role may then persist unchanged even if the perceived attitudes of the relevant other change or if the affective relationship between self and other change.

A NOTE ON EMPATHY

Of the many senses in which *empathy* has been used, five can be particularly related to our current discussion. (a) By most traditional usage empathy refers to nonreflexive identifying role-taking, in which the individual unwittingly puts himself in the position of another and adopts his standpoint. (b) Sometimes empathy is presented as an ability that is desirable in personnel relations, in which case it designates the ability to understand the role of another while retaining one's personal detachment. According to this usage, empathy includes all role-taking except that in which the standpoint of the other is adopted as one's own. (c) Empathy is sometimes used to designate the process of seeing one's self as others see one, the ability to react to one's own behavior as others are reacting to it. This usage makes empathy identical with reflexive role-taking, regardless of standpoint. (d) Empathic capacity is sometimes used synonymously with role-taking capacity, to include all the forms of the process we have described. (e) When empathy is distinguished from projection, it refers to one criterion for inferring the other-role. In this usage all our types would be included so long as the role-taking is not based upon projection.

To make a choice among these usages by fiat would be an empty gesture. However, there are at least three implications of our present discussion for the current work dealing with empathy. First, the *tendency* to empathize, in whatever sense this is meant, is at least as important a variable as the *ability* to empathize. Under what circumstances will a person employ such empathic abilities as he has rather than merely enact a rigidly predetermined role or react to the other's gestures with standardized responses? Second, given the tendency and ability to empathize (using the term in its broader senses), what relationship to the inferred other-role will determine its effect on the individual's behavior? The tendency and ability in role-taking must be seen in combination with the tendency to assume certain kinds of relations with relevant others. Third, the standpoint in role-taking operates to focus attention selectively on the role being taken. Consequently, certain aspects of the other-role are seen more clearly or are more salient than others, depending upon the standpoint governing the empathic process. Since empathy or role-taking is not normally performed in a vacuum, the accuracy of empathic behavior will vary according to the focus of attention supplied by the governing standpoint. Consideration of empathic ability might profit from taking this observation into account. A quite tentative suggestion from one study (Macfarlane, 1952) of empathic ability that empathy is more accurate with respect to reflexive than nonreflexive aspects of the other-role may tell something about the focus of attention in the role-taking process within a clinical counseling situation.

REFERENCE-GROUP BEHAVIOR

Two commentaries (Kelley, 1952; Shibutani, 1955) have recently pointed out different usages of the term "reference group." Both have noted that a reference group may mean a group with which one compares himself in making a self-judgment. This usage prevails in the original work of Hyman (1942) and the more recent discussion by Merton and Kitt (1950). Both commentaries have also noted an alternative usage of reference group to mean the source of an individual's vaules (Kelley, 1952) or perspectives (Shibutani, 1955; Sherif, 1948; Newcomb, 1950; and Hartley, 1951) have employed the concept chiefly in this sense. A third usage suggested by Shibutani refers to a group whose acceptance one seeks. In the literature, however, the desire to be accepted is depicted as the mechanism which leads to the adoption of the values and perspectives of the reference group (see Newcomb, 1950). These are not, therefore, separate usages of the term but merely definitions, on the one hand, in terms of the effect of the reference group and, on the other hand, in terms of the mechanism of the reference group.

When a reference group is the source of values and perspectives, the identity of meaning with role-taking is apparent. One takes the role of a member of the group, which is synonymous with having "a psychologically functioning membership" (Newcomb, 1951, p. 48) in the group, and one adopts the group's standpoint as one's own. Thus, except for emphasizing that the source of values need not be a group of which the individual is objectively a member, this use of reference group corresponds to one traditional usage of role-taking.

Reference group as a point of comparison corresponds partially to certain meanings of role-taking. The self-other relationship is essentially that which we have described as role-taking from a third-party standpoint. Merton and Kitt (1950) note the operation of a third-party standpoint in "the institutional definitions of the social structure which may focus the attention of members of a group or occupants of a social status upon certain *common* reference groups" (pp. 64–65). However, the actor may or may not take the role of a member of the reference group. So long as the actor is using the reference group only as a point of comparison in estimating his own social standing or in deciding whether to be satisfied or dissatisfied with his lot, external attributes of the other alone are involved. The role of the relevant other is not being taken. But when levels of aspiration, degrees of determination, and the like are being compared, the individual must necessarily take the role of the other in order to make a comparison.

In the preceding sense reference group as a point of comparison is a broader concept than role-taking from a third-party standpoint. However, in our discussion of role-taking we recognized that the standpoint of the third party might direct attention to the relevant other in more ways than simple comparison. Comparable relations of individual to group appear not to have been included in reference-group usages.

Dispute over the proper meaning of "reference group" seems to center about the acceptable generality of the concept. The limited usage which Sherif and Shibutani prefer, referring to the source of the individual's major perspectives and values, might well be named the *identification group*. The identification group is the source of values, since the individual takes the role of a member while adopting the member's standpoint as his own.

At the opposite extreme the individual's behavior is affected somewhat by groups whose members constitute merely conditions to his actions. The groups are neutrally toned to the actor; he must merely take them into account in order to accomplish his purposes. The manner in which he takes them into account may or may not require role-taking, and they may or may not constitute his membership group. Such a group might well be designated by some such neutral term as *interaction group*.

In between are those groups which acquire value to the individual because the standpoint of his identification groups designates them as points of reference. Conforming to the standpoint of his identification group (or of an autonomous self-image which has become stabilized independently of the identification group from which it was derived), the individual compares himself with certain groups or notes the impression he is making on them or in some other way takes account of them. Again, whether this relationship does or does not involve role-taking will depend upon the directive supplied by the identification group or self-conception. These groups might be called *valuation groups*, since their effect upon the individual's behavior is determined by the valuation which his more basic orientations lead him to place upon them.

Finally, if reference-group theory is to encompass the ways in which individual-group relationships shape the roles and role behaviors of the individual, we should note a dichotomy cross-cutting the preceding distinctions. Certain reference groups within each of the preceding types might usefully be regarded as *audience groups* to the individual. These are the groups by whom the actor sees his role performance observed and evaluated, and he attends to the evaluations and expectations which members of the group hold toward him. The actor takes the role of his audience reflexively. An individual's relations with his identification groups may place the latter on some occasions as his audience and on other occasions not. The reaction to the audience may be that of uncritical acceptance of their evaluations and expectations toward him, or the responses of his audience may be interpreted in an interactive context or as directed by his identification group or self-conception.

In general, then, it appears that the concepts of reference group and role-taking are closely related. In the broadest sense reference-group behavior is somewhat more inclusive than role-taking, since one may take account of a reference group without taking the role of a member. The terms "reference group" and "relevant other" refer to essentially the same phenomena. The reference group is a *generalized other* which is viewed as possessing member roles and attributes independently of the specific individuals who compose it. The same general differentiations seem applicable on the bases of standpoint and reflexiveness (audience). Likewise, the same theoretical problems apply, and a similar principle regarding the boundaries of the concepts seems applicable.

REFERENCES

Cooley, C. H., 1922. *Human nature and the social order* (Rev. ed.). New York: Scribner.

Coutu, W., 1951. Role-playing vs. role-taking: an appeal for clarification. *American Sociological Review*, **16**, 180–187.

Faris, E., 1937. *The nature of human nature*. New York: McGraw-Hill, pp. 144 ff.

Hartley, E. L., 1951. Psychological problems of multiple group membership. In J. H. Rohrer and M. Sherif (Eds.), *Social psychology at the crossroads*. New York: Harper and Row, pp. 371–386.

Hyman, H., 1942. The psychology of status. *Archives of Psychology*, No. 269.

Kelley, H. H., 1952. Two functions of reference groups. In G. E. Swanson, T. M. Newcomb, and E. L. Hartley (Eds.), *Readings in social psychology* (Rev. ed.). New York: Holt, pp. 410–414.

Macfarlane, T. G., 1952. Empathic understanding in an interpersonal interview situation. Unpublished doctoral dissertation, University of California, Los Angeles, pp. 115–116.

Mead, G. H., 1934. *Mind, self, and society*. Chicago: University of Chicago Press, pp. 149 ff.

Merton, R. K., and Kitt, Alice, 1950. Contributions to the theory of reference group behavior. In R. K. Merton and P. F. Lazarsfeld (Eds.), *Continuities in social research*. New York: The Free Press.

Newcomb, T. M., 1950. *Social psychology*. New York: Dryden, pp. 220–232.

Newcomb, T. M., 1951. Social psychological theory. In J. H. Rohrer and M. Sherif (Eds.), *Social psychology at the crossroads*. New York: Harper and Row.

Sarbin, T. R., 1943. The concept of role-taking. *Sociometry*, **6**, 273–285.

Sherif, M., 1948. *An outline of social psychology*. New York: Harper and Row, pp. 105–106, 123.

Sherif, M., 1953. The concept of reference groups in human relations. In M. Sherif and M. O. Wilson (Eds.), *Group relations at the crossroads*. New York: Harper and Row, pp. 203–231.

Shibutani, T., 1955. Reference groups as perspectives. *American Journal of Sociology*, **60**, 562–569.

Turner, R. H., 1952. Moral judgment: a study in roles. *American Sociological Review*, **17**, 70–77.

Turner, R. H., 1954. Self and other in moral judgment. *American Sociological Review*, **19**, 254–255, 258.

selection 15 Disability and Discrepancy of Expectations

BEATRICE A. WRIGHT

It is of far-reaching consequence that the expectations concerning the behavior and adjustment of persons with a disability are often discrepant with the apparent behavior and adjustment—that is, with what the subject observes. We shall call this the *expectation discrepancy*. The "subject" as used here will apply to the person whose expectations and other perceptions we are examining, be he the person with the disability or the person viewing him. The expectations can be worse than the apparent reality or better.

The subject who has these discrepant expectations will react with some feeling appropriate to the gap between the expected and apparent

Abridged from Chapter 3 of a book by the same author entitled *Physical Disability—A Psychological Approach*, 1960, New York: Harper and Row. Reprinted by permission of the author and Harper and Row. This investigation was supported by a grant from the Association for the Aid of Crippled Children.

state of affairs and to the direction of that gap. Where the expectations are worse than what he observes, he may be:

Surprised—"Despite their severe disabilities, the mental health of the veteran paraplegics as a group is surprisingly good."

Incredulous—"It's unbelievable, but he can even shave with those hooks!"

Where the expectations are better than the presenting facts, the subject may be:

Anguished—"I felt sick. The last hope that I might again see perfectly was gone."

Disappointed—"I had hoped this final operation would be successful, but she still can't bend her knee."

Assuredly, there is a wide gamut of emotional reactions to expectation discrepancy. Such feelings as amazement, wonder, curiosity, dismay, horror, frustration, futility, etc., could be added, but there is little in the way of research to assist us in delimiting the possibilities. It seems reasonable that if the direction of the expectation discrepancy is in accord with the subject's wishes, a positive affect emerges, such as "pleasant surprise" or hopefulness. If, however, the expectation discrepancy runs counter to his wishes, a negative feeling is experienced, such as disappointment and frustration.

Though it might appear that a positive reaction would be typical in cases where the state of affairs turns out to be better than anticipated, we must not forget that the subject, under certain conditions, might wish a worsening or a maintaining of the unfortunate situation. In the case of the person with a disability, this occurs when he does not wish to get well, when the secondary gains are contingent upon his remaining disabled. In the case of someone else, this occurs when the principle known as the "requirement of mourning" operates. Then it is that the subject may actually feel dismayed should he perceive the person with the disability as "better off" than he expected and quite content to find the reverse.

In addition to the subject's immediate reaction to the discrepancy between his expectation and presenting fact, he has a need to explain it, to fill in the gap, so that there is a reconciliation between the two halves of the equation, i.e., expectations on the one hand and the apparent reality on the other. How this reconciliation takes place also has important consequences for the evaluation of a person with a disability, but first we need to inquire as to the conditions giving rise to expectation discrepancy.

CONDITIONS UNDERLYING EXPECTATION DISCREPANCY

How does it happen that there is a discrepancy between what the subject expects of the behavior of a person with a disability and what at some later time he experiences of that behavior? Several conditions may be mentioned:

1. *Spread*—The subject perceives the person (or himself) as a "disabled person"; that is, the person is seen as disabled not only with respect to physique but with respect to other characteristics as well—for example, personality and adjustment. This spread appears to be particularly fluid when the subject is in a comparative frame of mind, that is, when he is evaluating the person with respect to some preconceived standard. Because of "spread," the subject *expects* the lot of the person with a disability to be *worse* than the apparent reality. Such spread, then, often accompanied by devaluation, becomes paradoxically a condition for the subsequent wonder and admiration at the proved accomplishments of the person with a disability.

2. *Position of the subject*—When the subject is in the position of an outsider—that is, when he is actually little concerned with the fate of the person with a disability—he will view the problems attendant upon the disability from his own perspective. This means that he will see the problems of the situation in terms of his own "equipment" as a person with the usual physical advantages and be unable to discover new ways of meeting these problems. In their insolubility the problems loom large indeed, and hence the expectations may be worse than the actuality. Were the subject closely aligned with the disability situation, either as the person with the disability himself or one close to him, then the necessity of meeting the problems of living would reveal to him the pertinent truth, "there is more than one way to skin a cat." When coping is enhanced, negative expectations are reduced and sometimes may even be underestimated.

3. *Requirement of mourning*—When the security of the subject depends upon physique as a high status value, he will tend to insist that the lot of a person with a disability is an unfortunate one. Exaggerated negative expectations are part and parcel of this need and point to an important source of expectation discrepancy.

4. *Wish for improvement*—Sometimes the wish that all will be well is so strong as to lead to unrealistic expectations of marked improvement

or eventual recovery. Even though current difficulties may be played down because of this same wish, the fact that the hopeful expectations cannot materialize means a discrepancy with reality that is at best disappointing and at worst heartbreaking. We should also expect that a person with such a strong wish would show other differentiating emotions; for example, he is less likely to be amazed or surprised at the positive adjustment and accomplishments of a person with a disability and more likely to be pleased than would the outsider who does not actively entertain the wish for improvement.

5. *Blurring of perception owing to anxiety*—Both the expectations and the apparent reality may remain obscure because of the tide of anxiety that keeps the subject, as it were, in a daze. Then it is that such emotions as worry, depression, antipathy take hold, and emotions arising from expectation discrepancy, such as anticipation, surprise, disappointment, etc., cannot appear until there is a clarification and differentiation of one's expectations and the apparent reality.

RECONCILING THE EXPECTATION DISCREPANCY

It is part of the nature of man to search for explanations and connections so that his experiences in the world about him become comprehensible. So it is in the case of expectation discrepancy. It is disturbing to the subject when his expectations do not match the presenting facts, and he feels a need to reconcile the two. This may be accomplished by such cognitive changes as *expectation revision*, *altering the apparent reality* and *anormalizing the person*. These means will be illustrated by several different cases of expectation discrepancy.

Let us consider the frequently occurring expectation discrepancy where the performance of the person outstrips the expectation of the subject. Assume that the subject in question is in the position of an outsider who, faced with the discrepancy, attempts to explain it. Because of this, he may cease ruminating about succumbing to the difficulties, i.e., emphasis on all the things the disability denies, and instead become concerned with the coping aspects, i.e., the ways in which the person has managed. In so doing, the subject begins to recognize the adjustment possibilities of a paraplegic, a blind girl, or an amputee, and is then able to agree with Miers (1953), for example, that ". . . . my athetosis . . . is not half the nuisance you think. Straws for drinking, a typewriter for putting my thoughts on paper, an electric razor, in the main cut down this disability to life size" (p. 7). Not only will the coping aspect of difficulties have become dominant, but the subject will have also shifted his position to that of the insider.

These two shifts give a new direction to the original amazement over the adjustment of the person with a disability. The *expectations* of the subject have been *revised* upward so that he is no longer incredulous. This does not mean that he is left with a simple nonchalance of fulfilled expectations. He may now, for example, feel respect for the persistence shown by the person with the disability in meeting his difficulties, or he may feel that it took courage or ambition or earthy common sense regarding the realities of life to do so. These positive feelings emerge when coping with, as against succumbing to, the difficulties in the field of concern.

Although this perceptual change for resolving the discrepancy is to be desired, the social-psychological position of the subject is not always conducive to such a shift in emphasis. For example, there may be little opportunity for the subject to learn just how the person with a disability does manage. This is particularly true if the subject is an outsider, for not only does he lack ready opportunity for coping discoveries but he has little need, other than that produced by the gap, to create such opportunities. Instead, the subject may seek other means at reconciliation.

He may, for example, *alter the apparent reality* by doubting the evidence concerning the adequate adjustment of the person with a disability. Thus, he may feel that the person is shamming, simply acting *as though* he were managing, when actually he is not. He may suppress evidence regarding the coping aspect of difficulties and high-light evidence bearing upon the succumbing aspects: for example, he may not "see" how well the child with braces gets around but may notice primarily that the child walks with a halting gait. He may tend to attribute all the discomforting aspects of the person's life to the disability, though they may have little actual connection and, in spite of all indications that the person has arranged his life in accord with his abilities and is living satisfactorily, he may insist that the person's lot is lamentable. Chevigny (1946), as a blind adult, sometimes could not help feeling that the world "doesn't want to be convinced that I am not altogether helpless, despite the plain evidence to the contrary" (p. 76). Unfortunately, this means of fitting together the expected state of affairs with the apparent state is probably not infrequent. Where the "requirement of mourning" is felt to insure the security of the subject, this method becomes a cunning maneuver. Altering the apparent reality requires some fluidity in the perception of the reality, i.e., what is perceived cannot be bound too tightly to the objective reality but must be responsive to the manipulations of the wishes and beliefs of the subject.

Finally, the discrepancy may be reconciled when the subject "*anormalizes*" the person, i.e., attributes to him certain unusual characteristics, even supernatural ones, so that the ordinary expectations do not apply. It is very much like the kind of anormalization one might experience in the event of winning the sweepstakes; the incredibility soon becomes cloaked with a strange feeling that one has been blessed or fated to win in the face of overwhelming odds. Similarly, when the subject expects the blind man to fumble and stumble and instead finds him well oriented, it is easy for him to chalk off this discrepancy by appraising the blind man's sensory apparatus as literally "out of this world."

Anormalization of persons who are deaf also occurs, as will be seen in the following fictionalized event:

In Gian-Carlo Menotti's contemporary opera, *The Medium*, the title character and fraud, Madame Flora, intones about the deaf-mute boy she has taken into her home: "just because he cannot speak we take him for a halfwit, but he knows a great deal. He knows more than we think. There is something uncanny about him. He sees things we don't see." Her vague apprehensions are ambiguously justified in the course of the opera. Assuming that the deaf-mute is the real medium for inexplicable phenomena, she is frightened into killing him, and thus brings about her own downfall. (Maisel, 1953, pp. 216–217.)

The person with a disability himself may feel a kind of supernatural intervention when he is carried through what appeared to be insuperable difficulties. Karsten Ohnstad (1942) describes the problem that confronted him when, in crossing a busy thoroughfare, his usual sound cues were disrupted by wind and the rumbling noises of trucks. Upon arriving safely at the curb, he felt that in some way he had been magically protected.

When Karsten gained thorough *control* over traffic hazards by using a white cane, the anormalization became even more a part of his very person:

. . . The cane was a nuisance, clattering against everything and catching in my trouser cuffs as I twirled it idly about like a baton; but at street corners it proved its worth. Car drivers saw it and stopped. I held it out before me and walked across the pavement with an assurance that I had never felt before. I was a worker of miracles. I was the Moses of the metropolis. I held out my staff over that roaring, honking sea, and lo! the traffic parted, and I stepped up on the opposite curb sound as a dollar. (Ohnstad, 1942, p. 69.)

The factor of personal control is probably conducive to the feeling of deification in contrast to the kind of anormalization in which the person is felt to be a pawn of fate or subject to control by other supernatural events. Such personal deification was experienced by Raymond Goldman (1947) when, unable to walk because of polio, he mastered the "unattainable" through the strength of his own will:

. . . Other children learn naturally and without conscious effort to move about and crawl and stand up. Not I. I had to achieve those things so deliberately, at the cost of so much pain and sweat and tears, that the attainment of each was a separate triumph. I stood almost in awe of my own power to accomplish. I was like a god (p. 38).

Anormalizing the person with a disability means that he transcends the laws of ordinary mortals so that expectations relevant to normal persons do not apply. There is one important difference between the quality of deified eminence and that of the esteem generated when, through concern over coping with difficulties, expectation revision takes place in which higher though entirely normal expectations are maintained. In the former case, the person with a disability is viewed as a different kind of person; he is set apart from normal persons and his accomplishments are seen as resulting from some kind of mystical intervention. In the latter case, the person with a disability is very much a part of the group of normal human beings, and his accomplishments are "understood" in terms of natural behavior.

Conditions for anormalizing the person appear to be favorable when the perceptions of the two sides of the equation are difficult to change. Again let us turn to blindness as an illustration: (a) When a sighted person has the position of an outsider with respect to blindness, he expects that the locomotion difficulties attendant upon blindness are insuperable. Moreover, this perception is difficult to change. (b) When such a subject sees a blind person unperturbably getting about there is a discrepancy with what he expected. Moreover, this perception is also difficult to change. Seeing is believing, and he cannot deny that the blind person has safely crossed the street, mounted the stairs, and located his books.

In these circumstances, it is perhaps comprehensible why the person who is blind should be looked upon with reverence and felt to be equipped with unusual powers. In fiction, the most frequent stereotype of the blind is that of the idealized and abnormally good person (Barker, Wright, Myerson, and Gonick, 1953). In religious practices, the blind have been accorded privileged positions (Barker *et al.*). Modern Turkey regards the sightless as indispensable assets to religious ceremonies and funerals (Maisel, 1953). In Greek legend many clairvoyants are blind (Hentig, 1948). Among the Koreans it is believed that the blind have acquired an inner vision and they are therefore held in high esteem (Maisel, 1953).

For a review of the factors important in resolving expectation discrepancy, the case of deafness serves well. Commonly, with respect to a person who is deaf, the subject holds higher expectations than are borne out by what ensues because the deaf person, looking just like anyone else, is expected to act like anyone else. The subject expects the person who is deaf, for example, to be able to communicate with him but discovers that he cannot.

Reconciliation of this expectation discrepancy is then initiated. Depending upon his social-psychological position with respect to the disability situation, the subject may revise his expectations downward. This is easier to do when the subject has an objective rather than a more personal, wishful interest in the welfare of the person. In such circumstances, the subject seeks honest understanding of "what is wrong" and may discover that his expectations were unrealistic in the light of the newly uncovered facts. If in the process of expectation revision the difficulties of deafness are seen in the light of coping rather than succumbing, positive evaluation of the person will occur.

However, there will undoubtedly be strong resistance against lowering the expectation level where there is an overpowering wish for the person to hear better, this not infrequently characterizing the subject who is in the position of an insider. In this case, the subject may alter the apparent reality. He may regard the discrepancy as a temporary one that will be erased through the efforts of continued cures; the apparent reality is looked upon as eventually rising upward to close the gap. In the meantime, insofar as the gap still gapes, the apparent reality will be perceived as progressively better. Thus the person with a hearing impairment and those close to him will after surgery tend to feel, as long as the apparent reality is sufficiently fluid, that there is an improvement, though this may not at all reflect the true state of affairs. Eventually, it is possible for the forces of objective reality to become so great as to make such mobility of the apparent reality difficult and the subject may then turn to a re-evaluation of the expectation level.

There are instances of expectation discrepancy in which both the expectations and the apparent reality resist change. This is true of some outsider subjects, where neither need nor opportunity exists for the comprehension of the difficulties incumbent upon deafness or for upward shift in the apparent reality. The discrepancy is resolved by anormalizing the person, and he is dubbed queer or strange or even bewitched. Anormalization that reconciles a discrepancy in which the expectations are lower than the apparent reality leads to sanctification, but where the expectations surpass the apparent reality anormalization leads to vilification.

This discussion has permitted, perhaps, some glimpse into the significance of expectation discrepancy for the social evaluation of persons with disabilities. Clearly, further investigation of the conditions underlying expectation discrepancy and its reconciliation is indicated. We have pointed out the probable significance of such factors as the position of the subject, his wishes, opportunity for re-evaluation, fluidity of apparent reality, direction of the gap, etc. Of course, the concepts have application to nondisability situations as well, just as do the concepts of marginal position, new situations, value systems, etc. The attitudes and behavior of adults toward children, for example, frequently can be understood in terms of expectation discrepancy. Recollection of such an incident with an analysis of possible conditions contributing to the expectation discrepancy and of the means taken toward its reconciliation is a worthwhile exercise. One must ponder apt illustrations from nondisability situations before one can realize with the conviction of fact rather than supposition that the social psychology of disability is truly a *general* social psychology, the laws of which have bearing upon diverse fields not restricted to problems of disablement.

REFERENCES

Barker, R. G., Wright, B. A., Myerson, L., and Gonick, M. R., 1953. *Adjustment to physical handicap and illness: a survey of the social psychology of physique and disability*. New York: Social Science Research Council, Bulletin 55, pp. 273, 274.

Chevigny, H., 1946. *My eyes have a cold nose*. New Haven, Conn.: Yale University Press.

Goldman, R., 1947. *Even the night*. New York: Macmillan.

Maisel, E., 1953. Meet a body. New York: Institute for the Crippled and Disabled. Unpublished manuscript.

Miers, E. S., 1953. Gosh I'm glad I'm handicapped. *The Crippled Child*, **31**, 4–7.

Ohnstad, K., 1942. *The world at my fingertips*. New York: Bobbs–Merrill, p. 68.

von Hentig, H., 1948. Physical disability, mental conflict and social crisis. *Journal of Social Issues*, **4**, 21–27.

selection 16 Role Conceptions, Organizational Size and Community Context

EDWIN J. THOMAS

The growth of organizations from modest-sized structures, often housed under one roof, to bureaucratic giants has brought a proliferation of administrative units and their dispersion over wide geographical areas. Although the units of these bureaucracies are generally part of the same organizational structure and are committed to achieving common objectives by means of uniformly applied operating procedures, the physical separation of bureaus and offices allows differences among them to germinate and grow. An important source of such differences is the number of persons in the local administrative units. These different sized units are a promising site for research on large-scale organizations because some of the characteristics that would normally vary freely in unrelated organizations are held equal.

Much still remains to be learned about the relations between the size of an organization and the behavior of its members.[1] A central question of practical and theoretical significance is the extent to which an organization's size facilitates or impedes efforts to attain its formally stated objectives. To answer this question research must be focused upon two related problems: delineation of the differences in behavior of members in organizations varying in size; and consideration of how these behavioral correlates of size affect the organization's capacity to achieve its goals. Such research should add to the further understanding of those non-formal characteristics of large organizations that affect organizational behavior.

This study compares the role conceptions, the degree of role consensus, and the quality of work of welfare workers in different sized organizational units of a state welfare department. The objectives of the welfare program and the formal requirements for the performance of roles were the same throughout the organization. In comparing small and large units in the department many formal characteristics of the welfare bureaus were thus held constant. Of course, not all of the possibly

[1] One of the few empirical studies of the size of organizations is Frederic W. Terrien and Donald L. Mills (1955). Discussions of organizational size are found in Theodore Caplow (1957); and Kenneth E. Boulding (1953).

The importance of size as a variable was noted long ago by Spencer, Durkheim, and Simmel, whose observations are well-known on this subject. Examples of recent laboratory work include: Robert F. Bales (1952), Robert F. Bales and Edgar F. Borgatta (1955), A. Paul Hare (1953).

Abridged from the *American Sociological Review*, 1959, **24**, 30–37, where the original title was, "Role Conceptions and Organizational Size." Reprinted by permission of the author and the American Sociological Association. The investigation was supported by funds from the State of Michigan, allocated through the University of Michigan.

influential variables were controlled because of differences in history and location of the bureaus.

Attention in the presentation of findings is given to the relationship of the variables to organizational size and, in the discussion of results, to interpretation of why the variables were associated with size and to the relationship of the size of the welfare bureau and their effectiveness in the attainment of one of the organizational goals.

THE ORGANIZATION

The Michigan State Department of Social Welfare administers a program of public assistance through bureaus located in 83 counties. Bureaus range in size from those of one person, who makes investigations and serves as bureau supervisor, to one with hundreds of employees. If sufficiently large, a bureau includes public assistance workers who investigate applications for financial assistance, case and bureau supervisors, and clerical personnel. Within a bureau the chain of authority runs from bureau supervisor to case supervisor and from case supervisor to public assistance worker, with each case supervisor generally supervising six to seven workers.

As noted earlier, the formal requirements of the role of public assistance worker are uniform throughout the organization. All workers have met the same minimal requirements for the job, all perform the same types of functions, and all follow the same rules and procedures as set forth in the manual of operation for the investigation of applications for assistance. At the same time, however, the role can be conceived and performed in different ways because of certain ambiguities in how it is defined (apart from other reasons). Consider, for example, the role of workers who handle cases in the Aid to Dependent Children program (these are the workers studied in this investigation). The federal laws define the ADC task too generally to be of much help in determining many concrete decisions. In contrast, the manual of operation, while very specific with respect to conditions of eligibility for financial assistance, does not cover numerous service problems met by the worker. Thus there is latitude for individual variability in performance and for different conceptions of the role.

PROCEDURE AND FINDINGS

The sample of 109 public assistance workers who handled ADC cases consisted largely of females, and most were married. A majority had worked in public assistance for less than four years, 22 per cent for less than a year. While three-quarters of the workers had college degrees, only nine per cent had specialized in social work and none had obtained a Master's degree in social work.

The sample was drawn from small, medium, and large administrative units. The "small" bureaus were those in which there were at least two but no more than five workers, and no more than a two-level hierarchy. A random sample of six small bureaus was drawn containing a total of 18 workers, all of whom participated in the study. The "medium-sized" bureaus were those that had six or more workers or a three-level hierarchy, but no more than three such levels. Five medium-sized bureaus were selected on a non-random basis, contributing 59 workers who handled ADC cases. The offices ranged in size from six to 22 workers and tended to be located in the more highly industrialized, urban counties. There was only one large bureau, Wayne County; it had a five-level hierarchy, with the positions of ADC division head and director above the level of case supervisor and below the level of bureau director. Thirty-two workers were selected from a pool of 96 ADC workers assigned to two different divisions by choosing four supervisory units at random. The mean number of workers in the small offices was 3.8; comparable figures for medium and large size were 17.4 and 45.5, respectively.

There was a direct relationship between the size of the bureaus and the number of hierarchically ordered strata, since bureaus in the sample were selected by criteria of size and number of strata. For the 83 bureaus in the state there was also a marked positive relationship between the number of employees and the number of strata.

The amount of specialization of function for the worker increased with size. Specialization for three of the four categories of cases was found in the largest bureau in the sample. In the two next largest ones, only a few of the workers had caseloads made up exclusively of ADC recipients, and for the remaining bureaus specialization by type of case was not found.

Characteristics of the workers in the units also differed by size. In the smaller administrative units there were found more older workers, more workers without college degrees, more who had married, more having children, and more workers with long experience in public assistance. The workers in the smaller units, as compared with the larger ones, moreover, lived in a more rural environment.

The personal characteristics of the workers were the only correlates that could be controlled statistically in the analysis of results reported below. There was no satisfactory way to separate the effects of specialization, degree of stratification, and population setting from those of the number of workers. Hence, even when the effects of personal characteristics were controlled, there was no way to determine whether it was the number of workers or some other factor that produced the effects. The results presented below were analyzed first without controls for variables operating concomitantly with size and, subsequently, with controls for the personal attributes of the workers. The different sized bureaus are labeled "small" or "large" as a matter of convenience; it should be understood that not merely the number of workers differentiates the offices.

Questionnaires were administered to the participating workers and to their case supervisors in the 12 administrative units. The questions referred to a wide range of variables. One of these, termed *role consensus*, is indicated by the degree of agreement between the public assistance worker and his supervisor about the importance of functions performed by workers. The amount of agreement was assumed to reflect the degree to which workers and supervisors shared a frame of

TABLE 1 PERCENTAGES OF WORKERS, SUPERVISORS, AND MEMBERS OF PROFESSIONAL ASSOCIATION SELECTING "CORRECT" ALTERNATIVES FOR ITEMS OF THE TEST OF COMMITMENT TO THE ETHICS OF PROFESSIONAL SOCIAL WORK

		Group		
Content of Item*	Inferred Underlying Value**	Workers (N=109)	Supervisors (N=26)	Members of Professional Group (N=75)
1. In interviewing, sacrifice directness *versus* ask direct questions	humanitarian *versus* utilitarian	49	54	63
2. Motivate by offering information *versus* urge directly	noncoercive *versus* coercive	72	88	97
3. When client is upset, discuss feelings *versus* ignore them	concern *versus* nonconcern for client's feelings	83	88	92
4. When client makes you angry analyze your anger *versus* ignore it	awareness *versus* nonawareness of self as an instrument of change	72	92	97
5. Financial aid given to all *versus* to those who use it wisely	help universally *versus* help selectivity	38	68	69
6. Illegitimacy demands focus on helping individual adjust *versus* changing individual	acceptance *versus* non-acceptance of deviance	28	38	74
7. Client making curtains in messy house, compliment *versus* mention housecleaning	positive *versus* negative methods to motivate	60	75	96

* The first of the alternatives for each item is the "correct" one.
** The first of the polarities of underlying values is the one matched to the "correct" alternative for its corresponding item.

reference regarding the importance of workers' functions. Eleven areas of knowledge and skill (for example, determining financial eligibility, job mechanics, and case-work methods) relevant to performance of the role of the public assistance worker were rated for importance on a seven-point scale by workers and supervisors and discrepancy scores were computed.

Another variable, termed *breadth of role conception*, refers to the number of activities or functions conceived as part of the role. In the questionnaire the workers were presented with nine activities (for example, budgeting and referral for vocational counselling) and were asked to indicate for each function whether they "always," "sometimes," or "never" performed it in cases for which that activity, as a type of service, *was needed*. Numerical values were assigned to responses and total scores were computed. The higher the score, the more broadly the role is conceived.

Another aspect of role, often implicit rather than formally defined, is the ethical commitment that it requires of individuals. In public welfare, as well as in other service fields, those responsible for giving the services are guided by ethical precepts. A test of *ethical commitment* was devised to measure some of these, more exactly termed a test of commitment to the ethics of professional social work, since it consists of items relating to seven ethical areas highly endorsed by a sample of 75 professionally trained social workers. The content of the items, given in Table 1, may be clustered into two categories: (a) how the worker should behave with a client, and (b) who should receive the benefits of social work services and under what conditions. To complete the validation, the responses of the professionally trained social workers were compared with those of the sample of public assistance supervisors and workers drawn in this study. In contrast to the professionally trained group, the majority of whom had obtained Master's degrees in social work, the public assistance workers generally had little such specialized training. Table 1 shows that the "correct" alternatives are most highly endorsed by the professional group and least highly endorsed by the workers, with the supervisors' responses falling between these extremes.

A final set of measures is related to the quality of the worker's performance on the job. It was possible to learn about the cognitive aspect of performance through evidence of the analytic skill of workers as indicated by their ability, first, to identify the problems of families and, second, to propose appropriate treatment plans. To measure the first item, the workers were asked to describe the problems they noted for the members of a family depicted in a case vignette; responses were transformed into a numerical score of diagnostic acuity.[2] To measure the second aspect of analytic skill, the workers were asked to describe what they would do for the individuals described in the case if they had the required time; responses were coded and scores were obtained for *appropriateness of treatment plans*.[3] A motivational aspect of performance was inferred from responses to a question about how much the worker would like to work on the case described in the vignette.[4]

RESULTS

Role Conceptions

Workers' conceptions of their roles differed according to the size of the welfare office. In the

TABLE 2 NUMBER OF WORKERS HAVING LARGE AND SMALL DISCREPANCY SCORES IN ROLE CONSENSUS, BY SIZE OF ADMINISTRATIVE UNIT

Size of Administrative Unit	Discrepancy Score: Small (0–1)	Discrepancy Score: Large (2–3)
Small	14	0
Medium	54	4
Large	21	11
	$\chi^2 = 15.00, p < .01$	

[2] Responses were coded into the following categories: non-existent problems (scored −2), superficially conceived problems (−1), problems manifest in the case (+1), and appropriately inferred underlying problems (+2). Scores were the algebraic sum. Kendall's *tau* is +.74 for the scores of two coders ($N = 20$).

[3] Responses were coded into plans inappropriate to the case (scored −2), plans to aid with manifest problems (+1), and plans to help with appropriately inferred underlying problems (+2). Scores were the algebraic sum. Kendall's *tau* is +.80 for the scores of two coders ($N = 20$).

[4] For the most part, the interrelationships among these variables are positive. Scores on diagnostic acumen are directly related to scores on appropriateness of treatment plans ($\chi^2 = 18.25$, $p < .001$) and on ethical commitment ($\chi^2 = 9.31$, $p < .01$); they bear no relationship, however, to motivation to help recipients. Scores on appropriateness of treatment plan are not related to those on ethical commitment, but are related to those of motivation to help recipients ($\chi^2 = 6.85$, $p < .01$). Scores on ethical commitment are positively associated with those on motivation to help recipients ($\chi^2 = 4.11$, $p < .05$).

smaller bureaus there was found to be greater *role consensus* between the worker and his supervisor about the importance of functions that workers performed (Table 2), greater *breadth of role conception* (Table 3), and *higher ethical commitment* (Table 4).

TABLE 3 NUMBER OF WORKERS CONCEIVING THEIR ROLES NARROWLY AND BROADLY, BY SIZE OF ADMINISTRATIVE UNIT

	Breadth of Role Conception	
Size of Administrative Unit	Narrow (0–4)	Broad (5–8)
Small	4	14
Medium	20	37
Large	18	14
	$\chi^2 = 6.48, p < .05$	

TABLE 4 NUMBER OF WORKERS SCORING HIGH AND LOW ON ETHICAL COMMITMENT, BY SIZE OF ADMINISTRATIVE UNIT

	Scores on Ethical Commitment	
Size of Administrative Unit	Low (1–4)	High (5–7)
Small	3	15
Medium	35	23
Large	26	6
	$\chi^2 = 20.04, p < .001$	

Quality of Performance

The size of the administrative unit was found to be associated with all indicators of the quality of the worker's performance. Those workers scoring high on the three measures are much more likely to be in the small bureaus than in the larger ones (Table 5).

The Effects of Personal Background Factors

Analyses were made with controls for age, education, experience on the job, marital status, and number of children. This procedure involved the relationship between organizational size and a dependent variable, holding constant the control factor whenever it was found that the control characteristic was associated with the dependent variable. The .05 level of significance was used as a choice point.

Using this technique, age is the only control factor related both to the size of bureaus and the magnitude of discrepancy of *role consensus*. Although the smaller bureaus had more older workers and more workers with small discrepancy scores, the effects of size remained with age held constant.

Two of the control factors are closely associated with the *breadth of role conception*. Broadly conceived roles were found more often for older workers and for those with lengthy experience in public assistance; the first relationship yields a χ^2 of 17.73, the second a χ^2 of 16.21, both giving p values of less than .001. When age and experience are controlled, size is no longer related to the *breadth of role conception*. Since there were more older workers and workers with longer experience in the smaller units, age and experience, and not other factors associated with size, account for the breadth of conception of roles.

TABLE 5 NUMBER OF WORKERS SCORING HIGH AND LOW ON MEASURES OF THE QUALITY OF PERFORMANCE, BY SIZE OF ADMINISTRATIVE UNIT

	Scores on Diagnostic Acuity		Scores on Appropriateness of Treatment Plan		Motivation to Help Recipients	
Size of Administrative Unit	High (4–8)	Low (0–3)	High (5–7)	Low (0–4)	High (3–7)	Low (1–2)
Small	13	5	14	4	15	3
Medium	23	36	21	38	21	38
Large	6	25	10	20	12	19
	$\chi^2 = 13.46, p < .01$		$\chi^2 = 11.26, p < .01$		$\chi^2 = 13.30, p < .01$	

Both the education and experience of workers are related to scores of *ethical commitment*. The less well educated and those with longer experience on the job most frequently show high as opposed to low scores on ethical commitment; the χ^2 is 8.51 for the former ($p < .01$) and 4.05 for the latter ($p < .05$). The effects of size remain, however, when education and experience are each held constant.

The only control variable found to be related to any of the three indicators of the quality of the worker's performance was the number of children the workers had; those workers having children had higher scores on motivation to help recipients than did those having no children ($\chi^2 = 5.40$, $p < .05$). The effects of size remained for workers with or without children.

DISCUSSION AND CONCLUSIONS

Why should the variables examined here be associated with organizational size? Like many others, size is not a "pure" variable—a single unitary phenomenon. Size is more like an index because of its relationship to a complement of variables associated with the number of persons in the organization. The findings of this study provide suggestions about these variables, but offer few clues about *why* they are associated with size or about their interrelationships. We now turn to these questions.

Most of our results may be accounted for plausibly in terms of the population and the community setting of the county in which the welfare bureau was located. The size of the bureau itself depends largely upon the population size of a county, since the more populous counties are likely to contain more individuals in need of welfare assistance. Although organizational size bears no necessary relationship to the population of the area in which the organization is located, one may be an index of the other to the extent that (a) the organizational unit serves a portion of the population, as does a welfare bureau, and (b) the unit is located by such arbitrary geographical criteria as county, state, or region.

The association of the workers' personal characteristics with the size of welfare bureaus probably indicates that the pool of potential employees in the counties with large populations differs from those with small populations. Available information indicates that some of the contrasts between workers in the smaller and the larger bureaus parallel those between rural residents and residents of cities.[5] This study provides no information about whether or not there is also selective retention of workers as a consequence of bureau size.

Roles were found to be more broadly conceived by workers in the smaller bureaus. The control analysis shows that age and experience account for the breadth of conception of roles. Welfare workers in rural areas change jobs less often than their urban counterparts, partly because there are fewer occupational alternatives and fewer welfare jobs from which to choose that pay as well or better than public assistance. Rural welfare workers therefore would be expected to be older and more experienced than urban ones. Furthermore, rural areas contain fewer specialized social services, making it necessary for the welfare worker in the rural areas to take over informally more functions as part of her role than her urban colleagues.

Another correlate of organizational size is the ethical commitment of workers. Differences in ethical commitment cannot be attributed to variations of professionalization, for none of the workers had had professional training in social work. The community setting of the welfare offices and the rural background of the workers account for the workers' ethical orientation most adequately. High scores on the test indicate a generally more positive approach to recipients—an approach probably growing out of a more intimate relationship with recipients in the smaller communities. The writer has been told by experienced welfare workers of the differences between working in the smaller and larger urban communities. In the small community they note that there is more frequent community contact with recipients; perception of recipients as individuals more often than as "clients"; less social distance between worker and recipient, due in part to similarity of ethnic background; and greater need to attend to more of the recipients' problems. Consequently, the worker in the small bureau is more likely to be willing to assume greater personal responsibility for the recipient and to have more compassion for the recipient as a person than the worker in an urban bureau.

The attitude of helpfulness toward others and

[5] Persons residing in rural areas are less well educated, more often married, generally more fertile and less mobile occupationally than urbanites (see Gist and Halbert, 1956).

the "positive" approach to recipients engendered by the small community probably explain why workers in the small bureaus evidenced performance of higher quality than those in the larger ones. The measures of quality of performance were skill in analyzing problems of recipients. appropriateness of treatment plans, and motivation to help recipients—all of which reflect the extent of the worker's willingness to do a complete and adequate job of helping recipients. That the rural workers are more willing than those in urban settings to help recipients and to put forth the extra effort needed to analyze thoroughly the recipient's problems and to propose suitable treatment is consistent with the earlier observations about the small community.

The community setting of the bureaus does not readily explain why size is related to role consensus. Past theoretical and empirical work indicates that consensus is likely to be greater in small than in large groups. The small group provides conditions well-suited to the development of consensus; there is likely to be a relatively rapid rate of interaction and a relatively smaller divergence of opinion and behavior, due to a smaller range of opinion and behavior than in large groups. In this study, size alone is therefore probably not the only organizational characteristic contributing to role consensus.

Another correlate of organizational size is the extent to which there was vertical and horizontal differentiation. Size enables differentiation to occur by providing a larger number of persons over whom functions may be distributed and by increasing the range of individual skill and ability needed to give feasibly different assignments to persons. In the organizational units studied here, differentiation in the larger bureaus was further facilitated by administrative policy stipulating the proportion of supervisory personnel required for a given number of workers and by the belief that specialized handling of cases is efficient only in the largest bureaus.

This discussion of the correlates of organizational size suggests that the number of workers may be a less potent variable in affecting the behavior of members than the community setting of the organizational unit. Studies of organizational units of an extended bureaucracy differing in size should be undertaken where it is possible to differentiate them in terms of the population size and type of community in which the units are located.

From another viewpoint, some of the variables used in this study can be said to reflect organizational effectiveness in providing services to families. These variables include the measures of the quality of work, ethical commitment, and breadth of role conception signified by the number of different services workers would perform for families were they needed. These three indications of service are negatively associated with the size of the organizational unit: the smaller bureaus show greater commitment to the ethics of professional social work, greater breadth of role conception, and better quality of work. To the extent that these variables reflect differences in performance of workers, the results indicate that the organizational goal of providing services to recipients was more effectively attained in the smaller welfare bureaus.

The findings of the study do not help to answer the question of how effectively the bureaus attained the organizational goal of determining eligibility for financial assistance.

Why were the small bureaus better able than the larger ones to provide services to families? If the interpretations of the findings presented above are correct, it is largely because the influences of the small community encourage a service orientation toward recipients. The impact of community setting thus may be viewed as reaffirming the significance of the secondary organizational goal, that of providing services, through orienting workers more toward the service aspects of their roles. The part played by the actual size of the welfare bureau is probably minimal, except insofar as it serves to mediate, through primary relationships, the service goal. The fact that role consensus was greater in the smaller bureaus may indicate greater cohesion of the primary groups and readier acceptance of the goal to provide service.

REFERENCES

Bales, R. F., 1952. Some uniformities of behavior in small social systems. In G. Swanson, T. M. Newcomb, and Eleanor Hartley (Eds.), *Readings in social psychology*. New York: Holt, pp. 146–159.

Bales, R. F., and Borgatta, E. F., 1955. Size of group as a factor in the interaction profile. In A. P. Hare, E. F. Borgatta, and R. F. Bales (Eds.), *Small groups: studies in social interaction.* New York: Knopf, pp. 396–413.

Boulding, K. E., 1953. *The organizational revolution.* New York: Harper and Row.

Caplow, T., 1957. Organizational size. *Administrative Science Quarterly*, **1**, 485–491.

Gist, N. P., and Halbert, L. A., 1956. *Urban society* (4th ed.). New York: Crowell.

Hare, A. P., 1953. Interaction and consensus in different sized groups. In D. Cartwright and A. Zander (Eds.), *Group dynamics: research and theory.* New York: Harper and Row, pp. 483–492.

Terrien, F. W., and Mills, D. L., 1955. The effect of changing size upon the internal structure of organizations. *American Sociological Review*, **20**, 11–14.

selection 17 Role Playing Variations and Their Informational Value for Person Perception

EDWARD E. JONES, KEITH E. DAVIS, AND KENNETH J. GERGEN

Largely under the impetus of Heider's (1944, 1958) persistent concern with phenomenological analysis, much of the recent research in social perception has addressed itself to the naïve psychology of the individual perceiver. How do individuals use the behavior of others to infer the probable existence of more enduring personal characteristics? What are the bases for social evaluation that in turn color the impressions one forms of another? What information is ignored and what information is made central in the formation of an impression? A number of investigators have sought a partial answer to these questions by assuming that a basic feature of naïve phenomenology is the assignment of observed behavior to psychological causes. It seems logical to propose, for example, that behavior whose locus of causation lies within the person is more relevant to inferences about his particular characteristics than behavior that is induced or constrained by external events. The present investigation was designed to demonstrate this proposition with specific reference to the adoption and performance of social roles.

Abridged from the *Journal of Abnormal and Social Psychology*, 1961, **63**, 302–310. Reprinted by permission of the authors and the American Psychological Association. This study was carried out under support from the National Science Foundation.

In the present paper, the concept of role refers to role demands rather than actual behavior. Role is herein treated as a set of expected behaviors implicit in the instructions to a stimulus person. These instructions define the impression the stimulus person should attempt to create in presenting himself to an interviewer, and variations in behavior given this role definition represent the major independent variable.

The present treatment of role is quite consistent with any other treatment that stresses the shaping of individual responses by social expectations or externally imposed norms. The point has often been made that general adherence to relevant sets of social norms is very important in facilitating social interaction. Particularly in organizational contexts, but by no means exclusively there, many social interactions can be effectively described in terms of the interplay of appropriate role behaviors. Jones and Thibaut (1958) have emphasized the economic significance of such interactions between roles as reducing the need for inferences about idiosyncratic personal characteristics. The complement of this point is that behavior appropriate to role expectations has little informational value in highlighting these individual characteristics.

To follow this line of reasoning a little further, roles facilitate interaction and the social cognitions that support it. The naïve person has his own repertory of role constructs that help to anchor his perceptions of the social environment and to endow it with the necessary stability for planful action. On the other hand, the performance of social roles tends to mask information about individual characteristics because the person reveals only that he is responsive to normative requirements. If these requirements are unclear or conflicting, of course, he may reveal something about himself by the way in which he defines and displays appropriate behavior. The stronger and more unequivocal the role demands, however, the less information is provided by behavior appropriate to the role. Following our introductory comments, this conclusion may be derived from considering probable differences in the attribution of phenomenal causality. When a person's behavior is very much in line with clear and potent social expectations, we tend to treat it as externally caused and uninformative with regard to a wide range of personal characteristics. When it departs from normative expectations, on the other hand, we tend to locate the cause for the departure in motivational forces peculiar to the person. We may assume, of course, that he misperceived the expectations, but we would then wish to push on to determine the motivational sources of this perceptual distortion.

From the perceiver's point of view, the behavior of a stimulus person which departs from role expectations takes on special significance for appraising the latter's personal characteristics. In assessing the motives behind such a departure from role, the perceiver must view the sample of behavior available against the background of role specifications. In general, our inferences from behavior to personality must take into account the stimulus conditions eliciting the behavior. This is no less true when the stimulus conditions consist of clearly established role expectations.

In attempting to predict the nature and direction of inferences, given a sample of behavior that departs from role expectations, a number of factors must be considered. For one thing, there may be tendencies for the perceiver either to minimize or maximize the nature of the departure. In organizing his impression of the stimulus person, the perceiver may assimilate the latter's behavior sample to the role specifications governing the situation, thus, avoiding the problem of inferring unique characteristics. Alternatively, there may be a contrast effect in that the behavior sample becomes cognitively salient and is recalled as departing even more from the role than was actually the case. We are not as yet in a position to choose between these alternative possibilities, or to specify the conditions favoring assimilation versus contrast. The present study does provide a measure of memory distortion, however.

Assuming that assimilation does not occur, or that it occurs incompletely, the perceiver's inferences about unique characteristics rest on his attempt to understand *why* the departure from role expectations took place. Undoubtedly, some departures are intended to achieve a humorous effect (the exchange of "friendly insults" between collaborators on a task); others are intended to play down role characteristics that might be offensive (the "soft-selling" salesman); still others stem from motives of rebellion and non-conformity. In the typical case, however, departure from role suggests a pattern of motivation and skill that is at variance with specific role requirements. The individual does not play the role because, somehow, he cannot or will not. In such cases, personality seems to override role expectations or to color role performance in a unique and significant way. The most probable inference from role departures of this type is that the person reveals something of his "true self" through his failure to perform the expected role.

The present investigation treats this last conjecture as a proposition. An experiment was designed in which stimulus persons were instructed in one of two patterns of role performance. The behavior of the stimulus person was arranged to be consistent with either the first or the second of these patterns, thus, creating two experimental treatments where the person's behavior was "in role" and two treatments where it was clearly "out of role." The general hypotheses prompting the study were:

1. Persons performing in line with role expectations reveal little of value for assessing their personal characteristics. When asked to describe such a person, subjects do so with little confidence and tend to avoid extreme statements.

2. Persons whose performance departs from role expectations reveal their personal characteristics through the direction and form of this departure. Their behavior is judged as internally caused and forms the basis for direct inferences about personal characteristics, characteristics that may be judged with confidence.

3. Roles do, however, serve as an organizing function in person perception. Because of its predictive value, in-role behavior is more accurately

recalled than behavior that departs from role expectations.

Note that no specific hypothesis was formulated concerning the possibilities of assimilation and contrast, but data bearing on these possibilities are to be presented.

METHOD

Subjects

One hundred and thirty-four male undergraduates participated as subjects in groups ranging in size from 5 to 20. Since the experimental design consisted of four treatment variations, an attempt was made to assign approximately equal numbers of subjects to each condition. The actual cell frequencies varied from 31 to 37.

Procedure Overview

Each experimental session began with a brief introduction in which the experimenter described the study as a problem solving task involving judgments of another person. Subjects were instructed to listen carefully to a tape recorded interview between a psychologist and a student, in which the student would be instructed to play a particular role. The tape recording began with the psychologist giving explicit instructions to the stimulus person (SP) about the interview to follow. Although the recordings were actually based on carefully constructed scripts, an attempt was made to convince the subjects that the SP was given no information about the interview and his role that did not appear on the tape. Thus, the taped instructions emphasized that the SP was to present himself in the interview in such a way as to impress the interviewer that he was ideally suited for a particular job. In interviews played to different groups of subjects one of two jobs requiring radically different personal qualifications was described. In this way the content of the role was manipulated. The SP was told in the recording to "be as honest as you can unless you think another answer would help your chances better of getting the job." In the interview that followed, SP answered some standard questions about his background in a neutral fashion and then responded to a series of choice items some of which were clearly relevant to the job for which he was applying. In responding to these items, the SP either gave answers appropriate to the job description he had been given, or answers which revealed markedly different preferences. Thus, the design involved presentation of four different stimulus patterns, two of which were "in-role" and two of which were "out-of-role."

After listening to the interview, each subject was asked to state his general impression of the SP and to fill out in succession the following dependent variable forms: given the same choice items to which the SP responded in the interview, subjects were asked to reconstruct from memory SP's response to each item; after this choice test form was collected the subject was handed an identical form and instructed to indicate how the SP would have responded if he were being completely honest in describing himself; finally, each subject was given a 16-item trait-rating scale and instructed to rate the SP, and indicate his subjective confidence for each rating. The stimulus materials and dependent variable forms are more fully described below.

Stimulus Variations

As implied by the foregoing discussion, the experimental design called for the construction of four separate tapes to be played as the stimulus pattern for independent groups of subjects. These tapes varied along two cross-cutting dimensions: on half of the tapes the job described was that of a submariner, on the remaining half the job was that of an "astronaut" in training for space flights; on half of the tapes the job description was followed by a set of responses appropriate for the submariner job (other-directed pattern), on the remaining half the responses were more appropriate for the astronaut job (inner-directed pattern). The four tapes were actually constructed by separately recording these four segments, always with the same person reading the part of the SP, and splicing them into the following combinations: Submariner–Other, Submariner–Inner, Astronaut–Inner, and Astronaut–Other.

Role Descriptions. Presentation of the submariner's role was prefaced by a reference to the capacities of atomic submarines and the corresponding qualities necessary for adjusting to the social conditions of submarine life. The following excerpts give both the flavor and some of the content of the role description:

People at the submarine school are pretty sure they know quite a bit about the kind of person who adapts well to submarine life . . . The main thing they work for is stability and good citizenship . . . constant cooperation with others is essential . . . willingness to tolerate routine . . . not supposed to think for himself . . . sticks to the rules . . . . Since submariners are in such constant contact with each other, it's important, of course, that the good submariner enjoys other people around, that he be relaxed and friendly and slow to irritate.

Presentation of the astronaut's role capitalized on the timely issue of sending a single man into space. The role description is suggested again by the following excerpts:

One of the most difficult requirements of space travel, at least in its early stages, is that it will most likely involve a man's being isolated from virtually all human contact for long periods of time . . . looking for men who don't need to have other people around . . . inner resources and the ability to maintain concentration without stimulation from others . . . alert, imaginative, resourceful . . . .

These particular role descriptions were designed, of course, without regard to truth value, solely to emphasize plausibly two sets of qualities that might best be described as other- versus inner-directed.

Behavior Samples. SPs on each of the four tapes responded in an identical fashion until they were asked by the interviewer to take a "choice test which has recently been devised to indicate how well a person will fit into various niches in life . . . ." The test that followed consisted of 22 items, each comprising a pair of statements. The SP was instructed to choose the member of each pair which was more characteristic of himself and to indicate his certainty on an 11-point scale. Half of the items were buffer items not specifically relevant to the difference between roles and always answered in the same manner by the SPs. The remaining 11 items were "critical" in reflecting the intended differences between inner- and other-directed response patterns. The following examples indicate some of the pair members endorsed by the SPs in the two behavior samples:

	Other-Directed	*Inner-Directed*
3.	I always like to support the majority.	I like to feel free to do what I want to do.
9.	I would like to be a door-to-door salesman.	I would like to be a forest ranger.
17.	When planning something I always seek suggestions from others.	When planning something I like to work on my own.
21.	I like to know how other people think I should behave.	I avoid situations where I am expected to behave in a conventional way.
22.	I like to settle arguments and disputes of others.	I like to attack points of view that are contrary to my own.

For each of these item pairs, the SP orally endorsed the statement appropriate to the condition and indicated the degree of his certainty. Degree of certainty was predetermined so that the same scale positions were endorsed the same number of times for each behavior sample. This was to equalize any tendency to regress toward or away from less certainty in the memory task.

Impression Rating Scale

The final task of the subjects was to record their impression of the SP in terms of a 16-item rating scale. Each item consisted of two polar adjectives separated by 10 scale points. To the right of each item was a 5-point confidence scale for that item. Thus, subjects were to indicate what they thought the SP was "really like" and how confident they were of each rating. Ten of the items were chosen to reflect five distinct clusters whose contents were relevant to the hypotheses being tested. Each cluster consisted of two items, each suggesting an aspect of cluster meaning but balanced for direction to inhibit tendencies toward response set. Thus the conformity cluster consisted of the pairs "conforming-independent" and "creative-unoriginal." Other clusters were affiliation, intelligence, motivation, and candor. The remaining six items were related to each other only in their strong evaluative tone: warm-cold, popular-unpopular, likable-irritating, etc.

In analyzing the results, cluster scores were derived simply by adding the scale placements for the two component items, naturally reversing the score of one item. Confidence scores were similarly derived by simple addition of scale values.

RESULTS

Predicted Differences in Perception

In line with the general hypotheses of the study, the first specific prediction was that SPs performing out-of-role (Astro-Others and Sub-Inners) would be perceived as revealing their true preferences in the simulated interview more than SPs performing in-role (Astro-Inners and Sub-Others). The most direct test of this hypothesis may be found in the data provided by subjects in trying to indicate how the SP would have responded in the interview if he was being completely faithful to himself. These data are summarized in Figure 1a and in Table 1. It is clear that the prediction is confirmed. The Astro-Other and the Sub-Inner SPs are both seen as revealing their true preferences, though there is a slight and understandable regression toward the mean. Interestingly enough, and quite in line with predictions, the two in-role groups locate the true answers of the SPs almost exactly halfway between the other-directed and the inner-directed pattern. Since behavior appropriate to powerful role requirements generally masks the characteristics of the actors, the perceivers apparently feel that their best guess is a completely neutral one.

The next issue to be raised is the extent to which these results are restricted to the particular pattern of items covered in the recorded interview. That is, do the highly significant results summarized in Table 1 merely reflect rational manipulations of the specific response scale used by the SP, or do they generalize to related measures of perception and inference? Recall that the subjects also filled out a bipolar adjective rating scale, in an attempt to express their appraisal of the SP's true characteristics. The items of this scale were members of small clusters of related traits, varying in their relevance to the dimension of inner-other directedness. Two of the most relevant clusters, by *a priori* judgment, were attempts to measure perceptions of affiliation and conformity. It was

TABLE 1 PREDICTIONS OF SP's TRUE RESPONSES (SUMMARY OF ANALYSIS OF VARIANCE[a] AND t TEST RESULTS)

Source	*df*	*MS*	*F*	Group	*N*	*Y*	*t*
A. Astro-Sub	1	1,554.73	63.56**	AO	33	91.12	5.32**
B. Inner-Other	1	1,764.91	64.27**	SO	31	69.26	
C. Mach[b]	2	18.81					
A × B	1	8.63		AI	33	69.15	5.98**
A × C	2	62.67		SI	37	43.92	
B × C	2	31.23					
A × B × C	2	22.84					
Error	122	27.46					
Total	133						

[a] Using the approximation technique for unequal cell frequencies (Snedecor, 1946).
[b] [Editors' Footnote—The experimental design included a treatment for Machiavelianism as measured by Christie's Mach IV (Christie and Merton, 1958). Interpretation of this treatment is omitted.]
** $p < .001$.

predicted that the two out-of-role SPs would be perceived to differ markedly in both affiliation and conformity and that the two in-role SPs would not. The results, as summarized in Table 2, clearly confirm this prediction. The Astro-Other is seen as significantly more affiliative and conforming than the Sub-Inner, and each is seen as differing significantly from its in-role control. Analyses of variance indicate that there are no significant interactions between role and behavior sample. This result seems to indicate that genuine perceptual decisions have been made that involve assessing the meaning of the behavior sample provided by the SP against the background of the role playing instructions imposed on him.

Since the predictions involving the direction and magnitude of perceptual rating differences have been borne out, the next relevant question concerns the confidence with which perceptual judgments were made. The general hypothesis, it will be recalled, predicted that in-role ratings would be less confidently made than ratings of out-of-role behavior. This prediction could be easily tested since the subject rendered a judgment of confidence with respect to each trait rated. The most precise test of the general prediction involves confidence ratings based on the two clusters most relevant to the differences between role: affiliation and conformity. When confidence ratings on these clusters are summed for each individual, the resulting pattern clearly confirms the hypothesis. As Table 3 shows, the interaction between role and behavior sample is highly significant. As for the individual mean comparison, in each case the subjects feel more confident about rating the SP who is behaving out of role

TABLE 2 PERCEPTIONS OF AFFILIATION AND CONFORMITY

	Astro-Other	Astro-Inner	Sub-Other	Sub-Inner	Comparisons	
N	33	33	31	37	Direction	*t*
Affiliation						
$\bar{X}$	15.27	11:12	12.00	8.64	AO > SO	4.02**
SD	2.92	3.81	3.53	4.73	AI > SI	2.12*
Conformity						
$\bar{X}$	15.91	13.09	12.58	9.41	AO > SO	4.02**
SD	3.22	3.42	3.39	4.95	AI > SI	3.65**

Note.—The higher the mean value, the greater the perceived affiliation or conformity. Comparisons between AO and SI are not tabled, but the differences between these conditions would of course be highly significant.
* $p < .05$.
** $p < .001$.

TABLE 3 CONFIDENCE RATINGS BY TREATMENTS (ANALYSIS OF VARIANCE[a] SUMMARY)

Source	df	Affiliation and Conformity	
		MS	F
A. Astro-Sub	1	.07	
B. Inner-Other	1	1.62	3.29
C. Mach[b]	2	.26	
A × B	1	8.58[c]	17.42**
A × C	2	.33	
B × C	2	.84	
A × B × C	2	.47	
Within	122	.49	
Total	133		

[a] Using the approximation technique for unequal cell frequencies (Snedecor, 1946).
[b] [Editors' Footnote—The experimental design included a treatment for Machiavelianism as measured by Christie's Mach. IV (Christie and Merton, 1958). Interpretation of this treatment is omitted.]
[c] Results of tests of individual mean comparisons: AO > SO, $t = 3.30$, $p < .01$; SI > AI, $t = 2.55$, $p < .02$.
** $p < .001$.

than the SP who is behaving the same way *in* role.

Differences in Recall

As one of their tasks, all subjects were asked to reproduce the responses made by the SP in the simulated interview. The fidelity of these attempts at recall was treated in two ways. First, a recall score was computed for each subject involving the degree of discrepancy in scale points for each item, summed without regard to direction. For convenience we may call these absolute error scores. Subjects were expected to make fewer errors in recalling the behavior samples of the in-role treatments than those in the out-of-role treatments. The assumption was that roles, like all categories that summarize relevant information, facilitate cognitive organization and enhance one's ability to predict behavior that is appropriate to the role. In the present case, the behavior sample available in the in-role treatments tended to confirm the expectations established by the role instructions. For subjects in the out-of-role treatments, the role instructions could not be used to organize and predict the behavior which occurred, except insofar as the subjects were led to adopt a clear negative expectation that the behavior was the opposite of that called for.

The results on this measure of absolute recall confirm the hypothesis. The responses of the in-role SPs (Astro-Inner and Sub-Other) are recalled with greater accuracy than the responses of the out-of-role SPs (Astro-Other and Sub-Inner). As Table 4 shows, the predicted interaction is significant ($p < .05$). Most of this interaction effect comes from the two cells in which the SP is other-directed (Sub-Other > Astro-Other, $t = 2.60$, $p < .01$; Astro-Inner > Sub-Inner, $t = .64$, $p < .50$). There is no obvious reason for this difference unless the submariner role was more helpfully predictive in organizing information about the other-directed behavior sample than was the astronaut role in organizing information about the inner-directed sample.

The recall data were also scored to take account of the direction of deviation from accuracy. These data are relevant for answering any questions dealing with the assimilation of recalled responses to categories implied by the roles. In fact, as Figure 1b shows, there was no evidence of either assimilation or contrast in directional recall of the SP's interview preferences. Those errors which the subjects did make (see the foregoing data on absolute errors) were quite evenly distributed on either side of the true scale position. As far as the mean directed error scores are concerned, then, the group recall accuracy was extremely high. Of course, we cannot state on the basis of these results that distortions from accurate recall of social behavior are always random distortions, but in the present case there is no evidence for

TABLE 4 ABSOLUTE RECALL ERRORS BY TREATMENTS (ANALYSIS OF VARIANCE[a] SUMMARY)

Source	df	MS	F
A. Astro-Sub	1	3.89	
B. Inner-Sub.	1	1.36	
C. Mach[b]	2	.30	
A × B[c]	1	9.59	6.23*
A × C	2	3.61	
B × C	2	.13	
A × B × C	2	1.40	
Within	122	1.54	
Total	133		

[a] Using the approximation technique for unequal cell frequencies (Snedecor, 1946).
[b] [Editors' Footnote—The experimental design included a treatment for Machiavelianism as measured by Christie's Mach. IV (Christie and Merton, 1958). Interpretation of this treatment is omitted.]
[c] The means for the four cells represented by this interaction were: $\bar{X}$ (Astro-Other) = 12.42; $\bar{X}$ (Sub-Other) = 9.52; $\bar{X}$ (Astro-Inner) = 10.00; $\bar{X}$ (Sub-Inner) = 10.56.
* $p < .05$.

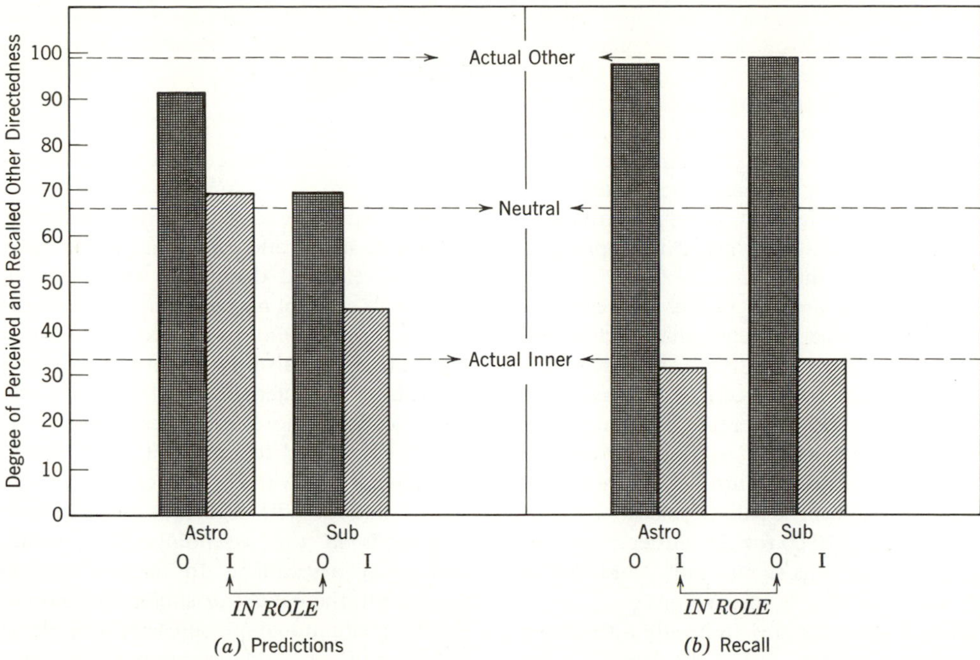

Figure 1. Degree of perceived and recalled other directedness. (*a*) Predictions of "true answer patterns" (means). (*b*) Recall of answers actually given (means).

directional errors either toward or away from the role category implied by the instructions to the SP.

Perception of Additional Characteristics

In planning the experiment, it seemed at least conceivable that many subjects would attribute the SP's out-of-role performance in the Astro-Other and Sub-Inner conditions to poor motivation, lack of intelligence, or both. If such were the case, then it would not necessarily follow that the behavior sample provided would be taken as a "true" reflection of the SP's affiliative and conforming tendencies (or the lack thereof). We have seen that most subjects did consider the out-of-role performance to be reflections of these tendencies, but it is still of interest to note their ratings of the SP on trait clusters tapping perceived motivation and intelligence. As Table 5 shows, the Sub-Other SP was seen as more highly motivated and intelligent than the Astro-Other SP ($p < .01$), but this expected trend was slightly reversed in the case of the two inner-directed SPs. It would appear, then, that the in-role SP is

TABLE 5 SELECTED TRAIT AND CLUSTER MEANS BY TREATMENTS WITH APPROPRIATE COMPARISONS

Clusters	Astro-Other $n=$ 33	Sub-Other $n=$ 33	Astro-Inner $n=$ 31	Sub-Inner $n=$ 37	Relevant Comparisons
Motivation					
$\bar{X}$	9.97	12.10	9.64	10.92	SO > AO, $p < .01$
SD	3.47	3.66	4.48	4.09	
Intelligence					
$\bar{X}$	8.00	11.13	9.39	9.84	SO > AO, $p < .01$
SD	3.35	4.15	3.72	3.94	
Candor					
$\bar{X}$	12.42	9.68	10.09	12.08	AO > SO, $p < .01$
SD	4.09	3.61	3.68	3.77	SI > AI, $p < .05$

judged to have greater motivation and intelligence only when the role involves volunteering for the submarine service. There is no obvious reason for this difference in response to the two roles. Perhaps the inner-directed pattern seemed more artificial or obvious in the context of astronaut instructions, or perhaps the meaning of motivation and intelligence became less situation-bound when subjects were asked to appraise a truly inner-directed man.

Also of interest are the ratings of perceived candor. It might be expected that performing out-of-role would be construed as evidence of the SP's frankness and sincerity. The results in Table 5 do show a clear difference between in-role and out-of-role SPs with regard to the perception of candor. As expected, the in-role SPs are judged by the average subject to fall at or near the midpoint of the scale (10.00 for the cluster); the out-of-role SPs are seen as significantly more candid in each variation of role instructions.

Results on the remaining traits add little to the picture already presented. For the most part the means fall into a pattern similar to those reflecting perceived affiliation and conformity. That is, the two in-role SPs are perceived to be relatively neutral on most of the evaluative trait dimensions; the Astro-Others are seen as significantly more likable (versus irritating), warm (versus cold), popular (versus unpopular), and helpful (versus disinterested) than the Sub-Inners. This pattern of findings might suggest the operation of a strong "halo" or "generosity" effect favoring those who are perceived as other directed. However, it must be recalled that the Astro-Other SP is seen as less highly motivated and less intelligent than the Sub-Other SP, personal attributes that are usually considered to be quite evaluative. Also, Astro-Other and Sub-Inner SPs are both seen as more candid than their in-role controls. It seems more likely, then, that evaluative traits like warm, popular, likable, and helpful are linked to other-directedness more by direct association than through an underlying decision that the Astro-Other SP is good and the Sub-Inner SP is bad. This conclusion is supported by two further results: to an extent that is nearly significant, the two out-of-role SPs are seen as more interesting (versus boring) than the two in-role SPs; also, the Astro-Inner SP is seen as significantly more conceited (versus self-effacing) than either the Astro-Other or the Sub-Inner SP. While these incidental findings are not all easy to rationalize, they do point up the complexity and subtlety of the cognitive impressions created by the experimental combinations of role and behavior sample.

DISCUSSION

The results of the present study are unequivocal. Starting from the assumption that individual characteristics are obscured when a person is exposed to strong and demanding stimulus forces, we have reasoned that social stimuli embraced by the role concept may operate in this same way. Thus a person who conforms to salient social expectations reveals little about his basic and distinguishing characteristics. On the other hand, one who rejects or ignores pressures to play a defined role is considered to reflect his true disposition and is perceived with confidence.

It is undoubtedly true that this reasoning is ubiquitous in the psychologist's approach to personality assessment. In many programs of assessment, the patient or subject is exposed to a variety of situational pressures and task demands. Of his responses to these situations, his nonmodal reactions are clearly more informative and carry the most interpretive weight. To take another example, psychological screening for desirable jobs must cope with the problems raised by this study in order to be effective. Since the role constraints for the applicant are often obvious, the interviewer or employer must penetrate to more subtle cues or fall back on projective devices which, though unreliable at best, at least produce the response variety essential for individualized judgment.

It is probably true that short-term social interactions can perfectly well proceed in line with established expectations defining reciprocal roles. If the interaction is self-limiting (as, say, between a hotel guest and his bellhop) there is little need for personalized information to sustain the interaction. When a relationship is more permanent, however, and involves the prospect of interactions in varied situations, such information rapidly increases in value. It is to the perceiver's advantage, in such cases, to be especially attuned to out-of-role behaviors and to create situations in which out-of-role behaviors can be most clearly observed. The results of the present study show that such behaviors, rightly or wrongly, are perceived to be peculiarly diagnostic of individual characteristics. Judgments about these personal qualities are presumably most important in governing the perceiver's behavior as he ventures into new situations with the SP.

SUMMARY

An experiment was designed to test the general proposition that behavior which is appropriate to a clearly specified role is relatively uninformative about personal characteristics. Subjects were asked to listen to a recorded interview in which the interviewee was heard being instructed, in two treatment conditions, to respond "as if" he very much desired to be accepted in the submarine service, and in two treatments as if he wished to qualify as a space astronaut. The qualifications of these two positions were described in such a way that dramatically different personal qualifications were required. As the interview proceeded, the interviewee either responded in line with the qualifications described for the astronaut position (inner-directedness) or with those for the submariner position (other-directedness). Thus, in a four-cell design there were two cells of in-role behavior to be judged (Astronaut-Inner and Submariner-Other) and two cells of out-of-role behavior (Astronaut-Other and Submariner-Inner). Reasoning from the importance of distinguishing between self-caused and externally induced behavior in person perception, the following predictions were made:

1. Out-of-role SPs are perceived to be revealing their true characteristics more than in-role SPs.

2. Out-of-role SPs are rated with greater confidence on the dimensions relevant to role performance.

3. The performance of in-role SPs is more accurately recalled than that of out-of-role SPs.

Each of these predictions was strongly confirmed by the results.

REFERENCES

Christie, R., and Merton, R. K., 1958. Procedures for the sociological study of the values climate of medical schools. *Journal of Medical Education*, **33**, 125–153.

Heider, F., 1944. Social perception and phenomenal causality. *Psychological Review*, **51**, 358–374.

Heider, F., 1958. *The psychology of interpersonal relations*. New York: Wiley.

Jones, E. E., and Thibaut, J. W., 1958. Interaction goals as bases of inference in interpersonal perception. In R. Tagiuri and L. Petrullo (Eds.), *Person perception and interpersonal behavior*. Stanford, Calif.: Stanford University Press, pp. 151–179.

Snedecor, G. W., 1946. *Statistical methods* (4th ed.). Ames, Ia.: Collegiate Press.

selection 18 Expectations and Behavior in Therapy

HENRY L. LENNARD AND ARNOLD BERNSTEIN

[It has been suggested that therapy as] a social system be conceived of as involving two subsystems, that of communication and that of expectations. Each system can be treated separately from the other [but one can demonstrate] interrelations between the systems of expectation and communication. We will try to document the hypothesis that asymmetry in the system of expectations (dissimilarities in role expectations) is reflected in asymmetry in the system of communication (communicational strain), and we will try to show how efforts are made in the latter system to resolve strain created by the former.

Abridged from Chapters 8 and 9 of a book by the same authors entitled *The Anatomy of Psychotherapy*, 1960, New York: Columbia University Press. Reprinted by permission of the authors and Columbia University Press.

EFFECT OF DISSIMILARITIES IN THERAPIST-PATIENT EXPECTATIONS UPON THE CONTENT OF COMMUNICATION

We will first introduce a set of quotations consisting of patient verbalizations which reflect unfulfilled (dissimilar) expectations in order to see how patients express their experience with a given expectational problem. Then in a series of subsequent excerpts we will show how therapists through their communication attempt to resolve the problem faced by the patients as a result of dissimilarity in expectations. Episodes of strain and role-teaching similar to these recur again and again throughout therapy.

Expectations Regarding Activeness

Patient Statements of Expectational Problem. Patient: A couple of seconds ago, uh, there was a silence in which I had nothing to say or I didn't say anything. And just before you said something I thought of this fact that, uh, I wonder *who's* going to talk first and *why*.

Patient: I was trying to arrive at a couple of things (*sigh*). The reaction of the analyst sitting and just staring at me, and waiting for me to say something or to think of something leads to two kinds of feelings in me. One, instead of coming forth and being able to think of things, is that I either draw a blank or, uh, have to fight to try and almost make up things to fill the void.

Patient: Well, actually, I haven't found this, uh, the kind of experience that I've anticipated. It's rather frustrating. It's difficult for me to carry on a one-man conversation with myself, something I've never been able to do.

Patient: I thought, uh, there would be more of a, uh, interaction, back and forth in trying to at least, get at your reactions to the kind of feeling I have.

Therapist Role Definition Responses. Therapist: You would like some reactions from me, is that it?

Patient: In a sense, yes.

Therapist: Why?

Patient: Well, what is the relationship we have? is it, do I get reactions from you or do I, what kind of a, an emotional learning process takes place if there is no reaction from you? I really don't know. Can I learn just by hearing myself?

Therapist: Look, it's easy for me to tell you some answers so you will know how you should behave . . . That way we don't find out anything about your motivations, your thinking, your emotions.

Therapist: Well, why don't we take it easy and wait till something occurs to you. We don't have to fill every second with sound.

Patient: . . . I suppose after a while it gets to be a game to see who can outstare the other.

Therapist: Is that what it feels like?

Patient: Well, I am trying to bring a humorous element into it.

Therapist: Hmm, that is a very difficult aspect of it though. It's sort of to get used to the nothing . . . that you're gonna come in and the doctor will just wait . . . he'd like to hear . . . what you have on your mind.

Therapist: No, that's what I hope you'll learn to do if you keep coming in, just sort of ramble on and let me try to—

Patient: Make sense out of it.

Therapist: Not to try to make sense, there'll be a lot of sense in it, but try to develop a sort of *pattern* or something like it.

Expectations Regarding Selectivity

Patient Statements of the Expectational Problem. Patient: All right now, would you say that I should try to talk about mostly what happens nowadays or mostly about whether it relates back?

Patient: Yeah, I don't know. Ah, well, I don't know what to talk about, I mean.

Patient: I am just thinking whether—what you're waiting for me to say?

Therapist Role Definition Responses. Patient: I guess it's generally your policy to have your patient talk as much as he wants and as freely as he wants.

Therapist: Well, the procedure is generally that you lie down and relax on the couch, and then put all your feelings, your memories, and your thoughts, into words so far as you can.

Patient: With no direction?

Therapist: With no direction and preferably with no selection. I know this is impossible, but so far as you can, you let me be the judge about what's important and what's not important. You just come in open-mindedly and report the data.

Patient: That's quite a thought, considering the data in any person's life takes up twenty-four hours every day.

Therapist: Well, since you needn't select, just say what's on top of your head.

Patient: . . . . I can't think of anything else that you'd be interested in.

Therapist: Talk about something that *you* would be interested in.

Patient: Nothing that would be significant in psychotherapy—

Therapist: Well, nothing that happens to you is insignificant in terms of our trying to get to know you, whether it's by accident or by design, whatever happens and what effects it has on you—

Patient: Yeah.

Therapist:—helps us to understand.

Patient: (35-*second pause*) That's all I can think of now.

Therapist: Talk about anything else that you want to. Any you listed as problems last time. You may want to go into detail with respect to some of them or take some other points up. I want you to feel free to talk about anything.

Expectations Regarding Temporal and Situational Differentiation

Patient Statements of the Expectational Problem. Patient: I wonder when, when you're going to, uh, start getting rough with me, probe—

Therapist: Speak with authority.

Patient: Yeah, speak with authority and, uh, bat me around a little bit, uh, snipe at me. Catch me up on things I say. So far the soliloquies I've indulged in—hasn't uncovered anything. (temporal)

Patient: I was thinking too that in the beginning you never said anything or occasionally a little "mm-hm" or "hmm." But now, ah, you're entering in more from a conversational viewpoint. (temporal)

Patient: I thought you'd be more sympathetic than you usually are, when you saw how upset I was. (situational)

Therapist Role Definition Responses. Therapist: I want to say something about me. You may ask any question you wish, but I may not answer them. I answer only those questions that I think are to your advantage to hear answers to, and I delay answering all others until such time as I feel it is appropriate. (temporal)

Therapist: I wish I could give you the answer right now, but it wouldn't do you any good if I presented you with an answer right now. (temporal)

Expectations Regarding Timing

Patient Statements of the Expectational Problem. Patient: No, I know that it will take quite a bit of time. But I was just hoping that I'd be started on the way to helping myself, improving these things. I really don't seem to know what I expect now. But I know it will take quite a bit of time.

Patient: I know you say you have to sorta sneak up on this thing, but I don't know. It's hard for me to grasp hold of that idea.

Therapist Role Definition Responses. Patient: I don't know, sometimes I feel so disgusted, I just feel like forgetting about the whole thing.

Therapist: That's what I mean. That's what I meant last time when I said it might take you a while to sort of get over the discouragement of feeling that psychotherapy is going to be something that's going to take *time and work*.

Therapist: Oh, I think you understand it very well, but it's just that I think you're kind of reluctant to accept it—because it means sort of that you're not going to be able to have a quick answer to all your problems.

Therapist: Well, this takes a good deal of time. Go slowly. What did you expect to get out of psychotherapy? And how fast did you expect to go? . . . Sometimes it takes months before you get anything out of this, because you can't hurry this along. You have, did you think that after a few visits, the heavens would open—

Patient: No.

Therapist:—as they do in the movies or in the short stories, and all your problems will be solved?

THERAPIST EXPECTATIONS REGARDING ACTIVENESS

To get at the therapists' activeness self-images and to assess their activeness expectations, each therapist was asked in a pre-therapy interview whether they considered themselves to be primarily an active or a passive participant in the therapeutic situation. They were asked, in general, how frequently they spoke during treatment. We have summarized their replies to these questions in Table 1. As can be seen, the responses to the questions place the therapists in about the same rank order for activeness. Activeness in the quantitative sense used here should not be confused with the issue of "directiveness." Activeness merely refers to the amount of verbal activity that the therapist engages in, not to the content

TABLE 1 THERAPISTS' RESPONSES TO QUESTIONS DEALING WITH THEIR ACTIVENESS IN THERAPY

Therapist	Active or Passive Participant	Frequency of Speaking
A	"Very active"	"Will speak a great deal depending on circumstances"
B	"Active in a nondirective sense"	"Somewhat less frequently than in ordinary conversation"
C	"Passive"	"Very infrequently"
D	"More Passive"	"Very infrequently"

of such verbal participation. Directiveness bears the connotation of direction and control over the patient's activities outside of therapy and often subsumes such categories of activities as value judgments, advice, and prescription.

Table 2 shows that there is a consistent relationship between the therapists' expectations as to how verbally active they would be, and their actual verbal activity during treatment as measured by the following three indices of activeness:

1. *Therapist Verbal Output*. This is defined as the number of therapist propositions in any given session or group of sessions. It is a measure of the *absolute* volume of the therapist's contribution.

2. *Therapist Proportion of Verbal Output*. This is defined as the number of therapist propositions divided by the total number of propositions obtained in a single session or group of sessions. It is a measure of the therapist's proportion of verbal activity during treatment and is

TABLE 2 THERAPISTS' CONCEPTION OF ACTIVENESS AND THEIR VERBAL OUTPUT DURING THE FIRST EIGHT SESSIONS OF TREATMENT

	Quantitative Measures of Verbal Activity		
Therapists in Rank Order of Self-Ratings on Activeness	Average Number of Propositions Per Session	Proportion of Total Verbal Output	Mean Number of Interactions Per Session
Therapist A:			
Patient 1	136	.30	78
Patient 2	166	.36	115
Mean	151	.33	96
Therapist B:			
Patient 1	114	.25	79
Patient 2	97	.21	61
Mean	106	.23	70
Therapist C:			
Patient 1	41	.14	36
Patient 2	75	.14	74
Mean	58	.14	55
Therapist D:			
Patient 1	44	.12	32
Patient 2	51	.17	37
Mean	48	.14	35
All Therapists:	91	.27	64

$n = 64$ sessions

one means of quantifying therapist-patient role differentiation.

3. *Rate of Interaction.* This is defined as the average number of exchanges or interactions that occur per session or per transcribed page, and it tells us how *often* the therapist speaks.

Thus our therapists were found to have a fairly clear and consistent conception of how verbally active they would be during treatment. Because these estimates of activeness were made prior to contact with the patients, and because inter-therapist variance in activity level was greater than inter-patient variance, it follows that at least in the early stages of therapy verbal activeness of therapists is largely (though obviously not entirely) a function of their experience and role expectations rather than of the expectations or activities of particular patients.

It seems to us that this congruence between therapists' expectations and certain quantitative aspects of their actual behavior during the first eight sessions of treatment may enable us to bridge the gap between the attitudinal and the behavioral aspects of the psychotherapy situation. It provides a sort of operational hold upon a particularly elusive problem and it provides a first-order approximation in quantitative terms as to what a therapist means when he says that he is an active or passive therapist. Thus we have found a direct relationship in psychotherapy between an expectational system and an action system.

EFFECTS OF DISSIMILARITIES IN THERAPIST AND PATIENT EXPECTATIONS

We shall now assess the hypothesis that dissimilarity between therapist and patient expectations in given areas disequilibrates the therapeutic system, and that mechanisms are consequently set in motion which are aimed at relieving the strain and restoring equilibrium. We consider socialization of the patient by the therapist to be one of these basic restorative mechanisms.

Therapist communications aimed at patient socialization deal with the process and goals of therapy, i.e., with the rights and obligations of therapist and patient vis-à-vis each other, and with the mechanisms and routines of this special social situation. They are communications concerned with "teaching" the patient the new system of reciprocal role relationships, which we hypothesized as essential to the restoration of system functioning whenever dissimilarities of expectation have created system strain.

We will now present data regarding the effect upon therapist performance of dissimilarities in one dimension of therapist-patient conceptions—that of "activeness."

An index of dissimilarity in conceptions of activeness was constructed, based on five parts of a question asked both of therapist and patient at the beginning of therapy.[1] The value of the index ranges from 0–10, with 0 indicating complete similarity and 10 the highest possible dissimilarity.

Table 3 shows the effect of dissimilarities in therapist-patient "activeness" expectations upon the occurrence of therapist primary system (socializing) communications during the first three hours of therapy.

We observe in Table 3 that our hypothesis is strongly documented. Comparing the two patients for each therapist, we find that whenever there is more dissimilarity with respect to activeness expectations, there is a greater number of therapist primary system references. Furthermore, as might be expected the amount of primary system reference generated by expectational dissimilarity is related to the level of activeness of each therapist. For instance when the index of dissimilarity reaches 3 for one of the active therapists (B), the proportion of his primary system references rises to .49. But for one of the less active therapists (C) when the index of dissimilarity reaches 3, his proportion of primary system references rises to only .20. We conceive the emergence of "role" information to be a direct consequence of dissymmetry in expectations. For purposes of dealing with this problem, we regard dissymmetry of expectation as one kind of disequilibrium and communication centered around the primary system as one form of attempted re-equilibration.

[1] The index was constructed as follows: The therapist is asked, "Consider the following list of activities—will you engage in them often, sometimes, or never, in the course of therapy with this particular patient?" The patient is asked, "Please indicate for each of the activities described below whether you think the therapist will engage in the activity often, sometimes, or never, during your therapy. The activities include: suggest what to talk about next; prohibit you from doing things he considers inadvisable; counsel or advise you in the management of day-to-day living; explain what therapy is all about." *Scoring*: The answers "often," "sometimes," and "never" are respectively given the numerical values of 3, 2, and 1. The arithmetical differences for any given item between therapist conception and patient conception are then added. The greater the value of the sum of the differences, the higher the dissimilarity in therapist-patient conception of therapist "activeness."

TABLE 3 DISSIMILARITIES BETWEEN THERAPIST-PATIENT EXPECTATIONS WITH REGARD TO THERAPIST ACTIVENESS AND THERAPIST PRIMARY SYSTEM REFERENCES

Therapist	Patient	Index of Dissimilarity (Ranging from 0–10, with High = Dissimilar)	Proportion of Therapist Primary System References during First Three Hours of Therapy
A	1	0	.09
	2	2	.27
B	1	1	.16
	2	3	.49
C	1	2	.05
	2	3	.20
D	1	3	.15
	2	4	.19

n = 24 sessions

Table 3 reflects the effect of *actual* dissimilarities in expectation. However, we also have data on *anticipated* dissimilarities, gathered to find out whether therapists' communicational acts are affected more by the state of the interaction system than by intra-personality system variables. In other words, will a therapist be more likely to give primary system information when the state of the system requires it (dissimilarity in actual state of expectations) or when he thinks it may be required (anticipated dissimilarity)? The extent to which the therapist anticipates that the patient's view is similar or dissimilar to his own is assessed by two questions consisting of five parts each, asked of the therapist at the beginning of therapy. The therapist is asked: "Consider the following list of activities—will you engage in them often, sometimes, or never in the course of therapy with this particular patient." He is then asked: "From what you know, does the patient think you will engage in these activities often, sometimes, or never?" On the basis of the therapist's answer, an index is constructed which reflects the extent of dissimilarity in expectations anticipated by the therapist. An index value of 0 indicates that the therapist anticipates that the

TABLE 4 THERAPIST ANTICIPATED DISSIMILARITIES IN EXPECTATION OF ACTIVENESS AND THERAPIST PRIMARY SYSTEM REFERENCES

Therapist	Patient	Index of Therapist Anticipated Dissimilarity (Ranging from 0–10, High = Dissimilar)	Proportion of Primary System References during the First Three Hours of Therapy
A	1	0	.09
	2	0	.27
B	1	1	.16
	2	4	.49
C	1	4	.05
	2	3	.20
D	1	2	.15
	2	1	.19

n = 24 sessions

patient's views are wholly like his own, while 10 indicates that he anticipates that they are wholly dissimilar.[2]

Table 4 shows to what extent the anticipation of dissimilarities bears upon the communication process between therapist and patient.

We observe that, except for therapist B, there is no relationship between anticipated dissymmetry and therapist primary references. Further, that the therapist allocates a good portion of his verbal output to the induction of the patient into the primary system even where he does not anticipate dissymmetry.

Comparing Tables 3 and 4 we note that the actual disequilibrium present in the system (dissimilarity of expectation) is highly associated with the extent to which the therapist emphasizes role discussion, but that anticipated disequilibrium on the part of the therapist does not show such a correlation. The therapist thus aligns his behavior with reference to the actual state of the system of expectations rather than with reference to an anticipated state.

We have shown previously that therapist expectations are reflected in communications, yet we now find that a discrepancy between his own expectations and those he attributes to the patient does not give rise to a change in his pattern of action. We suggest that this is due to the following interactive process. Patient role expectations reflect themselves in patient behavior (communications). Patient expectations that are dissimilar to those of the therapist tend to produce verbalizations indicating strain and disequilibrium. The therapist responds to these communications in such a way as to relieve the strain which they indicate, even though he may not have consciously re-evaluated his own estimate of the patient's expectations.

[2] The scoring is as follows: The answers "often," "sometimes," and "never" are respectively given the numerical values of 3, 2, and 1. The arithmetical differences between therapist expectations and therapist estimate of patient expectations are then added, irrespective of sign. The greater the value of the sum of the differences, the higher the index of therapist anticipated dissimilarity in expectations of activeness.

selection 19 Expectations of Psychotherapy in Patients of Lower Socioeconomic Class

BETTY OVERALL AND HARRIET ARONSON

There are many obstacles to psychotherapy with the patient of lower socioeconomic class. One of the greatest is such a patient's minimal involvement in the initial phases of treatment.

This problem became apparent in one of our psychiatric clinics in which the patient population consists almost entirely of individuals of lower socioeconomic class. A six-month survey of new patients revealed a dropout rate of 57 per cent after the initial interview, that is, only 43 per cent of the patients seen returned for a second appointment. This rate, while not notably different from that reported from comparable settings (Freedman, Engelhardt, Hankoff, Glick, Kaye, Buchwald, and Stark, 1958; Rosenthal and Frank, 1958), indicated a waste of time and effort sufficient to warrant an examination of the clinic population and the psychotherapeutic procedures followed.

The present study represents an attempt to define one of the factors that might have produced so high a rate of attrition. Since so many patients terminated after only one interview, it was felt that an important cause of dropouts might be the patient's negative evaluation of his initial interview in terms of his original expectations of treatment.

This study focuses on a general description of the treatment expectations of patients of lower socioeconomic class, and relates the fulfillment of these expectations to their returning or not returning for treatment.

Abridged from the *American Journal of Orthopsychiatry*, 1963, **33**, 421–430. Reprinted by permission of the authors and the American Orthopsychiatric Association. This study was supported in part by a grant from the National Institutes of Health.

For this purpose, three specific hypotheses were formulated:

1. Patients of lower social class expect the therapist to assume an active, medical role in the initial interview.
2. The actual conduct of the therapist during the interview is less active and medically oriented than the patient expects.
3. Those patients whose anticipations are less accurate will be less likely to return for further treatment; that is, those patients who do not return for treatment will have a greater discrepancy between their expectations and their perception of the interview.

Since the patient may evaluate the events of the interview in terms of his own reactions or even perceive them in a distorted manner, it appears reasonable to study the differences between a patient's and a therapist's perceptions. With this added dimension, a fourth hypothesis can be added:

4. The discrepancy between a patient's expectations and his perception of the interview is a better predictor of return to treatment than is the discrepancy between a patient's expectations and his therapist's perception of the interview.

METHOD

Setting

The locale of this study was a psychiatric clinic in the general outpatient department of a university hospital, but totally administered by the department of psychiatry. The therapists were fourth-year medical students, who were rotated through the clinic on a monthly basis. Supervision was by advanced residents and staff members, and the philosophy of the staff was dynamic. Patients received one or two initial interviews of an hour's duration. They were then seen for 15 to 20 minutes once every two or four weeks for the remainder of their treatment.

Subjects

The subjects were 40 patients who had come to the clinic for their first visit. Patients who were obviously psychotic or severely disoriented were screened out as untestable.

Although a student-therapist may have seen more than one intake patient during his rotation in the clinic, only his first was selected for examination. All further patients seen by the student-therapist were excluded from the study. The information was obtained, therefore, from 40 patients, each seen by a different student-therapist. Within these limits, the subjects were a random selection of those seen during a single school year.

The age range of the subjects was 16 to 66, with a mean age of 39.6. There were 26 females and 14 males; 27 Negro and 13 white patients. Thirty of the 40 patients declared themselves Protestant, and all but 2 were born in the South. Sixteen were married and 24 had no marital ties; that is, they were either single, separated, divorced or widowed.

Educational level ranged from second grade to completion of high school: 55 per cent had completed ninth grade or less, 37.5 per cent had completed 10 to 12 grades and 7.5 per cent (three) were students in high school at the time of the study. In terms of income: 33.3 per cent were recipients of public assistance, 41 per cent earned $50 or less weekly and 25.6 per cent earned more than $50 a week. The highest reported income was $85 a week.

Procedure

A questionnaire was constructed listing 35 statements of a therapist's possible behavior in an initial interview.[1] Each question was devised to tap one of five aspects of a therapist's behavior such that an affirmative response would indicate the presence of that aspect. Although the five points are not mutually exclusive, each question focuses on only one. The categories were:

1. Active—The therapist actively instructs or directs the patient, for example, "Do you think the doctor will tell you what is causing your trouble?"
2. Medical—The therapist focuses on the organic or physical problems of the patient, for example, "Do you think the doctor will be interested in your digestion?"
3. Supportive—The therapist avoids charged material in an attempt to bolster or comfort the patient, for example, "Do you think the doctor will try to get your mind off your troubles?"
4. Passive—The therapist leaves the direction of the discussion to the patient, encouraging all patient communications, for example, "Do you think the doctor will expect you to do most of the talking?"
5. Psychiatric—The therapist focuses on emotional or dynamic material, for example, "Do you think the doctor will want to know how you get along with people?"

A pilot study was conducted to be sure the questions were comprehensible and could differentiate among the subjects, that is, that no question was given the same response by all patients. The questionnaire was then revised to its present form.

Each patient was given the questionnaire orally by a psychiatric social worker on his first visit to the clinic, immediately preceding his interview with the therapist. The patient was asked to state whether he felt each statement was descriptive of the interview he

[1] A number of the questions were suggested by the Libo Preference Form P-D-A (Libo, unpublished test).

was about to have. At the conclusion of the initial interview, the patient was again given the questionnaire to obtain his perception of the therapeutic procedure. Three questions were also added:

"Do you like the doctor?"
"Do you think the doctor seemed to understand you?"
"Do you feel the doctor can help you?"

The face sheet data to determine social class (income, occupation, education, and so on) were obtained at this time.

The student-therapist completed a comparable questionnaire at the conclusion of the interview to determine his perception of the interview. There were four additional questions, asking:

"Would this type of patient benefit most by being seen for a few interviews only?"
"Do you think the interview went well?"
"Do you think the prognosis is good?"
"Do you think this patient can use psychiatric treatment?"

The therapist did not know the purpose of the questionnaire. He was told that the study was to investigate the kinds of therapeutic techniques necessary for the wide range of diagnostic problems seen in the clinic.

The patient's return for a second clinic appointment, scheduled for all patients, was the criterion for classification as Return or Non-Return.

RESULTS

Hypothesis 1. *Patients of lower social class expect the therapist to assume an active, medical role in the interview.*

Table 1 indicates the wording of the questionnaire and shows the percentage of affirmative responses to each question made by our subjects. Since there was no control group, it was arbitrarily considered a significant degree of affirmation when questions were answered affirmatively by 65 per cent or more of the subjects. Several categories are somewhat incompatible, yet only three questions are affirmed by less than 50 per cent of the subjects.[2] This could indicate a general set by the patients to answer Yes, or it could reflect an actual expectation that the therapist be simultaneously active, medical, supportive, passive and psychiatric, as these traits are defined above. The particularly high percentage of affirmative responses to questions in the psychiatric category strongly indicates that, contrary to the Hollingshead and Redlich (1958) conceptualization and to a much greater degree than we ourselves foresaw, these patients do generally anticipate that psychiatric issues will be raised.

At present, the degree to which the expectations reported here differ from those held by other socioeconomic groups must be left to the judgment of the reader.

Hypothesis 2. *The actual conduct of the therapist during the interview is less active and medically oriented than the patient expects.*

Table 1 shows the percentage of affirmative responses to the same statements made after the interview had been conducted. The patients' observations of the interview were significantly different from their expectations for 23 of the 35 questions when compared by the McNemar test for the significance of changes (Siegel, 1956). Figure 1 presents a graph of these differences in terms of the category of expectation indicated by an affirmative response. It shows that most of the discrepancy between expectation and observation lies in the categories of Active, Medical and Supportive, in each of which the therapist's behavior was generally less than the patient anticipated. In the Passive and Psychiatric categories, the tendency to expect more than was observed is not as clear-cut and the proportion of incorrect anticipation is generally smaller.

Hypothesis 3. *Those patients whose anticipations are less accurate will be less likely to return for further treatment*; *that is, those patients who do not return for treatment will have a greater discrepancy between their expectations and their perception of the interview.*

The 40 patients were subdivided into two groups: Return and Non-Return. There were 23 patients in the Return group and 17 in the Non-Return group. No significant differences were found between the two groups in terms of age, sex, race, income, education or marital ties; nor is this dropout rate of 42.5 per cent significantly different from that found through the six-month survey.

When the discrepancies between a patient's expectations and his view of the interview were totalled for the 35 questions, a single discrepancy score could be quantified for each patient. A Mann–Whitney U Test (Siegel, 1956) showed the discrepancy scores of the Non-Return group to be significantly greater than those of the Return group. The difference was significant at the .01 level, corroborating the hypothesis that those patients whose expectations were most inaccurate were less likely to return for treatment.

[2] [Editors' Note: See Figure 1 for the classification of questions in categories.]

Hypothesis 4. *The discrepancy between a patient's expectations and his perception of the interview is a better predictor of return to treatment than is the discrepancy between a patient's expectation and his therapist's perception of the interview.*

A single discrepancy score for each patient was also tabulated between the patient's expectations and the therapist's view of the actual conduct of the interview. The discrepancy scores of the Return and the Non-Return groups were then compared. In contrast to the significant difference noted above, no significant difference was found here ($p < .25$). Thus, our hypothesis that the patient's view is a better predictor of return is supported.

Since only three of the specific questions (namely, 9, 13 and 16, which are concerned with the adequacy of the medical history) show a significant difference between what the patient experienced and what the therapist felt had occurred, a Pearson product-moment correlation

TABLE 1 PERCENTAGE OF AFFIRMATIVE RESPONSES MADE BY PATIENTS BEFORE AND AFTER THEIR INITIAL INTERVIEWS AND BY STUDENT-THERAPISTS AFTER THE INITIAL INTERVIEWS†

Patients' before Do you think the doctor will . . .	*Patients' after* Did the doctor . . .	*Therapists' after* Did you . . .	
58%	50%	58%	1. give you medicine?
23	08	16	2. not ask questions about your personal life?
60	15**	08**	3. tell you what is wrong with you?
78	58*	54	4. try and cheer you up?
20	13	00	5. not want your opinions?
75	78	82	6. listen more than he talks?
68	18**	16**	7. give you definite rules to follow?
54	28*	29*	8. avoid subjects which might upset you?
80	43**	71	9. ask what medicines you have been taking?
78	43**	55	10. want to know what your childhood was like?
90	85	82	11. want to know what kinds of things make you unhappy?
63	15**	08**	12. tell you what is causing your trouble?
83	18**	45**	13. ask what physical illnesses have been in your family?
87	55**	47**	14. want you to look at the bright side of things?
85	88	100	15. want to know about your thoughts and feelings?
83	40**	82	16. want to know what other doctors you have seen lately?
70	55	50	17. ask you a lot of questions?
70	20**	24**	18. be interested in your digestion?
90	65*	84	19. want to know how you get along with people?
75	18**	13**	20. tell you ways to solve your problems?
65	08**	05**	21. have a list of things he will want to check over?
95	73*	82	22. want to know how happy you are?
68	85	95**	23. expect you to do most of the talking?
68	25**	24**	24. be particularly interested in your aches and pains?

TABLE 1—*continued*

Patients' before Do you think the doctor will . . .	*Patients' after* Did the doctor . . .	*Therapists' after* Did you . . .	
80%	63%**	39%**	25. try to get your mind off your troubles?
70	20**	29**	26. ask questions about any operations you have had?
88	100	100	27. be interested in hearing any personal problems you have?
70	15**	05**	28. tell you what is wrong with what you do?
50	83*	97**	29. not give you a physical examination?
78	45**	68	30. ask you to describe the physical illnesses you have had?
80	58*	74	31. want to know what your friends are like?
55	00**	00**	32. take your pulse and blood pressure?
93	95	100	33. listen to your troubles?
45	08**	08**	34. tell you what kinds of food you should eat?
98	83	100	35. be interested in knowing if some things make you afraid or nervous?
Patients' postinterview only:			
	97		36. Did you like the doctor?
	100		37. Do you think the doctor seemed to understand you?
	97		38. Do you feel that the doctor can help you?
Therapists' postinterview only:			
		50	36. This type of patient would benefit most by being seen for a few interviews only (Yes, No.)
		78	37. Do you think the interview went well?
		61	38. Do you think the prognosis is good?
		76	39. Do you think that this patient can use psychiatric treatment?

† The first 35 questions have been stated in the preinterview form given to patients. Appropriate changes of person or tense were made on the postinterview questionnaires. While the N is usually 40, omission of responses occasionally redueed the N to 38 or 39. Only one question was omitted by as many as three subjects. The results quoted are, of course, based on the actual number of responses obtained for each question.

* $p < .05$ (two-tailed) by means of the McNemar test for the significance of changes when compared with patients' preinterview responses.

** $p < .01$ (two-tailed) by means of the McNemar test for the significance of changes when compared with patients' preinterview responses.

(Peters and van Voorhes, 1940) was made between the two discrepancy scores described above, to determine the extent to which the patients disagreed with their therapists in terms of perception. The correlation was .72, which is significant at the level of 1 per cent. Thus, the patient and his therapist substantially agree on the interview, indicating that little distortion of the events had taken place.

General Questions

Of the 40 patients, only one answered No to the question, "Did you like the doctor?" and only one answered No to the question, "Do you feel that the doctor can help you?" Both patients were in the Non-Return group. All 40 patients answered Yes to, "Do you think the doctor seemed to understand you?" Apparently, questions such as these are of little value in understanding the dropout rate for the patients studied.

There was less unanimity in the student-therapists' responses. However, no differentiation between the Return and Non-Return patients was made on questions 36, 37 and 38. There was a

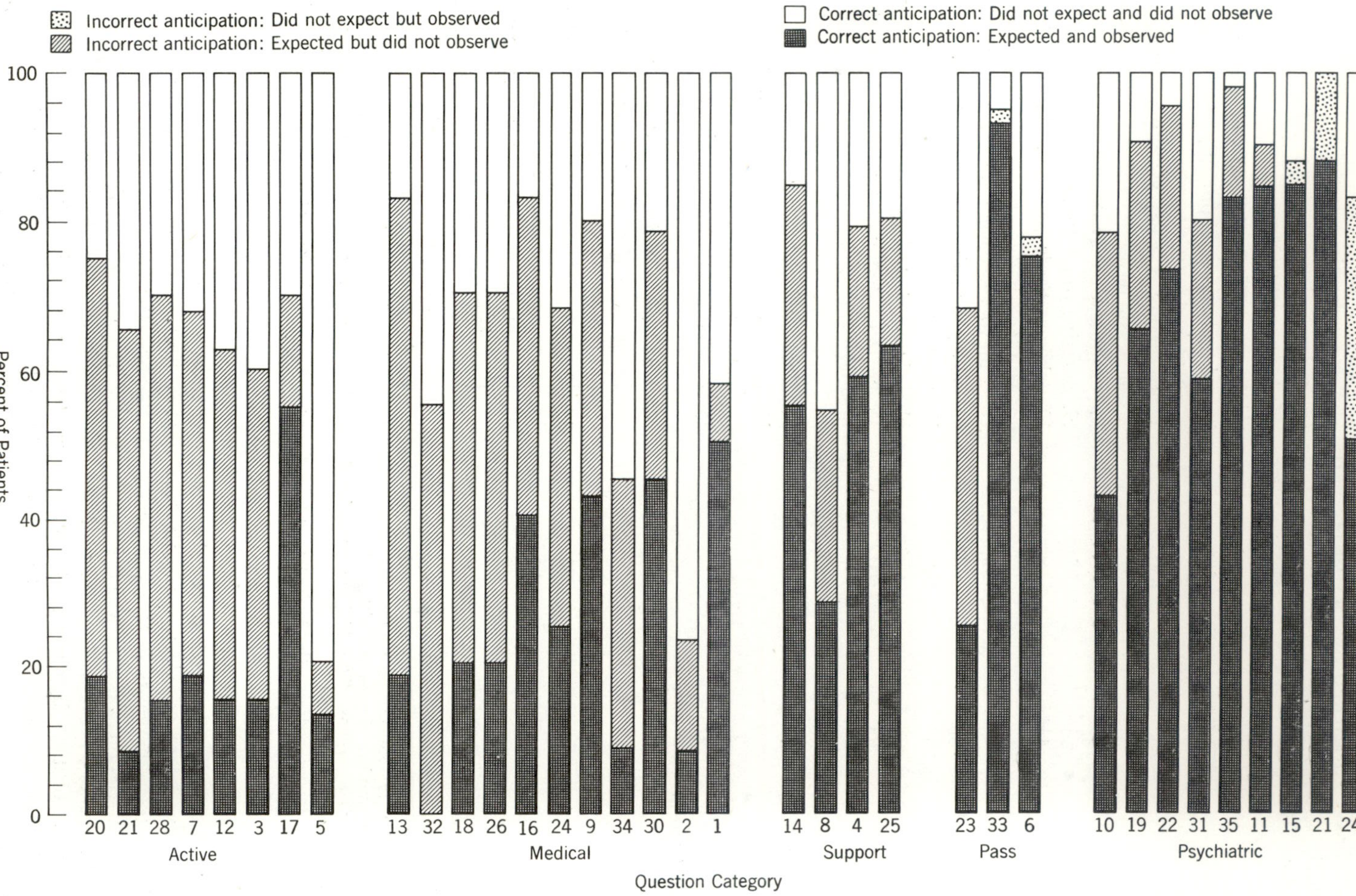

Figure 1. Comparison of patients' expectations prior to the initial interview with their reports directly after the interview.

significantly greater number of affirmative responses for the Return group, to, "Do you think that this patient can use psychiatric treatment?" ($p < .05$). There are two ways of interpreting this differentiation. The therapists could be discerning some difference between the groups, whatever this difference might be. However, it is also possible that the patients are able to perceive acceptance or rejection on the part of the therapist, and that this perception influences their decision to return.

DISCUSSION

The results of our study indicate that lower-class patients predominantly expect a medical-psychiatric interview with the therapist generally assuming an active but permissive role. They tend not to return when these expectations are not fulfilled. Such expectations may well be due to cognitive factors, and the problem, then, is to find some means by which these factors may be reduced. One way of reducing cognitive inaccuracies is to attempt, during the initial phases of treatment, to re-educate the patient as to both his own and the therapist's role in treatment. Since a great proportion of dropouts occur after the initial interview, it would seem particularly important to raise the question of expectations during the first hour. Moreover, it may be necessary to encourage a direct expression of expectations so that both patient and therapist can more easily view and modify their roles.

REFERENCES

Freedman, N., Engelhardt, D. M., Hankoff, L. D., Glick, B. S., Kaye, H., Buchwald, J., and Stark, P., 1958. Drop-out from outpatient psychiatric treatment. *A.M.A. Archives of Neurology and Psychiatry*, **80**, 657.

Hollingshead, A. B., and Redlich, F. C., 1958. *Social class and mental illness.* New York: Wiley.

Libo, L. M. Preference Form P-D-A. Unpublished test.

Peters, C. C., and van Voorhes, W. R., 1940. *Statistical procedures and their mathematical bases.* New York: McGraw-Hill.

Rosenthal, D., and Frank, J. D., 1958. The fate of psychiatric clinic outpatients assigned to psychotherapy. *Journal of Nervous and Mental Disease*, **127**, 330.

Siegel, S., 1956. *Nonparametric statistics for the behavioral sciences.* New York: McGraw-Hill.

part VI Performance and Interdependence

MUCH OF THE BEHAVIOR of the child at play, the employee at work, and the individual at home is *performance*. Such behavior is overtly manifested, has been learned previously, is goal directed, and displays apparent volition. Role analysts are concerned with such aspects of performance as its complexity, uniformity, adequacy, the bias with which it is presented, and the extent to which individuals are organismically engaged. Furthermore, most persons are interdependent with others in their performances and, as a consequence, an individual may incur rewards and costs and have his performance facilitated or hindered by the performance of others. Performance is also related to the personality characteristics of those performing, to the positions of which they are members, to the prescriptions for their behavior, among many other factors. The selections in this part relate variously to these aspects of performance.

In the first selection, Sarbin offers the concept of role enactment and elaborates on its various dimensions. The first of these is the number of roles simultaneously enacted by the individual, and this dimension is associated, in part, with the individual's social adjustment. The dimension of organismic involvement relates particularly to the intensity of enactment as it is manifested in the number of organic systems involved. Seven levels of organismic involvement are described—these ranging from a very low to a very high degree. For each level examples are provided. The paper concludes with a discussion of accessibility and the *as-if* dimension.

The selection by Goffman treats various aspects of the individual's presentation of performance. The important point is made that an individual's performance is made manifest to others so as to create particular impressions upon them and to realize the performer's personal objectives. These biases in the presentation of performance are identified and discussed. The notion of "front," for example, has reference to that part of the individual's performance that functions to define the situation for those who observe the performance. Dramatic realization, idealization, the maintenance of expressive control, and misrepresentation are among other important concepts identified by the author.

Mitchell elaborates upon an important type of bias in the presentation of performance in his characterization of interaction in a prison. The author suggests that instead of role-playing, prisoners engage in role calculation; that is, the prisoner intentionally simulates conformity behavior in order to "get by" in a social system in which participation is required by those in whose goals the individual does not share. Mitchell points out that the process of role calculation vitiates the goal of prison rehabilitation. This discussion has more general implications as well because most individuals must participate in nonvoluntary situations at various times in the course of their lives.

A central problem concerning the effects of role-playing is examined in the study reported in the selection by John and Carola Mann. The authors indicate that although in recent years there has been widespread use of role-playing as a means of training and therapy, the few empirical studies on the effects of role-playing have not adequately examined the basic assumptions upon which the technique is based. In an effort to attack these assumptions directly, the authors tested the hypotheses that: (1) role-playing improves future enactment of the role actually practiced,

(2) role-playing improves future role-playing, (3) role-playing improves the enactment of other roles. Findings supporting these hypotheses are presented.

The selection by Borg is a report of an experiment on the relationship between personality variables and role performance in the small group. On the premise that personality factors are among the determinants of role performance, the author finds relationships between such performance characteristics as popularity, followership, assertiveness, rigidity, creativity, and leadership, on the one hand, and the personality characteristics of assertiveness, power orientation, rigidity, and aggressive nonconformity, on the other hand. The findings of this study, and of others like it, serve as a reminder that role performance is not by any means solely determined by such factors as positional affiliation and prescriptions.

The important topic of interdependence is taken up in the selection by Thibaut and Kelley. The authors indicate that when individuals perform in interaction with others there are costs and rewards incurred for both the performer and his co-interactor; and, furthermore, that there are exogenous and endogenous determinants of the rewards and costs. In addition, performances may facilitate or interfere with one another. The strategies for avoiding interference include the synchronization of behavior sets and the elimination of the interfering sets. The authors also discuss the usefulness of role differentiation in larger groups, suggesting that it may make possible joint-cost cutting, joint consumption, mutual facilitation, and sequential patterns of interdependence.

The selection by Rapoport and Rosow is significant because it brings together a number of concepts relating to role and role performance in order to examine the performance of individuals in the context of the family. This thoughtful blending of ideas has theoretical as well as practical implications. The authors point out that success or failure in role performance is due to such factors as the positional membership of the individual, the fit of norms held for his performance, the emotional climate of the family, and the fit between the personality systems of the various members of the family. Along more practical lines, the authors discuss problems of role performance as they relate to the personality difficulties suffered by persons under psychiatric treatment. They contend that an understanding of the interdependence of members performing familial roles and of personality factors are significant in planning programs of therapy.

selection 20 Role Enactment

THEODORE R. SARBIN

Role enactment (equivalent to Newcomb's "role behavior," 1950) includes, among other segments of behavior, gross skeletal movements, the performance of verbal and motoric gestures, posture and gait, styles of speech and accent, the wearing of certain forms of dress and costume, the use of material objects, the wearing of emblems or ornamentation, including tattoos, etc. In short, role enactment embraces what may be called the mechanics of the role-taking process. These mechanics can be summarized by means of the following concepts: number of roles, organismic involvement, and accessibility or reportability.

NUMBER OF ROLES

The dimension, number of roles, is subject to observation and report, providing the actions which make up the roles are properly conceptualized. The ultimate in attaining ecological generality would occur if an observer followed a given subject for a representative number of days and recorded all instances of role behavior. The observer might also rate the intensity with which he enacted the various roles. This type of observational approach is not new to anthropologists (see, for example, Ford, 1938).

A less difficult approach for getting at the number of roles enacted by an individual is the use of small-group settings. The discussion group has been the focus of a number of research attempts in recent years and lends itself to the laboratory study of role behavior. Benne and Sheats (1948) have recognized and named a number of positions (systems of role expectations) which characteristically arise in the discussion group. Some examples are: the opinion-giver, the orienter, the encourager, the hostile critic, the aggressor, etc. It should be pointed out that such roles do not have the institutional support of the more traditional roles, such as mother, doctor, shortstop, etc. Nevertheless, they do emerge in the interaction process and can be described with the same formal characteristics as the traditional roles. Among the roles which emerge in the small group are various "leader" roles, such as initiator, coordinator, director, and so on. The dimension "number-of-roles" was applied to such leader roles in a recently completed study by Sarah Mazelis (1953). She addressed herself to the question: Is the productivity of a discussion work group related to the diffusion of leader roles among the members of the group? The leader roles were defined and categorized by actions. The observers recorded and counted the number of leader roles enacted by each person in each of four independent work groups. The hypothesis studied was: productivity will be greater among groups where the various leader roles are enacted by most of the group members; productivity will be less where the leader roles are enacted by a small proportion of the group members. The work products were rated on several criteria by experts in the field.

In a group task which required planning, the quality of the product, as rated by the judges, was directly related to the diffusion of the various leader roles among the group members. Spearman rank difference correlation between an index of role diffusion and production ratings was .75. Although the small number of groups makes this finding only suggestive, the method appears promising.

This number-of-roles dimension is implicit in the application of the role-taking approach to psychopathology. It is a widely accepted postulate that the more roles in a person's behavior repertory, the "better" his social adjustment—other things being equal. Cameron and Magaret (1951) have argued most convincingly that the absence of role-taking skills is influential in the development of paranoid disorders. Gough (1948) has also implicitly used number-of-roles as a dimension in his role-taking theory of psychopathy.

Abridged from a chapter by the same author entitled "Role Theory" in G. Lindzey (Ed.), *Handbook of Social Psychology*, Volume 1, 1954, Cambridge, Mass.: Addison–Wesley. Reprinted by permission of the author and Addison–Wesley.

Following Mead, he describes how the residuals of role enactments ("me's") are integrated into a self-conception, and how the ability to be self-critical is a function of the number of "me's" or the internalization of a "generalized other." Further, ". . . deficiency in role playing means the incapacity to look upon one's self as an object (Mead) or to identify with another's point of view . . ." (Gough, 1948, p. 363). Gough and Peterson (1952) have already utilized this conception in an empirical study of psychopathology.

ORGANISMIC DIMENSION

Any role may be enacted with different degrees of organismic involvement. This is essentially an intensity dimension, the intensity of the enactment being manifest in the number of organic systems involved. At the low end of the dimension would be the kind of interaction which occurs with little affect and with little effort. The role of the customer in today's supermarket involves only minimal participation—the saying of a few words, plus a few movements involved in the exchange of money. Contrast this role with the intensity involved in enacting the role of the mother of a sick child.

In daily life, of course, most roles are enacted with minimal organismic involvement. Behavior would be inefficient indeed if all roles were enacted with maximal intensity. Not only are cultures organized so that the number of maximally intense roles is few, but there are autonomic safeguards which limit the time span of roles that call for great mobilization of energy. The organismic dimension can be understood as applying to all organized actions. The illustrations we have chosen are reference behaviors against which more conventional roles may be compared for intensity (Figure 1).

Level I. The low end of the scale is labeled "role and self differentiated." The self, a cognitive structure (*v. infra*), and the role, also a cognitive structure, are minimally in contact. An example of a casual role, already given, is the customer in a supermarket. In fact, it is possible to perform this role at the motoric level while at the same time vicariously enacting other roles unrelated to the public role.

Level II. At the next level of organismic involvement, the reference is that of the dramatic actor who performs the motions necessary for the portrayal of the role assigned to him. In

Role and self differentiated
Minimal involvement
Few organic systems
Little effort

Role and self undifferentiated
Maximal involvement
Entire organism
Much effort

I. casual roles

II. dramatic role, mechanical acting

III. dramatic role, heated acting

IV. role of hypnotic subject

V. hysterical fugue, role of the amnestic

VI. roles involving ecstatic states; mystical experiences, possession, religious conversions, sexual climax

VII. role of the moribund person; object of sorcery and witchcraft (sometimes irreversible)

Figure 1

mechanical acting, the actor does not become involved; the self is relatively autonomous from the role. He must maintain a certain degree of consistency in the various response systems, which calls for more effort and precludes the degree of autonomy of the casual role. This degree of involvement is seen in many everyday interactions. For example, the employee who "puts on a good front" to impress the boss.

Level III. At the third level, "heated" acting is used as the illustrative reference behavior. Archer (1889) in his classical study of the psychology of acting, was able to discern this kind of acting from the more automatic and mechanical mentioned before. Commonly called "living the role," the actor behaves as if he *is* the character in the drama. Of course, the successful actor maintains some contact with his role as actor in order to change his tempo, amplitude, intensity, etc., as conditions warrant. His involvement includes some affective as well as motoric components. In order to portray anger, for example, the actor may work up a rage by violently shaking a ladder in the wings before appearing on the stage.

Level IV. The role of the hypnotic subject serves as a reference role for a moderate degree of organismic involvement. The classical behaviors of the hypnotic subject, the catalepsies, the compulsive post-hypnotic actions, sensory and motoric changes, and so on, illustrate more cogently the operation of the *as if* mechanism. In enacting the role of the hypnotized subject as perceived against a background of generalized and specific expectations, a person demonstrates that more of the organism is responding than in play acting. He behaves *as if* he is blind, or deaf, or fearful, or analgesic, or whatever the specific instructions call for.

The hypnotic situation provides a suitable laboratory model for the demonstration of organismic involvement. An experiment conducted by Lewis and Sarbin (1943) demonstrates this involvement. These investigators addressed themselves to the question: Can *as if* behavior, as observed in the role taking of hypnosis, influence a basic physiological process, namely, the hunger cycle. Ten volunteer subjects, demonstrating different degrees of hypnotizability, participated in the experiment. The apparatus was essentially the same as used by Carlson (1916) in his studies of gastric hunger contractions. Each subject appeared for the experimental period each morning without his breakfast. He was hooked up to the recording apparatus. He was hypnotized and given no further instructions. One full gastric hunger cycle was recorded. During the middle of the second cycle, he was given a fictitious meal. The results indicated that for subjects rated high on the role-taking aptitude (see below), i.e., the ability to participate in *as if* behavior, the gastric hunger contractions stopped. That is, taking the role of the eater was effective in reducing or eliminating the gastric contractions even though no food was ingested. For subjects who were not hypnotizable, who were limited in their ability to participate in this form of *as if* behavior, no effect was produced on the gastric cycle. Thus, a range of the dimension of organismic involvement was demonstrated.

Level V. The behaviors subsumed under the rubric hysteria may be used as a reference band on the organismic continuum. Responding *as if* one is afflicted with some organic dysfunction is the main characteristic of the hysteric. The range covered by hysteria overlaps considerably the range covered by hypnotic role taking. The organismic components in hysteria, however, are less self-limiting and more prolonged than in hypnosis. Descriptive cases may be found in any textbook of abnormal psychology. Common examples are hysterical seizures. hysterical anorexia, hysterical paralysis, and hysterical anesthesia. Both major varieties of hysteria, inactivation and autonomy (Cameron, 1947), show how the role of the invalid may involve the entire organism. In the same range of intensity of involvement is the couvade. In this custom the husband lies-in; the essence of the custom is the husband's taking the role of the wife (Crawley, 1902).

Level VI. Ecstasy, a condition usually involving suspension of voluntary action, illustrates organismic involvement to a degree which is not ordinarily observed in day-to-day social interaction. Obviously, such states cannot be prolonged over time without damage to the functioning of the body. Ethnologists' accounts of ecstatic trance experiences, possession, religious revivals, conversion experiences, and mystical unions show many of the characteristics of hysteria. But in addition to the greater involvement of the skeletal musculature, there is a greater involvement of the organs that are served by the autonomic nervous system.

In our own wider culture, such roles are taken by participants in revival meetings, by adolescent bobby-soxers who swoon upon hearing "the voice," by participants in sexual congress, by marathon dancers, etc. What is common to these events is the intensity of involvement, the apparent relationship of this intensity to the activities of the sympathetico-adrenal system, and the automatic equilibratory controls. All these activities are terminated through institutionalized rituals, fatigue and exhaustion, and/or autonomic regulation.

In *rites de passage* the role of the celebrant is characterized by high organismic involvement. The manifest purpose of the intense role behaviors of the ritual is to signify the change from one position to another in the society; the effect of the intensity of role enactment is to modify the participant's self-concept so that the new role, e.g., adult, may not be incongruent with the self. If, for example, strength is an expected property of the adult person, and the rites of passage from adolescent to adult includes passing a test of strength, then the successful completion of the test allows the person to add the adjective "strong" to his self-description. Thus he is better equipped to occupy the position of adult, not only because others know his strength, but because he conceptualizes the self as strong.

Level VII. The ultimate limit of the intensity dimension is an extension of the previous range. The effects of the sympathetico-adrenal system which is excessively activated in such role-taking sequences as described above may become irreversible under certain stimulus conditions. The end result of such a performance is death.

Well-authenticated cases of *Voodoo* death allow the employment of the descriptive phrase, taking-the-role-of-a-moribund person. Devereux (1939) has reported of the Mohave Indians that a person who learns that he has violated the incest taboo takes the role of the person who is about to die. Rivers (1924) reports of the Papuans and Melanesians: "Men who have offended one whom they believe to have magical powers sicken and die, as the direct result of their belief; and if the process has not gone too far they will recover if they can be convinced that the spell has been removed" (Rivers, 1924, p. 50).

The case of a man dominated by a death wish is described by Alexander (1943). Autopsy findings revealed no organic pathology. Apparently he took the role of the dying person so intensely that the equilibratory processes failed to work.

The eminent physiologist, Cannon (1942), has provided a description of the physiological and social events associated with taking the role of the doomed person. He uses the description of bone pointing among the Australian aborigines provided by Basedow (1925). This is a form of black magic in which the sorcerer points a sharpened bone at the intended victim.

Cannon explains the physiological events arising from the adoption of the victim's role. The fear response acts upon the soma in many ways. The sympathetico-adrenal system comes into action, exercising control over the viscera and blood vessels. The various internal changes render the organism ready for physical action (struggle or flight). If this state of extreme perturbation continues *without motoric discharge*, death may follow. But why do the equilibratory or internal constancy mechanisms fail to re-establish homeostasis, as in ecstatic experiences? One answer to this question is that the perturbation in the organism is maintained by the enactment of supporting roles by other members of the community (Warner, 1937).

These levels of organismic involvement are equivalent to, if not identical with, the concept of self-involvement. At one end of the continuum, we see relatively automatic responses, stereotyped habits, autonomous functioning of self and role. At the other end, we see the unitary functioning of self and role.

DIMENSION OF ACCESSIBILITY

Although it would be simpler to use the descriptive term "consciousness of role enactment," the writer prefers the term "accessibility," or reportability. The conscious-unconscious polarity carries with it connotations derived from psychoanalytic theory which assign motivational properties to so-called unconscious contents. Cameron (1947) has used the expression "not accessible to one's self-reactions," which carries the meaning that a person cannot make valid observations of his own role enactments.

This dimension applies to events in which the actor of the role reports his *actions*. One can immediately think of roles which are enacted automatically and where the person cannot recall his actions. The illustration given before about the person enacting the role of the customer in the supermarket can be applied here. He may perform all the actions necessary toward the selection and purchase of a wide variety of articles but be unable to report his actions. Another example is that of the hysterical amnesia victim. In enacting this role the patient does not recall events prior to the amnestic period. In Archer's (1889) study of acting, such a dimension was isolated. Some actors reported being relatively "unconscious" of self in certain roles, while in others they were extremely observant of their own role enactments.

In what is commonly called self-consciousness, the actor attends almost exclusively to his own actions rather than to the events occurring in the broader social field. The self-conscious person can report such events as the quivering of his voice, the shaking of his knees, the drying of his throat, etc. It is obvious that being greatly involved in the organismic features of the role enactment limits the possibility of observing the self as a social object. In general, one would expect to find a strong inverse relationship between the organismic dimension and the accessibility dimension. The two dimensions, however, should be characterized independently. Events that can be placed on the organismic dimension are available to the observation of others without the necessity of phenomenological report, while the accessibility dimension can be applied only to the actor's report of his own role behavior.

This dimension has not been studied empirically except in clinical settings and in hypnotic experiments. The value of this dimension of role enactment would lie in its application to the learning of social roles. Self-criticism of one's own actions could follow only if these actions were accessible or reportable. The therapeutic dictum, "making conscious what is unconscious" to effect behavioral changes, refers to the same events as making accessible to one's self-reactions inaccessible aspects of one's role enactments in order to modify or eliminate these actions. Bowman (1949) has utilized this notion in his description of the development of insight by virtue of practice in role enactment using the methods developed by Moreno (1934).

THE AS IF DIMENSION

It is by now a truism that the learning of social roles—in fact the learning of any concept—is associated with the ability to treat an object or event *as if* it is something else. One has to adopt the *as if* set in order to group apparently disparate objects or events into a common concept.[1]

In the *if statement*, or the conditional clause, something unreal, untrue, problematical, or fictive is stated. With this assumptive behavior is associated the *maintenance* of the assumption in spite of its fictive character. The maintenance of the assumption is possible only if the organism has developed verbal symbols and the capacity to bind time and tension. The imaginal processes, fantasy, identification, etc., are now seen to depend upon the capacity to engage in *as if* behavior. Between the *as* and the *if*, grammatically speaking, lies a whole sentence. The person must "hold the thought" or maintain the set established by the conditional fictive clause, while at the same time considering the independent clause. As stated earlier, this conceptual process cannot be performed if the person lacks the ability to bind time and tension, a function of the development of the self. Since roles are organized concepts, taking-the-role-of-the-other, then, is not possible without the *as if* ability.

This *as if* behavior can be treated as an aptitude or skill in the same way that we treat academic aptitude or skill. Operative in apparently diverse kinds of conduct, the *as if* formulation has been applied by the author (1950) to repression as an ego defense, impunitiveness as a response to frustration, and hypnotizability as a personality trait. These three variables (the "triadic hypothesis") have been found to be intercorrelated (Rosenzweig and Sarason, 1942). In repression the subject behaves *as if* an event threatening to the maintenance of the self-concept has not occurred; in impunitiveness the person acts *as if* the frustrating event were no longer frustrating; in hypnosis the person behaves *as if* certain qualities and events are different from what they actually are.

The *as if* skill applies to drama, hypnosis, fantasy, play—in fact, to all imaginative behavior. To test whether *as if* behavior has any appreciable effect on the performance of a subject, we can observe the overt action of persons under instructions to behave *as if* something is or is not occurring. Some experiments along this line have been reported. Jacobson (1938) and Schultz (1932) demonstrated the influence of the subject's imagining certain events upon bodily functions. Common experience illustrates how implicit imaginal processes are reflected in overt, muscular movements during the act of imagining. A person can feel his ears becoming red and his face becoming flushed when he imagines a former embarrassment. Similarly, he may experience nausea in imagining something extremely unpleasant or disgusting.

In an experiment on suggestibility Arnold (1946) relates hypnotic and suggestion effects to vividness of imagery. Her experiment allowed the inference that the more vivid the imaginative

[1] A full philosophical and logical treatment of the *as if* principle is given in Vaihinger (1924).

process, the more pronounced the overt movement associated with the imagined act. In a role-theoretical analysis of hypnotic phenomena, Sarbin (1950) has presented some evidence to support the hypothesis that enacting the role of the hypnotized person is a function of the veridicality of the role perception, congruence of the role with the self, and role-taking aptitude. The last-named item is defined as success in the use of *as if* behavior.

REFERENCES

Alexander, G., 1943. An unexplained death coexistent with death wishes. *Psychosomatic Medicine*, **5**, 188–194.

Archer, W., 1889. *Masks or faces*. New York: Longmans, Green.

Arnold, Magda B., 1946. On the mechanism of suggestion and hypnosis. *Journal of Abnormal and Social Psychology*, **41**, 107–128.

Basedow, H., 1925. *The Australian aboriginal*. Adelaide: Preece.

Benne, K. D., and Sheats, P., 1948. Functional roles of group members. *Journal of Social Issues*, **4** (2), 41–49.

Bowman, C. C., 1949. Role-playing and the development of insight. *Social Forces*, **28**, 195–199.

Cameron, N., 1947. *The psychology of behavior disorders*. Boston: Houghton-Mifflin.

Cameron, N., and Magaret, Ann, 1951. *Behavior pathology*. Boston: Houghton-Mifflin.

Cannon, W. B., 1942. "Voodoo" death. *American Anthropologist*, **44**, 169–181.

Carlson, A. J., 1916. *The control of hunger in health and disease*. Chicago: University of Chicago Press.

Crawley, A. E., 1902. *The mystic rose*. London: Methuen.

Devereux, G., 1939. Social and cultural implications of incest among the Mohave. *Psychoanalytic Quarterly*, **8**, 510–533.

Ford, C. S., 1938. The role of a Fijian chief. *American Sociological Review*, **3**, 541–550.

Gough, H. G., 1948. A sociological theory of psychotherapy. *American Journal of Sociology*, **53**, 359–366.

Gough, H. G., and Peterson, D. R., 1952. The identification and measurement of predispositional factors in crime and delinquency. *Journal of Consulting Psychology*, **16**, 207–212.

Jacobson, E., 1938. *Progressive relaxation* (Rev. ed.). Chicago: University of Chicago Press.

Lewis, J. H., and Sarbin, T. R., 1943. Studies in psychosomatics: the influence of hypnotic stimulation on gastric hunger contractions. *Psychosomatic Medicine*, **5**, 125–131.

Mazelis, Sarah, 1953. The relation of role-diffusion to work productivity. Unpublished manuscript.

Mead, G. H., 1934. *Mind, self, and society*. Chicago: University of Chicago Press.

Moreno, J. L., 1934. *Who shall survive?* Nervous and mental disease monograph series, No. 58. Washington, D.C.: Nervous and Mental Disease Publishing Company.

Newcomb, T. M., 1950. Role behaviors in the study of individual personality and of groups. *Journal of Personality*, **18**, 273–289.

Rivers, W. H. R., 1924. *Medicine, magic, and religion*. New York: Harcourt, Brace.

Rosenzweig, S., and Sarason, S., 1942. An experimental study of the triadic hypothesis: reaction to frustration, ego-defense, and hypnotizability. *Character and Personality*, **11**, 1–19.

Sarbin, T. R., 1950. Contributions to role-taking theory: I. Hypnotic behavior. *Psychological Review*, **57**, 255–270.

Schultz, J. H., 1932. *Das autogene training* (Kinzentrative selbstentspannung). Leipzig: Thieme.

Vaihinger, H., 1924. *The philosophy of "as-if."* London: Paul, Trench, Trubner.

Warner, W. L., 1937. *A black civilization: a social study of an Australian tribe*. New York: Harper.

selection 21 Presentation Biases

ERVING GOFFMAN

FRONT

Let us use the term "performance" to refer to all the activity of an individual which occurs during a period marked by his continuous presence before a particular set of observers and which has some influence on the observers. It will be convenient to label as "front" that part of the individual's performance which regularly functions in a general and fixed fashion to define the situation for those who observe the performance. Front, then, is the expressive equipment of a standard kind intentionally or unwittingly employed by the individual during his performance. For preliminary purposes, it will be convenient to distinguish and label what seem to be the standard parts of front.

First, there is the "setting," involving furniture, decor, physical layout, and other background items which supply the scenery and stage props for the spate of human action played out before, within, or upon it. A setting tends to stay put, geographically speaking, so that those who would use a particular setting as part of their performance cannot begin their act until they have brought themselves to the appropriate place and must terminate their performance when they leave it. It is only in exceptional circumstances that the setting follows along with the performers; we see this in the funeral cortége, the civic parade, and the dream-like processions that kings and queens are made of.

If we take the term "setting" to refer to the scenic parts of expressive equipment, one may take the term "personal front" to refer to the other items of expressive equipment, the items that we most intimately identify with the performer himself and that we naturally expect will follow the performer wherever he goes. As part of personal front we may include: insignia of office or rank; clothing; sex, age, and racial characteristics; size and looks; posture; speech patterns; facial expressions; bodily gestures; and the like. Some of these vehicles for conveying signs, such as racial characteristics, are relatively fixed and some sign vehicles are relatively mobile or transitory, such as facial expression.

It is sometimes convenient to divide the stimuli which make up personal front into "appearance" and "manner," according to the function performed by the information that these stimuli convey. "Appearance" may be taken to refer to those stimuli which function at the time to tell us of the performer's social statuses. These stimuli also tell us of the individual's temporary ritual state, that is, whether he is engaging in formal social activity, work, or informal recreation, whether or not he is celebrating a new phase in the season cycle or in his life-cycle. "Manner" may be taken to refer to those stimuli which function at the time to warn us of the interaction role the performer will expect to play in the oncoming situation. Thus a haughty, aggressive manner may give the impression that the performer expects to be the one who will initiate the verbal interaction and direct its course. A meek, apologetic manner may give the impression that the performer expects to follow the lead of others, or at least that he can be led to do so.

We often expect, of course, a confirming consistency between appearance and manner; we expect that the differences in social statuses among the interactants will be expressed in some way by congruent differences in the indications that are made of an expected interaction role. But, of course, appearance and manner may tend to contradict each other, as when a performer who appears to be of higher estate than his audience acts in a manner that is unexpectedly equalitarian, or intimate, or apologetic.

In addition we expect, of course, some coherence among setting, appearance, and manner. Such coherence represents an ideal type that provides us with a means of stimulating our attention

Abridged from Chapter 1 of a book by the same author entitled *The Presentation of Self in Everyday Life*, 1959, New York: Doubleday. Reprinted by permission of the author and Doubleday.

to and interest in exceptions. For example, a *New Yorker* profile on Roger Stevens (the real estate agent who engineered the sale of the Empire State Building) comments on the startling fact that Stevens has a small house, a meager office, and no letterhead stationery (Kahn, 1954).

DRAMATIC REALIZATION

While in the presence of others, the individual typically infuses his activity with signs which dramatically highlight and portray confirmatory facts that might otherwise remain unapparent or obscure. For if the individual's activity is to become significant to others, he must mobilize his activity so that it will express *during the interaction* what he wishes to convey. In fact, the performer may be required not only to express his claimed capacities during the interaction but also to do so during a split second in the interaction. Thus, if a baseball umpire is to give the impression that he is sure of his judgment, he must forgo the moment of thought which might make him sure of his judgment; he must give an instantaneous decision so that the audience will be sure that he is sure of his judgment (see Pinelli, 1953).

It may be noted that in the case of some statuses dramatization presents no problem, since some of the acts which are instrumentally essential for the completion of the core task of the status are at the same time wonderfully adapted, from the point of view of communication, as means of vividly conveying the qualities and attributes claimed by the performer. The roles of prize-fighters, surgeons, violinists, and policemen are cases in point. These activities allow for so much dramatic self-expression that exemplary practitioners—whether real or fictional—become famous and are given a special place in the commercially organized fantasies of the nation.

In many cases, however, dramatization of one's work does constitute a problem. The proprietor of a service establishment may find it difficult to dramatize what is actually being done for clients because the clients cannot "see" the overhead costs of the service rendered them. Undertakers must therefore charge a great deal for their highly visible product—a coffin that has been transformed into a casket—because many of the other costs of conducting a funeral are ones that cannot be readily dramatized (see Habenstein, 1954). Merchants, too, find that they must charge high prices for things that look intrinsically expensive in order to compensate the establishment for expensive things like insurance, slack periods, etc., that never appear before the customer's eyes.

IDEALIZATION

I want to consider here the tendency for performers to offer their observers an impression that is idealized in several different ways.

The notion that a performance presents an idealized view of the situation is, of course, quite common. Cooley's (1922) view may be taken as an illustration:

> If we never tried to seem a little better than we are, how could we improve or "train ourselves from the outside inward?" And the same impulse to show the world a better or idealized aspect of ourselves finds an organized expression in the various professions and classes, each of which has to some extent a cant or pose, which its members assume unconsciously, for the most part, but which has the effect of a conspiracy to work upon the credulity of the rest of the world. There is a cant not only of theology and of philanthropy, but also of law, medicine, teaching, even of science—perhaps especially of science, just now, since the more a particular kind of merit is recognized and admired, the more it is likely to be assumed by the unworthy (pp. 352–353).

Thus, when the individual presents himself before others, his performance will tend to incorporate and exemplify the officially accredited values of the society, more so, in fact, than does his behavior as a whole.

If an individual is to give expression to ideal standards during his performance, then he will have to forgo or conceal action which is inconsistent with these standards. When this inappropriate conduct is itself satisfying in some way, as is often the case, then one commonly finds it indulged in secretly, in this way the performer is able to forgo his cake and eat it too. We find that middle-class housewives sometimes employ—in a secret and surreptitious way—cheap substitutes for coffee, ice cream, or butter; in this way they can save money, or effort, or time, and still maintain an impression that the food they serve is of high quality. The same women may leave *The Saturday Evening Post* on their living room end table but keep a copy of *True Romance* ("It's something the cleaning woman must have left around") concealed in their bedroom. It may be added that recently the Kinsey reports have added new impetus to the study and analysis of secret consumption.[1]

[1] As Adam Smith (1853, p. 88) suggested, virtues as well as vices may be concealed:

It is important to note that when an individual offers a performance he typically conceals something more than inappropriate pleasures and economies. Some of these matters for concealment may be suggested here.

First, in addition to secret pleasures and economies, the performer may be engaged in a profitable form of activity that is concealed from his audience and that is incompatible with the view of his activity which he hopes they will obtain. The model here is to be found with hilarious clarity in the cigar-store – bookie-joint.

Secondly, we find that errors and mistakes are often corrected before the performance takes place, while telltale signs that errors have been made and corrected are themselves concealed. In this way an impression of infallibility, so important in many presentations, is maintained. There is a famous remark that doctors bury their mistakes.

Thirdly, in those interactions where the individual presents a product to others, he will tend to show them only the end product, and they will be led into judging him on the basis of something that has been finished, polished, and packaged. In some cases, if very little effort was actually required to complete the object, this fact will be concealed. In other cases, it will be the long, tedious hours of lonely labor that will be hidden.

A fourth discrepancy between appearance and over-all reality [is] that there are many performances which could not have been given had not tasks been done which were physically unclean, semi-illegal, cruel, and degrading in other ways; but these disturbing facts are seldom expressed during a performance. In Hughes's terms, we tend to conceal from our audience all evidence of "dirty work," whether we do this work in private or allocate it to a servant, to the impersonal market, to a legitimate specialist, or to an illegitimate one.

A fifth discrepancy between appearance and actual activity [is that] the activity of an individual is to embody several ideal standards, and if a good showing is to be made, it is likely then that some of these standards will be sustained in public by the private sacrifice of some of the others. Often, of course, the performer will sacrifice those standards whose loss can be concealed and will make this sacrifice in order to maintain standards whose inadequate application cannot be concealed. If attendants in a mental ward are to maintain order and at the same time not hit patients, and if this combination of standards is difficult to maintain, then the unruly patient may be "necked" with a wet towel and choked into submission in a way that leaves no visible evidence of mistreatment (Willoughby, 1953).

Finally, we find performers often foster the impression that they had ideal motives for acquiring the role in which they are performing, that they have ideal qualifications for the role, and that it was not necessary for them to suffer any indignities, insults, and humiliations, or make any tacitly understood "deals," in order to acquire the role. And so we find that clergymen give the impression that they entered the church because of a call of felt vocation, in America tending to conceal their interest in moving up socially, in Britain tending to conceal their interest in not moving too far down.

I have suggested that a performer tends to conceal or underplay those activities, facts, and motives which are incompatible with an idealized version of himself and his products. In addition, a performer often engenders in his audience the belief that he is related *to them* in a more ideal way than is always the case. Two general illustrations may be cited. First, individuals often foster the impression that the routine they are presently performing is their only routine or at least their most essential one. As previously suggested, the audience, in their turn, often assume that the character projected before them is all there is to the individual who acts out the projection for them. Secondly, performers tend to foster the impression that their current performance of their routine and their relationship to their current audience have something special and unique about them. The routine character of the performance is obscured (the performer himself is typically unaware of just how routinized his performance really is) and the spontaneous aspects of the situation are stressed.

"Vain men often give themselves airs of a fashionable profligacy, which, in their hearts, they do not approve of, and of which, perhaps, they are really not guilty. They desire to be praised for what they themselves do not think praiseworthy, and are ashamed of unfashionable virtues, which they sometimes practice in secret, and for which they have secretly some degree of real veneration."

MAINTENANCE OF EXPRESSIVE CONTROL

It has been suggested that the performer can rely upon his audience to accept minor cues as a sign of something important about his performance. This convenient fact has an inconvenient implication. By virtue of the same sign-accepting tendency, the audience may misunderstand the meaning that a cue was designed to convey, or may read an embarrassing meaning into gestures or events that were accidental, inadvertent, or incidental and not meant by the performer to carry any meaning whatsoever.

In response to these communication contingencies, performers commonly attempt to exert a kind of synecdochic responsibility, making sure that as many as possible of the minor events in the performance, however instrumentally inconsequential these events may be, will occur in such a way as to convey either no impression or an impression that is compatible and consistent with the over-all definition of the situation that is being fostered. When the audience is known to be secretly skeptical of the reality that is being impressed upon them, we have been ready to appreciate their tendency to pounce on trifling flaws as a sign that the whole show is false; but as students of social life we have been less ready to appreciate that even sympathetic audiences can be momentarily disturbed, shocked, and weakened in their faith by the discovery of a picayune discrepancy in the impressions presented to them. Some of these minor accidents and "unmeant gestures" happen to be so aptly designed to give an impression that contradicts the one fostered by the performer that the audience cannot help but be startled from a proper degree of involvement in the interaction, even though the audience may realize that in the last analysis the discordant event is really meaningless and ought to be completely overlooked. The crucial point is not that the fleeting definition of the situation caused by an unmeant gesture is itself so blameworthy but rather merely that it is *different* from the definition officially projected. This difference forces an acutely embarrassing wedge between the official projection and reality, for it is part of the official projection that it is the only possible one under the circumstances. Perhaps, then, we should not analyze performances in terms of mechanical standards, by which a large gain can offset a small loss, or a large weight a smaller one. Artistic imagery would be more accurate, for it prepares us for the fact that a single note off key can disrupt the tone of an entire performance.

In our society, some unmeant gestures occur in such a wide variety of performances and convey impressions that are in general so incompatible with the ones being fostered that these inopportune events have acquired collective symbolic status. Three rough groupings of these events may be mentioned. First, a performer may accidentally convey incapacity, impropriety, or disrespect by momentarily losing muscular control of himself. He may trip, stumble, fall; he may belch, yawn, make a slip of the tongue, scratch himself, or be flatulent; he may accidentally impinge upon the body of another participant. Secondly, the performer may act in such a way as to give the impression that he is too much or too little concerned with the interaction. He may stutter, forget his lines, appear nervous, or guilty, or self-conscious; he may give way to inappropriate outbursts of laughter, anger, or other kinds of affect which momentarily incapacitate him as an interactant; he may show too much serious involvement and interest, or too little. Thirdly, the performer may allow his presentation to suffer from inadequate dramaturgical direction. The setting may not have been put in order, or may have become readied for the wrong performance, or may become deranged during the performance; unforeseen contingencies may cause improper timing of the performer's arrival or departure or may cause embarrassing lulls to occur during the interaction.

As students we must be ready to examine the dissonance created by a misspelled word, or by a slip that is not quite concealed by a skirt; and we must be ready to appreciate why a near-sighted plumber, to protect the impression of rough strength that is *de rigueur* in his profession, feels it necessary to sweep his spectacles into his pocket when the housewife's approach changes his work into a performance, or why a television repairman is advised by his public relations counsels that the screws he fails to put back into the set should be kept alongside his own so that the unreplaced parts will not give an improper impression. In other words, we must be prepared to see that the impression of reality fostered by a performance is a delicate, fragile thing that can be shattered by very minor mishaps.

The expressive coherence that is required in performances points out a crucial discrepancy between our all-too-human selves and our socialized selves. As human beings we are presumably creatures of variable impulse with moods and energies that change from one moment to the next. As characters put on for an audience, however, we must not be subject to ups and downs. As Durkheim suggested, we do not allow our higher social activity "to follow in the trail of our bodily states, as our sensations and our general bodily consciousness do" (Durkheim, 1926, p. 272). A certain bureaucratization of the spirit is expected so that we can be relied upon to give a perfectly homogeneous performance at every appointed time.

MISREPRESENTATION

If [the] tendency of the audience to accept signs places the performer in a position to be misunderstood and makes it necessary for him to exercise expressive care regarding everything he does when before the audience, so also this sign-accepting tendency puts the audience in a position to be duped and misled, for there are few signs that cannot be used to attest to the presence of something that is not really there. And it is plain that many performers have ample capacity and motive to misrepresent the facts; only shame, guilt, or fear prevent them from doing so.

Sometimes when we ask whether a fostered impression is true or false we really mean to ask whether or not the performer is authorized to give the performance in question, and are not primarily concerned with the actual performance itself. When we discover that someone with whom we have dealings is an imposter and out-and-out fraud, we are discovering that he did not have the right to play the part he played, that he was not an accredited incumbent of the relevant status. The social definition of impersonation, however, is not itself a very consistent thing. For example, while it is felt to be an inexcusable crime against communication to impersonate someone of sacred status, such as a doctor or a priest, we are often less concerned when someone impersonates a member of a disesteemed, non-crucial, profane status, such as that of a hobo or unskilled worker. Further, while we may take a harsh view of performers such as confidence men who knowingly misrepresent every fact about their lives, we may have some sympathy for those who have but one fatal flaw and who attempt to conceal the fact that they are, for example, ex-convicts, deflowered, epileptic, or racially impure, instead of admitting their fault and making an honorable attempt to live it down. Also, we distinguish between impersonation of a specific, concrete individual, which we usually feel is quite inexcusable, and impersonation of category membership, which we may feel less strongly about. So, too, we often feel differently about those who misrepresent themselves to forward what they feel are the just claims of a collectivity, or those who misrepresent themselves for private psychological or material gain.

Finally, since there are senses in which the concept of "a status" is not clear-cut, so there are senses in which the concept of impersonation is not clear either. For example, there are many statuses in which membership obviously is not subject to formal ratification. Claims to be a law graduate can be established as valid or invalid, but claims to be a friend can be confirmed or disconfirmed only more or less. Where standards of competence are not objective, and where *bona fide* practitioners are not collectively organized to protect their mandate, an individual may style himself an expert and be penalized by nothing stronger than sniggers.

Let us try another approach to the understanding of misrepresentation. An "open," "flat," or barefaced lie may be defined as one for which there can be unquestionable evidence that the teller knew he lied and willfully did so. A claim to have been at a particular place at a particular time, when this was not the case, is an example. Those caught out in the act of telling barefaced lies not only lose face during the interaction but may have their face destroyed, for it is felt by many audiences that if an individual can once bring himself to tell such a lie, he ought never again to be fully trusted. However, there are many "white lies," told by doctors, potential guests, and others, presumably to save the feelings of the audience that is lied to, and these kinds of untruths are not thought to be horrendous. Further, in everyday life it is usually possible for the performer to create intentionally almost any kind of false impression without putting himself in the indefensible position of having told a clear-cut lie.

Formal recognition has been given to the shadings between lies and truths and to the embarrassing difficulties caused by this continuum. Organizations such as real estate boards develop explicit codes specifying the degree to which doubtful impressions can be given by overstatement, understatement, and omissions.

The law crosscuts many ordinary social niceties by introducing ones of its own. In American law, intent, negligence, and strict liability are distinguished; misrepresentation is held to be an intentional act, but one that can arise through word or deed, ambiguous statement or misleading literal truth, non-disclosure, or prevention of discovery (Prosser, 1941). Culpable non-disclosure is held to vary, depending on the area of life, there being one standard for the advertising business and another standard for professional counselors.

When we turn from outright impersonations

and barefaced lies to other types of misrepresentation, the common-sense distinction between true and false impressions becomes even less tenable. Charlatan professional activity of one decade sometimes becomes an acceptable legitimate occupation in the next (see McDowell, 1951). More important, we find that there is hardly a legitimate everyday vocation or relationship whose performers do not engage in concealed practices which are incompatible with fostered impressions. Although particular performances may place a performer in a position of having nothing to hide, somewhere in the full round of his activities there will be something he cannot treat openly. The larger the number of matters and the larger the number of acting parts which fall within the domain of the role or relationship, the more likelihood for points of secrecy to exist. Thus in well-adjusted marriages, we expect that each partner may keep from the other secrets having to do with financial matters, past experiences, current flirtations, indulgencies in "bad" or expensive habits, personal aspirations and worries, actions of children, true opinions held about relatives or mutual friends, etc. (see Dressler, 1953).

Perhaps most important of all, we must note that a false impression maintained by an individual in any one of his routines may be a threat to the whole relationship or role of which the routine is only one part, for a discreditable disclosure in one area of an individual's activity will throw doubt on the many areas of activity in which he may have nothing to conceal.

REFERENCES

Cooley, C. H., 1922. *Human nature and the social order* (Rev. ed.). New York: Scribner, pp. 352, 353.

Dressler, D., 1953. What don't they tell each other. *This Week*, September 13.

Durkheim, E., 1926. *The elementary forms of the religious life*. Translated by J. W. Swain. London: Allen and Unwin.

Habenstein, R. W., 1954. *The American funeral director*. Unpublished doctoral dissertation, University of Chicago.

Kahn, E. J., Jr., 1954. Closings and openings. *The New Yorker*, **29** (February 13), 37–56; **30** (February 20), 41–61.

McDowell, H. D., 1951. Osteopathy: a study of a semiorthodox healing agency and the recruitment of its clientele. Unpublished master's thesis, University of Chicago.

Pinelli, B., 1953. *Mr. Ump*, as told to Joe King. Philadelphia: Westminster Press, p. 75.

Prosser, W. L., 1941. Handbook of the law of torts. *Hornbook Series*, St. Paul, Minn.: West, pp. 701–776.

Smith, A., 1853. *The theory of moral sentiments*. London: Henry Bohn.

Willoughby, R. H., 1953. The attendant in the state mental hospital. Unpublished master's thesis, University of Chicago, p. 44.

selection 22 Cons, Square-Johns, and Rehabilitation

JOHN MITCHELL

The history of American prisons from its Quaker origins to the present-day advocates of rehabilitation through group-therapy reveals a consistent concern with not only the confinement of the offender but also with his "moral reform." One of the earliest "staff" positions established in prisons was that of the chaplain, who presumably was to provide "religious and moral" instruction to the inmate. The language of the corrections caseworker of today is replete with the terminology of psychotherapy, which is a secular version of the same thing. We are told that "prisoners are people," [and] that the true social function of prisons is rehabilitation, the "adjustment" of the offender to the going achievement-orientation of the middle-class. The warden of a large middle-western prison told the author:

> I believe that ninety per cent of the men here could go out and live clean lives and become decent citizens.

There is no intention on the part of the author of this paper to denigrate the underlying ethic of the prison reformer. It is an ethic rooted in a liberal humanitarianism with its doctrines of individualism, equality of opportunity, and the idea that what is good in man can be evoked under the proper set of circumstances. It is a catholic ethic conceived to be capable of indefinite extension. Like all closed systems of ideology, the ethic tries to explain "failures" in its own terms. In the case of the criminal, it is averred that the circumstances were not right. All men really want the same things and have the same motivations. The problem, then, is to get them to see themselves in the proper perspective. Where once there was a religious-salvation metaphor, there is now a medical-psychiatric metaphor. "Criminosis" is presumably "curable," and the grammar of values and attitudes can be manipulated by the astute practitioner.

Leaving aside the question of the validity of this value system, I want to show in this paper how the formal and informal structure of a prison limits the applicability of the ethic of reform. It will be urged in this discussion that there are real sociological factors, which nullify the effectiveness of the advocates of rehabilitation not only under a preponderantly security type of administration but also under a theoretically rehabilitative type of administration.

It is becoming a sociological commonplace that any large-scale institutional structure comprises formal and informal elements, and prisons are no exception to this observation. The Freudians have emphasized that human personality can be understood only in terms of conscious and unconscious components, which are the reciprocals of behavior. And the famous man-in-the-street differentiates pejoratively between how the books say something is to run, and how it actually runs. The formal structure of a prison is an officially designated pattern involving a division of labor, rank order of status, and areas of proper jurisdiction for staff and line. In short, there is the typical chain-of-command or table-of-organization which is authoritarian, impersonal, and vested with ultimate power over the prison population.

The fact that recidivism rates remain high is commonly explained as a result of the lack of funds, the size of the institution, or the type of personnel employed. Wardens point to the slim budgets on which they are forced to operate and their genuine difficulties in securing contracts for employing convicts on anything more than a sporadic basis. Classification officers usually bemoan the inadequate formal education of the guards, heavy case loads, and the lack of "diagnostic" centers. All these factors are seen by administrative personnel as militating against the

From a paper delivered at the annual meeting of the Midwest Sociological Society, 1957. Reprinted by permission of the author.

reform of prisoners. These explanations are seen in this paper as rationalizations derived from a particular system of ideological belief. It goes without saying that these explanations are genuine to the persons who adduce them.

It is a curious phenomenon, however, that administrative personnel, who daily work with the informal structure of the inmate body, fail to perceive that the informal culture negates the above explanations. The prison cannot operate without the cooperation of inmates, who are found in jobs ranging from chief clerk in the Deputy Warden's office to the porter in the industrial plants. Needless to say, the informal structure involves differentials in status, prestige, and power. As a consequence of this division of labor, there is a system of stratification recognized by the inmate body, which horizontally cuts the population into three levels; the Big Shots, the Con-wise, and the Hoosiers.

The Big Shots consist really of three groups: the Politicians, the Strategics, and the Hoodlums.[1] First in prestige and rank are the Politicians, who work either in the offices of the Deputy Warden and the Assistant Deputy, or as hall-tenders. The manifest function of these inmates is to provide clerical help to the designated officials and to aid in the management of the cell-blocks. While it is true that such inmates perform these duties, their chief function is to supply the type of information to the officials, which will enable them to maintain security measures effectively and conveniently.

The second type of "Shot," the Strategic, is a man who has some type of skill which is valued in the prison industries, or he is a person who has known certain officials over a long period of years. A man skilled in refrigeration mechanics is obviously valuable to the ice-plant; a man who knows typing and short-hand is unquestionably valuable to the doctor in the hospital; a good book-keeper is always in demand. Because many of these men come to know officials over a good many years, they understand and rely upon one another. Such an inmate is usually delegated a good deal of authority by the "square" personnel. It is a system which works to their mutual advantage. The civilian is protected in his dealing with his inmate workers and also with respect to the higher officials. The inmate in such a position is miraculously exempt from the petty, irksome rules of the institution, in addition to getting the better accommodations and a certain amount of recognition. Frequently, such inmates can get these officials to go to bat for them when they come up for parole through both formal and informal means.

The second echelon of inmates, the Con-wise are men who are either professional criminals, or men who have "pulled" enough time so that they are, as the saying goes, "prison-wise" or "con-wise." "They do their own time in their own way," maintaining a certain distance between themselves and the officials and also between themselves and the Shots and the Hoosiers. They prefer a relative anonymity, they abide by the rules selectively, and they carefully husband their "good time" against the day of release. In short, they know the ropes, and they are rarely tripped.

The lowest stratum of the inmate population is known as the Hoosiers. This class is made up of predominantly youthful offenders, who are considered by the two higher groups as ignorant, unstable, and transient. They are the men farthest down, to be "used" and exploited perhaps, but not to be treated as equals. It is the received opinion among the two higher echelons that the Hoosier is either a potential "rat" or the kind of person who can be easily "ribbed into a riot" by the Hoodlums.

I have delayed the introduction of the Hoodlums to the *dramatis personae* of the informal structure because they are a more openly predatory type of Big Shot, who are in conflict with the other types. The Hoodlums are a small, tightly knit, exploitative group. They consider themselves the true bearers of the "prison tradition" because of their anti-administration attitudes although they actually derive their prestige from strong-arm tactics against the remainder of the population. The Hoosier is believed to be extremely susceptible to the *charisma* of the Hoodlum leaders; that is, the Hoosier is conceived to be a type who is trying to build a "penitentiary reputation."

There is no question that many incoming inmates are strictly "square-johns" in that they abound in naiveté with regard to actual prison social structure. Most new arrivals, however, even the Hoosiers, are products of reformatories with not too dissimilar informal systems. If they have served previous "hitches," they already have some idea of what Joliet, Ft. Madison, or Jefferson

[1] Prisoners speak of Politicians and Rightos. The terms Strategic and Hoodlum are the author's. Incidentally, the role of the Hoodlums will not be discussed in sequence. Their place in the informal system is more easily understood in relation to the Hoosier.

City is like.[2] Much of convict shop-talk is concerned with rating various "joints" on a scale of "tight" to "loose" and the general standard of living afforded the inmate population. There is even an Old School Tie complex, a certain loyalty to past "joints," just as many soldiers have preferences in army camps. The writer has heard men expatiate at length on the relative merits of Menard, Jackson, McAlester, and Tennessee. A prison-intellectual summed it up this way:

There is a strange loyalty to past joints. You've heard them. This joint, yah! I wouldn't even admit—that'll be the gist of the conversation—I wouldn't even admit out in the street that I was ever in this joint. No self-respecting con would ever want to be identified with this place. But let me tell you about my old *alma mater* back in Ohio. Or let me tell you about such-and-such. Back in Ohio I heard men talk about this place. Wide-open joint, nothing but good joes, anything went. You come here, it's the same set-up.

This kind of shop-talk, however, does not mean that the convict population presents a solid phalanx of opposition to the administration. Anyone who has worked in a prison for any length of time knows that the famous "prison code" is notoriously weak and easily penetrated by custodial officials. The Con-wise will tell you, "The average inmate will sell his own mother." The solidarity of inmates is limited to particular cliques, which are in continual competition with other cliques in every segment of prison life. A clique may entrench itself in the hospital, but it has to be constantly on the alert for attempts to subvert it by other groups. The leader of a three-man group in the Catholic Chapel told the author:

We've got a nice set-up here. The law never comes in here because of the Father. But don't think some of the rightos wouldn't like to get in here if they could.

Within itself the clique may be "jam up," solid, but it is utterly treacherous with regard to outside groups or individuals. The same situation obtains in the cell-blocks, which are formally under the control of custodial officials, but actually are under the management of the hall-tender and his crew. Custody relies on these groups to run a "quiet hall." In return for this service the hall-tender's clique demands and gets privileges from the cell-block officials. In fact, there is a tendency to form a mutual defense league against higher custodial personnel. Over a period of time, informal arrangements are worked out for taking care of surprise inspections, cell assignments, and for "trouble-makers." In a word, the situation is analogous to the company commander's relationship with his top non-coms.

The socialization of the inmate, then, is a process of learning the informal structure. He is necessarily more concerned with this aspect of prison life because it is the one with which he is in daily contact. The ultimate power of the administration is present, it is true; but it is the proximate power of the informal structure with which the convict must come to terms, and the "wiser" he is the more effectively he deals with it.

The formal structure of the prison is characterized by the usual "staff" and "line" conflict. The classification officers are young college graduates with a social-work ideology. They are keenly aware of their almost purely ceremonial status in the formal structure, which, given the main thrust of their beliefs, causes them to stew in either futile frustration or to adopt (among themselves) a patent cynicism. Perforce, they must accommodate themselves to the dominance of the custodial force, which they regard as incompetent, illiterate, and, at times, almost irrelevant. One director of classification, who refers to himself as a "frustrated do-gooder" and an "institutional psychopath" puts it this way:

The fact is that we are only tolerated around here. Our only job is to listen to bitches from both custody and the cons.

If these men stay in prison-work for any length of time, there is a tendency for them to get "line-ized," to adopt the attitudes of the higher echelons of custody, as illustrated by this type of shop-talk:

You know, when I came here I thought it was terrible for a man to rack a con with a club. I used to wonder just what in the hell a criminal was, but now my attitude is that with most of these guys you have to kick 'em in the ass till their teeth rattle.
Do you really think that?
Oh, I don't know. I guess they're just a poor bunch of bums. We'd act just the same in the same situation.

However, even the most "line-ized" of the caseworkers are reminded every day by both the requirements of custody and the informal power of the Shots that they have only a ceremonial function in the prison. These quotidian barbs of reality leave the caseworker rotating about his skewered self-esteem in a state of futile ambivalence.

As for the custodial force, it is stratified in much the same way as the convict population. At the lower reaches of it, there is the same transiency

[2] [Editors' Note: This report is based upon a study of a mid-western prison.]

which is characteristic of the Hoosier level. The higher echelons of the line, however, are in effective control of the prison; they really run the institution along with their convict allies, the Big Shots. In fact, these two groups form a kind of nucleus, a cadre, which has common interests with regard to both the top administrative officials and the remainder of the inmate population. Directors of Corrections, Wardens, heads of industry, farms, and classification may come and go; the cadre outlasts them all. The cadre must deal with them; it must accommodate its interests to their demands; it must even, on occasion, surrender some of its prerogatives to them. But the cadre knows from experience that the "old system" will re-assert itself. After all, cadre-men have trained generation after generation of cons and square-johns.

What we have described thus far of the prison structure is the fact that on both sides of the line between administration and convict, there are congeries of groups with differential functions, power, and prestige. The formal structure is loosely co-ordinated and is characterized by transiency at both the upper and lower echelons, poor communication, and dependency upon certain segments of the inmate population for the smooth operation of the prison. The convict population is a largely transient population, foundering in a state of *anomie*, and it is dominated by relatively small cliques, which perpetuate their power as a means of self-preservation and even aggrandizement. At the operational center is a cadre, made up of both formal and informal complements, which locks the institution into a static equilibrium.

If the above analysis is approximately correct, I think we can then understand certain behavioral consequences noted by many observers in the field of penology. If we may define a community as a legitimate hierarchy of status emanating from a relatively stable matrix of consensus, the prison cannot be termed a community. A prison in its nature exemplifies a social system based on a maximum of compulsion, the corollary of which is a minimum of consensus. Now the compulsory segregation of random and transient individuals under an impersonal authority does not and cannot create consensus. The formal and informal power of the prison can compel conformity to its demands, but it cannot evoke unconscious and voluntary assent to them. By putting a man in such a situation, we are in effect locating him in a social system which is endemically anomic.

If we conceive of a system with a high degree of consensus, we may correctly infer that spontaneous, natural *role playing* will obtain within it. In an anomic system, however, role playing will be replaced by *role calculation*. Role calculation, as contrasted with role playing, we shall define as the conscious and deliberate simulation of conformity to the demands of power defined as real but not as moral to the persons under its control. With respect to the ultimate and proximate structure of power, the person conforms or appears to conform only to evade penalties or to maximize his own individual interest.

Role calculation is imminent in any situation of competition and conflict; as the saying goes, "all's fair in love and war." Conflict and hostility necessarily entail the expendability of unguarded sentiment, which is the penumbra of role playing in a system of consensus. Role calculation, as hereby conceived, is centered on interests stripped of spontaneous reciprocity. The man who has been through the process of arrest, who has bargained with prosecutors, who has accommodated himself to the informal structure of a prison, grows increasingly adept in the art of taking the measure of people with whom he has to deal. The term "deal" is appropriate because such relationships are almost purely symbiotic. Whatever the individual origins of his behavior may be, he becomes increasingly sophisticated in the art of dissimulation.

A person who has been habituated to a situation of *anomie* will perforce find moral appeals strange, if not, indeed, ludicrous. Even the square-john type of inmate, who has been catapulted into a pariah status, will discover that naked calculation rules the interactive process. If he is to survive, he must above all be shrewd. It is a case of "Jack be nimble, Jack be quick." The two most frequent words in his vocabulary will be "con" and "use," the reciprocals of the ethic of expediency. Nothing will ever be taken at its face value; everything will be suspect. As the process of socialization progresses, this emphasis becomes elaborated into an economy of distilled wariness. Needless to say, the sentiments are not completely erased, but they are carefully rationed to a chosen few. The inmate can be "jam up" only within a narrow horizon, with a buddy, or perhaps a clique. Even in this instance, however, his sense of security is easily and quickly undermined by habitual suspicion. The unwitting taking-for-grantedness, which allows people to play roles in a system of consensus, atrophies and disappears. The inmate does not play a role because he cannot. The calculus of interest having ravaged the sentiments, he feels abnormal, less than human. In a word, he is reduced to the Hobbesian minimum.

From interview material obtained over a period of months the following will illustrate the working of role calculation. A Negro lifer, speaking of the Hoodlums who had killed a "rat," stated:

There isn't one of them who hasn't ratted off himself. None of them is above suspicion.

The Protestant chaplain said matter-of-factly:

They'll con you, they'll use you every way they can. I've learned by bitter experience.

A three-time loser:

In the short three or four days I worked on the third floor of the hospital—I was trying to think the other night in my cell, how many men came to me to tell me that so-and-so was a rat. Now the man who tells me that, I watch. I've been working on the fourth floor since then, and I have yet to find a reliable man. I haven't yet found out what a good convict is in this joint. It's only within a clique that they're jam up, and even there you have to watch. That's why I prefer to stay isolated on the T.B. ward. I've learned to do my own time in my own way.

Vis-à-vis the square-john, especially the "sociologist," the inmate calculates his role with consummate skill. As many observers of the Negro have noted, he possesses a definite ability to conform consciously to the white man's stereotype of him. The white man has power over you, therefore flatter him, manipulate him, use him, but "get to" him at all events. In a somewhat analogous situation, missionaries in China were familiar with the "rice Christian." A two-time loser, a latter-day rice-Christian, in assessing the middle-class missionaries of "rehabilitation," stated:

I've got a ten year rap. I don't like this joint so I conform to their petty rules. If they want me to swallow all their crap about rehabilitation I'll do it—if it'll get me a parole.

A casual conversation with a lifer, who has spent thirteen years in prison, led to the following observation:

You see a convict has nothin' else to do but study the square-john. The square-john has got all kinds of things on his mind, his family, his friends, what he's goin' to do tonight, things like that. But a con, he's got nothin' else to do but think and study. He gets sharp at sizin' people up. He finds out a man's likes and dislikes, the way his mind works, is the way he thinks. You can tell by all kinds of things, the way he handles himself, the way he walks, his gestures, almost anything about him. So he knows how to act with this particular fellow. He may act different with another guy. When he talks to classification he talks one way. When he talks to a guard he talks another way. What a con is interested in is doin' easy time and gettin' out. And that's why he does it.

A nine-time loser related the following to a group of inmates among whom the author found himself:

One time I was pulling time in a Federal joint. Well, you know how it is, they called me up for a parole interview. What's the matter with you, Smith, they said. You seem to be intelligent, why can't you stay out of these places. You know, they just kept at it. But one of them gave me a lead. Is it drink, he said. Right away I saw an opening, so I gave 'em a song and dance about bein' an alcoholic, how I couldn't stay off the stuff, you know, down the line. Well, they said, maybe you ought to be interviewed by the psychiatrist. I put up a little resistance to that, but at last I gave in. Right away I went to the prison library where I worked and got out all the books on psychiatry they had. Well, you know the psychiatrist is a busy man so he asked me the questions I figured he was going to ask, and I gave him the answers he wanted. Believe it or not, I made a parole out of that deal.

If this process of role calculation as a response to an anomic social structure is operative among inmates, as I think it is, it is only logical that its effects will envelop the square-john. Line officials who deal with inmates everyday soon learn that conniving is elaborated to an almost incredible degree. The "contrast conception" which constitutes the stereotype of the convict and by which the line defines its relationship to him is not perceived as the result of a process of anomic interaction. It is "just the way they are." Hence the enormous contempt which these officials feel toward those "immature college boys" in the classification office.

The staff is only too keenly aware of the line's attitude, but it is the staff's continuing relationships with inmates which "line-izes" them. Caseworkers begin to say, "You know after all some of these guards are right about these characters." Their conflict with the guards progressively becomes a conflict involving the relative status or importance of their particular bailiwicks in the formal structure. It is a rare guard who becomes "staff-ized," but the reverse process is progressively common the longer the classification officer works in the prison. His feelings of futility and ambivalence continue to plague the remaining shreds of his social-work conscience, and he finally says:

> You and I know there isn't any solution to crime. The only thing you can do is to keep those who are dangerous to society. The man rehabilitates himself or it isn't done.

This discussion has attempted to delineate the formal and informal structure of a prison and the unintended social consequences which result from this type of institutional complex. That the formal and informal aspects of different prisons are different is not in question here, but the author believes that there are generic social processes operative in all of them which stem from common structural features. These characteristics may be stated in the following manner:

1. The formal structure is authoritarian, impersonal, and vested with ultimate power over the prison population.
2. The formal structure is dependent on an informal structure of power.
3. The actual operation of the prison is vested in a cadre, consisting of higher line officials and a convict élite.
4. The socialization of the inmate centers around the learning of the techniques of accommodation to the system of proximate power.
5. The institutional complex wields power, but it does not create consensus.
6. Role playing is displaced by role calculation.
7. Role calculation vitiates the goal of rehabilitation.

If the above analysis is valid, the problem of prisons as reformative institutions must be cast into new terms. Penologists have begun to emphasize better recreational programs, more vocational training, and "social education," but what this all amounts to from an inmate's point of view is a higher standard of living. The assumption of modern penology is that a higher standard of living will cause the inmate to redefine his self-conception so that he will cease to be a violator. The problem actually is one of consciously creating consensus under the most adverse circumstances: that of compulsion. The writer is skeptical about the consciously planned structuring of consensus, but it seems that it must be attempted if prisons are to be anything more than hostelries for an anomic population.

selection 23 The Effect of Role-Playing Experience on Role-Playing Ability

JOHN H. MANN AND CAROLA H. MANN

In recent years the use of role playing as a means of training and therapy has become increasingly popular. There have, however, been relatively few attempts to validate role-playing techniques. A recent review (Mann, 1956) of experimental evaluations of role playing has concluded that the majority of such studies simply attempts to demonstrate that role playing produces discernible attitudinal or behavioral changes. Few of these studies have been concerned with testing the assumptions that are made by role-playing practitioners to justify and explain their use of role playing. These assumptions are important because they help to provide a theoretical rationale for role playing and to relate role-playing procedures to role theory. A review of role-playing literature suggests that these assumptions can be formulated in the following terms:

1. Role-playing experience increases role-playing ability. (Role-playing ability is defined in terms of the size of the role repertoire and the effectiveness of the role enactments.)
2. Role-playing experience increases interpersonal adjustment. (Interpersonal adjustment is defined in terms of role-playing ability and the situational appropriateness of the roles that are performed.)

Abridged from *Sociometry*, 1959, **22**, 64–74. Reprinted by permission of the authors and the American Sociological Association.

3. Role-playing ability is positively related to interpersonal adjustment.

The present study is limited to a consideration of the first assumption. Among role theorists this assumption has found neither support nor rejection.

HYPOTHESES

In formulating the specific hypotheses of this study the authors were faced with the problem that the extent to which role-playing ability might be affected by role-playing experience is not clearly specified in role-playing literature. The relationship between role-playing experience and role-playing ability could take at least three different forms:

First, role playing a specific role might improve the performance of that role when it is enacted again at a later date. This assumption is made by trainers who teach individuals to take or improve their performance of a given role such as salesman, nurse, or foreman (Bavelas, 1957; Harrow and Haas, 1947).

Second, the performance of a number of roles in a given setting might improve all role performances in that setting. This assumption is made by practitioners (Moreno, 1953) who train professional role players (auxiliary egos). Training in the enactment of a variety of roles in the general context of the role-playing session is said to enable the role player to enact effectively any role that he may be called on to perform in such a session.

Third, role playing a limited number of roles in a series of role-playing sessions might improve an individual's ability to take other roles in other settings that had not been portrayed in the role-playing sessions. This assumption is made by practitioners who use role playing as a therapeutic method (Kline, 1957; Lawlor, 1957). Since the role therapist cannot anticipate all the life situations his client may encounter, he needs to assume that the enactment of certain roles in role-playing sessions will affect and improve his client's role performance in life situations not dealt with in the course of role therapy.

In order to determine whether role-playing experience affects role-playing ability in the various ways suggested above, the following hypotheses were formulated:

1. The enactment of a role in role-playing sessions improves the future enactment of that role.
2. The performance of a number of roles in a series of role-playing sessions improves role enactments in future role-playing sessions.
3. The performance of a number of roles in a series of role-playing sessions increases the number and improves the effectiveness of role enactments in a situation that was not specifically enacted in the role-playing sessions.

It is important to note that while hypothesis 1 is simply equivalent to the common sense notion that "practice makes perfect," this is not the case with hypotheses 2 and 3. These latter hypotheses are concerned with role-playing ability as it is generalized over situations. The existence of such a general ability, as indicated by the findings of Mouton, Bell, and Blake (1956), and the possibility that it is amenable to improvement through training, which was tested in the present study, are both of crucial importance for the formulation of a much needed sociologically oriented learning theory. Such a theory must consider the general ability to perform roles as the limiting condition imposed by individual personality and experience on social learning, and describe the procedures which are conducive to the development of this general ability. The implications of hypotheses 2 and 3, are therefore, more broad than may immediately be apparent, since they relate to important aspects of such a theory.

METHODS

Instruments

Hypotheses 1 and 2 were tested by means of a 5-point *Role-enactment Rating Scale* that was used by role-playing subjects to rate their own role performances as well as that of other group members on the effectiveness with which they took their respective roles. The rating scale used the categories of "fair," "good," "very good," "excellent," and "superb." In order to permit further testing of hypothesis 2, a 5-point *Role-playing Rating Scale* was used by judges to rate tape recordings of role-playing scenes on the "over-all effectiveness of the role enactments." The rating scale used the categories "below average," "average," "above average," "high," and "very high."

In order to test hypothesis 3, observers used a 5-point *Quality of Role Performance Rating Scale* to evaluate the "effectiveness of the subject's role performances" in a situational test. The rating categories used were identical with those utilized in the *Role-playing Rating Scale*. In addition, judges who listened to tape recordings of the situational test used a *Role Behavior List* to count the number of roles taken by the subjects. This list was based on Benne and Sheats' (1948) analysis of roles frequently taken in small discussion groups.

Subjects

The experimental sample consisted of 96 subjects drawn at random from a graduate course in education. Thirty-three of the subjects were male, 63 were female. The median age of the subjects was twenty-nine; the age range extended from nineteen to fifty-three years. Fifty-five of the subjects were white and 41 were Negro.

Procedure

The 96 subjects were divided into two groups of 48 subjects each, one group hereafter referred to as experimental group, the other as control group. Assignment to the groups was made by means of stratified random sampling that controlled for race and sex of subjects.

The experimental procedure was divided into the following three phases:

1. Both experimental and control groups were randomly subdivided into six groups of eight each. During the first two days of the experiment, all twelve groups were given a situational test that consisted of a 15-minute discussion of the topic "The Adequacy of Grades as a Measure of Ability in Graduate Study." Two observers rated the role behavior of each of the group members using the *Quality of Role Performance Rating Scale.*

2. After the first two days the 48 members of the experimental group were reassigned to groups of eight. The new assignment was made by means of stratified random sampling with race and sex again controlled. An additional restriction on random assignment was made to ensure that not more than two subjects who had been together in the situational test were in the same group under the new assignment. The same procedure was followed for the control group.

During this second phase each eight-man group of subjects met four times a week for one hour over a period of three weeks. The experimental groups were engaged in role-playing activity; three of the control groups met as discussion groups that were free to discuss whatever they wished; the remaining three control groups met as study groups to discuss assigned readings. Both the discussion and the study groups were planned as a control for the influence of the graduate course in which all the subjects participated and for the effect of group member interaction which by itself might produce certain changes in role behavior. The study groups were furthermore used as a control for task orientation.

An observer was present at each group meeting. He kept a running account of the meeting and ascertained that group members carried out their respective activities. Observers were rotated every three sessions in order to randomize any effect that their personalities might have had on the group.

During the first group meeting the subjects received instructions for their respective group activities. Role players were given some printed material about the nature and use of role playing. They were also given a demonstration of how role playing could be used and how they were expected to organize their hourly meetings. Discussion group members were encouraged to discuss subjects that came up in the general lecture session of the graduate course they were attending. Study group members were instructed to select six books from a book list issued in the general course and to discuss these books in their meetings.

The three group activities were planned so as not to require assigned leadership. Therefore the problem of distinguishing between the effects of (a) the leader's personality, (b) the leader's competence, and (c) the group activity itself did not arise in the interpretation of results.

3. At the conclusion of phase two the groups formed in the first phase of the experiment were reconstituted and the procedure described in that phase was repeated.

Procedure in Experimental Groups

In order to permit all role-playing subjects equal participation in role playing, each role-playing group was subdivided into two groups of four. This also ensured the presence of an audience for each role-playing scene since only one of the subgroups was actively engaged in role playing during any given role-playing scene. The initial subgroup assignments were made at random; they were changed from day to day so that each member spent approximately the same amount of time with each other member in role playing.

During the last 20 minutes of each meeting, subgroup assignments were rotated and the subjects in the new subgroups were asked to plan a role-playing situation for the following day. They were requested to fill out a Role Plan on which they had to identify what role each subgroup member was planning to take and the nature of the situation that was to be enacted. These Role Plans were given to the observer at the end of the session. At the beginning of each meeting each subgroup of four was allowed about 20 minutes for presenting its role-playing scene, so that there were two role-playing scenes each day, taking about 40 minutes. After each role-playing situation group members were asked to fill out the *Role-enactment Rating Scale* on which they rated the roles that had just been performed.

RESULTS AND DISCUSSION

A comparison of ratings received by role players on the *Role-enactment Rating Scale* for two different portrayals of the same role furnished the data for testing hypothesis 1. While group members were free to choose the roles they wished to play, they tended to repeat at least one role enactment during the course of the role-playing

TABLE 1 RATINGS OF ROLE PERFORMANCE OF THE SAME ROLE PERFORMED AT TWO DIFFERENT ROLE-PLAYING SESSIONS
($N = 47$)

	Pre		Post		
Criterion variable	Mean	SD	Mean	SD	Difference
Self-ratings	2.74	.65	3.13	.81	.39*
Role players' ratings of fellow players	3.13	.55	3.35	.61	.22*
Audience ratings of role players	3.06	.52	3.40	.64	.34*

* Significant at .05 level, by t test.

sessions. For each repeated role the difference between an individual's self-ratings, between the ratings made by fellow role players, and between the ratings made by audience members were analyzed. Separate analysis of the three sets of ratings was necessary because Rosenberg (1952) has reported that an active role player's perception of a role-playing scene differs from that of an observer. Analysis of the three types of ratings, as summarized in Table 1, indicated that the differences were found to be significant. The hypothesis was therefore supported.

Hypothesis 2 was tested by analyzing the significance of the difference between average ratings received by role players on the *Role-enactment Rating Scale* during the first three and the last three role-playing sessions. A threefold test of the hypothesis consisted again of an analysis of self-ratings, ratings by other role players, and ratings by audience members. The differences of the three sets of ratings were significant, as shown in Table 2, indicating that role players perceived a general improvement in role performance regardless of the roles performed. However, the subjects' ratings may have reflected expectation of improvement with continued role-playing experience rather than actual improvement in role-playing ability. In order to test the validity of group members' perceptions, five judges used the *Role-playing Rating Scale* to rate the quality of role performance in early and late sessions of each role-playing group from tape recordings. Since the judges did not know whether a given recording was made at the beginning or at the end of the experiment, their ratings could not be influenced by expectation of improvement. Analysis of the differences between the ratings of early and late sessions, as given in Table 2, indicated that the differences were significant, thus substantiating the validity of subjects' perceptions. Hypothesis 2 was therefore supported by the data.

Hypothesis 3 was tested in two parts. First, improvement in quality of role performance was determined by analyzing the significance of the

TABLE 2 PRE- AND POST-RATINGS OF ROLE PERFORMANCE IN ROLE-PLAYING SESSIONS
($N = 47$)

	Pre		Post		
Criterion variable	Mean	SD	Mean	SD	Difference
Role players' self-ratings	2.68	.63	3.10	.86	.42*
Role players' ratings of fellow role players	3.16	.50	3.36	.63	.20*
Audience ratings of role players	3.08	.53	3.31	.64	.23*
Judges' ratings of tape recordings	1.86	.63	2.78	.60	.92*

* Significant at .05 level, by t test.

TABLE 3 PRE-POST DIFFERENCE SCORES AND POST-RATINGS OF QUALITY OF ROLE PERFORMANCE IN THE SITUATIONAL TEST

	Experimental role playing ($N = 45$)		Control: Discussion ($N = 21$)		Control: Study ($N = 24$)		Difference between groups		
	Mean	SD	Mean	SD	Mean	SD	R–D	R–S	D–S
Pre-post difference score	1.04	.83	.47	.81	.16	.71	.57*	.88*	.31
Post score	3.19	1.03	2.71	.95	2.42	.98	.48*	.77*	.29

* Significant at .05 level, by *t* test.

TABLE 4 PRE-POST DIFFERENCE SCORES AND POST-SCORES OF NUMBER OF ROLES TAKEN IN THE SITUATIONAL TEST

	Experimental role playing ($N = 45$)		Control* discussion and Study ($N = 45$)		Difference between groups
	Mean	SD	Mean	SD	
Pre-post difference score	6.62	22.86	1.64	8.87	4.98†
Post score	14.80	40.25	8.44	22.60	6.36†

* Discussion and study group members were combined since judges listening to tape recordings of the situational test could not distinguish between them.
† Significant at .05 level, by *t* test.

difference between pre- and post-experimental ratings made by observers using the *Quality of Role Performance Rating Scale* in the situational tests. Interrater reliability of observers was found to be .62. Change in the performance of role players was compared with the corresponding change in the control groups that also took the situational tests. Observers were unaware of the group to which the subjects belonged.

Second, increase in number of roles was tested by comparing the number of roles taken by the subjects in the pre- and post-experimental situational tests. Interrater reliability of judges using the *Role Behavior List* was found to be .88. Change in the number of roles taken by role players in the situational tests was compared to the corresponding change among the control subjects.

The statistical treatment of the comparisons of role players and control subjects was designed to determine not only whether experimental and control groups differed significantly in amount of change, but also whether they differed significantly in their scores at the end of the experiment. The latter analysis was necessary to ensure that significance of difference in amount of change was not an artifact due to a regression effect. A regression effect could be responsible for a significantly greater change in the group with the lower initial rating; it could not, however, produce a significantly higher final rating for that group. Since experimental and control groups differed significantly both in amount of change and in final scores, as indicated in Tables 3 and 4, hypothesis 3 was supported by the data.

[In summary], since the three hypotheses of this study were supported by the data, the proposition that role-playing experience increases role-playing ability was substantiated in terms of one specific role enacted on two different occasions, in terms of a variety of roles enacted in several role-playing sessions, and in terms of roles enacted in a situation outside the context of role-playing sessions.

In order to interpret the findings of this study it is important to note that the experimental subjects were assigned arbitrarily to role-playing groups. Furthermore, no role-playing expert was provided to aid role players in their activity. These limitations, imposed on the subjects for the sake of experimental rigor, probably tended to reduce the effectiveness of role playing; they therefore add weight to the positive findings obtained in this study.

REFERENCES

Bavelas, A., 1947. Role playing in management training. *Sociometry*, **1**, 183–191.

Benne, K., and Sheats, P., 1948. Functional roles of group members. *Journal of Social Issues*, **4**, 41–50.

Harrow, Gertrude S., and Haas, R. B., 1947. Psychodrama in the guidance clinic. *Sociatry*, **1**, 70–81.

Kline, S., 1957. Psychodrama for mental hospitals. *Journal of Clinical Psychopathology*, **8**, 817–825.

Lawlor, G., 1947. Role therapy. *Sociatry*, **1**, 51–55.

Mann, J. H., 1956. Experimental evaluations of role playing. *Psychological Bulletin*, **53**, 227–234.

Moreno, J. L., 1953. *Who shall survive?* (Rev. ed.). New York: Beacon.

Mouton, Jane S., Bell, R. L., Jr., and Blake, R., 1956. Role playing skill and sociometric peer status. *Group Psychotherapy*, **9**, 7–17.

Rosenberg, Pearl P., 1952. Experimental analysis of psychodrama. Unpublished doctoral dissertation, Radcliffe College.

selection 24 Prediction of Small Group Role Behavior from Personality Variables

WALTER R. BORG

This study explores the degree to which a person's role in a small group problem solving seminar can be predicted from a battery of group administered tests which attempt to measure skills and personality characteristics observed to be important in small group situation. The specific hypothesis to be tested is that a person's scores on tests selected to give measures of assertiveness, rigidity, self orientation, and sociability will predict his role in a problem solving seminar.

METHOD

Subjects

The *S*s included 819 Air Force Majors and Lieutenant colonels in the Command and Staff School of the Air University, Class 1957. They were divided into 60 seminars of 12 to 14 officers each, and worked in the same seminar group for a period of two and one-half months. A large portion of the curriculum of the school is devoted to problem solving activities and discussions in the seminar groups. The problems dealt with by the seminars vary considerably in nature but for the most part, involve practical Air Force problems of a sort that might be encountered by a Wing Staff.

Variables and Measures

The first step in the research was the selection of tests to go into the predictor battery, which was to contain tests to measure variables related to patterns of behavior that had been found in observations of small group activity. A careful survey was made in order to identify variables that had occurred repeatedly in studies based on observations of small group interaction (Bass, 1951; Bass, McGehee, Hawkins, Young, and Gebel, 1953; Carter, 1951, 1954; Carter, Haythorn, and Howell, 1950; Carter, Haythorn, Shriver, and Lanzetta, 1951; Cattell and Stice, 1953; Haythorn, 1953; Sakoda, 1952; Schutz, 1955). The variables that appeared most frequently in these studies were:

Sociability. This variable, under different names, such as Personal Orientation, Group Sociability, and Social Adjustment, has been reported frequently in studies concerned with small group interaction.

Self orientation. Variations of this measure have appeared repeatedly under such names as Power

From the *Journal of Abnormal and Social Psychology*, 1960, **60**, 112–116. Reprinted by permission of the author and the American Psychological Association.

Orientation (Schutz, 1955) and Individual Prominence (Carter, 1954; Carter and Nixon, 1949).

Rigidity. Rigidity and related variables such as Authoritarianism, Conformity, and Dogmatism have been investigated in a number of relevant studies of small group behavior (Greer, 1955; Haythorn, Couch, Haefner, Langham, and Carter, 1956; Lippitt, 1940; McCurdy and Eber, 1954; Medalia, 1955).

Assertiveness. This variable has been employed with considerable success by Schutz (1955) and is somewhat similar to variables employed in other small group research such as Forceful Leadership, Surgency (Cattell, 1951), Ascendance (Bass et al., 1953), Physical Energy (Sakoda, 1952), and Individual Prominence (Carter, 1954).

The test selected to supply predictive measures of these characteristics included the following.

The FIRO test. This test was developed by Schutz (1955) and has been used by him with considerable success for predicting leadership behavior and organizing compatible groups. The form of the test employed in this research consisted of seven items, each of which was regarded as a separate score on the suggestion of Schutz. These items attempt to measure degree of power orientation, as compared with personal orientation and degree of assertiveness.

The California F Scale, Form 40. This form of the F scale employs the items that were found to be most discriminating in the original research at the University of California (Adorno, Frenkel-Brunswik, Levinson, and Sanford, 1950).

The Anxiety to Achieve Battery. This battery consisted of six group tests from the Cattell Objective Analytic Personality Battery (Cattell, 1955) and yielded a single factor score.

The Social Extroversion Score, from the Inventory of Factors STDCR (Guilford, 1945).

Eight factor scores from the Guilford Opinion Inventory (*Guilford*, 1951). This test was developed by Guilford from his factor analysis of the "interests" of Air Force officers. Factors used included: need for variety, orderliness, need for attention, physical drive, aggression, resistance to restriction, cultural conformity, self-reliance. The entire predictor battery yielded 18 scores.

Derivation of Factor Scores

After the battery was administered, results were subjected to centroid factor analysis. A total of four orthogonal rotations were made, yielding four factors. Rotated factor loadings may be found in Table 1. The factors were interpreted as follows:

Factor 1, Assertiveness, was loaded heavily on Schutz's Assertiveness scores, as well as Guilford's Physical Drive score and Social Extroversion score. A separate Sociability Factor, mentioned as an important variable in several studies, did not emerge. If additional Sociability measures had been included in the predictor battery, the factor may have emerged or may have loaded under Assertiveness as did Guilford's Social Extraversion score.

TABLE 1 ROTATED FACTOR LOADINGS EMPLOYED IN DEVELOPING WEIGHTED FACTOR SCORES

Variable	Loading
Factor 1: Assertiveness	
Schutz G-H, Assertiveness	.61
Schutz 5, Assertiveness	.66
Schutz 6, Success in Attaining Leadership	.57
Schutz 7, High Self-Estimate of Leadership Ability	.43
S Factor from Guilford's STDCR, Social Extroversion	.58
P Factor from Guilford's Opinion Inventory, High Level of Physical Drive	.36
Factor 2: Power Orientation	
Schutz A-B, Power Orientation	.43
G Factor from Guilford's Opinion Inventory, Self-Reliance	.40
Factor 3: Rigidity	
California F Scale, Authoritarianism	.56
S_0 Factor from Guilford's Opinion Inventory, Tendency toward Orderliness	.39
F Factor from Guilford's Opinion Inventory, Cultural Conformity	.53
Factor 4: Aggressive Nonconformity	
V_0 Factor from Guilford's Opinion Inventory, Need for Variety	.45
L Factor from Guilford's Opinion Inventory, Need for Attention	.54
Q Factor from Guilford's Opinion Inventory, Aggression	.62
M Factor from Guilford's Opinion Inventory, Resistance to Restriction	.43

Factor 2, Power Orientation, had loadings on Schutz's Power Orientation score, as well as Guilford's Self-Reliance variable.

Factor 3, Rigidity, seems clearly indicative of Rigidity, being loaded most heavily on the California F scale. Other significant loadings include Guilford's Cultural Conformity score and Orderliness score.

Factor 4, Aggressive Nonconformity, is more difficult to interpret. The heaviest loading on this factor was in Guilford's Aggression scores. Other variables loading on this factor included Guilford's Need for Variety score, Need for Attention score, and Resistance to Restriction score. Several interpretations of this factor were considered. In some respects it appeared quite similar to Cattell's Hypomanic Aggression. Another possible interpretation was that the factor was indicative of social immaturity, while a third interpretation was that it reflected frustration in the military environment. For several reasons, an interpretation of the factor as Aggressive Nonconformity seemed most plausible. First, the heavy weighting of Aggression and Need for Attention seemed to point in this direction. The loadings on Need for Variety and Resistance to Restriction suggest a negative reaction to the restrictions and conformity demands found in the military environment. Observations of the Command and Staff School, secondly, reveal that a significant number of students display overt aggressive attitudes towards the school. Some students also displayed considerable negativism concerning the testing itself. This negativism might well have been reflected in some of the test scores where it could have come to the surface. For example, some of the items on the Aggression test, such as those advocating punitive action, could give the *S* an indirect means of expressing aggression or negativism aroused by the testing situation. Weiss' [and Fine's] (1956) research dealing with the effect of the individual's immediate mood on attitude measures indicates that the individual's mood may be reflected to a significant degree in items where aggression can be displayed.

Weighted factor scores were computed including all variables loading over .30 and most heavily loaded on the given factor. These personality factor scores constituted the predictors against which to compare small group role scores (see Table 1).

Small Group Role Scores

The small group role scores were based on two peer nominations completed in the second and fifth weeks after the groups were organized. The first peer nomination contained six brief paragraphs describing typical small group behavior patterns. These paragraphs described popular-social behavior, good followers, assertive behavior, rigid behavior, creative behavior, and leadership. Each seminar member nominated the person (by code number) who best fitted each description and checked a five-point scale to indicate the degree to which the selected individual fitted the description. Each seminar member received a score for each of the six roles which was the sum his nominations weighted for degree of fit. These scores were then converted to standard scores.

The second peer nomination used the same six role descriptions but required the individual to select three seminar members most fitting the description and three least fitting the description. The individual's score for each role was the algebraic sum of his best fit and least fit nominations. Scores on the second peer nomination were converted to standard scores and combined with first peer nomination scores to give six composite role scores for each *S*.

RESULTS

In order to determine the degree to which the personality factor scores predicted small group role scores, samples of individuals who had made either high or low role scores were selected. The four individuals in each seminar who received the highest scores on a given role were selected as well as the four individuals with the lowest role scores. These cases were further screened to eliminate individuals from the top group who were not at least .6σ above the mean on both peer nominations and eliminating individuals from the bottom group who were not at least .6σ below the mean on both peer nominations. Thus, the persons chosen were not only at the extreme within their group but were at the extreme with respect to the entire sample on the role score under consideration.

A total of 24 specific hypotheses were then developed. The relationship of each of the four predictor factors to each of the six small group roles was hypothesized to be either positive, negative, or zero (see Table 2) based upon psychological theory and previous research results. Fourteen of these hypotheses were supported by the data. In all, 12 of the 24 widespread biserial correlations computed between the small group roles and the personality factors were significant at the .01 level.

It may be seen, however, in Table 2 that although many of the correlations were significant

TABLE 2 CORRELATIONS BETWEEN PREDICTOR FACTORS AND SMALL GROUP ROLE SCORES

Factor Scores	Popular-Social 1	Good Follower 2	Assertive 3	Rigid 4	Creative 5	Leader 6
1. Assertive	.245*	−.221*†	.422*†	.216*†	.423*†	.389*†
2. Power Orientation	−.044	.066	.012†	.008†	.020†	.020
3. Rigidity	.065†	.026†	−.114*	.012	−.176*†	−.158*†
4. Aggressive Nonconformity	.108	−.060	.141*†	−.020	.207*†	.175

* Significant beyond .01 level.
† Results as hypothesized.

TABLE 3 CORRELATIONS BETWEEN DIFFERENT PEER ROLES ON THE SECOND RATING

Variable	1	2	3	4	5	6
1. Popular-social	.000	.139	.255	−.348	.264	.252
2. Good Follower	.139	.000	−.251	−.404	.065	.105
3. Assertive	.255	—.251	.000	.452	.710	.599
4. Rigid	−.348	−.404	.452	.000	.207	.177
5. Creative	.264	.065	.710	.207	.000	.817
6. Leader	.252	.105	.599	.177	.817	.000

they were too small to permit prediction of the role of a given individual from his personality scores. By far the most promising of the predictor scores is Factor 1, Assertiveness. This score correlated significantly with all six role scores and yielded correlations around .40 with Assertiveness, Creativity, and Leadership roles. As Table 3 indicates, these three roles are moderately intercorrelated, suggesting that they are measuring a single broad leadership role. A combination of these three role scores correlates .46 with Factor 1. This correlation is sufficiently high to permit reasonably good selection for small group leadership if it is established that this role is stable from situation to situation.

DISCUSSION

The results shown in Table 2 generally support the findings of earlier research. Several studies have been reported that are concerned with relationships between personality and small group behavior. Some of these have analyzed small group observational data so as to yield personality factors. Some have explored relationships between peer or supervisor evaluations and small group behavior. Only a few, however, have attempted to predict small group behavior from personality test scores.

Leadership ratings of 20 sorority girls in a leaderless group discussion situation were compared with their scores on the Rorschach, Guilford-Zimmerman Temperament Survey and F scale by Bass, et al. (1953). In one study of this type Bass et al. found no significant results with the F scale, but did find that Ascendence and Sociability scores on the Guilford-Zimmerman and High Verbal Output on the Rorschach were significantly correlated with Leadership ratings. The Rorschach result is in all likelihood an artifact of Bass's LGD rating system, which depends to a considerable degree on Verbal Output (Bass, 1951). The correlation between Ascendency and Leadership in Bass's study, however, is almost identical to the correlation between Assertiveness and Leadership found in the research reported in this paper.

In another study of small group leadership (Cattell and Stice, 1953) leaders in 34 groups were compared in terms of scores on the 16 PF test. He found four variables that differentiated between leaders and nonleaders at the .05 level. These were Super Ego Strength, Adventurousness, Self Confidence, and High Self-Sentiment Formation. These variables, as described by Cattell, are similar in many respects to the Assertiveness and Power Orientation factors used as predictors in this paper. Richardson and Hanawalt (1944) compared two types of leaders and nonleaders on the basis of their scores on the Bernreuter Personality Inventory. They found their leader groups to be more dominant, extraverted, and self-sufficient than the nonleaders.

Thus, the few studies that have been done, despite the use of different personality measures, different leadership measures, and different types of *S*s, all agree to a considerable extent that leaders are significantly more assertive, self-confident, and extraverted than nonleaders.

Studies employing other personality variables as predictors of small group roles are much less conclusive.

Several workers have employed the F scale and related measures in small group research with varying results. The rigidity factor used in the research reported in this paper was correlated negatively to the variables in the broad leadership role, but the correlations, although significant, are too low to have much meaning. Some work has indicated that authoritarian leaders function effectively in authoritarian groups (McCurdy and

Eber, 1954). There is also evidence that different types of individuals emerge as leaders in authoritarian and equalitarian groups (Haythorn et al., 1956; Adorno et al., 1950). Some work has demonstrated a positive relationship between Authoritarian Leadership and Group Cohesiveness (Medalia, 1955), while other research has found a negative relationship between these variables (Lippitt, 1940). Unlike Assertiveness, which appears to be an important leadership variable in most groups, the importance of authoritarianism varies greatly with the group, the task, and the leader.

Four of Schutz's items loaded heavily in the Assertiveness factor and one in the Power Orientation factor identified in this research. The results of Schutz's experimental battery, particularly the Assertiveness items, were impressive but indicated a need for further development. Schutz's scores have rather low reliability as they are each based on only one item. The items aimed at measuring Assertiveness were found to correlate with each other from .19 to .47. Items measuring Power vs. Personal Orientation, however, correlated with each other −.09 to +.09, indicating little common variance. As Schutz's technique becomes more highly developed, the Power Orientation variable might become useful in role prediction.

SUMMARY AND CONCLUSIONS

A sample of 819 Air Force officers was administered a test battery designed to predict the individual's role in small group situations. This battery was factor analyzed, yielding four factors: Assertiveness, Power Orientation, Rigidity, and Aggressive Nonconformity. The sample was then divided into 60 small groups of 12 to 14 members and rated with respect to six small group roles. Twenty-four widespread biserial correlations were computed between the four predictor factors and the six small group roles. Twelve of these correlations were significant at the .01 level. The predictor factor "Assertiveness" was most successful, correlating .46 with a composite leadership role.

With regard to significance of these results for future work, it seems reasonable to conclude from the success in predicting the leadership composite that prediction of certain roles and behavior patterns in small group activity can be achieved by further developing predictor instruments along the lines indicated by this study. Further research may make it possible to analyze changes in the individual's role behavior that are attributable to differences in certain measurable characteristics of other group members in problem solving groups.

REFERENCES

Adorno, T. W., Frenkel-Brunswik, Else, Levinson, D. J., and Sanford, R. N., 1950. *The authoritarian personality.* New York: Harper and Row.

Bass, B. M., 1951. Situational tests: 2. Leaderless group discussion variables. *Educational and Psychological Measurement*, **2**, 196–207.

Bass, B. M., McGehee, C. R., Hawkins, W. C., Young, P. C., and Gebel, A. S., 1953. Personality variables related to leaderless group discussion behavior. *Journal of Abnormal and Social Psychology*, **48**, 120–128.

Carter, L. F., 1951. Some research on leadership in small groups. In H. Guetzkow (Ed.), *Groups, leadership and men.* Pittsburgh, Pa.: Carnegie Press, pp. 146–157.

Carter, L. F., 1954. Evaluating the performance of individuals as members of small groups. *Personnel Psychology*, **7**, 477–484.

Carter, L. F., Haythorn, W., and Howell, Margaret, 1950. A further investigation of the criteria of leadership. *Journal of Abnormal and Social Psychology*, **45**, 350–358.

Carter, L. F., Haythorn, W., Shriver, Beatrice, and Lanzetta, J., 1951. The behavior of leaders and other group members. *Journal of Abnormal and Social Psychology*, **46**, 589–595.

Carter, L. F., and Nixon, Mary, 1949. An investigation of the relationship between four criteria of leadership ability for three different tasks. *Journal of Psychology*, **27**, 245–261.

Cattell, R. B., 1951. Determining syntality dimensions as a basis for morale and leadership measurement. In H. Guetzkow (Ed.), *Groups, leadership and men.* Pittsburgh, Pa.: Carnegie Press.

Cattell, R. B., 1955. *Handbook for the objective-analytic personality test batteries.* Institute for Personality and Ability Testing, Champaign, Ill.

Cattell, R. B., and Stice, G. F., 1953. Four formulae for selecting leaders on the basis of personality. Urbana, Ill.: University of Illinois, Laboratory of Personal Assessment and Group Behavior. (*Human Relations*, 1954, **7**, 493–507.)

Greer, F. L., 1955. Small group effectiveness. Institute Report Number 6. Philadelphia, Pa.: Institute for Research in Human Relations.

Guilford, J. P., 1945. *Manual. An inventory of factors.* STDCR. Beverly Hills, Calif.: Sheridan Supply.

Guilford, J. P., 1951. *P. opinion inventory.* San Antonio, Tex.: Air Research and Development Command.

Haythorn, W., 1953. The influence of individual members on the characteristics of small groups. *Journal of Abnormal and Social Psychology*, **48**, 265–284.

Haythorn, W., Couch, A. S., Haefner, D., Langham, P., and Carter, L. F., 1956. The behavior of authoritarian and equalitarian personalities in groups. *Human Relations*, **9**, 57–74.

Lippitt, R., 1940. An experimental study of the effect of democratic and authoritarian group atmospheres. *University of Iowa Studies in Child Welfare*, **16**, 43–195.

McCurdy, H. E., and Eber, H. W., 1954. Democratic vs. authoritarian: a further investigation of group problem-solving. *Journal of Personality*, **22**, 258–269.

Medalia, N. Z., 1955. Authoritarianism, leader acceptance, and group cohesion. *Journal of Abnormal and Social Psychology*, **51**, 207–213.

Richardson, Helen M., and Hanawalt, N. G., 1944. Leadership as related to the Bernreuter Personality Measures: III. Leadership among adult men in vocational and social activities. *Journal of Applied Psychology*, **28**, 308–317.

Sakoda, J. M., 1952. Factor analysis of OSS situational tests. *Journal of Abnormal and Social Psychology*, **47**, 843–852.

Schutz, W. C., 1955. What makes groups productive? *Human Relations*, **8**, 429–465.

Weiss, W., and Fine, B. J., 1956. The effect of induced aggressiveness on opinion change. *Journal of Abnormal and Social Psychology*, **52**, 109–114.

selection 25 Performance Interdependence

JOHN W. THIBAUT AND HAROLD H. KELLEY

ANALYSIS AND CONCEPTS

Our conceptualization of a two-person relationship begins with an analysis of interaction and of its consequences for the two individuals concerned. The analytic technique used is a matrix formed by taking account of all the behaviors the two individuals might enact together. Each cell in this matrix represents one of the possible parts of the interaction between the two and summarizes the consequences for each person of that possible event. Although consequences can be analyzed and measured in many ways, we have found it desirable to distinguish positive components (*rewards*) from negative components (*costs*).

Abridged from Chapters 2, 4, and 11 of a book by the same authors entitled *The Social Psychology of Groups*, 1959, New York: Wiley. Reprinted by permission of the authors and Wiley.

Analysis of Interaction

The essence of any interpersonal relationship is *interaction*. By interaction it is meant that they emit behavior in each other's presence, they create products for each other, or they communicate with each other. In every case we would identify as an instance of interaction there is at least the possibility that the actions of each person affect the other.

There are many things that an individual can do in interaction with another person. It might be said that each person has a vast repertoire of possible behaviors, any one of which he might produce in an interaction.

Our unit for the analysis of behavior is referred to as the *behavior sequence* or *set*. Each unit to be identified consists of a number of specific motor and verbal acts that exhibit some degree of sequential organization directed toward the attainment of some immediate goal or end state. Typically, a sequence of this sort consists of some responses that are mainly instrumental in moving the person toward the final state. Other responses —perceptual, interpretive, consummatory in nature—can usually be identified as affording appreciation or enjoyment of the goal state.

The organization apparent in behavior sequences suggests that the person maintains a more or less constant orientation or intention throughout the sequence. We refer to this aspect of the behavior sequence as *set*, although loosely we use set and behavior sequence interchangeably. When a behavior sequence is observed, we may say that the individual has assumed a certain set. The probabilities of occurrence of the instrumental and appreciative behaviors comprising the sequence are heightened when the appropriate set is aroused. However, a set may be aroused without the corresponding behavior sequence being enacted. Thus the concept of set is useful in considering situations in which there is a tendency to produce a given sequence but in which this tendency does not, for various reasons, result in overt performance of the sequence. In this case we may still deduce the existence of a set if certain other manifestations (evidence of conflict or tension) are present. The specific set or sets aroused at any given time depend upon instigations, both from within the person (e.g., need or drive states) and from outside (incentives, problem situations or tasks confronting him, experimental instructions), and the reinforcement previously associated with enactment of the set. The stability of a set depends upon the temporal persistence of the stimuli that serve to instigate it.

Each person's repertoire of behaviors consists of all possible sets he may enact (or behavior sequences he may perform) and all possible combinations of these sets. Any portion of the stream of interaction between two persons can be described in terms of the items they *actually produce* from their respective repertoires.

The Consequences of Interaction. When the interactions of a number of persons are observed, it usually becomes quite apparent that interaction is a highly selective matter, both with respect to who interacts with whom and with respect to what any pair of persons interacts about. Not all possible pairs of individuals are observed to enter into interaction, and any given pair enacts only certain of the many behaviors they are capable of. Although there are several different ways of accounting for this selectivity, we assume that in part it indicates that different interactions in different relationships have different consequences for the individual. Some relationships are more satisfactory than others, and the same is true of some interactions within a given relationship. The selectivity observed in interaction reflects the tendency for more satisfactory interactions to recur and for less satisfactory ones to disappear.

The consequences of interaction can be described in many different terms, but we have found it useful to distinguish only between the rewards a person receives and the costs he incurs.

By rewards, we refer to the pleasures, satisfactions, and gratifications the person enjoys. The provision of a means whereby a drive is reduced or a need fulfilled constitutes a reward. We assume that the amount of reward provided by any such experience can be measured and that the reward values of different modalities of gratification are reducible to a single psychological scale.

By costs, we refer to any factors that operate to inhibit or deter the performance of a sequence of behavior. The greater the deterrence to performing a given act—the greater the inhibition the individual has to overcome—the greater the cost of the act. Thus cost is high when great physical or mental effort is required, when embarrassment or anxiety accompany the action, or when there are conflicting forces or competing response tendencies of any sort. Costs derived from these different factors are also assumed to be measurable on a common psychological scale, and costs of different sorts, to be additive in their effect.

The consequence or *outcomes* for an individual participant of any interaction or series of interactions can be stated, then, in terms of the rewards received and the costs incurred, these values depending upon the behavioral items which the two persons produce in the course of their interaction. For some purposes it is desirable to treat rewards and costs separately; for other purposes it is assumed that they can be combined into a single scale of "goodness" of outcome, with states of high reward and low cost being given high-scale values and states of low reward and high cost, low-scale values. Admittedly, such a scaling operation would be a very ambitious enterprise and would present a number of technical difficulties. However, the present interest is in the theoretical consequences of such an operation (real or imaginary) rather than in its technical properties or even its feasibility.

The Matrix of Possible Interactions and Outcomes. All portions of the interaction between two

TABLE 1. MATRIX OF POSSIBLE INTERACTIONS AND OUTCOMES

B's repertoire \ A's repertoire	a_1	a_2	···	a_n	$a_1\, a_2$	$a_1\, a_3$	···	$a_1\, a_2 \cdots a_n$
b_1	r_A, C_A / r_B, C_B	etc.	···					
b_2	etc.							
⋮	⋮							
b_n								
$b_1\, b_2$								
$b_1\, b_3$								
⋮								
$b_1\, b_2 \cdots b_n$								

persons, A and B, can be represented by the matrix shown in Table 1. Along the horizontal axis of this matrix are placed all the items in A's behavior repertoire and along the vertical axis, the items in B's repertoire. The cells of the matrix represent all possible events that may occur in the interaction between A and B, since at each moment the interaction may be described in terms of the items (consisting of one or more sets) that each one is *enacting*. (This assumes that each person is always in some set, even if only in a passive set in which he merely makes the responses necessary to observe, interpret, or appreciate what the other person is doing.) Although Table 1 presents the matrix in its most general form, for many purposes a much simpler matrix will provide an adequate description of the possibilities.

Entered in each cell of the matrix are the outcomes, in terms of rewards gained and costs incurred, to each person of that particular portion of the interaction. If rewards and costs are combined into a single scale of goodness of outcome, the matrix can be simplified as in Table 2.

Exogenous Determinants of Rewards and Costs

The reward and cost values entered in the matrix in Table 1 depend in the first place upon factors that are more or less external *to the relationship*. Each individual carries his values, needs, skills, tools, and predispositions to anxiety with him as he moves among the various relationships in which he participates. Hence we refer to them as *exogenous* factors.

The magnitude of rewards to be gained by the two members from the various elements will depend upon their individual needs and values and the congruency of the behaviors or behavioral products with these needs and values. Each person's rewards may be derived (a) directly from his own behavior and/or (b) from the other's behavior. The former consist of rewards the individual could produce for himself if he were alone. Any rewards he receives that depend in any way upon the other individual, even if only upon the presence of the other, will be considered as depending upon the other's behavior. For example, A obtains satisfaction from doing things for B.

TABLE 2. MATRIX OF POSSIBLE OUTCOMES, SCALED ACCORDING TO OVERALL GOODNESS OF OUTCOMES

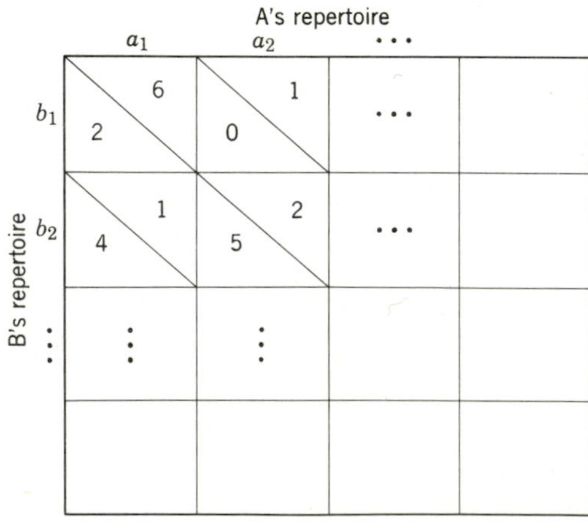

B's repertoire \ A's repertoire	a_1	a_2	···	
b_1	6 / 2	1 / 0	···	
b_2	1 / 4	2 / 5	···	
⋮	⋮	⋮		

We can interpret this to mean that B can produce rewards for A (probably at very low cost) by simply assuming a passive set in which he receives A's contributions and, perhaps, acknowledges receipt in some way.

In what might be characterized as a true trading relationship all of each person's rewards are derived from the other's efforts. More typical, perhaps, is the case in which each one's rewards depend in part upon his own behaviors and in part upon the other's behaviors.

When A produces an item from his repertoire, his costs depend on his skills and on the availability to him of efficient tools or instruments as well as on the degree to which anxiety or discomfort is associated with producing the various elements. Where A's actions are concerned, B's costs depend on the degree to which any of A's behaviors are punishing to him, whether by arousing anxiety or embarrassment or by causing physical harm.

Endogenous Determinants of Rewards and Costs

The second class of determinants of rewards and costs includes those intrinsic to the interaction itself, referred to as *endogenous* factors. The central point is that the specific values associated with a given item in A's repertoire depend upon the particular item in B's repertoire with which, in the course of the interaction, it is paired.

INTERFERENCE AND FACILITATION IN INTERACTION

Exogenous factors may be construed as setting the boundary conditions within which at any given moment other processes that are internal or endogenous to the relationship may operate to affect further the rewards and costs of the members. The maximum rewards and minimum costs potentially available under given boundary conditions are achieved only when certain endogenous factors are optimal. These endogenous factors, when they are less than optimal, attenuate the most favorable reward-cost possibilities. They are thought to arise mainly from particular combinations of sets, or response sequences, adopted by the members of the dyad.

A person often cannot do two things at the same time and do them efficiently and well. This is the phenomenon referred to as *response interference*, by which is meant that the performance of one response (or even the existence of a tendency to make that response) may be incompatible with the performance of another. Response interference is important in the analysis of dyadic interaction because for each individual the behaviors of the other constitute powerful instigations to responses. These may be incompatible with other responses which, by virtue of other instigations (events in the social or physical environment or internal events such as need or drive stimuli), the individual happens to be performing at that moment. Any two behavioral sets (or pairs of items) from the repertoires of A and B may be described in terms of their incompatibility. Set a_1 in A's repertoire is said to be *incompatible* with set b_1 in B's to the degree that when the two sets are simultaneously enacted a_1 instigates some response tendencies (or set) in B that interfere with his making the responses in b_1, and, vice versa, b_1 instigates some response tendencies (or set) in A that interfere with his performance of a_1.

Interference will frequently operate symmetrically in an interaction: if what A is doing interferes with B's activities, B will also often interfere with A's activities. If interference effects are symmetrical in this way, they would be expected to produce a correspondence between A's and B's outcomes over the various cells in the matrix; that is, a correlation tends to exist between the paired entries in each of the several cells in which such symmetry of interference occurs. It should be mentioned, though, that interference need not be symmetrical. In numerous situations such effects are asymmetrical: for example, when one participant to an interaction teases or criticizes the other or exhibits annoying mannerisms, such as scratching, belching, or snoring—in fact when any behavior is performed which interferes without being interfered with.

Before continuing with a discussion of the various effects of interference on the outcomes to the participants in an interaction, it should be emphasized (if it is not too obvious) that *facilitative* effects also occur in interaction. The husband's greeting is completed by the wife's countering in an appropriate way; hence the reward value to the husband of this bit of interaction is maximal only if the wife's response is satisfactory. The reader is asked to remember that these positive enhancing processes of the pairing of optimal responses are necessary if rewards are to be maximized. The concentration [here] on the effects of interference is based not on any conviction that facilitative effects are unimportant but rather on an impression that the effects of interference are more complex, hence require more careful analysis.

Effects of Response Interference

In specifying more exactly what we mean by interference we should first state that interference may exist at the level of the production of the behavior associated with a given set and also at the level of the consumption or appreciation of the behavior. On the production side, interference will be directly related to cost and will secondarily affect the quality or reward-value of the produced behavior. On the appreciation side, interference may affect both the perceiving or apprehending of the reward-value of behavior as well as the consummatory experience itself.

Return to the dyadic situation in which a person A is producing set a_1 from his repertoire while person B is enacting set b_1, from his. We will analyze the relationship from the point of view of A's production of behavior that is potentially rewarding to B with the understanding that the process would ordinarily be bilateral and that any conclusions about A's rewards for B would also apply to B's rewards for A.

Cost to A. The cost to A of set a_1 will be greater than minimum to the degree that there is interference from set b_1, that is, to the degree that set b_1 is incompatible with set a_1. To paraphrase, we are simply asserting that inhibiting or incompatible response tendencies accompanying the production of behavior increase the optimal cost of the behavior, whether in the form of annoyance, embarrassment, anxiety, or the increased effort required to make the appropriate responses.

The determinants of the amount of cost increase under conditions of set incompatibility are suggested by theoretical analyses of conflict. No doubt the reader will have noted a similarity between the present discussion of response interference and the usual treatment of conflict. We suggest that the excessive costs induced by interference are proportional to the amount of conflict produced by the situation. The tendency to avoid high costs, postulated here, is then another way of describing what might be called a "conflict-avoidance" drive.

Following Brown and Farber (1951) and Berlyne (1957), we take the amount of conflict to be an increasing function of four variables: (a) the number of competing responses, (b) their degree of incompatibility or interference, (c) their absolute strengths or intensities, and (d) the degree to which their strengths approach equality. From these considerations, it follows that A's costs when performing set a_1 are not likely to rise much if the incompatible response tendencies comprising the set instigated by B's activities are relatively weak. The husband's costs of watching an exciting boxing match on TV will be little affected if the wife only barely arouses in him an impulse to engage in whist. On the other hand, conflict will be maximal when both the original responses and the newly induced incompatible ones are very strong. Costs become high when both the boxing match and whist succeed simultaneously in instigating their "appropriate" sets.

Assuming the existence of a basic tendency to avoid high cost, we would expect A to take all available measures to avoid the arousal of incompatible sets. Stated more conventionally, A will avoid conflict-arousal. Assisting A in his reluctance to pay the increased costs of conflict is the fact that concentrated and intense enactment of the behaviors in a given set may prevent his receiving instigations from the other person's behavior. A wife thoroughly engrossed in a novel may not notice her husband's attempts at seductive flattery. Individuals can learn means of avoiding conflict and have numerous opportunities to do so. These include giving close attention to relevant stimuli and selectively excluding the irrelevant. The cues which tend to keep one in a single set may be multiplied and other cues avoided, either by surrounding oneself with appropriate behavioral "props" or by moving into an environment in which all cues act uniformly to support a single behavioral sequence.

In brief, because of cost considerations, individuals try to do "one thing at a time," and, to this end, they try to control their environments and perceptual responses so as to eliminate instigations to mutually interfering activities. However, there are limits to the effectiveness of these perceptual-selection and cue-control measures. The external cues presented to a person are in large part determined by other persons and the physical world. Moreover, some of the most powerful instigations to sets, in the form of need or drive stimuli, are internal to the individual and largely beyond his control.

Interference is, of course, a problem for both members of any dyad. If it exists for A, it will often exist at the same time for B, and the two are likely to share (though not necessarily to verbalize) a concern about avoiding the high costs incurred. Later we consider what the two might do jointly in the interests of reducing interference.

Reward Produced by A. Rewards may be considered from two points of view: first, in terms of the quality of the product created by A and, second, in terms of B's appreciation of the product created by A.

The reward value of set a_1 will be less than maximum to the degree that there is interference from set b_1 in the production of it. This statement is a prediction that the interferences (e.g., disturbances or distractions) will lower the quality of performance of the set. As we shall see shortly, this prediction will have to be severely qualified.

When the performance of a given set is interfered with by the partial or complete arousal of another, incompatible set, the result is conflict, manifested in tension, strain, and discomfort. The amount of conflict is a function of the degree of incompatibility of the two sets and of their intensities (which depend upon the strength of instigations to the sets).

Further, we have stated that increasing conflict leads to increasing costs, and, through a cost-minimization assumption, conflict will be avoided or reduced when possible. Conflict thus acts very much like a need or drive state: it tends to reduce itself.

We are now in a better position to evaluate the effects of incompatible sets on the reward-value produced by A. Any of the usual costly forms of conflict (anxiety, frustration, stress, fear, or intense self-consciousness) will generate high drive and lead A to produce behaviors of heightened intensity. Whether this will result in increased or decreased reward to B (or to A himself for that matter) is mooted by a further consideration. Any increase in drive will improve the performance of activities that are simple, easy, or well integrated (over-learned) but will lead to deteriorated performance of activities that are complex, difficult, or in general not well learned. This would seem to imply that for any given type of activity, such as speaking French, the greater A's skill, that is, the lower his costs of production, the more likely it is that an increase in drive (through conflict or any other source) will lead to improved performance; the less the skill the more likely that drive increases will impair his performance.

Thus it may be predicted that if the task is sufficiently simple and the appropriate behavior sufficiently automatic an increase in drive will lead to greater performance. The problem is to assess how pervasive this phenomenon is. In a summary of a large number of studies of the effects of stress and conflict on performance, Lazarus, Deese, and Osler (1952) conclude that: ". . . it does seem likely that some individuals will show a facilitation of performance under such conditions, but it also seems probable that these individuals will be in the minority in any randomly chosen sample of people" (p. 306). If this is a fair assessment of the evidence, we may conclude that the presence of incompatible sets or conflict will usually tend to lead to a deterioration in performance, and therefore, to lower rewards.

Appreciation by B. On the appreciation side, in general, the reward-value to person B of A's enactment of a_1 will be less than maximum to the degree that B does not make the appropriate attentive, interpretive, or consummatory responses. B's failure to make such responses is attributed to interference from the simultaneous arousal of response tendencies incompatible with them. The costs of making whatever appreciative responses he does make are likely also to be higher as a consequence of the interference.

Research evidence on interference with appreciative responses comes from several quarters. Music has been found to reduce reading efficiency (Henderson, Crews, and Barlow, 1945; Fendrick, 1937). The individual typically encounters difficulty in attending to two different streams of input to the same sensory modality.

It is obvious, perhaps, that the behaviors of other persons sometimes enhance one's enjoyment of other events. For example, more people laugh aloud at jokes heard over the radio when there are others listening in the same room. Similarly, most people feel radio humor to be improved if they can hear the laughter of a studio audience (Cantril and Allport, 1935). The importance of the appropriate setting and preliminaries for the enjoyment of sexual relations has been emphasized by marriage counselors and investigators of marital difficulties (Dickinson and Beam, 1931). These examples illustrate an important fact which the present emphasis on interference might lead one to overlook: on numerous occasions the behavior of another person serves to facilitate the full assumption of a set. In the absence of this or other instigations the set is likely to be enacted in a rather slack way and its reward-values to be less than maximal.

Means of Avoiding Interference in Interaction

If a dyadic relationship is to form and survive, it must provide minimally satisfactory reward-cost outcomes to its members. The preceding discussion suggests that the likelihood of the formation and survival of a relationship is, in part, contingent on the success of social interaction in providing for the participants combinations of sets that are compatible. A relationship might be expected to develop most cohesion and morale when the two individuals discover and employ some means of moving from one pair of compatible sets to another.

The question arises: How can compatible sets be attained in a relationship? Very generally, we can say that the presence of compatible sets in the relationship will depend on either of two processes. Sets incompatible with all or most other sets must be eliminated from the interaction, or pairs of sets must be synchronized so that incompatible sets will not be simultaneously aroused. In relationships that can be severely restricted as to the domain of relevant activity all incompatible sets might be eventually eliminated from the repertoire of interaction. However, in most relationships it would seem that a combination of mechanisms, including the elimination of some sets and the synchronizing of most sets would be used to reduce response interference.

Synchronizing Sets. Let us deal first with the ways in which synchronization of pairs of sets can take place. There seem to be two closely related types of factors that support synchronizing. The first of these has to do with the availability of synchronizing cues in the environment. More specifically, good synchronization would be expected to be found when the reciprocal sets are aroused by cues that occur at the same time, for example, when the social behavior associated with eating is aroused by the dinner bell. A variant of this would be observed when the cue is provided by one member of the pair and the other member is in the versatile set of adjusting to the cue, for example, in identification behavior (the doting mother) or when there are expectations of future rewards (the employment interview).

A further word is necessary to indicate the limits of probable success of this mechanism for synchronizing sets. It appears that we must distinguish between sets the instigations to which are beyond the control of the member (e.g., instigations from urgent and recurrent need states) versus those over which the member exercises a measure of control (e.g., instigations arranged for oneself by providing external cues, such as an appropriate work place, tools, clocks, and materials). Needless to say, synchronization will be more difficult to arrange when the sets of both members are governed only by strong need states, since the needs themselves are unlikely to be synchronized. But in the absence of such coercive needs, and by virtue of exercising control over instigation, moment-to-moment compatibility can often be achieved; that is, in many instances incompatibility can be converted at the next moment into compatibility. Thus, if one fails to instigate the other member to the appropriate set, one can adapt by providing self-instigations to the appropriate set.

A second way of achieving synchronization is provided by the rules for behavior specified in social roles. A main contribution of role to the achievement of set-compatibility is that roles frequently suggest (when they do not clearly specify) a synchronized order of interaction. We refer to the whole range of role attributes having to do with rights, privileges, responsibilities, precedence, seniority, and so forth. We define role in terms of norms and suggest that the activation of any given role often implies the coactivation of a role compatible with it. When this occurs, the cues that activate a given role in A also serve to activate a reciprocal role in B or the role behavior of A serves to activate reciprocal role behavior in B. Thus, because of the high serial dependence of items of behavior specified by a role, synchronization cues are necessary only to activate the roles and are not necessary on a moment-to-moment basis. This mode of synchronization probably occurs very widely and may be illustrated by such diverse situations as are observed in the interaction among factory workers on a production line and in that between doctor and patient.

Before leaving this discussion of social role, we should mention a further function which roles contribute in maintaining the reward positions of the members. We have noted that roles facilitate synchronization, but, should synchronization fail, there is another way in which roles can operate to avoid severe loss of rewards. This is the opportunity afforded by many roles for much rehearsal, hence for adequate overlearning of the behaviors specified by them. By virtue of this routinization of behavior, role behaviors should be less susceptible to interference; hence if any conflict-drive should arise from incompatible sets it might be expected to result in facilitated rather than deteriorated performance of the behavior. Some theory such as this appears to underlie the intensive practice and drill which soldiers, firemen, and policemen undergo in preparation for meeting emergency situations.

Eliminating Sets. We have said that one way to reduce the costly and reward-impairing effects of incompatible sets is by synchronization. Another more direct way is to eliminate such sets from the relationship. If it is true that a relationship does not survive if it provides chronically unfavorable reward-cost positions to its members, it is also true that there is a tendency for sets to be eliminated from a relationship when they persistently impair the members' reward-cost positions. Hence incompatible sets would tend to be eliminated from the flow of interaction, except when in spite of interference effects the incompatible sets yield reward-cost positions above the members' comparison levels for alternative relationships.

In suggesting that incompatible sets have low likelihood of survival in a relationship, we have in mind a model of "natural selection" of low-cost, high-reward sets rather than one of deliberate optimization through planful decisions at every moment. We do not deny that major decisions projecting optimizing strategies do occur, but they do so only at certain critical junctures in the lives of the members when major alternatives with long-term (contractual, irrevocable) consequences are clearly perceived. But routine day-to-day interaction consists more of coping with the immediate situation and accomplishing intermediate instrumental goals. We view this process as one in which pairs of sets and synchronizing conventions that are found to have satisfactory reward-cost consequences are retained (have high survival value) in the relationship, whereas those that prove to be unsatisfactory are eliminated from the relationship. Thus these endogenous processes may lead to a progressive restriction in the domain of paired sets operative in the relationship and to more or less ritualized modes of activating these sets.

Furthermore (role-prescribed) combinations of sets that are highly adaptive resultants of this endogenous process tend to be taught to the young of the next generation, thus providing exogenous means of eliminating incompatible sets even before they occur.

Although the above process would lead to a stabilization and rigidification of the content and style of the relationship, we can safely assume that any such stabilities will be intermittently upset or disrupted by exogenous influences (e.g., changes in other relationships, acquisition of new tastes or needs) as well as by unanticipated events in the interaction itself. Such shiftings and disruptions may be expected to provide for variety and innovation.

DIFFERENTIATION OF FUNCTION [IN LARGER GROUPS]

In any group it is possible for the various members to make qualitatively different contributions within the group. As group size increases from dyadic to triadic and larger relationships, a number of modes of raising a member's rewards in relation to his costs that are not possible in the dyad begin to appear. Let us consider the triad in some detail to illustrate these emergent possibilities. We begin with the problem of explaining the existence of the A-B-C triad. How is it that any given member, A, can be better off in the A-B-C relationship than in other relationships? Several specific examples may serve to clarify some of the possibilities.

Joint Cost-Cutting

Two persons may be able to cut A's costs when one alone cannot do so. For example, the adolescent girl, conflicted about sex, may be willing to go on dates with two boys but not with one. "Three's a crowd" if she's interested in sexual activities, but "there's safety in numbers" if she wants their company but not their advances.

A similar possibility is that two persons may cut each other's costs enough to enable them to interact with the third one. Two girls may be greatly concerned about visiting a fortune-teller alone but may be willing to do so together.

Joint Consumption

If A's behavioral products are such that the other members can simultaneously enjoy them without interference, then the total value of his product is increased in relation to his costs, and the others may be able together to provide sufficient rewards in return to make the relationship a viable one. For example, a father may take two children on a picnic with very little more effort than taking one. Or, if he can then get each of them to mow half the lawn, a trading agreement may be possible for the three of them, whereas no pair could have worked one out. A common example is the performer-audience relationship: the performer's jokes or songs may be enjoyed by each member of a large audience. In return, each can applaud or pay an admission fee, the cumulative effects of which may reimburse the performer for his costs. It is possible, of course, that the performer's costs will increase somewhat with the increasing size of his audience, but larger audiences are still desirable if the rate of this increase is less than the rate of increase in total return which increasing size makes possible.

Mutual Facilitation of Enjoyment

A further possibility is that members of the audience (e.g., two persons "consuming" the behavior of a third) may increase each other's enjoyment of the performance by mutual facilitation of appreciative and consummatory responses. The effects of comedy are probably particularly dependent upon social interactions within the audience.

Emergent Products

The behavioral products of B and C, taken separately, may be of little value to A, but, together, they may be greatly amplified. For example, their respective realms of knowledge may be partial and incomplete but complementary, so that B and C together can provide A with valuable advice and information about problem solutions; or, B's praise of A may be greatly increased in reward value if delivered in the presence of C.

Sequential Patterns of Interdependence

A pattern totally unknown in the dyad (hence unique to the triad and larger groups) is one in which A directs his contributions (in provision of rewards or cutting of costs) to one person and receives his outcomes from another. Consider this case: A has a supply of currency which is of value only to B, B has a different currency of value only to C, and C has a third type of currency of value only to A. This sets the conditions for the development of a circular pattern of currency exchange in which A agrees to pass some of his currency to B if B, by passing some of his to C, can induce C to provide some of his to A. Any of these links might, of course, consist of cost cutting rather than the provision of rewards for the next man in the chain. In general, the situation is one in which A is dependent upon C (or potentially so) but has nothing to offer C in return. There does exist, however, a third person who acts as an intermediary. In a sense, this intermediary (or so he appears from A's point of view) is somehow able to transform A's product into something of value to C.

REFERENCES

Berlyne, D. E., 1957. Conflict and choice time. *British Journal of Psychology*, **48**, 106–118.

Brown, J. S., and Farber, I. E., 1951. Emotions conceptualized as intervening variables—with suggestions toward a theory of frustration. *Psychological Bulletin*, **48**, 465–495.

Cantril, H., and Allport, G. W., 1935. *The psychology of radio*. New York: Harper and Row.

Dickinson, R. L., and Beam, L., 1931. *A thousand marriages*. Baltimore, Md.: Williams and Wilkins.

Fendrick, P., 1937. The influence of music distraction upon reading efficiency. *Journal of Educational Research*, **31**, 264–271.

Henderson, M. T., Crews, Anne, and Barlow, Joan, 1945. A study of the effect of music distraction on reading efficiency. *Journal of Applied Psychology*, **29**, 313–317.

Lazarus, R. S., Deese, J., and Osler, Sonia F., 1952. The effects of psychological stress upon performance. *Psychological Bulletin*, **49**, 293–317.

selection 26 An Approach to Family Relationships and Role Performance

RHONA RAPOPORT AND IRVING ROSOW

This paper concerns some problems in the general analysis of role relations in various institutional settings. It applies most clearly to small groups such as the family or work teams. A framework is presented for the collection and ordering of comprehensive data on familial (or other) relationships. Although the proposal may have wider uses, such as the analysis of group stability or sources of strain, it is discussed here in the specific context of family relationships and psychiatric rehabilitation. This clinical emphasis, however, should not obscure its broader relevance.

There is reason to believe that patients' family relationships may be a more significant condition of and limitation on successful rehabilitation than they may be in intensive, long-term individual psychotherapy. Accordingly, this paper reviews selected aspects of patients' family relationships that have crystallized out of work at one group centre, the Social Rehabilitation Unit of Belmont Hospital. The unit views patients less in terms of classical diagnostic categories or particular theoretical frameworks (such as the several Freudian schools) and more directly in terms of their immediate behaviour problems. Experience with these patients indicates that their behaviour problems reflect faulty interpersonal relations with others who are significant in the patient's normal roles—his spouse or children, supervisor or subordinates, employer or workmates, friends, relatives, neighbours, and others. His interpersonal difficulties at work and in his family almost invariably underlie the therapeutic problem. These can be specified in terms of "role failure" which requires correction and to which rehabilitative treatment can be oriented.

In exploring the nature of patients' role difficulties, at least three sets of factors had to be considered: (a) the *role* or position in which the failures occurred; (b) the *social norms* or the behaviour expected in that position (see Bott, 1954, 1955, 1956); and (c) the *personality* of the patient. We will review these elements in turn as they apply to the family situation.

First, in considering a patient's behavioural failures, it is important to know his *position* in the organization of the family. The meaning and consequences of a man's failure to hold a job will vary if he is single, if he is the sole support of invalid parents, if he has working brothers or sisters, if he is married but has no children, if his wife is working, if he is the father of a large family, or if he has grown children who are employed. Each situation implies different sets of obligations; there are different responsibilities and expectations of him and different opportunities for him to share these responsibilities with others. If he fails to work, different numbers of people will suffer in the various situations. In some circumstances there is another person to take up the slack of his unemployment while in others there is nobody else. So the expectations of him as son, brother, only child, husband, or father will vary primarily according to the role rather than to the particular person involved.

Second, a patient's behaviour can also be interpreted according to his definition of the situation, or according to the *social norms* which he thinks others attach to his family role, to the behaviour which they consider normal and appropriate for his position. Social norms, in the sense used here, may vary considerably from person to person. One person may feel that fathers should be disciplinarians of the children while mothers should be indulgent and warm. Others may feel that children should always be treated leniently while yet others may think that discipline is the proper environment for a child. Similarly, one may believe that it is improper for a wife to work while another may feel that wives should work. People's personal beliefs can be rationalized as

---

Abridged from *Human Relations*, 1957, **10**, 209–221. Reprinted by permission of the authors and *Human Relations*. The research program of which this paper is a part was financed by the Nuffield Foundation.

social norms particularly when there is a disagreement between husband and wife. Conflict between husband and wife may arise from disagreement about what social norms are, and from deviance from those norms. These conceptions of "proper" role behaviour are learned in childhood and in growing up are reinforced or modified by various adult experiences. People define proper behaviour in any family role according to various segments of society with which they identify themselves and which they take as a model. The identifications may be positive or negative and may involve real groups or projected constructs.

Finally, we need to relate behaviour itself to the pattern of *personality* needs that results from a patient's specific life history. Like social norms, personality needs develop from inter-personal experience with significant people during childhood, adolescence, and adult life. An emotionally rejected child may, as an adult, retain strong dependency needs to gain the reassurance that others love him. His inability to work for a living may be related to such dependency needs. Or a person with strong aggressive tendencies may use his family as a conspicuous outlet for the expression of his aggressive feelings. These personality elements affect participation in the family by organizing the patient's perception and interpretation of his immediate world, by mobilizing his system of needs and defences and by activating these strongly in the close quarters of family life. The family becomes a stage for the playing out of his emotional problems and the gratification or frustration of his deeper personality needs.

It became evident in the Unit, however, that the patient's *own* role, *his* social norms, and *his* personality organization *did not adequately account for his role failure*, or for the factors that precipitated his breakdown, or for his response to treatment. Similarly, changes in the patients' role performance, from before to after treatment, did not closely correspond with any apparent changes in their emotional make-up as a result of therapy. Experience rather indicated that patients with essentially *similar emotional problems* but with significantly *different family environments* seemed to adjust differently after treatment. Accordingly, the effort to restore adequate role performance and to rehabilitate these people solely with an eye to their personality pathology or to their deviant norms did not impress the Unit staff as markedly successful.

Other significant variables had to be taken into account. The most important of these was how well the patient's values and personality *fitted together* with the norms and personality needs of his family members. For example, while a passive, dependent husband might manage fairly well with a maternal, over-protective wife, incapacitating strains and tensions might develop for a similar patient whose wife wanted him to be dominant, decisive, and strong. Or a violently aggressive husband might thrive with a highly masochistic wife, while another family might be torn apart if the wife had strong needs to be protected from violence. Thus, the patient's participation in the family depends less upon his specific attributes alone than upon the *articulation* of his attributes with those of his family members.

The meaning of the patient's behaviour in relation to realistic therapeutic aims demands a fuller understanding of the larger family situation into which the patient fits. In the course of interviews with the families of several patients it became clear that the patient's role performance could be seen as a function of his relations with the other family members. Accordingly, a fruitful unit of analysis appeared to be the *relationship* between the patient and each of his significant intimates in his respective family roles. In order to locate and clarify possible sources of strain, these relationships were examined in three dimensions: (a) the *fit* between the norms of the patient and others about his proper role performance; (b) the fit between the personalities of the patient and other family members; (c) the emotional climate that developed from the intimate interaction of the patient and the family. We will consider some of the problems arising in this framework (see Ackerman, 1951; and Spiegel, 1954).

Fit of Norms about Role Performance. The degree of family consensus that may be expected about role standards is problematic, and obscures the contribution that conflicting norms make to role failure as such. The structure of the modern family permits a broad range of alternative role adjustments. Competing cultural values and flexible social norms increase the chance for personal preference to shape the organization of family life. Specific role content, the "proper" performance of different family members, and the preferred relationships between them are subject to flexible settlement which can vary considerably from one family to another. Consequently, idiosyncratic role adjustment may be specially marked in problem families, which may disproportionately display conflicting values and needs.

Though the limitations on free role adjustment

will vary in different classes, ethnic groups, neighbourhoods, and other social units, roles in the modern urban family generally tend to be more "fluid" and open to idiosyncratic definition than those of many non-urban, pre-industrial family systems. The content of a contemporary family position may embrace a wide variety of activities, obligations, and prerogatives that are subject to more personal choice than the highly prescribed behaviour patterns that are commonly defined and agreed upon in other social systems. There are many alternative patterns that different individuals prefer and rather fluid boundaries of "acceptable" behaviour. For example, wives may go out to work or not; husbands may help with the children or not; spouses may have an "egalitarian" relationship or a dominant-subordinate one, and so on. Since the culture prescribes role behaviour mainly within these loose limits, individual families can adjust rather freely within the most congenial of the available cultural alternatives. Spouses may work out a personally and socially acceptable marriage in various ways without being considered odd or unusual—and neither they nor anybody else will necessarily appreciate how much they differ from their fellows. A range of cultural values is available to rationalize different patterns that appeal to particular tastes.

While many possible adjustments are "acceptable," very few are positively prescribed as "musts" or clearly indicated as "strongly preferred." The leeway in acceptable role behaviour not only presents freedom of choice, but also creates numerous ambiguities of expectation which the spouses normally have to work out. Each has grown up in an environment that has shaped his images and expectations, his sometimes vague ideal picture of the life he wants, his fears and hopes. Each person brings to the marital relationship his own norms about appropriate behaviour in different family roles. Despite marked cultural endogamy, the spouses may have quite different norms. Their separate sets of norms have developed independently, and can, in the best of circumstances, only "fit" together with more or less imperfection. Their differences, rooted in separate definitions, must be reconciled or accommodated. This is commonly an intrinsic part of the process of marital adjustment, especially in its earlier phases. The initially different expectations that each spouse may have about a given role impart to their relationship a degree of *unclarity*, and they have to derive some shared definition of proper role behaviour or some common agreement about what is appropriate. Of course, the resolution of their initial differences does not always assure a good "terminal fit" of norms or a high and stable consensus of expectations.

The compatibility of norms affects reciprocal expectations about the patient's role performance. When there is consensus, role fulfilment is facilitated; when there is not, role performance may suffer or be negatively evaluated.

Fit of Personality Systems. The second major dimension of fit between the patient and other family members includes at least three elements: (a) their respective personality needs; (b) their characteristic modes of gratification; and (c) their typical defence mechanisms, or ways of dealing with anxiety and frustration, whether from real or fantasied causes.

The personality systems of any two people can fit together in various ways and have supportive or disruptive consequences on their relationship and their respective role performances. The effects of given personality fits will depend on the organization of the relationship. For example, a husband and wife who both have strong needs to dominate may be mutually supportive if they are highly identified with one another. But if they are not strongly identified, these similar needs might reduce them to a continuous rivalry. With firm identification patterns, a dominant husband and a submissive, dependent wife might enjoy a most compatible fit. In the first case, similar needs complement one another; in the second, they clash; and in the last, dissimilar needs are compatible. While it is commonly supposed that "opposite" or dissimilar personality characteristics constitute a good fit and similar attributes a poor fit (see Rosow, 1957), this obviously depends upon the conditions of the relationship. Two people's personality systems may reinforce each other by both similar and different qualities or by similar and different intensities of certain needs. Clearly, not all personality factors have reinforcing or disruptive effects. Some elements may be missing, some may simply be independent of one another, some may be congenial or mutually compatible without either complementing or clashing. The function of any pattern of fit can only be judged against the respective self-images, the personality systems, and the organization of the relationship itself.

It is clear that the variables of social norms and personality systems are not completely independent of one another. When possible role adjustments are loose and flexible, personality needs may shape role relationships which are then legitimized by appropriate cultural values. Therefore, the fit between people's personality systems may partially determine the fit between their social norms. The two variables are related to each other in as yet indeterminate ways.

Emotional Climate. The third major aspect of fit results from the interaction between people living together. The effects of this interaction gradually build up an emotional climate that may dominate the relationship. The initial fit between a couple's norms and between their personality needs sets the stage for the development of their relationship; their responses to the sustained interaction can alter the initial fit.

When the most basic cultural values are shared and supported by complementary personality systems of spouses, this tends to increase their commitment to and participation in the marriage, or how much of himself each person "puts into" his role performance. Conversely, to the extent that expectations are not shared or are undermined by antagonistic values or personality characteristics, there will be correspondingly less commitment to the marriage. These adjustments have direct effects on the motivations of role performance. The achievement of a reasonably stable family depends on some tolerable resolution of any discrepant norms or personality needs. While this adjustment initially requires some minimal "emotional maturity," it is further affected by the partners' ability to remain compatible through time, as they develop and change, separately and together, while the family goes through various experiences and stages of growth (Foote, 1956). In the face of an inability to adapt to one another, their frustrations and tensions may mount and hostility may accumulate. Although this results from the relations between the spouses, from their interaction, and from the fit between their values and needs, it may easily assume an independent force in its own right. As the accumulated strains pervade the emotional climate they reduce the solidarity of the relationship and impair the individuals' participation. The degree of disruptive qualities that develop (e.g., irritability, impatience, and aggressiveness gradually displacing sympathy, support, and cooperation) may ultimately discourage role fulfilment just as effectively as initially clashing values or personality systems.

While each set of fits can influence the emotional climate, our studies suggest that superficial psychotherapy can effect cognitive reorientation more easily than basic emotional changes. Hence, from the therapeutic viewpoint, the fit between social norms is more tractable than that between personality systems. A couple can achieve greater agreement on their most important cultural values more easily than they can adjust a poor fit in their personality needs. This is evident from case materials that illustrate the points in the preceding discussion:

Case 17. Jack Kelly came from an Irish background in which it was acceptable for a husband to spend the bulk of his leisure time in the pub drinking with his cronies, while his Cockney wife felt that husbands should spend more of their free time at home with their families than her husband did. Furthermore, in the sexual sphere, he indicated that, "Irish women, even though they are more religious and strait-laced [than Cockney women], they are more natural and healthy-minded about these things." His wife's views on sex apparently led her to avoid intercourse or undressing when intercourse did occur. While their differences about his free time had clear cultural roots, their different sexual orientation reflected personality determinants.

During treatment, the Kellys came to realize more clearly that they had quite different values in these two particular conflict spheres, and the emotional strains between them eased. They were able to achieve perceptibly closer agreement in their images of desirable role behaviour. Jack acknowledged that he had previously spent too much time away from his family drinking with friends. After treatment, he remained at home a good deal more, and when he went to the pub, he took his wife along to share his leisure. For her part, his wife realized that perhaps she had made herself sexually too inaccessible to him. Indeed, because of her new orientation, she had herself fitted with a contraceptive diaphragm.

Nonetheless, despite their new cognitive perspectives and their closer agreement on norms, the fit of their personality needs did not fundamentally change, and the improvement of the emotional climate proved short-lived. Their underlying needs proved too intractable and the relationship soon deteriorated to its previous state of strain, alienation, and defaulted role performance.

The foregoing discussion indicated that at least three aspects of the relations between a patient and his intimates may affect his role performance.

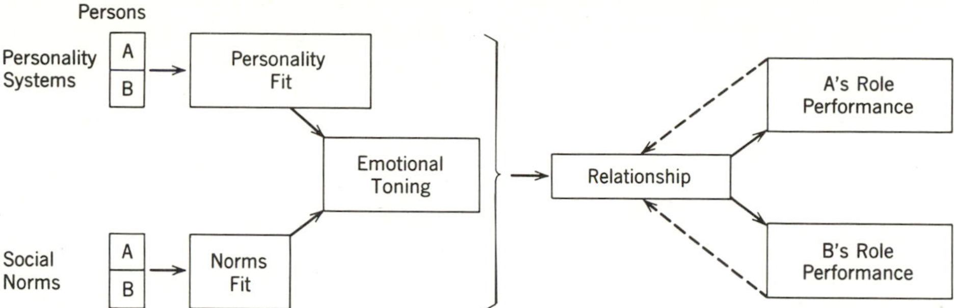

Figure 1. Model of relational analysis.

These variables include: (a) the fit between their social norms about their roles; (b) the fit between their personality systems, including needs, modes of gratification, and ways of dealing with anxiety or frustration; and (c) the emotional climate resulting from these fits in sustained intimate interaction. These three sets of variables may affect role performance by (i) increasing or decreasing consensus on expectations; (ii) stimulating or discouraging motivation to perform; and (iii) facilitating or reducing the opportunity to gratify needs and to perform adequately vis-à-vis common goals.

The relationship among these three sets of variables is schematized in *Figure 1*.

While this figure delineates a framework for a relational analysis, it does not specify particular variables within each category, e.g., of norms, personality, emotional toning. These can be varied according to different problems. For example, psycho-analytically derived categories of sexuality, aggression, and ego-defence mechanisms might be useful for typing personality dynamics. In the area of norms, regardless of the referents required for particular problems, it is essential to distinguish between people's norms of prescription and norms of personal option in order to localize therapeutic problem areas. Role performance might be expressed in terms of various prerogatives and responsibilities. In our own data, we have not yet gone beyond global judgments of strain and harmony in the analysis of emotional toning. The most useful subcategories in each of these dimensions depend on the nature of a particular therapeutic programme and the most problematic type of cases that warrant intensive study.

The paradigm has been presented here to illustrate the relations between two people. In practice, however, it is essential to have a full, accurate map of the therapeutic resources and weaknesses in a patient's larger family field. These data can be mobilized by a careful examination of the patient's relationships (in terms of the paradigm) with each of his intimates in turn, as *Figure 2* indicates. Thus *Figure 2* assimilates a series of analyses shown in *Figure 1*. Relations between the patient and his father in *Figure 1* would constitute the second cell in *Figure 2*. In this fashion one can examine the patient's total role behaviour as distributed among his array of family relationships, or what Merton has called a "role set." The analysis of his respective relationships allows an initial discrimination between pervasive and localized problems and the location of actual and potential sources of strain and support in the family environment. In this sense, the untapped therapeutic potentials (as well as the endemic irritants) in the family can be clarified and mobilized more systematically than usual into the treatment programme.

Of greater refinement and possibly greater therapeutic value is the extension of this mode of analysis to the patient's role performance in *three-person* relationships. We are here specially concerned with the patient's behaviour in relation to the interaction between two *other* family members. For example, how does he respond

Figure 2. Patient's role relation with:

	Father	Brother	Wife	Daughter
Mother			X	
Father				
Brother				
Wife				

Figure 3. Patient's role performance in response to relations between:

to the relations between his parents, between his wife and child, between his wife and mother, etc?

Such an analysis requires the extension of the simple interaction matrix of *Figure 2* to the next level of complexity. This is shown in *Figure 3*, whose cells indicate the interaction of two of the patient's significant others. The hypothetical family is that of a male patient living with his mother, father, brother, wife, and daughter. In this matrix, the other family members are represented as interacting with one another (in pairs in the respective cells), and the patient's responses to the network of relations in his environment can then be observed.

[In conclusion,] an orientation of the kind outlined here is useful as a common frame of reference for otherwise disparate clinical case reports, especially in combining the most relevant sociological and psychological materials into a single comprehensive picture. There is growing consensus that an effective understanding of even a single *special* area, such as patients' work relations, requires additional information about the patients' *other* relationships. The trend, especially in the social-psychiatric field, is away from treating the patient alone toward the development of techniques for treating the patients' relationships. The collection of research materials that systematically focus on the relationship as the unit of analysis may help to point the way for dealing clinically with patients' relationships as the unit of treatment.

REFERENCES

Ackerman, N. W., 1951. Social role and total personality. *American Journal of Orthopsychiatry*, **21**, 1–17.

Bott, Elizabeth, 1954. The concept of class as a reference group. *Human Relations*, **7**, 259–285.

Bott, Elizabeth, 1955. Urban families: conjugal roles and social networks. *Human Relations*, **8**, 345–384.

Bott, Elizabeth, 1956. Urban families: the norms of conjugal roles. *Human Relations*, **9**, 325–342.

Foote, N., 1956. Matching of husband and wife in phases of development. *Transactions of the Third World Congress of Sociology*, Vol. 4, London: International Sociological Association.

Rosow, I., 1957. Issues in the concept of need complementarity. *Sociometry*, **20**, 216–233.

Spiegel, J. P., 1954. The social roles of doctor and patient in psychoanalysis and psychotherapy. *Psychiatry*, **17**, 369–376.

part VII Differentiation, Specialization, and Division of Labor

IN ALL HUMAN AGGREGATIONS one finds differentiated behavior, the specialization of individuals in specific domains of behavior, and particular complements of specializations called the "division of labor." The concepts of differentiation, specialization, and division of labor are related but different concepts. Differentiation refers to behavior and means simply that behaviors are different, not similar; specialization has reference to the amount of, and the number of, differentiated behaviors engaged in by a particular individual; and the division of labor has reference to the particular complement of specializations. The differentiation of behavior is presupposed with specialization, and a variegated division of labor would be impossible without individuals engaging in different specializations. Despite the fact that each of the selections in this part is addressed mainly to one of these problems, the reader will not fail to observe the intimate relationship among these three factors. Many role analysts use the term "role differentiation" to refer to one or another of these separate problems, and some of the authors of the selections in this part follow this usage.

The first selection, by Parsons and Shils, is the only one devoted specifically to differentiation and specialization. The authors distinguish among instrumental, expressive, and integrative problems as bases for differentiated behavior and suggest that roles are specialized in terms of these functions. For example, instrumental activities suggest a variety of role specializations associated with the provision and distribution of facilities, among these being the supplier, consumer, collaborator, and source of income.

The remaining selections are addressed to the specializations and divisions of labor in legislatures, problem-solving groups, and families.

The selection by Wahlke, Eulau, Buchanan, and Ferguson is drawn from the authors' extensive study of role differentiation in four state legislatures. The authors offer a model of roles, role differentiation, and role sets for both upper and lower legislative chambers, and findings relating to the model as well. They distinguish among purposive, representational, areal, and pressure group roles. Among purposive roles are those of the ritualist, tribune, broker, and inventor. Representational roles include the trustee, delegate, and politico. Areal roles include the district-oriented, state-oriented and district-state oriented. Roles in regard to pressure groups include the facilitator, resister, and neutral. The model predicts which roles will be associated with others for any given legislator and the network of roles that one finds among the majority and minority members of upper and lower houses. Diagrams help the authors communicate their model and research findings.

With the selection by Bales we turn from the legislature to the small problem-solving group.

Bales surveys the findings from many of his studies and those of his associates in which problem-solving groups were observed using a standardized method of coding member behavior. Bales interprets the findings in terms of three alternative theories of leadership. In the first theory, that of a single-status order, the leader is viewed as distinguished from followers in terms of activity, task ability, and likability. The findings indicate that this theory is inadequate. The second theory is that there are two complementary leaders, one a task specialist and the other a social-emotional specialist. But this, too, is inadequate. The third theory says that there are three factors of leadership—activity, task-ability, and likability—and that various specializations in the areas may occur. A member high on all three of these corresponds to the traditional conception of the good leader, the "great man." There are other specializations, depending upon the relative rank of individuals on these three factors; thus such specializations as the "task specialist," "social specialist," "overactive deviant," and "underactive deviant" are identified.

Murdock's paper, which reports comparative data on the division of labor by sex, is the first of two papers relating to the division of labor in the family. Murdock's data are derived from ethnographic monographs on over two hundred (mostly primitive) societies from all parts of the world. The data concern the distribution of economic activities between the sexes. Activities included range from those that are exclusively masculine (metal working) through those that are overwhelmingly feminine (cooking, water carrying, and grain grinding). It is noteworthy that a large proportion of the activities are found to be performed to various degrees by both males and females.

The selection by Blood and Wolfe is a report on the specializations and division of labor in the contemporary American family. The traditional, highly specialized roles of the husband and wife are first discussed, and then the authors present data showing that contemporary role specializations exhibit mixed patterns of both specialization and nonspecialization. Thus it is found that the husband nearly always repairs things around the house and mows the lawn, while the wife typically straightens up the living room when company is coming. In contrast, both partners generally keep track of the money and bills and do the grocery shopping. The authors also discuss ethnic-group membership and rural-*versus*-urban living, as factors that affect specialization. They note also that whereas the American family appears committed to the concept of joint decision-making, the sheer expediency required to get a job done appears to be a significant factor affecting who specializes in what activities.

selection 27 The Content of Roles

TALCOTT PARSONS AND EDWARD A. SHILS

The allocative process does not determine the role structure of the social system or the content of the roles. It is necessary, therefore, to develop categories which make possible the analysis of the variability of the social system with respect to the content and organization of roles.

Role contents can be classified according to three sets of invariant points of reference. That is, there are three separate classes of problems that must be solved by all role occupants; if we classify the solutions to these problems generally enough, we will thereby have, in some sense, a classification of role contents. The three sets of problems (or invariant points of reference) are (a) problems of instrumental interaction, (b) problems of expressive interaction, and (c) integrative problems.

Problems of instrumental interaction concern relationships with alters which ego engages in, not primarily for their own sake, but for the sake of goals other than the immediate and direct gratification experienced in contact with the object. The social elaboration of instrumentally significant activities is what, in economic theory and its utilitarian philosophical background, has come to be called the division of labor. Problems of expressive interaction concern relationships with alters which ego engages in primarily for the immediate direct gratification they provide. Integrative problems are problems of a somewhat different order. They are the problems which arise when one would maintain proper relationships between roles with an eye to the structural integration of the social system.

It is inherent in the nature of human action that some goals should be sought instrumentally. It is consequently inherent in the nature of social systems that their members should perform certain mutually significant functions on the instrumental level—functions which require disciplined activity and in which the actor's interest in direct and immediate expression of gratification will not have primacy. But it is equally a precondition of the functioning of social systems that they should provide a minimum of essential gratifications direct and indirect to their members (i.e., to a sufficient proportion of them a sufficient proportion of the time). These direct gratifications of need-dispositions are so organized into a system of relationships that the structure of that system is just as vital to the actor's interest in expressive gratification as the structure of the instrumental system is to their instrumental interests. Moreover, the systems of gratification and instrumentality are intertwined in the same concrete system of social roles, and many of the factors that cause change emerge from this intertwining.

If we take the instrumental system first, we find there are four fundamental problems. The first derives from the fact that, given the division of labor, one or more alters must be the *beneficiaries* of ego's activities. In the terminology of economics, they must be the consumers of his product. In addition to the *technical* problem, then, of how ego is to organize his own resources, including his actions to produce the service or commodity, there is the further problem of determining the terms on which alter is allowed to become the beneficiary. This is a special case of the problem of the terms of exchange; specifically it is the problem of the terms of disposal. Thus, the problem of disposal is the first problem of instrumental interaction. Secondly, insofar as ego specializes in a particular type of instrumentally significant activity, he becomes dependent on the output of one or more alters for meeting his own needs. These may or may not be the same alters involved in the former relationship of disposal—in a complex economy they usually are not. At any rate there is an exchange problem here, too, growing out of the functional need, as it may be called, for ego to receive *remuneration* for his activities. Thus, the problem of remuneration is the second problem of instrumental interaction.

Third, only in a limiting case will all the facilities that ego needs to perform his instrumental functions be spontaneously available to him. It will be

Abridged from pages 208–216 of a book edited by the same authors entitled *Toward a General Theory of Action*, 1951, Cambridge, Mass.: Harvard University Press.

Problem of access to facilities (alters as *suppliers* of facilities)		Disposal problems (alters as *consumers*)
	Technical instrumental goal-orientation of ego	
Problem of collaboration (alters as *collaborators*)		Remuneration problems (alters as *sources* of income)

necessary for him to acquire or secure access to some of them through arrangement with one or more alters, involving still a third set of exchange relations and the associated standard incorporated into the terms of exchange. This third instrumental problem is that of access to facilities. Fourth, the product may not be capable of production by ego through his own unaided efforts. In this case he is dependent on still a fourth set of alters for collaboration in the joint instrumental process. The process requires organization in which ego and alters collaborate to produce a unitary result which is the object of instrumental significance. Thus, the fourth instrumental problem is the problem of co-operation or collaboration. These relations are set forth in the accompanying diagram.

In each of these relationships of ego and the alters, there is a problem of exchange, the solution of which is the settlement of the terms on which ego enters into mutually acceptable relations with the relevant alters. The settlement of the terms of exchange is a basic functional problem inherent in the allocative process of social systems. In addition to this, *exchange* implies a thing which changes hands. This entity may be called a *possession* and analysis will show that *possession* is always reducible to *rights*. Physical objects are significant insofar as one actor (individual or collective) has various types of control—acknowledged as legitimate—over them while others do not. The terms on which possessions are held, used, controlled, and disposed of is another focus of the functional problems of allocation: *property*.

We turn now to a somewhat different problem, also derivative from the division of labor. A most important range of variability occurs along the continuum of *fusion* and *segregation* of roles in instrumental relationships. The role allocated to ego may be confined to a technical instrumental content, such as the arrangement of the facilities through his own resources while assigning the "responsibility" for the execution of all four of the essential conditions of that role to the incumbents of the other roles. Such a *technical* role would be the extreme of segregation. This is the typical case of the functionally specific (specialized) roles within large-scale organizations in modern society. At the other extreme, is the type of role in which the incumbent has not only the responsibility for the technical performance but for all four associated functions—as in the case of the medieval craftsman, or the ideal type of independent general practitioner in medicine. This may be called the artisan[1] role.

The larger and more differentiated an instrumental system the more essential management or managed coördination becomes to keep the organization going as a functioning concern. With this, there emerge *executive* or managerial roles. In the executive role is centered the responsibility for the specification of roles to be performed, the recruitment of personnel to perform the roles, the organization and regulation of the collaborative relations among the roles, the remuneration of the incumbents for their performances, the provision of facilities for performance of the roles, and the disposal of the product. The organization of an instrumental complex into a corporate body which exists in a context of other individual actors and corporate bodies involves also the management of "foreign relations." Here rearrangements of the internal organization and the use of the power to gratify or deprive which the corporate body has at its disposal are available to the manager (as well as the invocation and interpretation of the common value-orientations which are shared with the "foreign" body).

Thus social systems may be further characterized by the extent to which they are made up of fused or segregated roles in an instrumental context or, more concretely, of technical, of artisan, and of executive roles.

Up to this point, our discussion has entirely passed over that aspect of the system of relation-

[1] The independent professional role is then defined as a special sub-type in which the technical competence of the incumbent includes the mastery of a generalized intellectual orientation. The professional role, too, is subject to a fairly high degree of segregation of its component elements, although some limits are imposed by the generalized intellectual orientation.

ships which is oriented primarily by interests in direct and immediate gratification. Within such a system of relationships oriented toward direct and immediate gratification the basic functional categories are homologous with those of the instrumental complex. In the first place, direct gratification in relation to a cathected social object is a relation to that object as a "consumer" of the impulse. It is not enough to have the need-disposition. An object must be available which is both "appropriate" for the gratification and "receptive." Alter must allow himself to be an object and not resist or withdraw.

Second, there is also a parallel to remuneration in the dependence of ego, not merely on the receptiveness but on what may be called the *response* of alter. Alter does not merely allow ego to *express* or gratify his need-disposition in the relationship; alter is also expected to act positively in such a way that ego will be the receptive object. These two types of functional preconditions for the gratification of need-dispositions are not always fulfilled by the same objects—where they are we may speak of a symmetrical attachment.

Third, gratification needs not merely an object but is also dependent on [a] set of circumstances which appear, in certain respects, to have functions homologous with those of facilities in the instrumental relationship (see Parsons and Shils, 1951, Ch. 2). [These circumstances or] occasions often center around relations to third parties, both because of the necessity of ego's distribution of his expressive orientations among the different objects in a system and because the prerequisite of giving gratification to and receiving it from certain actors in a system is a certain relationship with all other actors in the system.

Finally, if we take the need-disposition for gratification and not the object relation as the unit, there is an important functional parallel with coöperation in the instrumental complex. Some need-dispositions, like some technical performances, may be segregated into a separate object relation. But there is a strong tendency for ego to become attached to particular objects for the gratifications of a variety of different need-dispositions. We have called this kind of object relationship a diffuse "attachment." Such an attachment organizes need-disposition gratifications into a "coöperative" system. Putting these various elements together we derive the accompanying homologous paradigm of the structure of the system of relationships of direct and immediate gratifications or expressions. This paradigm analyzes the elementary structure of a social relationship system relevant to the actor's needs for direct gratification or expression. For *n* actors to participate in the same social system, the relationships involved in this paradigm must be organized and controlled, generally through institutionalization. There is in each case a problem of the settlement of the terms on which the gratifications in question can be attained, or in other terms, of the reciprocal rights and obligations to receive and to give various types and degrees of gratification, which is directly homologous with the problem of the settlement of the terms of exchange.

There is, furthermore, in the expressive system an important homologue to possessions in the instrumental system, since there are entities which can "change hands." The actor can acquire them from someone else or grant them to someone else and he can have, acquire, or relinquish rights in them. In the focal case where alter is the cathected object, this must mean the establishment of rights vis-à-vis the *action* of alter, that is, of a situation where ego can *count* on alter's actions. This will include exceptions of alter's overt behavior, but for the reasons which have already been discussed, the central interest will be in alter's *attitudes*. Such a right to a given attitude on alter's part may be called a relational possession. Relational possession in this sense constitutes the core of the reward system of a society and thus of its stratification, centering above all on the distribution of rights to response, love, approval, and esteem. (This also means that there will be an

Availability of appropriate occasions (depending on third parties)		Social objects as appropriate and receptive
	Specific gratifications of a particular need-disposition	
Diffuse attachments (coördinating particular need-dispositions)		Social objects as responsive

equivalent in the expressive system to the "terms of exchange.")

The expressive system of an actor will therefore, to a highly important degree, have to be organized in a system of relationships with other actors in appropriate roles. This system will regulate choice of objects, occasions—and what is primarily at issue in the present discussion—which objects have segmental significance, gratifying only one need-disposition at a time, and which other objects have diffuse significance, gratifying many need-dispositions at the same time. Here the two most obvious types of role would be on the one hand, segregated or specific gratification roles; on the other, diffuse attachment roles. A diffuse attachment then would involve gratification of a plurality of need-dispositions; it would place each object in both receptive and responsive roles and would involve the actor in a more or less continuous complex of appropriate occasions.

The instrumental complex and the complex of direct gratifications or expressions are both aspects of the total allocative mechanism of a concrete social system. The next step in our analysis, then, is to see how they both work in a single system. Instrumental and expressive functions may be segregated from each other, each being performed by distinctly separate objects in distinct roles, or they may be fused in the same objects and roles. Where there is segregation of the instrumental and need-gratifying roles and orientations toward objects, it does not necessarily mean that the need-dispositions are always frustrated. It means that the roles and objects which are instrumentally defined may be either neutral or negative as far as their capacity for the gratification of direct need-dispositions is concerned. There certainly can be and very frequently are cases of conflict where segregation is imperfect and positive fusion is impossible. In these cases there must be either frustration of the immediate and direct gratification of need-dispositions or the instrumental complex will be distorted because the instrumentally necessary actions will not be performed in accordance with instrumental role-expectations. In the total economy of the personality, however, adequate motivation of instrumental activities becomes impossible if the performance of instrumental roles imposes too heavy a sacrifice of the larger gratification interests of the personality.

It would be possible to carry out the classification of the possible combinations in this sphere to a high degree of elaboration. For our present purposes, however, it is sufficient to distinguish six major types of combination which are particularly relevant to the broader differentiations of role types. They are the following:

1. The segregation of specific expressive interests from instrumental expectations; for example, the role of a casual spectator at an entertainment.

2. The segregation of a diffuse object attachment from instrumental expectations; for example, the pure type of romantic love role.

3. The fusion of a specific expressive or gratificatory interest with a specific instrumental performance; for example, the spectator at a commercialized entertainment.

4. The fusion of a diffuse attachment with diffuse expectations of instrumental performances; for example, kinship roles.

5. The segregation of specific instrumental performances, both from specific expressive interests and attachments and from other components of the instrumental complex; for example, technical roles.

6. The fusion of a plurality of instrumental functions in a complex which is segregated from immediate expressive interests; for example, "artisan" and "executive" roles.

This classification has been constructed by taking the cases of fusion and segregation of the instrumental and direct gratification complexes and, within each of the segregated role orientations, distinguishing the segregation of role components from the fusion of role complexes. The technical role (5) and the executive role (6) are the two possibilities of segregation and fusion in the instrumental complex when it is segregated from the direct gratification complex. The role of casual spectator (1) and the romantic love role (2) are the two possibilities of segregation and fusion of the direct gratification complex when it has been segregated from the instrumental complex. There is a fusion of the two complexes in roles (3) and (4). In the role of the paying spectator there is segregation both in the direct gratification and in the instrumental orientation; in the role of member of a kinship group there is fusion of all role components in each orientation.

REFERENCES

Parsons, T., and Shils, E. A., 1951. *Toward a general theory of action.* Cambridge, Mass.: Harvard University Press.

selection 28 The Roles of Legislators in the Legislative Process

JOHN C. WAHLKE, HEINZ EULAU, WILLIAM BUCHANAN, AND LEROY C. FERGUSON

THE LEGISLATOR AS A DECISION MAKER: PURPOSIVE ROLES

Since "lawmaking" is accepted as the central function of American state legislatures, participation in the making of decisions is not only expected of the legislator but is authorized and legitimized by his occupancy of the official position. But "participation in lawmaking or decision making" is hardly a satisfactory characterization of the role of legislator. Rather it is role orientations which are the specifications of the legislative role, without which the central concept of "legislator" does not, and probably cannot, have much analytical meaning.

His role orientations are probably not unrelated to the legislator's perception of the power pattern of a political system and the kinds of functions which the legislature is called on to perform. For instance, in a party-disciplined legislature the individual legislator is unlikely to find much room for independence or inventiveness; the purely routine aspects of his job probably loom large in his legislative role orientations. In a legislature particularly exposed to the pulls and pressures of interest groups, role orientations are likely to derive from the need to arbitrate, compromise, and integrate group conflicts. In the legislature subservient to the whims and wishes of the electorate, the spokesman function is likely to be accentuated in legislative role orientations. In a legislature which enjoys relatively great independence from the executive, legislative role orientations may stress the creative, policy-making aspects of the job. Moreover, legislative role orientations need not occur in pristine singularity. Two and three, or even more, orientations may be held by a legislator.

The complexity of institutionally derived legislative role orientations becomes even more apparent if we place them in a historical perspective. They may be, and probably are, patterned by past as well as current configurations in the power structure of the political system. For as institutions, legislatures are phenomena in time, with memories of their own going beyond the limitations of time. These memories are transmitted by legislators themselves from generation to generation, consciously or unconsciously shaping the perceptions of the present. The past may thus continue to serve as a model for contemporary role orientations.

A legislature is the product of a long and slow growth over centuries, with a veritable maze of rules, procedures, privileges, duties, etiquettes, rituals, informal understandings and arrangements. Every phase of the lawmaking process—from the introduction of bills through their deliberation in committee and debate on the floor to the final vote—has gradually become circumscribed by appropriate strategies and tactics. The legislator was always expected to master the rules of parliamentary procedure and be familiar with available strategies. Hence the legislator could traditionally orient himself to the job of lawmaking in terms of the parliamentary rules and routines, rather than in terms of legislative functions as they may be shaped by the power situation in the political system. Parliamentary ritual rather than parliamentary goals would absorb his attention. One may call this orientation to the legislative role that of the *Ritualist*.

A second orientation is particularly deeply rooted in American political history. It was probably generated by the conflict between the British Crown, acting through the agency of the appointed governor, and the colonial legislatures. In the

---

Abridged from pages 245–422 of a book by the same authors entitled *The Legislative System: Explorations in Legislative Behavior*, 1962, New York: Wiley. Reprinted by permission of the authors and Wiley. This study was supported in part by a grant from the Committee on Political Behavior.

course of this conflict the legislature came to be viewed as the instrument through which colonial interests could be defended against what were perceived as royal encroachments on colonial rights. It does not matter, in this connection, that the colonists differed among themselves with regard to the proper object of legislative activity —whether the defense of property rights or the natural rights of man were the goals of colonial claims. The crucial point is that the legislature and legislators were expected to be advocates or defenders of popular demands. Wilfred E. Binkley has aptly described the role orientation of the colonial legislator—what we shall call the role orientation of *Tribune*: "The assemblyman, chosen by popular election as a representative of his neighbourhood . . . set forth to the provincial capital, commissioned, as he believed, to fight the people's battle against the governor" (Binkley, 1947, p. 4).

A third major orientation seems to have originated at a later stage of colonial-executive relations, the stage when the legislature asserted itself as an institution capable of performing independent, policy-making functions. As Alfred De Grazia has summarized this later development, "The Colonial legislatures already conceived of themselves as possessed of a positive legislative capacity removed from the ancient English idea of Parliament as an agency for wresting concessions from the Crown. They had learned well the lessons of the seventeenth century revolutions as well as those to be obtained from the Bill of Rights. Legislatures, they had come to realize, could govern" (De Grazia, 1951, p. 70). Once the colonial legislature was expected to be an instrument of governance, rather than an instrument of obstruction, a role orientation more appropriate to the legislature's new function was likely to emerge. We shall call this the orientation of *Inventor*. The legislator was now expected to be sensitive to public issues, discover potential solutions and explore alternatives, both with regard to means as well as ends. The problems of government were deemed soluble by way of rational deliberation and cogent argument in debate, partly because the issues were relatively simple, not requiring technical, expert knowledge; partly because the range of governmental activity was seen as very limited.

Just as the role orientation of inventor derived from the conception of the legislature as a creative, policy-making institution, a fourth orientation —we shall call it that of *Broker*—developed in response to the rise of interest groups and the increasing number of demands made on legislatures by pressure groups. The legislature became, in the course of the nineteenth century, a major integrating force in the pluralism of American political, social, and economic life. This development had been foreshadowed by the struggle of interests in the Constitutional Convention, in early Congresses and state legislatures, and had suggested to the authors of *The Federalist* the balancing function of legislative bodies. The role orientation of broker was probably implicit in Hamilton's notion of the disinterested representative (*The Federalist*, 35), and though everyday politics seemed to confirm this conception of the legislator's role as a working principle, it was not articulated in political theory until fairly recently.

This review of legislative role orientations, whether theoretically derived from the legislature's place in the power structure of the political system or historically reconstructed, has suggested four major types—ritualist, tribune, inventor, and broker. There may be others. For example, journalistic accounts suggest many legislators have an orientation which might be called *opportunist*—the legislator who holds the office without really "taking" the associated role, who accepts the bare minimum of expectations, such as voting on roll calls and attending committee meetings or sessions as a passive participant, but who mainly uses the legislative office, or "plays *at*" the legislative role while concealing that he is really playing other, essentially nonlegislative roles.

THE LEGISLATOR AS REPRESENTATIVE: REPRESENTATIONAL ROLES

The problem of representation is central to all discussions of the functions of legislatures or the behavior of legislators. For it is through the process of representation, presumably, that legislatures are empowered to act for the whole body politic and legitimized. And because, by virtue of representation, they participate in legislation, the represented accept legislative decisions as authoritative. It would seem, therefore, that legislation and representation are closely related. And if they are related, the functional relevance of representation to legislative behavior needs to be articulated.

But agreement about the meaning of the term "representation" hardly goes beyond a general consensus regarding the context within which it is appropriately used. In the following we shall describe [three] orientational types as they were defined by legislators themselves.

Trustee

The role orientation of trustee finds expression in two major conceptions of how decisions ought to be made. These conceptions may occur severally and jointly. There is, first, a moralistic interpretation. The trustee sees himself as a free agent in that, as a premise of his decision-making behavior, he claims to follow what he considers right or just, his convictions and principles, the dictates of his conscience. There is also a judgmental conception of the role of trustee. The trustee is not bound by a mandate because his decisions are his own considered judgments based on an assessment of the facts in each decision, his understanding of all the problems and angles involved, his thoughtful appraisal of the sides at issue.

A great variety of conceptions of representation are involved in the role orientation of the trustee. In particular, it seems that this orientation derives not only from a normative definition of the role of the representative, but that it is also often grounded in interpersonal situations which make it functionally inevitable. The condition that the represented do not have the information necessary to give intelligent instructions, that the representative is unable to discover what his clientele may want, that preferences remain unexpressed, that there is no need for instructions because of an alleged harmony of interests between representative and represented—all of the circumstances may be acknowledged as sources of the role orientation of trustee, at times even forced on the representative against his own predilection for a mandate if that were possible.

Delegate

Just as the trustee role orientation involves a variety of conceptions of representation, so does the orientation of delegate. All delegates are agreed, of course, that they should not use their independent judgment or principled convictions as decision-making premises. But this does not mean that they feel equally committed to follow instructions, from whatever clientele. Some merely say that they try to inform themselves before making decisions by consulting their constituents or others; however, they seem to imply that such consultation has a mandatory effect on their behavior: "I do ask them (i.e., constituents) quite often, especially where there's doubt in my mind." Others frankly acknowledge instructions as necessary or desirable premises in decision making: "I do what they want me to do. Being re-elected is the best test"; or, "A majority of the people always gets their way with me." Finally, there is the representative in the delegate role who not only feels that he should follow instructions, but who also believes that he should do so even if these instructions are explicitly counter to his own judgment or principles: "Some things I'm not particularly sold on but if the people want it, they should have it"; or, "Reflect the thinking of my district even if it is not my own private thinking."

What strikes one in the comments [of delegates], in contrast to those made by trustees, is the failure to elaborate in greater detail the problem of why the representative should follow instructions in his decision-making behavior. Delegates, it seems, have a simpler, more mechanical conception of the political process and of the function of representation in legislative behavior. Perhaps most noticeable, in contrast to the trustee orientation, is the omission of delegates to raise the question of political responsibility under conditions of strict instructions. Apparently, the problem is ignored by the delegate precisely because he rejects the possibility of discretion in his decision making. It is a matter of speculation whether the role orientation of delegate is based on a conscious majoritarian bias which he could elaborate and defend if necessary, or whether it simply reflects lack of political articulation and sophistication. On the other hand, the fact that the delegate seems to have so little doubt about this role suggests that, whatever his reasons and regardless of whether his decisions are really in accord with the views of different groups among his clientele, he is likely to be characterized by a fairly high sense of personal effectiveness in his approach to lawmaking.

Politico

As suggested earlier, the classical dichotomization of the concept of representation in terms of independent judgment and mandate was unlikely to exhaust the empirical possibilities of representational behavior. In particular, it would seem to be possible for a representative to act in line with both criteria. For roles and role orientations need not be mutually exclusive. Depending on circumstances, a representative may hold the role orientation of trustee at one time, and the role orientation of delegate at another time. Or he might even seek to reconcile both orientations in terms of a third. In other words, the representational-role set comprises the extreme orientations of trustee and delegate and a third orientation, the politico, resulting from overlap of these two. Within the orientational range called politico, the trustee and delegate roles may be taken simultaneously, possibly making for role conflict, or they may be taken seriatim, one after another as legislative situations dictate.

Because our data do not permit us to discriminate too sharply between these two possibilities, we shall speak of legislators who express both orientations, either simultaneously or serially, as politicos.

In general the politico as a representational-role taker differs from both the trustee and the delegate in that he seems to be more sensitive to conflicting alternatives, more flexible in the ways in which he tries to resolve the conflict among alternatives, and less dogmatic in his orientation towards legislative behavior as it is related to his representational role.

THE LEGISLATOR AND HIS DISTRICT: AREAL ROLES

Representation of geographical areas introduces a certain amount of ambiguity into the relationship between representative and represented. Part of this ambiguity involves the widely held expectation, contested by Edmund Burke but shared by many citizens and politicians alike, that the legislator is a spokesman of the presumed "interests" of his district. Implicit in this expectation is the assumption that a geographical unit has interests which are distinct and different from those of other units. This assumption has been challenged on a variety of grounds: that the geographical area as such, as an electoral unit, is artificial; that it cannot and does not generate interests shared by its residents; that it has no unique interests; and so on. Schemes of proportional or vocational representation have been advanced to make possible the representation of allegedly more "natural" interest groupings, such as minority, skill, or economic groups.

Yet, the assumption that geographical districts have unique interests which are, or ought to be, taken into consideration when legislative decisions are made, continues to be shared not only by voters, politicians, and others involved in policy making, but also by scientific students of the political process. It underlies many studies which seek to relate legislative roll-call votes to socio-economic characteristics of electoral districts, as well as those studies which analyze the socio-economic composition of legislatures.

Such an interpretation is most tenuous under modern conditions. Electoral districts tend to be so heterogeneous in population attributes, so pluralistic in the character of their group life, so diverse in the kinds of values and beliefs held, that whatever measures of central tendency are used to classify a district are more likely to conceal than to reveal its real character. The notion that elections are held as a method to discover persons whose attributes and attitudes will somehow mirror those most widely shared by people in their district appears to be of dubious validity. The function of representation in modern political systems is not to make the legislature a mathematically exact copy of the electorate.

But the difficulty of finding an identity between representative and represented does not mean that a legislator's point of reference in making decisions cannot be his district. It may or may not be, and whether it is or not is a matter of empirical determination. We may doubt that what orients a legislator towards his district rather than some other focus of attention is the similarity between his district's characteristics and his own. Or we may assume that a legislator incorporates in himself the characteristics of his district—which, for argument's sake, may be admitted when he comes from a relatively homogeneous area. But it is still an empirical question whether or not the legislator is subjectively concerned with his district and seeks to discover its "interests."

In spite of the considerations just mentioned, state legislators perceive representation of the interests of some geographical area as a proper function of their legislative activities. On the basis of their responses, we classified legislators into "district oriented," "state oriented," and "district–state oriented."

District Oriented

District-oriented legislators indicated two types of response patterns: some simply mentioned their district or county as an important focus of their areal role orientation; others explicitly placed district above state in defining this orientation.

A second major group of district-oriented legislators specifically pointed to the importance of placing the interests of their district above those of the state. Their concern with the state's interests usually appeared as an afterthought. But, as one respondent put it, "you cannot actually disassociate one from the other."

State Oriented

State-oriented legislators either mentioned the state alone as the salient focus of their areal orientation, or they also mentioned the district, but clearly tending to place the state above district in importance. Some of them emphasized the need for state policy or state program as an overriding consideration. A second group of state-oriented legislators pointed to both the state and the district as relevant foci of their role orientation, but tended to give the benefit of doubt to the state. Finally, some of the state-oriented legislators explicitly stressed the desirability of overcoming parochial considerations in favor of the state.

District–State Oriented

A third group of legislators who spontaneously concerned themselves with the areal focus of their legislative role mentioned both district and state as equally relevant to their legislative or service activities. Apparently, they did not envisage the possibility of conflict arising out of these orientations and thought that they could attend to the interests of both state and district without undue complications.

LEGISLATORS' ROLE ORIENTATIONS TOWARD PRESSURE GROUPS

Further insight into the character and function of pressure politics requires examination of individual legislators' postures toward pressure groups and their reasons for them—both "reasons" they adduce and correlations between legislators' postures and analytic variables established by analysts. We are concerned here, it should be emphasized, with the functioning of the legislative *institution* and not with unique historical events or outcomes. Similarly, we are concerned with legislators' orientations toward pressure groups as a *generic* class of "significant others," not with their particular individual group affiliations and identifications.

With respect to the bearing of pressure politics on the function of representation, the basic question is, how, and how much, are demands of interest groups considered by a legislature in the course of its decision making? In general some members will accommodate the demands of organized interest groups in the legislative process. Others will resist consideration or accommodation of these demands. Still others, presumably attuned to other persons or factors, will play a neutral or varying and indeterminate role toward such group demands.

It seems obvious that a legislator's reaction to the activities of pressure groups and lobbyists will depend in part upon his general evaluation of pressure politics as a mode of political activity in the world he lives in. It likewise seems obvious that legislators' reactions to pressure groups or lobbyists will vary with their different degrees of knowledge or awareness of group activities. The legislator who knows what the Municipal League is, what it wants, who speaks for it and when, will react differently to cues from the League than one who never heard of it and doesn't identify anyone as its spokesman.

Assuming, then, that any given legislator's behavior with respect to pressure groups will depend largely upon his general affective orientation toward pressure politics and his awareness of such activity when it occurs around him, one can construct the following very simple typology of legislators' role orientations toward pressure groups:

Facilitators: Have a friendly attitude toward group activity *and* relatively much knowledge about it.

Resistors: Have a hostile attitude toward group activity *and* relatively much knowledge about it.

Neutrals: Have no strong attitude of favor or disfavor with respect to group activity (regardless of their knowledge of it), or, have very little knowledge about it (regardless of their friendliness or hostility toward it).

THE NETWORK OF ROLES: AN IDEAL-TYPE CONSTRUCT

The analytical distinction between clientele, representational, and purposive roles is helpful in dissecting the legislator's total role. Actual behavior, however, is not a function of discrete roles, but of a system of roles. It is the network of interpenetrating roles which gives structure and coherence to the legislative process. Comparative analysis of the eight chambers of four states included in this study supports the notion that roles are meaningfully related to each other. Moreover, the patterning of observed relations and differences is such that it is possible to develop an ideal-type construct of the total network. Such an ideal-type construct is, of course, an exaggeration of empirical reality, but it can serve two valuable purposes: first, it can demonstrate the logic of the postulated network; and, second, it can serve as an independent criterion for comparing the concrete, empirical role systems.

Figure 1 presents a diagram of the ideal-type network of legislators' roles suggested by the clustering of role orientations empirically found in the four states and by the theoretical considerations. The diagram reflects the observed tendency of certain orientations in one sector to be associated with particular orientations in others. Thus, the upper half of the diagram idealizes the following pairs of role orientations: majority-state-oriented, majority-facilitator, state-oriented-facilitator, facilitator-politico, majority-politico, majority-broker, state-oriented-trustee, state-oriented-inventor/broker, facilitator-broker, broker-trustee/

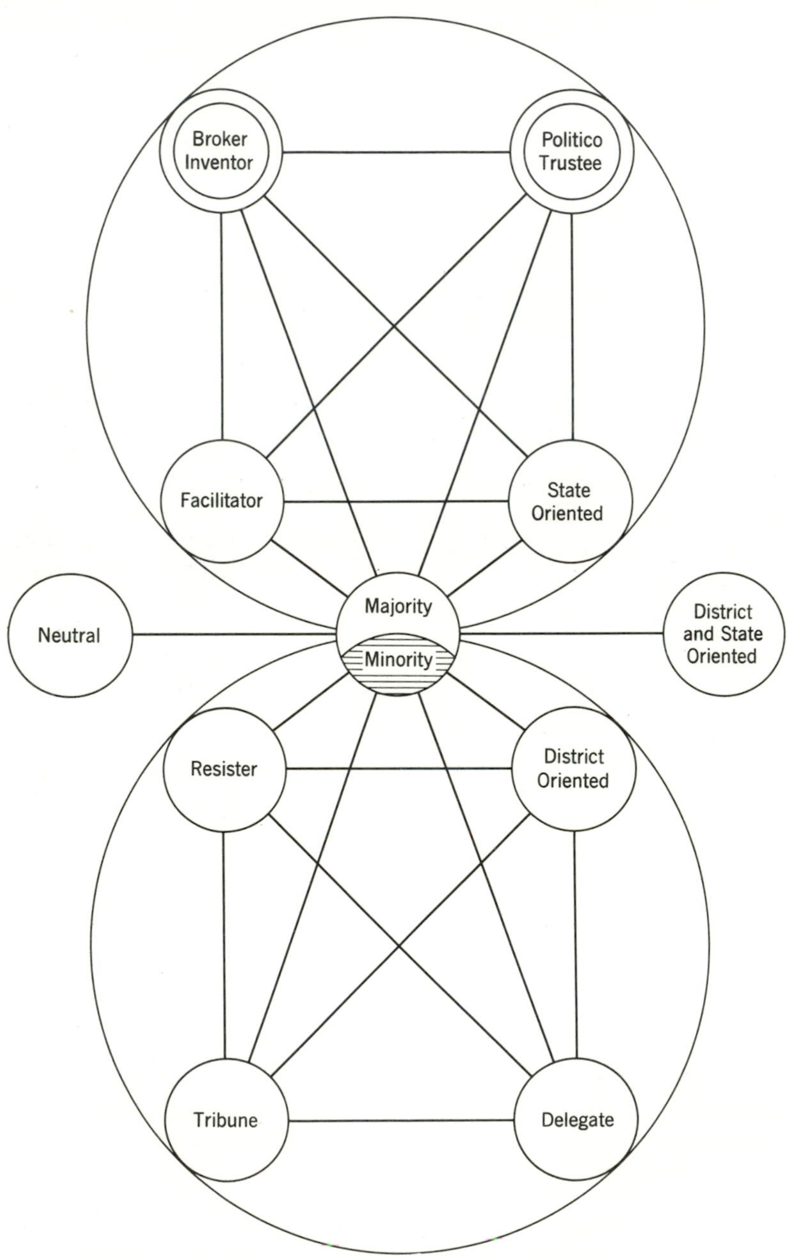

Figure 1. Ideal-type network of roles.

politico, and inventor-trustee. The lower half idealizes these pairs: minority-district-oriented, minority-resister, district-oriented-resister, resister-delegate, minority-delegate, minority-inventor/tribune, district-oriented-delegate, district-oriented-tribune, resister-tribune, and tribune-delegate. The diagram thus suggests two essentially reciprocal sets of relationships or dimensions, one represented in the upper, the other in the lower half of the diagram. The neutral and district-state orientations do not associate readily in theory with either of these, but, as the diagram shows, stand more or less outside and between them.

Any individual legislator is likely to be located more in one than another dimension of this network of available roles. Moreover, it is the network as such, rather than simple adoption of one orientation instead of another, which is crucial to the individual's behavior. That is to say, the difference between one role and another in a given subsystem—such as, for instance, the difference between facilitator and resister, or between trustee and delegate—is a function of the total network of roles. In such a network, each role is somehow related to every other role, and the character and extent of these relations gives any one empirical legislative role system its peculiar character.

We have not attempted to characterize the different patterns or clusterings of role orientation which might be manifested by the individual legislator, in terms of the ideal-type network

TABLE 1 PROPORTIONS OF DOMINANT ROLE PAIRS IN THE FOUR LEGISLATURES

Lower Chambers											
Ohio	*N* =	% =	N.J.	*N* =	% =	Calif.	*N* =	% =	Tenn.	*N* =	% =
Ma/Di-St	94	31	Ma/Di-St	38	34	Mi/Di	50	30	Ma/Di	38	42
Ma/Fa	125	32	Ma/Fa	57	28	Ma/Ne	68	26	Ma/Re	87	31
Di-St/Ne	89	19	Di-St/Fa	37	19	Di/Fa	44	27	Di/Re	38	23
Ma/Tr	94	35	Ma/Tr	39	41	Ma/Tr	37	30	Ma/Tr	61	59
St/Tr	75	20	Di-St/Tr	26	23	Di/De	23	30	Di/Tr	31	29
			St/Tr	26	23						
Fa/Tr	92	24	Fa/Tr	39	26	Ne/Tr	32	31	Ne/Tr	59	36
Ma/Br	130	36	Ma/Tri	58	47	Mi/Tri	78	28	Ma/Tri	89	48
Di-St/Br	95	27	Di-St/Tri	37	32	Di/Tri	49	47	Di/Tri	37	49
Fa/Br	125	24	Fa/Tri	57	23	Ne/Tri	68	22	Ne/Tri	87	28
Br/Tr	120	23	In/Tr	55	31	In/Tr	47	19	Tri/Tr	66	41
Senates											
Ma/Di-St	18	22	Ma/Di	16	25	Ma/Di	28	25	Ma/Di	8	50
Ma/Di	18	22	Mi/Di	16	25						
Mi/Di	18	22									
Ma/Fa	32	28	Ma/Fa	21	29	Mi/Fa	29	28	Ma/Re	29	38
Di/Fa	19	27	Di-/St/Fa	16	31	Di/Ne	24	21	Di/Re	8	38
Ma/Tr	20	50	Ma/Tr	15	33	Ma/Tr	12	33	Ma/Tr	17	76
Di/Tr	13	23	Di/De	13	31	Di-St/Tr	12	34	Di/Tr	5	80
St/Tr	13	23									
Ne/Tr	20	30	Fa/Po	15	27	Fa/Tri	12	50	Re/Tr	17	41
Ma/Br	32	28	Ma/In	21	38	Ma/Tri	35	34	Ma/Tri	31	42
Di/Tri	17	41	Di/Tri	16	44	Di/Tri	28	29	Di/Tri	8	63
						St/Tri	28	29			
Fa/Br	32	22	Fa/Tri	23	38	Ne/Tri	29	28	Re/Tri	29	28
In/Tr	24	25	In/Po	21	19	Br/Tr	17	24	Tri/Tr	18	50
Br/Tr	24	25	Tri/De	21	19	Tri/Po	17	24			

Key:
Ma = majority
Mi = minority
Br = broker
De = delegate
Di = district
Di-St = district-state
Fa = facilitator
In = inventor
Ne = neutral
Po = politico
Re = resister
Tri = tribute
Tr = trustee

illustrated in Figure 1. We have, instead, sought to characterize the system differences resulting from the various constellations of role orientation found to prevail in the four legislatures. In other words, although the diagram represents the coincidence of particular role orientations for the individual legislator, we are interested in it as a representation of the aggregates of role orientations and role relationships constituting a system of role relationships among legislators in particular legislatures. We wish to use the ideal-type construct of the network of roles to characterize differences among legislative systems. It is to this that we turn in the next section.

LEGISLATIVE ROLE STRUCTURES

Ideally, it would be desirable to identify and specify the entire matrix of all role combinations in a given legislative system. Unfortunately, even the largest chamber in this study includes too few cases to isolate empirically the theoretically possible matrix of roles in combination. However, we can construct a partial framework by dealing with the most frequent individual pairs of roles that are taken in a legislative chamber. Each of these "dominant pairs" may or may not be linked because any one role in one pair may also be linked with a third role in another pair.

Table 1 presents the dominant (i.e., the most frequent) pairs of roles in the two chambers of each state legislature. The base of the proportions is the total number of legislators whose individual roles appeared in the dominant pairs. For instance, of the California House members for whom data were available, 30 per cent are district-oriented minority members, 26 per cent are majority-neutrals, 27 per cent are district-oriented facilitators, and so on.

House Role Structures

The distributions in Table 1 yield some interesting results, but they are difficult to inspect and appraise. There are two ways in which we can simplify the emerging structures—one numerical, the other graphical. First, we can single out the number of times a given role appears in a dominant pair. Table 2 presents this alternative. The patterns for each role set are clear. They sensitize us to the significance of particular distributions in the more complex array of Table 1. In the first place, in the New Jersey and Ohio Houses, where "party government" has genuine meaning, the role of majority member appears among the dominant pairs, but the role of minority member does not. In California, where "party control" has little meaning, both the roles of majority and minority member are encountered in the dominant pairs. Tennessee represents a special case: although formally the role of "majority member" alone occurs in the dominant pairs, we know that the "majority" is factionalized and not a majority in the same sense as in the competitive party states. The Tennessee House is actually composed of competing "minorities," and though the role of majority member seems present in the dominant pairs, it cannot be taken in a literal sense.

TABLE 2 NUMBER OF TIMES A ROLE APPEARS IN COMBINATION WITH ANOTHER IN A DOMINANT PAIR, LOWER CHAMBERS

Role	Ohio	N.J.	Calif.	Tenn.
Party				
Majority member	4	4	2	4
Minority member	0	0	2	0
Representational				
Trustee	4	5	3	4
Politico	0	0	0	0
Delegate	0	0	1	0
Purposive				
Inventor	0	1	1	0
Broker	4	0	0	0
Tribune	0	3	3	4
Areal				
State oriented	1	1	0	0
District-State oriented	3	4	0	0
District oriented	0	0	4	4
Pressure group				
Facilitator	3	4	1	0
Neutral	1	0	3	2
Resister	0	0	0	2

Second, in the representational-role set, the role of trustee occurs in the dominant pairs almost exclusively, with the single exception of California, where the delegate role appears in one dominant pair. This role of trustee is, as we noted earlier, so universal that it is necessarily linked to any cluster in the total network of dominant pairs. In other words, it does not serve as a discriminating factor in a topology of role structures.

Third, in the purposive-role set, the Ohio House role structure differs from the other three lower chamber structures in the pervasiveness of the broker role in dominant pairs, while elsewhere the tribune role is more prominent, suggesting a more "populist" milieu than prevailed in 1957 in the Republican-dominated Ohio House.

Fourth, of the areal-role set, the district role is

present in dominant pairs in California and Tennessee, but not in Ohio and New Jersey. In the latter two states, the district-state role occurs in the dominant pairs, as does the state role in one pair, but neither of these two roles is present in the dominant California and Tennessee pairs. The pattern suggests that the areal-role orientations held by legislators may serve as critical discriminating devices in the characterization of legislative role structures.

Finally, the pressure-group-role set seems to perform a similar function. The facilitator role is prominent in Ohio's and New Jersey's dominant pairs, and the neutral role in California. Only in Tennessee does the resister role appear in dominant pairs, and it does so twice, while the facilitator

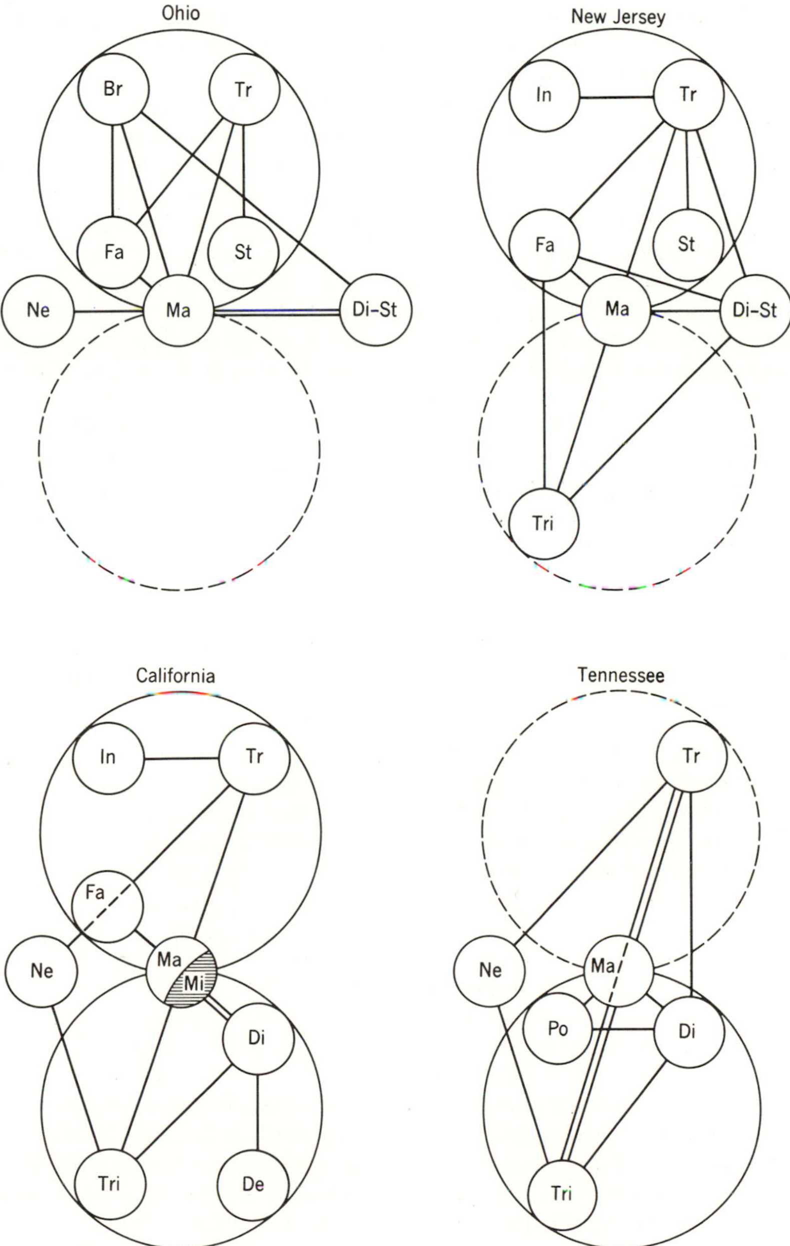

Figure 2. Role structures of four lower houses.

role is altogether absent from dominant pairs.

The frequency of a role's appearance in dominant pairs, and the pattern of occurrences from state to state, give a first view of what one might expect when the linkages between those roles which constitute the dominant pairs are constructed graphically. The diagrams of the House structures presented in Figure 2 can be readily compared with the ideal-type construct of [Figure 1]. This comparison makes it possible to develop an empirical typology of legislative role structures.

The Ohio diagram of Figure 2 shows a relatively highly integrated role cluster of what we may call the "majoritarian type." Almost all the ideal-type linkages are present, and where they are not they are replaced by "intermediate" roles in the dominant pairs (such as the district-state instead of the "pure" state role, or the neutral role instead of the facilitator role). But the linkages in no way penetrate into the reciprocal "minoritarian" cluster of the ideal-type model. Minority members are totally eclipsed as role takers in the dominant structure, as are such minority-linked roles of the ideal-type model as tribunes, resisters, delegates, and district oriented.

In The New Jersey House structure, also, the role of minority member and its ideally associated roles of delegate, resister, and district oriented are missing from the dominant majority-centered cluster. But, in contrast to Ohio, the tribune role of the minority cluster is linked three times to majority-anchored roles, and the reciprocal roles of the purposive-role set, ideally located in the majoritarian cluster, are not among the dominant pairs. With this one exception, then, the New Jersey House role structure is very similar to Ohio's. We can characterize the Ohio House structure as "broker-majoritarian" and the New Jersey House structure as "tribune-majoritarian."

By way of contrast, the California House role structure reveals a bipartisan pattern. The structure is not solely, as in the Ohio case, centered in the majority role (though the "majority" had organized the lower chamber), nor is it predominantly so centered as in the case of New Jersey. The California structure includes elements of both the ideal-type majoritarian and minoritarian clusters. And not only do both majority and minority member roles appear in the dominant pairs, but the linkages cut across the boundaries of the reciprocal sets of the ideal-type model. The "populist" component is outstanding: the tribune and district-oriented roles are linked across cluster boundaries, but the majority-related roles of inventor and facilitator each appear in dominant pairs. The California House role structure reflects the strongly "atomistic" orientation of California legislators, and it is indicative of the low salience of party roles as premises for legislative behavior. We may term the California House role structure "populist-bipartisan."

Finally, the Tennessee House role structure is altogether different from the previous types. Though formally "majoritarian," it is in fact minority geared: the tribune and district roles are most pervasive, and, alone among the four chambers, the role of resister appears in at least one dominant pair. At the same time, such majority-anchored roles as inventor or broker in the purposive-role set, facilitator, and state oriented are missing altogether in the Tennessee House structure. Only the trustee, ideally located in the majority cluster, is present. Apparently, it is a role which cannot be shed in contemporary empirical reality, even in a system which is so clearly minority geared. These results, we already suggested, are easy to explain, and they confirm that

TABLE 3 NUMBER OF TIMES A ROLE APPEARS IN COMBINATION WITH ANOTHER IN A DOMINANT PAIR, SENATES

Role	Ohio	N.J.	Calif.	Tenn.
Party				
Majority member	5	4	3	4
Minority member	1	1	1	0
Representational				
Trustee	6	1	4	4
Politico	0	2	1	0
Delegate	0	2	0	0
Purposive				
Inventor	1	2	0	0
Broker	3	0	1	0
Tribune	1	3	5	4
Areal				
State oriented	1	0	1	0
District-State oriented	1	1	1	0
District oriented	5	4	3	4
Pressure group				
Facilitator	3	4	2	0
Neutral	1	0	2	0
Resistor	0	0	0	4

the "majority" in Tennessee is only a pro forma majority. In fact, the "majority" Democrats are divided into competing fractions, none of which can permanently control the legislature, and which behave more like minority parties in a multiparty system. We can characterize this structure as "populist-minoritarian."

Senate Role Structures

Tables 1 and 3 show that in the four Senates more pairs are tied for dominance, making the over-all picture somewhat more complex. But a glance at Figure 3 will indicate that, in spite of the greater complexity, the general patterns observed in the role structures of the lower houses are maintained from state to state, but a number of differences may be noted.

In the first place, in the Ohio and New Jersey Senate the role of minority member seems to be somewhat more integrated into the dominant majority pattern than is the case in the respective Houses. This is quite plausible. In the smaller chambers, the minority is more likely to be in

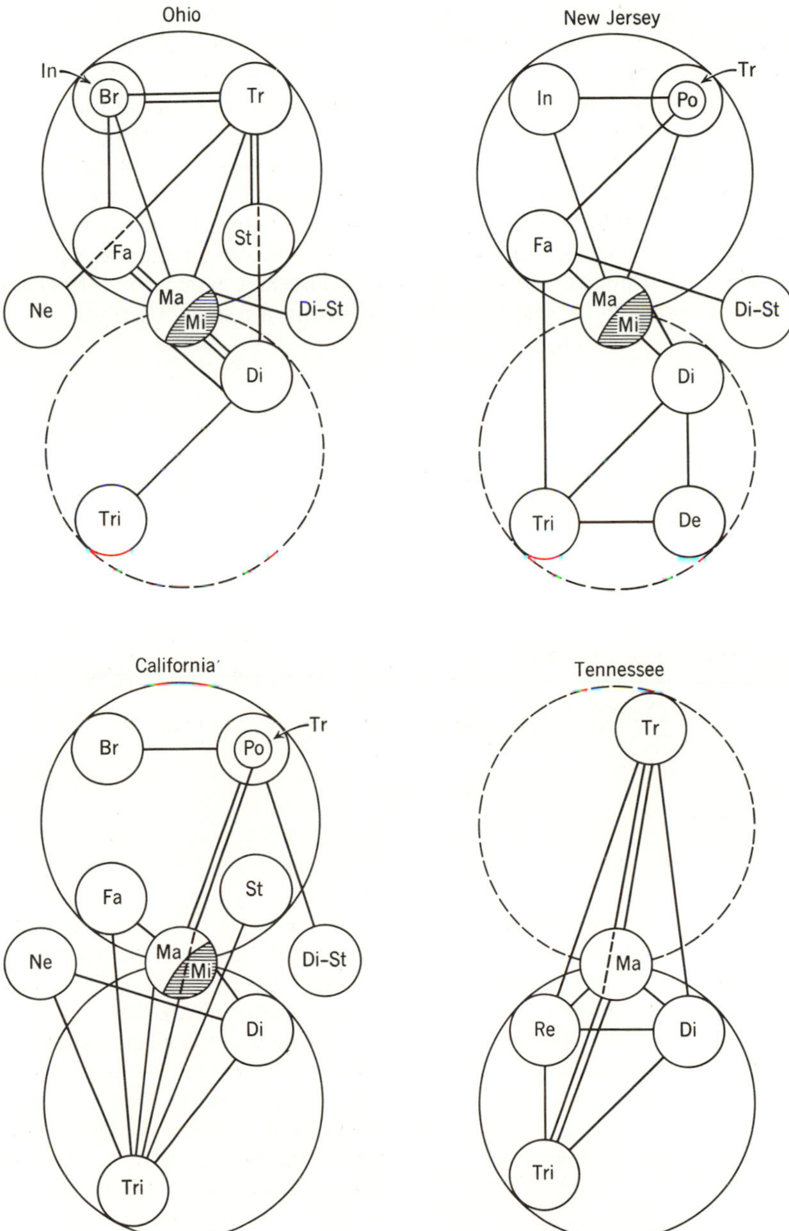

Figure 3. Role structures of four senates.

closer contact with the majority, it is more likely to be given attention, and it is more likely to play an active role in the legislative process. As a result, ideally minority-centered roles are likely to be more frequently linked to majority-anchored roles. In New Jersey, for instance, we may note that the facilitator-tribune combination among the dominant pairs, or in Ohio the facilitator-district pair.

Secondly, we note that in the Ohio and New Jersey Senates the district-oriented role appears in dominant pairs, while this is not the case in the respective Houses. Also, in New Jersey the delegate role and in Ohio the tribune role are paired with some other roles, while this pairing does not occur (with the exception of the tribune in New Jersey) in the lower chambers. These three roles—tribune, delegate, and district-oriented—seem to loom as latent premises of their behavior in Senators' self-conceptions of their legislative role in general. Senates have been historically looked on as performing more distinctly "ambassadorial functions" in the representative system. And though now popularly elected just as the members of the "popular" lower houses, the notion that Senates are, in part at least, conclaves of ambassadors from geographically-based constituencies may linger on in Senators' self-definitions. This, of course, we cannot prove, but as a hypothesis it is congruent with the fact that in the lower houses these "populist" roles are minority centered. Minority members are likely to perceive themselves as "ambassadors"—spokesmen of the "outs"—vis-à-vis the controlling majority with its predominant state orientation.

The "constructions" of legislative chambers as role structures suggest that through the use of non-conventional analytical categories, in our case derived from a role analysis of legislators, we can describe the structure of a legislative chamber, not as it is embodied in rules and bylaws (which are important parameters for behavior), but as it represents a system of action.

REFERENCES

Binkley, W. E., 1947. *President and congress.* New York: Knopf.
DeGrazia, A., 1951. *Public and republic, political representation in America.* New York: Knopf.
The Federalist, No. 35.

selection 29 Task Roles and Social Roles in Problem-Solving Groups

ROBERT F. BALES

During the last ten years, a number of laboratories for the study of social interaction within small groups and organizations have been started in university research centers, hospitals, clinics, and military installations. The studies and experiments I shall describe were conducted in one of these laboratories, which was established in 1947 at Harvard University.

From an article by the same author in Eleanor E. Maccoby, T. M. Newcomb, and E. L. Hartley (Eds.), *Readings in Social Psychology* (Third Edition), 1958, New York: Holt. Reprinted by permission of the author and Holt.

The laboratory consists of a large, well-lighted room for the group under study and an adjoining room for observers who listen and watch from behind windows with one-way vision. The subjects are told at the beginning that the room has been constructed for the special purpose of studying group discussion, that a complete sound recording will be made, and that there are observers behind the one-way mirrors. The purpose of the separation is not to deceive the subjects but to minimize interaction between them and the observing team.

Over a number of years we have evolved a more

or less standard type of group and task which has formed the setting for a number of studies. The data I shall report come from several studies, all done under essentially the same conditions, so that a description of the most recent investigation will serve in substance for the others.

PROCEDURES

The sample which provided data for the most recent investigation consisted of 30 five-man experimental groups. Subjects were 150 Harvard freshmen who were recruited by letters sent to a random sample of the entering class which briefly described the experiment as one concerned with group problem-solving and decision-making. Volunteers were offered a dollar an hour. The groups were randomly composed. Typically the members of a group did not know each other, nor were they introduced to each other. In effect, they were faced with the problem of getting organized as well as with the more obvious problem that was issued to them.

The more obvious problem, which we call the standard task, involved the discussion of a human-relations case, a five-page presentation of facts about a problem facing an administrator in his organization. Members were given separate identical copies of the case to read ahead of time and were told that, although each was given accurate information, we intended to leave them uncertain as to whether they each had exactly the same range of facts. The cases were collected after they had been read by the members individually, to prevent direct comparison of typed copies, although members were allowed to take notes. The task defined for each group was to assemble the information, to discuss why the people involved were behaving as they did, and to decide what should be recommended as action for the solution to the problem presented. The groups were asked to time themselves for 40 minutes and to dictate the group solution for the sound record in the final one or two minutes of the meeting.

While the group members began to organize themselves and to solve the case problem, the observers got to work in the observation room. They systematically recorded every step of the interaction, including such items as nods and frowns. Each observer had a small machine with a moving paper tape on which he wrote in code a description of every act—an act being defined essentially as a single statement, question, or gesture. Acts ordinarily occurred at the rate of 15 to 20 per minute. The recorded information on each act included identification of the person speaking and the person spoken to and classification of the act according to predetermined categories. The categories included attempts to solve either the organizational problems of the group or the task problems by the offering of information, opinions, and suggestions.

Questions and several types of positive and negative reactions completed the set of 12 categories (see Figure 1). This method is called "interaction-process analysis" (Bales, 1950). The categories are meant to have a general-purpose usefulness for group research and their use is not confined in any way to the laboratory conditions described here, although the best norms exist for the standard task and the group type described here (see Bales and Borgatta, 1955).

As Figure 1 shows, on the average about half (56 per cent) of the acts during a group session on the standard task fall into the categories of problem-solving attempts; the remaining 44 per cent are distributed among positive reactions, negative reactions and questions. In other words, the process tends to be two-sided, with the reactions serving as a more or less constant feedback on the acceptability of the problem-solving attempts. The following example will illustrate the pattern of interchange.

Member 1: I wonder if we have the same facts about the problem? [Asks for opinion.] Perhaps we should take some time in the beginning to find out. [Gives suggestion.]

Member 2: Yes [Agrees.] We may be able to fill in some gaps in our information. [Gives opinion.] Let's go around the table and each tell what the report said in his case. [Gives suggestion.]

Member 3: Oh, let's get going. [Shows antagonism.] We've all got the same facts. [Gives opinion.]

Member 2: (Blushes) [Shows tension.]

A number of interesting generalizations can be made about the way in which rates of activity in the various categories tend to differ according to group size, time periods within a meeting, development of a group over a series of meetings, pre-established status characteristics of members, and the like (see Bales, 1952). The present article, however, will be concerned with a particular set of problems in which the interaction data have played an important part—whether there are tendencies for persons to develop different roles during interaction, even though there are no pre-established status differences, and if so, what kind, and why? There are several plausible views

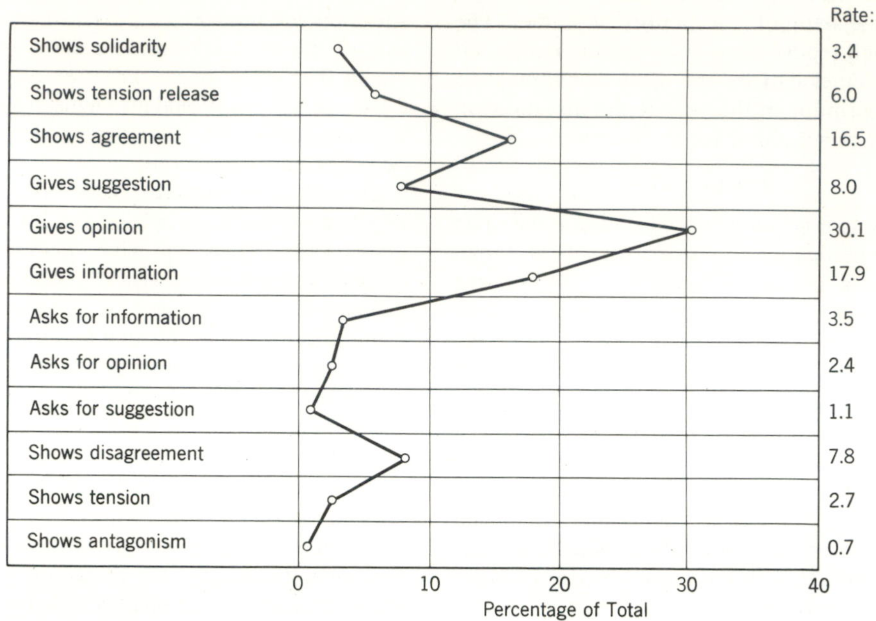

Figure 1. Types of interaction and their relative frequencies. This profile of rates is the average obtained on the standard task from 24 different groups, four of each size from two to size seven, each group meeting four times, making a total of 96 sessions. The raw number of scores is 71,838 (from Bales, 1955).

about this set of problems. The following account presents four distinguishable views and shows how research led from one view to another in the course of several studies.

THE HYPOTHESIS OF A SINGLE-STATUS ORDER

Perhaps the most ordinary conception of a group is that it consists of a leader and several followers who fall into a kind of status order from highest to lowest. The leader is the best-liked member of the group, participates most actively, and is felt to be the best performer of whatever task activities the group undertakes. No matter which of these criteria the researcher takes, he will come out with the same rank order of members. The expectation that most groups are structured like this and that departures from this simple form of organization may be treated as the result of special circumstances may be called the hypothesis of a "single-status order."

This is a plausible hypothesis. It underlies much research on leadership. It is congruent with the ideological position that for good leadership it is very important that a good leader should be an all-around "great man," and it assumes that there are such men, at least relative to the other members in a given group (see Borgatta, Couch, and Bales, 1954). This hypothesis assumes role differentiation but essentially only along a single quantitative dimension, leadership status.

Early in the research we began to ask group members about their likes and dislikes for each other, their opinions of who had the best ideas and who showed the most leadership, and other similar questions. We wanted to know how these questions related to each other and to our observations of interaction. The question as to whether or not there is role differentiation within a group can be reduced in part to whether group members show some consensus that certain members stand higher than others on a given criterion and whether different criteria give different status orders rather than a single-status order.

When I first began to examine data from our experimental groups, I worked under the assumption that there might be some such thing as a "simply organized group," that is, one in which the rank order of members on activity, task ability, and likeability would coincide, and that these groups would in some sense or other be the most successful or best satisfied (Bales, 1953).

Figure 2 shows the results which raised a most interesting set of questions. The total interaction initiated by one man in the course of a meeting establishes the basis for ranking him relative to the others on activity. If there is a strong tendency toward a single-status order, top men on activity should also rank highest in group-members' responses to such questions as "who has the best ideas," and should also receive the highest number of "liking" votes and lowest of "disliking."[1] The second man on activity should, on the average, be second highest on the other criteria of excellence, and so on. The rank order on each criterion should be highly correlated to the rank order on the other criteria.

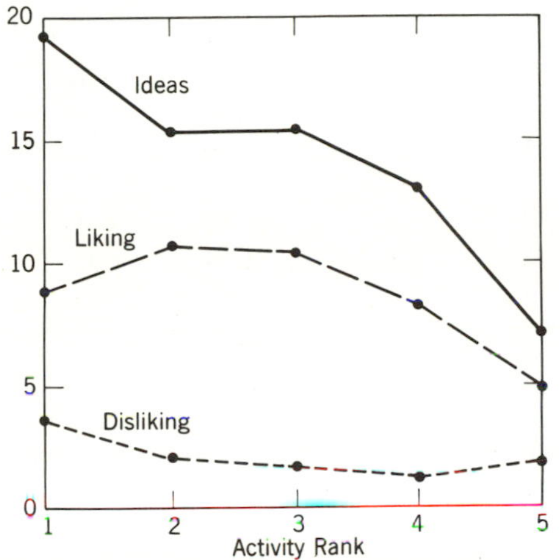

Figure 2. Average ratings received on ideas, liking, and disliking by men of each activity rank (from Bales, 1953, p. 146).

What does Figure 2 suggest? First, there seems to be a positive correlation between activity rank and idea rank, although the second man seems a little low. But on liking-received rank, there is a marked discrepancy. The top man on activity appears considerably lower than expected on liking received. Both the second and the third men are higher on the average than he. Is the top man doing something to lose likes and provoke dislikes? Here one notes the dislike curve. The differences are small and probably not significant but they suggest that the top man is possibly the highest on dislikes received. Liking seems to be centering on the second and third man in activity, and they both seem to be lower than expected on idea ranking. Can it be that these men are tending to avoid too heavy an emphasis on the task area for fear of being disliked?

On further investigation of this problem it turned out that something happened in groups over a series of four sessions that was equally thought-provoking. In the first sessions, if a given man held top position on the idea ranking by his fellow members, the probability was about 50–50 that he would *also* hold a top position on a likeability ranking. But in the second meeting the probability dropped markedly, and by the fourth meeting was only about one in ten. The percentage of cases in which the same man held the top position on liking and idea rankings at the same time, divided by session, may be charted as follows:

Sessions			
1	2	3	4
56.5	12.0	20.0	8.5

Could it be that there was something about arriving in a top-status position, owing to technical contribution to the task problems of the group, that tended to "lose friends and alienate people"? If so, was another man likely to arise who paid more attention to the social-emotional problems of the group and so tended to collect more liking? The idea that this happens with sufficient frequency that it can be viewed as typical may be called "the hypothesis of two complementary leaders."

THE HYPOTHESIS OF TWO COMPLEMENTARY LEADERS

Why, if at all, should groups tend to have two complementary leaders, one a task specialist, the other a social-emotional specialist?[2] Perhaps it would be helpful to look at the interaction of men highest on idea ranking received but not highest on liking received, and vice versa. It may be that men of these two types behave differently and the differences in behavior may give us some clues as to the reasons for the differences.

Table 1 shows the composite profiles of 44 matched session-pairs[3] of idea men (who were not best liked in their group) and best-liked men (who were not top in idea ranking). Slater, from whose paper the table is taken, comments: "The most

[1] The actual questions used are presented in Bales (1956). They are omitted in the present paper for the sake of brevity.

[2] A theory is advanced in R. F. Bales and P. E. Slater (1955).

[3] Although the number of *sessions* was 44, the number of separate individuals involved was not 88, since each group ran over four sessions, and some individuals were in the same position more than once.

TABLE 1 COMPOSITE PROFILES IN PERCENTAGES OF 44 TOP MEN ON IDEA RANKING AND 44 TOP MEN ON LIKE RANKING FOR THE SAME SESSIONS

		Initiated		Received	
	Interaction category	Idea men	Best-liked men	Idea men	Best-liked men
Area A: Positive reactions	Shows solidarity	3.68	4.41	2.57	3.15
	Shows tension release	5.15	6.98	7.95	9.20
	Shows agreement	14.42	16.83	23.29	18.27
Area B: Problem-solving attempts	Gives suggestion	8.97	6.81	7.01	7.22
	Gives opinion	32.74	28.69	25.52	31.09
	Gives orientation	18.54	17.91	14.06	14.54
Area C: Questions	Asks orientation	3.04	3.71	3.62	2.80
	Asks opinion	1.84	2.94	1.94	1.74
	Asks suggestion	.93	1.33	.85	.84
Area D: Negative reactions	Shows disagreement	8.04	7.60	10.65	9.35
	Shows tension increase	1.92	2.16	1.59	1.35
	Shows antagonism	.73	.63	.95	.45

From Philip F. Slater (1955, p. 305).

salient general difference in Table 1 is the tendency for the Idea man to initiate interaction more heavily in Area B (Problem-Solving Attempts) and the Best-liked man in Area A (Positive Reactions). The Idea man also seems to disagree somewhat more, and show a little more antagonism, while the Best-liked man asks more questions and shows more tension" (Slater, 1955).[4]

On the receiving end, the situation is largely reversed, with the idea man receiving more agreement, questions, and negative reactions, while the best-liked man receives more problem-solving attempts, and more solidarity and tension release. The general picture is thus one of specialization and complementarity, with the idea man concentrating on the task and playing a more aggressive role, while the best-liked man concentrates more on social-emotional problems, giving rewards and playing a more passive role.

The kind of complementarity that shows in the behavior, then, is a kind that occurs in short interchanges in conversations where a problem-solving attempt by one person is followed by an agreement or disagreement from some other, or where a pleasant remark or a joke by one is followed by a smile or a laugh from the other. Such a division of labor by type of act is very common and easily recognized. There may or may not be a specialization so that one person continues to produce more of one form of behavior than the other.

But now consider an important fact. Almost exactly the same sort of difference in interaction profile tends to be found between high participators and low participators (see Borgatta and Bales, 1953), even if one ignores the idea and like ratings. High participators tend to specialize in problem-solving attempts, low participators tend to specialize in positive or negative reactions or questions. Moreover, the proportion of problem-solving attempts increases when a man is placed with lower participators and decreases when he is working with higher participators (Borgatta and Bales, 1953). What do these facts suggest?

For one thing, these facts seem to imply that the qualitative differences in the type of act attributed to a given person may be more or less forced by the tendency of others in the group to talk a little or a great deal, thus giving him an

[4] It is not possible to state that all of the detailed differences indicated are significant, because rates in the various categories are interdependent. However, Slater shows that the two types are in general significantly different from each other.

opportunity to make the problem-solving attempts or leaving him only in a position to respond to the quicker or more valuable proposals of others.

Insofar as the ratings a man receives are based on the way he behaves, the ratings others give him will surely be dependent on how much he talks. Let us suppose that a man can receive a high rating on ideas only if he makes many problem-solving attempts. He can do this only by talking a good deal. Then, to receive a high rating on ideas he will have to talk a lot. Or, conversely, let us suppose that a man can receive a high rating on liking only if he rewards others by positive reactions. He can do this only if he permits them to make many problem-solving attempts, which in turn requires that he let the other(s) talk a lot. Then, to receive a high rating on liking he will have to talk less.

This line of reasoning seems to fit with the facts so far presented and, moreover, has a certain plausibility in terms of common organizational arrangements. The husband and wife in many families seem to play complementary roles of the sort described. Many administrators find cases from their experience where organizations in fact have two leaders, one who specializes on the task side, one on the social-emotional side. It is a kind of political maxim that it is almost impossible to elect the person who is technically best suited for an office—he is generally not popular enough. Surely there must be many persons in leadership positions who welcome any theory that explains to them that their lack of popularity is no fault of their own but a result of a specialization that is in the nature of things.

The problem now is that it might be inferred from this ideological version of the theory that there is no essential distinction between sheer activity and ratings received on goodness of ideas and, moreover, that there is a negative correlation between these two and liking received. Is it true that leaders must choose between task effectiveness and popularity?

THE HYPOTHESIS OF THREE ORTHOGONAL FACTORS

Fortunately, a number of studies in the literature bear on this question and the results of a number of researchers tend to converge on an answer. When members of small groups are asked to rate and choose each other on a wide variety of descriptive criteria or are assessed by observers, three factors or distinct dimensions generally tend to appear.

Carter (1954) indicates the frequency with which these factors are found in reviewing a series of factor analytic studies, such as those of Couch and himself (1952), Sakoda (1952), Wherry (1950), and Clark (1953). A recent study by Wispé (1955) may be added to the list.

Carter describes the factors as follows:

Factor I. *Individual prominence and achievement*: behaviors of the individual related to his efforts to stand out from others and individually achieve various personal goals.

Factor II. *Aiding attainment by the group*: behaviors of the individual related to his efforts to assist the group in achieving goals toward which the group is oriented.

Factor III. *Sociability*: behaviors of the individual related to his efforts to establish and maintain cordial and socially satisfying relations with other group members.

These factors seem to represent underlying dimensions in the evaluations persons make of each other, whether as observers or as fellow group members. It may be that the best way of looking at these factors is not as personality traits but as frameworks in which the perceiver responds to personality traits of others.

But the important thing to note is that in these studies the three factors, which I shall call "activity," "task ability," and "likeability," are not, in general, mutually exclusive: a high standing on one does not preclude or interfere with a high standing on the other. Nor are they mutually supportive in general but, rather, they tend to be uncorrelated.

The fact that they are uncorrelated in general does not necessarily mean, of course, that there are no dynamic relationships between the phenomena represented by the factors. It means that there is no simple linear relationship that tends to be found over all populations, so that knowing where a man stands on one does not allow for a prediction of his standing on either or both of the others. If there are dynamic relationships between the factors they must be more complicated, nonlinear, or circumstantial. What suggestions of relationships are there left?

THE HYPOTHESIS OF INDIVIDUAL DIFFERENCES IN OVERTALKING

Although it is not true that simply by talking a great deal one does guarantee a high rating on the quality of his ideas, it is still probably true that in groups of the sort we were studying it is very difficult to make a substantial contribution to the task without talking a great deal, especially in the first meeting, and overtalking may be resented by other members as a threat to their own status and a frustration of their own desire to talk. Results of other experimenters provided some findings that are congruent with this line of thought. Let us look for a moment at some of these results.

Leavitt and Mueller (1951) explored the effect of one-way communication in a restricted communication situation where the receiver of the information is given no opportunity to "feed back" acknowledgements, questions, or negative reactions to the sender. They find that an initial reaction of hostility toward the sender tends to appear.

Thibaut and Coules (1952) find that receivers who are not permitted to communicate to a person who has sent them an act of hostility show less post experimental friendliness to the sender than those permitted to reply.

A peripheral position in a restricted network approximates in some ways the position of a receiver with no opportunity for feedback. In an experiment where members were allowed to communicate only in written form through set channels on a task of assembling information, Leavitt (1947) finds that members in peripheral positions are less well satisfied with their jobs than those in central positions.

These results suggested to us that the relatively low average of likeability preferences received by top participators might be due to the presence of some men in the total population of top men who overtalk, in the sense that they do not allow an appropriate amount of feedback of objections, qualifications, questions, and countersuggestions to occur. Our method of observation allowed us to examine the amount of interaction a given man received in relation to the amount he initiated. We thus arrived at the hypothesis that the ratio of interaction received to that initiated might help distinguish between those top interactors who were proportionately well liked and those who were not.

In general, as has been indicated, activity, taskability ratings, and liking ratings appear in many studies as orthogonal factors, uncorrelated with each other over the total population assessed. It is important to recognize, however, that subparts of a population, or a different population, may show the variables related in a different way. It is the possibility that subparts of our population may show different relationships of these variables that we now explore.

We first make a basic division of the population according to the rank of each person within his own group on the gross amount of participation he initiated and call this his activity. Five ranks are thus recognized, since the groups were five-man groups.

The second division of the population is made within each rank. All the men of each rank are divided into three subpopulations according to their own ratio of amount of participation received from others to the amount of participation they initiate. This ratio is known as the R/I, or the feedback ratio. Within each rank, then, there are three subpopulations of ten men each, low, medium, and high on the feedback ratio.

Figure 3 shows the average values of ratings or ranking received for each of the subpopulations of ten men on liking, disliking, and ideas. The ratings or rankings were given to each man by his four fellow group members and have been converted for plotting in such a way that high numbers mean high average rankings received.

The point of greatest interest is the difference in the relations of liking to activity when the feedback ratio is taken into account. Figure 3 indicates that among the third of the population with a low feedback ratio, the top two men seem definitely lower than would be expected if liking received increased linearly in proportion to activity. The correlation between activity and liking received is near zero.

However, both the medium R/I and the high R/I thirds show a positive correlation. From these data it is still plausible to suppose that the top man even in the high R/I third shows a little less liking received than one would expect. But the effect is slight.

The data obtained by asking about dislikes present essentially the same picture. The highest participators among the third of the population with the lowest feedback ratio not only are less well liked but are more disliked than their less active colleagues in the same subpopulation. In this third of the population, the more the person talks, the more he is disliked. But in the opposite third of the population, those who have a high feedback ratio, there is no relation between how much a man talks and how much he is disliked.

With regard to idea rankings received, there is a definite indication that the highest participators in the third of the population with the low feedback ratio tend to suffer on idea rankings received, as they do on liking received, although the effect is not so marked. This effect seems to disappear completely in the medium R/I and high R/I groups.

It is plain, however, that there is an appreciable linear correlation between activity and idea rankings received over the total of the three subpopulations. This finding thus differs from other studies which find these two variables to be generally orthogonal. We attribute the correlation in our groups at least partly to the fact that we are dealing in this study with data from first meetings entirely. Data on groups running over four sessions indicate that this correlation tends to fall over time, especially in groups where the initial consensus as to who has the best ideas is low (Slater, 1955). The correlation between ideas and liking also tends to fall as indicated above in Table 1. In short, the three factors tend to separate out as independent more clearly in later meetings than in the first.

To summarize briefly: In the groups in this total sample there is only a weak correlation between liking received and activity, providing one makes no breakdown into subpopulations. But for about one-third of the population there is a positive and linear correlation between how much a man talks and how well he is liked. This is the third, who receive more interaction in proportion to the amount they initiate, that is, who have a high feedback ratio. The falling-off of liking received among the individuals who talk the most in total population is attributable especially to the other extreme third of the population, who talk proportionately most above the amount they receive. The same may be said for their rankings.

CONCLUSION

It appears that activity, task-ability ratings, and likeability ratings should be treated as three distinct factors, since over a large population of members, meetings, and groups they tend to be uncorrelated with each other. If one accepts this assumption a simple and very useful classification of role types in small groups suggests itself.

1. A member who is high on all three of the factors corresponds to the traditional conception of the good leader, or the "great man." Such men are found, but, if the factors are uncorrelated, are rare.

2. A member who is high on activity and task-ability ratings but less high on likeability is a familiar type who may be called the "task specialist." This type is not so rare as the first type and may operate effectively in cooperation with the third.

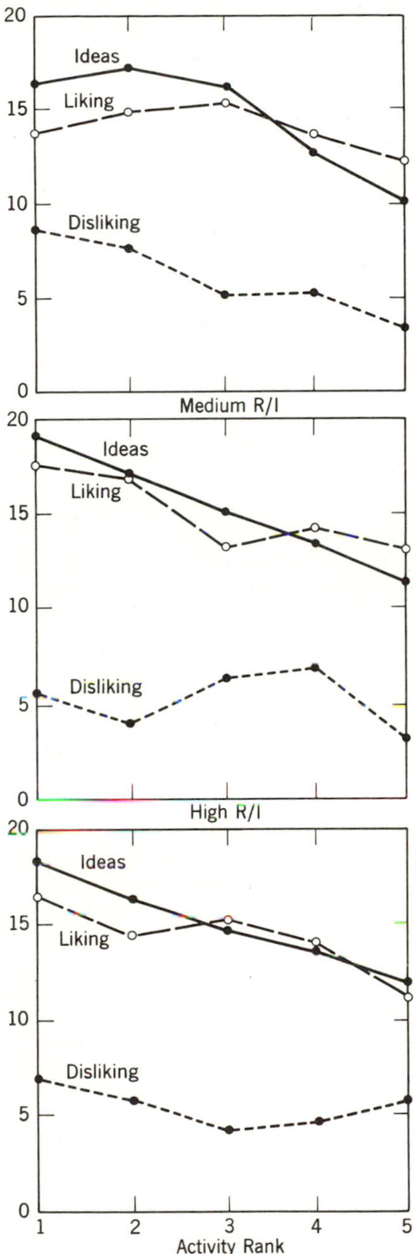

Figure 3. Average ratings[a] received on ideas, liking, and disliking by men of each activity rank, according to their feedback ratio (R/I) (condensed from Bales, 1956).

[a] Each entry at a given activity rank is the mean for ten persons. The idea index is not actually a rating but an index obtained by adding rankings received (including self-rankings) and subtracting the total from the highest possible, 25. The like and dislike indexes are average ratings, with the highest possible, 28.

3. A member who is high on likeability but less high on activity and task ability may be called the "social specialist." This type is much less rare than the first type and groups which operate under the dual leadership of a man of this type and of the second type are common.

4. A member who is high on activity but relatively low on task ability and likeability ratings may be called an "overactive deviant." This type is not rare. This is the person who, in the leadership literature, is said to show "domination" rather than "leadership."

5. A member who is low on all three may be called an "underactive deviant" and may indeed be a kind of scapegoat. On the assumption that the factors are uncorrelated this type should be as rare as the first type, but since the lack of correlation traces mainly to discrepancies at the upper end of the scales, this type is not actually so rare as the first type and is, in fact, probably very common.

Logically, of course, one can distinguish many additional types. Those mentioned, however, have a certain intuitive distinctness and for present purposes serve to summarize and harmonize the various views on role differentiation that have been examined in this paper.

REFERENCES

Bales, R. F., 1950. *Interaction process analysis: a method for the study of small groups.* Cambridge, Mass.: Addison-Wesley.

Bales, R. F., 1952. Some uniformities of behavior in small social systems. In G. E. Swanson, T. M. Newcomb, and Eleanor L. Hartley (Eds.), *Readings in social psychology* (Rev. Ed.). New York: Holt, pp. 146–159.

Bales, R. F., 1953. The equilibrium problem in small groups. In T. Parsons, R. F. Bales, and E. A. Shils (Eds.), *Working papers in the theory of action.* New York: The Free Press, pp. 111–161.

Bales, R. F., 1955. How people interact in conferences. *Scientific American*, **192** (3), 31–35.

Bales, R. F., 1956. Task status and likeability as a function of talking and listening in decision-making groups. In L. D. White (Ed.), *The state of the social sciences.* Chicago: University of Chicago Press, pp. 148–161.

Bales, R. F., and Borgatta, E. F., 1955. Size of group as a factor in the inter-action profile. In A. P. Hare, E. F. Borgatta, and R. F. Bales (Eds.), *Small groups: studies in social interaction.* New York: Knopf, pp. 396–413.

Bales, R. F., and Slater, P. E., 1955. Role differentiation in small decision-making groups. In T. Parsons, R. F. Bales, J. Olds, M. Zelditch, Jr., and P. E. Slater (Eds.), *Family, socialization, and interaction process.* New York: The Free Press, pp. 259–306.

Borgatta, E. F., and Bales, R. F., 1953. Interaction of individuals in reconstituted groups. *Sociometry*, **16**, 302–320.

Borgatta, E. F., Couch, A. S., and Bales, R. F., 1954. Some findings relevant to the great man theory of leadership. *American Sociological Review*, **19**, 755–759.

Carter, L. F., 1954. Recording and evaluating the performance of individuals as members of small groups. *Personality Psychology*, **7**, 477–484.

Clark, R. A., 1953. Analyzing the group structures of combat rifle squads. *American Psychologist*, **8**, 333.

Couch, A. S., and Carter, L. F., 1952. A factorial study of the rated behavior of group members. Paper read at the Eastern Psychological Association, March.

Leavitt, H. J., 1947. Some effects of certain communication patterns on group performance. In Eleanor E. Maccoby, T. M. Newcomb, and E. L. Hartley (Eds.), *Readings in social psychology* (3rd Ed.). New York: Holt, pp. 546–563.

Leavitt, H. J., and Mueller, R. A. H., 1951. Some effects of feedback on communication. *Human Relations*, **4**, 401–410.

Sakoda, J. M., 1952. Factor analysis of OSS situational tests. *Journal of Abnormal and Social Psychology*, **47**, 843–852.

Slater, P. E., 1955. Role differentiation in small groups. *American Sociological Review*, **20**, 300–310.

Thibaut, J. W., and Coules, J., 1952. The role of communication in the reduction of interpersonal hostility. *Journal of Abnormal and Social Psychology*, **47**, 770–777.

Wherry, R. J., 1950. Factor analysis of Officer Qualification Form QCL-2B. Columbus, Ohio: Ohio State University Research Foundation.

Wispé, L. G., 1955. A sociometric analysis of conflicting role-expectations. *American Journal of Sociology*, **61**, 134–137.

selection 30 Comparative Data on the Division of Labor by Sex

GEORGE P. MURDOCK

Certain data on the distribution of economic activities between the sexes, secured by the author and his students as a by-product of a research project in a graduate class in ethnology, are presented herewith as possibly of general interest. They were obtained in the course of abstracting material from the outstanding ethnographical monographs on two hundred and twenty-four tribes selected from all parts of the world with due regard to geographical distribution. A few higher civilizations were included in order to yield results representative of all types of culture.

The material is presented below in [Table 1]. The first column gives the number of tribes in which the particular activity is confined exclusively to males. The second enumerates those in which women engage in the occupation only relatively infrequently or in a subordinate capacity. The third column embraces the tribes in which the occupation is carried on indifferently by either sex or coöperatively by both. The fourth and fifth columns list the tribes in which the activity is, respectively, predominantly and exclusively feminine. The sixth column gives a rough index of the degree of masculinity of the occupation in general; the percentages were obtained by scoring tribes in the first five columns 100, 75, 50, 25, and 0 respectively and striking the average. Although errors have doubtless crept into the tabulation, the general result is probably not seriously distorted.

Complexes of activities have in many cases been split up. Thus agriculture is subdivided into the clearing of land, soil preparation and planting, and crop tending and harvesting; pastoral activities into the herding of large animals, the tending of fowls and small animals, and dairy operations; house building into the construction of permanent dwellings and the erection and dismantling of transportable shelters such as tents; the textile arts into weaving proper, the manufacture of non-textile fabrics such as barkcloth, etc. Other occupations might appropriately have been similarly subdivided. That fire making, for example, is often a masculine activity, whereas fire tending is feminine, is not revealed by the table.

The tendency among primitives to segregate economic activities according to sex is even stronger than the tabulation indicates, for in perhaps the majority of cases listed in the intermediate columns certain specific activities are regarded as masculine and others as feminine. For example, in a tribe where house building is listed as mutually pursued, the men may confine themselves to setting up the timbers and the women to preparing and affixing the roofing material. Of the various conclusions deducible from the table one of the most interesting is that, while a number of occupations are universally masculine, none is everywhere feminine: men have, here and there, taken to themselves even such predominantly feminine activities as cooking, the making of clothing, water carrying, and grain grinding.

From *Social Forces*, 1937, **15**, 551–553. Reprinted by permission of the author and The University of North Carolina Press.

TABLE 1 ACTIVITIES PERFORMED BY MALES AND FEMALES IN VARIOUS SOCIETIES

	M	M−	=	F−	F	Per-cent
Metal working	78	0	0	0	0	100.0
Weapon making	121	1	0	0	0	99.8
Pursuit of sea mammals	34	1	0	0	0	99.3
Hunting	166	13	0	0	0	98.2
Manufacture of musical instruments	45	2	0	0	1	96.9
Boat building	91	4	4	0	1	96.0
Mining and quarrying	35	1	1	0	1	95.4
Work in wood and bark	113	9	5	1	1	95.0
Work in stone	68	3	2	0	2	95.0
Trapping or catching of small animals	128	13	4	1	2	94.9
Work in bone, horn and shell	67	4	3	0	3	93.0
Lumbering	104	4	3	1	6	92.2
Fishing	98	34	19	3	4	85.6
Manufacture of ceremonial objects	37	1	13	0	1	85.1
Herding	38	8	4	0	5	83.6
House building	86	32	25	3	14	77.0
Clearing of land for agriculture	73	22	17	5	13	76.3
Net making	44	6	4	2	11	74.1
Trade	51	28	20	8	7	73.7
Dairy operations	17	4	3	1	13	57.1
Manufacture of ornaments	24	3	40	6	18	52.5
Agriculture—soil preparation and planting	31	23	33	20	37	48.4
Manufacture of leather products	29	3	9	3	32	48.0
Body mutilation, e.g., tattooing	16	14	44	22	20	46.6
Erection and dismantling of shelter	14	2	5	6	22	39.8
Hide preparation	31	2	4	4	49	39.4
Tending of fowls and small animals	21	4	8	1	39	38.7
Agriculture—crop tending and harvesting	10	15	35	39	44	33.9
Gathering of shellfish	9	4	8	7	25	33.5
Manufacture of non-textile fabrics	14	0	9	2	32	33.3
Fire making and tending	18	6	25	22	62	30.5
Burden bearing	12	6	33	20	57	29.9
Preparation of drinks and narcotics	20	1	13	8	57	29.5
Manufacture of thread and cordage	23	2	11	10	73	27.3
Basket making	25	3	10	6	82	24.4
Mat making	16	2	6	4	61	24.2
Weaving	19	2	2	6	67	23.9
Gathering of fruits, berries and nuts	12	3	15	13	63	23.6
Fuel gathering	22	1	10	19	89	23.0
Pottery making	13	2	6	8	77	18.4
Preservation of meat and fish	8	2	10	14	74	16.7
Manufacture and repair of clothing	12	3	8	9	95	16.1
Gathering of herbs, roots and seeds	8	1	11	7	74	15.8
Cooking	5	1	9	28	158	8.6
Water carrying	7	0	5	7	119	8.2
Grain grinding	2	4	5	13	114	7.8

selection 31 Division of Labor in American Families

ROBERT O. BLOOD AND DONALD M. WOLFE

This selection is concerned with the everyday tasks that have to be performed in every family in order to keep the home going. How do the husband and wife divide up or share the work around the house?

THE TRADITIONAL PATTERN

Traditionally, husbands did "men's work" and wives did "women's work." Men's work was strenuous and dangerous, the difficult tasks in field and woods which women were not considered strong enough to undertake. Women's work centered in the home, not only because women were incapable of the heaviest outside work but because women are the child-bearers. Pregnancy, childbirth, and breast feeding make it necessary and convenient for the woman to stay close to home. By a process of easy generalization, childbirth leads to childrearing, to feeding and clothing the children, to providing similar services for the husband. Thus the wife comes to be responsible for a large package of household tasks.

In recent years, there has been much discussion about the American family's alleged abandonment of this traditional division of labor. As more and more wives have taken jobs outside the home, there has been increased pressure on husbands to lighten the double load of job-plus-housework which falls on the working wife. Such assistance from the husband could come either by taking over some feminine tasks completely or by sharing tasks with his wife. In either case the new conception is one of sharing.

To a considerable extent, the idea of shared work is incompatible with the most efficient division of labor. Much of the progress of our modern economy rests upon the increasing specialization of its division of labor. A specialist is able to develop his particular skills in a way a jack-of-all-trades never can.

Family life has always required a multitude of skills of its practitioners, so that a husband or wife must necessarily perform many different tasks. Nevertheless, as long as the wife stuck to her cooking and the husband to his hunting, some of the advantages of specialization accrued. Such advantages would be lost if husband and wife were to merge their work completely.

The very threat of such a loss is one brake on the trend to undivided work. Individual preferences for particular tasks are another. The greatest preventative, however, is the continuing biological differences between men and women which even in the Israeli Kibbutz—with its ideological dedication to the abolition of sex roles within a communal framework—continue to influence the division of labor (Spiro, 1956).

It seems unlikely, therefore, that traditional sex roles in the home will be abandoned within the foreseeable future. At least they are still very much in evidence.

THE CONTEMPORARY PATTERN

To keep track of all the work done by a husband and wife has sometimes been attempted through the cooperation of small numbers of research-minded volunteer families. For a large-scale study of a cross section of a whole community, such comprehensive information is impossible to secure. One must be satisfied with a small group of family tasks as an index of the over-all division of labor. The eight tasks used in this research are:

1. Who repairs things around the house?
2. Who mows the lawn?
3. Who shovels the sidewalk?
4. Who keeps track of the money and the bills?
5. Who does the grocery-shopping?
6. Who gets the husband's breakfast on work days?

Abridged from Chapter 3 of a book by the same authors entitled *Husbands and Wives: The Dynamics of Married Living*, 1960, New York: The Free Press. Reprinted by permission of the authors and The Free Press.

TABLE 1 DIVISION OF LABOR, BY HOUSEHOLD TASKS

(731 Detroit Families)

Who Does It?	Task							
	Repairs	Lawn	Walk	Bills	Groceries	Break-fast	Living room	Dishes
1. Husband always	73%	66%	61%	19%	7%	16%	1%	1%
2. Husband more than wife	11	9	13	6	7	5	1	2
3. Husband and wife exactly the same	6	6	8	34	29	4	17	13
4. Wife more than husband	3	6	7	11	20	7	15	12
5. Wife always	3	7	7	30	36	66	65	70
N.A.	4	6	4	—	1	2	1	2
Total	100	100	100	100	100	100	100	100
Wife's mean task performance	1.46	1.71	1.81	3.27	3.72	4.04	4.44	4.52

7. Who straightens up the living room when company is coming?
8. Who does the evening dishes?

The questions were chosen because they concern tasks which most families perform.[1] (Since one third of the respondents have no children, childcare tasks could not be included.) They also are tasks which theoretically either partner could perform (hence the emphasis on *dinner* dishes since both partners are usually home in the evening).

Facets of the Division of Labor

The division of labor actually covers a variety of concepts. First is the amount of work done at home by each partner. This will be referred to as the *relative task participation* of the couple. Scores are computed in terms of the wife's mean task participation, with five points where she always does a task, four points for wife-more-than-husband, and so on (see Table 1).

In addition to knowing how *much* work is done by each partner, we must also know which tasks each does. Some of the eight tasks have been traditionally done by men and others by women. The degree of *adherence to male roles* refers to the extent to which the husband does the repairs, mowing, and shovelling. The degree of *adherence to female roles* is the extent to which the wife is responsible for the groceries, breakfast, living room, and dishes. Combined, these two indices provide a measure of the degree of *adherence to traditional sex roles* in the marriage.

Whereas the previous measures vary in degree, it is sometimes valuable to know how many tasks are done exclusively by the traditional partner. This gives a measure of the degree of *role stereotypy* in marriage; it may vary from none to a maximum of seven tasks performed exclusively according to the stereotyped pattern.

Closely related to stereotypy is the degree of *role specialization.* This is the number of tasks performed exclusively by one partner but not necessarily by the traditional partner. This refers to the degree of differentiation of roles between the two partners, rather than to their conformity to conventional patterns. In a completely specialized marriage, all eight of the battery of tests are performed unilaterally. The reciprocal of role specialization is the extent of *role-sharing.* This is restricted to the number of tasks out of the eight which are done by the husband and wife "exactly the same." These two measures of specialization and sharing deal with the extreme cases, ignoring those tasks which are partially shared, done by one partner more than the other.

Relative task performance, traditional role adherence and stereotypy, specialization and

[1] Those couples whose tasks are performed by children or servants were asked which partner they thought would do the task if no one else were available. Apartment dwellers similarly gave hypothetical answers about lawn and sidewalk. Since the hypothetical answers were few in number and were distributed in similar fashion to the "actual" answers, they were grouped together for purposes of analysis.

sharing provide a comprehensive series of perspectives on the division of labor in marriage. What is the American pattern today?

Who Does What?

Masculine Tasks. Table 1 shows that most husbands do the lawn-mowing, snow-shovelling, and repairing, while the wives do the dishes, straightening up, and cooking. The remaining two items are neither the husband's nor the wife's in a majority of families though they tend to be done more by wives.

The predominant picture reveals specialized task performance along traditional sex lines. The extent of this conformity to conventional patterns is greatest for the three male tasks, since the median Detroit husband performs over 90 per cent of them. Since grocery-shopping is less exclusively a feminine task, the median adherence to traditional feminine tasks is a bit less, but still substantial (76 per cent). Combined, the performance of these seven tasks follows traditional lines most of the time in the typical Detroit family.

If we pose the question, "How many families adhere completely to traditional sex lines?" the answer is only 6 per cent. However, the median family has a completely stereotyped allocation of five of the seven tasks, leaving only two for even marginal variation.

The reasons for this sharp division of labor along traditional sex lines are presumably those discussed already. Lawn-mowing and snow-shovelling exemplify tasks capitalizing on male musculature. Doing household repairs similarly utilizes the mechanical aptitude which men in our society possess more than women (Scheinfeld, 1944).

Feminine Tasks. The feminine tasks are less directly determined by biological or mental aptitudes, but are examples of the household "package" usually associated with the role of mother. Probably the number of husbands participating in grocery-shopping has increased since the neighborhood store gave way to supermarkets which can be reached only by car—husbands being the usual custodian of the American car.

Administrative Tasks. Keeping track of the money and bills lacks a generally accepted pattern of allocation. Handling the money is a sensitive operation, allied with such other household tasks as shopping but tied up, too, with the relative power of the husband and wife. Those wives who do more housework also tend to keep track of the money and bills. On the other hand, there is a high correlation between money-handling and decision-making. (Where the wife always keeps track of the money and bills the husband's mean power score is only 4.29, whereas husbands who always handle the money have a mean power of 6.13.)

Apparently keeping track of the money and bills is a crucial administrative function in the home, standing midway between the making of financial decisions and carrying them out through actual purchases. For all four of the financial decisions in this study, the partner who makes the decision is the one who is most apt to keep track of the money and bills. The relationship is especially marked in the case of decisions about how much money to spend on food and whether to buy life insurance, since these questions were phrased quite directly in financial terms. Clearly, the person who makes major financial decisions in marriage tends to be the one who follows through in seeing where the money goes and doling it out to the billing agencies. Apparently making decisions about money and keeping track of money are two functions which tend to reinforce each other. They are not easily separable between one partner as boss and the other as bookkeeper.

To summarize, the pattern of task performance is one of marked specialization. Taken task by task, six of the eight are usually performed in a completely specialized manner. Taken family by family, the median couple split up the same six tasks in the same specialized way. At the same time, the median couple share only one task fifty-fifty, leaving only one of the eight to be done primarily but not exclusively by one partner.

Doing and Deciding: The Structure of American Marriages

How does this division of labor compare with the pattern of decision-making in American marriage? Both are equalitarian in the sense that both husbands and wives participate. But whereas the division of labor is highly specialized, the process of decision-making is considerably less unilateral. The typical pattern in Detroit is to make only half the decisions unilaterally (compared to three-fourths of the tasks). Conversely, three decisions are typically shared equally by the two partners, compared to only one task. As a result of these differences, decision-making is also less stereotyped than task performance, there being substantially more variation from family to family in who decides than in who does things at home.

These differences are great enough to produce a general impression of flexible sharing in decision-making in contrast with stereotyped specialization in the division of labor. The typical family is therefore like a corporation which makes its decisions in staff conferences but executes them through technical experts.

Miller and Swanson (1958) have a name for this type of family. They call it the "colleague" family because it resembles co-workers "with equal, interdependent, but distinct and mutually recognized competencies." They speculate that the traditional American patriarchal family changed first into Burgess and Locke's "companionship family" which shared both decisions and tasks in an entrepreneurial competitive society. The companionship family then evolved into the colleague type as American husbands were increasingly employed in bureaucratic organizations.

However, Gold and Slater (1958) were unable to find any evidence at the present time of the predicted relationship between entrepreneurial occupations and companionship families or between bureaucratic occupations and colleague families. Perhaps a few ardent feminists did establish companionship-type families in the days of their "flaming youth" (the 1920's), but the major shift in American family patterns seems to be directly from the patriarchate to the colleague form.

DETERMINANTS OF THE DIVISION OF LABOR

Although the pattern of task allocation is rather inflexible for the community as a whole, it still differs appreciably from family to family. What social factors account for some of these variations between families? Under what circumstances do wives take a larger share of the work? Which families hew closest to the cultural line in task allocation and which are most radical?

Answers to these questions may be sought in three general directions: (a) What segments of the community follow traditional norms in their division of labor—just because they are traditional? (b) What situational factors affect the participation of husband and wife in household tasks? Especially, how important is the relative availability of the two partners? (c) What changes occur within marriages with the passage of time?

Where Is the Traditional Family?

A completely traditional family would be one in which the husband always did the male tasks (repairing, lawn-mowing, and snow-shovelling) and the wife always devoted herself to her traditional role (cooking, dish-washing, house-cleaning, and shopping). Since only six per cent of the families are this traditional, it is necessary to look for groups in the community which are simply more stereotyped than average. The standard of comparison here is the mean stereotypy score for the total sample (4.50). We expected immigrants, Catholics, and farm families to be the most traditional.

Immigrants? Since most immigrants were raised in traditional societies, they should be especially influenced by conventional norms. At first glance they are—for those couples where both partners were born overseas have a high stereotypy score of 4.97. However, this difference disappears when the age of the immigrants is taken into consideration. Most foreign-born Detroiters came to America a long time ago, and their division of labor is affected more by their age than by their place of birth. By contrast, young immigrants who have spent most of their life to-date overseas and have only recently arrived in America are less stereotyped (4.20) than average in their allocation of tasks. If it is true that immigrants do bring "old-fashioned" ideas with them to America, circumstances must outweigh those ideas in determining their division of labor.

Catholics? The same conclusion emerges from looking at Catholic and Protestant families. Catholics should follow the traditional division of labor more closely because Catholic teaching places special emphasis on prescribed roles for men and women. However Catholic stereotypy, at 4.46, is a shade less than average, and the Protestant average a shade higher (4.53). Moreover, devout Catholics are not more traditional but less so than inactive Catholics (4.39 versus 4.64).

Farmers? Farm families have the same median number of stereotyped task allocations (five) as the city families. So, again, there is no more adherence to tradition in a segment where it is rumored to exist.

[Summarizing,] traditional ideas do not seem to be an effective determinant of the division of labor. Rather than being motivated by ideological concerns, American families seem to be quite pragmatic in settling who does what around the house.

This doesn't mean that families cannot be found which are traditional in form. The question is whether they are traditional because of conven-

TABLE 2 UNILATERAL PERFORMANCE OF SPECIFIC HOUSEHOLD TASKS, BY FARM AND CITY WIVES

(178 Farm Families, 731 City Families)

Families Where Wife Only Performs Task*	Task							
	Repairs	Lawn	Walk	Bills	Groceries	Break-fast	Living room	Dishes
On farm	6%	13%	6%	25%	45%	86%	86%	88%
In city	3	7	7	30	36	66	65	70

* Reciprocal percentages of the 178 farm husbands and 731 city husbands help with those tasks at least occasionally.

tional beliefs and value patterns or for other reasons. The choice lies between culturological and dynamic theories. The culturological approach fails to account for variations between families, but pragmatic factors do provide workable interpretations. In the case of the division of labor, the general contemporary pattern happens to be traditional. While sheer conservatism may account for some of this behavior, the chief causes seem to be those bio-social factors which produced the tradition in the first place. Hence, the most traditionally patterned families in Detroit may not shape their division of labor from ideological considerations any more than the most unusually patterned families. Rather, both extremes reflect concrete, tangible factors at work in the interrelationships of husband, wife, and the community.

Resources for Getting Things Done

Nothing could be more pragmatic and non-ideological than the sheer availability of one partner to do the household tasks. This is precisely what seems to be the prime determinant of the division of labor.

Farm and City Schedules. Differential availability seems to explain why farm wives do so much more housework than city wives. Superficially one might expect farm husbands to do more around the house because they don't have to leave home to go to work. Yet Table 2 shows farm husbands doing less of everything except the farm-relevant account-keeping and shovelling a path to the barn. Not only do farm wives do more feminine tasks but they even do more of the other two masculine tasks.

How can this rural diligence be explained? In many ways, farm work is like woman's work—it's never done. Not only is there an endless amount of painting, fence-mending, and wood-chopping that could be done on the typical farm, but it's always so near at hand that it provides the husband with counterclaims to any demands that might come from the wife. The farmer's perennial involvement in his work makes him relatively unavailable for household tasks, whereas the city husband's separation from his place of work makes him highly available for part-time "employment" at home.

In Detroit, the differences between entire occupational groups are minor, although the business and professional group does have the highest task performance by the wife (5.49) and the low-blue-collar group the least (5.20). The big difference between city husbands is not between occupations as such but reflects the amount of involvement of the husband in his occupation.

Occupational Preoccupation. Two measures of the husband's success in his occupation are available. The first is the amount of income he earns. Presumably the more time and energy a man invests in his job, the more he is financially rewarded. The evidence is that high-income husbands do less work around the house.

A second measure of occupational success involves comparing the husband's occupation with that of his father before him. Those who now hold a better job have been "upward mobile," in comparison to those who have stayed in the same occupational stratum or moved downward.[2] The

[2] Occupations were rated on the National Opinion Research Center's scale of occupational prestige. "Stable" husbands were those who had not moved more than five percentile points from their father's rating.

TABLE 3 ROLE SPECIALIZATION, BY STAGE IN FAMILY-LIFE CYCLE

Mean Role Specialization	Stage in Family-Life Cycle					
Childrearing stages:		Preschool	Preadolescent	Adolescent	Unlaunched	
		5.13	5.22	5.47	6.01	
		(122)	(134)	(95)	(58)	
Childless stages:	Honeymoon				Postparental	Retired
	4.77				5.82	6.00
	(18)				(83)	(9)
Childless couples:		6.22	4.71	5.13		
		(9)	(28)	(8)		

differences are not great but they substantiate the generalization that the more successful the husband is in his occupation, the less the wife can count on his help at home.

Job-involved Wives. So far, only the husband's involvement outside the home has been mentioned. But since many wives also work, both partners' employment influences their availability for household tasks.

When the wife is away most of the day (nearly all working wives in Detroit have full-time jobs), she faces the potential burden of two jobs: paid work plus housework. Under these circumstances, the husband feels obliged to help out more at home and takes over an appreciably larger share of the housework. The working wife still has a more strenuous life than the housewife, no doubt, but the husband may come to her rescue sufficiently to cushion the physical strain on her and to minimize resentment against him.

However, his ability to come to her aid depends on the extent to which he works himself. If he is home all the time, he can pretty much take over the housework even if he is unable to hold a regular job. But if he has two jobs himself (as many overtime husbands do), there will be less reason and less possibility for him to help out with the wife's second area of responsibility.

The comparative availability of the husband has the same effect when the wife is not working—but it makes less difference then. If the wife is home all the time, she can do her traditional tasks without much help from the husband. Even if he's home full-time (as when neither partner works), he is not likely to invade her sphere as long as she is capable of doing her own traditional work. Most non-working couples involve a husband who has retired but spends his time largely in puttering around rather than in doing half of the housework.

This suggests a limitation on the principle of comparative availability: *under conditions of strain*, tasks will be reallocated in the direction of the more available partner. From this point of view, the full-time housewife whose husband is employed full-time is the normal pattern. She has full-time to devote to the feminine tasks and he has his spare-time in which to get around to the masculine tasks.

When the husband retires, there is no additional strain on the division of labor because the wife still has plenty of time to get her work done. Only if she takes a job does a stay-at-home husband come under pressure to change his role.

On the other hand, if the husband works evenings and weekends, it may be difficult for him to accomplish even the traditional male tasks—so the wife who is home all the time may find herself taking over his tasks.

For the husband to work overtime puts less strain on the traditional division of labor than for the wife to go outside the home to work. This is a simple question of the number of hours in the week. Husbands rarely put in as much as forty hours overtime but this is the usual outside investment of the wife who goes to work.

Changes in the Division of Labor

The resources which the husband and wife bring to the family are partly skills acquired before the couple get married. Partly they are resources of time which the partners are able to contribute to marriage by default of external involvements or by intentional interest in the family.

Role Differentiation. Still other differences between families stem from the internal dynamics of family living. One of these is a type of change

TABLE 4 RELATIVE TASK PERFORMANCE, BY STAGE IN FAMILY-LIFE CYCLE

Wife's Mean Task Performance	Stage in Family-Life Cycle						
Childrearing stages:		Preschool	Preadolescent	Adolescent	Unlaunched		
		5.14	5.58	5.53	5.56		
		(122)	(134)	(95)	(58)		
Childless stages:	Honeymoon					Postparental	Retired
	4.55					5.47	5.50
	(18)					(83)	(10)
Childless couples:		5.00	5.11	5.25			
		(9)	(28)	(8)			

which is likely to affect any group over the course of time—gradually the members become specialists along differentiated but complementary lines.

Table 3 shows that the honeymoon period of role experimentation involves more sharing of tasks than any later stage. For most couples, the honeymoon period is followed quickly by the retirement of the wife from work to housewifery, enabling her to begin specializing despite the newness of her tasks. As the children become less of a burden and more of a resource, role differentiation between husband and wife increases at an accelerated pace, reaching its peak when the wife has fully trained children at her disposal, or the retired husband unlimited time to perform his own tasks.

Relative Participation in Tasks. Similar trends occur with respect to the amount of work done by each partner, although specialization and task performance are not identical phenomena.

Whereas age of wife alone gives a somewhat irregular picture of the changing amount of work, stage in the family-life cycle reflects age, the wife's employment, and the burden of preschool children sufficiently to provide a clearer trend line. Table 4 shows that the young wife without children does the least work at home. However, the coming of the first child does not deprive her completely of her husband's assistance since she needs his help in adjusting to the increased demands of her new role as mother. By the time her oldest child gets into grade school, she settles into a *hausfrau* pattern, carrying the main responsibility for tasks about the home. Even when the last child leaves, the ending of the mother role hardly affects the wife's share in the performance of household tasks.

In general, the division of labor in the modern family coincides with the division of labor in the traditional family. The reason is not so much that contemporary Americans are conservative in principle—for they have altered their pattern of decision-making to fit the times. Rather the same bio-social reasons which shaped the traditional family still supply differential resources which men and women bring to marriage. But where resources differ from man to man or woman to woman, the modern family adjusts its division of labor accordingly. If it clings to traditional patterns under altered circumstances, the condemnation of spouse and observers alike is incurred. For the criterion which governs the contemporary division of labor is not custom but equity, and an equitable division of labor depends on the resources of time, energy, and skill which each family member can contribute to the common task.

REFERENCES

Gold, M., and Slater, Carol, 1958. Office, factory, store—and family: a study of integration setting. *American Sociological Review*, **23**, 64–74.

Miller, D. R., and Swanson, G. E., 1958. *The changing American parent: a study in the Detroit area.* New York: Wiley.

Scheinfeld, A., 1944. *Women and men.* New York: Harcourt, Brace.

Spiro, M. E., 1956. *Kibbutz: venture in utopia.* Cambridge, Mass.: Harvard University Press.

part VIII Consensus and Conflict

THE CHILD MAY HAVE a different role conception of himself than does his teacher, parents may expose a child to conflicting prescriptions, an employee may evaluate his performance more highly than does his supervisor, or a friend's sanction may be different from that of some representative of society. These are examples of conflicts for descriptions, prescriptions, evaluations, and sanctions, respectively. Although everyone has had experience with such conflicts, it is often assumed by some social theorists that there exists a high degree of consensus in society. Actually, the degree of consensus varies from near maximum disagreement (dissensus), through polarization (conflict), to virtually unanimous agreement (consensus). Studies in recent years have amply documented that various conditions of agreement and disagreement may be found for aspects of role.

The importance of consensus and conflict may be illustrated by considering some of the effects of conflicting prescriptions. An individual exposed to conflict obviously has two or more courses of action prescribed. He cannot behave consistently with both sets of prescriptions at the same time, and thus complete conformity, considering both sets of expectations, is impossible. But were there consensus of the prescriptions, he could conform. Furthermore, conflict may create personal confusion, anxiety, and ambivalence for the individual, to say nothing of the many possible social dysfunctions of the conflict. Prescriptive consensus, in contrast, not only allows complete conformity, but probably fosters it as well, because of the sheer force of the shared prescriptions and because conformity behavior is less ambiguously defined. The selections in this part explore both the antecedents and the effects of consensus and conflict.

Problems of role conflict are discussed in the first selection, by Parsons. The author describes sources of role conflict and some of its functions and dysfunctions for individuals and the society.

The selection by Kahn, Wolfe, Quinn, Snoek, and Rosenthal is also a general discussion of role conflict with particular emphasis upon conflict in an organizational context. In their model, the role episode is identified as including four factors: the role expectations and pressures characteristic of a role sender, and the psychological conflict and coping efforts characterizing a focal person for whom the conflict exists. Direct effects of role pressures are identified as well as the effects associated with the individual's response to the conflicting role expectations. The role episode is then considered in a model in which organizational, personality, and interpersonal factors are viewed as impinging upon various aspects of it.

Merton's selection is addressed to particular forms of articulation and disarticulation in the role set. The author observes that individuals are bound to have a variety of role relationships even when occupying a single position, and that these relationships are very likely to lack complete articulation, partly because role partners are differently located in the social structure. Merton suggests various mechanisms in dealing with disarticulation, among these are the variation in intensity of role involvement, the use of power, the insulation of role activity from observability, the increase of observability of the conflicting demands, the social support by others, and the disruption by role relationships.

Factors affecting the resolution of role conflict is the subject of the selection authored by Gross, McEachern, and Mason. Role conflict is defined in terms of school administrators' perceptions of conflicting prescriptions held for them by others. Role conflict resolution is given by what the administrators said they chose to do under such conditions. An example of one of the regions of conflicts studied is the size of increase in salary for teachers, where administrators perceived a conflict between the norms of the school board and the teachers. Three types of behavior are identified as possible courses of action in the face of conflict; these are preferential selection of one alternative or the other, compromise, or avoidance. Three factors are studied as possible sources of influence in determining the mode of resolving role conflict. One is the legitimacy of the expectations, another is perception of the sanctions that others may apply for nonconformity, and the third is the personal propensity of the administrators to respond differentially to legitimacy and sanctions. It was found that a remarkably high proportion of the specific modes of resolving role conflict could be predicted from the knowledge of these three variables.

The selection by Jacobson is a report of research relating to consensus and conflict of marital partners. The study indicated that divorced couples exhibited greater disparities than did married couples in their attitudes toward the roles of husband and wife in marriage. Although it was not clear from the study whether it was dissensus or some other factor that led to divorce, the findings highlight the importance of role consensus in families and offer suggestions for the counseling of marital partners.

One of the social mechanisms discussed by Merton is that pattern "in which the individual members of a group *assume* that they are actually alone in holding the attitudes and expectations they do, all unknowing that others privately share them." The phenomenon of "shared inaccuracy" is the object of study in the selection by Biddle, Rosencranz, Tomich, and Twyman. In this study of the role of the public school teacher, evidence is adduced from norms, attributed norms, and reported teacher performances which indicates that conservative standards are attributed by respondents to both the "public" and the school officials for public behavior by teachers. These conservative standards are also attributed to school officials who, alone, are aware of the actual liberal attitudes they hold. In discussing these results, the authors speculate that mechanisms of shared inaccuracy often function to restrict communication and observation of role behavior.

selection 32 Role Conflict and the Genesis of Deviance

TALCOTT PARSONS

The consequences of the factors in the genesis of deviant motivation and behavior may be compounded by the factor of role conflict. By this is meant the exposure of the actor to conflicting sets of legitimized role expectations such that complete fulfillment of both is realistically impossible. It is necessary to compromise, that is, to sacrifice some at least of both sets of expectations, or to choose one alternative and sacrifice the other. In any case the actor is exposed to negative sanctions and, so far as both sets of values are internalized, to internal conflict. There may, of course, be limited possibilities of transcending the conflict by redefining the situation, as well as of evasion as for example through secrecy, and segregation of occasions.

Role conflict in this sense is continuous with elements of uncertainty and malintegration. This is particularly true of the conflict of rules, and of exposure to alters who though not explicitly deviant, "stretch a point" in their reaction to ego. The beginnings of a role conflict may thus be present in the difficulty of living up both to the expectations of one alter who interprets a norm in the direction of a "perfectionistic" compulsive conformity pattern, and those of another who is also in close interaction with ego, and who stretches the same normative pattern to the verge of active rebellion, both of them expecting active reciprocation from ego.

There is a certain endemic potentiality of role conflict inherent in the fact that any actor has a plurality of roles, which involve differences of pattern, thus of relations to alters whose interests and orientations mesh with ego's in different ways. These differences have to be adjusted by an ordering or allocation of the claims of the different role-expectations to which the actor is subject. This ordering occurs by priority scales, by occasion, e.g., time and place, and by distribution among alters. There are thus always a variety of activities which have their appropriate partners, which would not be appropriate with other partners, and which have their appropriate time and place. This allocative ordering of any given actor's role-system is often delicately balanced. Any serious alteration in one part of it may encroach on others and thus necessitates a whole series of adjustments.

In the present context it is particularly important to note that a deviant motivation component relative to one set of role-expectations will have a tendency to upset this delicate balance. Thus a compulsive need to excel in an occupational role may cause the actor to encroach on times appropiately allocated to kinship roles, and make him feel that he is exposed to a conflict of expectations as between his boss and his wife. This may in turn accentuate elements of strain in his marital relationship with the possibility that this should lead to stimulation of the deepening of the vicious circle from there on.

But the source of the conflict may not be ego-made. It may be imposed upon the actor from the malintegration of the social system itself. Not all social malintegration belongs in this category, there may for example be conflicts between groups with no overlapping membership. But, even here, in the pattern sense, there may well be role conflict because only part of the role-pattern defining participation in each group justifies the expectations of the group vis-à-vis the adversary group. This would, for example, be the case in white-Negro relations in the South (and in less accentuated form throughout the United States). This may be put as a conflict of roles in that for example the white man has in his role as American citizen internalized participation in the universalistic values of the wider society, the "American creed," but also as a Southerner in the pattern of

From pages 280–283 of a book by the same author entitled *The Social System*, 1951, New York: The Free Press. Reprinted by permission of the author and The Free Press.

"white supremacy." The conflict can, however, be mitigated in that he relatively seldom has to act in roles where the significant alters hold up the conflicting expectations to him in such a way that he must directly choose. He deals universalistically in some contexts for example vis-à-vis white colleagues in his occupational sphere, and particularistically vis-à-vis Negro-white situations. This segregation is essential to minimize the strain. This situation may be regarded as a main basis of the Southern resentment against "Northern interference" in the race problem. It introduces an active conflict of the expectations of significant alters whose differences cannot be ignored. This forces a decision which the segregation of contexts has tended to make it possible to evade.

The significance of role conflict as a factor in the genesis of alienative motivation should be clear from the above. Exposure to role conflict is an obvious source of strain and frustration in that it creates a situation incompatible with a harmonious integration of personality with the interaction system. There must be external frustrations, internal conflicts or both, in the more severe cases always both. Indeed what, on the interaction level if not the fully developed social role level, is exposure to conflicting expectations of some kind may be presumed to be the generic situation underlying the development of ambivalent motivational structures with their expression in neuroses, in deviant behavior or otherwise.

When, however, the element of conflict is present on the level of institutionalized role-expectations, a further element is introduced which can be of great significance. The fact that both sides of the conflicting expectations are institutionalized means that there is the basis for a claim to *legitimacy* for both patterns. As distinguished then from alienative need-dispositions which are clearly stigmatized by the moral sentiments common to ego and alter, and later, hence are the foci of feelings of guilt and shame, there is the possibility of the justification of the alienative as well as the originally conformative motivation.

On one level this should serve as a factor in the intensification of internal conflict, and therefore call for greater pressure to resort to defensive and adjustive mechanisms. An example would be the "touchiness" of the Southern white with regard to outside interference. But the obverse of intensification of conflict is that in a certain sense the defenses against overt deviance are greatly weakened if the alienative need-disposition (from the point of view of one of the given expectation patterns) is given a basis of legitimation. Both internal sanctions and those from significant alters are weakened. Then on the one hand role conflict can be seen to be very important as a source of motivations leading to social change, through some sort of undermining of the motivational bases of an established order which includes the provision of motivationally acceptable alternatives. On the other hand this possibility is potentially so dangerous to the stability of a given institutional system that it may be presumed that one of the major functions of the mechanisms of social control is to forestall the establishment of a claim to legitimacy for the expression of need-dispositions which are alienative relative to the major institutionalized patterns of the social system. Of course the establishment of such a "functional need" of the social system does not in any way explain the actual structures and processes related to it. But it does serve to focus our attention on certain points in the motivational equilibrium of the social system in such a way that our attention will be called to certain problems of the determination of processes which might otherwise have been overlooked.

selection 33 Adjustment to Role Conflict and Ambiguity in Organizations

ROBERT L. KAHN, DONALD M. WOLFE, ROBERT P. QUINN, J. DIEDRICK SNOEK, AND ROBERT A. ROSENTHAL

FACTORS INVOLVED IN ROLE CONFLICT AND AMBIGUITY

An adequate understanding of processes of adjustment to stresses in organizations must take into account many factors. Organizations are complex and the interdependencies among members are both potent and subtle. The personalities of members, especially those whose adjustments are to be investigated, must be considered, as must be the pattern of social relations among the members. Processes of communication and social influence are of major concern, and so are the intrapsychic processes involved in coping with psychological conflict, tension, and anxiety. Moreover, these many variables tend to be related in complex ways. A theoretical model, providing a general orientation to the interactions of the major groups of variables, is essential.

Figure 1 presents the core of such a model, built around the notion of a role episode; that is, a complete cycle of role sending, response by the focal person, and the effects of that response on the role senders.

The four boxes represent *events* that constitute a role episode. The arrows connecting them imply a causal sequence. Role pressures are assumed to originate in the expectations held by members of the role set. Role senders have expectations regarding the way in which the focal role should be performed. They also have perceptions regarding the way in which the focal person is actually performing. They correlate the two, and exert pressures to make his performance congruent with their expectation. These pressures induce in the focal person an experience which has both perceptual and cognitive properties, and which leads in turn to certain adjustive (or maladjustive) responses. The responses of the focal person are typically observed by those exerting the pressures and their expectations are correspondingly adjusted. Thus, for both the role senders and the focal person, the episode involves experience and the response. Let us look at the

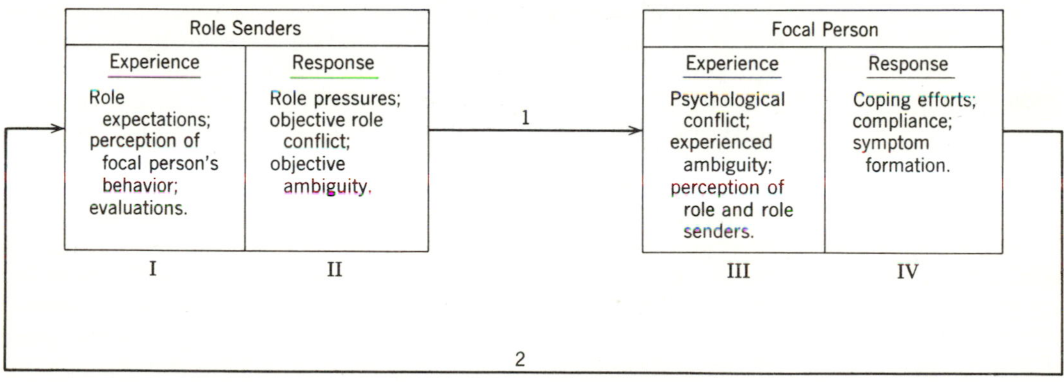

Figure 1. A model of the role episode.

Abridged from pp. 26–34 of a book by the same authors entitled *Organizational Stress: Studies in Role Conflict and Ambiguity*, 1964, New York: Wiley. Reprinted by permission of the authors and Wiley. The research upon which this report was based was financed by a grant from the National Institute of Mental Health.

contents of these four boxes and their relations in more detail.

The episode starts with the existence of a set of role expectations held by role senders about a focal person and his behavior on the job. The experience of the role senders includes perceptual, cognitive, and evaluative components. Speaking of role senders as a group is a matter of convenience. In fact, each role sender behaves toward the focal person in ways determined by his own expectations and his own anticipations of the focal person's responses. Under certain circumstances, the role sender, responding to his own immediate experience, expresses his expectations overtly; he attempts to influence the focal person in the direction of greater conformity with his expectations. It is not uncommon for a role sender to be relatively unaware that his behavior is in fact an influence attempt. Even mild communications about actual and expected role performance usually carry an evaluative connotation. Role expectations [often] lead to role pressures, but there is no simple isomorphism between them.

To determine the likelihood and nature of sent role pressures, the expectations of each role sender must be investigated separately. To understand the degree of conflict or ambiguity in the role, the total pattern of such expectations and pressures must be considered. A thorough investigation into all the role expectations held at a given moment by all the members of the role set should yield an indication of the potential in the situation for conflict. The actual degree of objective role conflict will depend on the configuration of role pressures actually exerted by role senders on the focal person. His experience of this conflict will in turn depend upon its objective magnitude and on certain characteristics of the focal person himself. Likewise, the potential degree of clarity or ambiguity in a role can be assessed by investigating the availability of relevant information within the role set. The degree of objective ambiguity for a focal position will depend, of course, on the availability of that information to the position. The experienced ambiguity of the occupant of that position will reflect the objective situation as it interacts with relevant properties of the person (for example, need for cognition).

Direct Effects of Role Pressures

Arrow 1 indicates that the total set of role pressures affects the immediate experience of the focal person in a given situation (Box III). This experience typically has both perceptual and cognitive aspects. It would include, for example, the focal person's perception of the demands and requirements placed on him by his role senders and his awareness or experience of psychological conflict. In general, we expect the focal person's experience of a situation to be a function of the objective demands and pressures to which he is subjected at that moment. When his associates are generally supportive of his present performance, we expect them to be so perceived and the response to be primarily one of satisfaction and confidence. When pressures from associates are especially strong and directed toward changes in the behavior of the focal person, or when they are contradictory to one another, the experience is apt to be fraught with conflict and ambiguity, and to evoke responses of tension, anger, or indecision. These, however, are general predictions; we do not expect them to hold alike for all focal persons.

The specific reactions of each focal person to a situation are immediately determined by the nature of his experience in that situation. For example, the likelihood of his attempting rational problem solving will depend on the opportunities he perceives for creating changes in the situation or in his own behavior which will be acceptable to all concerned. On the other hand, as conflict and tension become more severe, he is more likely to become ego-defensive and to fall back on other coping techniques, some of which may be maladaptive in the long run because they tend to create greater pressures or increased tension.

The person who is confronted with a situation of role conflict must respond to it in some fashion. One or more of role senders are exerting pressure on him to change his behavior, and he must cope somehow with the pressure they are exerting. Whatever pattern of response he adopts may be regarded as an attempt to attain or regain an adequately gratifying experience in the work situation. Of special significance to us are certain identifiable coping responses. These include direct attempts at solving the objective problem by compliance or by persuading role senders to modify incompatible demands. Coping will also take the form of attempts to avoid the sources of stress, and the use of defense mechanisms which distort the reality of a conflictual or ambiguous situation in order to relieve the anxiety of the undistorted experience. There is also the possibility that coping with the pressures of the work will involve the formation of affective or physiological symptoms. Regardless of which of these, singly or in combination, the focal person uses, his behavior can be assessed in relation to the expectations and sent pressures of each of his role senders.

Effects of Response on Role Expectations

The degree to which the focal person's behavior conforms to the expectations held for him will affect the state of those expectations at the next moment. If his response is essentially a hostile counter-attack, his role senders are apt to think of him and behave toward him in ways quite different than if he were submissively compliant. If he complies partially under pressure, they may increase the pressure; if he is obviously overcome with tension and anxiety, they may "lay-off." In sum, the role episode is abstracted from a process which is cyclic and ongoing: the response of the focal person to role pressures "feeds back" on the senders of those pressures in ways that alter or reinforce them. The next role sendings of each member of the set depend on his evaluations of the response to his last sendings, and thus a new episode begins.

In order to understand more fully the causal dynamics of such episodes and their consequences for the person's adjustment, the model must be extended to include three additional classes of variables—organizational and ecological factors, personality factors, and the character of interpersonal relations between the focal person and his role senders. Taken in combination, these factors represent the context within which the episode occurs.

ADJUSTMENT TO ROLE CONFLICT AND AMBIGUITY

At this point we move to a somewhat different level of analysis. In Figure 1 the boxes represent events—occurrences at a given moment in time. The directed lines represent a causal sequence: sent pressures (II) lead to experienced conflict (III), which leads to coping responses (IV); these are perceived and evaluated in relation to expectations (I), and the cycle resumes. Figure 1 also forms the core of Figure 2. However, the circles in Figure 2 represent not momentary events but enduring states of the organization, the person, and the interpersonal relations between focal person and role senders. An analysis of these factors will make more understandable the sequence of events in a role episode. The properties and traits which make up the organization, the person, and social relationships are for the most part abstractions and generalizations based upon recurrent events and behaviors, for example, characterizing a relationship as friendly means simply that the parties to the relationship think well of each other and behave in a pleasant supportive manner toward one another. It is such repetitions and patterns of behaviors and events which give us a basis for understanding each new event.

Organizational Antecedent of the Person's Role

To a considerable extent, the role expectations held by the members of a role set—the prescriptions and proscriptions associated with a particular position—are determined by the broader organizational context. The organizational structure, the functional specialization and division of labor, and the formal reward system, which may have been specified by the organization's directors and are now matters of record and policy, dictate the major content of a given office. What the occupant of that office is "supposed" to do, with and for whom, is given by these and other properties of the organization itself. Although other human beings are doing the "supposing" and the rewarding, the structural properties of organization are sufficiently stable so that we can treat them as independent of the particular persons in the role set. For such properties of size, number of echelons, and rate of growth, the justifiable abstraction of organizational properties from individual behavior is even more obvious.

The organizational circle (A) in Figure 2, then, represents a set of variables. Some of them characterize the organization as a whole, e.g., its size, number of rank or status levels, the products it produces, or its financial base. Other variables in this set are ecological, in that they represent the relation of a certain position or person to the organization, e.g., his rank, his responsibilities for certain services in the division of labor, or the number and positions of others who are directly concerned with his performance.

Arrow 3 asserts a causal relationship between various organizational variables and the role expectations and pressures which are held about and exerted toward a particular position. For example, a person in a liaison position linking two departments is likely to be subjected to many conflicting role pressures because his role set consists of persons in two separate units, each having its own goals, objectives, and norms. In general, the organizational conditions surrounding and defining the positions of one's role

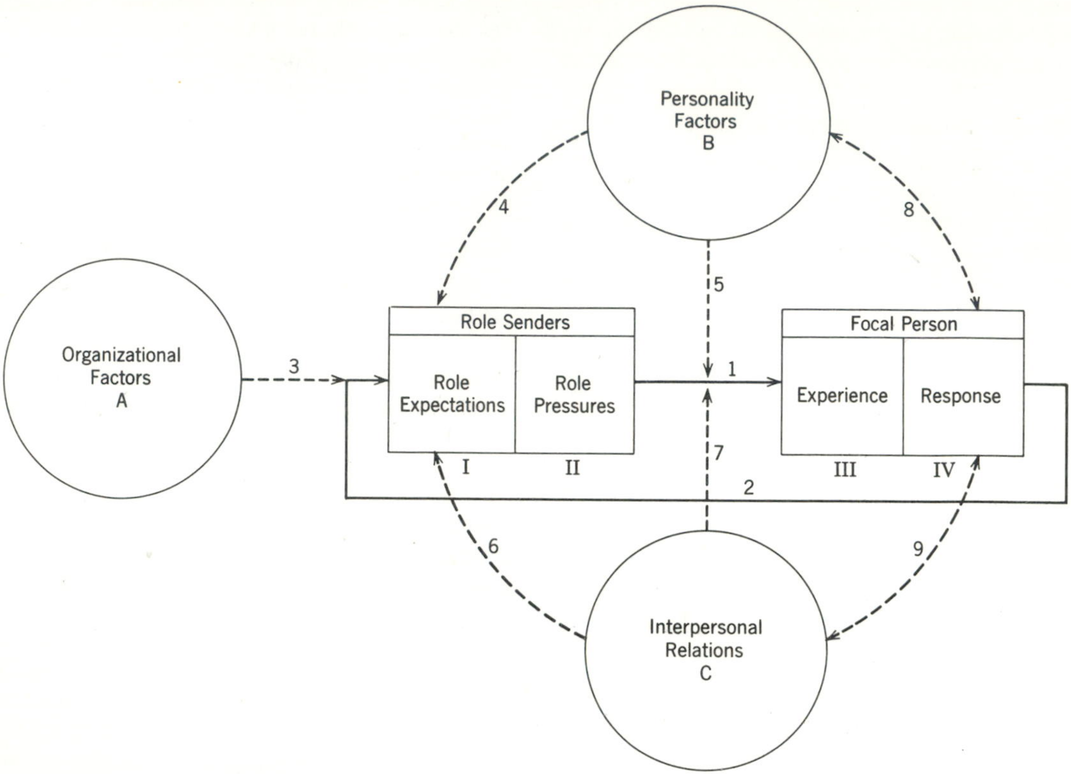

Figure 2. A theoretical model of factors involved in adjustment to role conflict and ambiguity.

senders will determine in part their organizational experience, their expectations, and the pressures they impose.

Personality Factors

The term "personality" is used broadly to refer to all those factors that describe a person's propensities to behave in certain ways, his motives and values, his sensitivities and fears, his habits, and the like. Such factors affect role episodes in several ways. First, some traits of the person tend to evoke or facilitate certain responses from his role senders (Arrow 4). For example, a volatile, aggressive personality may elicit strong pressures because only strong pressures have a lasting effect on him, while a more rigid person may so successfully resist influence that many associates give up trying to influence him. Second, it is likely that some persons will experience role pressures differently than others (Arrow 5); that is, personality factors will act as conditioning variables in the relationship between the objective and experienced situations. For example, a highly sensitive person may experience more emotional tension under mild pressures than a more "thick-skinned" person will under intense pressures. Finally, we are interested in the extent to which personality predispositions lead to the use of certain kinds of coping responses. The intra-punitive person, for example, may blame and hold himself responsible when faced with conflict and frustration; and an aggressive, extra-punitive person would perhaps respond to the same situation with overaggression against others whom he tends to blame for his difficulties. Preferences for certain styles of coping with tension and anxiety also tend to be rooted in personality structure.

In sum, personality factors are seen as important determinants of both differential elicitations of role pressures and differential reactions to role pressures.

The Involvement of Interpersonal Relations

We will use the term "interpersonal relations" to refer to the more or less stable patterns of interaction between a person and his role senders and to their orientations toward each other. These patterns of relationships may be characterized along several dimensions, some of them stemming from the formal structure of the organization, others from informal interaction and the sharing of common experiences. The following dimensions are seen as particularly important in the present context: (a) *power* or ability to influence, (b) *affective bonds*, such as respect, trust in the cooperativeness and benevolence of the other, and attraction or liking, the bonds of friendship, (c) *dependence* of one on the other, and (d) the style of *communication* between the focal person and his associates.

As Figure 2 indicates, interpersonal relations fulfill some functions parallel to those described in connection with personality factors. The kind of pressures exerted by role senders upon the focal person depends to some degree upon the nature of relations between them (Arrow 6). Role senders who are superior in the formal hierarchy will present their demands in a different manner than subordinates or peers. In like manner, pressures will be interpreted differently depending on the affective bonds between focal person and role senders (Arrow 7). For example, pressures from trusted associates may arouse more tension than similar pressures from others. Also, the nature of a person's behavioral reactions to a given experience may be affected by interpersonal relations in the situation. For example, some kinds of coping responses (like overt aggression) may be virtually ruled out when the pressures are exerted by a hierarchial superior. On the other hand, strong bonds of trust and respect may encourage a response of shared problem-solving.

Coping Responses and "Feedback" Cycles

There are several ways in which reactions to conflicts may produce changes in other sets of variables in Figure 2. As noted above, the extent to which a focal person complies with his role senders' demands is one example of his behavior that will directly affect future role sending behavior (Arrow 2). When he is seen as resisting influence, the pressures upon him may be temporarily increased; when he is seen as unable or unwilling to comply with the requirements of his job, a whole new set of pressures may be brought to bear. Another kind of feedback occurs when the focal person attempts to initiate communication with his role senders about the problems he encounters in the performance of his job; such feedback may lead to immediate modifications in the demands that are made of him, to changes in informal collaborative arrangements, or even to alterations in the formal division of labor.

Two other feedback cycles affect the total process of role sending—one through the effects of the focal person's responses upon his own personality, and one through the effects of his responses upon his relations with each of his role senders. For example, immediate changes in the focal person's feelings and behavior toward his role senders (Arrow 9), such as a loss of trust or respect, are likely in the long run to create significant changes in the enduring pattern of relations between them. Such a change in interpersonal relations will in turn affect future role sender behavior (Arrow 6) as well as the focal person's response to it (Arrow 7). Three kinds of reactions seem of particular significance in this process. First, tensions and frustrations of the focal person may arouse in him hostile feelings, which in turn give rise to aggressive actions and communications to his role senders. These actions may result in a decrease in pressures; just as often, depending on circumstances and personalities, aggression results in stronger and more restrictive demands by role senders. Second, the focal person may attempt to reject or avoid those role senders whose demands he has difficulty in meeting. As with hostility, his rejection and withdrawal may or may not reduce his difficulties, depending on how his role senders respond in return. Finally, response of the focal person to a situation of conflict may be to approach his role senders, increasing the effectiveness of communication with them and perhaps the likelihood of joint problem solving. If this increases the amount of supportive behavior by associates, it may lead to a reduction in tensions of the focal person, even in cases where pressures continue to be strong.

Certain reactions to role experiences also may lead to modifications in the personality organization (Arrow 8) of the focal person. Such changes are relevant for two reasons. First, they may be symptomatic of good or bad mental health, affecting his ability to carry on all the normal functions of living. Second, such changes may have specific effects upon his performance in the work situation, including his ability to handle pressures and tensions. Let us imagine, for example, a person whose continual inability to meet the demands of his environment threatens his self-esteem. In attempting to cope with the anxiety aroused by this threat he may be forced to rely more and more on the use of defense mechanisms that distort the realities of his situation, so that his behavior becomes less and less adaptive (Arrow 5). Other kinds of changes in the person, such as changes in his level of aspiration or the development of symptoms of ill health, may affect his associate's behavior toward him directly (Arrow 4), creating a change in the role pressure.

Both adjustive and maladjustive cycles are comprehended by this framework. That is, we have considered cycles in which responses to role experiences increase the likelihood of future experiences which are basically pleasant and gratifying or basically unpleasant and frustrating. This model is presented to provide a sort of cognitive map, a way of thinking about a large set of factors and conditions in a complex interaction. The model becomes a theory when the specific variables in each panel are delineated and the causal connections among them are specified.

selection 34 Instability and Articulation in the Role-Set

ROBERT K. MERTON

A particular social status involves, not a single associated role, but an array of associated roles. This is a basic characteristic of social structure. This fact of structure can be registered by a distinctive term, *role-set*, by which I mean that *complement of role relationships which persons have by virtue of occupying a particular social status*. As one example: the single status of medical student entails not only the role of a student in relation to his teachers, but also an array of other roles relating the occupant of that status to other students, nurses, physicians, social workers, medical technicians, etc. Again: the status of public school teacher has its distinctive role-set, relating the teacher to his pupils, to colleagues, the school principal and superintendent, the Board of Education, and, on frequent occasions, to local patriotic organizations, to professional organizations of teachers, Parent-Teachers Associations, and the like.

STRUCTURAL SOURCES OF INSTABILITY IN THE ROLE-SET

It would seem that the basic source of disturbance in the role-set is the structural circumstance that any one occupying a particular status has role-partners who are differently located in the social structure. As a result, these others have, in some measure, values and moral expectations differing from those held by the occupant of the status in question. The fact, for example, that the members of a school board are often in social and economic strata quite different from that of the public school teacher will mean that, in certain respects, their values and expectations differ from those of the teacher. The individual teacher may thus be readily subject to conflicting role-expectations among his professional colleagues and among the influential members of the school board and, at times, derivatively, of the superintendent of schools. What is an educational frill for the one may be judged as an essential of education by the other. These disparate and inconsistent evaluations complicate the task of coming to terms with them all. What holds conspicuously for the status of the teacher holds, in varying degree, for the occupants of other statuses who are structurally related, in their role-set, to others who themselves occupy diverse statuses.

As things now stand, this appears to be the major structural basis for potential disturbance of a stable role-set. The question does not arise, of course, in those special circumstances in which all those in the role-set have the same values and same role-expectations. But this is a special and,

Abridged from pages 369–379 of a book by the same author entitled *Social Theory and Social Structure* (Rev. ed.), 1957, New York: The Free Press. Reprinted by permission of the author and The Free Press.

perhaps historically rare, situation. More often, it would seem, and particularly in highly differentiated societies, the role-partners are drawn from diverse social statuses with, to some degree, correspondingly different social values. To the extent that this obtains, the characteristic situation should be one of disorder, rather than of relative order. And yet, although historical societies vary in the extent to which this is true, it seems generally the case that a substantial degree of order rather than of acute disorder prevails. This, then, gives rise to the problem of identifying the social mechanisms through which some reasonable degree of articulation among the roles in role-sets is secured or, correlatively, the social mechanisms which break down so that structurally established role-sets do not remain relatively stabilized.

Social Mechanisms for the Articulation of Roles in the Role-Set

1. *The mechanism of differing intensity of role-involvement among those in the role-set*: Role-partners are variously concerned with the behavior of those in a particular social status. This means that the role-expectations of those in the role-set are not maintained with the same degree of intensity. For some, this role-relationship may be of only peripheral concern; for others, it may be central. As an hypothetical example; the parents of children in a public school may be more directly engaged in appraising and controlling the behavior of teachers than, say, the members of a local patriotic organization who have no children in the school. The values of the parents and of the patriotic organization may be at odds in numerous respects and may call for quite different behavior on the part of the teacher. But if the expectations of the one group in the role-set of the teacher are central to their concerns and interests, and the expectations of the other group, only peripheral, this eases the problem of the teacher seeking to come to terms with these disparate expectations.

There is patterned variation in the scope and intensity of involvement of group members in their statuses and roles. Such variation serves to cushion the disturbance to a role-set involving conflicting expectations of the behavior of those occupying a particular status. The teacher, for whom this status holds primary significance, is in this degree better able to withstand the demands for conformity with the differing expectations of those in his role-set for whom this relationship has only peripheral significance. This is not to say, of course, that teachers are not vulnerable to these expectations which are at odds with their professional commitments. It is only to say that they are less vulnerable than they would otherwise be (or sometimes are) when the powerful members of their role-set are only little concerned with this particular relationship. Were all those involved in the role-set of the teacher *equally* concerned with this relationship, the plight of the teacher would be considerably more sorrowful than it presently is.

2. *The mechanism of differences in the power of those involved in a role-set*: A second mechanism which affects the stability of a role-set is potentially provided by the distribution of power. By power, in this connection, is meant nothing more than the observed and predictable capacity for imposing one's own will in a social action, even against the resistance of others taking part in that action.

The members of a role-set are not apt to be equally powerful in shaping the behavior of occupants of a particular status. However, it does not follow that the individual, group, or stratum in the role-set which is *separately* most powerful uniformly succeeds in imposing its expectations upon the status-occupants—say, the teacher. This would be so only in the circumstance when the one member of the role-set has an effective monopoly of power, either to the exclusion of all others or outweighing the combined power of the others. Failing this special situation, the individuals subject to conflicting expectations among the members of their role-set can effect, deliberately or unwittingly, *coalitions of power* among them which enable these individuals to go their own way. The conflict is then not so much between the status-occupants and the diverse members of their role-set as between the members of the role-set itself. The counterpoise to any one powerful member of the role-set is at times provided by a coalition of lesser powers in combination. The familiar pattern of "balance of power" is not confined to power struggles among nations; in less easily visible form, it can be found in the workings of role-sets generally, as the child who succeeds in having his father's decision offset his mother's contrasting decision has ample occasion to know. When conflicting powers in the role-set neutralize one another, the status-occupant has relative freedom to proceed as he intended in the first place.

Thus, even in those potentially unstable structures in which the members of a role-set hold distinct and contrasting expectations of what the status-occupant should do, the latter is not wholly at the mercy of the most powerful among them. Moreover, a high degree of involvement in his status reinforces his relative power. For to the extent that powerful members of his role-set are not primarily concerned with this particular relationship in the same degree as the status-occupant, they will not be motivated to exercise their potential power to the full. Within wide margins of his role-activity, the status-occupant will then be free to act, uncontrolled because unnoticed.

This does not mean, of course, that the status-occupant subject to conflicting expectations among members of his role-set is in fact immune to control by them. It is only to say that the power-structure of role-sets is often such that the status-occupant more nearly has autonomy than would be the case if this structure of competing powers did not obtain.

3. *The mechanism of insulating role-activities from observability by members of the role-set*: The occupant of a status does not engage in continuous interaction with all those in his role-set. This is not an incidental fact, but is integral to the operation of role-sets. The interaction with each member (individual or groups) of the role-set is variously limited and intermittent; it is not equally sustained throughout the range of relationships entailed by the social status. This fundamental fact of role-structure allows for role-behavior which is at odds with the expectations of some in the role-set to proceed without undue stress. For effective social control presupposes an appreciable degree of *observability* of role-behavior. To the extent that the role-structure insulates the status-occupant from direct observation by some of his role-set, he is not uniformly subject to competing pressures. It should be emphasized that we are dealing here with a fact of social structure, not with individual adjustments whereby this or that person *happens* to conceal parts of his role-behavior from certain members of his role-set.

The structural fact is that social statuses differ in the extent to which some of the associated role-behavior is insulated from ready observability by all members of the role-set. Variations in this structurally imposed attribute of social statuses accordingly complicate the problem of coping with the disparate expectations of those in the role-set. Thus, occupants of all occupational statuses sometimes face difficult decisions which involve their sense of personal integrity, i.e. of living up to the norms and standards basically governing the performance of their occupational role. But these statuses differ in the extent of ready observability of occupational behavior. As Senator [the late President] Kennedy notes—few, if any, occupations face such difficult decisions "in the glare of the spotlight as do those in public office. Few, if any, face the same dread finality of decision that confronts a Senator facing an important call of the roll" (1956, p. 8).

In contrast, other social statuses have a functionally significant insulation from easy observability by some of those in the role-set. The status of the university teacher provides one example. The norm which holds that what is said in the class-rooms of universities is privileged, in the sense of being restricted to the professor and his students, has this function of maintaining a degree of autonomy for the teacher. For if this were uniformly made available to all those comprising the role-set of the teacher, he might be driven to teach not what he knows or what the evidence leads him to believe, but what will placate the numerous and diverse expectations of all those concerned with "the education of youth." This would soon serve to lower the level of instruction to the lowest common denominator. It would be to transform teaching and place it on the plane of the television show, concerned to do whatever is needed to improve its popularity rating. It is, of course, this exemption from observability from all and sundry who may wish to impose their will upon the instructor which is an integral part of academic freedom, conceived as a functional complex of values and norms.

More broadly, the concept of privileged information and confidential communication in the professions—law and medicine, teaching and the ministry—has the same function of insulating clients from ready observability of their behavior and beliefs by others in their role-set. If the physician or priest were free to tell all they have learned about the private lives of their clients, they could not adequately discharge their functions. If the facts of all role-behavior and all attitudes were freely available to anyone, social structures could not operate. What is sometimes called "the need for privacy"—that is, insulation of actions and thoughts from surveillance by others—is the individual counterpart to the functional requirement of social structure that some measure of exemption from full observability be provided for. Otherwise, the pressure to live up to the details of all (and often conflicting) social norms would become literally unbearable; in a complex society, schizophrenic behavior would become the rule rather than the formidable exception it already is. "Privacy" is not merely a personal predilection; it is an important functional requirement for the effective operation of social structure. Social systems must provide for some appropriate measure, as they say in France, of *quant-à-soi*—a portion of the self which is kept apart, immune from social surveillance.

The mechanism of insulation from observability can, of course, miscarry. Were the politician or statesman fully removed from the public spotlight, social control of his behavior would be correspondingly reduced. Anonymous power anonymously exercised does not make for a stable structure of social relations meeting the values of the society, as the history of secret police amply testifies. The teacher who is fully insulated from observation by peers and superiors may fail to live up to the minimum requirements of his status. The physician in his private practice who is largely exempt from the judgment of competent colleagues may allow his role-performance to sink below tolerable standards. The secret policeman may violate the values of the society, and not be detected.

All this means that some measure of observability of role-performance by members of the role-set is required, if the indispensable social requirement of accountability is to be met. This statement obviously does not contradict earlier statements to the effect that some measure of insulation from observability is also required for the effective operation of social structures. Instead, the two statements, taken in conjunction, hold again that there is some optimum of observability, difficult as yet to identify in measurable terms and doubtless varying for different social statuses, which will simultaneously make for accountability of role-performance and for autonomy of role-performance, rather than for a frightened acquiescence with the distribution of power that happens, at a given moment, to obtain in the role-set. Varying patterns of observability can operate to enable the occupants of social statuses to cope with the conflicting expectations among members of their role-sets.

4. *The mechanism making for observability by members of the role-set of their conflicting demands upon the occupants of a social status*: This mechanism is implied by the two foregoing accounts of the power structure and patterns of insulation from observability; it therefore needs only passing comment here. As long as members of the role-set are happily ignorant that their demands upon the occupants of a status are incompatible, each member may press his own case upon the status-occupants. The pattern is then many against one. But when it is made plain that the demands of some members of the role-set are in full contradiction with the demands of other members, it becomes the task of the role-set, rather than the task of the status-occupant, to resolve these contradictions, either by a struggle for exclusive power or by some degree of compromise. As the conflict becomes abundantly manifest, the pressure upon the status-occupant becomes temporarily relieved.

In such cases, the occupant of the status subjected to conflicting demands and expectations can become cast in the role of the *tertius gaudens*, the third (or more often, the nth) party who draws advantage from the conflict of the others. The status-occupant, originally at the focus of the conflict, virtually becomes a more or less influential bystander whose function it is to high-light the conflicting demands by members of his role-set and to make it a problem for them, rather than for him, to resolve *their* contradictory demands. Often enough, this serves to change the structure of the situation.

This social mechanism can be thought of as working to eliminate one form of what Floyd H. Allport described as "pluralistic ignorance" (1924; see also Schanck, 1932), that is, the pattern in which individual members of a group *assume* that they are virtually alone in holding the social attitudes and expectations they do, all unknowing that others privately share them. This is a frequently observed condition of a group which is so organized that mutual observability among its members is slight. This basic notion of pluralistic ignorance can, however, be usefully enlarged to take account of a formally similar but substantively different condition. This is the condition now under review, in which the members of a role-set do not know that their expectations of the behavior appropriate for the occupants of a particular status are *different* from those held by other members of the role-set. There are two patterns of pluralistic ignorance—the unfounded assumption that one's own attitudes and expectations are unshared and the unfounded assumption that they are uniformly shared.

Confronted with contradictory demands by members of his role-set, each of whom assumes that the legitimacy of his demands is beyond dispute, the occupant of a status can act to make these contradictions manifest. To some extent, depending upon the structure of power, this redirects the conflict so that it is one between members of the role-set rather than, as was at first the case, between them and the occupant of the status. It is the members of the role-set who are now in a position in which *they* are being required to articulate their role-expectations. At the very least, this serves to make evident that it is not willful misfeasance on the part of the status-occupant which keeps him from conforming to all of the contradictory expectations imposed upon him. In some instances, the replacing of pluralistic ignorance by common knowledge serves to make for a re-definition of what can properly be expected of the status-occupant. In other cases, the process serves simply to allow him to go his own way, while the members of his role-set are engaged in their conflict. In both instances, this making manifest of contradictory expectations serves to articulate the role-set beyond that which would occur, if this mechanism were not at work.

5. *The mechanism of social support by others in similar social statuses with similar difficulties of coping with an unintegrated role-set*: This mechanism presupposes the not unusual structural situation that others occupying the same social status have much the same problems of dealing with their role-sets. Whatever he may believe to the contrary, the occupant of a social status is usually not alone. The very fact that it is a *social status* means that there are others more or less like-circumstanced. The actual and potential experience of confronting conflicting role-expectations among those in one's role-set is to this extent common to occupants of the status. The individual subject to these conflicts need not, therefore, meet them as a wholly private problem which must be handled in a wholly private fashion. Such conflicts of role-expectations become patterned and shared by occupants of the same social status.

These facts of social structure afford a basis for understanding the formation of organizations and normative systems among those occupying the same social status. Occupational and professional associations, for example, constitute a structural response to the problems of coping with the power structure and (potentially or actually) conflicting demands by those in the role-set of the status. They constitute social formations designed to counter the power of the role-set; of being, not merely amenable to these demands, but of helping to shape them. The organization of status-occupants—so familiar a part of the social landscape of differentiated societies—serves to develop a normative system which anticipates and thereby mitigates the conflicting demands made of those in this status. They provide social support to the individual status-occupant. They minimize the need for his improvising private adjustments to conflict situations.

It is this same function, it might be said, which also constitutes part of the sociological significance of the emergence of professional codes which are designed to state in advance what the socially supported behavior of the status-occupant should be. Not, of course, that such codes operate with automatic efficiency, serving to eliminate in advance those demands judged illegitimate in terms of the code and serving to indicate unequivocally which action the status-occupant should take when confronted with conflicting demands. Codification, of ethical as of cognitive matters, implies abstraction. The codes still need to be interpreted before being applied to concrete instances. Nevertheless, social support is provided by consensus among status-peers as this consensus is recorded in the code or is expressed in the judgments of status-peers oriented toward the code. The function of such codes becomes all the more significant in those cases in which status-occupants are vulnerable to pressures from their role-set precisely because they are relatively isolated from one another. Thus, thousands of librarians sparsely distributed among the towns and villages of the nation and not infrequently subject to censorial pressures received strong support from the code on censorship developed by the American Library Association in conjunction with the American Book Publishers Council.[1] This kind of social support for conformity to the requirements of the status when confronted with pressures by the role-set to depart from these requirements serves to counteract the instability of role-performance which would otherwise develop.

6. *Abridging the role-set: disruption of role-relationships*: This is, of course, the limiting case in modes of coping with incompatible demands

[1] For the code, see *The Freedom to Read* (1953); for an analysis of the general issue, see Richard P. McKeon, R. K. Merton, and Walter Gellhorn, *Freedom to Read* (1957).

upon status-occupants by members of the role-set. Certain relationships are broken off, leaving a consensus of role-expectations among those that remain. But this mode of adaptation is possible only under special and limited conditions. It can be effectively utilized only in those circumstances where it is still possible for the status-occupant to perform his other roles, without the support of those with whom he has discontinued relations. Otherwise put, this requires that the remaining relationships in the role-set are not substantially damaged by this device. It presupposes that social structure provides the option to discontinue some relations in the role-set as, for example, in a network of personal friendships. By and large, however, this option is far from unlimited, since the role-set is not so much a matter of personal choice as a matter of the social structure in which the status is embedded. Under these conditions, the option is apt to be that of the status-occupant removing himself from the status rather than that of removing the role-set, or an appreciable part of it, from the status. Typically, the individual goes, and the social structure remains.

REFERENCES

Allport, F. H., 1924. *Social psychology*. Boston: Houghton Mifflin.

American Library Association, 1953. *The freedom to read.* Chicago.

Kennedy, J. F., 1956. *Profiles in courage: decisive moments in the lives of celebrated Americans.* New York: Harper and Row.

McKeon, R. P., Merton, R. K., and Gellhorn, W., 1957. *Freedom to read.* New York: Bowker, for the National Book Committee.

Schanck, R. L., 1932. A study of a community and its groups and institutions conceived of as behaviors of individuals. *Psychological Monographs*, **43**, 2.

selection 35 Role Conflict and Its Resolution

NEAL GROSS, ALEXANDER W. McEACHERN, AND WARD S. MASON

In certain situations an individual may find himself exposed to conflicting expectations: some people expect him to behave in one way, others in another, and these expectations are incompatible. How will individuals behave when faced with such conflicts? This is the problem with which our paper is concerned. Later we shall offer a theory of role-conflict resolution and present a test of its usefulness. Before doing this it is necessary to try, first, to clarify the meaning of role conflict and introduce definitions of the concepts we shall employ; second, to present the methods we used in a study of role conflicts of school superintendents; and third, to describe their behavior when they perceived their exposure to conflicting expectations.

From an article by the same authors in Eleanor E. Maccoby, T. M. Newcomb, and E. C. Hartley (Eds.), *Readings in Social Psychology* (3rd. ed.), 1958, New York: Holt. Reprinted by permission of the authors and Holt. This article represents a condensed and simplified version of the analysis of role conflict which may be found in N. Gross, W. S. Mason, and A. W. McEachern, *Explorations in Role Analysis: Studies of the School Superintendency Role*, 1957, New York: Wiley.

CONCEPTS

An examination of the literature concerned with "role conflict" reveals that this term has been given different meanings by different social scientists. Some have used it to denote incompatible expectation situations to which an actor is exposed, whether he is aware of the conflict or not. Other social scientists use "role conflict" to mean situations in which the actor *perceives* incompatible expectations. A foreman's subordinates and his boss may hold quite opposite expectations for his behavior but he may or may not be aware of this discrepancy.

Some formulations of role conflict specify that the actor must be exposed to conflicting expectations that derive from the fact that he occupies two or more positions simultaneously. For example, a young man may occupy simultaneously the positions of son and a member of a fraternity, and his father and his fraternity brothers may hold contradictory expectations for his "drinking behavior." Other formulations include in role conflict those contradictory expectations that derive from an actor's occupancy of a single position. A professor may be expected to behave in one way by his students, in another way by his dean.

Some writers limit role conflict to situations in which an actor is exposed to conflicting *legitimate* expectations or "obligations" whereas others do not make this restriction.

In view of these differences it is necessary to specify the way we defined and limited our problem. First, our interest was in role conflicts which were *perceived* by the individuals subject to them. Second, we were concerned with incompatible expectations resulting from an actor's occupancy of single as well as of multiple positions; *intra-role* as well as *inter-role* conflicts were within the focus of inquiry. Third, the analysis was not restricted to incompatible expectations which were perceived as legitimate. Attention was directed to situations involving both legitimate and illegitimate incompatible expectations.

Limiting the problem in this way the following definitions of basic concepts were used. A *role congruency* is a situation in which an actor as the incumbent of one or more positions perceives that the same or highly similar expectations are held for him. A school superintendent who perceived that his teachers, principals, students, and school board all expected him to handle a discipline problem in the same way would be confronted with a role congruency.

There are situations, however, in which an actor perceives that he is exposed to expectations which are incompatible. A school superintendent may think teachers and parents hold conflicting expectations for his behavior in dealing with a truant child. Any situation in which the incumbent of a position perceives that he is confronted with incompatible expectations will be called a *role conflict*.

The person for whom an expectation is held may consider it to be *legitimate* or *illegitimate*. A legitimate expectation is one which the incumbent of a position feels others have a right to hold. An illegitimate expectation is one which he does not feel others have a right to hold. An expectation which is felt to be legitimate will be called a *perceived obligation*. One which is felt to be illegitimate will be called a *perceived pressure*.

A *sanction* is either a reward or a punishment, conditional on how an individual behaves. For our analysis we will not be concerned with negative sanctions, nor will we be concerned with *actual* sanctions, but rather with an individual's *perceptions* of the sanctions others may apply to him. Whether or not the perceived and actual sanctions are the same in any given situation is an empirical problem which will not be relevant to these analyses.

METHODOLOGY

One hundred and five school superintendents were included in the study. They represented a 48 per cent stratified random sample of all school superintendents in Massachusetts in 1952–53. The data to be reported were obtained from each of these superintendents in the course of an eight-hour interview conducted in the staff research offices.

After considerable experimentation with various methods of isolating the role conflicts to which superintendents were exposed, the following procedure was developed. Four situations were presented to the superintendent, each involving problems with which all superintendents must deal and which, on the basis of the pretests, were judged likely to arouse incompatible expectations. They concerned (a) the hiring and promotion of teachers, (b) the superintendent's allocation of his after-office hours, (c) salary increases for teachers, and (d) the priority the superintendent gives financial or educational needs in drawing up the school budget. For each situation we offered three alternative expectations that incumbents of relevant counterpositions might hold. For example, in the situation which is concerned with teachers' salaries these three expectations were described:

A. Expect me to recommend the highest possible salary increases for teachers so that their incomes are commensurate with their professional responsibilities.
B. Expect me to recommend the lowest possible salary increases for teachers.
C. Have no expectations one way or another.

Eighteen potentially relevant groups or individuals were then listed, and each of the superintendents was asked to indicate which of the three statements most nearly represented what each of the groups or individuals expected the superintendent to do in the situation. If he said that one or more individuals held expectation A and one or more held expectation B, then he was reporting incompatible expectations from incumbents of positions counter to his own.

In addition, the superintendents were asked whether or not they felt that the expectations they said others held were "legitimate." Furthermore, if incompatible expectations were perceived by the superintendent, the interviewer probed with open-end questions to discover how much anxiety was thus created, how the conflict was resolved, and what sanctions the superintendent thought would result from selecting one or the other of the incompatible alternatives.

An example of a city superintendent's responses to the role conflict instrument illustrates the exact method of securing the data for this analysis. Table 1 summarizes the responses of this superintendent to the question of which groups or individuals held which expectations for him with respect to salary increases for teachers.

It is clear that he perceived incompatible expectations. He perceived that labor unions, the Parent-Teacher Association (PTA) and parent groups, some teachers, some of his personal friends, some service clubs, some of the school-board members, and his family expect him to recommend the highest possible salary increases. A number of other groups and individuals hold the contrary expectation; these are politicians, religious groups, some parents, some personal friends, taxpayers' association, economic influentials, service clubs, some school-board members, the town finance committee and the press.

In four cases some members of a given category held one expectation, according to the superintendent, while others in the same category held the contrary expectation. School-board members, parents, personal friends, and service clubs were all described by the superintendent in this way.

THE INCIDENCE AND RESOLUTION OF ROLE CONFLICT

In view of space limitations it is necessary to limit consideration of the incidence and resolution of role conflict to only one of the four situations studied. The teacher-salary issue will be used. An examination of this potential area of role conflict will serve as a background to the theory of role-conflict resolution and yield part of the data with which one test of it can be made.

That the teacher-salary issue is a fertile source of role conflict is clear from the fact that 88 per cent of the superintendents perceived that they were exposed to conflicting expectations in this

TABLE 1 A SAMPLE QUESTIONNAIRE THREE ATTITUDES OF VARIOUS GROUPS AND INDIVIDUALS WHICH ONE SUPERINTENDENT PERCEIVED IN HIS COMMUNITY

	A	B	C
1. Politicians		×	
2. Church or religious groups		×	
3. Farm organizations			×
4. Business or commercial organizations			×
5. Labor unions	×		
6. Parents (PTA)	×	×	
7. Teachers	×		
8. Personal friends	×	×	
9. Taxpayers' association		×	
10. Individuals influential for economic reasons		×	
11. Service clubs	×	×	
12. Fraternal organizations			×
13. Veterans' organizations			×
14. Individual school-committee members	×	×	
15. Town finance committee		×	
16. My wife, family	×		
17. Chamber of commerce			×
18. The press		×	
19. Other ________			

TABLE 2 PERCENTAGE OF SUPERINTENDENTS WHO PERCEIVED PARTICULAR EXPECTATIONS FROM SPECIFIED GROUPS AND INDIVIDUALS WITH RESPECT TO THEIR SALARY RECOMMENDATIONS

Group or individual	A. High salary expectation (percent)	B. Low salary expectation (percent)	C. Mixed expectation (percent)	D. No expectation (percent)	N*
1. Politicians	14	51	6	29	105
2. Church or religious groups	34	6	3	57	104
3. Farm organizations	12	17	2	69	62
4. Business or commercial organizations	15	34	4	47	105
5. Labor unions	63	2	2	33	53
6. Parents (PTA)	78	1	9	12	105
7. Teachers	99	0	1	0	105
8. Personal friends	57	1	5	37	105
9. Taxpayers' association	9	77	4	11	61
10. Individuals influential for economic reasons	11	45	7	37	105
11. Service clubs	35	7	7	50	87
12. Fraternal organizations	19	3	3	74	93
13. Veterans' organizations	27	5	4	64	104
14. Individual school-committee members	70	14	14	2	105
15. Town finance committee or city council	18	60	11	10	103
16. My wife, family	71	0	0	29	103
17. Chamber of commerce	20	27	7	47	65
18. The Press	28	25	2	45	88

* When N is less than 105 it is usually because the group or individual did not exist in a number of communities; the "no answers" when the group or individual did exist are also excluded.

area. Table 2 reports the proportions of superintendents who perceived that incumbents of each of the listed counter-positions held: (a) the expectation that he recommend the highest salary increases possible; (b) the expectation that he recommend the lowest salary increases possible; (c) mixed expectations (that is, some held the A and others the B expectation); (d) no expectations regarding this issue.

Whereas 99 per cent of the superintendents perceived that their teachers expected them to recommend the highest salary increases possible, 75 per cent of those with taxpayers' associations in their communities reported that these associations held the opposite expectation (column 2). Similarly a majority of the superintendents said that their town finance committee or city council and local politicians expected them to minimize salary increases for teachers. In addition to reporting that their teachers expected them to recommend the highest possible salary increases, a majority of the superintendents reported that labor organizations, parents and the PTA, personal friends, individual school-board members, and their wives held the same expectation. Relatively few superintendents, however, are confronted with the "mixed" expectation from members of the same group or category, school-board members obtaining the highest percentage (14 per cent in column 3) and town finance-committee members the next highest (12 per cent in column 3).

From these data it is possible to conclude not only that superintendents are frequently confronted with role conflicts with respect to their teacher salary recommendations, but also that these conflicts may stem from different groups and individuals or from groups and individuals of the same kind. For the 88 per cent of the superintendents who perceived that they were exposed to incompatible expectations, there is clearly a problem which must be resolved. How do superintendents act when they perceive that some groups or individuals expect them to behave in a contradictory manner?

When a superintendent had indicated that he was exposed to incompatible expectations, he was asked how he resolved the dilemma implied by this condition. Of the 92 superintendents (88 per cent) who were exposed to role conflict in this situation (13 were not), seven gave insufficient information to permit coding their behavior, 54 conformed to the expectation of recommending the highest possible salary increases (64 per cent of the 85 who told us what they did), eight recommended the lowest possible increases (9 per cent of 85), and 23 (27 per cent of 85) adopted some kind of strategy which did not require them to make an unequivocal choice between the two incompatible alternatives. Before we turn to an effort to predict which people will resolve the conflict in which way, let us examine briefly the different resolution techniques of those 23 superintendents who did not make a definite choice but developed a procedure whereby they could to some degree satisfy (18 or 21 per cent) or ignore (5 or 6 per cent) both demands.

One of the five superintendents who ignored both demands was not yet on tenure and perceived that his school board members, the town finance committee, the taxpayers' association, and individuals who were economically influential expected him to recommend the lowest possible salary increases, whereas his teachers held the contrary expectation. He described his situation in this way:

> I put it all in the hands of the school committee. It's a hot potato so I let the school committee handle it. The teachers feel I should represent them; the school committee feels I should represent them: I'd hang myself by getting involved. But I go along with the school committee recommendation one hundred per cent, whatever they decide.

Four of the 18 superintendents who compromised assumed the position of negotiator when confronted with this dilemma. They apparently worked on the assumption that, although the expectations they face conflict, it is their duty to negotiate "a settlement" that will be most satisfactory to everyone. One superintendent perceived that his teachers, the school board, and the PTA expected him to recommend high salary increases to hold and attract competent personnel, while the town finance committee and taxpayers' association expected him to recommend the lowest increases, because they felt that the town was approaching a financial crisis. This superintendent says: "I use the salesman's technique. I tell the town, 'You don't want cheap teachers if you want a good school system.' I tell the teachers they have to be reasonable, that there has to be a compromise . . . if I completely agreed with the teachers, I'd be out of a job."

Three of the superintendents who compromised rejected both sets of expectations and substituted a new criterion in making their recommendations. They took the position that since they could not fully conform to both sets of expectations they try to develop a defensible rationale for their recommendations which is independent of the incompatible expectations of others. One of the superintendents recommended that the salary increases be contingent on a cost of living index. The others recommended an increase that would keep their school system in a competitive position with those of comparable size and wealth. One superintendent said he tried ". . . to do what's fair in light of what other communities are doing. I don't want my teachers to be at a disadvantage, but neither do I want our system to be a leader in the salaries we pay."

Ten of the 18 superintendents who compromised resolved the salary dilemma by trying to modify the conflicting expectations of one group so that they more nearly approximated the expectations of other groups. This technique differs from that of the superintendents who tried to adopt the position of negotiator, in that no attempt was made by these ten to modify both sets of expectations, and additionally, once one group's expectation had been modified, the superintendents gave their clear support to it. One superintendent told his teachers that if they gave him ". . . a reasonable request, I'll fight for it. If it's unreasonable, I won't. Then I tell them what I think is reasonable according to the town's ability to pay . . . It's the realistic way to support the profession."

The remaining superintendent who compromised combined several of the previously described strategies. His primary objective was to obtain the maximum salary increases possible.

According to his assessment, however, the way to do this was a little at a time. This superintendent said that he worked on this principle: "He who fights and runs away, lives to fight another day." He went on to say that ". . . it's a give and take matter. If your goal isn't damned you haven't lost. I have friends operating for better salaries for teachers who are on the town finance committee. This is the effective way to get results over time, if done consistently. You have to make compromises, and get part of what you want one year and part the next. You can't move too fast. The idea is to make steady progress."

The above excerpts from interviews have illustrated strategies of compromise or avoidance. We saw earlier that while some superintendents compromised, others made a clear choice between the two kinds of behavior expected of them. What determines the choice an individual will make in resolving role conflict?

THE THEORY

The starting point for this theory of role-conflict resolution is the actor's definition of the situation. We assume that actors will have perceptions of whether or not the expectations to which they are exposed are legitimate. Furthermore, we assume that they will have perceptions of the sanctions to which they would be exposed if they did not conform to each of the expectations. In addition, we assume that individuals may be differentiated into three types according to whether they are primarily oriented toward legitimacy or sanctions in making decisions.

The first type characterizes the person who, when faced with a role conflict, gives most weight to the legitimacy of expectations. His definition of the situations places stress on *the right* of others to hold their expectations and de-emphasizes the sanctions he thinks will be applied to him for nonconformity to them. We shall say such a person has a *moral* orientation to expectations. He will be predisposed to behave in a role-conflict situation in such a way that he can fulfill legitimate expectations and reject illegitimate ones. If one of the incompatible expectations is viewed as legitimate and the other is not, he will be predisposed to conform to the legitimate expectation, regardless of what sanctions are involved. If both are legitimate he will adopt a compromise behavior in order to conform, at least in part, to both of them. If both are perceived as illegitimate, he will be predisposed to conform to neither of them and will adopt in consequence some type of avoidance behavior. In short, for an individual with a moral orientation to expectations we will ignore his perceptions of the probable sanctions in making predictions about his behavior. From his definition of the legitimacy of the expectations we can make predictions about his behavior, and in Table 3 these predictions are specified.

The second type of orientation to expectations may be called *expedient*. An individual who has this orientation is one who gives priority to the sanctions others will bring to bear if he does not conform to their expectations. Such a person, we will assume, will act so as to minimize the negative sanctions involved in the role-conflict situation. He will try to provide the best defense for himself in view of the relative severity of the sanctions he feels others will apply to him for nonconformity to their expectations. Whether others have a right to hold certain expectations is irrelevant or of secondary importance to him. When he perceives strong sanctions for nonconformity to one expectation and weaker sanctions for nonconformity to the other, he will conform to the expectation which would result in the stronger sanctions for nonconformity. If he perceives that equally strong sanctions result from both, he will compromise in order to minimize sanctions. If he perceives no sanctions for nonconformity to either of the expectations, then the sanctions dimension will be of no value as a predictor of his behavior. Under this condition the other factor in the model, the legitimacy dimension, would be the only basis for predicting his behavior. In Table 4 the predictions for expedients are specified.

A third type of orientation to expectations will be called *moral-expedient*. A person who has this orientation does not give primacy to either the legitimacy or sanctions dimensions but takes both relatively equally into account and behaves in accordance with the perceived "net balance." For some role-conflict situations the decisions of an individual with a moral-expedient orientation are relatively simple since both the legitimacy and sanctions elements lead him to the same behavior. If, for example, expectation A is perceived as legitimate and expectation B illegitimate and if he perceives greater sanctions for nonconformity to expectation A than for nonconformity to B, he will conform to expectation A. In general, if the legitimacy dimension leads him to the same behavior indicated by the sanctions dimension,

TABLE 3 PREDICTED AND ACTUAL BEHAVIORS OF MORALISTS IN 16 TYPES OF ROLE CONFLICT

Types of role conflict							
Superintendent's Perception of:							
Expectation A		*Expectation B*					
Is it legitimate?	Sanctions for non-conformity?	Is it legitimate?	Sanctions for non-conformity?	Predicted behavior*	Number of moral superintendents exposed to each type of conflict	Frequency of actual behavior	Proportion of correct predictions
1. Yes	Yes	Yes	Yes	*c*	2	$c = 2$	2/2
2. Yes	No	Yes	Yes	*c*	1	$c = 1$	1/1
3. Yes	Yes	Yes	No	*c*	0	—	—
4. Yes	No	Yes	No	*c*	0	—	—
5. Yes	Yes	No	Yes	*a*	4	$a = 3; c = 1$	3/4
6. Yes	No	No	Yes	*a*	4	$a = 4$	4/4
7. Yes	Yes	No	No	*a*	7	$a = 7$	7/7
8. Yes	No	No	No	*a*	1	$a = 1$	1/1
9. No	Yes	Yes	Yes	*b*	0	—	—
10. No	No	Yes	Yes	*b*	0	—	—
11. No	Yes	Yes	No	*b*	0	—	—
12. No	No	Yes	No	*b*	0	—	—
13. No	Yes	No	Yes	*d*	0	—	—
14. No	No	No	Yes	*d*	0	—	—
15. No	Yes	No	No	*d*	0	—	—
16. No	No	No	No	*d*	0	—	—
				Total:	19		18/19 (.95)

* The abbreviations used in this column are as follows: a = conformity to expectation A, b = conformity to expectation B, c = compromise, and d = avoidance.

no problem exists for him. Either criterion leads him to the same behavior.

By comparing Tables 3 and 4 and observing which types of role conflict lead moralists and expedients to the same behavior we can easily isolate all the non-problematic situations for the moral-expedients.

What is required as a basis for predicting his behavior in the remaining types of role conflict? A person with a moral-expedient orientation is one who takes both the legitimacy and sanctions dimensions into account and is predisposed to adopt a behavior that emerges from a balancing of these two dimensions. Thus, if expectations A and B are both viewed as legitimate but he perceives greater negative sanctions for non-conformity to A than to B, he will conform to expectation A. Weighing the two dimensions would result in clear-cut resolutions of the role conflict in types 2, 3, 5, 9, 14, and 15 of Table 5. In each of these instances on the basis of the sanctions and legitimacy dimensions there are two predispositions to one of the behaviors and only one to the other.

How would a moral-expedient behave when the sanctions and legitimacy dimensions lead him to conform to opposite expectations, as in types 6 and 11? In type 6, the legitimacy dimension would require conformity to expectation A, but the sanctions dimension would lead to conformity to expectation B. Since the actor is a moral-expedient he will try to do both or compromise because this seems to be the best balancing of the two dimensions when they lead to opposite behaviors; he is predisposed to do A on the basis of legitimacy and B on the basis of sanctions, and is, therefore, predisposed to both A and B, or to a compromise of the two.

We are left with one additional type in Table 5, type 13. In this case neither of the expectations

TABLE 4 PREDICTED AND ACTUAL BEHAVIORS OF EXPEDIENTS IN 16 TYPES OF ROLE CONFLICT

Types of role conflict							
Superintendent's perception of:							
Expectation A		*Expectation B*					
Is it legitimate?	Sanctions for nonconformity?	Is it legitimate?	Sanctions for nonconformity?	Predicted behavior*	Number of expedient superintendents exposed to each type of conflict	Frequency of actual behavior	Proportion of correct predictions
1. Yes	Yes	Yes	Yes	*c*	3	$c = 1; d = 2$	1/3
2. Yes	No	Yes	Yes	*b*	2	$b = 2$	2/2
3. Yes	Yes	Yes	No	*a*	2	$a = 2$	2/2
4. Yes	No	Yes	No	*c*	0	—	—
5. Yes	Yes	No	Yes	*c*	3	$c = 3$	3/3
6. Yes	No	No	Yes	*b*	4	$b = 4$	4/4
7. Yes	Yes	No	No	*a*	7	$a = 7$	7/7
8. Yes	No	No	No	*a*	0	—	—
9. No	Yes	Yes	Yes	*c*	0	—	—
10. No	No	Yes	Yes	*b*	0	—	—
11. No	Yes	Yes	No	*a*	0	—	—
12. No	No	Yes	No	*b*	0	—	—
13. No	Yes	No	Yes	*c*	1	$c = 1$	1/1
14. No	No	No	Yes	*b*	0	—	—
15. No	Yes	No	No	*a*	1	$a = 1$	1/1
16. No	No	No	No	*d*	0	—	—
				Total:	23		21/23(.91)

* The abbreviations used in this column are as follows: a = conformity to expectation A, b = conformity to expectation B, c = compromise, and d = avoidance.

is viewed as legitimate but nonconformity to both is perceived as leading to strong negative sanctions. The legitimacy dimension leads him to an avoidance behavior and the sanctions dimension suggests a compromise. It seems clear that he will not conform to expectation A or to B. To minimize sanctions he would compromise or try to conform to both A and B, and to emphasize legitimacy he would avoid or fail to conform to both A and B. It is clear that an avoidance reaction does not conform at all to either A or B; but it seems equally clear that a compromise fails to conform in part to both A and B and, therefore, is partially an avoidance. Consequently, the most probable resolution of situations of this kind by moral-expedients would be a compromise, which in part avoids and in part conforms to both expectations.

In Table 5 the predictions made on the basis of legitimacy and sanctions for "moral-expedients" are specified. Tables 3, 4, and 5 together describe all of the predictions made on the basis of the theory.

The Data for a Test of the Theory

If the superintendent's responses to the salary instrument revealed that contradictory expectations were held for his behavior, we designated the situation as a role conflict. On the basis of his answers to the interview questions, each of the superintendents was then coded on (a) his perception of the legitimacy or illegitimacy of the expectations, (b) the perceived sanctions for noncompliance with each expectation, and (c) how he resolved the role conflict.

The remaining element of the theory that requires consideration is the superintendent's orientation to expectations, that is, whether he was a moralist, expedient or moral-expedient. The superintendent's responses to another and completely independent instrument provided the data used for this categorization. Each item in

TABLE 5 PREDICTED AND ACTUAL BEHAVIORS OF MORAL-EXPEDIENTS IN 16 TYPES OF ROLE CONFLICT

Types of role conflict							
Superintendent's perception of:					Number of		
Expectation A		*Expectation B*		Pre-	moral-expedient		
Is it legiti-mate?	Sanctions for non-conformity?	Is it legiti-mate?	Sanctions for non-conformity?	dicted behav-ior*	superintendents exposed to each type of conflict	Frequency of actual behavior	Proportion of correct predictions
1. Yes	Yes	Yes	Yes	*c*	6	$c = 5; d = 1$	5/6
2. Yes	No	Yes	Yes	*b*	2	$b = 2$	2/2
3. Yes	Yes	Yes	No	*a*	6	$a = 6$	6/6
4. Yes	No	Yes	No	*c*	1	$c = 0; d = 1$	0/1
5. Yes	Yes	No	Yes	*a*	4	$a = 3; c = 1$	3/4
6. Yes	No	No	Yes	*c*	3	$c = 2; d = 1$	2/3
7. Yes	Yes	No	No	*a*	20	$a = 19; c = 1$	19/20
8. Yes	No	No	No	*a*	1	$a = 1$	1/1
9. No	Yes	Yes	Yes	*b*	0	—	—
10. No	No	Yes	Yes	*b*	0	—	—
11. No	Yes	Yes	No	*c*	0	—	—
12. No	No	Yes	No	*b*	0	—	—
13. No	Yes	No	Yes	*c*	0	—	—
14. No	No	No	Yes	*b*	0	—	—
15. No	Yes	No	No	*a*	0	—	—
16. No	No	No	No	*d*	0	—	—
				Total:	43		38/43(.88)

* The abbreviations used in this column are as follows: a = conformity to expectation A, b = conformity to expectation B, c = compromise, and d = avoidance.

this instrument refers to expectations that could be applied to a superintendent. For the 37 items in this instrument, he was asked: "As a school superintendent, what obligation do you feel that you have to do or not to do the following things?" The response categories were: absolutely must; preferably should; may or may not; preferably should not; absolutely must not.

We reasoned that a person who would typically react to expectations in terms of "it depends" is one who possesses an *expedient* orientation to expectations. In operational terms he would respond to the expectation items with the "preferably should," "preferably should not," or "may or may not" response categories.

On the other hand, a person whose typical response is not a contingent one but is in terms of "absolutely must" or "absolutely must not" carry out expectations is one who is primarily oriented toward their rectitude. He does not think in terms of factors in the situation that would lessen his obligations. Such a person would be predisposed "to honor" legitimate expectations regardless of the sanctions involved in the situation. Such a person would be a moralist.

One who shows no "typical" response to expectations but vacillates between the conditional and mandatory categories in his reactions to expectations would possess the characteristic required for the moral-expedient orientation. This lack of consistency in orientation to expectations suggests that he is the type of person who would tend to take *both* the sanctions and legitimacy dimensions into account in reacting to perceived expectations.

This line of reasoning led to the following procedure. Each superintendent was given a score of 1 for each item in this instrument for which he gave a mandatory response (absolutely must, or absolutely must not). This provided a range of scores from 1 through 30 for the 37 items in the instrument. The estimated reliability of these scores is .884. These scores were then split into the following three categories: 1–9, 10–18, and 19–30. On the reasoning outlined above those superintendents who fell into the low mandatoriness group (1–9) were defined as expedients, those who fell into the high mandatoriness group (19–30) were considered moralists, and those who fell in the middle category (10–18) were categorized as moral-expedients.

A TEST OF THE THEORY

If we accept each of these operational indexes as adequately representing the variables and conditions described by the theory of role conflict resolution, we can use our data to perform an exploratory test of the theory. We have 48 possible "types" of situations. That is, the moralists, expedients, and moral-expedients can each be subdivided into four groups according to their judgments about the legitimacy of the expectations directed toward them (i.e., both expectations legitimate; both illegitimate; A legitimate and B illegitimate, and A illegitimate and B legitimate). Each of the resulting 12 groups can be further subdivided into four categories according to whether the subject believed sanctions would be forthcoming for nonconformity to A, B, both, or neither.

By comparing the behavior predicted on the basis of the theory for each of these 48 types with the actual behavior of the superintendents who fell within these categories, we may say whether or not the theory has led in each case to the correct prediction.

As can be seen in Tables 3, 4, and 5 for 77 (91 per cent) of the 85 role-conflict cases the theory led to the correct prediction. In order to test the theory it is necessary to ask whether the proportion of correct predictions obtained could have occurred by chance. To answer this question, the numbers of correct and of incorrect predictions were compared with the numbers expected on the basis of chance. Statistical details are presented elsewhere (see Gross, Mason, and McEachern, 1957). The theory led to significantly more correct predictions than would be expected by chance (at the .01 level). We are consequently led to the conclusion that the findings provide significant support for the theory in the teacher-salary role-conflict situation.

A review of the predictions made for moralists, moral-expedients, and expedients will reveal that for many of the types of role conflict the theory leads to exactly the same prediction no matter what the orientation of the individual involved. It is particularly interesting, therefore, to ask how well the theory does in the "difficult" cases. How well will the theory do in predicting the behavior in only those cases of role conflict where it makes a difference (according to the theory) what the orientation of the individual is? It would be inappropriate to apply a significance test to only those cases, but it is nevertheless revealing of the power of the theory to consider them separately.

Let us consider those cases for moralists and those for expedients in which the theory makes a prediction which differs from the one made in the case of the moral-expedient orientation. In types 2, 6, 11, 13, 14, and 15 of the moralist orientation and types 5, 6, 9, and 11 of the expedient orientation the theory leads to a prediction which differs from the one to which it leads for the moral-expedients. There were 12 school superintendents with either a moralist or expedient orientation who experienced role conflicts of these types. For how many of these did the theory lead to the correct prediction? For how many would the correct prediction have been made by assuming that their resolution of role conflict would be the same as that of moral-expedients? The answer is that in all 12 cases (as may be verified by reviewing the appropriate types of conflict in Tables 3 and 4) the theory led to the correct prediction, and in none of these cases would the correct prediction have been made on the basis of the assumption that these moral or expedient individuals resolved their conflicts in the same way as do moral-expedients.

In this paper we have not been able to consider a number of questions that the critical reader would ask about the theory. How does this theory differ from others? What accounts for the errors in the predictions? Have we ignored certain variables which affect the resolution of certain types of role-conflict situations? We have tried to consider these problems elsewhere (Gross, Mason, and McEachern, 1957).

REFERENCES

Gross, N., Mason, W. S., and McEachern, A. W., 1957. *Explorations in role analysis: studies of the school superintendency role*. New York: Wiley.

selection 36 Conflict of Attitudes toward the Roles of the Husband and Wife in Marriage

ALLVAR HILDING JACOBSON

Family disorganization has been, and is, the subject of considerable attention in both popular and scientific literature. Attitudes of, and attitude differences between, married and divorced persons toward their respective spouses' marital roles may be significantly related to marital rifts.[1] Because divorce rates are high, and because little or no empirical analysis has been done in the field of differences in attitudes toward marital roles between spouses,[2] this study was undertaken with the assumption that additional insight into the total problem of family disorganization might be obtained or suggested. The hypothesis to be tested is: *Divorced couples exhibit a greater disparity in their attitudes toward the roles of the husband and wife in marriage than do married couples.*

CONSTRUCTION OF THE ATTITUDE SCALE

Since this study is concerned with *attitude* toward *role* of spouses in marriage, these two terms were defined. A review of the literature indicates that these terms are employed variously, depending upon the problem at hand. However, for purposes of this study, *attitude* refers to the response consistencies of the respondents toward the role of spouses in marriage as revealed in the totality of their responses to items employed as a scale. *Role* refers to a culturally ascribed pattern of behavior, including duties, expected or required of persons behaving in specific social situations; i.e., the behavior expected of husband and wife in marriage situations.

Commencing in 1941 and extending through 1947, exclusive of the war years, 62 case histories of married and divorced persons were collected from which common attitudes toward marriage roles were selected to provide bases for items to be included in a scale designed to measure attitudes toward the roles of the husband and the wife in marriage.[3] A preliminary scale of 60 items was constructed from this information. This scale was revised and reduced to fifty items by consultation with three "experts"—two sociologists and one psychologist—who were requested to judge each item on the basis of: the quality of expressing an attitude, relevance to the role of spouses in marriage, clarity, and, as nearly as possible, expression in the vernacular. This 50-item scale was then given to 30 divorced and 30 married couples whose responses were subjected to a method of measuring internal consistency whereby the scale was reduced to 28 items—retained because of their comparatively high critical ratios (Sletto, 1937). Relative reliability of the 28-item scale is indicated by the fact that a test-retest comparison produced a coefficient of correlation of .79; and the split-half method employing

[1] "Each young man who marries brings with him, both consciously and unconsciously, his idea of the part to be played by himself as husband and the part to be played by his wife as his wife. Similarly, the young woman enters marriage with a preconceived notion of the roles of wife and husband. . . . If the conceptions of both are reasonably fulfilled, we can expect a satisfactory adjustment. . . . We should remember, however, that we enter marrriage with definite expectations, and if reality falls short of them, dissatisfaction follows. . ." c.f. Hill and Becker (1942; pp. 316-317).

[2] H. L. Ingersoll's article (1948) was the only article relating specifically to role in marriage which the writer could find, although other studies such as the work of Burgess and Cottrell (1939) incidentally treated this problem. [Editors' Note—Others have appeared since, of course.]

From the *American Sociological Review*, 1952, **17**, 146–150. Reprinted by permission of the author and the American Sociological Association.

[3] Additional details concerning methodology and analysis are presented in the writer's doctoral dissertation (1950), in which Appendix A includes a summary of the case history data, plus sample reasons given for getting married or divorced.

the Kuder–Richardson formula produced an uncorrected coefficient of correlation of .90. These two coefficients of correlation were computed from the responses of 80 persons equally divided by sex and marital status. The test-retest interval was twenty days.

In order to express "the quantity of a quality" an arbitrary system of weights ranging from one to five was assigned to the verbal response positions ranging from Strongly Agree to Strongly Disagree. A low score indicates the traditional male-dominant or conservative attitude and a high score indicates the emergent feminine-equalitarian or liberal attitude. The lowest possible score on the 28-item scale is 28, or a completely male-dominant attitude, compared to the highest possible score of 140, indicating the opposite extreme. The complete schedule of 28 attitude statements[4] includes ten personal data items used for description of the respondents and for analyses of possible relationships between attitude configurations thus measured and the items such as marital status, sex, age, occupation, education and the like.

THE SAMPLE

The sample was obtained by interviews with 400 persons, 100 divorced and 100 married couples, living in or around Chillicothe, Ohio during the duration of this study. The sample of 100 divorced couples was obtained from the total of 393 divorces recorded in Chillicothe (Ross County seat) from January 1, 1947 to July 1, 1949. Use of the City Directory, local personnel rosters, acquaintance with local leaders and the like produced the names of 312 divorced men assumed to be residing in the area and available for interview; from which 130 were selected for interview by use of Tippett's random sampling numbers (Pearson, 1927). A total of 117 numbers was used to obtain 200 complete cases, i.e., complete schedule responses from 100 divorced men and their respective former wives. The sample of 100 married couples was obtained in the same manner, with this important difference: the married couples selected for random numbering were chosen from the marriage records; a minimum of two couples being selected for each divorced couple, selected on approximately the same date that the respective divorced couples had been married. Thus, the control was based on the respective married and divorced couples having married on approximately the same date. A total of 118 numbers was used before 200 complete married cases were obtained. The data presented here were obtained by personal interview with each of the 400 persons in on-the-job and at-home situations from July 1, 1949 through April 30, 1950. Each person was interviewed in the absence of spouse or former spouse.

Characteristics of the 400-person sample, other than sex and marital status, were: median age, 25.2; median education, 9.4; median years since marriage, 3.5; 100 per cent native white; 14 per cent rural residence; six per cent Catholic; of the males, 37 per cent were common laborers, 13 per cent farm laborers, 22 per cent semi-skilled, 16 per cent skilled, and 6.5 per cent were engaged in professional, semi-professional or business administrative occupations. Table 1 presents the characteristics of the 400-person sample and it is evident that this is a more representative group than either the Burgess–Cottrell (1939) or Terman (1938) samples.

FINDINGS AND ANALYSES

By use of the product moment method of linear correlation of ungrouped data, the responses of the 400 persons yielded the following general results: (a) No statistically significant coefficients of correlation were found to exist between attitude scores of the various sex and marital status categories and such attributes as age, education and occupation, which would indicate possible sample error; (b) A high positive coefficient of correlation was found between married couples' attitude scores and, also between divorced couples' attitude scores—suggesting that persons holding similar attitude levels tend to marry or that these attitudes converge after marriage. A summary of the various coefficients of correlation between attitudes and variables is presented in Table 2.

By use of analysis of the significance of the difference between mean scores of the various sex and marital status groups, some statistically significant results were found which inspection of the ranges and mean scores had suggested (see Table 3).

Two facts stand out in this particular analysis: (a) The divorced males had the lowest scores which then rose among the married males, married females, to the divorced females; (b) The difference between mean scores for the divorced

[4] Some sample statements: The husband should help with the housework. If the husband insists, the wife should quit a needed job. If a husband runs around, so can his wife. The husband should wear the pants. It's okay for the wife to earn as much as her husband.

TABLE 1 CHARACTERISTICS OF THE SAMPLE BY MARITAL STATUS AND SEX

	Divorced		Married		Total		
Characteristics	Male n=100	Female n=100	Male n=100	Female n=100	Male n=100	Female n=100	TOTAL
Median Age	27.7	23.7	26.8	22.8	27.2	23.2	25.2
Median Education	9.1	9.6	9.2	9.8	9.1	9.7	9.4
Per Cent Employed	100	85	100	38	100	61.5	80.7
Occupations (per cent) of males							
Common Labor	38		35		36.5		
Farm Labor	11		16		13.5		
Semi-Skilled	21		22		21.5		
Skilled	16		15		15.5		
Professional, Semi-Professional and Business Administration	7		6		6.5		

TABLE 2 SUMMARY OF COEFFICIENTS OF CORRELATION BETWEEN ATTITUDES OF VARIOUS GROUPS AND OTHER VARIABLES

Variables	Sex and Marital Status Categories					
	Divorced		Married		Couples	
Correlation Between	Male	Female	Male	Female	Divorced	Married
Score and Age	+.10	+.19	−.01	−.08	....	....
Score and Education	+.09	+.03	−.15	−.10	....	....
Score and Occupation	−.10	....	+.01	....	....	....
Differences in Score and Differences in Age					−.06	+.09
Differences in Score and Years Married					+.04	−.11
Male Score and Female Score					+.86	+.80

TABLE 3 RANGE OF SCORES, MEAN SCORES, AND DIFFERENCES BETWEEN MEAN SCORES BY SEX AND MARITAL STATUS

Group	Range	Mean Scores	Differences between Means
Divorced Males	34–118	66.16	....
Divorced Females	52–129	93.86	27.70
Married Males	41–120	75.18	....
Married Females	39–126	81.82	6.64

TABLE 4 SIGNIFICANCE OF THE DIFFERENCES BETWEEN MEAN ATTITUDE SCORES OF THE VARIOUS SEX AND MARITAL STATUS CATEGORIES

Paired Groups	Mean Scores	Difference	Standard Error of Difference	Critical Ratio
Divorced Female	93.86	....	....	
Married Female	81.82	12.04	2.40	5.01
Married Male	75.18	....	....	
Divorced Male	66.16	9.02	1.80	5.01
Divorced Female	93.86	....	....	
Divorced Male	66.16	27.70	2.27	12.20
Married Female	81.82	....	....	
Married Male	75.18	6.64	1.97	3.37
Total Female	87.84	....	....	
Total Male	70.67	17.17	1.70	10.10
Div. Cples Mn. Dif.	27.70	....	....	
Mrd. Cples Mn. Dif.	6.64	21.06	2.32	11.01

couples was approximately four times as great as that for the married couples.

It is evident that a large difference in mean scores exists between divorced husbands and their former wives, and a somewhat smaller difference exists between the married couples. A measure of the significance of the difference between these means was obtained by using a standard formula.[5]

By applying this formula to the attitude scores of the various sex and marital status categories we find differences that are statistically significant, by virtue of large critical ratios, between the following groups: mean scores of the married men and their wives; mean scores of the divorced men and their former wives; mean scores of the divorced and married men; mean scores of the divorced and married women; and, finally, the combined mean score of the men compared with the combined mean score of the women. Table 4 contains this information in detail.

Thus far there appear to be significant differences between the attitudes of men and women toward the roles of spouses in marriage. These differences, however, cannot be considered as sex differences alone, because equally significant differences were found between married and divorced males and between married and divorced females, suggesting that marital status is an important factor. The nature of the scale is such as to measure sex differences in attitudes toward their respective roles in marriage. The division of labor by sex in our culture and a general tendency for each sex to learn different role attitudes may account for much of the difference.

Additional evidence of the significance of differences is revealed in Table 5. Every divorced female had a higher, or more equalitarian attitude score than her respective former husband, and the actual differences ranged to 60 points higher on the scale. In contrast, 25 of the married females had lower, or more conservative, attitude

TABLE 5 DISTRIBUTION OF DIFFERENCES IN ATTITUDE SCORES BETWEEN COUPLES

Difference in Score	Married Couples	Divorced Couples	All Couples
−39 to −20	2	0	2
−19 to −10	5	0	5
− 9 to 0	18	0	18
0 to 9	30	1	31
10 to 19	36	16	52
20 to 29	5	48	53
30 to 39	4	23	27
40 to 49	0	9	9
50 to 60	0	3	3
Total	100	100	200
Range of Difference	−30 to +35	+4 to +60	−30 to +60

[5] $\sigma_d = \sqrt{\frac{\sigma 2_1}{N_1} - \frac{\sigma 2_2}{N_2}}$

scores than their respective husbands and the actual differences ranged from minus 39 to plus 25 points on the scale. The sign of the difference is plus when the wife's score is higher, since the difference as calculated is the wife's score minus that of her husband.

These outstanding differences were probably affected by various factors involved in this study, such as the interview method. Divorced persons may have overstated their attitudes as a result of playing the role of divorcée in the presence of the interviewer. Similarly, it is possible that some married persons may have overstated their attitudes; the net result being a larger difference than might have developed by use of a questionnaire method. In spite of this possible bias, it would appear that differences, although smaller, would still be found.

SUMMARY AND CONCLUSIONS

Statistically significant attitude differences toward the marital roles of husband and wife were found to be related to sex (the males were more conservative) and to marital status (differences in attitudes between divorced couples were on the average four times as great as those between married couples). No significant relationships were found to exist between attitudes of the various sex and marital status groups and variables such as age, education and occupation. Thus, within the limits of this study the hypothesis: *Divorced couples exhibit a greater disparity in their attitudes toward the roles of the husband and wife in marriage than do married couples*, was found to be true.

As usual, research tends to create more problems than are solved, and this study is no exception. The relationships found here may be greatly influenced by many factors, including poor sampling and faulty analysis. In any event, replication might serve to verify the results found here. Meanwhile, it is suggested that this or similar attitude scales might be useful in counseling situations, especially if used in conjunction with other instruments measuring such factors as personality deviation which, in itself, may be the most fruitful area of inquiry with relation to the nature of marital discord.

REFERENCES

Burgess, E. W., and Cottrell, L. S., Jr., 1939. *Predicting success or failure in marriage*. Englewood Cliffs, N.J.: Prentice-Hall.

Hill, R., and Becker, H. (Eds.), 1942. *Marriage and the family*. Boston: Heath.

Ingersoll, Hazel L., 1948. Transmission of authority patterns in the family. *Marriage and Family Living*, **10**, 36.

Jacobson, A. H., 1950. *A study of conflict in attitudes toward the roles of the husband and wife in marriage*. Unpublished doctoral dissertation, Columbus, Ohio: Ohio State University.

Pearson, K. (Ed.), 1927. *Tracts for computers*. London: Cambridge University Press, No. 15.

Sletto, R. F., 1937. *Construction of personality scales by the method of internal consistency*. Hanover, N. H.: Sociological Press.

Terman, L. M., Buttenwieser, P., Ferguson, W., Johnson, B., and Wilson, D. P., 1938. *Psychological factors in marital happiness*. New York: McGraw-Hill.

selection 37 Shared Inaccuracies in the Role of the Teacher

BRUCE J. BIDDLE, HOWARD A. ROSENCRANZ, EDWARD TOMICH, AND J. PASCHAL TWYMAN

It is often assumed in social theories that social stability depends on the accuracy with which roles are perceived. Thus, persons are presumed both to be aware of, and to share, standards for behaviors that are appropriate for persons who are members of social positions. Should people disagree, by chance, about what behaviors are appropriate, they must at least be aware of the others' thinking in order to plan intelligent activity with those others.

In contrast with this broad assumption, a small group of commentators has stressed the usefulness of deception (Bettelheim, 1943; Goffman, 1959), ignorance (Moore and Tumin, 1949), and partial information (von Neumann and Morgenstern, 1947). In the view presented by these latter authors, social relations may often be designed around or benefit from inaccuracies of role perception. At the very least, inaccurate and nonshared perceptions are not only indigenous to some forms of social relationships, they are often necessary or desirable.

Despite these latter assertions, clear empirical studies of situations involving shared distortions of role are difficult to find in the literature. Perhaps the first such study was that of Schanck (1932) who discovered in an isolated community evidence for agreed-upon norms which were attributed widely to members of the community but which were not matched by the privately held norms of individuals nor by their actual (secret) behaviors. A different example was provided by Wheeler (1961). In this study, the author demonstrated that inmates and prison officials both inaccurately judged norms held by the other group for themselves—both tending to exaggerate normative disparities.

In the Schanck and Wheeler studies it is assumed that shared inaccuracies on role concepts attributed are a social phenomenon, that they are the results of processes acting jointly on a number of individuals, and that they are stable despite the problems they imply for persons involved. Thus, these examples are distinct from studies of "social perception" in which the misperception of social events is treated as an individual phenomenon (see Gage and Cronbach, 1955; and Cronbach, 1958).

The purpose of this paper is to examine and interpret evidence for the existence of shared inaccuracies in the role of the public school teacher. It will be shown that teachers and those with whom they interact have distorted ideas of one anothers' norms and that those distortions imply problems for all concerned.

SHARED INACCURACIES IN ROLE

In order to discuss the problem of shared inaccuracies in role attribution, it is necessary that we adopt certain verbal conventions. *Shared inaccuracy of role attributions will be said to exist whenever two or more subject persons share mistaken concepts about covert processes characterizing an object person or position.* Several implications of this definition are worth noting. First, while people may often be mistaken about the overt performance of others—particularly when they don't have a chance to observe the performances in question—we focus on the mistaken concepts people have of covert processes taking place in others (mistaken concepts of others' norms, values, or concepts, etc.).

Second, there are usually two or more classes of object persons referenced in role attributions. It is easiest to demonstrate this property with an example: "Americans hold mistaken concepts

Reproduced by permission of the authors. The research reported herein was performed pursuant to contracts with the Cooperative Research Program, Office of Education, Department of Health, Education, and Welfare and the Office of Naval Research (Group Psychology Branch) at the Universities of Kansas City and Missouri.

about the norms held by Russians for women." Such a statement has the logical form of a statement about a norm; thus it exhibits three classes of persons. The *subjects* are those persons who share the attributed concepts in question (Americans). The *objects* are those persons to whom are attributed covert processes (Russians). Finally, the *secondary objects* are those persons for whom covert processes attributed to object persons are presumably held (women). Subjects must of course be real persons, while objects and secondary objects are but referenced and may be either real or fictitious. However, in order to judge the accuracy of an attributed concept it is necessary to find a real group of object persons who match the object designation appearing in the attribution.

This brings up the problem of operationalizing a shared inaccuracy. In order to judge accuracy of role attributions it is necessary to obtain an overt expression from both subject and object persons. The accuracy of an attributed norm, for instance, may only be judged when we have an expression of both the norm attributed by the subject and the norm actually held by the object person.

Finally, it should be clear that norms held by subjects, norms attributed by subjects to object persons, norms held by objects, and actual performances by secondary object persons are all independently defined and independently measurable. Whether these phenomena are related—and how—depends on the nature of the relationships among subject, object, and secondary object persons. For instance, groups of persons who are separated from one another by physical or social distance may often hold quite distorted views of one another without engendering immediate problems. However, when subject and object persons are called upon to interact with each other, distortions of one anothers' views are likely to pose problems for both parties and to be maintained only through systemic activity. In the study described here, public school teachers constitute the secondary object position, and norms are attributed and reported by persons representing various positions that interact with teachers.

SHARED INACCURACIES IN TEACHER ROLE ATTRIBUTION

The data to be reported here were gathered as part of a two-and-one-half hour group interview study consisting of five different instruments that were administered to 927 respondents from the Kansas City metropolitan area.[1] Respondents represented a number of social positions defined in relationship with the public school systems and were sampled through schools. In this paper, we report data from four subject groups—98 teachers, 261 parents, 237 pupils, and 67 school officials.

Among other tasks, respondents were asked to give their own norms and then to attribute norms to three object positions: People in General, Teachers, and School Officials. Each respondent was given a set of ten situations in which a teacher (secondary object) performance was placed. For instance, Item 1 read, "Watching pupils during a study period." Five alternate degrees of teacher performance were then specified ranging from: (1) Teachers should do little or no "watching pupils" (or other behavior specified), to (5) Teachers should do a great deal of "watching pupils." Respondents were asked to choose one of the five scaled behavioral alternatives to indicate their own norms, the norms of People in General, and so on. In all, four normative responses were collected for each behavioral item from each respondent—one that was their own and three that were attributed to others. Finally, teacher respondents (only) were asked to give an additional response in which they reported their *own* performance for the item.

In order to cover a broad spectrum of teacher performance, three different forms were used. Thus, a total of thirty performance items was covered in all, while any given item was seen by only a third of the total group of respondents. Items were derived from prior studies in which respondents had volunteered their concerns for teacher role. Items were chosen to represent regions of inter-positional conflict.

Analysis of these data was performed on a computer. For each type of comparison (for instance, norms attributed by parents to School Officials versus norms revealed by school officials) the difference in central tendency was assessed by the Mann-Whitney z_U. This statistic is roughly equivalent to a t test of mean differences but is appropriate for use with rank-order data. It should be noted that all findings reported in this paper were significant at $p < .05$ or less (using the Mann-Whitney z_U), but that numerical differences reported are mean differences.

[1] Additional reports of this study may be found in Biddle (1961, 1964); Biddle, Rosencranz, and Rankin (1961); Biddle, Twyman, and Rankin (1962); Rosencranz and Biddle (1964); and Twyman and Biddle (1963, 1964).

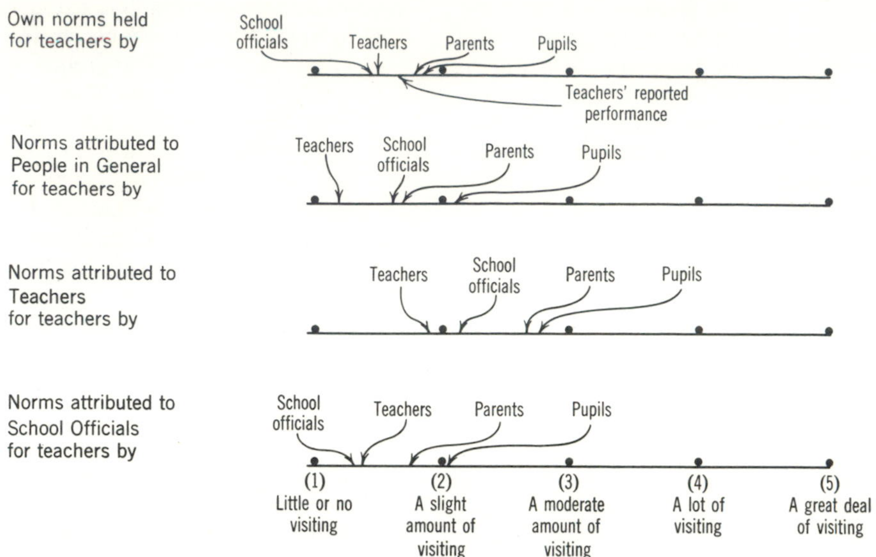

Figure 1. Mean normative responses for Item 11, "Visiting with other teachers during study period."

Examples of Inaccurate Attributions

It is best to begin with two items exemplifying distinct patterns of shared inaccuracy in the attribution of norms. Figure 1 displays the mean own and attributed norms given by respondents for Item 11—Visiting with Other Teachers During Study Period. Figure 2 presents similar information for Item 12—Watching for Cheaters During a Classroom Test. On the first lines of these two figures are displayed the mean responses of the four respondent positions when giving their own norms. On the second line, norms attributed to People in General are displayed; on the third, norms attributed to Teachers; on the fourth, norms attributed to School Officials. Mean teacher reported performance is indicated by an entry underneath the first line.

If we turn first to Figure 1, it will be seen that norms attributed to People in General (line 2) and School Officials (line 4) are within the same general range as the norms actually held by these groups (line 1). By way of contrast, however, norms attributed to Teachers (line 3) are displaced to the right; that is, towards the self-indulgent end of the scale. As a generalization, respondents attributed to teachers norms for greater amounts of self-indulgence than teachers revealed in norms they held for themselves (line 1). Moreover, the performances reported by teachers (underneath line 1) matched the own norms reported by teachers rather than the norms erroneously attributed to Teachers by respondents.

The third line of Figure 1, thus, provides an example of shared, inaccurate attribution of norms. Respondents generally attributed to Teachers norms (for teachers) that were more self-indulgent than were norms actually held by teachers themselves. It should also be noted that teachers responded to the "problem" of differential standards by conforming to their own norms rather than to the norms attributed to them by others. Finally, pupil respondents were the least accurate in norms attributed to Teachers, followed by parent, school official, and teacher respondents in that order.

A somewhat more complex picture of shared inaccuracy appears in Figure 2. In this latter figure it will be seen that while respondents generally assigned to Teachers (line 3) norms that were similar both to their own and those actually held by teachers (line 1), the norms attributed to People in General and School Officials show a different story. Norms attributed to People in General (line 2) are displaced in a conservative direction—towards the right—by all respondents except parents. Additionally, all respondents except school officials attributed similar, conservative norms to School Officials. If we compare these two sets of attributed norms with the own

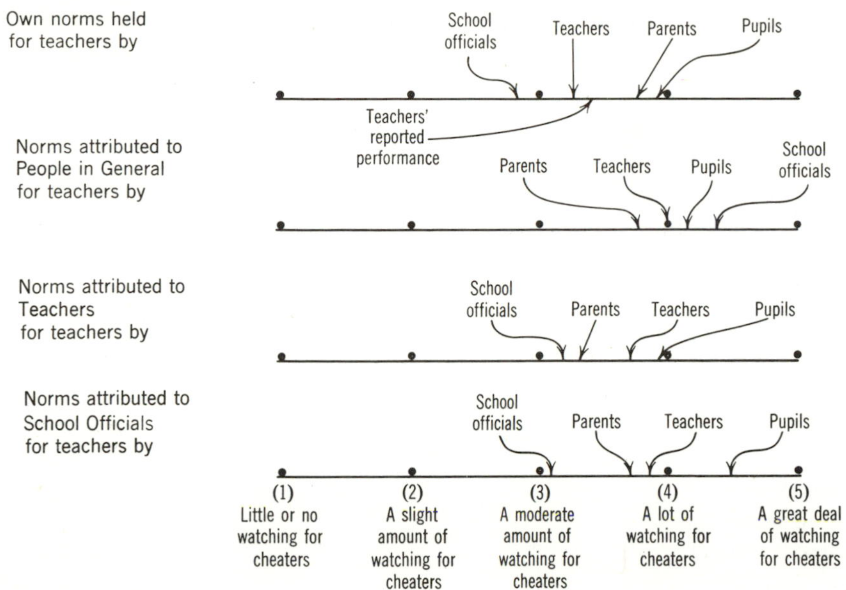

Figure 2. Mean normative responses for Item 12, "Watching for cheaters during a classroom test."

norms held by parents[2] and school officials respectively, it is evident that both are distorted. Figure 2, thus, exhibits two examples of shared inaccuracies in role attribution: respondents were generally mistaken about norms held by both People in General and School Officials; moreover, the mistakes made about these two object positions were similar. Note, however, that parents made the least error in attributing norms to People in General; and school officials, who made the greatest error in attributing to People in General, were the least inaccurate in attributing norms to School Officials.

The Extent of Shared Inaccuracies

But how significant and wide-spread were these findings of shared inaccuracies in teacher role? Tables 1 and 2 attempt to answer this question by presenting significances and mean differences for selected items that show clear patterns similar to those of Items 11 and 12. (Items not included in these tables presented little evidence of shared inaccuracies in teacher role, although they were productive of other findings. Altogether, 23 percent of all comparisons checked for shared inaccuracy were statistically significant at $p < .05$; while 38 percent of all comparisons for shared inaccuracy reported in Tables 1 and 2 are similarly significant.)

Table 1 presents findings for items involving teacher self-indulgence. The reader will note that significant differences appear in this table between norms attributed to Teachers and those actually held by teachers (part A) and between norms attributed to Teachers and the performances reported by teachers (part B). Interestingly enough, although distorted when compared with teacher-held norms, norms attributed to Teachers are not generally significantly different from norms actually held by subjects (part C). Again, it must be concluded that (particularly parental and pupil) respondents are incorrectly convinced that Teachers hold self-indulgent norms for themselves —norms that are not matched by teacher reported performances, and that are reasonably similar to norms actually held by respondents themselves.

Table 2 presents findings for items involving teacher discipline and control of pupils. The major pattern appearing in Table 2 is of shared

[2] The equivalence of parents (a subject position) with People in General (an object position) is questionable. The parental sample was obviously not a demographic sample of the public. However, it may well have been a sample of the "public that takes action on school matters." In addition, in a pilot study we were unable to find *any* significant differences between attributions to Parents and to People in General.

TABLE 1 MEAN DIFFERENCES AND LEVELS OF SIGNIFICANCE FOR ITEMS INVOLVING TEACHER SELF-INDULGENCE

	Norms Attributed to People in General by				Norms Attributed to Teachers by				Norms Attributed to School Officials by			
	Teachers	Parents	Pupils	School Officials	Teachers	Parents	Pupils	School Officials	Teachers	Parents	Pupils	School Officials
A. Differences between Norms Attributed to Object Persons and Norms Actually Held by Them												
Item 9. Visiting with other teachers on the playground	−.48*					.54**	.78**	.71**	−.58*			
Item 11. Visiting with other teachers during study period	−.50*				.48*	1.00***	1.11***	.94**			.63*	
Item 21. Reading own books during study period	−.97**		.82*			1.15***	1.70***				1.59**	
Item 22. Leaving the room during a classroom test						.33*	.58*					
Item 23. Grading papers during a classroom singing period						.84**	1.13**				1.02*	
B. Differences between Norms Attributed to Object Persons and Reported Teacher Performances												
Item 9. Visiting with other teachers on the playground									−.58*			
Item 11. Visiting with other teachers during study period			.61*			.95***	1.05***	.89**				
Item 21. Reading own books during study period			1.75*			1.31*	1.85*				1.60*	
Item 22. Leaving the room during a classroom test												
Item 23. Grading papers during a classroom singing period						.98*						
C. Differences between Norms Attributed to Object Persons and Norms Held by Subjects												
Item 9. Visiting with other teachers on the playground				−.54*								
Item 11. Visiting with other teachers during study period					.48*	.51**	.59**	.76*				
Item 21. Reading own books during study period												
Item 22. Leaving the room during a classroom test												
Item 23. Grading papers during a classroom singing period						.38*						

Note: All figures to be found in Tables 1 and 2 are signed mean differences that were statistically significant. Significance was computed using the Mann-Whitney z_U and is indicated as follows: * = $.01 < p < .05$, ** = $.001 < p < .01$, *** = $p < .001$.

TABLE 2 MEAN DIFFERENCES AND LEVELS OF SIGNIFICANCE FOR ITEMS INVOLVING DISCIPLINE AND PUPIL CONTROL

	Norms Attributed to People in General by				Norms Attributed to Teachers by				Norms Attributed to School Officials by			
	Teachers	Parents	Pupils	School Officials	Teachers	Parents	Pupils	School Officials	Teachers	Parents	Pupils	School Officials
A. Differences between Norms Attributed to Object Persons and Norms Actually Held by Them												
Item 1. Watching pupils during study period				*** .76						* .53	* .59	
Item 7. Policing the halls	* −.51			* .65		* .60	*** .90			** .89	** .80	
Item 8. Disciplining pupils during basketball games in gym						* .52	*** 1.21			* .74	*** 1.05	
Item 12. Watching for cheaters during a classroom test			** .60	* .65					** 1.20	** 1.11	*** 1.46	
Item 14. Telling misbehaving pupils in classroom to stop talking						* .43	*** .86			** .90	*** 1.15	
Item 19. Supervising on the playground				* .51			** .72			** .88		
Item 24. Threatening pupils misbehaving in classroom						** .87				** 1.22	** 1.45	
B. Differences between Norms Attributed to Object Persons and Reported Teacher Performances												
Item 1. Watching pupils during study period				** .85						* .43	* .49	
Item 7. Policing the halls		** .67	* .61	*** 1.44			** .78		* .58	*** 1.04	*** .95	
Item 8. Disciplining pupils during basketball games in gym		** .95	** 1.08			* .61	** 1.20			** 1.05	*** 1.36	
Item 12. Watching for cheaters during a classroom test	* .65		** .77	* .83			** .63		* .61	* .53	*** .87	
Item 14. Telling misbehaving pupils in classroom to stop talking		* .54	* .63				** .72				** .71	
Item 19. Supervising on the playground	* .60	*** .83		*** 1.10						** .68	** .71	** .85
Item 24. Threatening pupils misbehaving in the classroom			* 1.25			* 1.17						

TABLE 2—*continued*

	Norms Attributed to People in General by				Norms Attributed to Teachers by				Norms Attributed to School Officials by			
	Teachers	Parents	Pupils	School Officials	Teachers	Parents	Pupils	School Officials	Teachers	Parents	Pupils	School Officials
C. Differences between Norms Attributed to Object Persons and Norms Held by Subjects												
Item 1. Watching pupils during study period			* .60	* .77			* .52			** .34	*** .80	
Item 7. Policing the halls			* .55	*** 1.21			** .72		** .70		*** .89	* .58
Item 8. Disciplining pupils during basketball games in gym										* .39		
Item 12. Watching for cheaters during a classroom test				** 1.28					** .75			
Item 14. Telling misbehaving pupils in classroom to stop talking			* .37	* .93			** .46				* .45	
Item 19. Supervising on the playground	** .87		* .42			** —.62	* .45	* 1.05	** .77		*** .72	
Item 24. Threatening pupils misbehaving in the classroom								* .83				

inaccuracy in norms attributed to School Officials, primarily by parents and pupils. These respondents are in agreement that School Officials hold conservative norms for teacher disciplining and controlling of pupils—norms that are not in fact held by school officials. It should also be noted that school-official respondents (and to a lesser extent others) attributed similar, inaccurate, conservative norms to People in General. Finally, performances reported by teachers did not match the inaccurate, conservative norms attributed to School Officials and People in General (part B); and, interestingly, the falsely inaccurate norms attributed tended to be significantly more conservative than norms actually held by subjects themselves (part C).

Interpretation

An understanding of these findings requires that one answer several questions. How did these shared inaccuracies get set up? By what means are these inaccuracies maintained? What problems do these inaccuracies impose on teachers and those with whom they interact?

The appearance of inaccurate attributions to teachers favoring self-indulgence would appear to pose few problems of origin or effect. It may be assumed that most occupations or professions will be judged, by outsiders, to be self-indulgent; if only as a means of ego defense for those who are not members. If this interpretation is correct, we will find similar norms approving self-indulgence attributed to doctors, lawyers, coal miners, policemen, indeed anyone with a defined occupation. It should also be noted that our data show few significant differences between norms attributed to Teachers for self-indulgence and norms actually held by subjects themselves—suggesting that respondents are for the most part attributing to Teachers but a modification of their own norms. Attributed norms involving self-indulgence would pose a problem for the teacher only if associated with a general denigration of the profession. There seems to be little evidence for this here.

The problem of conservative standards for the teacher-pupil relationship is considerably more complex. One must assume that education today is faced with rapid social change paired with the legitimizing of public outcry from heel-draggers. Many persons may assume that the public continues to think of teachers in terms of the values of small-town America when they listen to the criticisms of the super-patriots and those interested in a "classical" education. Assuming this explanation, similar conservative inaccuracies should be observable for many public values (such as sexual mores), particularly when they are supported by public outcry from but a single faction (as in the case of Southern Whites speaking on desegregation of schools).

It may also be true that teachers are particularly vulnerable to conservative inaccuracies due to their ambiguous position of giving personal service in a public institution and their inability to form strong professional organizations that would set and enforce standards for their profession. This latter interpretation suggests that conservative inaccuracies would be likely to appear for nurses, social workers, government officials, and other professions having similar liabilities.

Whatever its etiology, conservative inaccuracies for the teacher are probably maintained through restriction of both communication and performance observation. It may be noted that teacher performance in the school is rarely observed by anyone other than the teacher herself and her pupils. School officials and teachers must rely upon hearsay for a description of (other) teachers' classroom performance, while parents depend upon the reporting of their own children. Many schools are also notable in the slight degree to which they discuss standards for teacher performance.

It is also probable that the conservative inaccuracy attributed to School Officials is facilitated by duplicity. It should be noted that school officials are the most mistaken of all respondents in the norms they attribute to People in General. The school official, then, is faced with the problem of "representing" a public whose standards run counter to his own. This should result in a double standard of performance; conservative values for teacher behavior supported and enforced in public—liberal standards held in private. Thus, through lack of information about actual public opinion on teacher role, the school official is not only forced into upholding standards he does not share, but he adds to his burdens by appearing as an authoritarian "fuddy-duddy" in the eyes of teachers, parents, and pupils alike.

But not only the school official suffers from conservative, mistaken, attributed norms. Parents and teachers are constrained from expressing opinions which they believe run counter to norms of school officials and (sometimes) public opinion. (Note the number of significant differences between the own norms of subjects and those attributed to others.) Teachers, also, who in fact share many norms with school officials, appear unaware of this commonality of role and are burdened with satisfying a set of standards which they don't believe in and which are not shared by school officials.

It is possible that shared inaccuracies of a conservative type are endemic to the maintenance of authority within an hierarchically ordered institution. It is also possible that contemporary leaders will generally tend to underestimate the degree to which their constituents are ready for change. One wonders, however, what would happen if school officials were apprised that public opinion was generally more liberal than they gave credit for; or a serious attempt was made by the school system to sample public opinion regarding teacher role on a regular basis. It is possible that changes might be wrought for the role of teacher, and that the professions of teacher and school administrator might become more attractive.

FORMS OF SHARED INACCURACY

The example of shared inaccuracy presented here differs from those of both the Schanck and Wheeler examples previously cited. In Schanck's original study shared inaccuracies were presented for the case in which subjects attributed to a position of which they were members norms for themselves (which were in error). In the Wheeler example, subjects attributed to a different object position norms for themselves (which were in error). In our example, subjects (for instance, parents) attributed to a different object position (for instance, School Officials) norms for a third position (teachers).

Certain logical properties differentiate these cases from one another. For instance, in both the Wheeler and our examples, it is possible to study the effect of social distance between subjects and objects on the prevalence of shared inaccuracy. In our data, note that there is not a single significant case in which parents attributed inaccurate norms to People in General nor school officials to themselves, and there is but one case where teachers were mistaken about Teacher norms. In addition, but two cases exist where pupils were mistaken about the norms of People in General, but two in which school officials were mistaken about Teachers, and but two in which teachers misjudged School Officials. In contrast, pupils and parents were often in error about Teacher and School Official norms, while school officials were in error about the norms of People in General. Note also that the greatest number of mistakes were made by pupils. It would seem from these data that shared inaccuracies were more likely with immature subjects and with increased social distance between subject and object positions. (Wheeler reports related findings.)

Despite differences among these three studies, Schanck, Wheeler, and we have suggested that not only do shared inaccuracies pose problems for those who interact but also that stable patterns of inaccuracy may persist in some situations. In fact, where shared inaccuracies are supported through deception and the hiding of one's true norms, it would appear that shared inaccuracies are generating the very conditions that would guarantee their perpetuation. This suggests that stable social forms may sometimes be organized around the perpetuating of partial or distorted communication systems. To the best of our knowledge, no systematic discussion has yet appeared of the forms of distortion-protecting interaction.

It should be clear, for instance, that the Schanck, Wheeler and our examples do not exhaust the forms of shared inaccuracy; nor are we yet informed about the conditions creating or supporting such forms, nor the extent to which they create problems for participants. Shared inaccuracies exist, nevertheless, in many role relationships. Investigators should be sensitized to recognize shared, inaccurate role attributions and to seek out the various ways in which they effect our lives.

REFERENCES

Bettelheim, B., 1943. Individual and mass behavior in extreme situations, *Journal of Abnormal and Social Psychology*, **38**, 417–452.

Biddle, B. J., 1961. *The present status of role theory*. Columbia, Mo.: University of Missouri Press (mimeographed).

Biddle, B. J., 1964. Roles, goals and value structures in organizations. In W. W. Cooper, J. J. Leavitt, and M. Shelly (Eds.), *New perspectives in organization research*. New York: Wiley.

Biddle, B. J., Rosencranz, H. A., and Rankin, E. F., Jr., 1961. *Studies in the role of the public school teacher* (5 volumes). Columbia, Mo.: University of Missouri Press (mimeographed).

Biddle, B. J., Twyman, J. P., and Rankin, E. F., Jr., 1962. The role of the teacher and occupational choice, *School Review*, **70**, 191–206.

Cronbach, L. J., 1958. Proposals leading to analytic treatment of social perception scores. In R. Tagiuri and L. Petrullo (Eds.), *Person perception and inter-personal behavior*. Stanford, Calif.: Stanford University Press.

Gage, N. L., and Cronbach, L. J., 1955. Conceptual and methodological problems in interpersonal perception, *Psychological Review*, **62**, 411–422.

Goffman, E., 1959. *The presentation of self in everyday life*. New York: Doubleday.

Moore, W. E., and Tumin, M. M., 1949. Some social functions of ignorance, *American Sociological Review*, **14**, 787–795.

Rosencranz, H. A., and Biddle, B. J., 1964. The role approach to teacher competence evaluation. In B. J. Biddle and W. J. Ellena (Eds.), *Contemporary research on teacher effectiveness*. New York: Holt.

Schanck, R. L., 1932. A study of a community and its groups and institutions conceived of as behaviors of individuals, *Psychological Monograph*, **43**, No. 2.

Twyman, J. P., and Biddle, B. J., 1963. Role conflict for public school teachers, *Journal of Psychology*, **55**, 183–198.

Twyman, J. P. and Biddle, B. J., 1964. *The uses of role conflict*. Stillwater, Okla.: Oklahoma State University Monographs in Social Science.

von Neumann, J., and Morgenstern, O., 1947. *Theory of games and economic behavior* (2nd. ed.). Princeton, N.J.: Princeton University Press.

Wheeler, S., 1961. Role conflict in correctional communities. In D. R. Cressey (Ed.), *The prison: studies in institutional organization and change*. New York: Holt.

part IX Sanctioning and Conformity

SANCTIONING IS BEHAVIOR engaged in by individuals with the intention of achieving an alteration of another's behavior; this alteration is generally toward greater conformity. Sanctions may or may not be effective in achieving an actual alteration of the behavior in question. Indeed, conformity may occur without any sanctioning whatever. The relationships between conforming and nonconforming behavior and the sanctioning of such behavior are complex and not well explored. The writings included in this part are addressed to some of the conditions under which conformity behavior will occur. In this connection, many variables are identified that relate to the extent to which behavior is controlled by prescriptions, by sanctions, and by other factors as well.

In his paper on norm commitment, conformity, and sanctioning, Goode points out that conformity is necessary for the smooth operation of institutions, and that generally individuals conform because of their motivation to do so. In the course of socialization, Goode observes that the individual acquires a commitment to norms and also comes to accept the rightness of applying a particular norm in a specific situation. This theme is pursued in his comments on norm commitment in contemporary society and on the interlocking of role relationships. Sanctioning is not only necessary to enforce role conformity, he asserts, but acts of sanctioning become the obligations, and hence, the role, of others.

Skinner's selection on the control of behavior by persons, groups, and culture is a general discussion of conformity. The techniques for controlling individual behavior include physical force, manipulation of stimuli, reinforcement, aversive stimulation, punishment, deprivation and satiation, emotion, and use of drugs. Skinner speaks as well of the various controlling agencies in society, these being government, law, religion, education, and culture. The characteristic controlling techniques used by these agencies are discussed.

The complexity and subtlety of conformity processes are highlighted in Foa's conceptualization of, and research on, relationships between norms and behavior in the dyad. In this selection, Foa points out that each of the two persons involved in a dyad may act, observe, and be a person for whom a perception is ascribed; and that each of these three functions takes place on the actual and normative level. By considering various relationships between combinations of these functions, such concepts as relevance, consonance, and homovalence are identified. A general theorem is stated about the balance of the system of norms, and hypotheses are derived dealing with perception by the actors and relationships among the various subsystems. Foa then presents results from a study designed to test his hypotheses. He discovers that there is (1) a tendency toward balancing rewards in both intra-personal and inter-personal systems, (2) a tendency for the actor to choose behavior that will improve communication of reward, and (3) a tendency to choose the behavior that is perceived and associated with reward. Additional hypotheses evolving from the model are developed.

The relationship between role expectations (prescriptions) and performance was the subject of the study of Dinitz, Angrist, Lefton, and Pasamanick. In this selection the authors report on the relationship between the role expectations of family members and the performance of female mental patients following their discharge from a mental hospital. The findings indicate a direct relationship between the expectations and the performance, i.e., the higher the expectations held for the patient's role performance, the higher the level of the patient's actual performance. In their discussion of the results, the authors recognize an important problem, namely, that it is not clear whether the patients conformed in their behavior to the norms held for them or whether the norms held for the patient were adjusted to match the actual performance of the patients. It is possible that only one of these alternatives is correct, or even that both are, to some extent. Many apparent correspondences between prescriptions and the behavior prescribed in real life are assumed to derive only from the operation of prescriptions, and this study reveals the naiveté of this assumption.

selection 38 Norm Commitment and Conformity to Role-Status Obligations

WILLIAM J. GOODE

[This paper is concerned with] the relationship between role-status conformity and variations in norm commitment. Although role conformity may be approached through the theorem of institutional integration, that is, that individuals carry out institutional tasks because they have been reared to want to do so, this theorem is only an orientation and not a precise hypothesis. Many do not discharge their responsibilities while wanting to do so. The road to hell is paved with good intentions: conformity to a set of norms is not a simple function of norm commitment.

Indeed, the theorem asserts only that social norm and individual desire by and large have the same *direction*. This rephrasing of the theorem discloses, however, that it is merely self-evident. Since individual desires were created or shaped by the socialization experience in the society, and since that experience was precisely the inculcation of social norms in the individual, any other *general* direction of relationship would be surprising. As against that general influence, however, particular experiences of socialization may lead the individual to accept norms counter to those which are more widely accepted. Doubtless, too, there are "need dispositions" which are socially shaped but which may not be easily reducible to moral rules or directives.

As against such limitations, the theorem does serve the useful purpose of rejecting a primitive hedonistic theory, so characteristic of Western notions about sin, which views human action as arising from a choice between individual desire and the norms which oppose such desires. Such a view is erroneous, then, because almost all the individual's desires are in conformity with *some* norm or another.

But the substitution of the theorem of institutional integration in the place of a primitive hedonism fails to add much in an understanding of role-status conformity. The individual who fails in a role obligation may have chosen among several alternative norms, but the alter who censures him feels that he did not apply the *appropriate* norm for the particular role context (MacIver and Page, 1949). On the other hand, the *content* of a given role is partly an organization of norms, that is, a connection among several norms, as applicable to a particular type of situation. This organization checks the individual's tendency to range too widely in his selection of possible norms, some of which would require less of him but would yield less for institutional or alter's needs.

According to this view, the significance of socialization is thus not only that the individual acquires a commitment to the norms of the society, that is, internalizes the norms, but that he accepts the rightness of applying a particular norm or norms to a specified situation. This acceptance is, in turn, based upon an important characteristic of the socialization experience, that the censure and rewards of socialization focus on the role relationship as a unit, far more than on conformity with a single norm. The reasons are several: (a) There is no concrete norm to be observed, but there are many concrete role models (e.g., "boy," "girl," "daddy's helper"). Consequently, the process of conceptualization is made easier for the child. (b) Many of the broad norms must be modified by reference to the particular role relationship: "respect for elders" is in some contexts different toward uncles and aunts from that toward grandparents. (c) Especially in the earlier years the child is more likely to be punished for failure in his role performance toward a person, so that deviation from the norm is censured through the pressures of persons, that is, roles or organization of norms rather than a single norm. The norm has no independent,

Abridged from the *American Journal of Sociology*, 1960, **66**, 246–258. Reprinted by permission of the author and the University of Chicago Press. This selection was partially completed under a National Institute of Mental Health Grant.

original source of power other than persons, and their spontaneous censure usually focuses on the role relationship.

ADULT RESOCIALIZATION

Socialization is not merely a childhood experience: as adults we are all being continually *re*socialized, that is, reaffirmed in our normative commitment, by the alters in our total role network. (I use the term "socialization" in the technical sense even when applied to adults, i.e., the inculcation or internalization of values or norms, not merely learning cognitively which actions will be punished or rewarded.) Of course, the influence of these alters is greater, because the high emotional and cognitive significance of the various alters in ego's childhood develops a continuing emotional and cognitive sensitivity to others' reactions. This sensitivity is of great importance in resocializing ego, that is, in maintaining the intensity of his commitment to the appropriate role performance. The process is also facilitated by a structural fact about roles: they are "public" in several ways: (a) Fundamentally, they require action, including the action that is an expression of emotion. Such actions are at least partially observable by others. (b) Role obligations are defined, either in outline or in part, by other people—"third parties" with whom ego and alter are in interaction and who therefore have a real concern with ego's and alter's behavior. (c) Still more concretely, though ego's duty may be accepted by both ego and alter, both also know that some third party, group, or community also knows about and evaluates both behavior and normative commitment. (d) A consequence, then, is that, even when alter has no strong emotional commitment to holding ego to his obligations, he may do so in fact because of his sensitivity to outside reactions. Alter has, then, an obligation to other alters to censure ego. Therefore, even when third parties do not censure either ego or alter openly, both will know how such people actually do feel and will be responsive to presumed unexpressed censure, for example, "what the neighborhood thinks."

NORM COMMITMENT IN MODERN SOCIETY

The individual's emotional commitment to an adequate discharge of his role duties, and thus his behavioral consistency, derives ultimately from his experiences of censure and reward in his role relationships. However, such internal commitments are not sufficient to maintain even a single role relationship. Ample commentary, both literary and historical, exists to show that under certain types of situations men will abandon even well-learned role responsibilities: the nearly treasonable behavior of many American troops in Chinese prison camps during the Korean war (Strassman, Thaler, and Schein, 1956; Schein, 1956), the similarly self-oriented behavior of inmates in some Nazi concentration camps (Bettelheim, 1943), the mass flight of soldiers in various battles, the breakdown of discipline in some shipwrecks or among Europeans under jungle or polar conditions or the infrequent near-savagery of shipwreck survivors. Such disintegration of roles may occur when the appropriate alters are absent, but the underlying variable is rather that the appropriate alters no longer have the power to censure or reward ego effectively. In turn, ego cannot perform adequately.

The social theory which deals with societies as [a] whole fits primitive societies best and has laid greatest stress on the individual's commitment to the values and norms of the society and the value consensus among its members. Modifications of it to fit a complex civilization have not been stated clearly; for example, how intense must the commitment be, and how complete the consensus, to insure what measure of individual conformity and societal stability? For a precise analysis we need to measure, for a wide range of societies, the actual level of emotional and behavioral conformity with various role obligations within them. We know that ego may feel much or little emotional commitment to a given norm, that ego's appropriate alter may care more or less whether ego does conform, and that people in their social networks but outside that specific role relationship may also care more or less whether ego or alter conforms or insists upon the other's conformity. In addition, in all three of these "layers" there may be some individuals who assert a counternorm.

Many individuals in our own society do not feel strongly committed to various important norms—Catholic dogma, the appropriate behavior of husband and wife, private property, etc. (see Jones, 1941; Fichter, 1951; Fichter, 1957; Stouffer, 1949; Gross, Mason, and McEachern, 1957; Baumert, 1952). Public opinion surveys show that almost every question about appropriate role behavior elicits a wide range of answers (Hyman, 1953). If there is consensus, it seems to be loose. Moreover, observation shows that a considerable proportion of the population violates one or another important norm at some time (see Kinsey, Pomroy, and Martin, 1948; Sutherland, 1949; Kinsey, Pomroy, Martin, and Gebhard, 1953; Fichter, 1957). Of course, we may fail to comply with a role prescription when we do *not* assert a counternorm or even when we *do* feel committed to the prescription, and we may assert a counternorm or feel a low commitment *without* deviating in behavior from what others expect of us. Moreover, the norm does not lose its ordering power in a social structure merely because some people disobey it. Indeed, as Durkheim (1893) saw, the reactions of others—the counter-sanctions of alters—may then strengthen the cohesion of the group and its fidelity to the existing social structure.

NORM COMMITMENT AND CONFORMITY RATE

With reference to norm commitment and rate of conformity, several very general propositions can be stated: (a) When there is a low rate of conformity and an increasing rate of assertion of a counternorm, the older norm begins to lose its power and official standing. (b) In addition, if alters do not punish egos for their role failure, then only the norm commitment of egos is left to assure their conformity. No part of the social structure can long survive even a moderate rate of violation of norms if there is a substantial rate of alter's failure to punish ego for his violation or of failure to punish alter for his failure to punish (e.g., the gradual breakdown of the Prohibition Amendment). (c) Further, if their social network does not support the punishment, the relationship between ego and alter will change or dissolve. (d) Perhaps, similarly, the dissolution of a norm will occur when a relatively small group asserts a counternorm and punishes its violation in others without being punished in turn (e.g., the Nazis in the late 1920's).

Perhaps the social structure is under no threat under modern conditions of apparently weak consensus if the conformity to which ego is pressed is merely of a "general" nature, that is, the norms permit a wide range of rough approximations to the ideal. But whether norms in fact are general is not easy to determine. Which is in fact "the" norm? You should not lie (only a loose conformity is demanded); or you may tell lies of the following types in these situations but not in others, and the wrongness of other lies is to be ranked in the following order. The first is a general norm, and of course there will be only a rough conformity with it, but it is not a correct description. The second would be empirically more accurate, but no one has established such a matrix of obligations on empirical evidence.

In addition, though a broad societal norm might require only loose conformity, the subgroups or individual role relationships of which the individual is a member require conformity to their specific versions and modifications of that norm; a rough conformity to the general norm is not likely to be acceptable. To say "general conformity is all that is required" means only that *individuals at some distance from us* in the social network demand from us only a loose conformity; those who are closer define the norm itself more specifically and require a more specific performance.

INTERLOCKING OF ROLE RELATIONSHIPS

Pursuing the problem of role conformity in a complex society, we noted earlier that role relationships embody three main sources of pressures toward fulfillment of role obligations: (a) ego is socialized to have an autonomous emotional commitment to his appropriate role behavior; (b) alter may in turn require that behavior of ego; and (c) other concerned individuals may censure the behavior of either ego or alter. Thus, even if ego's norm commitment is weak, alter may demand conformity. And, even if alter is willing to demand little of ego, still others—members of a reference group, family, neighbors—may press alter to make the appropriate demands upon ego. A social structure can tolerate, perhaps, a substantial number of individuals who are not strongly committed to a given role norm, since those additional safeguards exist. Moreover, since the third parties, those in interaction with ego and alter who may concern themselves with how ego and alter carry out the relationship, is made up of a much larger number of people and role nexuses, the chances are reduced that weakly committed ego, weakly demanding alter, and entirely non-censoring, related outsiders would come together simultaneously. Without considering more empirical data, however, it is not yet possible to specify how weak these forces can be without undermining the social structure. (d) An additional interlocking support is that an individual finds it difficult to fail in any important role obligation without failing in other, related roles and thus incurring sanctions from more than one alter (if as a student I do not study, I fall short of the expectations of both my teacher and my family). (e) In addition, individuals in many statuses have also the obligation of serving as models for others (parents for children, officers for enlisted men, professors for graduate students). Their behavior has motivational consequences, and thus, even when they do not feel a strong commitment to fulfilling the normative requirement, they may nevertheless conform. Their peers or superiors may press them to conform at least outwardly, and especially in formal situations, so that their alters will follow their model. This pressure is lessened, of course, when they are less likely to be identified as belonging to that status (the officer in civilian clothes, parents at a party away from children). Here, then, the roles are interlocked through ties between the two central statuses and an indirect link between a third party and the "subordinate" status (student, child) through the superordinate status (professor, parent). (f) A last proposition is that the sanctions in such interlocking patterns need not be, and usually are not, powerful; they need only be recurring and generally unidirectional, that is, pressing toward the same kind of behavior, even when they originate in different persons.

MORAL APPROVAL OF ROLE REPRISALS

The main day-to-day support for appropriate role behavior is not direct punishment or reward but alter's choice over whether he will live up to his obligations to ego, if ego fails in his own. Aside from ego's "sensitivity" to alter's feelings, ego's effective action toward his own goals depends on the supporting activities of alter, and eventually alter may not act properly if ego does not. Moreover, the opinion and behavior of the relevant third parties, or "third layer," underlie this set of expectations about failure. For not only are these interested, outside people able to predict (cognitively) that any alter is likely to reject his role obligation if ego continues to fail in his, but they approve that rejection. Even a rejection of maternal obligation, perhaps the duties which are supposed to embody the most forbearance in our society, will be approved if the child is flagrantly abusive or derelict. The rules of the game are basically set by a group or network, and they include the penalties for role failure which alter may properly impose upon ego for ego's possible role failures. And, in turn, ego's perception of both these empirical possibilities (alter's deliberate counterfailure and the group's support of it) arouses ego's anxiety or other emotional response to such eventualities.

ROLE FAILURE: EMOTION VS. ACTIVITY

Ego may fail in role performance by not carrying out the overt activities prescribed or by not feeling the prescribed emotions. He may, for example, either fail to go to his kinsman's funeral or show that he is unconcerned about his kinsman's death. Several propositions grow from a consideration of the relation between covert and overt performance of roles.

First, of course, failure in role is more likely if, in fact, ego does not care, does not have the appropriate emotions. This seems to be no more than a corollary of the integration theorem. Alter, on the other hand, is less likely to know that there has been failure in attitude if the behavior follows the prescription. Indeed, if an individual expresses an intense norm commitment or the appropriate emotion but *acts* contradictorily (the professor who "loves learning" but shows no evidence of it), his appropriate alters will usually doubt the reality of his emotional commitment. Expressions of condolence are accepted as expressions of real sorrow or sympathy; salutations, gestures, the use of titles, and overt deference are accepted as indexes of real respect. Alter may, then, evaluate incorrectly the intensity of ego's real emotion. However, alter is motivated to judge accurately and does have some ability to judge, while ego cannot always hide his emotion or its absence. In addition, where there are two or more role partners who owe role performances to the same alter (e.g., two children in relations with their parent or two bureaucratic subordinates in relations with the same superior), either of the two may know that the other does not have the prescribed attitudes, but they may and do attempt to measure the other's "sincerity."

Precisely because the appropriate emotional response in the role is the day-to-day working origin of our appropriate role performance—that is, because people "feel" the appropriate emotions, they do the appropriate thing—role failure in this dimension arouses more disapproval than does mere failure in role activity. And when the activity is not carried out because the emotion is lacking, alter disapproves still more. Groups have long recognized the functional importance of the underlying emotional commitment (e.g., the Church can afford to be more indulgent to the sinner than to the heretic). When the individual fails to carry out the appropriate acts or gestures, he can later assert his repentance, or his disappointment in his own weakness, or the validity of other claims. But to admit that he did not "care" is to deny that either punishment or repentance is appropriate or that the group values are the right ones.

On the other hand, because alter (whether group or individual) does respond more intensely to a failure in the appropriate emotion, ego will try to avoid letting either alter know about it or any other individual who stands in a similar relationship to alter.

A further proposition is that few or no specific techniques can be used to punish ego's failure in emotion alone. The techniques of socialization —shame, physical punishment, anxiety, etc.— do not aim at actional or emotional conformity as separable goals. As noted earlier, role behavior is taught mainly in role units. Indeed, if these two goals were separated in socialization, then their disjunction would occur more often in adulthood, and, as a consequence, role conformity would be rarer. The external pressures toward conformity would not be backed as often by internal emotional commitment.

Of more theoretical significance for an understanding of role maintenance in our type of society is a further proposition, which restates within the given propositional context a notion implied in the preceding section: in a secularized society, with perhaps weak commitment to norms or role emotion, role or norm conformity may depend far more on the greater sensitivity of ego to alter's response than it does in other types of societies. This is not to assert that high sensitivity is inversely correlated with high intensity of role commitment or emotion. Rather, when there is a low intensity, there must be a correlative increase of sensitivity to "alter opinion" or to "community opinion" (outsiders related to alter and ego) if role obligations are to be met generally.

This last proposition may be seen, in the foregoing context, as a structural-functional basis for the emergence or wider distribution in certain strata, groups, and statuses, or the "urban" or "other-oriented" type which observers from Plato to Riesman have described. Moreover, it suggests why the type is more likely to appear in those particular groups or strata—that is, where the appropriate emotions are mild, counternorms are not generally proclaimed, but alters are highly vigilant in the matter of these emotions. (Perhaps it also explains why these segments emphasize a sort of mild "friendship" as the ideal working relationship: friendliness permits enough close observations of others to check on their behavior, but its shallowness prevents any real probe into the intensity of emotions felt by others.)

Finally, if this line of theoretical analysis is empirically valid, then we can suppose that in such segments or groups there can be rapid social change, that is, changes in role patterns and therefore in social structures. For, although ego's guesses about alter's probable responses will hold ego in general to a proper role activity, the fact that neither is intensely committed to their mutual role obligations, while both are attentive to each other's opinions, suggests at least the possibility of a "double revelation." When both alter and ego learn that neither really cares, much of the motive power behind the relationship is removed, and their subsequent decisions about conformity may become rational calculations of an essentially hedonic sort, whereby they seek their best advantage together and ignore or evade moral demands. Under such structural circumstances, slight shifts in the balance of advantages and disadvantages to a class of individuals might lead to large shifts in their social behavior.

REFERENCES

Baumert, G., 1952. *Deutsche Familien nach dem Kriege*. Darmstadt: Roether, pp. 176–177.

Bettelheim, B., 1943. Individual and mass behavior in extreme situations. *Journal of Abnormal and Social Psychology*, **38**, 417–452.

Durkheim, E., 1893. *De la division du travail social.* (The division of labor in society.) Paris: F. Alcan. Translated by George Simpson, 1949. New York: The Free Press, p. 98 ff.

Fichter, J. J., 1951. *Southern parish, Vol. I: Dynamics of a city church.* Chicago: University of Chicago Press.

Fichter, J. J., 1957. The marginal Catholic: an institutional approach. In M. J. Yinger (Ed.), *Religion, society and the individual.* New York: Macmillan.

Gross, N., Mason, W. S., and McEachern, A. W., 1957. *Explorations in role analysis.* New York: Wiley, pp. 48–69.

Hyman, H., 1953. The value systems of different classes. In R. Bendix and S. M. Lipset (Eds.), *Class, status, and power.* New York: The Free Press, pp. 426–442.

Jones, A. W., 1941. *Life, liberty, and property.* Philadelphia: Lippincott.

Kinsey, A. C., Pomroy, W. B., and Martin, C. E., 1948. *Sexual behavior in the human male.* New York: Dutton.

Kinsey, A. C., Pomroy, W. B., Martin, C. E., and Gebhard, P. H., 1953. *Sexual behavior in the human female.* New York: Saunders.

MacIver, R. M., and Page, C. H., 1949. *Society.* New York: Holt, pp. 197 ff.

Schein, E. H., 1956. The Chinese indoctrination program for prisoners of war: a study of attempted "brainwashing." *Psychiatry*, **61**, 149–172.

Stouffer, S. A., 1949. An analysis of conflicting social norms. *American Sociological Review*, **14**, 707–717.

Strassman, H. D., Thaler, Margaret B., and Schein, E. H., 1956. A prisoner of war syndrome: apathy as a reaction to severe stress. *American Journal of Psychology*, **61**, 998–1003.

Sutherland, E. H., 1949. *White collar crime.* New York: Dryden.

selection 39 Control of Behavior by Persons, Groups, and Culture

B. F. SKINNER

PERSONAL CONTROL

Let us look at a social episode from the point of view of one of the participants. *A* behaves in a way which alters *B*'s behavior because of the consequences which *B*'s behavior has for *A*. We say, colloquially, that *A* is *deliberately* controlling *B*. Our task is to evaluate the various ways in which one person controls another.

Techniques of Control

Physical Force. Physical force is the most immediately effective technique available to those who have the necessary power. In its most immediately personal form it is exemplified by the wrestler who suppresses the behavior of his opponent through sheer physical restraint. The most extreme form of restraint is death: the individual is kept from behaving by being killed. Less extreme forms include the use of handcuffs, strait-jackets, jails, concentration camps, and so on.

Abridged from pages 313–355, 403–407, and 415–419 of a book by the same author entitled *Science and Human Behavior*, 1953, New York: Macmillan. Reprinted by permission of the author and Macmillan.

The use of force has obvious disadvantages as a controlling technique. It usually requires the sustained attention of the controller. It is almost exclusively concerned with the prevention of behavior and hence is of little value in increasing the probability of action. It generates strong emotional dispositions to counterattack. It cannot be applied to all forms of behavior; handcuffs restrain part of a man's rage but not all of it. It is not effective upon behavior at the private level, as we suggest when we say that one cannot imprison a man's thoughts.

For all these reasons, control through physical restraint is not so promising a possibility as it may at first appear. It is, of course, never available to those who lack the necessary power. In the long run the use of force usually gives way to other techniques which employ genuine processes of behavior. Here the controller need not have the power to coerce or restrain behavior directly but may affect it indirectly by altering the environment.

Manipulating Stimuli. Most of the techniques of self-control through the manipulation of stimuli may be directly extended to the behavior of others. We present unconditioned or conditioned stimuli to *elicit* reflex responses when we give an emetic to induce vomiting; and we arrange *discriminative occasions* for behavior when we display merchandise in a store in such a way that the customer is more likely to purchase it. We use stimuli to *eliminate* behavior by evoking incompatible responses. When women employed in a factory created a hazard by hurrying down a corridor at the end of the day, the manager put mirrors along the corridor to evoke responses of adjusting wearing apparel and applying cosmetics. This behavior proved to be incompatible with hurrying. We use *supplemental stimuli* to induce behavior when we "interpret a situation favorably," as when the salesman assures the potential buyer that he will enjoy or profit from a purchase, or when we encourage someone to join us on a given occasion by assuring him of enjoyable consequences. A particularly effective mode of stimulation evokes the imitative repertoire: the businessman who is resorting to alcohol as a technique of control induces his prospect to have another drink by ordering another himself.

Reinforcement as a Technique of Control. If the individual possesses money or goods, he may use them for purposes of reinforcement in the form of wages, bribes, or gratuities. If he is in a position to do someone a favor, he can reinforce accordingly. He may also be able to offer his own physical labor, either to an employer in return for wages or to a friend in return for a particular action. Sexual stimulation is a common form of reinforcement and is widely used in personal control.

In practice many of these reinforcers are preceded by more immediate conditioned reinforcers. Money is itself a conditioned reinforcer, but primary reinforcement may be further postponed when a check is given which is later converted into cash. Contracts and verbal promises are other forms of conditioned reinforcers available in personal control. Minor examples include praise and thanks. These deferred reinforcements are likely to be unreliable, however. Praise may give way to flattery, checks may not be honored, and promises may be made in bad faith. But it may be some time before the interlocking social system deteriorates to the point at which there is no longer a reinforcing effect.

Aversive Stimulation. Negative reinforcement is employed in personal control in the aversive cry of the child and the nuisance value of the behavior of an adult. Control is achieved by making the withdrawal of these aversive stimuli contingent upon the response to be strengthened. Forgiveness and acquittal are similarly reinforcing. The bully who pommels another boy until he cries "Uncle!", the police who employ the third degree to obtain a confession, and the nation which makes war until the enemy surrenders, exemplify the same use of aversive stimulation. *Conditioned* aversive stimulation used in the same way is exemplified by the "dare" or by other ways of shaming someone into acting.

Punishment. The individual who is able to present a positive reinforcement or withdraw a negative is usually also able to present the negative or withdraw the positive and is therefore able to punish. Punishment is not to be confused with physical restraint or the use of aversive stimulation. All three forms of control are usually available to the same individual because of the nature of the power of control, but confining a man in jail to keep him from behaving in a certain way or to induce him to behave in a certain way in order to be released is not the same as confining him in order to reduce his tendency to behave in that way in the future. In the control of psychotic patients confinement is a means of restraint rather than punishment; and, conversely, some forms of punishment involve at best only momentary restraint. Punishment as a technique of control has all the disadvantages of physical restraint and, in addition, all the weaknesses. Moreover, it generates emotional dispositions which may be disadvantageous or even dangerous to both controller and controllee.

Punishment as the removal of positive reinforcers, conditioned or unconditioned, is exemplified by cutting a dependent off "without a cent," refusing to supply food or shelter previously given, imposing economic sanctions, and refusing customary sexual contact. Another important example is withholding customary social stimulation, as in snubbing an acquaintance or "putting a schoolboy on silence." Lesser degrees of such punishments are social neglect and inattention. None of these are punishments in their own right, but only when made contingent upon behavior.

Punishment in the form of presenting aversive stimuli is commoner. Physical injury is exemplified by spanking a child, striking an adult, and attacking a nation. Conditioned aversive stimuli, many of them verbal, are exemplified by disapproval and criticism, by damning and cursing, by ridicule, and by the carrying of bad news. These again are punishments only when contingent upon behavior. We have seen that it is questionable whether they permanently reduce any tendency to behave. They all generate emotional dispositions which are particularly disorganizing and which may in turn call for further remedial control.

Pointing Up Contingencies of Reinforcement. It is possible to use techniques based upon reinforcement and punishment without being able to control the events in question. A considerable effect may be achieved simply by clarifying the relation between behavior and its consequences. The instructor in sports, crafts, or artistic activities may directly reinforce the behavior he is trying to establish, but he may also simply point up the contingency between a given form of behavior and the result—"Notice the effect you get when you hold the brush this way," "Strike the key this way and see if it isn't easier," "If you swing the club this way, you won't slice the ball," and so on. The controller may make use of reinforcing events which have occurred without his intervention by making the contingencies more likely to modify the behavior of the controllee. Punishing consequences are pointed up by such expressions as "Now, see what you've done," "This is costing you money," or "You are responsible for all this." Other techniques of emphasizing reinforcing contingencies consist of arranging various schedules of reinforcement—"Play this passage until you can play it without a mistake"—and programs of differential reinforcement—"When you can clear the bar at this height, move it one inch higher."

Deprivation and Satiation. If we are controlling a child's behavior through reinforcement with candy, it is well to make sure that little candy is received at other times. Deprivation may also be used to control behavior which has been strengthened by generalized reinforcers. To evoke behavior which has been reinforced with money, one procedure is to deprive the individual in such a way as to strengthen behavior which can be executed only with money. For example, a man is made susceptible to bribery by encouraging him to follow a mode of living in which money is an important requirement. Satiation is a common technique of control which is particularly effective in eliminating unwanted behavior. A child stops teasing for candy when he is given all he will eat. One may satiate an aggressor by submitting to him—by "turning the other cheek."

Emotion. We are sometimes interested in controlling the reflex responses characteristic of emotion, as in making someone laugh, blush, or cry. We are more likely to be interested in establishing emotional *predispositions.* We have noted the important case in which someone is "favorably inclined" toward a particular person or set of circumstances. Building morale is usually concerned with generating such a predisposition. The effect often follows from the same events which reinforce behavior. Gratuities, for example, serve as a mode of control not only through reinforcement but by generating "favorable attitudes." More specific predispositions are also generated with appropriate stimuli—as when Christmas music is played in a store to encourage "good will toward men" and the purchase of gifts. Other techniques of altering emotional predispositions are suggested by terms like "jollying," "cajoling," "haranguing," "seducing," "inciting," "allaying fear," and "turning away wrath." The actual variables responsible for a given predisposition need to be analyzed in each case.

The Use of Drugs. The drug most commonly used in personal control is alcohol. Like certain emotional operations it is often used to dispose an individual toward favorable action. It appears also to act directly in reducing anxieties or alarm and may be used for that reason—for example, in closing a business deal or in getting someone to talk about a confidential matter. It is also used as a positive reinforcer. As a habit-forming drug it makes possible a special form of deprivation, in which behavior which has been reinforced with alcohol may be made so powerful that the individual will "do anything" for a drink. Such drugs as morphine and cocaine have been used to create the possibility of using other powerful deprivations for the same purpose. Other drugs are employed in the control of psychotic behavior and in connection with governmental or police functions—for example, the so-called truth serums.

GROUP CONTROL

The principal technique employed in the control of the individual by any group of people who have lived together for a sufficient length of time is as follows. The behavior of the individual is classified as either "good" or "bad" or, to the same effect, "right" or "wrong," and is reinforced or punished accordingly.

The group as a whole seldom draws up a formal classification of behavior as good or bad. We infer the classification from our observations of controlling practices. A sort of informal codification takes place, however, when the terms themselves come to be used in reinforcement. Perhaps the commonest generalized reinforcers are the verbal stimuli "Good," "Right," "Bad," and "Wrong." These are used, together with unconditioned and other conditioned reinforcers such as praise, thanks, caresses, gratuities, favors, blows, blame, censure, and criticism, to shape the behavior of the individual.

The actual controlling practices are usually obvious. Good behavior is reinforced, and bad behavior punished. The conditioned aversive stimulation generated by bad behavior as the result of punishment is associated with an emotional pattern commonly called "shame." The individual responds to this when he "feels ashamed of himself." Part of what he feels are the responses of glands and smooth muscles recorded by the so-called lie detector. The relevance of this instrument to lie detection is based upon the fact that lying is frequently punished. Another part of the reaction of shame is a conspicuous change in normal dispositions—the social offender acts in a shamefaced manner. Any or all of these emotional conditions may be directly or indirectly aversive, in which case they combine with other conditioned aversive stimulation in providing for the reinforcement of behavior which displaces or otherwise reduces the probability of the punished response. The best example of such behavior is self-control. The group also directly reinforces practices of self-control.

CONTROLLING AGENCIES

The group exercises an ethical control over each of its members mainly through its power to reinforce or punish. The power is derived from sheer number and from the importance of other people in the life of each member. Usually the group is not well organized, nor are its practices consistently sustained. Within the group, however, certain *controlling agencies* manipulate particular sets of variables. These agencies are usually better organized than is the group as a whole, and they often operate with greater success. The agencies to be considered are chosen from the fields of *government*, *religion*, and *education*.

Techniques in Government Control

Where the group classifies behavior as "right" or "wrong" for purposes of ethical reinforcement, the governing agency adopts a distinction between "legal" and "illegal." The terms are defined roughly in relation to the source of power of the agency. Under an absolute ruler behavior is illegal if it has aversive consequences for the agency. To the extent that the power of the government derives from the group, the definitions approach those of "right" and "wrong." Since the governmental agency operates principally through the power to punish, however, the emphasis is upon "wrong." A government uses its power to "keep the peace"—to *restrain* behavior which threatens the property and persons of other members of the group. A government which possesses only the power to punish can *strengthen* legal behavior only by making the removal of a threat of punishment contingent upon it. This is sometimes done, but the commoner technique is simply to punish illegal forms of behavior.

Some governmental punishments consist of removing positive reinforcers—for example, dispossessing a man of property, fining him, taxing him punitively, or depriving him of contact with society through incarceration or banishment. Other common punishments consist of presenting negative reinforcers—for example, inflicting physical injury as in flogging, threatening injury or death, imposing a sentence at hard labor, exposing the individual to public ridicule in the stocks, and aversively stimulating the individual in minor ways as by requiring him to report in person to a police station where the principal punishment is simply the time and labor consumed in reporting. In practice, these punishments are made contingent upon particular kinds of behavior in order to reduce the probability that the behavior will occur again. A direct weakening as the opposite effect of reinforcement is, as we have seen, unlikely. Instead, conditioned aversive stimuli are produced, one effect of which resembles the "sense of shame" of group control. When this results from governmental punishment, the commoner term is "guilt." The process provides for the automatic reinforcement of responses which are incompatible with illegal behavior. As the net effect of governmental control, then, illegal behavior comes to generate aversive stimuli which make the individual "feel guilty" and which provide for the automatic positive reinforcement of behaving legally.

A controlling technique usually associated with an emphasis upon punishment is the establishment of *obedient* behavior. This is often a characteristic of personal control—for example, in the relation between parent and child. It is seen as a by-product of auxiliary techniques in the field of education when the pupil is taught obedience to his teacher. It is a staple product of governmental control. In the broadest sense the controlled individual is obedient to the dictates of the agency if he behaves in conformity with its controlling practices, but there is a special form of obedience in which a particular response is brought under the control of a verbal command. As a verbal stimulus a command serves a double function. It specifies behavior to be carried out, and it generates an aversive condition from which only that behavior will bring escape. The command is, of course, a familiar feature of military training. A selected repertoire of responses is brought under the control of appropriate verbal stimuli, which may then be used to time or otherwise coordinate the behavior of the members of a group. The civilian shows a comparable repertoire when he obeys traffic signals or a traffic policeman. But obedience to the government is more than a selected repertoire. Any behavior commanded by the government—in actual fact by "persons in authority" who are able to exert governmental control—is eventually carried out within the range of the verbal history of the individual. The group exercises a control of this sort to the extent that the imperative mood prevails in everyday discourse. By establishing obedient behavior, the controlling agency prepares for future occasions which it cannot otherwise foresee and for which an explicit repertoire cannot, therefore, be prepared in advance. When novel occasions arise to which the individual possesses no response, he simply does as he is told.

Law. An important point in the development of a governmental agency is the codification of its controlling practices. The study of law or jurisprudence is usually concerned with the codes and practices of specific governments, past or present. It is also concerned with certain questions upon which a functional analysis of behavior has some bearing. What is a law? What role does a law play in governmental control? In particular, what effect does it have upon the behavior of the controllee and of the members of the governmental agency itself?

A law usually has two important features. In the first place, it specifies behavior. The behavior is usually not described topographically but rather in terms of its effect upon others—the effect which is the object of governmental control. When we are told, for example, than an individual has "committed perjury," we are not told what he has actually said. "Robbery" and "assault" do not refer to specific forms of response. Only properties of behavior which are aversive to others are mentioned—in perjury the lack of a customary correspondence between a verbal response and certain factual circumstances, in robbery the removal of positive reinforcers, and in assault the aversive character of physical injury. In the second place, a law specifies or implies a consequence, usually punishment. A law is thus a *statement of a contingency of reinforcement maintained by a governmental agency.* The contingency may have prevailed as a controlling practice prior to its codification as a law, or it may represent a new practice which goes into effect with the passage of the law. Laws are thus both descriptions of past practices and assurances of similar practices in the future. A law is a *rule* of conduct in the sense that it specifies the consequences of certain actions which in turn "rule" behavior.

To show how the individual actually comes to abide by a code, we should have to analyze how he learns not to lie, not to steal, not to assault others, and so on. The governmental agency may codify its controlling practices and maintain the contingencies thus set forth but it seldom attempts to make the code effective in any other way. The individual is directly affected by only a small fraction of prevailing contingencies. In asserting that "ignorance of the law is no excuse," the governmental agency leaves the actual conditioning of the individual to others. Parents and friends establish minor contingencies which keep behavior within legal bounds, and the governmental function may also be actively supported by the ethical group and by religious and educational institutions with their appropriate techniques.

The governmental agency often conceals its neglect of this important step in control by claiming to have an educational effect. The individual is said to be affected by witnessing the punishment of others. But the effect of punishment as a deterrent to those who are not themselves punished is neither simple nor inevitable. The question is not peculiar to governmental contingencies. A boy may see a companion fall from a tree and may then see that the companion behaves in a manner characteristic of strong aversive stimulation. Through at least two stages of respondent conditioning any subsequent move on the part of the boy himself to climb trees generates conditioned aversive stimulation, a reduction in which reinforces competing behavior. The process is the same, although the effect is not of the same magnitude, as when the boy himself falls and is hurt. The same aversive stimulation—from trees and from boys in trees—explains why the boy may stop others who start to climb trees and why he may call climbing trees "wrong" or "bad." In the same way a man who has observed illegal behavior and the punishment contingent upon it may act to keep himself from such behavior and to prevent others from behaving in the same way. In doing so, he supports governmental control. But it is rare that an individual witnesses both the behavior and the punishment of another person. The effect of the contingency expressed in a law is usually mediated by complex verbal processes, which cannot be fully analyzed here. The law itself is a verbal device, and it is in furthering these intermediate processes that codification of governmental practices helps most. A code supports the verbal behavior which bridges the gap between instances of punishment and the behavior of others. Nevertheless, it is only a slight step toward a recognition of the behavioral processes through which governmental control is usually exerted.

Other Types of Governmental Control. Since governmental agencies have been particularly committed to the use of punishment, the change to other forms of control has been especially slow. Modern governments, however, have it in their power to use other techniques and do so extensively. If wealth is accumulated—through taxation, for example—economic control is then available. This is used as a form of positive reinforcement in subsidies and bonuses. The citizen is thus induced to act legally rather than deterred from acting illegally. Although it is theoretically possible to control agricultural production through punishment by making the cultivation of certain crops illegal, a government with economic power achieves the same effect through positive reinforcement with subsidies. The educational control of legal behavior is another alternative technique. Where it is theoretically possible to induce a soldier to fight entirely through coercion—by arranging matters so that he must fight or be still more severely punished than in battle—a modern government is likely to generate an inclination to fight through educational devices. Variables in the fields of respondent conditioning, motivation, and emotion are arranged to increase a disposition to fight. These practices lead eventually to far more effective behavior than coercion. Unfortunately, educational techniques in the field of government are represented most conspicuously by propaganda, where variables are manipulated for an effect which is concealed or disguised, often in a way which is aversive to many people. But education may be effective even when the result is clearly indicated.

Similar alternative techniques are available in preventing illegal behavior, but the processes are more complicated and are not yet well explored. A start has been made at the level of minor offenses. Motorists are usually induced to obey traffic signals by a familiar process. A certain percentage of those who go through stop signs, for example, are punished. An alternative procedure which has been tried successfully is to commend or otherwise reinforce motorists who obey signs. This is clearly not an adequate technique for all drivers, but it has a measurable effect upon many who might otherwise be only partially controlled by traffic signals. Educational programs which point up the contingencies between reckless driving and its consequences —injury or death—should in the long run be more effective than a program of arrests and fines.

Techniques of Religious Control

The principal technique is an extension of group and governmental control. Behavior is classified, not simply as "good" and "bad" or "legal" and "illegal," but as "moral" and "immoral" or "virtuous" and "sinful." It is then reinforced or punished accordingly. Traditional descriptions of Heaven and Hell epitomize positive and negative reinforcement. The features vary from culture to culture, but it is doubtful whether any well-known positive or negative reinforcer has not been used. To a primitive people who depend upon forest and field for their food, Heaven is a happy hunting ground. To a poverty-stricken people primarily concerned with the source of the next meal, it is a perpetual fish fry. To the unhappy it is relief from pain and sorrow or a reunion with departed friends and loved ones. Hell, on the other hand, is an assemblage of aversive stimuli, which has often been imaginatively portrayed. In Dante's *Inferno*, for example, we find most of the negative reinforcers characteristic of social and nonsocial environments. Only the electric shock of the psychological laboratory is missing.

The reinforcers portrayed in Heaven and Hell are far more powerful than those which support the "good" and "bad" of the ethical group or the "legal" and "illegal" of governmental control, but this advantage is offset to some extent by the fact that they do not actually operate in the lifetime of the individual. The power achieved by the religious agency depends upon how effectively certain verbal reinforcements are conditioned—in particular the promise of Heaven and the threat of Hell. Religious education contributes to this power by pairing these terms with various conditioned and unconditioned reinforcers which are essentially those available to the ethical group and to governmental agencies. The relation between the agency and the communicant, or between God and man, is often made more effective by being characterized as such a familiar mundane relation as that between a father and his sons, a king and his subjects, or a military commander and his men—where again the primary reinforcing contingencies do not differ greatly from those used in ethical and governmental control.

In actual practice a threat to bar from Heaven or to consign to Hell is made contingent upon sinful behavior, while virtuous behavior brings a promise of Heaven or a release from the threat of Hell. The last is a particularly powerful technique. The agency punishes sinful behavior in such a way that it automatically generates an aversive condition which the individual describes as a "sense of sin." The agency then provides escape from this aversive condition through expiation or absolution and is thus able to supply a powerful reinforcement for pious behavior.

Other techniques are, of course, encountered in religious control. Insofar as the agency controls other variables, it can use other processes. It may acquire wealth and operate eventually through *economic* control. It may train and support teachers to achieve *educational* control. It may utilize *ethical* or *governmental* techniques in addition to those within its own sphere. This is especially likely when its controlling practices coincide with those of the group as a whole. In short, all the techniques described under self-control and under personal control are available to the agency possessing the necessary power.

The use of physical restraint by a religious agency is exemplified by actual incarceration, as in the treatment of women in Moslem countries. Relevant environmental conditions are manipulated when the stimuli which elicit or set the occasion for sinful behavior are weakened or removed and when the stimuli which elicit or serve as the occasion for virtuous behavior are pointed up. Suggested regimens of simple fare, unseductive clothing, limited personal contact, and the other features of the cloister or the "sheltered life" follow this pattern. Religious agencies are likely to favor censorship of movies, plays, and books, the enforcement of laws governing modesty of dress, the prohibition of the sale of alcoholic beverages, and so on, because these measures reduce occasions for sinful behavior. Satiation and deprivation are also manipulated. St. Paul defended marriage as a measure which reduces licentious behavior, and periods of fasting and regimens of exercise may be employed for the same effect. Ritualistic techniques which affect the physiology of the organism are common—in Hindu practices, for example. Some religions encourage substitute forms of behavior to reduce sexual or other tendencies; the practice is based upon the transferred satiation. Since emotion is usually an important means of religious control, respondent conditioning is important. Religious art, music, and pageantry generate emotional responses by portraying the suffering of martyrs, the torments of the damned, the tender emotions of the family, and so on. These responses are transferred to stimuli, verbal or nonverbal, which are later used by the agency for purposes of control. Some religious agencies resort to the use of drugs, either to induce appropriate emotional or motivational conditions or to produce effects which seem to support the claim of a supernatural connection.

Educational Reinforcement

The reinforcers used by established educational institutions are familiar: they consist of good grades, promotions, Phi Beta Kappa keys, diplomas, degrees, and medals, all of which are associated with the generalized reinforcer of approval. The spelling bee is a familiar device which makes approval or other social reinforcers explicitly contingent upon scholastic behavior. The same technique is represented by modern quiz programs in which "knowledge is reinforced for its own sake." A certain exchange value is evident when the recently educated individual is offered a job or is automatically admitted to membership in certain controlling groups. The educational agency usually wields no economic power itself, however, except for prizes, fellowships, and scholarships. Some reinforcers may be available in the form of privileges. The institution may also have the support of the family which makes primary or conditioned reinforcers contingent upon a level of scholastic achievement

—for example, by granting a special allowance to the student who maintains a certain average.

The venerable place of punishment in educational control is represented by the birch rod and the cane, as well as by the condoning of certain forms of disciplinary violence—for example, hazings. Extreme forms of physical punishment have now been generally abandoned, but we have noted the general rule that when one aversive consequence is dropped, another is often created to take its place. Just as wages paid on a fixed-interval schedule may eventually be used to supply aversive stimulation in the form of a threat of dismissal, so the teacher of small children who does not spank may nevertheless threaten to withdraw approval or affection in a form of aversive control. In the same way, the positive reinforcers available to schools and colleges are often used as the basis for conditioned aversive stimulation in the form of a threat of failure or dismissal.

By-products of control through punishment have always been conpicuous features of educational institutions. Hell-raisings, riots, hazings, and truancy are forms of counteraggression or escape. Somewhat more neurotic by-products are common. The advantages to be gained in turning to other techniques of control are therefore obvious. But one mode of control cannot be given up until something else is ready to take its place, and there is evidence that the educational institution at the moment lacks adequate control. Not only has the educator relinquished the birch rod; he can no longer borrow discipline from family practices based on aversive control. As more and more people are educated, the honorific reinforcements of education are weakened; fewer special advantages are now contingent upon education. With increasing social security the economic consequences of an education are also less important; relatively fewer students are out to "make good" in amassing wealth or at least in escaping the threat of a destitute old age.

Educational institutions have, therefore, turned to alternative methods of control. The teacher, often unwillingly, uses the sources of power available to him in personal control to make himself or his teaching interesting; in other words, he becomes an entertainer. Textbooks are supplied with pictures and diagrams which resemble expositions of the subject matter in magazines or the press, and lectures are supplemented with demonstrations and "visual aids." Especially favorable circumstances for the execution of the behavior to be controlled by the educational institution are arranged: libraries are designed to make books more readily accessible, laboratories are expanded and improved, facilities are provided for field trips and periods of study in especially favorable locations. Subjects which are not easily adapted to these techniques are often minimized or discarded.

The term "progressive education" roughly describes a concerted effort to find substitutes for the spurious reinforcements of educational control. Consequences of the sort which will eventually govern the behavior of the student are brought into the educational situation. Under the traditional system the student who is reinforced for speaking French correctly by an A is eventually reinforced, if at all, when he enjoys books written in French or communicates effectively in a French-speaking community. In progressive education, these "natural" or "functional" reinforcements are employed by the educational agency as soon as possible. Similarly, the student who is studying science is reinforced as soon as possible by his increasing competence in dealing with nature. By permitting a wider choice of what is to be studied, the probability is increased that scholastic behavior will receive such noneducational reinforcement at an early date. It has perhaps always been characteristic of good education to introduce "real" consequences, but progressive education has made an effort to do this as often and as soon as possible. A common objection has been that certain fields of study are thus unduly emphasized at the expense of others in which disciplinary training with merely educational reinforcement cannot be avoided.

The conditioned reinforcers of the educational agency may be made more effective by pointing up the connection with natural contingencies to be encountered later. By informing the student of the advantages to be gained from education, education itself may be given reinforcing value. Many educational institutions have therefore turned to counseling and various forms of therapy as auxiliary techniques.

CULTURE AND CONTROL

Manners and Customs

In addition to ethical behavior, the individual acquires from the group an extensive repertoire of *manners* and *customs*. What a man eats and drinks and how he does so, what sorts of sexual behavior he engages in, how he builds a house or draws a picture or rows a boat, what subjects he talks about or remains silent about, what music he makes, what kinds of personal relationships he enters into and what kind he avoids—all depend in part upon the practices of the group of which he is a member. The actual manners and customs of many groups have, of course, been extensively described by sociologists and anthropologists. Here we are concerned only with the kinds of processes which they exemplify.

Behavior comes to conform to the standards of a given community when certain responses are reinforced and others are allowed to go unreinforced or are punished. These consequences are often closely interwoven with those of the nonsocial environment. The way in which a man rows a boat, for example, depends in part upon certain mechanical contingencies; some movements are effective and others ineffective in propelling the boat. These contingencies depend upon the construction of the boat and oars—which are in turn the result of other practices observed by the boatmakers in the group. They also depend upon the type of water, which may be peculiar to a group for geographical reasons, so that the manner in which a boat is rowed in an inland lake district is different from that along the seacoast even when boat and oars are of the same type. The educational contingencies established by the group are still another source of difference. The individual is reinforced with approval when he adopts certain grips, postures, kinds of strokes, and so on, and punished with criticism when he adopts others. These variables are especially important in determining the "style" which eventually becomes characteristic of a group.

There remains the fact that the community as a whole often establishes conforming behavior through what are essentially educational techniques. Over and above the reciprocal reinforcements which sustain verbal behavior, for example, the community extends the classification of "right" and "wrong" to certain forms of that behavior and administers the generalized reinforcements of approval and disapproval accordingly. In many groups a mistake in grammar or pronunciation is followed by more aversive consequences than, say, minor instances of lying or stealing. The group also supports educational agencies which supply additional consequences working in the same direction. But why is such deviant behavior aversive? Why should the group call an ungrammatical response "wrong" if the response is not actually ambiguous? Why should it protest unconventional modes of dress or rebuke a member for unconventional table manners?

One classical answer is to show that a given form of deviant behavior must have been aversive for good reason under an earlier condition of the group. Foodstuffs are in general selected by contingencies which follow from their physical and chemical properties. Foods which are unpalatable, inedible, or poisonous come to be left alone. A child who starts to eat such a food receives powerful aversive stimulation from the group. "Good" and "bad" foods are eventually specified in ethical, religious, or governmental codes. When, now, through a change in climate or living conditions, or as the result of changing practices in the preparation and preservation of food, a "bad" food becomes safe, the classification may nevertheless survive. There is no longer any current return advantage to the group to explain why eating a particular food is classified as bad. The classification may be especially puzzling if the group has meanwhile invented an explanation for it.

We may also show indirect, but presumably none the less effective, current consequences. In his *Theory of the Leisure Class*, Thorstein Veblen demonstrated that customs or manners which seemed to have no commensurate consequences, and which were explained in terms of doubtful principles of beauty or taste, had an important effect upon other members of the group. According to Veblen we do not necessarily wear "dress" clothes or speak useless languages because the clothes are beautiful or the languages "cultured," but because we are then accepted by a group in which these achievements are a mark of membership and because we gain prestige in controlling those who are unable to behave in the same way. According to this theory, a modern American university builds Gothic buildings not because the available materials resemble those which were originally responsible for this style of architecture, or because the style is beautiful in itself, but because the university then commands a more extensive control by resembling medieval educational institutions. The practices of the group which perpetuate a "good" style of architecture are thus as easy to explain as those which perpetuate modes of construction which are "good" for mechanical reasons.

Perhaps the simplest explanation of the differential reinforcement of conforming behavior is the process of induction. The forces which shape ethical behavior to group standards are powerful. The group steps in to suppress lying, stealing, physical assault, and so on, because of immediate consequences to its members. Its behavior in so doing is eventually a function of certain characteristic features of the "good" and "bad" behavior of the controlled individual. Among these is lack of conformity to the general behavior of the group. There is thus a frequent association of aversive properties of behavior with the property of nonconformance to a standard. Nonconforming behavior is not always aversive, but aversive behavior is always nonconforming. If these properties are paired often enough, the property of nonconformance becomes aversive. "Right" and "wrong" eventually have the force of "conforming" and "nonconforming." Instances of behavior which are nonconforming but not otherwise aversive to the group are henceforth treated as if they were aversive.

No matter how we ultimately explain the action of the group in extending the ethical classification of "right" and "wrong" to manners and customs, we are on solid ground in observing the contingencies by virtue of which the behavior characteristic of a particular group is maintained. As each individual comes to conform to a standard pattern of conduct, he also comes to support that pattern by applying a similar classification to the behavior of others. Moreover, his own conforming behavior contributes to the standard with which the behavior of others is compared. Once a custom, manner, or style has arisen, therefore, the social system which observes it appears to be reasonably self-sustaining.

selection 40 Behavior, Norms, and Social Rewards in a Dyad

URIEL G. FOA

The relationship between actual behavior and norms has been an object of attention by the social psychologist, the student of personality and also by the therapist. It has been often stressed that harmony between the perceived self and the ideal self is of great relevance to the mental health of the individual. The ideal self is, in essence, a product of the socialization process, shaped by the primary groups in which the individual grows and socializes. Yet the ideal self of childhood may not fit the requirements of other groups encountered later in life. It is indeed recognized that differences in role expectation between members of such small groups as the family or a working team may lead to behavior problems and maladjustment (Rapoport and Rosow, 1957).

According to psychoanalytic theory the ideal self is an introjection of the norms of the socializing agents. Compliance with these norms has been associated with reward since the early childhood period (Dollard and Miller, 1950). It seems, therefore, that the individual becomes conditioned: (a) to associate reward with compliance with the norm of the other; (b) to generalize from the norm of the other to the norm of the self and, therefore; (c) to associate reward with compliance with the norm of the self (Whiting and Child, 1953). Thus compliance with norms seems to be associated with certain rewards in the socialized individual: the reward coming from compliance with his own norm and the reward expected from compliance with the norm of the other. These may be called *social* rewards to distinguish them from other kinds of rewards such as those based on the satisfaction of biological needs.

Later, when the individual comes in contact with other groups and acquires new roles, he is likely to discover that the norm of the other is

From *Behavioral Science*, 1958, **3**, 323–334. Reprinted by permission of the author and *Behavioral Science*. This paper is an outgrowth of a program of research in interpersonal relations in industry, supported in part by the Ford Foundation.

sometimes different from his own. Then he has to choose between losing the reward associated with compliance with his own norm or losing the reward asociated with compliance with the norm of the other. One of the possible ways for solving the conflict is through imitation (Dollard and Miller, 1950), i.e., the individual may choose the same solution which appears to be also chosen by the other.

The foregoing discussion of the relationship between behavior, norms and associated social rewards is relatively simple since it refers to the situation as perceived by one individual. Truly enough this individual has an image of the perception of behavior and of the norm of the other. Nevertheless the perception of the other, of the same situation, may be different. In order to obtain a complete view both pictures of the situation should be considered and compared. This is precisely what our formal model attempts to do. The model is concerned with the relationship between norm and actual behavior. The assumption that compliance with norm is associated with social rewards is not essential to the formal development of the model. But, if such assumption is accepted, the model can be viewed as a system for the production and distribution of social rewards in the dyadic relationship. We turn now to the description of the model.

Let us consider two interacting individuals, a dyad. Each one of the two persons of the dyad may be regarded as performing three kinds of functions as follows:

1. acting, i.e., being an *actor*;
2. perceiving behavior (of himself or of the other), i.e., being an *observer*;
3. being ascribed a certain perception, i.e., being an *alias*.

These three functions take place on two different levels: the actual and the normative.

Each person can be actor, observer, and alias. In a dyad there are, therefore, two actors, two observers, and two aliases. The observer is a potential informer for the researcher. A given act is perceived by the two observers (the actor himself and the other) and ascribed, by each observer, to each one of the two aliases (the alias of the observer himself and that of the other). Through ascription to the other, the observer obtains a picture of the behavior of the actor, as apparently perceived by the other observer.

Ascription consists in assigning the perceived stimulus to a given type of behavior. It is assumed that types of behavior are exhaustive and mutually exclusive. That is, for every ascription there always exists one type of behavior, and one only, to which the stimulus can be assigned. An example of the construction of a list of types of behavior, appropriate for wide classes of social psychological problems, has been given in an earlier paper (Foa, 1955).

Two given ascriptions may or may not be assigned to the same type of behavior. This identification of two ascriptions with the same or different types of behavior may be relevant in certain cases or for certain research purposes, and irrelevant in certain other cases, or for other research purposes. For the purpose of the present model it is relevant to know whether an actual action by a given actor, perceived by a given observer, and ascribed to a given alias, does or does not belong to the same type of behavior as the corresponding norm. That is, two ascriptions are said to be *relevant* to each other when their levels are different (one actual and one normative), but the actor, observer and alias are the same. Otherwise, the two ascriptions are said to be *irrelevant*.

Two relevant ascriptions are in a state of *consonance* when they belong to the same type of behavior. Otherwise they are in a state of *dissonance*. It is assumed that an action is rewarding when it is consonant with the norm and not rewarding when it is dissonant with it. This way of comparing the behavior types of different ascriptions may be regarded as a special case of Festinger's Theory of Dissonance (1957). A clear definition of "relevance" for this special case has been provided above.

CLASSIFICATION OF STATES

We shall use valence as a generic term for consonance and dissonance. Thus any pair of relevant ascriptions has a valence. A valence is characterized by a given actor, a given observer and a given alias. Consonant valence indicates reward; dissonant valence lack of reward. The reward specified by the valence is produced by the actor, received by the observer and attributed to the alias. For example, the valence for actor 1, observer 2, alias 2, indicates the reward that observer 2 attributes to himself from the action of actor 1. The valence for actor 1, observer 2, alias 1 indicates the reward that observer 2, attributes to the other for his own action. It has been indeed suggested that an individual gives reward to himself when he behaves according to his own norm and gives reward to the other when he behaves according to the norm of the other.

Let us consider the two valences for a given actor, a given observer and the two aliases. These two valences indicate how the reward produced by the actor and received by the observer is distributed between the two aliases. There are four mutually exclusive possibilities (see Table 1):

TABLE 1 STATES OF A GIVEN OBSERVER FOR A GIVEN ACTOR

State	Description	Valence For Actor	Valence For Non-actor
C	Consonant	+	+
D	Dissonant	−	−
A	Actor—consonant	+	−
O	Other (non-actor)—consonant	—	+

Note. Consonance is indicated by +, dissonance by −.

1. The observer perceives the action as consonant with both the norm of the actor and the norm he ascribes to the non-actor. This is the consonant, or *C* state. The action is seen as rewarding for both the actor and the non-actor.

2. The observer perceives the action as dissonant with the norm of the actor as well as with that of the non-actor. This is the dissonant, or *D* state. The action is not seen as rewarding neither for the actor, nor for the non-actor.

3. The observer perceives the action as consonant with the norm of the actor and dissonant with that of the non-actor. This is the actor-consonant, or *A* state. The action is seen as rewarding for the actor and not rewarding for the non-actor.

4. The observer perceives the action as dissonant with the norm of the actor and consonant with that of the non-actor. This is the other-consonant, or *O* state. The action is seen as not rewarding for the actor and rewarding for the non-actor.

Each one of these four states describes the valences of the two aliases as seen by a given observer with reference to a given actor. The first two states are *homovalent*: the same valence is attributed to the two aliases. The last two states are *heterovalent*: a different valence is attributed to the two aliases. Homovalence indicates that the reward produced by the actor and received by the observer is equally distributed between the two aliases. Heterovalence indicates that, either because of differences in the ascribed perceptions of the action, or because of differences in the ascribed norms, or for both reasons, the action cannot produce reward for both aliases; reward for one person leads to lack of reward for the other. There exists, in heterovalent states, a problem of choice between the two rewards. In homovalent states the identity between the norm of the self and the norm of the other, established during childhood training, is maintained. In heterovalent states the individual is faced with a new conflicting situation.

Each state is characterized by a given actor and a given observer. In a dyad there are two actors and two observers and this makes a total of four (2×2) states. Namely: state for actor 1 and observer 1; state for actor 2 and observer 1; state for actor 1 and observer 2; state for actor 2 and observer 2. State for actor 1 and observer 1 and state for actor 2 and observer 1 constitute the *intrapersonal subsystem* of observer 1. The other two states constitute the intrapersonal subsystem of observer 2.

State for actor 1 and observer 1 and state for actor 1 and observer 2 constitute the *interpersonal subsystem* for actor 1. The other two states constitute the interpersonal subsystem for actor 2.

The Intrapersonal Subsystem

The intrapersonal subsystem of a given observer gives a picture of the production and distribution of rewards of the dyadic system as seen by this observer. The rewards produced by the two actors of the subsystem are distributed by the observer between the two aliases. The states of the subsystem indicate the amount of reward received by each alias and its source. These states, and the corresponding pattern of valences are listed in table 2.

Table 2 shows whether the conflict between rewarding the self and rewarding the other is present for both, neither, or one actor only. When both states of the subsystem are homovalent there is no conflict for either actor. This happens in states *CC*, *DD*, *CD*, and *DC*. When both states are heterovalent the conflict occurs for both actors (states *AA*, *OO*, *AO*, and *OA*). In all the other cases one state is homovalent and the other heterovalent and the conflict occurs for the actor in the heterovalent state only.

Table 2 also indicates whether or not the relationship between rewarding the other and being rewarded by him is preserved. In order to

TABLE 2 THE INTRAPERSONAL SUBSYSTEM OF OBSERVER 1

State		Valence Pattern			
		For Actor 1		For Actor 2	
For Actor 1	For Actor 2	Alias 1	Alias 2	Alias 1	Alias 2
C	*C*	+	+	+	+
D	*D*	−	−	−	−
C	*D*	+	+	−	−
D	*C*	−	−	+	+
A	*A*	+	−	−	+
O	*O*	−	+	+	−
A	*O*	+	−	+	−
O	*A*	−	+	−	+
C	*A*	+	+	−	+
C	*O*	+	+	+	−
D	*A*	−	−	−	+
D	*O*	−	−	+	−
A	*C*	+	−	+	+
A	*D*	+	−	−	−
O	*C*	−	+	+	+
O	*D*	−	+	−	−

know this we need to observe the fourth and fifth columns of the table. When the two entries of these columns are of the same sign the relationship is preserved, otherwise it is not preserved. The relationship exists, for example, in state *CC*: here observer 1 perceives that his own action is rewarding for the alias of 2. At the same time the action of 2 is perceived as rewarding for the alias of 1. In state *DD* the relationship likewise exists, albeit in negative form: the observer perceives that his own action is not rewarding for the other and the action of the other is not rewarding for him. Also in states *AA*, *OO*, *CO*, *DA*, *AD*, and *OC* the relationship is found to exist. When there is conflict and it is solved in the same manner for both actors (states *AA* and *OO*) the relationship between reward given and reward obtained is preserved. In the first six states of Table 2 either there is no conflict for either actor or it is solved in the same manner for both actors. In all these cases the total reward attributed to one alias is equal to the total reward attributed to the other alias. In state *CC* both aliases are rewarded by both actors. In state *DD* neither alias is rewarded by either actor. In state *CD* both aliases are rewarded by actor 1 only. In state *DC* both aliases are rewarded by actor 2 only. In state *AA* each alias is rewarded by his own actor. In state *OO* each alias is rewarded by the other actor.

These states will be called *balanced.* In all the other ten states the total reward received by one alias is different from the total reward received by the other alias. These states will be called *unbalanced.*

In conclusion the intrapersonal subsystem is balanced when both its states are either homovalent or both are heterovalent *and* equal.

The Interpersonal Subsystem

We turn now to the interpersonal subsystem for a given actor. This is the subsystem formed by the states of both observers for a given actor. The 16 possible combinations of states of this subsystem are given in Table 3. Let us consider the state of observer 1. We know already that this state indicated whether this observer does or does not perceive a conflict between rewarding himself (alias 1) and rewarding the other (alias 2). In order to know whether the conflict really exists one needs to compare the valence of observer 1 for alias 1 with the valence of observer 2 for alias 2. When these two valences are different, then the conflict really exists. Otherwise it may be merely perceived by observer 1. Indeed the valence of observer 1 for alias 2 is nothing but the image that this observer has of the reward of the other.

This comparison between the existence of the conflict and its perception by a given observer suggests four classes of states for this observer:

1. The conflict exists and is not perceived. This is the class of projection or *P* class: the observer projects on the alias of the other his own valence and fails to judge correctly the valence of the other. For example, in state *CD* of Table 3, the valence that observer 1 attributes to the alias of 2 (column *6*) is positive and identical with the valence that this same observer attributes to his own alias (column *5*), but different from the valence that observer 2 attributes to his own alias (column *8*). In consequence the valence of column *5* is different from the valence of column *8*, i.e., the conflict really exists. Likewise the valence that observer 2 attributes to the alias of 1 (column *7*) is equal to the valence that the same observer attributes to his own alias (column *8*). Thus in state *CD* both observers are in the *P* class, i.e., both observers fail to perceive the existing conflict.

2. The conflict exists and is perceived. The observer judges correctly the valence of the other which is different from his own. This is the *empathic* or *E* class. In state *AA*, for example, both observers are in the empathic class.

TABLE 3 THE INTERPERSONAL SUBSYSTEM FOR ACTOR 1

State and Class				Valence Pattern			
Of Observer 1		Of Observer 2		Of Observer 1		Of Observer 2	
State (1)	Class (2)	State (3)	Class (4)	For Alias 1 (5)	For Alias 2 (6)	For Alias 1 (7)	For Alias 2 (8)
C	*B*	*C*	*B*	+	+	+	+
D	*B*	*D*	*B*	−	−	−	−
C	*P*	*D*	*P*	+	+	−	−
D	*P*	*C*	*P*	−	−	+	+
A	*E*	*A*	*E*	+	−	+	−
O	*E*	*O*	*E*	−	+	−	+
A	*R*	*O*	*R*	+	−	−	+
O	*R*	*A*	*R*	−	+	+	−
C	*B*	*O*	*R*	+	+	−	+
D	*B*	*A*	*R*	−	−	+	−
O	*E*	*C*	*P*	−	+	+	+
A	*E*	*D*	*P*	+	−	−	−
O	*R*	*D*	*B*	−	+	−	−
A	*R*	*C*	*B*	+	−	+	+
D	*P*	*O*	*E*	−	−	−	+
C	*P*	*A*	*E*	+	+	+	−

3. The conflict neither exists nor is perceived. The valence attributed to the alias of the other is equal to both the valence of the alias of the self and the valence attributed by other observer to his own alias. Here one has *both* empathy and projection, or the *B* class. This happens, e.g., in state *CC* for both observers.

4. The conflict does not exist but is perceived. The valence attributed to the other is different from both the valence of the self and the valence of the other. The last two valences are, of course, equal. This is the class of *rejection* or *R* class.

When there is no real conflict the valences of the two observers for their respective aliases (columns *5* and *8*) are identical and each observer can be in either class *B* or class *R*. This will be called the *similarity condition.* When there is conflict the valences of columns *5* and *8* are different and each observer is either in class *P* or in class *E*. This will be called the *dissimilarity condition.* It follows that when one observer is either in class *P* or class *E*, the other observer must also be in one of these two classes. When one observer is in class *B* or in class *R*, the other observer must also be in one of these two classes. Similarity or dissimilarity, i.e., the absence or presence of real conflict in the distribution of rewards, applies equally well to both observers.

The class of one observer does not depend on the specific state of this observer alone, but also on the state of the other observer. In particular the following necessary relationships between states and classes exist:

1. When the states of both observers are homovalent and identical (*CC* or *DD*), both observers are in the projective-empathic class.
2. When the states of the two observers are homovalent but different (*CD* or *DC*), both observers are in the projective class.
3. When the states of the two observers are heterovalent and alike (*AA* or *OO*), both observers are in the empathic class.
4. When the states of the two observers are heterovalent and different (*AO* or *OA*), both observers are in the rejective class.

An interpersonal subsystem is *balanced* when the states of both observers are either homovalent or heterovalent. Otherwise the subsystem is *unbalanced.* The eight states mentioned above appear in the upper half of Table 2, and are all balanced. In these states both observers belong to the same class. Therefore:

Theorem. *When the interpersonal subsystem is balanced, the two observers belong to the same class. When the subsystem is unbalanced, the two observers belong to a different class. In unbalanced subsystems when one observer is in the empathic class the other must be in the projective class. When one observer is in the rejective class the other must be in the empathic-projective class.*

Let us disregard the fact that empathy may or may not be accompanied by projection, depending on the presence or absence of a real conflict in the distribution of reward. Then the states of the two observers, for a given actor, are balanced when either both observers or neither are empathizing. In the first case, the balance is achieved, so to speak, through good communication on both sides. In the second case, it is precisely the lack of communication that produces balance: each observer perceives his own social "reality" with little regard for the perception of the other.

On the other hand, when only one observer empathizes neither isolation nor full mutual understanding is possible: the symmetric balance is broken. If one of the two observers is a better empathizer than the other (for example, he might be the leader of the dyad), one cannot expect balance in this particular subsystem. However, it seems possible that the leader might use his superior judgment of the interpersonal situation in order to manipulate it, i.e., strive toward a given balanced state.

The Psychological Meaning of Balance

An *intrapersonal* subsystem has been defined as balanced when both its states are either homovalent or heterovalent and equal. An *interpersonal* subsystem has been said to be balanced when both its states are either homovalent or heterovalent.

The dyadic system will be said to be balanced when all its subsystems are balanced. We may also agree that a state will be called balanced when its two valences are equal, i.e., when the state is homovalent.

All these definitions of balance rest on formal properties of the system. Yet they reveal clear-cut psychological differences between balance and imbalance. These differences can be summarized as follows:

1. In the state for a given observer and actor, balance or homovalence, indicated lack of conflict between self reward for the acting person and reward for the other person.
2. In the intrapersonal subsystem balance refers to the distribution of rewards between the two aliases. When the subsystem is balanced both aliases receive the same amount of reward. When the subsystem is unbalanced one alias is rewarded more than the other.
3. In the interpersonal subsystem balance refers to the communication between the two observers. When the subsystem is balanced the communication from observer 1 to observer 2 is equally good as the communication from observer 2 to observer 1. Either each observer judges correctly the perception of the other, or both misjudge it. Imbalance indicates that while one observer empathizes with the other, the other does not empathize with him.

In the whole system balance refers both to distribution of rewards and to communication. When the whole system is balanced there exists a necessary relationship between the classes of the two observers relative to both actors and their respective perception of the distribution of rewards. In particular:

1. When both observers are in the empathic (or empathic-projective) class, with respect to both actors, their respective perceptions of the distribution of rewards are balanced and alike.
2. When neither observer is in the empathic (or empathic-projective) class, with respect to both actors, the respective perceptions of the distributions of rewards are balanced but different.

Mutual empathy is therefore a necessary and sufficient condition for the two observers to have the same perception of reward and distribution. Lack of empathy, on both sides, is a necessary and sufficient condition for the two observers to have different perceptions of the reward distribution.

The formal concept of balance used in this paper is somewhat more restricted than the concept developed by Cartwright and Harary (1956), following certain hypotheses of Heider (1946), and Newcomb (1953). The reason for adopting here more restricted definition of balance may be found in the fact that our system extends over three dimensions: actor, observer, and alias. Each subsystem covers two of these dimensions. A given valence in a certain subspace does not necessarily balance an equal valence in another subspace.

HYPOTHESES

There are four possible states for each observer and for a given actor. This makes 16 states for each observer and both actors, and $16 \times 16 = 256$ states for the dyad as a whole. The purpose of empirical hypotheses is to predict which states are more likely to appear in practice and which are less likely. To put it differently, we are concerned here with the possible relationship between the state of one observer for a given actor and that of the same observer for the other actor; between the state of one observer for a given actor and that of the other observer for the same actor, etc. It is evident that, if these states are interdependent, the frequencies of the 256 possible states will vary and some states may not appear at all.

The General Balance Hypothesis

Newcomb (1953) and Heider (1946) have suggested that systems tend toward a balanced state. This might be interpreted to indicate that, in a given population of systems, it can be expected that the frequency of the balanced states will be higher than that of the unbalanced states. This general hypothesis, in terms of the present model, suggests the following two specific hypotheses:

1. A person tends to perceive that he and the other get the same amount of reward for their relationship (balanced intrapersonal subsystem).
2. A person tends to judge correctly the rewards perceived by the other to the extent that the other succeeds in judging correctly the rewards perceived by him (balanced interpersonal subsystem).

If these predictions should prove true, it will be necessary to explain the transition from balanced to unbalanced states, and vice versa. One possible explanation is that the system may move from an unbalanced state to a balanced state (or to another unbalanced state), but not vice versa: Once the system is balanced it does not return to an unbalanced state. Thus the unbalanced state would be identical with the transient state of the mathematicians (Feller, 1950). The balanced state would operate something like a trap: one can get into it, but he cannot get back to the unbalanced state again. If this explanation is accepted, one would predict that the frequency of balanced states will increase with the age of the system: the longer the system has been in existence, the higher the frequency of balanced states.

An alternative explanation is as follows: unbalanced states are states of passage from one balanced state to another. The system, in order to move from one balanced state to another, must pass through an unbalanced state. Moving to an unbalanced state is somewhat like getting into an automobile in order to reach a different place. Some formal support for this hypothesis is found in the valence pattern of Table 3. Consider the pattern of any balanced state; it is evident that if one, and only one, of the valences changes, the pattern becomes unbalanced. Vice versa, any single change of valence in an unbalanced pattern makes it balanced. According to this explanation, therefore, going into an unbalanced state is a necessary intermediate step toward a different balanced state. The identification of imbalance with state of change suggests that interpersonal subsystems are more likely to be unbalanced under conditions of dissimilarity than under conditions of similarity; imbalance seems more likely when there is a real conflict between the rewards that the two observers attribute to their respective aliases.

Thus one might formulate the following:

Hypothesis: *In interpersonal subsystems, states of balance are associated with similarity, and states of unbalance with dissimilarity.*

Under conditions of dissimilarity the possible classes of the two observers are *P* and *E*, the projective and the empathic. The state is unbalanced when the class combinations of the two observers are *PE* or *EP*. If the two observers are in the same class (*PP* or *EE*), the state is balanced. Now, under conditions of dissimilarity and unbalance, which observer will more likely be in the *E* class and which one in the *P* class? It is proposed that the one of the two observers, who is also the actor, is more likely to be in the *E* class than the other observer. Being in this class enables the actor-observer to ascribe correctly the valence of the other, which is a prerequisite of any attempt to change this valence. One possible way of changing it is through behavior. Thus the actor, in order to decide which behavior is required to change the valence of the other, must be in the empathic class, i.e., he must know the present valence of the other. Therefore, it seems possible to suggest the following:

Hypothesis: *In interpersonal subsystems, the frequency of the class combination* EP *is higher than that of the combination* PE (*as usual, the first letter indicates the class of the actor, and the second that of the non-actor*).

This hypothesis seems to contrast with earlier findings showing that ego-involvement hampers empathy (Foa, 1957b; Nagle, 1954). It should be noted, however, that empathy as discussed here refers neither to perception of behavior nor to the norm, but to the *relationship* between them. Although ego-involvement may produce misjudgment of the behavioral perception of the other and/or of this norm, it does not necessarily follow that it should also cause misjudgment of the valence between perception of behavior and the norm. Mistakes in judging perception and the norm might cancel out each other and result in a correct judgment of the relationship between them.

The Dissonance Hypothesis

Festinger (1957) has suggested that dissonance is associated with pressure to reduce or eliminate such dissonance. In our system dissonance between perception of action and norm is identical with lack of reward. Thus Festinger's hypothesis would indicate that a behavior perceived as producing an increase of reward is more likely to occur than a behavior producing a perceived decrease.

On the other hand, it might be supposed that a relationship is more likely to continue the larger the amount of reward it produces. The relationship will tend to cease when the system is characterized by a large number of dissonances, i.e., by little or no reward. In summary: either the dissonance will change to consonance or the relationship will tend to terminate. In both cases it may be expected that:

Hypothesis: *In a population of dyads the frequency of the state of each subsystem is inversely related to the number of its dissonances.*

This hypothesis is in agreement with the principle of modern behavior theory that a given behavior tends to cease unless it is rewarded.

The Actor Hypothesis

It is suggested that, in heterovalent states, consonance will tend to be associated with the observer's own behavior more than with the behavior of the other. This is more or less equivalent to saying that one is more likely to follow the behavior that gives reward to him than the behavior that rewards the other.

PROCEDURE

A group of 361 factory workers and their respective 51 foremen were administered the Test of the Foreman-Worker Relationship (Foa, 1957a). This test consists of two sets of picture stories, with eight stories in each set. One set refers to the behavior of the foreman, and the other set to that of the worker. Foremen and workers alike were requested to complete each story by choosing an appropriate picture from four alternatives. Respondents were requested to indicate both the picture which depicts what usually happens in practice in their department, and the picture which shows what ought to happen in ideal conditions. Thus for each respondent four sets of eight responses each were obtained, referring respectively to the actual behavior of the worker, the actual behavior of the foreman, the ideal behavior of the worker, and the ideal behavior of the foreman.

Furthermore, each worker was asked to guess the responses of his foreman, while the foreman was asked to guess the modal responses of his workers.

The valence of a given respondent for each story was determined by observing whether the response at the actual level was the same as or different from the corresponding response at the normative level. Thus eight valences were obtained for each set of eight stories. Obviously there were three possibilities: (a) the frequency of consonances was higher than that of dissonances; (b) the frequency of dissonances was higher than that of consonances; (c) the two frequencies were equal (four consonances and four dissonances).

In the first two cases the valence with the modal frequency was accepted as the prevailing valence of the respondent. In the third case the prevailing valence was said to be uncertain. Further, for the respondents with a prevailing valence, the state of each respondent was determined by observing the prevailing valence of the responses he ascribed to himself and the prevailing valence of those he ascribed to the other. This determined the prevailing state of the respondent for the behavior of the actor to whom the set of stories referred. The respondents with at least one uncertain valence were said to be in an uncertain state.

This procedure established the prevailing or modal state for each respondent. It would have been possible, instead, to find the frequency distribution of the various states for each respondent. It was felt, however, that because of the

TABLE 4 PERCENTAGE OF BALANCED STATES BY "AGE" OF DYAD

Subsystem	Percentage of Balanced States for Various "Ages" of Dyad				
	Less than One Year	1–1½ Years	1½–3 Years	More than 3 Years	All Ages
	%	%	%	%	%
1	78	52	75	66	72
2	100	100	99	66	82
a	63	75	73	64	70
b	33	55	54	50	51

preliminary nature of the present analysis and in view of the relatively small number of cases, a full analysis of the frequency distribution would have been premature. Respondents of uncertain state are not included in the present analysis.

RESULTS[1]

In presenting the results, the states of the *worker*, relative to both his own behavior and that of the foreman will be referred to as *subsystem 1* or the intrapersonal subsystem of the worker. The states of the foreman relative to both his own behavior and that of the worker will be referred to as *subsystem 2*, or the intrapersonal subsystem of the foreman.

The states of both the worker and the foreman relative to the behavior of the *worker* will be referred to as *subsystem a*, or the interpersonal subsystem for the worker's behavior. The states of both the worker and the foreman relative to the behavior of the *foreman* will be referred to as *subsystem b*, or the interpersonal subsystem relative to the behavior of the foreman.

The General Balance Hypothesis

In each one of the four subsystems the frequency of the balanced states is always higher than that of the unbalanced states. In subsystem b, however, the two frequencies are almost identical (see Table 4).

The breakdown by "age" of the dyad shows that:

1. Dyads in the first year of existence have a relatively high intrapersonal balance (subsystems 1 and 2) and a relatively low interpersonal balance (subsystems a and b).
2. Dyads in the second and third years of existence have a higher interpersonal balance and a lower intrapersonal balance.
3. Dyads older than three years show a certain downward trend in balance in all four subsystems.

The small number of cases in each cell makes these results highly tentative. They seem to indicate, however, that balance does not tend to increase with time, and therefore do not support the hypothesis that unbalanced states are transient states.

Relationship Between Balance and Similarity

In the two interpersonal subsystems, a and b, the frequency of the balanced states is significantly higher under conditions of similarity than under conditions of dissimilarity (see Table 5).

TABLE 5 PERCENTAGE OF BALANCED STATES FOR DIFFERENT CONDITIONS OF SIMILARITY

Condition	Percentage Frequency of Balanced States	
	Subsystem a	Subsystem b
Similarity	76	81
Dissimilarity	52	32

These results sustain the hypothesis relative to the existence of a positive relationship between balance and similarity. Conditions of similarity are more frequent for the behavior of the worker (75 per cent of the cases) than for that of the foreman (37 per cent of the cases).

[1] All the differences reported as significant are significant at the 1 per cent level at least. Actually almost all the differences are significant at the .01 per cent level. The chi-square test was used.

Relative Frequency of the *EP* and *PE* Classes

In subsystem a the frequency of the *EP* class is almost four times that of the *PE* class. In subsystem b the frequency of the *EP* class is more than twice that of the *PE* class. These significant differences seem to sustain the hypothesis that, under conditions of dissimilarity and imbalance, the actor is more likely to be in the *E* class than is the non-actor.

The Dissonance Hypothesis

Table 6 shows that in all of the subsystems except for subsystem b, the frequency of each state is inversely related to the number of its dissonances. This relationship is particularly clear-cut in subsystem 1 and a. In subsystem b the relationship does not appear. A possible explanation is suggested by the intermediate position of the foreman in the social structure of the factory. The behavior of the foreman is influenced not only by the needs of his relationship with the worker but also by his contact with management.

TABLE 6 PERCENTAGE FREQUENCY OF STATES WITH A GIVEN NUMBER OF DISSONANCES

Number of Dissonances	Frequency in Subsystem 1	2	a	b
0	54	82	53	25
1	20	18	25	43
2	14	—	15	25
3	7	—	4	7
4	5	—	3	—
All states	100	100	100	100
Absolute frequency	151	23	159	159

Note. The difference between the absolute frequencies given above and the total number of workers and foremen gives the number of cases, in each subsystem, for which there was no prevailing state for at least one of the two states of the subsystem.

In general the results reported in Table 5 seem to sustain the hypothesis that dissonance either changes to consonance or tends to produce a discontinuance of the relationship. In other terms: the likelihood of a dyad to continue is positively related to the amount of reward it produces.

Actor Hypothesis

According to this hypothesis the frequency of state *A* should be higher than that of state *O*, and especially so for the foreman's behavior. The data do not sustain this hypothesis. They suggest instead that the relative frequency of states *A* and *O* is related to the observer rather than to the actor. In the worker the frequency of state *A* (for the behavior of the worker and the foreman combined) is two-and-a-half times the frequency of state *O*. In the foreman on the contrary, the frequency of state *O* is double that of state *A*. These differences are highly significant. Thus the manner of distribution of the perceived rewards seems to be a characteristic of the observer rather than of the actor.

The main findings may be summarized as follows:

1. Both the intrapersonal and the interpersonal subsystems tend to be balanced. That is (a) Each member of the dyad tends to perceive that he and the other get the same amount of reward from the relationship; and (b) Each member of the dyad tends to judge correctly the rewards perceived by the other to the extent that the other succeeds in judging correctly the rewards perceived by him.

2. The frequency of the balanced states does not increase with the age of the relationship. This finding supports the hypothesis that imbalance is a state of transition from one balanced state to another.

3. In the interpersonal subsystem balance is positively related to similarity; imbalance to dissimilarity. This finding suggests that the interpersonal subsystem is more likely to be unbalanced, or in the process of changing, when the reward perceived by one observer is different from the reward perceived by the other observer with regard to the same action.

4. Under conditions of dissimilarity and imbalance the actor is more likely to be in the empathic class than the non-actor. That is: each one of the two persons of the dyad is more likely to judge correctly the reward received by the other when the reward is produced by the behavior of this same person than when it is produced by the behavior of the other person.

5. The frequency of a given state of a subsystem tends to be inversely related to the number of its dissonances. This finding suggests that a dyadic relationship is more likely to continue the larger the amount of reward it produces.

6. The relative frequency of states *A* and *O* is related to the observer rather than to the actor. This finding suggests that the way of solving the conflict between rewarding the self and rewarding

of the other is related to the perception of behavior rather than to behavior in itself.

DISCUSSION: TOWARD A STOCHASTIC THEORY

The empirical results seem to suggest the existence of three main tendencies in the model:

1. A tendency toward balancing rewards both intra- and interpersonally.
2. A tendency of the actor to choose the behavior that will improve communication of reward, that is the behavior that will be perceived by the other in the same way as it is perceived by the actor.
3. A tendency to choose the behavior which is perceived as associated with reward rather than the behavior perceived as nonassociated with reward.

If the choice of future behavior will be determined by these tendencies, it seems that findings are suggestive of new hypotheses concerning the probabilities of transition from one given state to another. This may provide a contribution toward a stochastic theory of interpersonal behavior.

In order to formulate these new hypotheses, let us assume that the operation of moving from one state to another consists in changing the sign of one of the valences of the state, and of one valence only.

It then follows immediately that:

1. There is zero probability of moving from a balanced state to another balanced state, and from an unbalanced state to another unbalanced state.

The findings on the frequencies of balanced and unbalanced states suggest that:

2. The probability of being in a balanced state is higher than that of being in an unbalanced state.

The findings relative to the relationship between balance and similarity suggest that:

3. Under conditions of similarity an unbalanced state has a relatively high probability of moving to a balanced state.

4. Under conditions of dissimilarity a balanced state has a relatively high probability of moving to an unbalanced state.

The findings relative to the relationship between the number of dissonances of the state and its frequency suggest that:

5. A valence change from dissonance to consonance is more probable than one from consonance to dissonance.

The findings relative to the relationship between the *E* class and the actor suggest that:

6. In a move from a balanced to an unbalanced state a change in the valence of the actor is more probable than a change in the valence of the nonactor. Further: a change in the valence attributed to the other (the non-observer) is more probable than a change in the valence attributed to the self (the observer).

7. In a move from an unbalanced to a balanced state a change in the valence of the non-actor is more probable than a change in the valence of the actor. Further: a change in the valence attributed to the self is more probable than a change in the valence attributed to the other.

While the above hypotheses, as they stand, lend themselves to experimental verification, it seems that further conceptual work is required in order to integrate them into a stochastic theory of interpersonal behavior.

REFERENCES

Cartwright, D., and Harary, F., 1956. Structural balance: A generalization of Heider's theory. *Psychological Review*, **63**, 277–293.

Dollard, J., and Miller, N. E., 1950. *Personality and psychotherapy*. New York: McGraw-Hill, pp. 38, 92.

Feller, W., 1950. *An introduction to probability theory and its applications*. New York: Wiley, p. 323.

Festinger, L., 1957. *An introduction to the theory of dissonance*. New York: Harper and Row.

Foa, U. G., 1955. The foreman-worker interaction: A research design. *Sociometry*, **18**, 226–244.

Foa, U. G., 1957a. A test of the foreman-worker relationship. *Personnel Psychology*, **9**, 469–486.

Foa, U. G., 1957b. Relation of worker's expectation to satisfaction with supervisor. *Personnel Psychology*, **10**, 161–168.

Heider, F., 1946. Attitudes and cognitive organization. *Journal of Psychology*, **21**, 107–112.

Nagle, B. F., 1954. Productivity, employee attitude and supervisor sensitivity. *Personnel Psychology*, **7**, 219–233.
Newcomb, T. M., 1953. An approach to the study of communicative acts. *Psychological Review*, **60**, 393–404.
Rapoport, Rhona, and Rosow, I., 1957. An approach to family relationships and role performance. *Human Relations*, **10**, 209–221.
Whiting, J. W. M., and Child, I. L., 1953. *Child training and personality*. New Haven, Conn.: Yale University Press, p. 241.

selection 41 Instrumental Role Expectations and Posthospital Performance of Female Mental Patients

SIMON DINITZ, SHIRLEY ANGRIST, MARK LEFTON, AND BENJAMIN PASAMANICK

This paper attempts to test the proposition, derived in part from role theory, that the behavior of former mental patients tends to be consistent with the expectations of their significant others (Sarbin, 1954; Merton, 1957; Gross, Mason, and McEachern, 1958). This proposition consists of two assumptions. First, in any reciprocal relationship each of the actors adjusts his performance to the perceived expectations of the other. Were this not so, there would cease to be any rationale for the continuation of the relationship and behavior would become idiosyncratic. Second, the expectations of others are founded not only on common and shared experiences with the actor but on the ability of the actor to perform his role (Gullahorn and Gullahorn, 1959). Since this ability may at times be impaired to a greater or lesser extent, the expectations of others with regard to the performance of the patient should continually be in a limited state of flux. That is, it is possible for the significant others to expect more or less of the actor over time and within limits. In short, the assumption here is that not only does performance tend to measure up to expectations but conversely, expectations also tend to reflect performance. In these reciprocal relations between actor and significant others it is therefore impossible to specify which of the two variables —expectations and performance—is independent and which dependent.

From *Social Forces*, 1962, **40**, 248–254. Reprinted by permission of the authors and the University of North Carolina Press. The research was supported by a grant from the National Institute of Mental Health.

Granting, for the moment, the validity of these assumptions, certain hypotheses with regard to the posthospital functioning of former mental patients can be derived and tested. These are:

1. There is a positive relationship between the expectations of significant others and the posthospital functioning of patients. The higher the expectations of significant others, the better the performance of the patients.
2. The self-expectations for performance of the patients are also positively related to their actual performance as reported by the significant others. Again, it is not possible to specify which is cause and which effect. The likelihood is that the expectations of the patient reflect previous performance rather than the reverse.
3. Agreement on role expectations between patient and significant other is positively related to high posthospital performance and disagreement to poor performance.

There is still another facet to this problem of the relationship between expectations and performance which requires explanation. This aspect concerns the relationship between prehospital and hospital psychiatric and social factors and posthospital expectations for performance.

With regard to this latter aspect it was hypothesized that the expectations of significant others would have been affected by the length, severity and type of illness of the patient prior to and during hospitalization. The more severe the impairment, the lower the expectations for performance. Severe previous disability, it was thought, would carry over into lower expectations even after discharge.

Again, regardless of the degree of patient disability prior to and during hospitalization, social class variables would have an important bearing on expectations. The higher the socioeconomic status of the patient and significant other, the higher the expectations for posthospital performance. Lastly, expectations for performance are viewed as varying with the necessity for performance. To the extent that the significant other is able to rely upon himself or others to perform the functions normally associated with the patient's role, there is less reason to expect the former patient to do so. Therefore, it is suggested that expectations vary inversely with the availability of role replacements and directly with the necessity for performance.

METHOD

In the period, December, 1958 through June, 1959, a total of 376 female patients were released from the Columbus Psychiatric Institute and Hospital, a short-term, heavily staffed, intensive therapy hospital affiliated with Ohio State University Medical Center.

Of these 376 consecutive releases, 89 were excluded from the study for one of two reasons or both. First, some were returned to a community outside the area served by the hospital. Second, others failed to remain in the community a minimum of 15 days before reinstitutionalization or were transferred directly upon discharge to another hospital. The removal of these 89 cases left 287 patients in the study. Within six months after discharge, 41 patients had been rehospitalized leaving 246 patients in the community.

Every former patient and a significant other of each was interviewed six months after discharge. All of the interviewing was done by psychiatric social workers who had been specifically trained for the purpose. A structured interview schedule was utilized in the interviewing. Additional information was obtained from case records and other official reports as well as from an examination of a sample of the patients by two psychiatrists.

The interview for significant others contained indices designed to measure various aspects of patient posthospital functioning including psychological and domestic performance and social participation. A total functioning index was derived as a composite of these three indices. Another section of the schedule pertained to the significant others' expectations for the instrumental role performance of the patients. A precisely similar index was used with the former patients. This index contained 14 items resulting in a score of 14 to 42 points. The higher the score, the greater the expectation for performance. On the basis of these expectation scores, patients and significant others were divided into three groups which arbitrarily were classed as low, medium and high expectation categories.

FINDINGS

The results indicate that there is a positive relationship between level of expectation for instrumental performance and the level of actual functioning of former patients. The greater the expectations of significant others and of the patients themselves, the higher the level of posthospital patient functioning. In addition, the greater the agreement in expectations between patient and significant other, the greater the tendency for better posthospital performance.

Significant Other Expectations and Patient Performance

Significant others were asked to indicate whether or not they expected the patient to perform each of 14 behaviors normally associated with the female role. These included the performance of such mundane tasks as cleaning, shopping, preparing meals and caring for the children as well as exhibiting some degree of interpersonal competence such as that involved in participating in social activities, visiting, entertaining and simply getting along with neighbors and with other family members.[1] Significant others and patients differed in their level of expectations and particularly in the specific aspects of functioning which they expected. There was, on the one hand, the almost universal expectancy among significant others that the former patient ought to provide adequate care for the children, a lesser expectancy that she perform the routine household tasks and still less that she function socially.

[1] We are indebted to Howard E. Freeman and Ozzie G. Simmons for use of this measure of expectations.

TABLE 1 LEVEL OF SIGNIFICANT OTHER EXPECTATIONS AND PATIENT DOMESTIC, SOCIAL AND PSYCHOLOGICAL PERFORMANCE

Expectation Category	N	Domestic Performance		Social Participation		Psychological Functioning	
		Mean	σ	Mean	σ	Mean	σ
Low	75	13.7	3.2	52.6	8.9	83.2	9.1
Moderate	90	17.9	2.2	56.7	7.9	87.3	6.0
High	65	18.1	2.2	57.4	8.2	87.6	6.5

Mean differences between Low and High Expectation Categories for each performance measure are significant (C.R.'s < .01).

On the basis, then, of their over-all expectations, 75 significant others were classed as having low expectations, 90 as having medium or moderate expectations and 65 as having high expectations. Table 1 indicates that patient domestic performance, social participation and psychological functioning increased significantly from the low to the high expectation groups. For example, the actual seven item domestic performance score of patients varied from a mean of 13.7 in the low expectancy group to a mean of 18.1 in the high category. Similarly, on the 11 item scale of social participation, the mean score of patients whose significant others held low instrumental expectations was 52.6 and for those with high expectations the mean score was 57.4. The strongest case that can be made on logical grounds for the role of expectations and its influence on behavior concerns the 32 item index of posthospital psychological functioning which is less contaminated by instrumental role expectations than are domestic functioning and social participation. Here again, low expectation significant others had low functioning former patients as spouses or relatives and the reverse held for high expectation significant others. Finally, not only did the means differ significantly in each of these comparisons but the variation in scores was also consistently lower in the high expectation group.

Patient Expectations and Performance

As with significant others, and again more strongly in this instance since patients did not evaluate their own functioning, patient expectations were positively related to their performance as determined by their significant others and largely independently corroborated by two staff psychiatrists. As indicated in Table 2, the higher the patient's expectations for her role behavior, the higher her level of functioning. This was statistically significant for domestic and psychological functioning and for her social participation. This would tend to indicate that the more she expects of herself, the more competent her performance or the better her performance, the greater her self-expectations or both.

TABLE 2 LEVEL OF PATIENT EXPECTATIONS AND PATIENT DOMESTIC, SOCIAL, AND PSYCHOLOGICAL PERFORMANCE

Patient Expectation Category	N	Domestic Performance		Social Participation		Psychological Functioning	
		Mean	σ	Mean	σ	Mean	σ
Low	88	14.8	3.1	52.7	8.8	84.7	8.6
Moderate	76	17.5	2.6	57.5	7.5	86.5	6.5
High	60	18.2	2.5	57.5	8.0	87.5	6.9

Mean differences between Low and High Expectation Categories for each performance measure are significant (C.R.'s for Domestic and Social Participation < .01, but < .05 for Psychological Functioning).

TABLE 3 PERCENT OF FORMER PATIENTS AND THEIR SIGNIFICANT OTHERS WHO AGREE ON SPECIFIC EXPECTATION ITEMS

Item	N	Agree*	Disagree: Former Patient Expects More	Disagree: Significant Other Expects More
Dust, sweep and do other usual cleaning	225	90.2	9.4	.4
Help with the family shopping	225	85.3	11.6	3.1
Entertain people at home	225	76.8	11.6	11.6
Dress and take care of herself	225	98.7	1.3	0.0
Handle the grocery money	225	82.2	12.0	5.8
Prepare the morning and evening meals	225	88.0	9.3	2.7
Take care of laundry and mending	225	88.9	9.8	1.3
Dress and bathe the children†	68	95.6	2.2	2.2
Make sure the children get to school on time‡	84	100.0	0.0	0.0
Go visit friends and relatives	225	84.4	7.1	8.5
Get along with family members	225	94.7	2.2	3.1
Get along with the neighbors	225	92.4	4.9	2.7
Go to parties and other social activities	225	68.0	16.4	15.6
Hold a job full time or part time	225	84.0	12.4	3.6

* Agreement here means that the former patient and her significant other agree on whether the woman should or should not perform each task.
† This item applies only to former patients with children aged 1-5 in the household.
‡ This item applies only to former patients with children aged 6-18 in the household.

Agreement in Expectations and Patient Performance

Table 3 reveals that there was a great deal of agreement between significant other and patient in their expectations for her role performance. The level of agreement ranged from complete agreement in expecting the former patient to get the children ready to go to school on time to 68 percent agreement in the patient's involvement in social activities. In general, where disagreement in expectations did exist it was the patient who expected more of herself than was expected of her by the significant other, indicating greater tolerance on the part of the latter.

The agreement thesis was not, however, as clearly related to performance as were the individual expectations of patient and significant other. The low agreement category of patients and others scored lower on domestic performance, social participation and psychological functioning but significantly so only on the former. The best performers on all three dimensions seemed to be drawn from the moderate agreement group indicating that flexibility and minor differences in expectations may be conducive to more adequate functioning than the rigidity imposed by nearly complete agreement in expectations whether these are high or low.

Since expectations have been demonstrated as being a pertinent variable in assessing posthospital performance, the question becomes one of determining the degree to which other variables impinge upon expectations. To what extent, for example, are the high expectation significant others justified in holding these high expectations in terms of the patients' previous histories of illness? To what extent, on the other hand, is the level of expectations relatively independent of the psychiatric history and dependent upon such variables as socioeconomic status and education? In short, the question really amounts to determining and evaluating the rationale underlying expectations.

Psychiatric Variables and Expectations

In dealing with the psychiatric and social correlates of expectations a preliminary analysis revealed that each of the variables associated with the expectations of significant others was also related to patient expectations. Factors associated with level of expectations seem to be almost equally operative for both the significant other and the patient. The implication of this finding is that expectations for posthospital functioning are grounded in the reality of previous experience.

Four psychiatric variables seemed to be sufficiently related to the level of expectations to merit some attention. These included diagnosis, the duration of illness prior to hospital admission, case complications such as alcoholism and drug addiction and the therapists' prognosis at discharge.

Significant other and patient expectations were lowest for the cases diagnosed to be organically impaired. The highest expectations were found when the diagnosis was listed as being either a psychoneurosis or a characterologic disturbance. Similarly, the average length of illness prior to admission varied inversely with expectations. The low expectation group averaged 7.0 years of reported previous illness, the moderate expectation group had a mean of 6.2 years and for the high expectation group the mean was 5.0 years. There was also a tendency for the cases complicated by drug addiction or alcoholism to be concentrated in the low expectation group. Finally, the more favorable the prognosis at discharge, the higher the subsequent level of expectations.

None of the other psychiatric variables seemed to bear any kind of relationship to posthospital expectations. This was particularly the case with hospital treatment variables including the length of hospital stay, the use of drug or electroconvulsive therapy or the type of discharge.

Social Factors and Expectations

The level of patient and significant other expectations could also be understood in sociological terms. Variables such as age, marital status, living group to which the patient was returned, composition of the household, education, and other socioeconomic factors were highly correlated with posthospital expectations.

1. *Age.* The age of the patient was found to have an inverse relationship to expectations. The mean age of patients in the low expectation group was 46 years, in the moderate group 37.7 years and in the high expectation category 36.7 years. There was also a tendency for an inverse relationship to exist between age of patient and significant other agreement in expectations. The patients in the low agreement group averaged 42.7 years of age and in the high agreement group the mean age was 38.7 years.

2. *Family Type.* The data indicate that husbands have higher expectations for the performance of their wives than do any other types of significant others. Married ex-patients have higher expectations for their own role performance than do single, divorced, separated or widowed women. By the same token, the conjugal household contains the greatest percentage of high expectation persons. Parents, in particular, hold very low expectations and this seems to be reflected in the expectations, and it should be noted, in the actual functioning of the former patients. Conjugal households in which young children are present contain an even higher percentage of high expectation former patients and significant others. Finally, conjugal households with young children present and other adult females—role replacements—absent contain an overwhelming preponderance of the high expectation patients and significant others.

In summary, it would appear that high expectations for instrumental performance occur precisely in those family situations in which the need for the adequate performance of the routine female role is most necessary. The lowest expectations are found in those family situations in which others are available to serve as role substitutes for the former patient.

3. *Socioeconomic Variables.* Sociologists have long contended that expectations vary with class factors such as education, occupation, and zone of residence. These data certainly support this contention. For example, college educated former patients had a significantly greater level of expectations than did those with only a grade school education. The significant others of the former had comparably higher expectations than did those of the latter. Similarly, using the Warner ISC instrument as a composite measure of class, expectations were found, on the part of the former patient and of the significant other, to increase with class level. Upper middle class persons had the highest expectations, as anticipated, and lower class persons the lowest expectations for patient role performance.

These results relating class to expectations, though significant in and of themselves, do require some tempering. The fact is that the class factor becomes rather unimportant in expectations when performance is held constant whereas level of performance, controlling for class, remains significant for expectations. For example, at all performance levels—low, medium and high—expectations are slightly but not significantly higher among the college educated and are lower for those with only a grade school education. When appropriate controls for class are made, however, expectations continue to vary significantly with performance.

SUMMARY AND CONCLUSIONS

The empirical evidence presented above tends to substantiate the general and specific hypotheses concerning the relationship between expectations for performance and actual performance. There is a positive relationship, with or without controlling for class factors, between, (a) the expectations of significant others and the functioning of former patients and (b) between patient expectations and patient functioning. Although positive, the relationship between expectation agreement of patient and significant other and patient performance was of a lesser order. Also, where disagreement between patient and other existed, it was the patient expectations which were generally greater, indicating that significant others may tend to be somewhat more realistic in their demands on the patient than former patients are of themselves.

Further, in assessing the psychiatric and social variables underlying differential expectations—both significant other and patient—it was found that a diagnosis other than organic psychosis and without alcoholism and drug addiction, a shorter history of illness and a more favorable prognosis at discharge were associated with high expectations. Similarly, younger, married, patients living in conjugal households, having minor children, and of relatively higher social class status had greater expectations as did their significant others.

This analysis while supporting the hypotheses and the previous work of others (Adler, 1953; Brown, 1959; Freeman and Simmons, 1958, 1959a, and 1959b) nonetheless fails to settle the central issue with regard to posthospital expectations and performance—namely, the degree and direction of influence of these two reciprocally related factors on each other. Two assumptions, as previously indicated, are possible. The first, that "corrosion" in expectations follows inevitably from poor performance is certainly tenable. The second possible assumption is that performance is adjusted to expectations.

For the present it is safe to conclude that forcing the recovered former patient to maintain the "sick" role by lessening the role demands upon her may well be self-defeating—as self-defeating as placing excessive demands upon former patients who return from the hospital still mildly or moderately impaired.

REFERENCES

Adler, Leta M., 1953. The relationship of marital status to incidence of and recovery from mental illness. *Social Forces*, **32**, 185–194.

Brown, G. W., 1959. Experiences of discharged chronic schizophrenic patients in various types of living groups. *Milbank Memorial Fund Quarterly*, **37**, 105–131.

Freeman, H. E., and Simmons, O. G., 1958. Mental patients in the community: family settings and performance levels. *American Sociological Review*, **23**, 147–154.

Freeman, H. E., and Simmons, O. G., 1959a. Familial expectations and posthospital performance of mental patients. *Human Relations*, **12**, 233–242.

Freeman, H. E., and Simmons, O. G., 1959b. Social class and posthospital performance levels. *American Sociological Review*, **24**, 345–351.

Gross, N., Mason, W. S., and McEachern, A. W., 1958. *Explorations in role analysis.* New York: Wiley.

Gullahorn, J. T., and Gullahorn, Jeanne B., 1959. A model for role conflict analysis. Paper presented at the American Sociological Association Annual Meeting in Chicago.

Merton, R. K., 1957. The role set: problems in sociological theory. *British Journal of Sociology*, **8**, 106–121.

Sarbin, T. R., 1954. Role theory. In G. Lindzey (Ed.), *Handbook of social psychology*. Cambridge, Mass.: Addison-Wesley, pp. 223–258.

part X Learning and Socialization

ROLE BEHAVIOR is in large measure learned behavior; and, as such, the learning processes pertaining to the acquisition, maintenance, and extinction of behavior become proper subjects of interest. Because much of role behavior occurs in natural contexts in which numerous variables operate in complex combination, it has been difficult to apply the methodology and knowledge of the learning psychologist to an elucidation of how role behavior is learned. What is known about the learning of role behavior derives largely from a different tradition of thought and inquiry; this other focus, called "socialization," is concerned particularly with the learning of socially relevant behavior at various stages of the life cycle. It is probably fair to say that studies of socialization have revealed more descriptive information about behavior of individuals and groups at different points of the life cycle than they have discovered information about the processes by which such behavior appears, remains, and disappears from one's repertoire. The selections in this part provide information about the characteristic behaviors of males and females at different ages, as well as about some of the processes that enter into the learning of such behavior.

One of these processes of socialization is discussed in the selection by Merton. In this paper the notion of anticipatory socialization is developed as a concept having reference to the fact that individuals may acquire new behaviors characteristic of a position of which they are not currently a member, but into which they are about to move, through anticipating what these new behaviors are. Movement from one position to another, and particularly from a lower to a higher status, is common in contemporary society, Merton observes. Through anticipatory socialization, the individual becomes prepared for the new position and thereby eases his movement into it. This process is not without its difficulties, however. Merton notes that the individual often becomes marginal to both the group of his present membership and the group to which he aspires; and because individuals may defect from the norms of the group in which they currently have membership, anticipatory socialization of departing members may be dysfunctional for this group.

Another feature of learning in unstructured, natural situations is that the person who serves as the "teacher" often performs in a characteristic way. The role of the coach, described in the selection by Strauss, is one example. In addition to describing the forms, motivations, and functions of coaching, Strauss describes some of the subtle ways in which the coach shapes the behavior of a neophyte. For instance, the coach explains the sequence of learning experiences to the beginner, interprets the signs of his behavior, provides immediate correction for mistakes, and manipulates the environment. This discussion has general relevance because numerous socializing agents may be viewed as engaging in a coaching role.

Ruth Hartley's paper discusses the development of female sex-role identification. Concepts such as molding, canalization, symbolic manipulation, and activity exposure are among the mechanisms she identifies as important in sex-role development. Another portion of the selection is descriptive of the phases of the development of sex-roles, and here the author presents findings from a study of sex-role development among young girls. Among the findings is evidence that sex-roles are different for subjects of different social classes.

Rich findings pertaining to the development of children's conceptions of interfamilial sex and age roles are offered in Emmerich's selection. On the basis of information relating to the family role concepts of two hundred and twenty-five children of six to ten years of age, the author found that there was by no means high consensus in the ways in which boys and girls of different ages conceived of familial roles. The basis of sex-role discrimination differed for boys and girls, and these differences were related to age; the father's sex-role was seen as more powerful than the mother's; and in the discrimination of parent roles, it was found that there was greater consensus on judgments of relative power than of positive or negative attitudes. These are but a few of the findings reported in this study.

Joan and William McCord report the effects of a parental role model on the behavior of children. The authors are concerned with the genesis of criminality and present data from a study of predelinquent youths. Three factors are considered in predicting the likelihood of a boy becoming delinquent: parental role model (whether or not the father was a criminal), attitude of each parent toward the child (warm, passive, or rejecting), and methods of discipline (punitive, love-oriented, consistent, erratic). The authors show that complex relationships obtain among these factors in the genesis of criminality; that the effect of a criminal father is dependent upon other factors in the family; and that paternal rejection, absence of maternal warmth, or maternal deviance are likely to support the appearance of a criminal pattern of behavior. The authors conclude that the role modeling adage "like father, like son" is overly simple and that the development of adult roles depends upon a complex interrelationship of many causative factors.

The final selection, by Landy and Wechsler, is concerned with rehabilitation and the use of pathway organizations. The authors point out that in the case of psychiatric rehabilitation, the problem of rehabilitation may not only be one of relearning the skills of "normality," but may also be a task of habilitation, i.e., the acquisition of skills and behavior that the person never had previously. Pathway organizations are those specifically set up for rehabilitation, and their operations are characterized by continuity of the rehabilitative process, delaying action, and specific activities leading to resocialization. The authors distinguish between open and closed settings, between organizations that are professional or lay, between the dependence and independence involved, and between the roles of the patient and nonpatient. Throughout, emphasis is placed upon problems of adult (re)socialization in the operation of pathway organizations.

selection 42 Anticipatory Socialization

ROBERT K. MERTON

In considering the possible consequences of pattern of conformity to non-membership group norms, it is advisable to distinguish between the consequences for the individual exhibiting this behavior, the sub-group in which they find themselves, and the social system comprising both of these.

For the individual who adopts the values of a group to which he aspires but does not belong, this orientation may serve the twin functions of aiding his rise into that group and of easing his adjustment after he has become part of it. That this first function was indeed served is the gist of the finding in *The American Soldier* (Stouffer, Suchman, DeVinney, Star, and Williams, 1949; Stouffer, Lumsdaine, Lumsdaine, Williams, Smith, Janis, Star, and Cottrell, 1949) that those privates who accepted the official values of the Army hierarchy were more likely than others to be promoted. The hypothesis regarding the second function still remains to be tested. But it would not, in principle, be difficult to discover empirically whether those men who, through a kind of *anticipatory socialization*, take on the values of the non-membership group to which they aspire, find readier acceptance by that group and make an easier adjustment to it.

It appears that anticipatory socialization is functional for the individual only within a relatively open social structure providing for mobility. For only in such a structure would such attitudinal and behavior preparation for status shifts be followed by actual changes of status in a substantial proportion of cases. By the same token, the same pattern of anticipatory socialization would be dysfunctional for the individual in a relatively closed social structure, where he would not find acceptance by the group to which he aspires and would probably lose acceptance, because of his outgroup orientation, by the group to which he belongs. This latter type of case will be recognized as that of the marginal man, poised on the edge of several groups but fully accepted by none of them.

Thus, the often-studied case of the marginal man and the case of the enlisted man who takes the official military mores as a positive frame of reference can be identified, in a functional theory of reference group behavior, as special cases of anticipatory socialization. The marginal man pattern represents the special case in a relatively closed social system, in which the members of one group take as a positive frame of reference the norms of a group from which they are excluded in principle. Within such a social structure, anticipatory socialization becomes dysfunctional for the individual who becomes the victim of aspirations he cannot achieve and hopes he cannot satisfy. But precisely the same kind of reference group behavior within a relatively open social system is functional for the individual at least to the degree of helping him to achieve the status to which he aspires. The same reference group behavior in different social structures has different consequences.

To this point, then, we find that positive orientation toward the norms of a non-membership group is precipitated by a passage between membership-groups, either in fact or in fantasy, and that the functional or dysfunctional consequences evidently depend upon the relatively open or closed character of the social structure in which this occurs. And what would, at first glance, seem entirely unrelated and disparate forms of behavior—the behavior of such marginal men as the Cape Coloured or the Eurasian, and of enlisted men adopting the values of military strata other than their own—are seen, after appropriate conceptualization, as special cases of reference group behavior.

Although anticipatory socialization may be functional for the *individual* in an open social system, it is apparently dysfunctional for the solidarity of the *group* or *stratum* to which he belongs. For allegiance to the contrasting mores of another group means defection from the mores of the in-group. And accordingly, as we shall

Abridged from pages 265–271 of a book by the same author entitled *Social Theory and Social Structure* (Rev. ed.), 1957, New York: The Free Press. Reprinted by permission of the author and The Free Press.

presently see, the in-group responds by putting all manner of social restraints upon such positive orientations to certain out-group norms.

From the standpoint of the larger social system, the Army as a whole, positive orientation toward the official mores would appear to be functional in supporting the legitimacy of the structure and in keeping the structure of authority intact. (This is presumably what is meant when the text of *The American Soldier* refers to these conformist attitudes as "favorable from the Army's point of view.") But manifestly, much research needs to be done before one can say that this is indeed the case. It is possible, for example, that the secondary effects of such orientations may be so deleterious to the solidarity of the primary groups of enlisted men that their morale sags. A concrete research question might help clarify the problem: are outfits with relatively large minorities of men positively oriented to the official Army values more likely to exhibit signs of anomie and personal disorganization (*e.g.*, non-battle casualties)? In such situations, does the personal "success" of conformists (promotion) only serve to depress the morale of the others by rewarding those who depart from the in-group mores?

[The] imputations of legitimacy to social arrangements seem functionally related to reference group behavior. They apparently affect *the range of the inter-group or inter-individual comparisons* that will typically be made. If the structure of a rigid system of stratification, for example, is generally defined as legitimate, if the rights, perquisites and obligations of each stratum are generally held to be morally right, then the individuals within each stratum will be the less likely to take the situation of the other strata as a context for appraisal of their own lot. They will, presumably, tend to confine their comparisons to other members of their own or neighboring social stratum. If, however, the system of stratification is under wide dispute, then members of some strata are more likely to contrast their own situation with that of others, and shape their self-appraisals accordingly. This variation in the structure of systems and in the degree of legitimacy imputed to the rules of the game may help account for the often-noticed fact that the degree of dissatisfaction with their lot is often less among the people in severely depressed social strata in a relatively rigid social system, than among those strata who are apparently "better off" in a more mobile social system. At any rate, the *range of groups* taken as effective bases of comparison in different social systems may well turn out to be closely connected with the degree to which legitimacy is ascribed to the prevailing social structure.

In the course of considering the functions of anticipatory socialization, we have made passing allusion to social processes which sustain or curb this pattern of behavior. Since it is precisely the data concerning such processes which are not easily caught up in the type of survey materials on attitudes primarily utilized in *The American Soldier*, and since these processes are central to any theory of reference group behavior, they merit further consideration.

As we have seen, what is anticipatory socialization from the standpoint of the individual is construed as defection and nonconformity by the group of which he is a member. To the degree that the individual identifies himself with another group, he alienates himself from his own group. Yet although the field of sociology has for generations been concerned with the determinants and consequences of group cohesion, it has given little *systematic* attention to the complementary subject of group alienation. When considered at all, it has been confined to such special cases as second-generation immigrants, conflict of loyalties between gang and family, etc. In large measure, the subject has been left to the literary observer, who could detect the drama inherent in the situation of the renegade, the traitor, the deserter. The value-laden connotations of these terms used to describe identification with groups other than one's own definitely suggest that these patterns of behavior have been typically regarded from the standpoint of the membership group. (Yet one group's renegade may be another group's convert.) Since the assumption that its members will be loyal is found in every group, else it would have no group character, no dependability of action, transfer of loyalty to another group (particularly a group operating in the same sphere of politics or economy), is regarded primarily in affective terms of sentiment rather than in detached terms of analysis. The renegade or traitor or climber—whatever the folk-phrase may be—more often becomes an object of vilification than an object of sociological study.

The framework of reference group theory, detached from the language of sentiment, enables the sociologist to identify and to locate renegadism, treason, the assimilation of immigrants, class mobility, social climbing, etc., as so many special forms of identification with what is at the time a non-membership group. In doing so, it affords the possibility of studying these, not as *wholly* particular and unconnected forms of behavior, but as different expressions of similar processes under significantly different conditions. The transfer of allegiance of upper class individuals from their own to a lower class—whether this be in the pre-revolutionary period of 18th century France or of 20th century Russia—belongs to the same family of sociological problems as the more familiar identification of lower class individuals with a higher class, a subject which has lately begun to absorb the attention of sociologists in a society where upward social mobility is an established value. Our cultural emphases notwithstanding, the phenomenon of topdogs adopting the values of the underdog is as much a reference group phenomenon lending itself to further inquiry as that of the underdogs seeking to become topdogs.

In such defections from the in-group, it may turn out, as has often been suggested, that it is the isolate, nominally in a group but only slightly incorporated in its network of social relations, who is most likely to become positively oriented toward non-membership groups. But, even if generally true, this is a static correlation and, therefore, only partly illuminating. What needs to be uncovered is the process through which this correlation comes to hold. Judging from some of the qualitative data in *The American Soldier* and from other studies of group defection, there is continued and cumulative interplay between a deterioration of *social relations* within the membership group and positive *attitudes* toward the norms of a non-membership group.

What the individual experiences as estrangement from a group of which he is a member tends to be experienced by his associates as repudiation of the group, and this ordinarily evokes a hostile response. As social relations between the individual and the rest of the group deteriorate, the norms of the group become less binding for him. For since he is progressively seceding from the group and being penalized by it, he is the less likely to experience rewards for adherence to the group's norms. Once initiated, this process seems to move toward a cumulative detachment from the group, in terms of attitudes and values as well as in terms of social relations. And to the degree that he orients himself toward out-group values, perhaps affirming them verbally and expressing them in action, he only widens the gap and reinforces the hostility between himself and his in-group associates. Through the interplay of dissociation and progressive alienation from the group values, he may become doubly motivated to orient himself toward the values of another group and to affiliate himself with it. There then remains the distinct question of the objective possibility of affiliating himself with his reference group. If the possibility is negligible or absent, then the alienated individual becomes socially rootless. But if the social system realistically allows for such change in group affiliations, then the individual estranged from the one group has all the more motivation to belong to the other.

This hypothetical account of dissociation and alienation, which of course only touches upon the processes which call for research in the field of reference group behavior, seems roughly in accord with qualitative data in *The American Soldier* on what was variously called brown-nosing, bucking for promotion, and sucking up. Excerpts from the diary of an enlisted man illustrate the interplay between dissociation and alienation: the outward-oriented man is too sedulous in abiding by the official mores—"But you're *supposed* to [work over there]. The lieutenant said you were supposed to."—this evokes group hostility expressed in epithets and ridicule—"Everybody is making sucking, kissing noises at K and S now"—followed by increasing dissociation within the group—"Ostracism was visible, but mild . . . few were friendly toward them . . . occasions arose where people avoided their company"—and more frequent association with men representing the non-membership reference group—"W, S and K sucked all afternoon; hung around lieutenants and asked bright questions." In this briefly summarized account, one sees the mechanisms of the in-group operating to curb positive orientation to the official mores as well as the process through which this orientation develops among those who take these mores as their major frame of reference, considering their ties with the in-group as of only secondary importance.

REFERENCES

Stouffer, S. A., Lumsdaine, A. A., Lumsdaine, Marion H., Williams, R. M., Jr., Smith, M. B., Janis, I. L., Star, Shirley A., and Cottrell, L. S., Jr., 1949. *The American soldier: Combat and its aftermath*, Vol. **2**. Princeton, N.J.: Princeton University Press.

Stouffer, S. A., Suchman, E. A., DeVinney, L. C., Star, Shirley A., and Williams, R. M., Jr., 1949. *The American soldier: Adjustment during Army life*, Vol. **1**. Princeton, N.J.: Princeton University Press.

selection 43 Coaching

ANSELM STRAUSS

When passages of status are more or less well regulated, those who have gone through the recognized steps stand ready to guide and advise their successors. This guidance is essential, for even regulated passage is perhaps more hazardous than my account has indicated.

In the well known novel, *The Late George Apley*, J. P. Marquand (1940) portrays the well ordered life of George as it follows the traditional Bostonian upper class pattern of growing up and growing old. As a young man, George is in danger of being drawn off the track, when he becomes fond of an Irish girl far below him in social position. He is brought to heel through family pressure and by being shown how this incident "really" fits into his entire expected life cycle. Natural as it is for him to dally with such a girl, the "escapade" is not to be treated as a serious venture. The great danger of such an escapade is that through it some George Apley—if not this one—will be drawn off expected paths and lost to family and social class. However, the counsel of elders is requisite to status passages for reasons other than hazard, since all the future steps are clear only to those who have traversed them. Certain aspects of what lies over the horizon are blurred to the candidate, no matter how clear may be his general path. This forces his predecessors not only to counsel and guide him, but to prepare and coach him beforehand. Coaching is an integral part of teaching the inexperienced—of any age.

Abridged from pages 100–118 of a book by the same author entitled *Mirrors and Masks*, 1959, New York: The Free Press. Reprinted by permission of the author and The Free Press.

Once we see this function of "the coach," we are prepared to discuss coaching quite apart from regularized status steps, and within wider contexts than athletics or professional drama. A coaching relationship exists if someone seeks to move someone else along a series of steps, when those steps are not entirely institutionalized and invariant, and when the learner is not entirely clear about their sequences (although the coach is). The football coach attempting to turn out a good half-back, Iago seeking to induce Othello along the path of jealousy, the piano teacher trying to make a concert pianist out of a young man, the revivalist trying to work his audience into a frenzy of conversion, the psychiatrist carefully maneuvering his patient back to better psychological integration, and the confidence man manipulating his victim through sequential steps of involvement in an illicit deal: all are instances of coaching relationships, albeit each has different aspects. In each instance there is a man who has yielded himself (whether he knows it or not) to a teacher who guides him along at least partly obscure channels. Since every field in which such teaching goes on has its own prescriptions and rules of thumb, my discussion of coaching quite obviously must be very general, and will be pointed particularly toward those changes of identity that take place during coaching.

The general features of the coaching relationship flow from the learner's need for guidance as he moves along, step by step. He needs guidance not merely because in the conventional sense he needs someone to teach him skills, but because some very surprising things are happening to him that require explanation. The coach stands ready to interpret his responses, which may otherwise only have the status of ambiguous signs. If you look at something as non-psychological as learning a physical skill, perhaps you can see the point more easily. The learner leans upon the coach's expert advice, for instance, whether a given muscular movement is going to lead forward, or down a false path; and without the coach he may not even notice his own movement. The coach literally calls attention to new responses: "Look, this is the first time you have managed to do this." Likewise, the coach explains away responses, saying "pay no attention" for what is happening either should be regarded as of no importance or as something that happens only "at this stage." The next steps are pointed out ("Don't worry, wait, this will happen"). In sum: because the sequences of steps are in some measure obscure, and because one's own responses become something out of the ordinary, someone must stand prepared to predict, indicate, and explain the signs.

But the tutor generally assigns himself a far more active role than I have suggested. He does not merely wait for the student to develop new responses; he throws him into situations so as to elicit certain responses from him. This provides an opportunity to indicate, interpret, and predict. Understandably, this involves the coach in a certain kind of duplicity upon occasion (as when a fencing teacher allows his pupil to hit him for the first time); the coach's position also requires that he may have to function like a playwright, arranging episodes, setting scenes, getting supporting characters to act in a certain way. Of course the pupil, by virtue of his acquisition of new skills or new perspectives, can be counted upon to engage other persons in new interactions. Like the infant who upon learning his first words encounters his parents differently, the learner's recently gained skills will throw him into novel situations. Some outcomes will be gratifying, but of course others can be terrifying or at least frightening. The coach utilizes both kinds of outcomes to retain control, occasionally even allowing him his head so as to be able to say—"I told you so, now then you see. . . ." The point is that the untutored cannot see until he has tried for himself, just as generally he cannot visualize much of the proper path beforehand.

In malevolent kinds of coaching—as in seduction, or in conning by confidence men—the relationship is one of trapper and victim. However, in almost all coaching there appears to be a strong element of inducement, temptation, and behind-the-scenes action. The con man baits, tempts, induces; but so does, although in less obvious ways, the art teacher, the basketball coach, or the psychiatrist. Abstractly stated, the coach not only works on current desires to get action directed along given paths, but seeks to create new desires and aims. He seeks to create a new identity for the pupil—or the victim—and to do this involves him in a variety of canny maneuvers.

In general, we should be struck by the importance of timing in all coaching. Because the pupil is being guided in his moves—muscularly, psychologically, socially—the coach is preoccupied with teaching him certain things at correct places and times. To begin with, the coach may be rejected if he forces too fast a pace, especially at the outset. The pupil may lose face or become frightened or otherwise distressed. In psychiatric coaching the patient may go elsewhere for help or, if the relationship is involuntary as when he is committed to a mental hospital, simply withdraw psychologically. On the other hand, the pupil (whether a patient, victim, or convert) may be lost to his mentor if the latter moves too slowly—lost through boredom, shattering of faith, or other reasons. Of course, the teacher may call attention to his superior experience and wisdom, as well as draw upon the resources of trust placed in him by the other, in order to set the pace; but he does so always at some risk. This risk is unavoidable and can only be minimized by shrewd tactics. The coach has to know when to force his man over a hurdle, and when to let him sidle up to it; when to schedule definite moves, and when to allow a period of relative free play. The coach must skillfully balance between two poles: he must not pressure the student by his own impatience; yet he must force movement at those junctures when the fellow appears ready but reluctant to move, is in fact really "there" but does not realize it.

Crucial tactics in this delicately balanced process are the prescription, the schedule, the challenge, the trial, and the accusation. Prescriptions for action are sometimes called "routines" or "exercises" or "lessons"; they are traditional step-by-step progressions that prepare the way for further movement. When the coaching relationship is well-institutionalized, such routine practices become a very visible and sometimes hampering part of the coaching profession. The schedule is also an integral aspect of the coaching process; notions arise of how fast or how slowly the pupil should move, and at what points he should move slower or faster. There is at least an implicit set of norms governing how quickly he should progress through certain stages. Recently, a psychologist has suggested to a group of psychiatrists how a standardized set of norms might be used to measure the progress of their patients. In the coaching relationship, a considerable potential strain exists because the coach must control his own impulses to standardize schedules too greatly.

Challenges or dares are also an invariant aspect of coaching. Since a person is being asked to relinquish old modes of doing and seeing, he is in effect being asked to do and say and even think things that look risky or dangerous. I recently heard a psychiatrist say to a patient, "It is now time to do. . . . You may fail but you are likely not to; it is a risk worth taking." Of course, there are clever and institutionalized ways of cushioning failure, but the important thing is that the person by meeting the challenge receives an indication of how far he has progressed. His overcoming of a challenge provides a marker, a milestone of his development.

Essential also to coaching is the accusation, hurled or insinuated. The coach will conceive of his pupil on occasion as backsliding, as giving in to old habits, old temptations, and therefore must be frankly reprimanded. The pupil will also be accused of loss of faith or trust: "How can you benefit from what I have to teach you if you do not trust me now." From the learner's perspective, the coach may be neglecting his job, ruining one's talents, breaking faith, even engaging in betrayal. Accusations both block the process of learning and are vitally important for those reconciliations that mark turning points on the road forward.

I have mentioned the elements of risk and trust involved in the coaching relationship, although they loom as more obvious in some kinds of relationships than in others. The novice airplane pilot literally puts his life at the disposal of his instructor. In seduction or in confidence games the secret motivations that are involved highlight the risk and danger. Even in such mundane pursuits as piano and voice teaching or training for track meets, the pupil's potential level of performance may be greatly endangered by improper counsel. Insofar as the coaching process also leads to great changes of identity—as in G. B. Shaw's apocryphal drama *Pygmalion*—you, as a pupil, are in large measure ceding an unknown destiny to a mentor who presumably knows where he is taking you. A special danger is that the relationship may be broken off midstream, before "the treatment" is completed, with potential danger to both but particularly to the learner.

The reverse side of great risk and danger is trust and faith. To this should be added what the psychoanalysts call "identification"; that is, a very close modeling of self after the other, or after certain of his aspects. The coach is not only a partial model ("do as I do"), but in certain stages may become almost a total model ("be as I am" or "wish to be what I am"). The tutor, of course, may consciously utilize this desire or propensity. On the other hand, in many types of coaching, particularly after the earlier stages of learning, mere imitation is not sufficient for progress.

Let us now consider more explicitly the shifts of identity brought about through coaching, as against the mere acquisition of skill. One cannot, of course, discuss risk, trust, identification, duplicity, challenge, and merely talk of the acquisition of skill. In some coaching, the person may be taken as a *tabula rasa*, as if he had no previous commitments of the kind the coach is now about to build; the task is simply to build upon unimpeded ground. More often this is not a realistic stance for the coach to take. The learner has something to unlearn, to cope with, and this will enter the trajectory of his learning early and often stay with him until very late. This is perhaps another way of saying that the coach must challenge old modes of doing, seeing, and thinking, as well as point out new modes. When the learning and re-learning is extreme there must be massive and frontal attack upon identities. In less drastic kinds of change, through the agency of coaches, a man is requested also to turn his back upon his past, to discount previous accomplishments, to divest himself of earlier prides, to disidentify himself with old practices, old allies, and even old loves.

One may sometimes observe during the initial sessions of a new coaching relationship how the participants gingerly hold back from much involvement until they are "sure." This is especially true of the student, but the teacher also may have provisos. Traditionally, the early phases may be coached in terms of "make-believe" or "not for keeps"; and institutionally they may take the form of not yet counting the score or recording the performance. All this, in a sense, represents a trial period; one is involved, but without much commitment to his own performance, and can retreat with honor and dignity. It is as if there were a kind of moratorium, during which effort is great but during which both sides ceremonially ignore negative performances. Of course, such a moratorium and such make-believe run all through the coaching process, perhaps particularly during the new phases in cycles of learning, when the person is particularly sensitive to criticism and must be encouraged and must encourage himself to chance certain endeavors. You can see this procedure operating in reverse when young art students are so jealous of their paintings, so serious about their performances, that they bridle when the teacher lays a brush upon their work.

In his fondest moments, the coach may believe that he has total control over the progress of his pupil. But the very character of coaching is likely to set into motion unpredictable changes of identity. The best model for visualizing this learning is not as a steady progression through a series of stages, mostly known to the coach, but rather to imagine a tree with many branches and twigs. The pupil moves along certain branches until he reaches alternatives, and the coach stands ready to guide or channel his movement until the next set of alternatives arises. But the best pupils, like the best children, get out from under the control and the vision of the best teachers, and the best teachers are pleased that this is so. At the outer limits of learning, the stages can no longer be as standardized as at the beginning; and the pupil discovers his own style, whether we are talking of religious conversion, musical composition, or anything else. For the coach, too, the process may be open-ended; he too may end with a different identity. This mutual change may be, as Nelson Foote has suggested, "a winning pattern for each" (1957, p. 38), but unfortunately it may also be mutually destructive or end happily for one but not for the other.

Something should now be added to counteract the notion that coaching is merely a two-way relationship between a coach and a coached person, for many if not most coaching processes occur in organization or institutional contexts. Thus the teacher hands on pupils to higher or more famous teachers, saying "I can teach you no more, you are now beyond me—or at least it is said that you are beyond me." Although I shall not develop the point, you ought to recognize that the organizational framework within which the coaching goes on vitally affects the process and outcome of coaching. In some organizational contexts the coach may move his students too quickly or his coaching may become standardized or he may handle his pupils far too impersonally. He may bind his students too closely to himself for their rapid or maximum development or he may fail to sustain proper trust of himself. Since coaching is thus linked with social structure and with the positions and careers of both the coaches and the coached, one can scarcely speak of process as divorced from structure. My discussion of process has been exceedingly general and its details must be spelled out in relation to particular structures and worlds. This is a task for meticulous and thoughtful research.

REFERENCES

Foote, N., 1957. Concept and method in the study of human development. In M. Sherif and M. O. Wilson (Eds.), *Emerging problems in social psychology*. Norman, Okla.: University of Oklahoma Book Exchange.

Marquand, J. P., 1940. *The late George Apley*. New York: The Modern Library.

selection 44 A Developmental View of Female Sex-Role Identification

RUTH E. HARTLEY

This paper discusses aspects of the development of female sex-roles in childhood. I wish to discuss some problems of early childhood development, to review selected findings bearing on these problems, and to add some bits of information derived from our recent studies of school-age children, aspects of which have been reported elsewhere (Hartley, 1960, 1961a, 1961b, 1964; Hartley and Hardesty, 1962; Hartley and Klein, 1959).

By "sex-role" I refer to those sets of related cognitions (Biddle, 1961) maintained by subjects for objects designated as members of the female sex. These cognitions may be first order (i.e., perceptions of what females do) or second order (attributed expectations, such as what females like to do). Definition of the female sex-role consists of the complex of behaviors considered characteristic of or appropriate to persons occupying the female status, and the attributed expectations concerning those behaviors. Implementation of the female sex-role will be defined by the subjects' preferences for sex-role activities.

Sex-role definitions involve also age-role definition. The female sex-role at age 5 is specific to the attributes of the five-year-old and different from the female sex-role at 25. At each developmental level a sex-role specified for that level is implemented. Role cognitions and expectations may, however, develop in anticipation of future statuses by perception of role-implementations by older persons, much like the development of "cognitive maps" of Tolman's rats (1948). Thus, although sex-role implementation can be assessed only at the current age-status of the subject, sex-role definitions proceed on a multiple track (Duvall, 1955; Finch, 1955; Hartley, 1960, 1961a, 1964; Hartley and Klein, 1959), depending on the perceptibility of the differences among sex-age-status behaviors and the variety of exposure of the subjects. In this discussion, time will permit dealing with sex-role definition on a single track only.

Attempting to trace the processes by which sex-role definition comes about early in life we are hampered by a paucity of empirical data for ages younger than three years. Since evidence for sex-role differentiation exists for four years of age (Abel and Shahin Kaya, 1962; Brown, 1956; Emmerich, 1959; Hartley, Frank, and Goldenson, 1952; Rabban, 1950), it seems reasonable to expect that some relevant preliminary processes must take place earlier. I am assuming on the basis of evidence that these are some sort of learning processes, rather than inevitable maturational components of the biological process. The function of these processes would be to specify the appropriate behaviors out of a matrix of all possible behaviors, to stabilize the appearance of these behaviors, and to inhibit the appearance of inappropriate behaviors. A search of the literature and a widespread inquiry by correspondence having been singularly unavailing with respect to systematically collected empirical data which could blueprint such processes, I shall venture to suggest some of them hypothetically, on the basis of unsystematically collected and inadequately controlled empirical data.

MOLDING AND CANALIZATION

One widely accepted point of view about sex-role specification holds that some of the related behaviors are developed as integral personality functions, without awareness on the part of the subject of their sex-status connection. For example, little girls may be "gentled" as infants and little boys "roughhoused," with ensuing

Abridged from a paper delivered at the biennial meeting of the Society for Research in Child Development, Berkeley, California, 1963. Reprinted by permission of the author. A slightly amended version of this paper appears in the *Merrill–Palmer Quarterly*, 1964, **10**, 3–16.

built-in personality dimensions. The sex-differentiated disciplinary techniques noted by Sears, Maccoby, and Levin (1957), would fall into this category of event.

An informal survey of sex-typing techniques used during the early years (about one year to five years of age) in 22 young families revealed several kinds of handling by which generalized molding may take place. For convenience, we shall call one of these socialization by manipulation. For example, young mothers of female run-arounds report they "fuss with" the baby's hair, dress them "feminine," and tell them how pretty they are. If we apply to this situation Piaget's concept of imitation through indifferentiation (Piaget, 1952, 1962), we can see how it could lead to self-manipulation of the same kind, and, as personal differentiation takes place, to the incorporation of its quality as a basic element in the self-concept. This seems to me not far removed in effect from the passive "molding" of infants described by Mead in her reports on Bali (1954).

Canalization (Murphy, 1947) also seems to play its part as a subtle delimiting process. For example, dolls and carriages are almost invariably mentioned as among the toys specifically made available to little girls (as differentiated from toys furnished to both sexes). Opportunities to manipulate these with satisfaction, to incorporate them into early imitative sequences, provides the basis for both heightened awareness and anticipation of pleasure in relation to similar objects. Piaget and others have indicated that sheer familiarization can provoke positive responses (Krugman, 1943; Piaget, 1952). This emotional toning becomes part of the total perception of the familiar objects, giving them a competitive advantage against more neutral candidates for attention. If this result were not reinforced, it might not endure against the counterpressures of satiation and novelty. For girls it *is* reinforced, however, by repetitions of the toys in novel forms and by constant encouragement to more complex manipulation by the availability of a continuous stream of variegated accessories. If perceptual stimuli for appropriate imitative acts also are present in the home, the intrinsic reinforcement value of manipulating these objects is intensified by their participation on the child's ludic assimilation of the external world to the ego. This process of perceptual priority and manipulatory reinforcement should obtain for all objects or aspects of objects (such as color) which are selectively made available to the child early in life and which are perceptually meaningful. Thus, preferences for pastel colors (now available in electric trains), for feminine types of clothing, for certain qualities of movement, as well as for games and playthings can theoretically develop without specific extrinsic reinforcement and without awareness of sex-status relevance on the part of the subject.

SYMBOL MANIPULATION

Another type of limiting sex-directional training of the child takes place early in life through parental applications of sex-appropriate verbal appelations. Starting some time in the first year, the child hears frequently expressions like "That's a good girl"; "Don't be a bad girl"; "Where's daddy's girl?"; "There, now, —— is a pretty girl." Coming before the child is capable of forming concepts, before consensual meaning is acquired, before real classification on any stable basis is possible, before discriminative learning is likely to have taken place, before ego differentiation has developed, what *can* the repetition of the sex-designating terms mean to the child? We suggest that it serves as a sign leading to self-identity, much as a name does, and is comprehended syncratically as representing whatever complex of sensation and emotion is experienced at the time of its use. It would be logical to expect it to be built into the self-concept as a symbolic self-designation. As such, it might serve later as a "signalizer" to raise the perceptual saliency of girl-specific references and referrents. As the child is exposed to others who are similarly designated, the common reference should both encourage the identification (self-generalization) of indifferentiation and serve as a basis for the formation of a concept of a general category of being to which one belongs, as perceptually distinctive and specified others also belong. These results would then be useful, through heightened selective awareness, in developing the cognitions necessary for implementing appropriately one's sex-role at childhood levels. That such selective awareness is indeed developed is indicated by data reported respectively by Hartley (1964) and by Baum (1957).

An early step in the perception of adult sex-appropriate behaviors seems to be the parental practice of encouraging indifferentiated identification by the frequent use of the expression "just like mommy." Little girls are told they will grow up to be ladies "just like mommy" if they eat up all their food. Nail polish is applied to tiny nails so that they are "just like mommy's." Perceptual similarity is heightened by mother-daughter dresses, with appropriate verbal attention-arousal. Kits of "dress-up" clothing are supplied with high-heeled shoes "just like mommy's." The young child's tendency to pan-identification and pan-imitation seems to be given specific directional limitation by this device, resulting in a more pronounced "self-clumping" with the mother than with the father (disregarding for the moment the factor of uneven exposure). This would logically lead to a relatively favored position for the mother, as compared with the father, in the attention of the young girl. That this occurs is indicated by the preschool girl's greater information about the mother's activities (Baum, 1957), by attributions to the mother of more activities than to the father (Baum, 1957; Emmerich, 1959), and by attribution to her of own-sex preference in relation to children (Hartley and Hardesty, 1962). Since this anti-differentiation technique seems to be employed earliest in the feeding situation, when children are still being fed by their mothers, it would appear to be among the earliest sex-typing indoctrination devices used, leading to a symbiotic-like relationship with the same-sex parent (MacFarland, 1960).

Around the time toilet training is becoming well established, when the child is beginning to manage her own toileting behavior, a similar device with more stringently limiting implications, one facilitating discrimination learning, comes into use. The observant little girl who wants to urinate from an erect position is told, "No, little girls don't do that. You must sit, like mommy. Only Daddies and boys stand." This may be the first direct negatively phrased sex-oriented limitation the young female has encountered. It not only emphasizes further her kinship with women, but calls attention insistently to her separation from men.

Parallel with this phase, or a little later, another divisive note is struck when the girl wants to shave as her daddy does. She is usually told, "Girls don't shave—only daddies do." At the same time she is permitted to imitate her mother in applying cosmetics and using perfume, both apparently intrinsically attractive activities. She is also often supplied with her own cosmetic kit, her own perfume, her own shampoo and toilet water, her own bath fragrance, so that what starts as symbolic imitation at two or three becomes reality activity by four or five.

Similarly, not only is the small girl invited to participate in household tasks, but she is supplied with the tools to imitate sequences of female house-keeping behavior. This is not a preparation for future roles, but is part of the female child's age-status role from about two years on. If Piaget (1962) is correct in his analysis of the importance of imitation for perceptive activity, which in turn creates the memory image on which deferred imitation (symbolic play or dramatic play) is based, furnishing the girl child with the tools for imitating traditional female activities is a basic step in sex-typing, for this encourages practice in selected sequences of behavior, resulting in the satisfaction of mastery and further repetition for the sheer pleasure of repeating what has been mastered. Continued exteriorization of the image, leads, furthermore, to greater accommodation of the image to reality.

If imitation is, as Piaget contends, always a continuation of understanding, that which is more repetitively imitated, with continued access to the model, is better understood. If, in addition, it is true that there is imitation of visual models only in so far as they are understood, access to the tools of imitative activity takes on further significance. The importance of sensory-motor activity in developing "understanding" early in life suggests that appropriate tools with which one can go through perceived movements easily and achieve perceptible effects endow the original evocative perceptions with meaning beyond that inherent in the partial imitation possible without appropriate objects to manipulate. This effect has impact, in addition to encouraging the continuation of the "practice" into ages when manipulating completely symbolic objects is no longer relished.

ACTIVITY EXPOSURE

I have made no mention of the concentrated exposure to women's traditional activities which in itself could account for a preference for imitating these activities through the reinforcing effects of familiarization and repetition *per se*, because little boys are similarly exposed, and often invited to participate. To my mind significant differential emphasis is furnished by unhindered access to the means for continuing the activity on a deferred basis, encouraging both assimilation of the percepts to the ego, thus endowing them with more positive affect, and accommodation of the imitation to more clearly perceived reality as ego-differentiation proceeds.

With imitative activity filling the gap until the child is able to participate meaningfully as a partner in the home centered behaviors, the definition of this aspect of the female sex-role seems to proceed without interruption and with continuous reinforcement almost from the cradle on. With the advantage of primacy as well as continuity-amid-change, with the impact of positive self-reinforcement through satisfaction in perfected performance, the traditional domestic female role seems to have an advantage over other aspects of role definition which may account partially for the apparent single-minded purposiveness with which the newly adult female seeks to achieve the status connected with it.

There is, however, another aspect to female sex-role definition in childhood. Middle class mothers rarely feel strongly about *limiting* their young daughters to "feminine" toys or about inhibiting motor behavior. Girls who are given houseplay equipment are also given tricycles and guns and baseball bats if they wish them. While there seems to be a tendency to discourage girls from fisticuffs, most other interests and behaviors are viewed tolerantly during the preschool years. One mother's comment, "There's no point to making an issue of it—when they need to be feminine they grow out of their tomboyish ways," seems to reflect a pervasive attitude. Hence, although some aspects of femininity are emphasized by techniques of evocation, these are not necessarily exclusive nor restrictive. From the young subject's point of view, sex-role, child-role and self-definition are blended in an unselfconscious complex of unobstructed behavior. If little girls are permitted to play with guns as well as with dolls, playing with guns is part of the female sex-role definition. If they meet no specific strictures *against* playing with trains or trucks, even though these objects may not be customarily supplied to them, expressing interest in them in no way violates their implementation of their sex-role, as they perceive it. To interpret such choices, on a one-session basis as occurs in most "tests" of early sex-identification, as "masculine-striving" is to suggest a lack of understanding of both developmental milieu and individual personal dynamics.

THE DEVELOPMENT OF PREFERENCES

The gradual nature of the development of limitation and specification in toy preferences by female children, as reported by several investigators (Brown, 1956; Hartup and Zook, 1960; Rabban, 1950), may logically have multiple determinants such as a continuation of the narrowing influences of canalization, the cumulative effect of differential awareness and the parallel personality and cognitive processes of ego differentiation and concept formation alluded to earlier. It seems no accident that accurate sex-status self-identity (Rabban, 1950), early initial empirical evidence of limited sex-appropriate toy preferences (Hartup and Zook, 1960; Rabban, 1950), intense preoccupation with imitative houseplay (Hartley, Frank, and Goldenson, 1952), and indications of the beginnings of concept formation (Ausubel, 1958; Rabban, 1950) all occur at about the same time—around four years. Awareness of one's own sex-identity would appear to be crucial for the conscious rejection of nonappropriate play objects, and Rabban's data support such an hypothesis. He finds consistently increasing sex-oriented limitation of toy choices with increase in awareness of own sex, from age three through age six (Rabban, 1950).

The first limited, adult-imitative phase of female sex-role definition seems to come to a peak around five years (Brown, 1956; Fauls and Smith, 1956; Rabban, 1950). Both Rabban and Brown report a broadening of toy choices after five years, while Rabban also finds a decrease in the relationship between own-sex awareness and toy preference at eight years.

The sex-differentiating cognition and implementations which define her sex-role for the eight-year-old girl, reported separately by Hartley (1964) and by Sutton-Smith, Rosenberg, and Morgan (1961), indicate both continuity and change. The Hartley data, based on primary cognitions, and gathered from 45 eight-year-old and 45 11-year-old girls, indicate that while the traditional houseplay toys are included in the female child's role, they are joined by many of the actual household services they represent. Helping mother hang clothes, caring for a baby, dusting, washing and drying dishes, clearing the table, going to get groceries are seen consensually (with significantly more than 50 per cent of the girls agreeing) as activities girls engage in and that boys do not.

Between eight and 11 years there is no significant change in cognition in relation to these specific domestic items. The change from early childhood comes with the addition of activities that are specifically age-appropriate as well as sex-related and that are independent of traditional adult female sex-role activities. These include the addition of jacks, jump-rope and dancing lessons (from the Hartley data) and (from Sutton-Smith et al.) apparent broadening of imitative play to include other-than-home foci (store, church, actors, actresses) more vigorous motor performances (skating, cartwheels), as well as a plethora of group games (farmer in the dell, drop the handkerchief, etc.) that adults do not engage in.

The Hartley data report two types of sex-role information: cognitions, indicating knowledge of what girls *do* (that boys do not), and preferences, which indicate what girls *like* to do. The Sutton-Smith, et al. data report only implemented preferences. From a combination of the two groups of *preference* data, the following picture emerges: a steadily increasing inclusivity of interest in every variety of nonutilitarian game, sport and exercise of skill, along with a partial withdrawal of interest from "houseplay," sewing, cooking, knitting and a variety of actual household tasks like washing dishes and emptying wastebaskets. At the same time, at 11, there is greater rejection of certain traditionally masculine playthings, such as wagons, trucks and toy soldiers. Viewed broadly, the female sex-role definition of middle childhood maintains a specifically domestic core, while it extends to include a wide variety of non-domestic activities, most of which are also specific to an age status. This development suggests the reflection of multiple role activity, with greater emphasis on a peer-group focus.

Some investigators have suggested a rejection of femininity during this period, but our material does not support such a view. Of all the activities consensually identified by our female subjects as being implemented by girls, none were consensually rejected. Of all the activities consensually identified as being implemented by boys, only one (playing with electric trains) was given consensual preference by girls. Activities definitely recognized as male-appropriate tended to be avoided, not desired, by the majority of our female subjects.

Our data emphasize the need to distinguish between historical trends and personal dynamics. While girls may now be doing more of the sorts of things boys only were doing earlier (Sutton-Smith and Rosenberg, 1961), for each girl growing into a specific age-sex status currently, these behaviors are clearly included within her cognitions of the female role and do not indicate cross-sex role intrusions.

LATER DEVELOPMENT

The dynamics of the shift from the limited domestic imitative focus of the preschool years to the broadly competitive and skill-centered later years need present no mystery. The imitative activity continues, with the priority of the old models challenged by the introduction of new. As the child is forcibly separated from home by school, the focus of exposure is diluted while new requirements for adjustment intensify the perceptual saliency of new models, both adult and child. At the same time, continuing ego differentiation, with its implicit burden of awareness of self-limitations, forces awareness of similarity to other children while it intensifies awareness of difference from adults. The child's ability to categorize, to distinguish parts from wholes, appearing close to the time of school entrance, would facilitate the simultaneous multiple classification needed to perceive accurately both similarities and differences related to sex-age statuses. Once this perception is achieved, it can become a basis for specified imitative behavior designed to emphasize differentiation from one category of beings (adults) and similarity to another (children). One need only take into account the attraction of novelty, relative recency of exposure for many girls, the lack of inhibiting restrictions, and the newly developed priority of child-models (compared to adults) as an aspect of advanced ego-differentiation to accept as logical the findings of Sutton-Smith, et al. (1961) concerning 3rd grade girls who show an increase in interest in playing Indians, cops and robbers, and other "immature" boyish games. The female peer-group esteem extended to daring and to motor skills is sufficient to reinforce these and to extend their manifestations. Historically these values may have had a basically masculine connotation, but to the school age girl growing up today they are simply part of the behavior of the admired own-sex model. As evidence on this point, an informal series of pilot interviewers with preadolescents conducted in 1961 suggested that no girl today wants to be a "sissy." For the girls, the term has lost its sex-status connotation, and implies quite simply certain undesirable qualities of behavior.

SOCIAL CLASS AND SEX-ROLE SPECIFICITY

I have been talking until now as if sex-specific barriers to behavior do not exist for girls.

Obviously, this is not true. The various reports of attempts to measure female sex-role behavior in childhood emphasize greater variability among girls than among boys and increasing variability with age. This suggests more variation in the sex-role expectations individual girls meet than is the case with boys. Rabban has described the difference in degree of direction and restriction exercised respectively by parents of upper and of lower economic groups in their children (Rabban, 1950). Our own small family survey referred to earlier confirms his findings. From these, we would expect middle class girls to define their sex-roles much more broadly and inclusively than working class girls.

Our data, comparing small matched groups of upper middle class and lower middle class girls (N=40) do not support this hypothesis in general. Of 18 behavior items (Hartley, 1964) assigned by our total female sample (N=90) consensually to girls, the upper middle class group claimed significantly greater sex-status exclusivity to two items (taking dancing lessons and playing with jacks) and disowned none. Of 22 items assigned by the total female sample to boys consensually (Hartley, 1964), the upper middle differed from the lower middle significantly on only one item—climbing trees. The former saw this as something for both boys and girls, rather than for boys alone. In terms of primary cognitions they differed little from the lower economic group.

If we consider *preference*, however, the picture changes. On the female child-role measure mentioned earlier (made up of 10 selected items) the upper middle group made significantly lower scores than the lower middles. They rejected significantly more often *washing and drying dishes*, *clearing the table*, *helping mother with the washing*. Other activities, not included in the short measure, for which they showed significantly more dislike were *tidying a room*, *emptying wastebaskets*, *helping carry packages*, *protecting a frightened younger child*, *playing with toy dishes* and *with a toy carpet sweeper*, and *playing with a little boy*. They also showed significantly less liking for *playing in country fields* and *carrying wood into the house*.

What we see here seems to refer less to sex-role rejection than to rejection of *work-roles*. In terms of the activities we used, the upper middle class subjects seems to prefer a narrower range of activities than the lower economic group. It is highly likely, however, that what we are faced with here is not literally a narrowing of role preferences but an attitudinal forerunner of differential class-based sex-role implementation.

Pertinent here may be Piaget's warning that imitative behavior occurs only when the models are esteemed and the behavior is both meaningful and perceived as related to the child's interests. It is a matter of general knowledge that domestic roles are differently implemented in different economic groups. Since our upper middle class girls tended to reject not only the tasks of domesticity, but the toys that represented them, we might infer that the domestic core of service activities were not as meaningfully present for them as for the lower middle class girls. The activities marked perceptually by the women of whom the upper group were most meaningfully aware may have been implemented in areas not sufficiently represented in our investigatory tools.

We do know that their secondary cognitions or attributed expectations (i.e. perceptions of preferences) of *adult* female roles follows a similar pattern, with significantly more dislike of traditional household tasks attributed to "most women" than is reflected by girls from less prosperous homes (Hartley, 1961a, 1961b). Since Komarovsky found dissatisfaction with domestic roles more characteristic of young college-trained females than of working class wives (1962), this attribution is apparently both accurately reflective and predictive. What we seem to need now to fill in the picture are some *positives*—we know how upper middle class girls do *not* define their sex-roles—the detail of how they *do* define them and when and how the differentiation begins may have to wait on future studies specifically focused on this end.

Such studies should not be very difficult. For a start, carefully controlled observations of the content of the dramatic play of preschool girls from different socio-economic backgrounds might be helpful in clarifying this picture. The techniques, described elsewhere (Hartley, 1960, 1961b), that we used to gather the data on the secondary cognitions of school age girls work well with five-year-olds, too—a comparatively small effort could fill a significant gap by extending our data downward in age. We also have interview data, not yet analyzed, from the mothers of our subjects which could show illuminating differences in the patterns of daily living for the two socio-economic child groups. A little cooperative endeavor at this time could yield high dividends in this area.

SUMMARY

Three points deserve emphasis. First, sex-role differentiation takes place through a *variety* of highly complex processes, each of which contributes to a particular facet of status-related personality formation, perceptual sharpening and response reinforcement. Second, for females, significant class-based differences in definition seem to exist, starting early in life. And third, in relation to research approaches, it seems clear that secondary cognitions must parallel primary cognitions for meaningful data, and, finally, definitions of role must be referred to the subjects for valid interpretation of the meaning of any specific style of sex-role implementation.

REFERENCES

Abel, H., and Shahin Kaya, R., 1962. Emergence of sex and race friendship preferences. *Child Development*, **33**, 939–943.

Ausubel, D. P., 1958. *Theory and problems of child development*. New York: Grune and Stratton.

Baum, P., 1957. Identification in pre-school children. Unpublished master's thesis, University of California.

Biddle, B. J., 1961. *The present status of role theory*. Columbia, Mo.: University of Missouri Press.

Brown, D. G., 1956. Sex-role preference in your children, *Psychological Monographs*, **70** (14).

Duval, Elise, B., 1955. Conceptions of mother roles by five- and six-year-old children of working and non-working mothers. Unpublished doctoral dissertation, Florida State University.

Emmerich, W., 1959. Parental identification in young children. *Genetic Psychological Monographs*, **60**, 257–308.

Fauls, Lydia B., and Smith, W. D., 1956. Sex-role learning of five-year-olds. *Journal of Genetic Psychology*, **89**, 105–117.

Finch, Helen M., 1955. Young children's concepts of parent roles. *Journal of Home Economics*, **47**, 99–103.

Hartley, Ruth E., 1960. Children's concepts of male and female roles. *Merrill-Palmer Quarterly*, **6**, 83–91.

Hartley, Ruth E., 1961a. Current patterns in sex-role: children's perspectives. *Journal of the National Association of Women's Deans and Counselors*, **25**, 3–13.

Hartley, Ruth E., 1961b. Sex-roles and urban youth: some developmental perspectives. *Bulletin on Family Development*, **2**, 1–12.

Hartley, Ruth E., 1964. Children's perceptions of sex-role activity in childhood. *Journal of Genetic Psychology*, **105**, 43–45.

Hartley, Ruth E., Frank, L., and Goldenson, R., 1952. *Understanding children's play*. New York: Columbia University Press.

Hartley, Ruth E., and Hardesty, F., 1962. Children's perceptions and expression of sex-preferences. *Child Development*, **33**, 221–227.

Hartley, Ruth E., and Klein, A., 1959. Sex-role concepts among elementary school girls. *Marriage and Family Living*, **21**, 59–64.

Hartup, W. W., and Zook, Elsie, A., 1960. Sex-role preferences in three- and four-year-old children. *Journal of Consulting Psychology*, **24**, 420–426.

Komarovsky, Mirra, 1962. The homemaker: a comparative view. *American Association of University Women Journal*, **55**, 226–229.

Krugman, H. E., 1943. Affective response to music as a function of familiarity. *Journal of Abnormal and Social Psychology*, **38**, 388–392.

MacFarland, Margaret B., 1960. Personal communications, December 30, 1959, and February 29.

Mead, Margaret, 1954. Age patterning in personality development. In W. Martin and C. Stendler (Eds.), *Readings in child development*. New York: Harcourt, Brace, pp. 170–176.

Murphy, G., 1947. *Personality*. New York: Harper and Row.

Piaget, J., 1952. *The origins of intelligence in children*. New York: International Universities Press.

Piaget, J., 1962. *Play, dreams and imitation in childhood*. New York: W. W. Norton.

Rabban, M., 1950. Sex-role identification in young children in two diverse social groups. *Genetic Psychological Monographs*, **42**, 81–158.

Sears, R. R., Maccoby, Eleanor E., and Levin, H., 1957. *Patterns of child rearing*. New York: Harper and Row.

Sutton-Smith, B., and Rosenberg, B. G., 1961. Sixty years of historical change in the game preferences of American children. *Journal of American Folklore*, **74**, 17–46.
Sutton-Smith, B., Rosenberg, B. G., and Morgan, E. E., 1961. Sex differences in role preference for play activities and games. Paper read at Society for Research in Child Development, University Park, Pa.
Tolman, E. C., 1948. Cognitive maps in rats and men. *Psychological Review*, **55**, 189–208.

selection 45 Family Role Concepts of Children Ages Six to Ten

WALTER EMMERICH

A number of social scientists have emphasized the importance of role perception as a determinant of social action (Asch, 1952; Gross, Mason, and McEachern, 1958; Mead, 1934; Parsons, 1955; Sarbin, 1954). It is believed that role discriminations help define the constancies anticipated in each person's behavior during the ensuing interaction. Insofar as such anticipations function to mediate and guide purposeful activity, a thorough understanding of their nature is essential for predicting behavior. Very little is known about the dimensions children use to define dyadic relationships within the family. In an earlier study by the writer (Emmerich, 1959b), this problem was investigated in children of 4½ to 6 years. The present study extends the investigation to an older sample, with the purpose of describing intragroup role consensus and differences in consensus among subgroups classified according to sex and age.

The descriptive aim of this study is pertinent to several areas of developmental social psychology. First, any subgroup regularities in role perception will in part describe the typical child's social space and thereby become parameters in predicting his behavior. Second, the functioning of a social system is presumably dependent upon the extent of agreement on role definitions among its members. By comparing normative data on children and parents, it should be possible to determine characteristic areas of definitional agreement and disagreement between parent and child and to relate these to indices of family integration. Third, sex and age variations in role consensus have bearing on theories of developmental change in the cognition of social structures, such as that of Parsons (1955). Fourth, if role conceptions are influenced by cultural arrangements which vary with such factors as social status, sex, and age, it becomes necessary to have subgroup norms in order to evaluate properly the degree of "normalcy" of a particular individual's role perceptions. Finally, as Parsons (1955) and Brim (1957) point out, knowledge about specific intrafamilial role relationships is essential for understanding the precise nature of more complex role processes. To illustrate this point, consider the commonly held belief that sex-identity is ordinarily acquired by the child's taking one of his parents as a model. Assuming that this belief is correct, the problem still remains of specifying which role relationships serve as referents of the modeling process. For example, in the case of the girl who takes her mother as a model in play, to what extent does her play behavior reflect the mother's relationship with the girl, the father, a sibling, a person outside the family, or some combination of these? Suppose that the girl discriminates age roles, but not sex roles. Then she might take the mother-girl relationship as a model, but she cannot do so for the mother-father relationship because she does not discriminate sex roles. The assessment of children's role concepts, then, is believed to be prerequisite to the analysis of identification patterns acquired through a process of role modeling.

From *Child Development*, 1961, **32**, 609–624. Reprinted by permission of the author and the Society for Research in Child Development. The investigation was supported by grants from the National Institute of Health.

It is important to select for study those role dimensions which are likely to be salient for both sexes over an extended age period. The literature indicates that *relative power* and *attitudinal direction* are two dimensions which meet this criterion (Barker and Wright, 1955; Gardner, 1947; Kagan, 1956; Kagan and Lemkin, 1960). Relative power is defined here as the amount of implied or explicit control each person has over the outcome of an interaction. Attitudinal direction is defined as the extent of implied or explicit agreement (positive) or disagreement (negative) with respect to the means and/or goals of an interaction. Other definitions used in the study are as follows. A *role* is defined as the behaviors (performances) characteristic of the incumbent of one position toward the incumbent of another position in a social structure. This definition is similar to Gross, Mason, and McEachern's (1958) concept of "role behavior sector." A *role concept* is defined as the discrimination of a particular position on a specific behavioral dimension. The referent of a *person concept* is distinguished from that of a *role concept*. A person concept is derived from a particular person's performances of a variety of roles, whereas a role concept is derived from the performance of a typical person or many persons in a single role. There are at least two criteria for operationally distinguishing person and role concepts. For a role, but not for a person concept, there is: (a) generalization to the population of persons who hold the same position; (b) intra-group consensus on the behavior characteristic of a position, when each group member judges a different occupant of the position. This study relies primarily upon the second of these criteria.

METHOD

Subjects

Subjects were 225 elementary school children from middle-class families unbroken by separation, death, or divorce. None was adopted. Age groups were formed in such a way as to create nonoverlapping age ranges, approximately the same mean age for both sexes within each age level, and approximately equal *N*s in all subgroups. Six age groups resulted, henceforth called the 6, 6½, 7, 8, 9, and 10 year groups. Subgroup sizes and age statistics are given in Table 1. Approximately 79 per cent of the sample came from socioeconomic levels 1 or 2 in Warner, Meeker, and Eels' (occupational) classification scheme (1949), and approximately 76 per cent of the sample had either one or two siblings.[1]

Materials

Stylized figure drawings, described in detail elsewhere (Emmerich, 1959b), were prepared on 6¼ by 3¼ in. Hunter Card Master cards in the following pairs: mother-girl, father-boy, mother-father, and girl-boy. Each member of a pair appeared on the left and right sides of the cards half the time. The 48 cards were presented to subjects by means of the Hunter Card Master, Model 340.

Procedure

Subjects were tested individually. *S* sat in front of the exposure window of the Card Master, with *E* seated beside him. *E* pointed to the exposed

TABLE 1 DESCRIPTION OF SUBJECTS

	N	Age (in Months) *Mean*	*Range*	*SD*
6 *Year Group*				
Girls	21	71.5	66– 75	2.7
Boys	17	70.4	64– 75	3.4
Total	38	71.0	64– 75	3.1
6½ *Year Group*				
Girls	18	78.9	76– 82	2.0
Boys	19	79.7	76– 82	1.8
Total	37	79.3	76– 82	1.9
7 *Year Group*				
Girls	19	87.9	83– 91	2.8
Boys	20	86.8	83– 91	2.9
Total	39	87.3	83– 91	2.8
8 *Year Group*				
Girls	17	96.2	92–104	3.7
Boys	21	96.4	92–103	3.2
Total	38	96.3	92–104	3.7
9 *Year Group*				
Girls	20	108.7	105–116	3.7
Boys	16	108.7	104–115	3.5
Total	36	108.7	104–116	3.5
10 *Year Group*				
Girls	16	121.1	117–131	3.7
Boys	21	121.6	117–129	3.3
Total	37	121.4	117–131	3.4
Total				
Girls	111	93.2	66–131	17.2
Boys	114	94.4	64–129	17.6
Total	225	93.8	64–131	17.4

[1] These figures are based upon the 157 cases for which exact data were available on socioeconomic level and number of siblings. The remaining 68 subjects were very similar to this group in both respects.

boy-father card and said, "Do you see these people here? Let's play a game with them. Okay? Who says, 'I'm the boy'?" After *S* pointed to the correct figure, *E* said, "Yes, that's a boy just like you," if *S* was a boy, or "Yes, that's a boy just your age," if *S* was a girl. *E* then asked, "Who says, 'I'm the father'?" After *S* pointed to the correct figure, *E* exposed the next card which was the girl-mother pair. Experimenter then asked, "Who says, 'I'm the girl'?" After *S* pointed to the correct figure, *E* said, "Yes, that's a girl just like you," if *S* was a girl, or, "Yes that's a girl just your age," if *S* was a boy. *E* then asked, "Who says, 'I'm the mother'?" In order to give some initial practice with behavior descriptions similar to the actual test items, the girl-boy card was presented next, with the item, "I want it." The mother-girl card was then presented with the item, "Stop doing that." The test proper then began and consisted of presenting the 48 pairs in a prearranged order, designed to control for a variety of possible response sets. Either pointing to a figure or naming it was an acceptable response. *S* was given as much time as he wanted, and *E* repeated the item whenever *S* did not respond after several seconds or responded ambiguously. Each child was told that he did very well at the completion of testing.

In order to have partial control over the influences of examiner characteristics on the children's responses, a male and a female tested approximately half the subjects in each of the 12 subgroups.

Measures

The items were similar to those used in the previous study (Emmerich, 1959b) and are classified in Table 2 according to relative power and attitudinal direction. Items having corresponding numbers across columns and rows are role reciprocals on the power and attitude dimensions, respectively. All items were used to assess age-role discriminations of the mother-girl and father-boy pairs. Because of limited time for testing and because of the tendency for younger subjects to assign high and lower power items to the adult and child generations, respectively (Emmerich, 1959b), high power items only were used to assess sex-role discriminations of the mother-father pair, while low power items only were used to assess sex-role discriminations of the girl-boy pair. For the mother-girl and father-boy comparisons, the *power discrimination measure* was the total number of assignments of high power items to adult figures and low power items to child figures. For the mother-father comparison, this measure was the number of times the father was chosen on high power items, and, for the girl-boy comparison, this measure was the number of times the girl was chosen on low power items. For the mother-girl and father-boy comparisons, the *attitude discrimination measure* was the total number of assignments of positive items to adult figures and negative items to child figures. For the mother-father and girl-boy comparisons, this measure was the total number of assignments of positive items to female figures and negative items to male figures.

The above measures were based upon the assumption that all items contributed to both dimensions according to the scheme presented in Table 2. A number of scale characteristics, such as small variances and skewed distributions, made it impossible to estimate scale homogeneities and

TABLE 2 CLASSIFICATION OF ITEMS ACCORDING TO RELATIVE POWER AND ATTITUDINAL DIRECTION

High Power	*Low Power*
Positive Attitude	
1. You can have it.	1. I want it.
2. That's nice. You did what I asked.	2. I'll do what you say.
3. You made that very well.	3. I made it very well.
4. You did what was right.	4. I'll do what is right.
Negative Attitude	
1. You can't have it.	1. Give me what I want.
2. You'd better do as I say.	2. No. I won't do it.
3. You didn't make it very well.	3. I can't make it very well.
4. You did something that is wrong.	4. I'll do something that is wrong.

the discrimination power of items with precision. However, crude analyses of part-whole association were performed, using the extremes of those subgroups having maximal variability on the scales. All items were found to contribute to both scales applied to each of the four paired comparisons. The chi square probabilities associated with the 32 phi coefficients ranged from .20 to .001, with a median of .01.

RESULTS AND DISCUSSION

Nonparametric statistics were used in all analyses, and a finding is interpreted if it was significant beyond the .05 level. For analyses of intragroup consensus, chi square was used to determine if more than half the *S*s fell either above or below the scale point representing equal assignment of both ends of a dimension to each person in a pair. This point on the scale shall henceforth be referred to as "chance." The median test or its extension to several independent variables in a single analysis (Wilson, 1956) was applied to differences among subgroups. The sign test was used in the analyses of differential item sensitivities. The index of association was *C* (significance levels only are reported), with distributions divided at or near the median.

Discrimination of Age Roles by Relative Power

There was a marked tendency for the whole sample to use the power dimension to discriminate the mother-girl and father-boy pairs. Scores for these two pairs combined could vary from 0 to 32, with 16 representing chance. Ninety-nine per cent of the whole sample had scores above 16, and the median was 29.5. It is clear that the power dimension is used by children of this age to discriminate age roles, as is the case for younger children (Emmerich, 1959b). This result is highly consistent with Barker and Wright's (1955) survey of actual parent-child interactions, in which it was found that dominance and nurturance are the most frequent parent behaviors, whereas appeal, submission, and resistance are the most frequent child behaviors.

Girls discriminated age roles on the power dimension somewhat more than boys ($p < .05$), and this difference did not vary with age. Although this finding is consistent with those suggesting that girls are more sensitive to age grading than boys (Emmerich, 1959a; Hartley, Frank, and Goldenson, 1952; Sears, Maccoby, and Levin, 1957) or that boys are more successful than girls in defying parental commands and restrictions (Radke, 1946), it does not very strongly support either of these interpretations, since boys clearly discriminated age roles by power, and the difference between the sexes was only about one point on the scale. Further, this sex difference did not appear in younger children (Emmerich, 1959b).

Age changes in age-role discrimination by power are presented in Figure 1. The tendency for scores to increase with age is significant for the father-boy ($p < .001$), but not for the mother-girl comparison. There was no interaction between sex and age of child for either comparison. These findings are subject to several possible interpretations. If it is assumed that the age trend for the (nonassessed) father-girl comparison would have been similar to that found for the father-boy comparison, then the results signify that children age-type maternal relationships earlier than paternal relationships. Several factors could account for this possibility. Since mothers interact more frequently with children of this age than fathers (Barker and Wright, 1955), there is more opportunity for children to learn appropriate age roles in their maternal relationships. However, there is little evidence indicating that the frequency of father-child interactions increases with age during this period (Barker and Wright, 1955; Tasch, 1952), as did the father-boy discrimination. Or, if the mother is (or is perceived as) more nurturant or powerful than the father in socializing the younger child, then the child may be more motivated to overlearn appropriate age roles in the maternal relationship. Again, however, although some studies support this interpretation (Barker and Wright, 1955; Brim, 1957; Radke, 1946) others do not (Brim, 1957; Gardner, 1947; Kagan, 1956; Kagan and Lemkin, 1960). Another possibility is that the child's awareness of the father's high power in other roles increases with age and generalizes to the father-child relationship. This interpretation gains support from the finding, discussed in more detail later, that amount of power attributed to the father *vis-à-vis* the mother also increases rapidly between the sixth and eighth year (*see* Figure 2). On the other hand, if it is assumed that the age trend for the (nonassessed) mother-boy comparison would have been similar to that found for the father-boy comparison, then the findings signify that children of both sexes perceive that girls age-type earlier than boys. A number of studies do suggest that girls perceive, accept, or are expected to learn age-appropriate child and adult roles earlier than boys (Emmerich, 1959a; Hartley, Frank, and Goldenson, 1952; Meltzer, 1943; Radke, 1946; Sears, Maccoby, and Levin, 1957). Further study is needed to determine which of these interpretations is most valid.

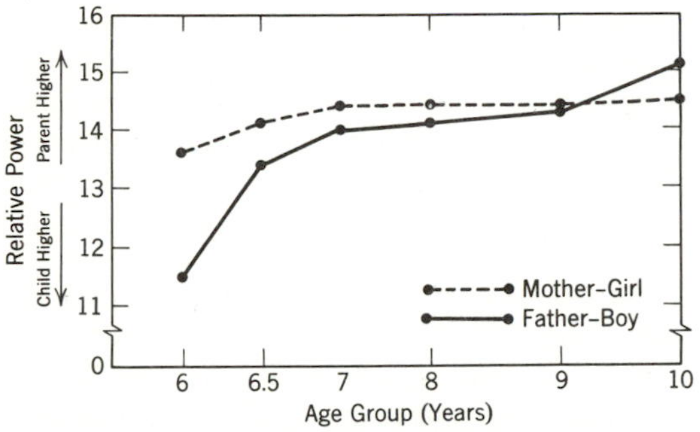

Figure 1. Discrimination of age roles by power.

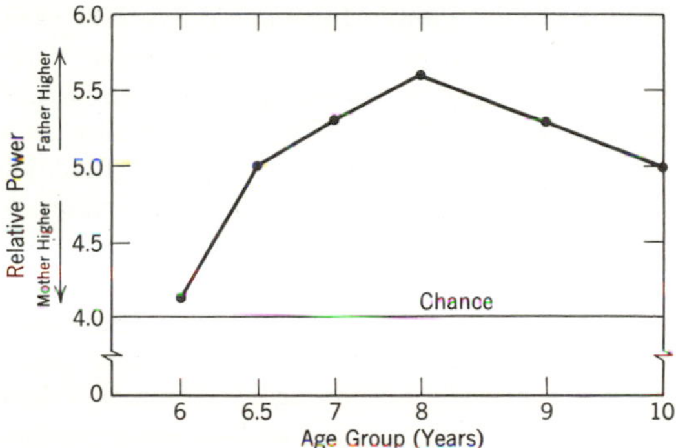

Figure 2. Discrimination of parent sex roles by power.

There was a greater tendency to assign high power items to parents than to assign low power items to children ($p < .001$), and this difference showed no consistent variation with sex or age. This is a replication of an earlier finding and is discussed elsewhere (Emmerich, 1959b).

Parsons (1955) has hypothesized that there are developmental changes in the specific cues used by the child to discriminate family roles. His discussion suggests the following developmental sequence of age-role discriminations: (a) *Response:* The child is primarily an object having needs; the parent is an agent of gratification or frustration of these needs. (b) *Acceptance:* The child is capable of meeting specific norms governing the parent-child relationship; the parent praises the child when he conforms, and controls the child when he deviates. (c) *Approval:* The child is capable of meeting universal standards of achievement; the parent responds positively to the child's successes and criticizes his failures. (d) *Esteem:* The child is capable of acting according to broad standards of conduct; the parent recognizes appropriate behavior and reproves inappropriate behavior.

The four kinds of items in each cell of Table 2 were formulated to correspond to each of these presumed developmental levels. It was hypothesized that age-role discrimination by power is a function of the interaction between item type and age of child; i.e., lower level items would be age-typed more by younger children, whereas higher level items would be age-typed more by older children. The results did not support this hypothesis, as age-role discrimination by power increased with age at about the same rate for all four types of items. Rather, certain items were more sensitive to this dimension, irrespective of the child's sex or age. Specifically, the scores on items 2 and 4 were significantly higher than those on items 1 and 3 ($p < .01$ for each of the four comparisons), and the differences between items within these pairs were not significant.

Do items 2 and 4 possess some quality lacking in items 1 and 3 which might account for the former pair's greater sensitivity to the power dimension? Whereas item 1 involves the exchange of an object and item 3 the exchange of meanings with reference to an objective standard of performance, items 2 and 4 seem to connote an exchange of affect directed toward the interacting persons themselves. If this analysis is correct, then it would suggest that children are more sensitive to personalized "love-oriented" than to "object-oriented" relationships (Sears, Maccoby, and Levin, 1957) in their age-typing. Perhaps the kinds or patterning of rewards and punishments associated with love-oriented socialization techniques provide the child with greater incentive to learn age-role discriminations. This interpretation should be viewed with caution, however, for several reasons. Little is known about the differential incentive values of the rewards associated with each of the four types of items. Further, in view of the importance of achievement in middle-class society, particularly in boys, it is surprising that item 3 did not have stronger affective implications. Also, item affect saturation may vary among respondent populations, so that specification of affect criteria without reference to these populations would be misleading. It might be expected, for example, that item 1 would have stronger affective implications in a lower-class sample.

The failure of this study to confirm Parsons' hypothesis of developmental stages in children's age-role concepts should not be viewed as strong evidence against the theory. Parsons' discussion of levels (1955) is not sufficiently detailed to be certain that the items used are highly representative of their respective level universes. Also, item differences on other dimensions, such as affect, may have masked the predicted interaction. Finally, since the hypothesis refers to changes in role perception which presumably begin during the first year, the present study may not have sampled age groups which are young enough for the effect to appear.

Discrimination of Age Roles by Attitudinal Direction

The median of the whole sample on the attitude age-role discrimination scale did not differ from chance. There were no significant variations from chance within any of the 12 subgroups, either for the separate mother-girl and father-boy comparisons or for these comparisons combined. It would appear that attitudinal direction is not a dimension in children's age-role discriminations. It should be noted, however, that the power and attitude discrimination scores for the same pair are not completely independent. The fact that the children used the power dimension so intensively and extensively made it less likely, though not impossible, for significant age-role discriminations to occur on the attitude dimension. Nevertheless, if some subjects had relied heavily upon the attitude dimension, or if many had used this dimension a little more frequently, significant intra-group consensus or group differences could have appeared on this as well as on the power dimension. Therefore, it is reasonable to conclude that power is at least relatively more pertinent than attitude as a dimension of age-role discrimination during this age period.

Discrimination of Adult Sex Roles

The whole sample assigned more high power items to the father than to the mother ($p < .001$), and, as seen in Figure 2, there was a curvilinear relation between this tendency and age ($p < .05$). There was no interaction between sex and age on this measure. With respect to the attitude dimension, the median of the whole sample for mother-father discrimination did not differ from chance, and there was no significant variation with age. Although intragroup consensus on this measure was not significant for either sex, there was a difference between sex groups. Girls perceived the mother as somewhat more positive than the father, whereas boys perceived the converse ($p < .05$).

It is most striking that, for the sample as a whole, consensus again occurred on the power dimension, and not on the dimension of attitudinal direction. This finding, together with those on age-role discrimination, indicates that power is the more basic dimension in children's discriminations of parent roles, at least during this age period. If this conclusion is correct, then several interesting implications might follow. Although the importance of power has been recognized in the analysis of intrafamilial relationships (Baldwin, Kalhorn, and Breese, 1945; Barker and Wright, 1955; Hoffman, 1960; Kagan and Lemkin, 1960; Mussen and Distler, 1959; Parsons, 1955; Radke, 1946; Symonds, 1939), many investigators, including the present writer, have assumed that the attitude dimension is at least equally important in parent role differentiation (Brim, 1957; Emmerich, 1959a; Emmerich, 1959b; Kagan, 1956; Kagan and Lemkin, 1960; Mussen and Distler, 1959; Parsons, 1955; Sears, Maccoby, and Levin, 1957). In view of the present results, the latter assumption seems questionable, at least for children of this age. It should be noted, however, that this conclusion does not imply lack of salience of the attitude dimension at other levels, such as that of *person perception*, but only that this dimension may not be pertinent at the level of *role consensus*. Indeed, other results of the present study suggest that several levels need to be considered in a theory of the perceptual factors which guide interpersonal behavior in the child. For example, consider the findings that both sexes perceive the father's sex role as more powerful than the mother's but that girls perceive the mother as more positive, whereas boys perceive the father as more positive. Heider's analysis of benefit and sentiment (1958) suggests that a powerful person is seen as benevolent if he is also perceived as positive or as malevolent if he is also perceived as negative; whereas a nonpowerful person is differentiated less sharply in terms of potential benefit. In the present example, it might follow that the father's sex role is perceived as more benevolent by boys and as more malevolent by girls, but that the mother's sex role is not perceived by either sex so clearly in terms of potential benefit or harm.

The amount of power attributed to the father increased with age between the sixth and eighth year in both the father-boy and mother-father comparison (Figures 1 and 2, respectively), indicating that this period is particularly significant in the development of father-role concepts. Comparison of these two curves also suggests that while there is generalization across the sex- and age-role components of the father role during this period, differentiation of these role components begins to occur between the eighth and tenth year.

The pattern of results for the mother-father comparison differs in several respects from that found in the study of subjects ages 4½ to 6 (Emmerich, 1959b). The younger sample as a whole discriminated parent sex roles on the attitude dimension, whereas the power dimension was used in the present older sample. The obvious interpretation of this difference is that there is a dimension crossover at about the age of 6. The fact that the 6-year-olds of the present study did not discriminate the mother-father pair on the power dimension is consistent with this interpretation. However, this group did not discriminate parent sex roles by attitude either. Further, the girls of the younger sample perceived the mother as more powerful than the father. It is difficult to account for these discrepancies on any basis other than age, since the procedures of the two studies were very similar and the subjects were selected from the same school in successive years. However, in view of the potential importance of a dimension crossover at about the age of 6, it would be desirable to replicate this aspect of the studies in a group ranging in age from 4 to 8 years.

It has been assumed throughout this discussion that the mother-father discrimination measure was derived independently of the measures of age-role discrimination discussed earlier. However, if upon presentation of the mother-father pair, the child imaginatively placed himself into the situation, then this measure could reflect differential parental behaviors toward the child, rather than toward each other. That such confounding may have occurred was suggested by the (non-significant) positive association found between amount of power attributed to the father in the mother-father and father-boy comparisons. However, other evidence indicates that this type of confounding did not occur extensively, if at all. First, about a dozen subjects were asked, "Who does he (she) say that to?" after the child responded to a mother-father comparison. In every instance, the child reported that the parent "said" the item to the other parent, not to an imaginatively introduced child. Second, although children perceived the father as significantly more powerful than the mother on the mother-father comparison, they did not attribute greater power to the father in the father-boy comparison than to the mother in the mother-girl comparison. Third, attribution of power to the father in the mother-father comparison was positively correlated with attribution of power to the mother in the mother-girl comparison ($p < .05$), a result opposite to that expected if confounding had occurred. It is also of interest that the mother-girl and father-boy comparisons were positively correlated ($p < .001$). It would appear that attribution of higher power to the father's sex role covaries positively with attribution of higher power to adult roles. Thus, rather than reflecting confounding, the pattern of correlations among the three measures indicates that children's use of the power dimension tends to generalize to both the sex- and age-role components of parent roles.

Discrimination of Child Sex Roles

Girls perceived the girl role as more positive (and less negative) than the boy role ($p < .001$), whereas boys did not consistently discriminate child sex roles by attitude. There were no significant variations with age for either sex. This finding is in essential agreement with that for children of 4½ to 6 years (Emmerich, 1959b), although differences in the patterns of findings in the two studies lead to somewhat different interpretations. In the study of the younger sample, the fact that girls also discriminated adult sex roles on this dimension led to the conclusion that girls had developed sex-role concepts which generalize across the generations. This conclusion is not warranted in the present study, since girls did not discriminate adult sex roles by attitude. Perhaps this discrepancy between the studies reflects a true developmental change. However, for reasons discussed earlier, it would be important to replicate the findings on adult sex-role perception during the years 4 to 8 in order to evaluate this interpretation.

An interesting pattern of sex differences appears when this measure is broken down into its component items. As seen in Table 3, girls attributed more positive (and less negative) content to the girl role on all four items, particularly on items 2, 3, and 4. Boys, however, used the dimension significantly on fewer items, and not always in the same direction. The fact that both sexes attributed greater achievement competence (item 3) to themselves than to their opposite-sex peers is subject to two interpretations. It may signify a true sex difference in consensus on the definition of child sex roles with respect to achievement competence. Or it may reflect the child's wish to attribute greater competence to himself than to another child, irrespective of the other child's sex. The latter explanation seems plausible in view of the achievement pressures placed upon middle-class children of both sexes. However, the same argument fails to account for the fact that boys did not perceive themselves as significantly more positive than girls on any of the other items. Indeed, on item 4, there was consensus within both sexes that girls are more likely than boys to do the "right thing" and to avoid trouble. What is clear from this pattern of findings is that both sexes use the attitude dimension to discriminate child sex roles, but, whereas girls apply it in the same way to a variety of settings, boys apply it more selectively and in a direction that varies among situations.

TABLE 3 SEX ATTRIBUTED POSITIVE CONTENT ON EACH ITEM FOR GIRL–BOY COMPARISONS

Item Number	Sex of Subject: Girls		Boys	
1	Girl	ns	Boy	ns
2	Girl	<.01	Girl	ns
3	Girl	<.02	Boy	<.001
4	Girl	<.001	Girl	<.01

The whole sample assigned more low power items to the boy's sex role than to the girl's sex role ($p < .02$), and this tendency did not vary significantly with the child's sex or age. This result is difficult to explain, as it contradicts rather well-established facts on sex differences in children's social behavior (Terman and Tyler, 1954). It is also inconsistent with the finding on adult sex-role discrimination by power. The implausibility of this result raises a question about the validity of the power measure when applied to child sex-role discriminations. It will be recalled that low power items only were included in this measure because it seemed reasonable to use those items typically assigned to a particular generation when assessing discriminations within that generation. Perhaps this procedure resulted in loss of information that would have provided a more plausible finding, although the same procedure led to quite reasonable findings in the case of adult sex-role discriminations. Another possibility is that the power dimension collapses when the low end is applied to sex-role discriminations within the child generation. If this were the case, the measure could still consistently reflect a dimension, but one that differs from the intended dimension of power. Inspection of the low power items suggests that this measure might have reflected self-centeredness, or simply differential social activity levels. It should be noted that the same question can also be raised about the dimensionality of the power measure applied to adult sex-role discriminations despite the fact that the findings on this measure were more plausible. Further study is required to resolve this problem.

SUMMARY

This study investigated the development of children's conceptions of intrafamilial sex and age roles. The family role concepts of 225 middle-class children of 6 to 10 years of age were assessed by means of a modified paired-comparison procedure. The sample was divided into 12 subgroups based upon the child's sex and age. Intragroup and between group analyses of role consensus revealed the extent of use of the dimensions of relative power (high vs. low) and attitudinal direction (positive vs. negative) to discriminate intrafamilial roles. The major findings were as follows:

1. In the discrimination of parent roles, there was much greater consensus on the power dimension than on the dimension of attitudinal direction.
2. Children discriminated age roles by assigning high power actions to the adult and low power actions to the child.
3. With increasing age, there was an increasing tendency to discriminate male but not female age roles by power.
4. Some age-role relationships were more differentiated by power than others. It was suggested that children age-type love-oriented more than object-oriented relationships.
5. The father's sex role was seen as more powerful than the mother's sex role.

6. There was a curvilinear relation between the child's age and the extent to which the father's sex role was perceived as more powerful than the mother's sex role.

7. Positive correlations were found among the measures of parent sex- and age-role discrimination by power, suggesting that use of the power dimension to discriminate parent roles generalizes across role situations.

8. Girls discriminated child sex roles by assigning positive actions to the girl and negative actions to the boy. In boys, the discrimination of child sex roles by attitude varied according to the specific interaction situation.

REFERENCES

Asch, S. E., 1952. *Social psychology*. Englewood Cliffs, N.J.: Prentice-Hall.

Baldwin, A. L., Kalhorn, Joan, and Breese, Fay H., 1945. Patterns of parent behavior. *Psychological Monographs*, **58** (268), 1–75.

Barker, R. G., and Wright, H. F., 1955. *Midwest and its children*. New York: Harper and Row.

Brim, O. G., Jr., 1957. The parent-child relation as a social system: I. Parent and child roles. *Child Development*, **28**, 343–364.

Emmerich, W., 1959a. Parental identification in young children. *Genetic Psychological Monographs*, **60**, 257–308.

Emmerich, W., 1959b. Young children's discriminations of parent and child roles. *Child Development*, **30**, 403–419.

Gardner, L. Pearl, 1947. An analysis of children's attitudes toward fathers. *Journal of Genetic Psychology*, **70**, 3–28.

Gross, N., Mason, W. S., and McEachern, A. W., 1958. *Explorations in role analysis*. New York: Wiley.

Hartley, Ruth E., Frank, L. K., and Goldenson, R. M., 1952. *Understanding children's play*. New York: Columbia University Press.

Heider, F., 1958. *The psychology of interpersonal relations*. New York: Wiley.

Hoffman, M. L., 1960. Power assertion by the parent and its impact on the child. *Child Development*, **31**, 129–143.

Kagan, J., 1956. The child's perception of the parent. *Journal of Abnormal and Social Psychology*, **53**, 257–258.

Kagan, J., and Lemkin, Judith, 1960. The child's differential perception of parental attributes. *Journal of Abnormal and Social Psychology*, **61**, 440–447.

Mead, G. H., 1934. *Mind, self and society*. Chicago: University of Chicago Press.

Meltzer, H., 1943. Sex differences in children's attitudes to parents. *Journal of Genetic Psychology*, **62**, 311–326.

Mussen, P., and Distler, L., 1959. Masculinity, identification, and father-son relationships. *Journal of Abnormal and Social Psychology*, **59**, 350–356.

Parsons, T., 1955. Family structure and the socialization of the child. In T. Parsons, R. F. Bales, and Associates, *Family, socialization, and interaction process*. New York: The Free Press, pp. 35–131.

Radke, Marian J., 1946. The relation of parental authority to children's behavior and attitudes. *University of Minnesota Institute of Child Welfare Monographs*, No. 22.

Sarbin, T. R., 1954. Role theory. In G. Lindzey (Ed.), *Handbook of social psychology*. Vol. 1. Cambridge, Mass.: Addison-Wesley, pp. 223–258.

Sears, R. R., Maccoby, Eleanor E., and Levin, H., 1957. *Patterns of child rearing*. New York: Harper and Row.

Symonds, P. M., 1939. *The psychology of parent-child relationships*. New York: Appleton-Century-Crofts.

Tasch, R. J., 1952. The role of the father in the family. *Journal of Experimental Education*, **20**, 319–361.

Terman, L. M., and Tyler, L. E., 1954. Psychological sex differences. In L. Carmichael (Ed.), *Manual of child psychology*. New York: Wiley, pp. 1064–1114.

Warner, W. L., Meeker, Marcia, and Eels, K., 1949. *Social class in America*. Chicago: Science Research Associates.

Wilson, K. V., 1956. A distribution-free test of analysis of variance hypotheses. *Psychological Bulletin*, **53**, 96–101.

selection 46 The Effects of Parental Role Model on Criminality

JOAN McCORD AND WILLIAM McCORD

Those who are at all familiar with criminology no longer question the importance of the family environment in the causation of crime. Among the many factors in the home which are known to be related to crime are the parents' attitudes toward their children, their methods of discipline, and their attitudes toward society. This last factor, the parental role model—the behavior and attitudes of the parents—is the focus of this paper. Many criminologists have emphasized the importance of the parental role model in the making of criminals (see Healy and Bronner, 1926; Glueck and Glueck, 1950). The aim of this paper is a more detailed investigation of the ways in which parental role models affect criminality.

[METHOD]

The present research is an outgrowth of the Cambridge-Somerville Youth Study, designed by Dr. Richard Clark Cabot for the prevention of delinquency. In 1935, Dr. Cabot and his staff selected 650 lower- and lower-middle-class boys from Cambridge and Somerville, Massachusetts, as participants in the project. Half of these boys were referred to Dr. Cabot as pre-delinquents, and the other half (added to avoid stigmatizing the group) were considered "normal" by their teachers and community officers. The average age of these boys was seven. After interviews, physical examinations, and psychological testing, each boy was matched to another as nearly similar in background and personality as possible. One from each pair (determined by toss of a coin) was placed in a treatment group; the remaining boys constituted the control group.

The treatment program began in 1939 and continued (on the average) for five years. Counselors gathered information from teachers, ministers, parents, and neighbors detailing the backgrounds of each of their boys. More importantly, the counselors repeatedly visited the boys and their families. Although two books have been written which point to the failure of this treatment as a preventative to crime (Powers and Witmer, 1951; McCord and McCord, 1959), the comprehensive reports written by the counselors provide a fund of information on the backgrounds of these boys who are now men.

Seventy-two boys who died, moved away from the area, or were dropped from the project near its beginning have been omitted from the present study. For the remaining 253 boys, running records had been kept which depicted each boy as he acted in his family and among his peers. The records describe conversations overheard by the counselors and discussions with the counselors; they report casual and formal interviews with or about the boys and their families.

In 1955 a staff of trained workers read these voluminous case records and recorded data pertaining to the behavior of each boy's parents. Thus, information on family background was based on direct, repeated observations by a variety of investigators, over an extended period of time.

Also in 1955, the names of the subjects and their parents were sent through the Massachusetts Board of Probation. In this way, we learned which of our subjects and which of their parents had acquired criminal records either in Massachusetts or Federal courts. For the purpose of this study, we defined as criminal anyone who had been convicted at least once for a crime involving violence, theft, drunkenness, or sexual violations. We recognize, of course, the deficiencies in this standard: some criminals may escape detection, and a number of cultural variables intercede between the committing of a crime and subsequent conviction. Nevertheless, we believe that this is the most objective standard available.

The information produced by the Cambridge-Somerville Youth Study enabled a unique longitudinal analysis of the causes of crime: the

From the *Journal of Social Issues*, 1957, **13**, 66–75. Reprinted by permission of the authors and the Society for the Psychological Study of Social Issues.

boys averaged seven years of age when the data were first collected, while their average age was twenty-seven when their criminal records were gathered. Moreover, since all of the boys came from the relatively lower-class, disorganized urban areas, they were all exposed to the delinquent subculture. Since this factor was held constant, we could concentrate our attention on those variables which differentiate among boys living in transitional areas.

In the study of the relation between role models and crime, we focused on three interacting variables in the familial environment of the boys: the role model of the parents, the attitudes of the parents toward the child, and the methods of discipline used by the parents.

The *parental role model* was, of course, our basic variable. Information about this factor was ascertained from two sources. First, the verbatim records kept by the observers contained direct evidence of the everyday behavior of the parents. Second, reports from the Boston Social Service Index and the Massachusetts Board of Probation reported all contacts between the parents and community agencies. We classified each parent into one of three groups: (a) those who had been convicted by the courts for theft or assault or who had spent time in a state or Federal prison; (b) those who, though they were non-criminal by our definition, were known to be alcoholic (many had records for repeated drunkenness) or were sexually promiscuous in a blatant fashion; and (c) those who were neither criminal nor alcoholic nor sexually unfaithful. These we considered as non-deviant. Two raters independently checking the same randomly selected cases agreed on 90 per cent.

In addition, information was gathered concerning the *attitudes of each parent toward the subject*. Previous research has linked parental rejection and crime; consequently, we expected that the influence of the parental role model might well depend on the emotional relation between the child and his parents. A parent was considered "warm" if he or she generally enjoyed the child and showed affectionate concern for him. A parent was considered "passive" if he or she had very little to do with the child. And a parent was considered "rejecting" if he or she gave primarily negative attention to the child. Finally, of course, there were a number of absent parents. (We rated step-parents in families where they had replaced the natural parents.) Using these classifications, three judges agreed in their ratings on 84 per cent of the fathers and on 92 per cent of the mothers in the cases selected at random from the sample.

Disciplinary methods, as well as parental attitudes, have often been cited as an important variable in the causation of crime. Since discipline can be regarded as the mediator between parental values and the child's learned behavior, we naturally wished to investigate the importance of this factor. The classification of discipline rested upon a theoretical division between techniques which depended upon the physical strength of the parent for effectiveness, and those techniques which utilized withdrawal of love. Verbal or physical attacks upon the child—beatings, displays of violent anger, and aggressive threats—constituted our "punitive discipline" category. Use of approval and verbal disapproval, reasoning, and withholding privileges were considered "love-oriented" discipline. If both parents regularly used one or the other of these basic methods, we classified the discipline as consistent. If one or both parents were erratic in their discipline or if they disagreed in their techniques, we considered the discipline inconsistent. Only if there was evidence that almost no restraints of any kind were used by the family did we consider the discipline to be "lax." Thus we arrived at five classifications of discipline: (a) consistently punitive, (b) consistently love-oriented, (c) erratically punitive, (d) erratically love-oriented, and (e) lax. Three raters agreed in the classification of 88 per cent of the cases they read.

[RESULTS]

In our sample of 253 subjects, we found that 45 boys had been raised by criminal fathers, and of these boys 56 per cent had themselves been convicted of crimes. Sixty-nine boys had alcoholic or sexually promiscuous fathers, and of these boys 43 per cent had themselves been convicted of crimes. Of the remaining 139 boys, only 35 per cent had received criminal convictions. These differences are significant at the .05 level.

Clearly, paternal deviance tends to be reflected in criminality among the sons. As a next step, we wished to determine whether paternal rejection of the son aggravated or hindered the boy's tendency to imitate the father. Two conflicting hypotheses appeared reasonable. One might hypothesize that boys would be more likely to imitate or "identify" with their fathers if these fathers were affectionate towards them. (If this were true, the highest criminal rates would appear among boys having criminal, but "warm" fathers.) On the other hand, one could hypothesize that criminality is primarily an aggressive response to emotional deprivation—and that a criminal model serves to channel aggression against society. (If this second hypothesis were true, one would expect the highest criminal rates among boys having criminal, rejecting fathers.) To check which hypothesis was more adequate, we held constant the fathers' attitudes toward their sons and found the following pattern:

TABLE 1 PER CENT CONVICTED OF CRIMES

Father's Attitude Toward Boy	Father's Role Model: Criminal	Alcoholic or Promiscuous	Non-deviant
Warm	(N: 13) 46	(N: 15) 27	(N: 67) 33
Passive	(N: 6) 50	(N: 15) 40	(N: 16) 13
Rejecting	(N :13) 85	(N: 25) 60	(N: 30) 40

(Absent fathers and 8 about whom there was inadequate information are omitted.)

This analysis suggests that *both* paternal rejection and a deviant paternal model tend to lead to criminality. Holding constant rejection by the father, sons of criminals had a significantly[1] higher incidence of criminality than did sons of non-deviants. Holding constant paternal criminality, subjects raised by rejecting fathers had a significantly higher rate of criminality than did those raised by warm or passive fathers. *Criminal rates were highest among paternally rejected boys whose fathers were criminal.*

What effect does the mother's attitude have on the boy's tendency to imitate his father's behavior? One would naturally assume that rejecting mothers would have a relatively high proportion of criminal sons. Two theories might account for this expected result: either maternal rejection tends to "push" a boy toward greater closeness with his father, or maternal rejection increases aggression and a criminal role model channels aggression against society. Because the criminal rates for sons of passive women approximated those for maternally rejecting women, the second explanation seems more adequate:

[1] Tests of significance were two-tailed using $P < .05$ as the minimum standard for asserting significance.

TABLE 2 PER CENT CONVICTED OF CRIMES

Mother's Attitude Toward Boy	Father's Role Model: Criminal	Alcoholic or Promiscuous	Non-deviant
Warm	(N: 27) 41	(N: 45) 42	(N: 102) 28
Passive	(N: 6) 83	(N: 4) 25	(N: 12) 50
Rejecting	(N: 9) 89	(N: 19) 53	(N: 19) 53

(Absent mothers and 2 about whom there was inadequate information are omitted.)

The importance of maternal warmth to the process of gaining acceptance to the rules of society can be seen in Table 2. Even among boys whose fathers presented non-deviant role models, absence of maternal warmth resulted in significantly higher criminal rates.

From this analysis we conclude: (a) Maternal affection decreases criminality, while maternal rejection or passivity increases criminal tendencies. (b) The criminal-producing effect of a criminal role model is aggravated by absence of maternal warmth. The combination of a criminal father and a passive or rejecting mother is strongly criminogenic.

Next, we investigated the effects of disciplinary methods upon the child's tendency to imitate his father's behavior. One of the questions we had in mind concerned the conscious values of criminal fathers. Assuming that discipline accorded with conscious values, we could test the nature of these values through analysis of the interrelationship of discipline and role model. If the conscious values of criminals supported criminality, one would anticipate that the highest criminal rates would occur among sons of criminals who were disciplined consistently. If the conscious values of criminals supported the non-criminal values of society, however, one would expect relatively low criminality among this group.

A second question we hoped to answer dealt with the relative effectiveness of punitive as opposed to love-oriented techniques in the prevention of criminality. While the evidence generally supports the theory that love-oriented techniques have superior effectiveness in transmitting the values of society, we wished to check the relationship of disciplinary technique to criminality among our sample of (largely) lower-class subjects who were exposed to a deviant subculture.

The figures which help to answer both of these questions are presented in Table 3.

TABLE 3 PER CENT CONVICTED OF CRIMES

Discipline	Father's Role Model: Criminal	Alcoholic or Promiscuous	Non-deviant
Consistent:			
Punitive	(N: 2) 0	(N: 1) 100	(N: 11) 18
Love-oriented	(N: 11) 18	(N: 8) 25	(N: 41) 29
Erratic:			
Punitive	(N: 17) 76	(N: 26) 54	(N: 41) 44
Love-oriented	(N: 3) 67	(N: 14) 43	(N: 23) 26
Lax	(N: 12) 75	(N: 20) 35	(N: 20) 50

Quite clearly, this analysis indicates that the conscious values of criminals support the non-criminal values of society. Of those boys raised by criminal fathers, a significantly *lower* proportion whose discipline had been consistent became criminal.

Unfortunately, the distribution according to techniques of discipline permits only very tentative answers to our second question. Although there is a tendency, holding constant erratic administration, for punitive techniques to correspond with higher criminal rates, the difference is not statistically significant. Comparing criminal rates between the two techniques in instances where these were administered consistently, we find a tendency for punitiveness to result in lower criminal rates (though this difference, too, is not statistically significant). The relationship between techniques of discipline and consistency is, however, very strong and may, perhaps, account for some previous findings which have indicated that love-oriented discipline tends to deter criminality.

Our results suggest: (a) Conscious values, even within a deviant sub-culture, support the non-criminal values of general society. (b) Consistent discipline effectively counteracts the influence of a criminal father. (c) Consistency of discipline is more strongly related to transmission of values than is the technique of discipline.

In these analyses of the effect of the paternal role model in the causation of crime, we have seen that the father's criminal behavior, paternal rejection, absence of maternal warmth, and absence of consistent discipline are significantly related to high crime rates. To ascertain the interrelationship among these factors, we computed the criminal rates for each category of familial environment.

Several interesting relationships emerge from this chart:

1. Boys reared by parents both of whom were loving were generally not criminal. In this group of boys, neither the paternal role model nor disciplinary methods bore a significant relation to crime.
2. Boys reared in families where only one parent was loving were strongly affected both by methods of discipline and by the parental role model.
3. In families where neither parent was loving, the crime rate reached a high level regardless of the paternal model.
4. Among subjects whose discipline had not been consistent, parental affection seemed to have a stronger influence on criminality than the paternal model. Holding constant paternal criminality, crime rates among sons of two loving parents were significantly lower than for those who had only one or neither parent loving.

Thus, we see that consistent discipline or love

TABLE 4 PER CENT CONVICTED OF CRIMES

Father's Role Model	Two Loving Parents Discipline: Consistent	Erratic or Lax	One Loving Parent Discipline: Consistent	Erratic or Lax	No Loving Parent Discipline: Consistent	Erratic or Lax
Criminal	(N: 5) 40	(N: 8) 38	(N: 8) 0	(N: 9) 100		(N:12) 92
Alcoholic or Promiscuous	(N: 5) 40	(N:16) 38	(N: 5) 20	(N:28) 43		(N:15) 60
Non-deviant	(N:29) 28	(N:37) 30	(N:18) 13	(N:30) 37	(N:3) 33	(N:16) 75

(Passive fathers were considered as "loving"; passive mothers were grouped with absent and rejecting women.)

from both parents mediates against criminality, whereas absence of parental love tends to result in crime. The paternal role model seems to be most crucial for boys who are raised by only one loving parent and whose discipline is not consistent.

Theoretically, one might assume that the father's role model would be more important than the mother's in determining the criminal behavior of the sons. In the above analyses, we have not considered the influence of the mother's role model. Yet criminal rates, computed on the basis of the mother's role model, indicated that this might be a critical variable.

Fifteen of our subjects had mothers who were criminal, by our definition, and of these boys 60 per cent had themselves been convicted of crimes. Thirty boys had mothers who were alcoholic or promiscuous, and 67 per cent of these boys had received criminal convictions. Of the remaining 208 boys, only 36 per cent had criminal convictions. These differences are significant at the .01 level.

The interaction of the mother's and father's role model can be seen clearly in Table 5. In this table mothers who were criminal, alcoholic, or promiscuous are grouped together as "deviant."

TABLE 5 PER CENT CONVICTED OF CRIMES

Mother's Role Model	Father's Role Model		
	Criminal	Alcoholic or Promiscuous	Non-deviant
Deviant	(N: 16) 88	(N: 17) 59	(N: 12) 42
Non-deviant	(N: 29) 31	(N: 52) 42	(N: 127) 34

If either the mother or the father was non-deviant, crime rates were not significantly related to the role model of the other parent. Yet, if the mother was deviant, crime rates varied significantly according to the father's role model; and if the father was criminal, the mother's role model seemed to be strongly influential in determining the behavior of the son.

As a summary of these many factors which mediate between the parental role model and criminality, let us see in Table 6 the interrelationships of these variables as they affect criminality.

This final analysis regarding the relationship of the parental role model to criminality suggests several conclusions:

1. If the father is criminal and the mother is also a deviant model, criminality generally results regardless of parental affection.

2. If the father is criminal but the mother is non-deviant, and only one parent is loving, consistent discipline apparently deters the son from becoming criminal.

3. If the father is criminal but the mother is non-deviant (holding discipline constant), parental affection seems to be crucial: two loving parents apparently counteract the criminogenic force of a criminal father.

4. If the father is criminal and both parents are loving, the mother's deviance greatly increases the likelihood of criminality.

To put these conclusions regarding the influence of a criminal father in another form, one could say that the son is extremely likely to become criminal unless either (a) both parents are loving and the mother is non-deviant, or (b) parental discipline is consistent and one parent is loving. *Twenty-four of the twenty-five boys whose fathers were criminal and whose backgrounds evidenced neither of these mitigating circumstances had criminal records as adults.*[2]

SUMMARY

This paper, an outgrowth of a larger longitudinal study of the causes of crime, has been concerned with the effects of the parental role model on crime. Over a five year period, observations were made of the day-to-day behavior of 253 boys and their families. These observations are relatively valid, for the investigators had no chance of learning the eventual outcome of their subjects' lives. Twenty years later, the criminal records of these boys, now adults, were examined. The backgrounds of the men were independently categorized and compared to their rates of crime. All of the men came from relatively lower-class, urban areas; thus one major factor in the causation of crime, the influence of a delinquent subculture or tradition, was held constant.

The following conclusions emerge from this paper:

1. The effect of a criminal father on criminality in the son is largely dependent upon other factors within the family.

2. If paternal rejection, absence of maternal

[2] Although the distribution of other factors among alcoholic or promiscuous fathers is quite poor, we may perhaps stretch the evidence to suggest that paternal alcoholism and promiscuity are not nearly so criminogenic as popular literature would have us believe.

TABLE 6 PER CENT CONVICTED OF CRIMES

Parental Role Model	Two Loving Parents Discipline: Consistent	Two Loving Parents Discipline: Erratic or Lax	One Loving Parent Discipline: Consistent	One Loving Parent Discipline: Erratic or Lax	No Loving Parent Discipline: Consistent	No Loving Parent Discipline: Erratic or Lax
Father Criminal; Mother Deviant	(N: 1) 100	(N: 3) 100	(N: 1) 0	(N: 4) 100		(N: 7) 86
Father Criminal; Mother Non-deviant	(N: 4) 25	(N: 5) 0	(N: 7) 0	(N: 5) 100		(N: 5) 100
Father Alcoholic or Promiscuous; Mother Deviant	(N: 1) 0	(N: 1) 0	(N: 1) 0	(N: 5) 60		(N: 9) 78
Father Alcoholic or Promiscuous; Mother Non-deviant	(N: 4) 50	(N:15) 40	(N: 4) 25	(N:23) 39		(N: 6) 33
Father Non-deviant; Mother Deviant	(N: 3) 33	(N: 4) 25	(N: 1) 0	(N: 2) 50		(N: 2) 100
Father Non-deviant; Mother Non-deviant	(N:26) 27	(N:33) 30	(N:17) 18	(N:28) 36	(N: 3) 33	(N:14) 71

warmth, or maternal deviance is coupled with a criminal role model, the son is extremely likely to become criminal.

3. Consistent discipline in combination with love from at least one parent seems to offset the criminogenic influence of a criminal father.

4. The conscious values, even among criminals, seem to support the non-criminal norms of society. These conscious values are transmitted through consistent discipline.

More generally, we conclude:

First, the old adage, "like father, like son," must be greatly qualified—at least when one is talking about criminality. Children imitate their father's criminality when other environmental conditions (rejection, maternal deviance, erratic discipline) tend to produce an unstable, aggressive personality.

Second, in terms of crime, it seems fallacious to assume that sons imitate their criminal fathers because they have established an affectionate bond with their fathers and "identify" with them. Rather, it would appear that rejection by the father creates aggressive tendencies in the child who, having witnessed a criminal model in childhood, tends to channel aggression into criminal activities.

Third, again in terms of crime, the parents' conscious values can affect the child's behavior if these values are impressed upon the child by consistent discipline. Even though the actual behavior of the parent contradicted his conscious values, the consistently disciplined son tended more often to follow the expressed values, instead of the behavior, of the parent. This finding opposes those who maintain that children will follow their parents' values only if the parents' actions reinforce their values.

Thus, this study casts serious doubt on some of the more popular opinions concerning the causes of crime.

REFERENCES

Glueck, S., and Glueck, Eleanor T., 1950. *Unraveling juvenile delinquency.* New York: The Commonwealth Fund.

Healy, W., and Bronner, Augusta F., 1926. *Delinquents and criminals.* New York: Macmillan.

McCord, W., McCord, Joan, and Zola, I., 1959. *Origins of crime.* New York: Columbia University Press.

Powers, E., and Witmer, Helen, 1951. *An experiment in the prevention of delinquency.* New York: Columbia University Press.

selection 47 Rehabilitation, Socialization and Pathway Organizations

DAVID LANDY AND HENRY WECHSLER

The behavioral sciences, and the field of psychiatric rehabilitation have as yet been unable to provide an adequate theoretical framework for the study and description of the rehabilitation process; but one must be provided before that part of the rehabilitative process concerning the patient's departure from the mental hospital and re-entrance into the community is to be understood. An attempt is made here, inadequate though it obviously must be, to establish a crude framework from existing concepts in the above fields, for the study of rehabilitation as a social process.

CULTURAL MOVEMENTS

In the broadest sense one may view rehabilitation as a process in *acculturation*, though not in the strict sense of change resulting from cultural contact and interaction, as this term has been used in anthropology and sociology. Perhaps a better way to characterize the process from the cultural standpoint is to view it as a series of *cultural movements* for the patient, or *enforced cultural conformity* from the viewpoint of the social institutions involved in bringing the patient "back to normality."

The process begins the moment the troubled individual becomes ill; he is viewed as taking on the role attributes of a sick or deviant person in his family and community. As the illness becomes so intense that the victim is unable to tolerate family living and/or the family is unable to accommodate to his sick behavior, the first cultural movement and dislocation takes place as he leaves home to enter the hospital. He must adapt to the cultural milieu of the hospital, must find a place for himself in its way of life. In the process he first must learn to accept the fact that he is ill and then, as his symptoms begin to remit, to begin to accept more "normal" or "well" ways of behaving. As he learns something of the "well" role, he may be deemed ready for transfer to the community—or, if such conditions as unhealthy family situation, lack of family or friends, lack

Abridged from two articles by the same authors, appearing in the *Journal of Social Issues*, 1960, **16**, 3–7 and 70–78. Reprinted by permission of the authors and the Society for the Psychological Study of Social Issues.

of financial resources, regressed social adaptational techniques, and so on, seem to block the patient's path back to the general society, one of a number of different pathways, involving the use of various types of transitional facilities, may be brought into play. Again a significant cultural movement and dislocation occurs. He must now adapt to the subculture of the transitional agency, and to some extent learn to play a new role there—convalescing patient or expatient. In all such facilities the patient continues to be known, at least to members of the agency, as an expatient. In some, as in voluntary membership in an expatients' club, he decides to continue, at least for the period of membership, the role of expatient, in contrast to patients who leave the hospital directly for the community, and, more often than not, "pass" into the society without the identifying stigmata of the expatient role (see Wechsler, 1960).

Each phase of the rehabilitation process, then, presents a potential cultural discontinuity for the patient. At any point along the way his steps may falter and he may return or regress to an earlier phase. He may be unable even to place his foot upon any community-directed pathway in some cases. But in any event, the task of diverse rehabilitators in hospital, transitional agency and community is to help smooth the passage through these exchanges of cultural environments so that the patient may learn successfully to accommodate to them and live with and in them. The process is complicated by the fact that the stages are overlapping so that the patient may have to play more than one role at one time. Unlike socialization of the child, discussed below, the stages have no discrete markers such as age.

SOCIALIZATION

A somewhat less broad approach, and a more viable one for the study of rehabilitation, is to see the whole process, from the patient's viewpoint, as one in *socialization or resocialization*—of learning and relearning ways of personal and interpersonal behavior in a series of potentially therapeutic or antitherapeutic situations in which the patient must learn to live with himself and with others at every step of the way. In this view the rehabilitators become teachers and/or enablers. Through various kinds of assistance, from role-modeling of nurses and other staff and patients on the ward to guidance of the psychiatrist in the complexities of the psychotherapeutic process, the patient is either learning new ways of perception and behavior, or relearning old ways from an altered perspective. Theoretically as he moves from one social role to another—well person to sick person to patient to convalescent patient to expatient to well person—he must learn or relearn the functional aspects of these statuses and their requisite roles. Relearning and social readaptation has been referred to as *rehabilitation*; new learning and adaptation *habilitation*. The extent to which a patient must be habilitated or rehabilitated depends upon his own resources, the depths of his illness and degree of impairment of interpersonal skills, and the resources and capabilities of hospital, transitional agency and community.

In a recent study we have attempted to see rehabilitation on the hospital ward as a process of socialization or resocialization (see Mishler, Landy, and Guiness, 1959). The nurse is seen as an authority figure, in some respects functioning as a parent-surrogate to the patient. Student nurses and attendants similarly may be seen in family-surrogate roles (parents, siblings, other relatives). Other patients are viewed as comprising the peer group to which the patient must affiliate in some manner. The patient is viewed as analogous to the child in learning the ways of his society in family and peer group, each acting as agents of cultural movement and influence. In this sense the patient is for the most part a learner in the process—but he is also to some extent a teacher of other patients (and the staff, as it frequently will admit, in turn learns from him, also!).

The patient, nevertheless, is not to be confused with the child. He already has had some experience, however his growing may have been a pathologically distorted process, in learning the ways of his society and reference groups. No matter how deprived he may have been, no matter how asocial a warped socialization may have rendered him, he is not simply facing life de novo. Each situation he encounters in the rehabilitation process may appear new to him, but he adapts to it in terms of his previously learned response repertory. (Even though a goal of psychotherapy may be the modification of his behavioral response mechanism, these have been learned earlier—and can only be unlearned, which is a difficult process, or changed.) Authority figures (staff personnel) and peer group figures (fellow patients) serve, therefore, not only as direct teachers or inculcators but as role models for the proper relearning of older roles, or the learning of newer more socially appropriate, more "adult" roles.

In the ideally successful case of rehabilitative resocialization, the patient will have learned how to modify his old behavior modes, or learned new ones which are acceptable to hospital—and later transitional agency—authorities, and therefore also acceptable to the larger society. What the authorities transmit and model are values and practices of the particular segment of society in which they have themselves been socialized. In most cases they will be oriented toward middle-class values and practices, since these are, to the staff, "second-nature," and underlie and motivate their instrumental and expressive behaviors. Obviously, therefore, where the patient comes from a similar background, and his values are fairly consonant with those of the staff—or with relatively minimal conflict brought into line with these values—the chances for successful rehabilitation would seem to be greatest. However, as we shall see in the study of a halfway house, it is not only middle-class patients who, having been treated in the hospital and transitional agency, become able to function adequately in the community. Lower-class patients also are often able to accomplish the transition from illness back to health, from desocialization back to socialization, successfully. One could hypothesize that in such cases the lower-class patient already has, or has been enabled to accommodate to, a set of middle-class value orientations. It is possible that he may be able to effect changes toward a middle-class orientation among his relevant others, but this whole question compels further exploration and study.

For child or patient, the end-point or major goal of socialization is the internalization of the values and practices which define and direct his culture. When he has been able to internalize these values and practices, he has also identified with authority figures and peers (identification with the latter may involve reinforcement of authority identification or rebellion against it).

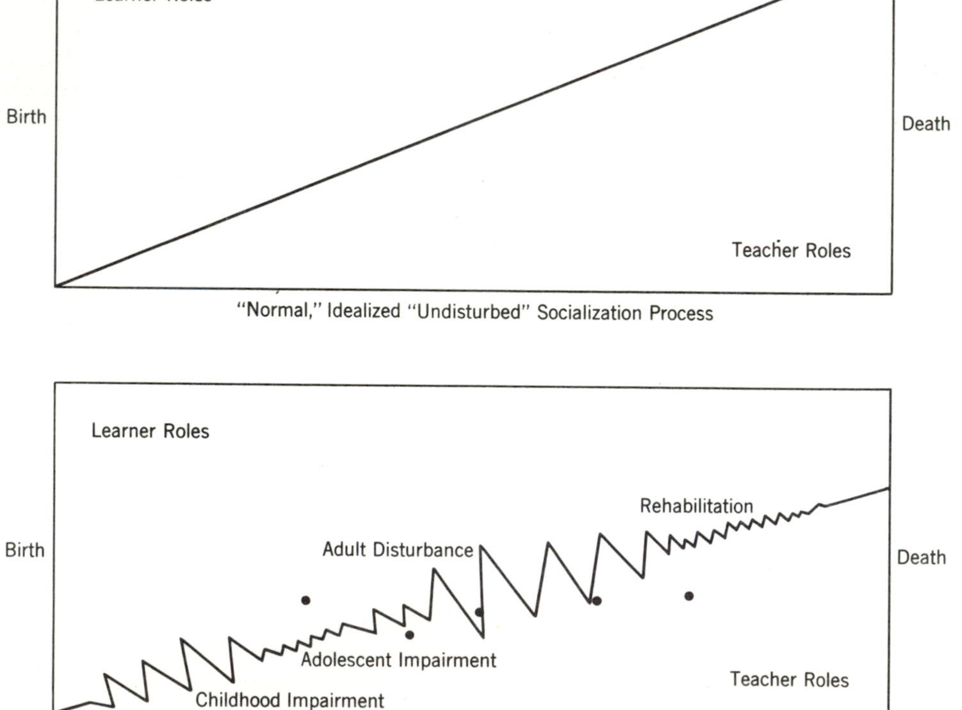

Figure 1. Paradigms of idealized "normal" and "pathological" life cycles in terms of socialization process (adapted from Landy, 1959, pp. 6–13).

Identification then means that the individual has learned how to behave like the person or persons with whom he identifies and is capable of such behavior *in the absence of the persons who acted as teachers and models.* Whether or not he is aware of it or wishes it, every participant in the socialization process thus becomes to some degree a model (positive or negative) with whom the child or patient identifies.

Use of a socialization paradigm has permitted us not only to view sick people and others trying to help them get well, but people behaving in specific ways in specified social systems and cultural milieux. The use of this framework helps us to see not simply a set of persons behaving in strange and bizarre fashion and another set of persons attempting to cope with such actions, but persons behaving in ways that, while defined as deviant by their society, are never completely outside its pale. The hospital is itself a social institution and its ways are defined by the culture in which it is a participant; the same may be said for the day hospital, halfway house, expatient club, protected workshop, or other posthospital rehabilitative operation. Sick behavior as much as well behavior is culturally defined. This does not deny the possibility of biological bases of etiology, but states that getting well, and the process of making sick persons well, take place in given social and cultural contexts and this must be made explicit in understanding processes of health and disease. From this viewpoint the hospital and its staff, and "pathway" agencies and their staffs, are seen as community agents attempting to restore to adequate social functioning these socially impaired members of the community.

COMMON ASSUMPTIONS OF PATHWAY AGENCIES

Irrespective of their form, location, size and other factors, all pathway agencies appear to make common assumptions about their part in the rehabilitative process. These may be grouped as follows:

1. *Continuity of Rehabilitation.* As in sociocultural models of socialization, in rehabilitation it is deemed desirable that the process be as smooth as possible. In this sense, the transition agencies serve to anticipate and eliminate potential discontinuities or abrupt gaps between parts of the process, particularly the movement from hospital to community. The psychiatric assumption is that the patient will be less likely to relapse or regress if, in some cases, he is not placed immediately upon discharge into a socially and psychologically demanding environment.

2. "*Delaying Action.*" To avoid possible socially and psychologically noxious effects of an abrupt thrust into the outside world, the pathway facilities are viewed for some patients as kinds of "decompression chambers," that aid passage through the stages of rehabilitation. Thus possible effects of the usually heavy pressures of community living are postponed temporarily by the delaying action of the lighter (but more "realistic" than hospital) pressures of the transitional agency. It is assumed that the delaying action or decompression effect is best achieved within the context of a milieu which is relatively nonrestrictive, nonthreatening, loosely structured, and hierarchy-reducing; that is, a *sheltered environment.*

3. *Socialization and/or Resocialization.* It is assumed that the mentally ill individual is socially impaired in part, at least, because of a pathologically distorted socialization into his family and society. To restore him to, or retrain him for, an adequate level of interpersonal competence, it is believed that he needs to live for a period in a protected social environment in which he may learn to interact effectively with peer and authority figures. The peer group is comprised of others who have shared the common experience of illness and hospitalization, and are sharing the common experience of group living and moving toward normal community status. The authority figures are the rehabilitative "enablers" who in the ideal case attempt to reduce social barriers between themselves and the patients while setting up "realistic" limits for behavior, thus serving as "normal" role models.

DIMENSIONS OF PATHWAY ORGANIZATIONS

Pathway organizations tend to vary along several dimensions structurally and functionally in terms of the kinds of solutions designed to meet needs of various patient populations in various settings. As schematized below, these dimensions are seen as possible alternative modes of transitional care.

1. *Closed and Open Systems.* Rehabilitation may take place in a series of institutional settings that may be conceptualized as ranging from the closed, custodial type of institution to the open,

presumably therapeutic type. One index of the degree of openness of the institutional system is the proportion of involvement of the member's life-space in it, or the extent to which it is responsible for, and seeks to control, the total life of the patient. A frequent rehabilitative sequence along this continuum is that which begins with the person's admission to a closed ward while he is in an acutely disturbed state, continues with his transfer to an open or convalescent ward as his symptoms remit, thence to a day hospital, which places him back into community residence while continuing a hospital program. From this stage he may be discharged directly into the community or placed in one of a number of transitional facilities such as those discussed herein. The assumption of rehabilitators is that as the patient is able to take on more responsibilities and pressures of social life, he is placed into situations which permit a greater proportion of openness of choice and decreasing pathological involvement.

2. *Professional and Lay Orientation.* Pathway facilities differ in terms of the extent of their professional or lay emphasis, both in outlook and in terms of the use of personnel. The professional to lay continuum can be seen as extending from the rather totally professional-medical orientation of the day hospital to the partially professional, essentially nonmedical orientation of most halfway houses and sheltered workshops, to the lay orientation of member-run, autonomous expatient groups. Differences along this dimension reflect basically the view of the facility regarding the amount of responsibility, initiative and freedom that the expatients whom it serves need and are prepared to accommodate. Pathway organizations select members on the basis, in part, of whether the amount of professional-medical supervision available is sufficient for the patient's requirements. The traditional mental hospital has few criteria for selection other than mental illness (except legal requirements), whereas sheltered workshops and halfway houses tend to exclude patients who appear to need constant supervision and care.

3. *Dependence and Independence.* All rehabilitative agencies, including those with a transitional function, are faced with the paradox that while a major objective is the enabling of the patient to achieve sufficient independence to operate autonomously, the supports provided by the sheltered milieu may perpetuate the dependency that the patient brings with him, or stimulate latent dependent needs. To minimize such effects some facilities have established mechanisms such as time-limit on residence in certain halfway houses or on jobs, as in the case of the transitional employment program of Fountain House. Another impetus toward the shedding of dependency are the constant reminders of staff that the member is there only temporarily, and the proffering of their assistance in obtaining work and other means of achieving independent, community status. Where such mechanisms are not present, or do not operate effectively, fears have been expressed that the facility becomes a "dumping ground" for unrehabilitatable patients.

4. *Patient Role and Nonpatient Role.* The objective of the rehabilitation process seen sociologically, and also one of the objectives of the process seen psychiatrically, is for the patient to surrender his role in favor of that of nonpatient. An assumption of pathway facilities that influences their structure and design is that they are constructed on more "realistic" or "normal" bases than the hospital by fostering family-like or work-like situations analogous to those the patient will experience in the larger society. Experiencing the ways of transitional facilities should, in the ideal case, enable him gradually to relinquish the "abnormal" attributes of the patient role and resume or re-acquire attributes of a non-patient or "normal" role. However, being a member of a pathway agency involves the assumption of an expatient role. To the extent that he is not able to wean himself from the facility, he clings to this alternative to nonpatienthood. A question is raised as to whether the rehabilitative process has succeeded where the patient assumes the expatient role indefinitely.

SOME CRUCIAL PROBLEMS FACING TRANSITIONAL AGENCIES

Currently all facilities engaged in easing the community restoration of the discharged mental patient are groping, more or less intuitively, toward answers to problems of practice that in some degree affect all of them. While systematic research is necessary for definitive knowledge, it seems possible that by raising and objectively facing these questions in terms of knowledge of everyday practices and policies tentative answers may be found. The authors are aware of the fact that no agency can succeed in its operations without a high level of "therapeutic enthusiasm" on the part of its staff. Practitioners must believe in what they are doing for their practices to have beneficial effects. But optimism, however necessary to the therapeutic and rehabilitative process, is in itself no guarantee that the goals of the agency are being reached. Obscuring defects and playing up successes in a "best-of-all-possible-worlds" manner can only serve in the long run to deceive clients, sponsors, public and the agency itself. Honest appraisal of the procedures and weighing of shortcomings may not always serve to make the agency a sensational "success," but it will insure that its future operations will be based on sounder knowledge and undoubtedly increase the probability of true success. Some crucial problems to be faced, it seems to us, are these:

1. *Length of stay.* While there are differences in individual needs, each agency eventually must learn a range of optimal length of stay. This must be considered in terms of balancing benefits accruing from the delaying or decompression effect as against possible undesirable accretions of dependency. The goal is to maintain the transitional nature of the facility while serving as many clients as possible, and at the same time providing maximum benefits to each.

2. *Readmissions.* To our knowledge, no agency has yet squarely faced this problem and little accurate information exists of readmission rates to transitional agencies. The fact of readmission, or even a series of readmissions through time, does not in itself indicate "failure" on the part of the agency, any more than discharge without subsequent readmission indicates "success." The question is the degree to which the facility wishes to take on aspects of a "permanent sanctuary," a friendly, protected environment easily accessible to its graduate clients. This latter is an ideal of some social psychiatrists, who feel that the provision of such a sanctuary would eliminate the need for formal recommitment to mental hospitals and insure ultimate success of the rehabilitative aims.

3. *Selection.* Most facilities tend to operate on the basis of negative selective criteria (i.e., no alcoholics, homosexuals, psychopaths, etc.) and use only vague positive criteria (i.e., rehabilitation potential, work tolerance, etc.). Consequently they have not developed systematic admission policies and depend primarily upon current or recent experiences to inform them. Three effects are possible: (a) the success of the agency cannot be evaluated if only "good risks" are admitted while "poor risks" are omitted. (b) Certain types of needy expatients may be ineligible for all existing facilities. (c) Facilities may not be aware of the extent of homogeneity of the patient population they serve and therefore may not set up appropriate procedures for staff selection, activity programming, physical plant, and relationships with referring and cooperating agencies.

4. *Costs.* It is not apparent to us that so far pathway organizations have in fact been able to operate more cheaply than hospitals and existing social agencies. To say that a facility "saves money" by using an already constructed building, or by "borrowing" personnel or consultants, is using black ink on the red side of the ledger. If indeed these facilities operate more economically, then the yardstick must be the extent of decrease or prevention of hospital readmission, forestalling of effects of chronic illness, and maintaining former patients in productive and gratifying community roles.

5. *Determination of Need.* While there is a general assumption that widespread needs exist among psychiatric patients for the types of facilities discussed herein, few attempts have been made to determine the scope and extent of such need. It has been traditional for social agencies to determine need of their services by community-wide surveys, but it is not at all clear to what extent the needs which have been measured are the ones actually being fulfilled by the agencies. The problem of determination of need can be approached from the viewpoint of sampling surveys of patients near discharge, or capable of discharge, from hospitals and clinics, if rigorous criteria for the measurement of needs can be set up; or it could be approached through using a number of readmissions within a year to hospitals and clinics as an index of need; or some combination or variation of these approaches could be utilized. At present, however, aside from the belief of some administrators and clinicians that such needs exist, there is little objective knowledge of whether such beliefs are well-founded.

REFERENCES

Landy, D., 1959. *Tropical childhood: cultural transmission and learning in a rural Puerto Rican village.* Chapel Hill, N. C.: University of North Carolina Press.

Mishler, Anita L., Landy, D., and Guiness, V., 1959. Rehabilitation on a mental hospital ward: a process in socialization. Unpublished paper prepared for the Rehabilitation Project, Massachusetts Mental Health Center, pp. 1–36.

Weschler, H., 1960. The expatient organization: a survey. *Journal of Social Issues*, **16**, 47–53.

Bibliography on Role Theory

THE ROLE BIBLIOGRAPHY presented here is intended to be a relatively complete listing of published theoretical and empirical contributions to the role literature. It was prepared by reviewing in a systematic fashion approximately 250 journals and standard reference sources from both the United States and elsewhere. Its coverage runs from the early precursors of role theory through to contributions appearing in September, 1964. Included in it are legitimately published journal articles, monographs, and books. Excluded are unpublished doctoral dissertations, reports of supported research programs, university-sponsored monographs, papers delivered at professional meetings, and all other forms of quasi-publication.

Although coverage in any bibliography reflects necessarily some of the prejudices of its compilers, certain criteria have guided the preparation of this list. Our intention was to compile a bibliography of serious contributions to role theory, and hence we have favored theoretical and empirical contributions and omitted much practitioner literature, particularly that pertaining to role taking, role playing, psychodrama, and the like. We have also excluded hortative materials, off-the-cuff descriptions, and popularizations—unless these were buried in empirical or theoretical studies. Many studies in related fields, such as symbolic interactionism, ego psychology, aptitude research, cognitive dissonance, rigidity, authoritarianism, social influence, social perception, leadership, human performance, and learning, have also been omitted because they were not phrased in role terms.

Abbott, M. G., 1960. Values and value perceptions in superintendent-school board relationships. *Administrator's Notebook*, **9** (4).

Ackerman, N. W., 1951. "Social role" and total personality. *American Journal of Orthopsychiatry*, **21**, 1–17.

Ackerman, N. W., 1958. *Psychodynamics of Family Life*. New York: Basic Books.

Adams, J. K., & Adams, Pauline A., 1961. Realism of confidence judgments. *Psychological Review*, **68**, 33–45.

Adams, J. S., & Romney, A. K., 1959. A functional analysis of authority. *Psychological Review*, **66**, 234–251.

Adams, S., 1953. Status congruency as a variable in small group performance. *Social Forces*, **32**, 16–22.

Adler, A., 1928. Neurotisches Rollenspiel. (Neurotic role playing.) *Internationale Zeitschrift für Individual Psychologie*, **6**, 427–432.

Albert, R. S., & Whitslam, P., 1963. Role of the critic in mass communications. *Journal of Social Psychology*, **60**, 153–156.

Alfert, Elizabeth, 1958. Two components of assumed similarity. *Journal of Abnormal and Social Psychology*, **56**, 135–138.

Allardt, E., 1960. Internal and external criteria of behaviour regularities. *Acta Sociologica*, **4**, 29–41.

Allen, A. T., & Seaberg, D. I., 1964. Teachers-in-the-becoming. *Elementary School Journal*, **64**, 332–338.

Allport, F. H., 1924. *Social Psychology*. Boston: Houghton Mifflin.

Allport, F. H., 1934. The *J*-curve hypothesis of conforming behavior. *Publications of the American Sociological Society*, **28**, 124–125.

Allport, F. H., 1938. Occupational and societal roles studied with relation to the human behavior pattern. *Psychological Bulletin*, **35**, 693–694.

Allport, F. H., 1962. A structuronomic conception of behavior: individual and collective I. Structural theory and the master problem of social psychology. *Journal of Abnormal and Social Psychology*, **64**, 3–31.

Allport, G. W., 1943. The ego in contemporary psychology. *Psychological Review*, **50**, 451–478.

Anderson, A. R., & Moore, O. K., 1957. The formal analysis of normative concepts. *American Sociological Review*, **22**, 9–17.

Anderson, H. H., & Anderson, Gladys L., 1961. Image of the teacher by adolescent children in seven countries. *American Journal of Orthopsychiatry*, **31**, 481–492.

Anderson, W. A., 1943. Family-member roles in social participation. *American Sociological Review*, **8**, 718–720.

Anderson, W. A., 1946. Family social participation and social status self-ratings. *American Sociological Review*, **11**, 253–258.

Angell, R. C., 1958. *Free Society and Moral Crisis*. Ann Arbor: University of Michigan Press.

Angell, R. C., 1962. Preferences for moral norms in three problem areas. *American Journal of Sociology*, **67**, 650–660.

Archer, W., 1889. *Masks or Faces*? London: Longmans Green.

Arelson, L. J., 1963. Marital adjustment and marital role definitions of husbands of working and non-working wives. *Marriage and Family Living*, **25**, 189–195.

Argyle, M., 1952. The concepts of role and status. *Sociological Review*, **44**, 39–52.

Argyle, M., 1957. Social pressure in public and private situations. *Journal of Abnormal and Social Psychology*, **54**, 172–175.

Argyris, C., 1957. *Personality and Organization: The Conflict between System and the Individual*. New York: Harper.

Argyris, C., 1961. Explorations in consulting-client relationships. *Human Organization*, **20**, 121–133.

Arkoff, A., & Shears, Loyda, 1961. Conceptions of "ideal" leadership in accepted and rejected principal training candidates. *Journal of Educational Research*, **55**, 71–74.

Arkoff, A., Meredith, G., & Dong, Janice, 1963. Attitudes of Japanese-American and Caucasian-American students toward marriage roles. *Journal of Social Psychology*, **59**, 11–15.

Arnold, Magda B., 1946. On the mechanism of suggestion and hypnosis. *Journal of Abnormal and Social Psychology*, **41**, 107–128.

Arnold, Mary F., 1962. Perception of professional role activities in the local health departments. *Public Health Reports*, **77**, 80–88.

Aronson, G. J., 1959. Treatment of the dying person. In H. Feifel (Ed.), *The Meaning of Death*. New York: McGraw-Hill. Pp. 251–258.

Arthur, Bettie, 1963. Role perceptions of children—ulcerative colitis. *General Psychiatry*, **8**, 536–545.

Asch, S. E., 1940. Studies in the principles of judgments and attitudes: II. Determination of judgments by group and by ego standards. *Journal of Social Psychology*, **12**, 433–465.

Asch, S. E., 1948. The doctrine of suggestion, prestige and imitation in social psychology. *Psychological Review*, **55**, 250–276.

Asch, S. E., 1951. Effects of group pressure upon the modification and distortion of judgments. In H. Guetzkow (Ed.), *Groups, Leadership and Men*. Pittsburgh: Carnegie Press. Pp. 177–190.

Asch, S. E., 1952. *Social Psychology*. New York: Prentice-Hall.

Asch, S. E., 1956. Studies of independence and conformity: I. A minority of one against a unanimous majority. *Psychological Monographs*, **70**:9, 1–70.

Aubert, V., 1956. The housemaid—an occupational role in crisis. *Acta Sociologica*, **1**, 149–158.

Aubert, V., 1959. Norske sakførere 1932–1950. (Norwegian attorneys 1932–1950.) *Norsk Sakförerblad*, **26**, 73–82.

Aubert, V., 1961. Løsning av konflikter i par og trekant. (Conflict resolution in dyads and triads.) *Tidsskrift for Samfunnsforskning*, **2**, 89–102.

Aubert, V., Haldorsen, Gerthe, & Tiller, P. O., 1956. Laerernes holdning til yrkesrollen og oppdragelsesspørsmôal. (The attitudes of teachers toward occupational roles and educational problems.) *Norsk Pedagogisk Tidsskrift*, **40**, 81–114.

Aubert, V., & Messinger, S., 1958. The criminal and the sick. *Inquiry*, **1**, 137–159.

Aubert, V., Torgersen, U., Tangen, K., Lindbekk, T., & Pollan, Sonja, 1960. Akademikere i norsk samfunnsstruktur. (Academic professions in Norwegian social structure.) *Tidsskrift for Samfunnsforskning*, **1**, 185–204.

Axelson, L. J., 1963. Marital adjustment and marital role definitions of husbands of working and non-working wives. *Marriage and Family Living*, **25**, 189–195.

Babchuck, N., 1962. Role of the researcher as participant observer and participant-as-observer in the field situation. *Human Organization*, **21**, 225–228.

Babchuck, N., & Bates, A. P., 1962. Professor or producer: the two faces of academic man. *Social Forces*, **40**, 341–348.

Back, K. W., 1951. Influence through social communication. *Journal of Abnormal and Social Psychology*, **46**, 9–23.

Backman, C. W., & Secord, P. F., 1962. Liking, selective interaction and misperception in congruent inter-personal relations. *Sociometry*, **25**, 321–335.

Backman, C. W., Secord, P. F., & Pierce, J. R., 1963. Resistance to change in the self-concept as a function of consensus among significant others. *Sociometry*, **26**, 102–111.

Baker, B. O., & Block, J., 1957. Accuracy of interpersonal prediction as a function of judge and object characteristics. *Journal of Abnormal and Social Psychology*, **54**, 37–43.

Baker, B. O., & Sarbin, T. R., 1956. Differential mediation of social perception as a correlate of social adjustment. *Sociometry*, **19**, 69–83.

Baldwin, J. M., 1891. *Handbook of Psychology*. London: Macmillan.

Baldwin, J. M., 1897. *Le Développement mental Chez l'Enfant et dans la Race*. (Mental Development in the Child and in the Race.) London: Macmillan.

Baldwin, J. M., 1899. *Interprétation Sociale et Morale des Principes du Développement Mental: Etude de Psychosociologie*. (A Social and Ethical Interpretation of the Principles of Mental Development: A Study in Social Psychology.) London: Macmillan.

Bales, R. F., 1950. A set of categories for the analysis of small group interaction. *American Sociological Review*, **15**, 257–263. (a)

Bales, R. F., 1950. *Interaction Process Analysis: A Method for the Study of Small Groups*. Cambridge, Mass: Addison-Wesley. (b)

Bales, R. F., 1958. Task roles and social roles in problem-solving groups. In Eleanor E. Maccoby, T. M. Newcomb, & E. L. Hartley (Eds.), *Readings in Social Psychology* (3rd ed.). New York: Holt. Pp. 437–447.

Bales, R. F., & Borgatta, E. F., 1955. A study of group size: size of group as a factor in the interaction profile. In A. P. Hare, E. F. Borgatta, & R. F. Bales (Eds.), *Small Groups: Studies in Social Interaction*. New York: Alfred Knopf. Pp. 396–413.

Bales, R. F., & Slater, P. E., 1955. Role differentiation in small decision-making groups. In T. Parsons & R. F. Bales, *Family, Socialization and Interaction Process*. Glencoe, Ill.: The Free Press. Pp. 259–306.

Bales, R. F., & Slater, P. E., 1957. Notes on "role differentiation in small decision-making groups"; reply to Dr. Wheeler. *Sociometry*, **20**, 152–155.

Bales, R. F., & Strodtbeck, F. L., 1951. Phases in group problem-solving. *Journal of Abnormal and Social Psychology*, **46**, 485–495.

Balma, M., Maloney, J., & Lawshe, C., 1958. The role of the foreman in modern industry: I. The development of measurement of management of identification. *Personnel Psychology*, **11**, 195–205. (a)

Balma, M., Maloney, J., & Lawshe, C., 1958. The role of the foreman in modern industry: II. Foreman identification with management, work group productivity, and employee attitude toward foreman. *Personnel Psychology*, **11**, 367–378. (b)

Balma, M., Maloney, J., & Lawshe, C., 1958. The role of the foreman in modern industry: III. Some correlates of foreman identification with management. *Personnel Psychology*, **11**, 535–544. (c)

Banton, M., 1964. *The Policeman in the Community*. London: Tavistock.

Barch, A. M., Trumbo, D., & Nangle, J., 1957. Social setting and conformity to a legal requirement. *Journal of Abnormal and Social Psychology*, **55**, 396–398.

Barker, R. G., 1942. The social interrelations of strangers and acquaintances. *Sociometry*, **5**, 169–179.

Barker, R. G., & Wright, H. F., 1955. *Midwest and its Children*. Evanston, Ill.: Row, Peterson.

Barnard, C. I., 1938. *The Functions of the Executive*. Cambridge, Mass.: Harvard University Press.

Barnard, C. I., 1946. Functions and pathology of status systems in formal organizations. In W. F. Whyte (Ed.), *Industry and Society*. New York: McGraw-Hill. Pp. 46–83.

Barnard, C. I., 1948. *Organization and Management*. Cambridge, Mass.: Harvard University Press.

Baron, G., & Tropp, A., 1961. Teachers in England and America. In A. H. Halsey, Jean Floud, & C. A. Anderson (Eds.), *Education, Economy and Society: A Reader in the Sociology of Education*. New York: The Free Press. Pp. 545–557.

Barron, F., 1952. Some personality correlates of independence of judgment. *Journal of Personality*, **21**, 287–297.

Bass, B. M., 1956. Development and evaluation of a scale for measuring social acquiescence. *Journal of Abnormal and Social Psychology*, **53**, 296–299.

Bates, A. P., 1952. Some sociometric aspects of social ranking in a small, face-to-face group. *Sociometry*, **15**, 330–341.

Bates, A. P., & Cloyd, J. S., 1956. Towards the development of operations for defining group norms and member roles. *Sociometry*, **19**, 26–39.

Bates, F. L., 1956. Position, role, and status: a reformulation of concepts. *Social Forces*, **34**, 313–321.

Bates, F. L., 1957. A conceptual analysis of group structure. *Social Forces*, **36**, 103–111.

Bates, F. L., 1960. Institutions, organizations, and communities: a general theory of complex structures. *Pacific Sociological Review*, **3**, 59–70.

Bates, F. L., 1962. Some observations concerning the structural aspect of role conflict. *Pacific Sociological Review*, **5**, 75–82.

Bavelas, A., 1947. Role playing and management training. *Sociatry*, **1**, 183–191.

Bavelas, A., 1948. A mathematical model for group structures. *Applied Anthropology*, **7**, 16–30.

Bavelas, A., 1950. Communication patterns in task oriented groups. *Journal of the Accoustical Society of America*, **22**, 725–730.

Beale, H. K., 1936. *Are American Teachers Free*? New York: Scribner.

Becker, E., 1962. Toward a theory of schizophrenia. *General Psychiatry*, **7**, 170–181.

Becker, H. P., 1960. Normative reactions to normlessness. *American Sociological Review*, **25**, 803–810.

Becker, H. S., 1951. The professional dance musician and his audience. *American Journal of Sociology*, **57**, 136–144.

Becker, H. S., 1952. The career of the Chicago public school teacher. *American Journal of Sociology*, **57**, 470–477.

Becker, H. S., 1953. The teacher in the authority system of the public school. *Journal of Educational Sociology*, **27**, 128–141.

Becker, H. S., 1955. Schools and systems of social status. *Phylon Quarterly*, **16**, 159–170.

Becker, H. S., 1962. The career of the schoolteacher. In S. Nosow & W. H. Form (Eds.), *Man, Work, and Society*. New York: Basic Books. Pp. 321–329.

Becker, H. S., & Carper, J. W., 1956. The development of identification with an occupation. *American Journal of Sociology*, **61**, 289–298. (a)

Becker, H. S., & Carper, J. W., 1956. The elements of identification with an occupation. *American Sociological Review*, **21**, 341–348. (b)

Becker, H. S., & Geer, Blanche, 1952. The fate of idealism in medical school. In E. G. Jaco (Ed.), *Patients, Physicians and Illness*. Glencoe, Ill.: The Free Press. Pp. 300–307.

Becker, H. S., Geer, Blanche, Hughes, E. C., & Strauss, A. L., 1961. *Boys in White: Student Culture in Medical School*. Chicago: University of Chicago Press.

Becker, H. S., & Strauss, A. L., 1956. Careers, personality, and adult socialization. *American Journal of Sociology*, **62**, 253–263.

Becker, W. C., 1960. The relationship of factors in parental ratings of self and each other to the behavior of kindergarten children as rated by mothers, fathers, and teachers. *Journal of Consulting Psychology*, **24**, 507–527.

Belanger, P., & Jumeau, A., 1961. Les Maîtres de l'Enseignement primaire: Etude socio-culturelle. (Elementary school teachers: A socio-cultural study.) *Recherches Sociographiques*, **2**, 55–68.

Bell, D., 1953. Crime as an American way of life. *Antioch Review*, **13**, 131–154.

Bell, G. B., & French, R. L., 1950. Consistency of individual leadership position in small groups of varying membership. *Journal of Abnormal and Social Psychology*, **45**, 764–767.

Bell, R. R., & Buerkle, J. V., 1963. Mothers and mothers-in-law as role models in relation to religious background. *Marriage and Family Living*, **25**, 485–486.

Beloff, H., 1958. Two forms of social conformity: acquiescence and conventionality. *Journal of Abnormal and Social Psychology*, **56**, 99–104.

Ben-David, J., 1958. The professional role of the physician in bureaucratized medicine: a study in role conflict. *Human Relations*, **11**, 255–274.

Bender, I. E., & Hastorf, A. H., 1950. The perception of persons: forcasting another person's responses on three personality scales. *Journal of Abnormal and Social Psychology*, **45**, 556–561.

Benedict, Ruth, 1938. Continuities and discontinuities in cultural conditioning. *Psychiatry*, **1**, 161–167.

Benne, K. D., & Bennis, W., 1959. The role of the professional nurse. *American Journal of Nursing*, **59**, 196–198. (a)

Benne, K. D., & Bennis, W., 1959. What is real nursing? *American Journal of Nursing*, **59**, 380–383. (b)

Benne, K. D., & Sheats, P., 1948. Functional roles of group members. *Journal of Social Issues*, **4**, 41–50.

Bennett, Edith B., 1955. Discussion, decision, commitment, and consensus in group decision. *Human Relations*, **8**, 251–273.

Bennett, J. W., & Tumin, M. M., 1948. *Social Life: Structure and Function.* New York: Knopf.

Bennis, W. G., 1959. Leadership theory and administrative behaviors: the problem of authority. *Administrative Science Quarterly*, **4**, 259–301.

Bennis, W. G., Berkowitz, N. H., Affinito, M., & Malone, Mary F., 1958. Authority, power and the ability to influence. *Human Relations*, **11**, 143–155.

Bennis, W. G., Berkowitz, N. H., Malone, Mary F., & Klein, M. W., 1961. *The Role of the Nurse in the Outpatient Department.* New York: American Nurses' Foundation.

Bennis, W. G., & Shepard, H. A., 1956. A theory of group development. *Human Relations*, **9**, 415–437.

Benoit-Smullyan, E., 1944. Status, status types, and status interrelations. *American Sociological Review*, **9**, 151–161.

Benson, L. G., 1955. Family social status and parental authority evaluations among adolescents. *Southwestern Social Science Quarterly*, **36**, 46–54.

Berenda, Ruth W., 1950. *The Influence of the Group on the Judgments of Children.* New York: King's Crown Press.

Berg, J., 1955. Cooperation without communication and observation. *Journal of Social Psychology*, **41**, 287–296.

Berge, A., 1959. La prise de conscience des rôles dans la structuration familiale. (Becoming aware of roles in family structure.) *Revue de Neuropsychiatrie Infantile et d'Hygiène Mentale de l'Enfance*, **7**, 1–18.

Berger, A., & Waters, T. J., 1956. The psychologist's concept of his function in institutions for the mentally retarded. *American Journal of Mental Deficiency*, **60**, 823–826.

Bergson, H. L., 1889. *Essai sur les Données Immédiates de la Conscience.* (An Essay on the Immediate Data of the Conscience.) Paris: F. Alcan.

Bergson, H. L., 1900. *Le Rire.* (Laughter.) Paris: F. Alcan.

Berkowitz, Joanne E., & Berkowitz, N. H., 1960. Nursing education and role conception. *Nursing Research*, **9**, 218–220

Berkowitz, L., 1954. Group standards, cohesiveness, and productivity. *Human Relations*, **7**, 509–519.

Berkowitz, L., 1956. Group norms among bomber crews: patterns of perceived crew attitudes, "actual" crew attitudes, and crew liking related to air-crew effectiveness in Far Eastern combat. *Sociometry*, **19**, 141–153. (a)

Berkowitz, L., 1956. Personality and group position. *Sociometry*, **19**, 210–222. (b)

Berkowitz, L., 1957. Effects of perceived dependency relationships upon conformity to group expectations. *Journal of Abnormal and Social Psychology*, **55**, 350–354. (a)

Berkowitz, L., 1957. Liking for the group and the perceived merit of the group's behavior. *Journal of Abnormal and Social Psychology*, **54**, 353–357. (b)

Berkowitz, L., & Howard, R. C., 1959. Reactions to opinion deviates as affected by affiliation need (n) and group member interdependence. *Sociometry*, **22**, 81–91.

Berkowitz, L., & Macaulay, Jacqueline R., 1961. Some effects of differences in status level and status stability. *Human Relations*, **14**, 135–148.

Bernard, J., 1941. Normative collective behavior: a classification of societal norms. *American Journal of Sociology*, **47**, 24–38.

Bernard, J., 1957. Parties and issues in conflict. *Journal of Conflict Resolution*, **1**, 111–121.

Bernard, J. S., 1957. *Social Problems at Midcentury: Role, Status and Stress in a Context of Abundance*. New York: Dryden Press.

Bernberg, R. E., 1955. A measure of social conformity. *Journal of Psychology*, **39**, 89–96.

Bernberg, R. E., 1956. Personality correlates of social conformity: II. *Journal of Social Psychology*, **43**, 309–312.

Biber, Barbara, & Lewis, Claudia, 1949. An experimental study of what young school children expect of their teachers. *Genetic Psychology Monographs*, **40**, 3–97.

Bible, B. L., & Brown, E. J., 1963. Role consensus and satisfaction of extension advisory committee members. *Rural Sociology*, **28**, 81–90.

Bible, B. L., & McComas, J. D., 1963. Role consensus and teacher effectiveness. *Social Forces*, **42**, 225–232.

Bible, B. L., Nolan, Francena L., & Brown, E. J., 1961. Consensus on role definition of the county executive committee member. *Rural Sociology*, **26**, 146–156.

Bicz, R., 1952. Rolle und Szene im menschlichen Dasein. (Role and Scene in Human Existence.) *Psychologische Rundochau*, **3**, 281–290.

Biddle, B. J., 1964. The integration of competence research. In B. J. Biddle and W. J. Ellena (Eds.), *Contemporary Research on Teacher Effectiveness*. New York: Holt. (a)

Biddle, B. J., 1964. Roles, goals and value structures in organizations. In W. W. Cooper, H. J. Leavitt, & J. M. Shelly (Eds.), *Organization Theory*. New York: Wiley. Pp. 150–172. (b)

Biddle, B. J., Twyman, J. P., & Rankin, E. F., Jr., 1962. The role of the teacher and occupational choice. *School Review*, **70**, 191–206.

Bidwell, C. E., 1955. The administrative role and satisfaction in teaching. *Journal of Educational Sociology*, **29**, 41–47.

Bidwell, C. E., 1957. Some effects of administrative behavior: a study in role theory. *Administrative Science Quarterly*, **2**, 163–181.

Bidwell, C. E., 1961. The young professional in the Army: a study of occupational identity. *American Sociological Review*, **26**, 360–372.

Bieri, J., 1953. Changes in interpersonal perceptions following social interaction. *Journal of Abnormal and Social Psychology*, **48**, 61–66.

Bieri, J., 1955. Cognitive complexity-simplicity and predictive behavior. *Journal of Abnormal and Social Psychology*, **51**, 263–268.

Bieri, J., & Blacker, E., 1956. The generality of cognitive complexity in the perception of people and inkblots. *Journal of Abnormal and Social Psychology*, **53**, 112–117.

Bieri, J., & Lobeck, Robin, 1959. Acceptance of authority and parental identification. *Journal of Personality*, **27**, 74–86.

Bierstedt, R., 1950. An analysis of social power. *American Sociological Review*, **15**, 730–738.

Binet, A., 1900. *La Suggestibilité*. (Suggestibility.) Paris: Schleicher Frères.

Bird, Grace E., 1917. Pupils' estimates of teachers. *Journal of Educational Psychology*, **8**, 35–40.

Bishop, Barbara M., 1951. Mother-child interaction and the social behavior of children. *Psychological Monographs*, **65** (238).

Bjerstedt, Å., 1958. A field-force model as a basis for predictions of social behavior. *Human Relations*, **11**, 331–340.

Black, M. (Ed.), 1961. *The Social Theories of Talcott Parsons*. Englewood Cliffs, N. J.: Prentice-Hall.

Blake, Judith, & Davis, K., 1964. Norms, values and sanctions. In R. E. L. Faris (Ed.), *Handbook of Modern Sociology*. Chicago: Rand McNally. Pp. 456–484.

Blake, R. R., 1954. Social standards and individual conduct. *Southwestern Social Science Quarterly*, **35**, 11–24.

Blake, R. R., Helson, H., & Mouton, Jane S., 1957. The generality of conformity behavior as a function of factual anchorage, difficulty of task, and amount of social pressure. *Journal of Personality*, **25**, 294–305.

Blake, R. R., & Mouton, Jane S., 1957. The dynamics of influence and coercion. *International Journal of Social Psychiatry*, **2**, 263–274.

Blake, R. R., Rosenbaum, M., & Duryea, R. A., 1955. Gift-giving as a function of group standards. *Human Relations*, **8**, 61–73.

Blau, P. M., 1962. Operationalizing a conceptual scheme: the universalism-particularism pattern variable. *American Sociological Review*, **27**, 159–169. (a)

Blau, P. M., 1962. Patterns of choice in interpersonal relations. *American Sociological Review*, **27**, 41–55. (b)

Blau, P. M., 1963. Formal organization: dynamics of analysis. *American Journal of Sociology*, **63**, 58–69.

Blau, P. M., & Scott, W. R., 1962. *Formal Organizations*. San Francisco: Chandler.

Blizzard, S. W., 1955. The roles of the rural parish minister, the Protestant seminaries, and the sciences of social behavior. *Religious Education*, **50**, 383–392.

Blizzard, S. W., 1958. The parish minister's self-image of his master role. *Pastoral Psychology*, **9**, 25–32.

Blizzard, S. W., 1959. The parish minister's self-image and variability in community culture. *Pastoral Psychology*, **10**, 27–36.

Blocher, D. H., 1963. Dilemma of counselor identity. *Journal of Counseling Psychology*, **10**, 344–349.

Block, J., 1952. The assessment of communication; role variations as a function of interactional context. *Journal of Personality*, **21**, 272–286.

Block, Jeanne, & Block, J., 1952. An interpersonal experiment on reactions to authority. *Human Relations*, **5**, 91–98.

Blondel, C. A. A., 1914. *La Conscience Morbide: Essai de Psycho-pathologie Générale*. (The Awareness of Death: An Essay in General Psychopathology.) Paris: F. Alcan.

Blondel, C. A. A., 1927. *Introduction à la Psychologie Collective*. (Introduction to Collective Psychology.) Paris: Armand Colin.

Blondel, C. A. A., 1932. *La Psychographie de Marcel Proust*. (The Psychography of Marcel Proust.) Paris: J. Vrin.

Blood, R. O., Jr., & Wolfe, D. M., 1960. *Husbands and Wives: The Dynamics of Married Living*. Glencoe, Ill.: The Free Press.

Bogen, I., 1954. Pupil-teacher rapport and the teacher's awareness of structures within the group. *Journal of Educational Sociology*, **28**, 104–114.

Bolda, R. A., & Lawshe, G. H., 1962. Evaluation of role playing. *Personnel Administration*, **25**, 40–42.

Bolton, C. D., 1958. Behavior, experience, and relationships: a symbolic interactionist point of view. *American Journal of Sociology*, **64**, 45–58.

Book, W. F., 1905. The high school teacher from the pupil's point of view. *Pedagogical Seminary*, **12**, 239–288.

Borg, W. F., 1960. Prediction of small group role behavior from personality variables. *Journal of Abnormal and Social Psychology*, **60**, 112–116.

Borg, W. R., & Silvester, J. A., 1964. Playing the principal's role. *Elementary School Journal*, **64**, 324–331.

Borgatta, E. F., 1954. Analysis of social interaction and sociometric perception. *Sociometry*, **17**, 7–32.

Borgatta, E. F., 1955. Analysis of social interaction: actual, role-playing, and projective. *Journal of Abnormal and Social Psychology*, **51**, 394–405. (a)

Borgatta, E. F., 1955. Attitudinal concomitants to military statuses. *Social Forces*, **33**, 342–347. (b)

Borgatta, E. F., 1960. Rankings and self-assessments: some behavioral characteristics replication studies. *Journal of Social Psychology*, **52**, 279–307. (a)

Borgatta, E. F., 1960. Role and reference group theory. In L. S. Kogan (Ed.), *Social Science Theory and Social Work Research*. New York: National Association of Social Workers. Pp. 16–28. (b)

Borgatta, E. F., 1961. Role-playing specification, personality and performance. *Sociometry*, **24**, 218–233.

Borgatta, E. F., 1962. A systematic study of interaction process scores, peer and self assessments, personality, and other variables. *Genetic Psychology Monographs*, **65**, 219–291.

Borgatta, E. F., & Bales, R. F., 1953. The consistency of subject behavior and the reliability of scoring in interaction process analysis. *American Sociological Review*, **18**, 566–569. (a)

Borgatta, E. F., & Bales, R. F., 1953. Task and accumulation of experience as factors in the interaction of small groups. *Sociometry*, **16**, 239–252. (b)

Borgatta, E. F., Cottrell, L. S., Jr., & Mann, J. H., 1958. The spectrum of individual interaction characteristics: an inter-dimensional analysis. *Psychological Reports*, **4**, 279–319.

Bossard, J. H. S., & Boll, Eleanor S., 1947. The role of the guest: a study in child development. *American Sociological Review*, **6**, 192–201.

Bossard, J. H. S., & Boll, Eleanor S., 1955. Personality roles in the large family. *Child Development*, **26**, 71–81.

Bott, Elizabeth, 1955. Urban families: conjugal roles and social networks. *Human Relations*, **8**, 345–384.

Bott, Elizabeth, 1956. Urban families: the norms of conjugal roles. *Human Relations*, **9**, 325–342.

Bott, Elizabeth, 1957. *Family and Social Network: Roles, Norms, and External Relationships in Ordinary Urban Families.* London: Tavistock Publications.

Bovard, E. W., Jr., 1951. Group structure and perception. *Journal of Abnormal and Social Psychology*, **46**, 398–405.

Bovard, E. W., Jr., 1953. Conformity to social norms and attraction to the group. *Science*, **118**, 598–599.

Bowman, C. C., 1949. Role playing and the development of insight. *Social Forces*, **28**, 195–199.

Brandt, R. M., 1958. The accuracy of self-estimate: a measure of self-concept reality. *Genetic Psychology Monographs*, **58**, 55–99.

Braude, L., 1961. Professional autonomy and the role of the layman. *Social Forces*, **39**, 297–301.

Bray, D. H., 1962. Study of personal attributes and roles favoured by boys and girls aged eleven to thirteen years. *British Journal of Educational Psychology*, **32**, 308–310.

Bray, D. W., 1950. The prediction of behavior from two attitude scales. *Journal of Abnormal and Social Psychology*, **45**, 64–84.

Brayfield, A. H., & Crockett, W. H., 1955. Employee attitudes and employee performance. *Psychological Bulletin*, **52**, 396–424.

Brehm, J. W., & Festinger, L., 1957. Pressures toward uniformity of performance in groups. *Human Relations*, **10**, 85–91.

Brehm, J. W., & Lipsher, D., 1959. Communicator-communicatee discrepancy and perceived communicator trustworthiness. *Journal of Personality*, **27**, 352–361.

Brenner, D. J., Crumley, Wilma, Schores, D. M., & Biddle, B. J., 1962. Views of prospective teachers and non-teachers in a journalism graduate class toward teaching. *Journalism Quarterly* **41**, 253–258.

Brim, O. G., Jr., 1957. The parent-child relation as a social system: I. Parent and child roles. *Child Development*, **28**, 343–364.

Brim, O. G., Jr., 1958. Family structure and sex role learning by children: a further analysis of Helen Koch's data. *Sociometry*, **21**, 1–16.

Brim, O. G., Jr., 1960. Personality development as role-learning. In I. Iscoe, & H. W. Stevenson (Eds.), *Personality Development in Children.* Austin, Texas: University of Texas Press. Pp. 127–159.

Brodbeck, A. J., Nogee, P., & Di Mascio, A., 1956. Two kinds of conformity: a study of the Riesman typology applied to standards of parental discipline. *Journal of Psychology*, **41**, 23–45.

Brookover, W. B., 1943. The social roles of teachers and pupil achievement. *American Sociological Review*, **8**, 389–393.

Brookover, W. B., 1955. Research on teacher and administrator roles. *Journal of Educational Sociology*, **29**, 2–13.

Brooks, E., 1955. What successful executives do. *Personnel*, **32**, 210–225.

Brown, D. G., 1958. Sex-role development in a changing culture. *Psychological Bulletin*, **55**, 232–242.

Brown, D. G., 1962. Sex-role preference in children: methodological problems. *Psychological Reports*, **11**, 477–478.

Brown, J. C., 1952. An experiment in role-taking. *American Sociological Review*, **17**, 587–597.

Brown, W., 1960. *Exploration in Management: A Description of the Glacier Metal Company's Concepts and Methods of Organization and Management.* New York: Wiley.

Browne, C. G., 1950. Study of executive leadership in business. II. Social group patterns. *Journal of Applied Psychology*, **34**, 12–15.

Browne, C. G., & Cohn, T. S., 1958. *The Study of Leadership.* Danville, Ill.: Interstate Printers and Publishers.

Brownfain, J. J., 1952. Stability of the self-concept as a dimension of personality. *Journal of Abnormal and Social Psychology*, **47**, 597–606.

Bruhn, J. G., 1962. An operational approach to the sick-role concept. *British Journal of Medical Psychology*, **35**, 289–298.

Bruner, J. S., Postman, L., & Rodriguez, J., 1951. Expectation and the perception of color. *American Journal of Psychology*, **64**, 216–227.

Bruner, J. S., & Tagiuri, R., 1950. The perception of people. In G. Lindzey (Ed.), *Handbook of Social Psychology*, v. 2. Cambridge, Mass.: Addison-Wesley. Pp. 634–654.

Brun-Gulbrandsen, S., & Ås, Berit, 1960. Kjønnsroller og ulykker. (Sex roles and accidents.) *Tidsskrift for Samfunnsforskning*, **1**, 65–79.

Bruun, K., 1959. Significance of role and norms in the small group for individual behavioral changes while drinking. *Quarterly Journal of Studies on Alcohol*, **20**, 53–64.

Bryer, S. J., & Wagner, R., 1963. The didactic value of role-playing for institutionalized retardates. *Group Psychotherapy*, **16**, 177–181.

Buerkle, J. V., Anderson, T. R., & Badgley, R. F., 1961. Altruism, role-conflict, and marital-adjustment: a factor analysis of marital interaction. *Marriage and Family Living*, **23**, 20–26.

Burchard, W. W., 1954. Role conflicts of military chaplains. *American Sociological Review*, **19**, 528–535.

Burke, R. L., & Bennis, W. G., 1961. Changes in perception of self and others during human relations training. *Human Relations*, **14**, 165–182.

Burns, T., 1954. The directions of activity and communication in a departmental executive group. *Human Relations*, **7**, 73–97.

Burns, T., 1955. The reference of conduct in small groups: cliques and cabals in occupational millieux. *Human Relations*, **8**, 467–486.

Burnstein, E., Roubert, M., & Liberty, P., Jr., 1963. Prestige vs. excellence as determinants of role attractiveness. *American Sociological Review*, **28**, 212–219.

Burwen, L. S., & Campbell, D. T., 1957. The generality of attitudes toward authority and non-authority figures. *Journal of Abnormal and Social Psychology*, **54**, 24–31.

Bush, G., & London, P., 1960. On the disappearance of knickers: hypotheses for the functional analysis of the psychology of clothing. *Journal of Social Psychology*, **51**, 359–366.

Bush, R. N., 1954. *The Teacher-Pupil Relationship*. Englewood Cliffs, N.J.: Prentice-Hall.

Byrne, D., & Buehler, J. A., 1955. A note on the influence of propinquity upon acquaintanceships. *Journal of Abnormal and Social Psychology*, **51**, 147–148.

Cameron, N., 1947. *The Psychology of Behavior Disorders, a Bisocial Interpretation*. Boston: Houghton Mifflin.

Cameron, N., 1950. Role concepts in behavior pathology. *American Journal of Sociology*, **55**, 464–467.

Cameron, N., & Magaret, Ann, 1951. *Behavior Pathology*. Boston: Houghton Mifflin.

Campbell, E. Q., & Pettigrew, T. F., 1959. Racial and moral crisis: the role of Little Rock minister. *American Journal of Sociology*, **64**, 509–516.

Cannon, W. B., 1942. "Voodoo" death. *American Anthropologist*, **44**, 169–181.

Cantril, H., 1957. Perception and interpersonal relations. *American Journal of Psychiatry*, **114**, 119–126.

Cantril, H., 1962. The nature of faith. *Pastoral Psychology*, **13**, 38–47.

Carlson, R. O., 1961. Variation and myth in the social status of teachers. *Journal of Educational Sociology*, **35**, 104–118.

Carper, J. W., & Becker, H. S., 1957. Adjustment to conflicting expectations in the development of identification with an occupation. *Social Forces*, **36**, 51–56.

Carter, H. D., 1944. The development of interest in vocations. *Yearbook of the National Society for the Study of Education*, **43**, Part I, 255–276.

Carter, L. F., 1954. Recording and evaluating the performance of individuals as members of small groups. *Personnel Psychology*, **7**, 477–484.

Cattell, R. B., 1957. A mathematical model for the leadership role and other personality-role relations. In M. Sherif & M. O. Wilson (Eds.), *Emerging Problems in Social Psychology*. Norman, Okla.: University of Oklahoma Book Exchange Duplicating Service. Pp. 207–227.

Cattell, R. B., 1961. Group theory, personality and role: a model for experimental researches. In F. Geldard (Ed.), *Defense Psychology*. New York: Pergamon.

Cattell, R. B., 1963. Personality, role, mood, and situation-perception: a unifying theory of modulators. *Psychological Review*, **70**, 1–18.

Catton, W. R., 1959. A theory of value. *American Sociological Review*, **24**, 310–317.

Caudill, W., 1958. *The Psychiatric Hospital as a Small Society*. Cambridge, Mass.: Harvard University Press.

Cavan, Ruth S., 1962. Self and role in adjustment during old age. In A. M. Rose (Ed.), *Human Behavior and Social Process*. Boston: Houghton Mifflin. Pp. 526–536.

Champlin, D., 1931. Attributes desired in college instructors. *School and Society*, **33**, 89–90.

Chance, Erika, 1957. Mutual expectations of patients and therapists in individual treatment. *Human Relations*, **10**, 167–178.

Chance, Erika, 1959. Mutuality of role expectations as a necessary basis of the treatment relationship. In Erika Chance (Ed.), *Families in Treatment*. New York: Basic Books. Pp. 151–154.

Chance, June E., & Meaders, W., 1960. Needs and interpersonal perception. *Journal of Personality*, **28**, 200–209.

Chansky, N. M., 1958. The attitudes students assign to their teacher. *Journal of Educational Psychology*, **49**, 13–16.

Chapin, F. S., & Tsouderos, J. E., 1955. Formalization observed in ten voluntary associations: concepts, morphology, process. *Social Forces*, **33**, 306–309.

Chapin, F. S., & Tsouderos, J. E., 1956. The formalization process in voluntary associations. *Social Forces*, **34**, 342–344.

Charters, W. W., & Waples, D., 1929. *The Commonwealth Teacher-Training Study*. Chicago: University of Chicago Press.

Charters, W. W., Jr., 1952. The school as a social system. *Review of Educational Research*, **22**, 41–50.

Charters, W. W., Jr., 1953. Social class analysis and the control of public education. *Harvard Educational Review*, **23**, 268–283.

Chartier, Barbara, 1950. The social role of the literary elite. *Social Forces*, **29**, 179–186.

Chase, F. S., & Guba, E. G., 1955. Administrative roles and behavior. *Review of Educational Research*, **25**, 281–289.

Cheek, Frances, 1964. A serendipitous finding: sex roles and schizophrenia. *Journal of Abnormal and Social Psychology*, **69**, 392–400.

Chilcott, J. H., 1961. The school teacher stereotype: a new look! *Journal of Educational Sociology*, **34**, 389–390.

Child, I. L., 1943. The use of interview data in quantifying the individual's role in the group. *Journal of Abnormal and Social Psychology*, **38**, 305–318.

Chowdhry, K., & Newcomb, T. M., 1952. The relative abilities of leaders and non-leaders to estimate opinions of their own groups. *Journal of Abnormal and Social Psychology*, **47**, 51–57.

Christensen, H. T., & Carpenter, G. R., 1962. Value-behavior discrepancies regarding pre-marital coitus in three western cultures. *American Sociological Review*, **27**, 66–74.

Clark, B. R., 1956. Organizational adaptation and precarious values: a case study. *American Sociological Review*, **21**, 327–336.

Clark, E. T., 1963. Sex role preference in mentally retarded children. *American Journal of Mental Deficiency*, **67**, 606–610.

Clark, R. A., & McGuire, C., 1952. Sociographic analysis of sociometric valuations. *Child Development*, **23**, 129–140.

Cline, M. G., 1956. The influence of social context on the perception of faces. *Journal of Personality*, **25**, 142–158.

Clinton, R. J., 1930. Qualities college students desire in college instructors. *School and Society*, **32**, 702.

Cloward, R., & Ohlin, L. E., 1960. *Delinquency and Opportunity: a Theory of Delinquent Gangs*. Glencoe, Ill.: The Free Press.

Cobb, P. R., 1952. High school seniors' attitudes toward teachers and the teaching profession. *Bulletin of the National Association of Secondary School Principals*, **36**, 140–144.

Cohen, A. R., 1960. Attitudinal consequences of induced discrepancies between cognitions and behavior. *Public Opinion Quarterly*, **24**, 297–318.

Cohen, B. P., 1958. A probability model for conformity. *Sociometry*, **21**, 69–81.

Collins, S., 1960. The school teacher in his role as leader in West Indian and African societies. *Civilization*, **10**, 315–325.

Colombotos, J., 1963. Sex-role area professionalism: a study of high-school teachers. *School Review*, **71**, 27–40.

Connor, Ruth, Johannis, T. B., Jr., & Walters, J., 1955. Family recreation in relation to role conceptions of family members. *Marriage and Family Living*, **17**, 306–309.

Conrad, F. A., 1962. Sex roles as factors in longevity. *Sociology and Social Research*, **46**, 195–262.

Consinet, R., 1936. Le monologue enfantin. (The infantile monologue.) *Journal de Psychologie Normale et Pathologique*, **33**, 28–39.

Conyers, J. E., 1961. An exploratory study of employers' attitudes toward working mothers. *Sociology and Social Research*, **45**, 144–156.

Cook, L. A., Almack, R. B., & Greenhoe, Florence, 1938. Teacher and community relations. *American Sociological Review*, **3**, 167–174.

Cook, L. A., & Almack, R. B., 1939. The community participation of 2,870 Ohio teachers. *Educational Administration and Supervision*, **25**, 107–119.

Cook, W. W., Leeds, Carroll H., & Callis, R., 1949. Predicting teacher-pupil relations. In The Association for Student Teaching, *The Evaluation of Student Teaching*, 1949th Yearbook, Lock Haven, Pa.: State Teachers College. Pp. 66–80.

Cooley, C. H., 1902. *Human Nature and the Social Order*. New York: Scribner's. (Revised ed., 1922.)

Cooley, C. H., 1909. *Social Organization: a Study of the Larger Mind*. New York: Scribner's.

Copeland, M. T., 1952. *The Executive at Work*. Cambridge, Mass.: Harvard University Press.

Corey, S. M., 1937. Attitudes toward teaching and professional training. *Educational Administration and Supervision*, **23**, 521–527.

Corwin, R. G., 1961. The professional employee: a study of conflict in nursing roles. *American Journal of Sociology*, **67**, 604–615. (a)

Corwin, R. G., 1961. Role conception and career aspiration: a study of identity in nursing. *Sociological Quarterly*, **2**, 69–86. (b)

Corwin, R. G., Taves, M. J., & Haas, J. E., 1960. Social requirements for occupational success: internalized norms and friendships. *Social Forces*, **39**, 135–140.

Coser, L. A., 1956. *The Functions of Social Conflict*. Glencoe, Ill.: The Free Press.

Coser, L. A., 1962. Some functions of deviant behavior and normative flexibility. *American Journal of Sociology*, **68**, 172–181.

Coser, Rose L., 1961. Insulation from observability and types of social conformity. *American Sociological Review*, **26**, 28–39.

Cottrell, L. S., Jr., 1933. Roles and marital adjustment. *Publications of the American Sociological Society*, **27**, 107–115.

Cottrell, L. S., Jr., 1942. The adjustment of the individual to his age and sex roles. *American Sociological Review*, **7**, 617–620. (a)

Cottrell, L. S., Jr., 1942. The analysis of situational fields in social psychology. *American Sociological Review*, **7**, 370–382. (b)

Cottrell, L. S., Jr., 1950. Some neglected problems in social psychology. *American Sociological Review*, **15**, 705–712.

Couch, C. J., 1958. The use of the concept "role" and its derivatives in a study of marriage. *Marriage and Family Living*, **20**, 353–357.

Couch, C. J., 1962. Family role specialization and self-attitudes in children. *Sociological Quarterly*, **3**, 115–121.

Coult, A. D., 1964. Role allocation, position structuring, and ambilineal descent. *American Anthropologist*, **66**, 29–40.

Cousins, A. N., 1951. Social equilibrium and the psycho-dynamic mechanisms. *Social Forces*, **30**, 201–209.

Coutu, W., 1951. Role-playing versus role-taking: an appeal for clarification. *American Sociological Review*, **16**, 180–187.

Craig, H., 1960. The teacher's function: some observations on an aspect of the teacher's job in Scotland. *Journal of Educational Sociology*, **34**, 7–16.

Crandall, V. C., 1963. Reinforcement effects of adult reactions and nonreactions on children's achievement expectations. *Child Development*, **34**, 335–354.

Cronbach, L. J., 1955. Processes affecting scores on "Understanding of others" and "Assumed similarity." *Psychological Bulletin*, **52**, 177–193.

Crow, W. J., 1957. The effect of training upon accuracy and variability in interpersonal perception. *Journal of Abnormal and Social Psychology*, **55**, 355–359.

Crow, W. J., & Hammond, K. R., 1957. The generality of accuracy and response sets in interpersonal perception. *Journal of Abnormal and Social Psychology*, **54**, 384–390.

Crozier, M., 1961. Human relations at the management level in a bureaucratic system of organization. *Human Organization*, **20**, 51–64.

Culbertson, Frances M., 1957. Modification of an emotionally held attitude through role playing. *Journal of Abnormal and Social Psychology*, **54**, 230–233.

Curle, A., 1947. Transitional communities and social reconnection: a follow-up study of the civil resettlement of British prisoners of war: Part I. *Human Relations*, **1**, 42–68.

Curle, A., & Trist, E. L., 1947. Transitional communities and social reconnection: a follow-up study of the civil resettlement of British prisoners of war: Part II. *Human Relations*, **1**, 240–288.

Dahl, R. A., 1957. The concept of power. *Behavioral Science*, **2**, 201–215.

Dahlke, H. O., 1953. Determinants of sociometric relations among children in the elementary school. *Sociometry*, **16**, 327–338.
Dahrendorf, R., 1958. Homo sociologicus: an essay on the history, meaning and critique of social role, Part I. *Kölner Zeitschrift für Soziologie und Sozial-Psychologie*, **10**, 178–208. (a)
Dahrendorf, R., 1958. Homo sociologicus: continuation and conclusion. *Kölner Zeitschrift für Soziologie und Sozial-Psychologie*, **10**, 345–378. (b)
Dallolio, Helen C., 1955. Teachers on trial: group of pupils tell what they like in teachers. *Clearing House*, **29**, 497–499.
Dalton, M., 1950. Conflicts between staff and line managerial officers. *American Sociological Review*, **15**, 342–351.
Daniels, M. J., 1959. Relational status and the role concept. *Pacific Sociological Review*, **2**, 41–48.
Daniels, M. J., 1960. Affect and its control in the medical intern. *American Journal of Sociology*, **66**, 259–267.
Daniels, M. J., 1962. Levels of organization in the role position of the staff nurse. *Social Forces*, **40**, 242–248.
Davies, J. E., 1933. What are the traits of the good teacher from the standpoint of junior high school pupils? *School and Society*, **38**, 649–652.
Davis, F. J., 1954. Conceptions of official leader roles in the Air Force. *Social Forces*, **32**, 253–258.
Davis, F. J., 1963. *Passage Through Crisis: Polio Victims and Their Families*. New York: Bobbs-Merrill.
Davis, F. J., Hagedorn, R., & Larson, J. R., 1954. Scaling problems in a study of conceptions of Air Force leader roles. *Public Opinion Quarterly*, **18**, 279–286.
Davis, F. J., & Olesen, V. L., 1963. Initiation into a woman's profession: identity problems in the status transition of coed to student nurse. *Sociometry*, **26**, 89–101.
Davis, J. A., 1956. Status symbols and the measurement of status perception. *Sociometry*, **19**, 154–165.
Davis, J. A., 1957. Correlates of sociometric status among peers. *Journal of Educational Research*, **50**, 561–569.
Davis, J. A., 1961. Compositional effects, role systems, and the survival of small discussion groups. *Public Opinion Quarterly*, **25**, 574–584. (a)
Davis, J. A., 1961. *Great Books and Small Groups*. New York: The Free Press. (b)
Davis, K., 1940. The sociology of parent-youth conflict. *American Sociological Review*, **5**, 523–535.
Davis, K., 1942. A conceptual analysis of stratification. *American Sociological Review*, **7**, 309–321.
Davis, K., 1949. *Human Society*. New York: Macmillan.
Davison, W. P., 1961. A public opinion game. *Public Opinion Quarterly*, **25**, 210–220.
Davitz, J. R., 1955. Social perception and sociometric choice of children. *Journal of Abnormal and Social Psychology*, **50**, 173–176.
Deasy, L. C., 1964. *Social Role Theory: Its Component Parts, and Some Applications*. Washington: The Catholic University of America Press.
DeCharms, R., & Rosenbaum, M. E., 1960. Status variables and matching behavior. *Journal of Personality*, **28**, 492–502.
DeJung, J. E., & Gardner, E. F., 1962. Accuracy of self-role perception: a developmental study. *Journal of Experimental Education*, **31**, 27–42.
DeLucia, L. A., 1963. The toy preference test: a measure of sex role identification. *Child Development*, **34**, 107–118.
DeSoto, C. B., & Basley, J. J., 1962. The cognitive structure of a social structure. *Journal of Abnormal and Social Psychology*, **64**, 303–307.
DeSoto, C. B., & Kuethe, J. L., 1959. Subjective probabilities of interpersonal relationships. *Journal of Abnormal and Social Psychology*, **59**, 290–294.
Deutsch, M., 1949. An experimental study of the effects of cooperation and competition upon group processes. *Human Relations*, **2**, 199–232.
Deutsch, M., & Gerard, H. B., 1955. A study of normative and informational social influences upon individual judgement. *Journal of Abnormal and Social Psychology*, **51**, 629–636.
Deutscher, I., & Montague, Ann, 1956. Professional education and conflicting value systems: the role of religious schools in the educational aspirations of nursing students. *Social Forces*, **35**, 126–131.
Devereux, G., & Weiner, F. R., 1950. The occupational status of nurses. *American Sociological Review*, **15**, 628–634.

DeVos, G., & Wagatsuma, H., 1961. Value attitudes towards role behavior of women in two Japanese villages. *American Anthropologist*, **63**, 1204–1230.

Dewey, J., 1899. *The School and the Society*. Chicago: University of Chicago Press.

Dewey, J., 1922. *Human Nature and Conduct: An Introduction to Social Psychology*. New York: Carlton House.

Dexter, L. A., 1956. Role relationships and conceptions of neutrality in interviewing. *American Journal of Sociology*, **62**, 153–157.

Diggory, J. C., 1962. Sex-differences in judging the acceptability of actions. *Journal of Social Psychology*, **56**, 107–114.

Dinitz, S., Angrist, Shirley, Lefton, M., & Pasamanick, B., 1962. Instrumental role expectations and post-hospital performance of female mental patients. *Social Forces*, **40**, 248–254.

Dinitz, S., Mangus, A. R., & Pasamanick, B., 1959. Integration and conflict in self-other conceptions as factors in mental illness. *Sociometry*, **22**, 44–55.

Dittes, J. E., 1959. Attractiveness of group as function of self-esteem and acceptance by group. *Journal of Abnormal and Social Psychology*, **59**, 77–82.

Dittes, J. E., & Kelley, H. H., 1956. Effects of different conditions of acceptance upon conformity to group norms. *Journal of Abnormal and Social Psychology*, **53**, 100–107.

DiVesta, F. J., 1948. The relationship between values, concepts, and attitudes. *Education and Psychological Measurement*, **8**, 645–659.

Dodd, S. C., 1949. Note on an index of conformity. *Science*, **110**, 233–235.

Donahue, Wilma, Orbach, H. L., & Pollack, O., 1960. Retirement: the emerging social pattern. In C. Tibbitts (Ed.), *Handbook of Social Gerontology: Societal Aspects of Aging*. Chicago: University of Chicago Press. Pp. 298–330.

Donovan, Frances R., 1938. *The Schoolma'am*. New York: Frederick A. Stokes.

Downing, J., 1958. Cohesiveness, perception, and values. *Human Relations*, **115**, 157–166.

Doyle, L. A., 1958. Convergence and divergence in the role expectations of elementary teachers. *Michigan State University College of Education Quarterly*, **4**, 3–9.

Dreyer, A. S., 1954. Aspiration behavior as influenced by expectation and group comparison. *Human Relations*, **7**, 175–190.

Driver, E. D., 1962. Caste and occupational structure in central India. *Social Forces*, **41**, 26–30.

Dunphy, D. C., 1963. Social structure of urban adolescent peer groups. *Sociometry*, **26**, 230–246.

Durkheim, E., 1893. *De la Division du Travail Social*. (The Division of Labor in Society.) Paris: F. Alcan.

Durkheim, E., 1894. *Les Règles de la Méthode Sociologique*. (The Rules of Sociological Method.) Paris: F. Alcan.

Durkheim, E., 1897. *Le Suicide*. (Suicide.) Paris: F. Alcan.

Dwyer, R. J., 1953. The Negro in the U.S. Army, his changing role and status. *Sociology and Social Research*, **38**, 103–112.

Dyer, W. G., 1962. Analyzing marital adjustment using role theory. *Marriage and Family Living*, **24**, 371–375.

Dymond, Rosalind F., 1949. A scale for the measurement of empathic ability. *Journal of Consulting Psychology*, **13**, 127–133.

Dymond, Rosalind F., 1950. Personality and empathy. *Journal of Consulting Psychology*, **14**, 343–350.

Eaton, J., 1963. Role expectations: the social worker looks in the mirror. *Public Administration Review*, **23**, 170–175.

Edmonston, W. E., Jr., 1962. Hypnotic age-regression: an evaluation of role-taking theory. *American Journal of Clinical Hypnosis*, **5**, 3–7.

Eggert, M. A., 1937. *Person und Rolle*. (Person and Role.) Endingen-Kaiserstuhl: Wild.

Ehrlich, H. J., Rinehart, J. W., & Howell, J. C., 1962. The study of role conflict: explorations in methodology. *Sociometry*, **25**, 85–97.

Eisenstadt, S. N., 1954. Studies in reference group behavior, I: reference norms and the social structure. *Human Relations*, **7**, 191–216.

Eisenstadt, S. N., 1956. *From Generation to Generation*. Glencoe, Ill.: The Free Press.

Ellemeers, J. E., 1953. Het interview als rol-ontmeeting. (The interview as a role-encounter.) *Sociologische Gids*, **1**, 26–29.

Emerson, R. M., 1954. Deviation and rejection: an experimental replication. *American Sociological Review*, **19**, 688–693.

Emerson, R. M., 1962. Power-dependence relations. *American Sociological Review*, **27**, 31–41.

Emmerich, W., 1959. Young children's discrimination of parent and child roles. *Child Development*, **30**, 403–419.

Emmerich, W., 1961. Family role concepts of children ages six to ten. *Child Development*, **32**, 609–624.

Emmerich, W., 1962. Variations in the parent role as a function of the parent's sex and the child's sex and age. *Merrill-Palmer Quarterly*, **8**, 3–11.

Engelman, H. O., 1962. Social psychological issues in the theory of social organization. *Sociological Quarterly*, **3**, 286–295.

English, O. S., 1954. The psychological role of the father in the family. *Social Casework*, **35**, 323–329.

Epstein, R., 1963. Verbal conditioning and sex-role identification in children. *Child Development*, **34**, 99–106.

Erikson, K. T., 1957. Patient role and social uncertainty—a dilemma of the mentally ill. *Psychiatry*, **20**, 263–274.

Eulau, H., Wahlke, J. C., Buchanan, W., & Ferguson, L. C., 1959. The role of the representative: some empirical observations on the theory of Edmund Burke. *American Political Science Review*, **53**, 742–756.

Evan, W. M., 1963. Role strain and the norm of reciprocity in research organizations. *American Journal of Sociology*, **68**, 346–354.

Evan, W. M., & Zelditch, M., Jr., 1961. A laboratory experiment on bureaucratic authority. *American Sociological Review*, **26**, 883–893.

Exline, R. V., 1957. Group climate as a factor in the relevance and accuracy of social perception. *Journal of Abnormal and Social Psychology*, **55**, 382–388.

Exline, R. V., 1960. Effects of sex, norms, and affiliation motivation upon accuracy of perception of interpersonal preferences. *Journal of Personality*, **28**, 397–412.

Exline, R. V., & Ziller, R. C., 1959. Status congruency and interpersonal conflict in decision-making groups. *Human Relations*, **12**, 147–162.

Fallding, H., 1961. The family and the idea of a cardinal role. *Human Relations*, **14**, 329–350.

Fallers, L., 1955. The predicament of the modern African chief: an instance from Uganda. *American Anthropologist*, **57**, 290–305.

Fanshel, D., 1961. Studying the role performance of foster parents. *Social Work*, **6**, 74–81.

Farber, B., & Blackman, L. S., 1956. Marital role tensions and number and sex of children. *American Sociological Review*, **21**, 596–601.

Farina, A., 1960. Patterns of role dominance and conflict in parents of schizophrenic patients. *Journal of Abnormal and Social Psychology*, **61**, 31–38.

Faris, R. E. L., 1937. The social psychology of George Mead. *American Journal of Sociology*, **43**, 391–403.

Faris, R. E. L., 1952. *Social Psychology*. New York: Ronald Press.

Fauls, Lydia B., & Smith, W. D., 1956. Sex-role learning of five-year-olds. *Journal of Genetic Psychology*, **89**, 105–117.

Fava, Sylvia F., 1960. The status of women in professional sociology. *American Sociological Review*, **25**, 271–276.

Favez, G., 1947. *Les Personnes et les Rôles*. (Persons and Roles.) Lausanne: Rot.

Feffer, M. H., & Gourevitch, Vivian, 1960. Cognitive aspects of role-taking in children. *Journal of Personality*, **28**, 383–396.

Fenchel, G. J., Monderer, J. H., & Hartley, E. L., 1951. Subjective status and the equilibration hypothesis. *Journal of Abnormal and Social Psychology*, **46**, 476–479.

Fensterheim, H., & Tresselt, M. E., 1953. The influence of value systems on the perception of people. *Journal of Abnormal and Social Psychology*, **48**, 93–98.

Festinger, L., 1942. Wish, expectation, and group standards as factors influencing level of aspiration. *Journal of Abnormal and Social Psychology*, **37**, 184–200.

Festinger, L., 1947. The role of group belongingness in a voting situation. *Human Relations*, **1**, 154–180.

Festinger, L., 1950. Informal social communication. *Psychological Review*, **57**, 271–282.

Festinger, L., 1954. A theory of social comparison processes. *Human Relations*, **7**, 117–140.

Festinger, L., 1957. *A Theory of Cognitive Dissonance*. Evanston, Ill.: Row, Peterson.

Festinger, L., Back, K., Schachter, S., Kelley, H. H., & Thibaut, J., 1950. *Theory and Experiment in Social Communication*. Ann Arbor: Research Center for Group Dynamics, Institute for Social Research.

Festinger, L., Gerard, H. B., Hymovitch, B., Kelley, H. H., & Raven, B., 1952. The influence process in the presence of extreme deviates. *Human Relations*, **5**, 327–346.

Festinger, L., Pepitone, A., & Newcomb, T. M., 1952. Some consequences of de-individuation in a group. *Journal of Abnormal and Social Psychology*, **47**, 382–389.

Festinger, L., Schachter, S., & Back, K., 1950. *Social Pressures in Informal Groups*. New York: Harper.

Festinger, L., & Thibaut J., 1951. Interpersonal communication in small groups. *Journal of Abnormal and Social Psychology*, **46**, 92–99.

Festinger, L., Torrey, Jane, & Willerman, B., 1954. Self-evaluation as a function of attraction to the group. *Human Relations*, **7**, 161–174.

Fey, W. F., 1957. Correlates of certain subjective attitudes towards self and others. *Journal of Clinical Psychology*, **13**, 44–49.

Fiedler, F. E., 1953. The psychological-distance dimension in interpersonal relations. *Journal of Personality*, **22**, 142–150.

Fiedler, F. E., 1954. Assumed similarity measures as predictors of team effectiveness. *Journal of Abnormal and Social Psychology*, **49**, 381–388.

Fiedler, F. E., Warrington, W. G., & Blaisdell, F. J., 1952. Unconscious attitudes as correlates of sociometric choice in a social group. *Journal of Abnormal and Social Psychology*, **47**, 790–796.

Field, M. G., 1953. Structured strain in the role of the Soviet physician. *American Journal of Sociology*, **58**, 493–502.

Filer, R. J., 1952. Frustration, satisfaction, and other factors affecting the attractiveness of goal objects. *Journal of Abnormal and Social Psychology*, **47**, 203–212.

Finer, H., 1959. The tasks and function of the legislator. In J. C. Wahlke and H. Eulau (Eds.), *Legislative Behavior*. Glencoe, Ill.: The Free Press. Pp. 281–284.

Finestone, H., 1957. Cats, kicks and color. *Social Problems*, **5**, 3–13.

Fishbein, M., & Raven, B. J., 1962. The AB Scales—an operational definition of belief and attitude. *Human Relations*, **15**, 35–44.

Fishburn, C. E., 1962. Teacher role perception in the secondary school. *Journal of Teacher Education*, **13**, 55–59.

Fisher, S., & Lubin, A., 1958. Distance as a determinant of influence in a two-person serial interaction situation. *Journal of Abnormal and Social Psychology*, **56**, 230–238.

Flament, C., 1956. Influence des changements de réseaux de communication sur les performances des groupes. (The influence of changes in the network of communications upon the performance of groups.) *Psychologie Française*, **1**, 12–13.

Fleming, Charlotte M., 1957. *Teaching: A Psychological Analysis*. New York: Wiley.

Foa, U. G., 1957. A test of the foreman-worker relationship. *Personnel Psychology*, **9**, 469–486.

Foa, U. G., 1958. Behavior, norms, and social rewards in a dyad. *Behavioral Science*, **3**, 323–334. (a)

Foa, U. G., 1958. The contiguity principle in the structure of interpersonal relations. *Human Relations*, **11**, 229–238. (b)

Foa, U. G., 1961. Convergences in the analysis of the structure of interpersonal behavior. *Psychological Review*, **68**, 341–353.

Foa, U. G., 1962. The structure of interpersonal behavior in the dyad. In J. H. Chrisswell, H. Solomon, and P. Suppes (Eds.), *Mathematical Methods in Small Groups Processes*. Stanford, Calif.: Stanford University Press. Pp. 166–179.

Foley, A. S., 1944. The status and role of the Negro priest in the American Catholic clergy. *American Catholic Sociological Review*, **15**, 83–93.

Foote, N. N., 1954. Changes in American marriage patterns and the role of women. *Eugenic Quarterly*, **1**, 254–260.

Ford, C. S., 1938. The role of a Fijian Chief. *American Sociological Review*, **3**, 541–550.

Frank, A. G., 1964. Administrative role definition and social change. *Human Organization*, **22**, 238–242.

Freeman, H. D., & Simmons, O. G., 1958. Mental patients in the community: family settings and performance levels. *American Sociological Review*, **23**, 147–154.

Freeman, H. D., & Simmons, O. G., 1963. *The Mental Patient Comes Home*. New York: Wiley.

French, J. R. P., Jr., 1944. Organized and unorganized groups under fear and frustration. *University of Iowa Studies in Child Welfare*, **20**, 231–308.

French, J. R. P., Jr., Israel, J., & Ås, D., 1960. An experiment on participation in a Norwegian factory: interpersonal dimensions of decision-making. *Human Relations*, **13**, 3–19.

French, J. R. P., Jr., & Kahn, R. L., 1962. A programmatic approach to studying the industrial environment and mental health. *Journal of Social Issues*, **18**, 1–47.

French, J. R. P., Jr., Morrison, H. W., & Levinger, G., 1960. Coercive power and forces affecting conformity. *Journal of Abnormal and Social Psychology*, **61**, 93–101.

French, J. R. P., Jr., & Raven, B., 1959. The bases of social power. In D. Cartwright (Ed.), *Studies in Social Power*. Ann Arbor, Mich.: Institute for Social Research. Pp. 150–167.

French, J. R. P., Jr., & Zajonc, R. B., 1957. An experimental study of cross-cultural norm conflict. *Journal of Abnormal and Social Psychology*, **54**, 218–224.

French, K. S., 1962. Research interviewers in a medical setting: roles and social systems. *Human Organization*, **21**, 219–224.

French, R. L., & Mensh, I. N., 1948. Some relationships between interpersonal judgments and sociometric status in a college group. *Sociometry*, **11**, 335–345.

Freud, Anna, 1952. The role of the teacher. *Harvard Educational Review*, **22**, 229–234.

Fromm-Reichmann, Frieda, 1940. Notes on the mother role in the family group. *Bulletin of the Menninger Clinic*, **4**, 132–148.

Fulton, R. L., 1961. The clergyman and the funeral director: a study in role conflict. *Social Forces*, **39**, 317–323.

Gage, N. L., 1953. Accuracy of social perception and effectiveness in interpersonal relationships. *Journal of Personality*, **22**, 128–141.

Gage, N. L., & Chatterjee, B. B., 1960. The psychological meaning of acquiescence set: further evidence. *Journal of Abnormal and Social Psychology*, **60**, 280–283.

Gage, N. L., & Cronbach, L. J., 1955. Conceptual and methodological problems in interpersonal perception. *Psychological Review*, **62**, 411–422.

Gage, N. L., & Exline, R. V., 1953. Social perception and effectiveness in discussion groups. *Human Relations*, **6**, 381–396.

Gage, N. L., Leavitt, G. S., & Stone, G. C., 1956. The intermediary key in the analysis of interpersonal perception. *Psychological Bulletin*, **53**, 258–266.

Gage, N. L., Leavitt, G. S., & Stone, G. C., 1957. The psychological meaning of acquiescence set for authoritarianism. *Journal of Abnormal and Social Psychology*, **55**, 98–103.

Gallagher, J. J., 1958. Social status of children related to intelligence, propinquity, and social perception. *Elementary School Journal*, **58**, 225–231.

Galtung, J., 1959. A model for studying images of participants in a conflict: Southwille. *Journal of Social Issues*, **15**, 38–43. (a)

Galtung, J., 1959. Expectations and interaction processes. *Inquiry*, **2**, 213–234. (b)

Gardener, B. B., & Whyte, W. F., 1945. The man in the middle: position and problems of the foreman. *Applied Anthropology*, **4**, 1–28.

Gates, Georgina S., 1924. The effect of an audience upon performance. *Journal of Abnormal and Social Psychology*, **18**, 334–344.

Gebel, A. S., 1954. Self-perception and leaderless group discussion status. *Journal of Social Psychology*, **40**, 309–318.

Gebhard, Mildred E., 1948. The effect of success and failure upon the attractiveness of activities as a function of experience, expectation and need. *Journal of Experimental Psychology*, **38**, 371–388.

Gerard, H. B., 1953. The effect of different dimensions of disagreement on the communication process in small groups. *Human Relations*, **6**, 249–271.

Gerard, H. B., 1954. The anchorage of opinions in face-to-face groups. *Human Relations*, **7**, 313–325.

Gerard, H. B., 1956. Some factors affecting an individual's estimate of his probable success in a group situation. *Journal of Abnormal and Social Psychology*, **52**, 235–239.

Gerard, H. B., 1957. Some effects of status, role clarity and group goal clarity upon the individual's relations to group process. *Journal of Personality*, **25**, 475–488.

Gerard, H. B., 1958. Some effects of involvement upon evaluation. *Journal of Abnormal and Social Psychology*, **57**, 118–120.

Gerver, I., 1957. The social psychology of witness behavior with special reference to the criminal courts. *Journal of Social Issues*, **13**, 23–29.

Getzels, J. W., 1952. A psycho-sociological framework for the study of educational administration. *Harvard Educational Review*, **22**, 235–246.

Getzels, J. W., 1963. Conflict and role behavior in the educational setting. In W. W. Charters, Jr., and N. L. Gage (Eds.), *The Social Psychology of Education*. Boston: Allyn & Bacon. Pp. 309–318.

Getzels, J. W., & Guba, E. G., 1954. Role, role conflict, and effectiveness: an empirical study. *American Sociological Review*, **19**, 164–175.

Getzels, J. W., & Guba, E. G., 1955. Role conflict and personality. *Journal of Personality*, **24**, 74–85. (a)

Getzels, J. W., & Guba, E. G., 1955. The structure of roles and role conflict in the teaching situation. *Journal of Educational Sociology*, **29**, 30–40. (b)

Getzels, J. W., & Guba, E. G., 1957. Social behavior and the administrative process. *School Review*, **65**, 423–441.

Ghiselli, E. E., & Barthol, R., 1956. Role perceptions of successful and unsuccessful supervisors. *Journal of Applied Psychology*, **40**, 241–244.

Ghiselli, E. E., & Lodahl, T. M., 1958. Patterns of managerial traits and group effectiveness. *Journal of Abnormal and Social Psychology*, **57**, 61–66.

Gieber, W., & Johnson, W., 1961. The city hall "beat": a study of reporter and source roles. *Journalism Quarterly*, **38**, 289–297.

Gilbert, Doris, & Levinson, D. J., 1957. Role performance, ideology and personality in mental hospital aides. In M. Greenblatt, D. J. Levinson, & R. H. Williams (Eds.), *The Patient and the Mental Hospital*. Glencoe, Ill.: The Free Press. Pp. 197–208.

Ginzberg, E., Ginsburg, S. W., Axelrad, S., & Herma, J. L., 1951. *Occupational Choice: An Approach to a General Theory*. New York: Columbia University Press.

Gioscia, V., 1961. A perspective for role theory. *American Catholic Sociological Review*, **22**, 142–150.

Glasser, P. H., & Glasser, Lois N., 1962. Role reversal and conflict between aged parents and their children. *Marriage and Family Living*, **24**, 46–51.

Goffman, E., 1957. Alienation from interaction. *Human Relations*, **10**, 47–60.

Goffman, E., 1959. *The Presentation of Self in Everyday Life*. New York: Doubleday.

Goffman, E., 1961. *Encounters: Two Studies in the Sociology of Interaction*. Indianapolis: Bobbs-Merrill.

Goffman, E., 1963. *Behavior in Public Places*. New York: The Free Press.

Goffman, I. W., 1957. Status consistency and preference for change in power distribution. *American Sociological Review*, **22**, 275–281.

Goldberg, S. C., 1954. Three situational determinants of conformity to social norms. *Journal of Abnormal and Social Psychology*, **49**, 325–329.

Goldberg, S. C., 1955. Influence and leadership as a function of group structure. *Journal of Abnormal and Social Psychology*, **51**, 119–122.

Goldberg, S. C., & Lubin, A., 1958. Influence as a function of perceived judgment error. *Human Relations*, **11**, 275–281.

Goldstein, A. P., 1962. Participant expectancies in psychotherapy. *Psychiatry*, **25**, 72–79. (a)

Goldstein, A. P., 1962. *Therapist-Patient Expectancies in Psychotherapy*. New York: Pergamon. (b)

Goldstein, B., & Dommeanuth, P., 1961. The sick role cycle: an approach to medical sociology. *Sociology and Social Research*, **46**, 36–47.

Goldstein, S. I., 1953. The roles of an American Rabbi. *Sociology and Social Research*, **38**, 32–37.

Golovensky, D. I., 1952. The marginal man concept: an analysis and critique. *Social Forces*, **30**, 333–339.

Gone, M. S., 1961. Husband-wife and mother-son relationships. *Sociological Bulletin*, **11**, 91–102.

Gonya, G. G., & Warman, R. E., 1962. Differential perceptions of the student dormitory counselor's role. *Personnel and Guidance Journal*, **41**, 350–355.

Goodacre, D. M., III., 1953. Group characteristics of good and poor performing combat units. *Sociometry*, **16**, 168–179.

Goode, W. J., 1956. *After Divorce*. Glencoe, Ill.: The Free Press.

Goode, W. J., 1960. A theory of role strain. *American Sociological Review*, **25**, 483–496. (a)

Goode, W. J., 1960. Norm commitment and conformity to role-status obligations. *American Journal of Sociology*, **66**, 246–258. (b)

Gordon, C. W., 1955. The role of the teacher in the social structure of the high school. *Journal of Educational Sociology*, **29**, 21–29.

Gordon, C. W., 1959. *The Social System of the High School: A Study in the Sociology of Adolescence*. Glencoe, Ill.: The Free Press.

Gordon, L. V., 1960. *Survey of Interpersonal Values*. Chicago: Science Research Associates.

Gordon, L. V., & Mensh, I. N., 1962. Values of medical school students at different levels of training. *Journal of Educational Psychology*, **53**, 48–51.

Gottlieb, D., 1961. Processes of socialization in American graduate schools. *Social Forces*, **40**, 124–131.

Gouhier, M. L., 1955. Une discussion de groupe. (A discussion of the group.) *Bulletin de Psychologie*, **8**, 383–388.

Gouldner, A. W., 1957. Cosmopolitans and locals: toward an analysis of latent social roles: I. *Administrative Science Quarterly*, **2**, 281–306. (a)

Gouldner, A. W., 1957. Cosmopolitans and locals: toward an analysis of latent social roles: II. *Administrative Science Quarterly*, **2**, 444–480. (b)

Gouldner, A. W., 1959. Reciprocity and autonomy in functional theory. In L. Gross (Ed.), *Symposium in Social Theory*. Evanston, Ill.: Harper & Row. Pp. 241–270.

Gouldner, A. W., 1960. The norm of reciprocity: a preliminary statement. *American Sociological Review*, **25**, 161–178.

Gouldner, A. W., & Gouldner, Helen, 1963. Roles, identities and categories. In R. K. Merton (Ed.), *Modern Sociology*. New York: Harcourt Brace. Pp. 179–190.

Grace, H. A., 1951. Effects of different degrees of knowledge about an audience on the content of communication. *Journal of Social Psychology*, **34**, 111–124.

Grace, H. A., 1954. Conformance and performance. *Journal of Social Psychology*, **40**, 333–335.

Graham, D., 1962. Experimental studies of social influence in simple judgment situations. *Journal of Social Psychology*, **56**, 245–269.

Gray, H., 1962. Trapped housewife. *Marriage and Family Living*, **24**, 179–182.

Greco, M., 1950. *Group Life: The Nature and Treatment of Its Specific Conflicts*. New York: Philosophical Library.

Greenhoe, Florence, 1940. Community contacts of public-school teachers. *Elementary School Journal*, **40**, 497–506.

Greer, F. L., Galanter, E. H., & Nordlie, P. G., 1954. Interpersonal knowledge and individual and group effectiveness. *Journal of Abnormal and Social Psychology*, **49**, 411–414.

Greer, S., 1953. Situational pressures and functional role of the ethnic labor leader. *Social Forces*, **32**, 41–45.

Griffiths, W., 1959. A study of work role perceptions: the community health worker on the Navajo Indian reservation. *Journal of Psychology*, **48**, 167–180.

de Groat, A. F., & Thompson, G. G., 1949. A study of the distribution of teacher approval and disapproval among sixth-grade pupils. *Journal of Experimental Education*, **18**, 57–76.

Gronlund, N. E., 1956. Generality of teachers' sociometric perceptions: relative judgment accuracy on several sociometric criteria. *Journal of Educational Psychology*, **47**, 25–31. (a)

Gronlund, N. E., 1956. The general ability to judge sociometric status: elementary student teacher's sociometric perceptions of classmates and pupils. *Journal of Educational Psychology*, **47**, 147–157. (b)

Gronseth, E., 1955. The political role of women in Norway. In M. Duverger (Ed.), *The Political Role of Women*. Paris: UNESCO. Pp. 194–221.

Gross, N., & Mason, W. S., 1953. Some methodological problems of eight-hour interviews. *American Journal of Sociology*, **59**, 197–204.

Gross, N., Mason, W. S., & McEachern, A. W., 1957. *Explorations in Role Analysis: Studies of the School Superintendency Role*. New York: Wiley.

Gross, N., McEachern, A. W., & Mason, W. S., 1958. Role conflict and its resolution. In Eleanor E. Maccoby, T. M. Newcomb, & E. L. Hartley (Eds.), *Readings in Social Psychology* (3rd ed.). New York: Holt. Pp. 447–459.

Grossack, M. M., 1953. Cues, expectations, and first impressions. *Journal of Psychology*, **35**, 245–252.

Grossack, M. M., 1955. Effects of variations in teacher role behavior on student-teacher relationship. *Journal of Educational Psychology*, **46**, 433–436.

Gruen, W., 1962. Tolerance for idiosyncratic roles in group cohesion. *Psychological Reports*, **11**, 432.

Grusky, O., 1957. A case for the theory of familial role differentiation in small groups. *Social Forces*, **35**, 209–217.

Grusky, O., 1959. Role conflict in organization: a study of prison camp officials. *Administrative Science Quarterly*, **3**, 452–472.

Grusky, O., 1960. Administrative succession in formal organizations. *Social Forces*, **39**, 105–115.

Guetzkow, H., 1960. Differentiation of roles in task-oriented groups. In D. Cartwright & A. Zander (Eds.), *Group Dynamics: Research and Theory* (2nd ed.). Evanston, Ill.: Row, Peterson. Pp. 683–704.

Guetzkow, H., & Simon, H. A., 1955. The impact of certain communication nets upon organization and performance in task-oriented groups. *Management Science*, **1**, 233–250.

Guillaume, P., 1925. *L'imitation chez L'enfant.* (Imitation in the Child.) Paris: F. Alcan.

Gullahorn, J. T., 1956. Measuring role conflict. *American Journal of Sociology*, **61**, 299–303.

Gullahorn, J. T., & Gullahorn, Jeanne E., 1963. Role conflict and its resolution. *Sociological Quarterly*, **4**, 32–48.

Gustafson, J. M., 1954. An analysis of the problem of the role of the minister. *The Journal of Religion*, **34**, 187–191.

Gynther, Ruth A., 1957. The effects of anxiety and of situational stress on communicative efficiency. *Journal of Abnormal and Social Psychology*, **54**, 274–276.

Gyr, J., 1951. Analysis of committee member behavior in four cultures. *Human Relations*, **4**, 193–202.

Haas, J. E., 1956. Role, position, and social organization: a conceptual formulation. *Midwest Sociologist*, **19**, 33–37.

Haas, J. E., 1964. *Role Conception and Group Consensus.* Columbus: Ohio State University, Bureau of Business Research.

Haas, R. B., 1947. A role study from pupil motivations: students evaluate their English instructors. *Sociometry*, **10**, 200–210.

Habenstein, R. W., & Christ, E. A., 1955. *Professionalizer, Traditionalizer, and Utilizer.* Columbia, Mo.: University of Missouri Press.

Hacker, Helen M., 1951. Women as a minority group. *Social Forces*, **30**, 60–69.

Haer, J. L., 1953. The public views the teacher. *Journal of Teacher Education*, **4**, 202–204.

Haggard, W. W., 1943. Some freshmen describe the desirable college teacher. *School and Society*, **58**, 238–240.

Haire, M., 1955. Role perceptions in labor-management relations: an experimental approach. *Industrial and Labor Relations Review*, **8**, 204–216.

Haire, M., Ghiselli, E. E., & Porter, L. W., 1963. Cultural patterns in the role of the manager. *Industrial Relations*, **2**, 95–118.

Haire, M., & Grunes, Willa F., 1950. Perceptual defenses: processes protecting an organized perception of another personality. *Human Relations*, **3**, 403–412.

Hall, G. S., 1891. The contents of children's minds on entering school. *Pedagogical Seminary*, **1**, 139–173.

Hall, G. S., 1898. Some aspects of the early sense of self. *American Journal of Psychology*, **9**, 351–395.

Hall, R. L., 1955. Social influence on the aircraft commander's role. *American Sociological Review*, **20**, 292–299.

Halleck, S. L., 1960. The criminal's problem with psychiatry. *Psychiatry*, **23**, 409–412.

Halpin, A. W., 1954. The leadership behavior and combat performances of airplane commanders. *Journal of Abnormal and Social Psychology*, **49**, 19–22.

Halpin, A. W., 1955. The leader behavior and leadership ideology of educational administrators and aircraft commanders. *Harvard Educational Review*, **25**, 18–32. (a)

Halpin, A. W., 1955. The leadership ideology of aircraft commanders. *Journal of Applied Psychology*, **39**, 82–84. (b)

Hammond, S., 1952. Stratification in an Australian city. In G. E. Swanson, T. M. Newcomb, & E. L. Hartley (Eds.), *Readings in Social Psychology* (Rev. ed.). New York: Holt. Pp. 288–299.

Hanlon, T. E., Hofstaetter, P. R., & O'Connor, J. P., 1954. Congruence of self and ideal self in relation to personality adjustment. *Journal of Consulting Psychology*, **18**, 215–218.

Hanson, E. M., & Umstattd, J. G., 1937. Mores and teacher selection in Minnesota. *School and Society*, **45**, 579–582.

Hanson, P. G., Morton, R. B., & Rothaus, P., 1963. The fate of role stereotypes in two performance appraisal situations. *Personnel Psychology*, **16**, 269–280.

Hanson, R. C., 1962. System linkage hypothesis and role consensus patterns in hospital-community relations. *American Sociological Review*, **27**, 304–313.

Harary, F., 1959. A criterion for unanimity in French's theory of social power. In D. Cartwright (Ed.), *Studies of Social Power.* Ann Arbor: University of Michigan Press. Pp. 168–182.

Harary, F., 1959. Status and contrastatus. *Sociometry*, **22**, 23–43.

Hardy, K. R., 1957. Determinants of conformity and attitude change. *Journal of Abnormal and Social Psychology*, **54**, 289–294.

Hare, A. P., 1952. A study of interaction and consensus in different sized groups. *American Sociological Review*, **17**, 261–267.

Harris, R. P., 1946. Students' reactions to the educational profession. *Educational Administration and Supervision*, **32**, 513–520.

Harrison, R., Tomblen, D. T., & Jackson, T. A., 1955. Profile of the mechanical engineer, III. Personality. *Personnel Psychology*, **8**, 469–490.

Hartley, E. L., & Hartley, Ruth E., 1952. *Fundamentals of Social Psychology*. New York: Knopf.

Hartley, E. L., & Krugman, Dorothy C., 1948. Notes on children's social role perception. *Journal of Psychology*, **26**, 399–405.

Hartley, E. L., Rosenbaum, M., & Schwartz, S., 1948. Children's perceptions of ethnic group membership. *Journal of Psychology*, **26**, 387–398. (a)

Hartley, E. L., Rosenbaum, M., & Schwartz, S., 1948. Children's use of ethnic frames of reference: an exploratory study of children's conceptualizations of multiple ethnic group membership. *Journal of Psychology*, **26**, 367–386. (b)

Hartley, Ruth E., 1959. Sex-role pressures and the socialization of the male child. *Psychological Reports*, **5**, 457–468. (a)

Hartley, Ruth E., 1959. Some implications of current changes in sex role patterns. *Merrill-Palmer Quarterly*, **6**, 153–164. (b)

Hartley, Ruth E., 1960. Children's concepts of male and female roles. *Merrill-Palmer Quarterly*, **6**, 83–91. (a)

Hartley, Ruth E., 1960. Norm compatibility, norm preference, and the acceptance of new reference groups. *Journal of Social Psychology*, **52**, 87–95. (b)

Hartley, Ruth E., 1961. Current patterns in sex roles: children's perspectives. *Journal of the National Association of Women Deans and Counselors*, **25**, 3–13. (a)

Hartley, Ruth E., 1961. Sex roles and urban youth: some developmental perspectives. *Bulletin of Family Development*, **2**, 1–12. (b)

Hartley, Ruth E., 1962. Personal characteristics and acceptance of secondary groups as reference groups. *Journal of Individual Psychology*, **13**, 45–55.

Hartley, Ruth E., 1964. A developmental view of female sex-role definition and identification. *Merrill-Palmer Quarterly*, **10**, 3–16.

Hartley, Ruth E., & Klein, A., 1959. Sex-role concepts among elementary-school-age girls. *Marriage and Family Living*, **21**, 59–64.

Hartup, W. W., & Zook, Elsie A., 1960. Sex-role preferences in three- and four-year-old children. *Journal of Consulting Psychology*, **24**, 420–426.

Harvey, O. J., 1953. An experimental approach to the study of status relations in informal groups. *American Sociological Review*, **18**, 357–367.

Harvey, O. J., 1956. An experimental investigation of negative and positive relations between small groups through judgmental indices. *Sociometry*, **19**, 201–209.

Harvey, O. J., & Beverly, G. D., 1961. Some personality correlates of concept change through role playing. *Journal of Abnormal and Social Psychology*, **63**, 125–129.

Harvey, O. J., & Consalvi, C., 1950. Status and conformity to pressures in informal groups. *Journal of Abnormal and Social Psychology*, **60**, 182–187.

Harvey, O. J., Kelley, H. H., & Shapiro, M. M., 1957. Reactions to unfavorable evaluations of the self made by other persons. *Journal of Personality*, **25**, 393–411.

Harvey, O. J., & Rutherford, J., 1960. Status in the informal group: influence and influencibility at differing age levels. *Child Development*, **31**, 377–385.

Hastorf, A. H., & Bender, I. E., 1952. A caution respecting the measurement of empathic ability. *Journal of Abnormal and Social Psychology*, **47**, 564–576.

Hatfield, Agnes B., 1961. An experimental study of the self-concept of student teachers. *Journal of Educational Research*, **55**, 87–89.

Havighurst, R. J., 1954. Flexibility and the social roles of the retired. *American Journal of Sociology*, **59**, 309–311.

Hawkes, G. R., Burchina, L. G., & Gardner, B., 1957. Pre-adolescents' views of some of their relations with their parents. *Child Development*, **28**, 393–399.

Hawkes, R. W., 1961. The role of the psychiatric administrator. *Administrative Science Quarterly*, **6**, 89–106.

Hayward, R. S., 1935. The child's report of psychological factors in the family. *Archives of Psychology*, **28**: 189, 1–75.

Heider, F., 1953. *The Psychology of Interpersonal Behavior*. New York: Wiley.

Heilbrun, A. B., Jr., 1963. Sex-role identity and achievement motivation. *Psychological Reports*, **12**, 483–490.

Heilbrun, A. B., Jr., 1964. Parental model attributes, nuturant reinforcement, and consistency of behavior in adolescents. *Child Development*, **35**, 151–167.

Heine, R. W., & Trosman, H., 1960. Initial expectations of the doctor-patient interaction as a factor in psychotherapy. *Psychiatry*, **23**, 275–278.

Heinicke, C., & Bales, R. F., 1953. Developmental trends in the structure of small groups. *Sociometry*, **16**, 7–38.

Heiss, J. S., 1962. Degree of intimacy and male-female interaction. *Sociometry*, **25**, 197–208.

Helfrich, Margaret L., 1961. The generalized role of the executive's wife. *Marriage and Family Living*, **23**, 384–387.

Helson, H., 1947. Adaptation-level as frame of reference for prediction of psychophysical data. *American Journal of Psychology*, **60**, 1–29.

Helson, H., 1948. Adaptation-level as a basis for a quantitative theory of frames of reference. *Psychological Review*, **55**, 297–313.

Helson, H., 1964. *Adaptation-Level Theory: An Experimental and Systematic Approach to Behavior.* New York: Harper & Row.

Hencley, S. P., 1960. The conflict patterns of school superintendents. *Administrator's Notebook*, **8**:9.

Henry, A. F., 1956. Family role structure and self blame. *Social Forces*, **35**, 34–38.

Henry, A. F., 1957. Sibling structure and perception of the disciplinary roles of parents. *Sociometry*, **20**, 67–74.

Henry, A. F., & Borgatta, E. F., 1953. A comparison of attitudes of enlisted and commissioned Air Force personnel. *American Sociological Review*, **18**, 669–671.

Henry, W. E., 1949. The business executive: the psycho-dynamics of a social role. *American Journal of Sociology*, **54**, 286–291.

Herbert, Eleanore L., 1961. The use of group techniques in the training of teachers. *Human Relations*, **14**, 251–263.

Herbst, P. G., 1952. The measurement of family relationships. *Human Relations*, **5**, 3–35.

Herman, S. N., & Schild, E., 1960. Ethnic role conflict in a cross-cultural situation. *Human Relations*, **13**, 215–228.

Hetzler, S. A., 1955. Variations in role-playing patterns among different echelons of bureaucratic leaders. *American Sociological Review*, **20**, 700–706.

Higgin, G., 1954. The effect of reference group functions on social status ratings. *British Journal of Psychology*, **45**, 88–93.

Hiller, E. T., 1937. The social structure in relation to the person. *Social Forces*, **16**, 34–43.

Hiller, E. T., 1947. *Social Relations and Structures.* New York: Harper & Row.

Hilton, T. L., 1960. Alleged acceptance of the occupational role of teaching. *Journal of Applied Psychology*, **44**, 210–215.

Hites, R. W., & Campbell, D. T., 1950. A test of the ability of fraternity leaders to estimate group opinion. *Journal of Social Psychology*, **32**, 95–100.

Hobart, C. W., 1958. Some effects of romanticism during courtship on marriage role opinions. *Sociology and Social Research*, **42**, 336–343.

Hobart, C. W., & Klausner, W. J., 1959. Some social interaction correlates of marital role disagreement and marital adjustment. *Marriage and Family Living*, **21**, 256–263.

Hoffman, Lois W., 1960. Effects of the employment of mothers on parental power relations and the division of household tasks. *Marriage and Family Living*, **22**, 27–35.

Hoffman, Lois W., Rosen, S., & Lippitt, R., 1960. Parental coerciveness, child autonomy, and child's role at school. *Sociometry*, **23**, 15–22.

Hoffman, M. R., 1963. Parent discipline and the child's consideration for others. *Child Development*, **34**, 573–588.

Hogbin, H. I., 1934. *Law and Order in Polynesia.* New York: Harcourt, Brace.

Hollander, E. P., 1958. Conformity, status, and idiosyncrasy credit. *Psychological Review*, **65**, 117–127.

Hollander, E. P., 1960. Competence and conformity in the acceptance of influence. *Journal of Abnormal and Social Psychology*, **61**, 365–369.

Hollander, E. P., 1961. Some effects of perceived status on responses to innovative behavior. *Journal of Abnormal and Social Psychology*, **63**, 247–250.

Holliday, J., 1964. Ideal traits of the professional nurse described by graduate students in education and in nursing. *Journal of Educational Research*, **57**, 245–249.

Hollingshead, A. B., & Rogles, L. H., 1962. Lower socioeconomic status and mental illness. *Sociology and Social Research*, **46**, 387–396.

Holter, Harriet G., 1960. Sosialarbeiderens yrkesrolle. (The occupational role of social workers.) *Tidsskrift for Samfunnsforskning*, **1**, 28–49.

Holter, Harriet G., 1961. Kjønnsforskjeller i skole—og arbeidsprestasjoner. (Sex differences in performance at school and work.) *Tidsskrift for Samfunnsforskning*, **2**, 147–161.

Holter, Harriet G., *et al.*, 1955. Posisjon og innstillinger hos industriarbeidere. (Status and attitudes among industrial workers.) *Nordisk Psykologis Monografiserie*, **6**.

Homans, G. C., 1950. *The Human Group*. New York: Harcourt, Brace.

Homans, G. C., 1953. Status among clerical workers. *Human Organization*, **12**, 5–10.

Homans, G. C., 1961. *Social Behavior: Its Elementary Forms*. New York: Harcourt, Brace.

Horwitz, M., 1958. The veridicality of liking and disliking. In R. Tagiuri & L. Petrullo (Eds.), *Person Perception and Interpersonal Behavior*. Stanford, Calif.: Stanford University Press. Pp. 191–209.

Huang, L. J., 1963. Re-evaluation of the primary role of the Chinese woman: the homemaker as the worker. *Marriage and Family Living*, **25**, 162–166.

Hughes, E. C., 1937. Institutional office and the person. *American Journal of Sociology*, **43**, 404–413.

Hughes, E. C., 1938. Position and status in a Quebec industrial town. *American Sociological Review*, **3**, 709–717.

Hughes, E. C., 1945. Dilemmas and contradictions of status. *American Journal of Sociology*, **50**, 353–359.

Hughes, E. C., 1946. The knitting of racial groups in industry. *American Sociological Review*, **11**, 512–519.

Hughes, E. C., 1956. Social role and the division of labor. *Midwest Sociologist*, **17**, 3–7. (a)

Hughes, E. C., 1956. The making of a physician—a general statement of ideas and problems. *Human Organization*, **14**, 21–25. (b)

Hughes, E. C., Hughes, Helen M., & Deutscher, I., 1958. *20,000 Nurses Tell Their Story*. Philadelphia: Lippincott.

Huitt, R. K., 1959. A case study in Senate norms. In J. C. Wahlke & H. Eulau (Eds.), *Legislative Behavior: A Reader in Theory and Research*. Glencoe, Ill.: The Free Press. Pp. 284–294. (a)

Huitt, R. K., 1959. The roles of congressional committee members. In J. C. Wahlke & H. Eulau (Eds.), *Legislative Behavior: A Reader in Theory and Research*. Glencoe, Ill.: The Free Press. Pp. 317–322. (b)

Huitt, R. K., 1961. The outsider in the Senate: an alternative role. *American Political Science Review*, **55**, 566–575.

Hulett, J. E., Jr., 1940. The social role and personal security in Mormon polygamy. *American Journal of Sociology*, **45**, 542–553.

Hulett, J. E., Jr., 1943. The social role of the Mormon polygamous male. *American Sociological Review*, **8**, 279–287.

Hulett, J. E., Jr., 1944. The person's time perspective and the social role. *Social Forces*, **23**, 155–159.

Hunt, D. E., 1955. Changes in goal-object preference as a function of expectancy for social reinforcement. *Journal of Abnormal and Social Psychology*, **50**, 372–377.

Hurvitz, N., 1960. The marital roles inventory and the measurement of marital adjustment. *Journal of Clinical Psychology*, **16**, 377–380.

Hurvitz, N., 1961. Components of marital roles. *Sociology and Social Research*, **45**, 301–309.

Hyman, H. H., 1942. The psychology of status. *Archives of Psychology*, **38**: 269, 1–94.

Ichheiser, G., 1943. The structure and dynamics of interpersonal relations. *American Sociological Review*, **8**, 302–305.

Inkeles, A., & Levinson, D. J., 1963. Personal system and the socio-cultural system in large-scale organizations. *Sociometry*, **26**, 217–229.

Irwin, F. W., 1944. The realism of expectations. *Psychological Review*, **51**, 120–126.

Irwin, F. W., 1953. Stated expectations as functions of probability and desirability of outcomes. *Journal of Personality*, **21**, 329–335.

Ishiyama, T., Denny, J. M., Prada, R., & Vespe, R., 1962. The role of the psychologist on mental hospital wards as defined by the expectant-others. *Journal of Clinical Psychology*, **18**, 3–10.

Israel, J., 1956. *Self-Evaluation and Rejection in Groups*. Uppsala, Sweden: Almqvist & Wiksell.

Israel, J., 1960. The effect of positive and negative self-evaluation on the attractiveness of a goal. *Human Relations*, **13**, 33–47.

Jackson, J. M., 1960. Structural characteristics of norms. In N. B. Henry (Ed.), *The Dynamics of Instructional Groups: Sociopsychological Aspects of Teaching and Learning*. Yearbook of the National Society for the Study of Education, **59**, Part II. Pp. 136–163.

Jackson, J. M., & Saltzstein, H. D., 1958. The effect of person-group relationships on conformity processes. *Journal of Abnormal and Social Psychology*, **57**, 17–24.

Jackson, P. W., & Moscovici, F., 1963. Teacher-to-be: a study of embryonic identification with a professional role. *School Review*, **71**, 41–65.

Jacobs, R. C., & Campbell, D. T., 1961. The perpetuation of an arbitrary tradition through several generations of a laboratory microculture. *Journal of Abnormal and Social Psychology*, **62**, 649–658.

Jacobson, A. H., 1952. Conflict of attitudes toward the role of the husband and wife in marriage. *American Sociological Review*, **17**, 146–150.

Jacobson, E., Charters, W. W., Jr., & Lieberman, S., 1951. The use of the role concept in the study of complex organizations. *Journal of Social Issues*, **7**, 18–27.

Jahoda, Marie, 1959. Conformity and independence, a psychological analysis. *Human Relations*, **12**, 99–120.

James, W., 1890. *The Principles of Psychology*, New York: Holt.

Janet, P., 1928. *L'Évolution de la Mémoire et de la Notion de Temps*. (The Evolution of Memory and the Idea of Time.) Paris: Chahine.

Janet, P., 1929. *L'Évolution Psychologique de la Personnalité*. (The Psychological Evolution of Personality.) Paris: Chahine.

Janet, P., 1932. Les Sentiments dans le délire de persécution. (Sentiments in persecution delirium). *Journal Psychologique Française*, **29**, 161–195.

Janet, P., 1936. *L'Intelligence avant le Langage*. (Intelligence before Language). Paris: Flammarion.

Janet, P., 1937. Les troubles de la personnalité sociale. (The disorders of the social personality). *Année de Médicine—Psychologique Française*, **95**, 149–200 and 421–468.

Janis, I. L., & King, B. T., 1954. The influence of role playing on opinion change. *Journal of Abnormal and Social Psychology*, **49**, 211–218.

Janoska-Bendel, J., 1962. Probleme der Freiheit in der Rollenanalyse. (Problems of freedom in role analysis.) *Kölner Zeitschrift für Soziologie und Sozialpsychologie*, **14**, 459–475.

Jansen, Mathilda J., 1963. Een experimentele Studie van Rollenspel in een inrichting. (An experimental study of role play in an institution.) *Psychologie en Haar Grensgebieden*, **18**, 186–219.

Jaques, E., 1952. *The Changing Culture of a Factory*. London: Tavistock.

Jaques, E., 1953. On the dynamics of social structure. *Human Relations*, **6**, 3–24.

Jaques, E., 1956. *Measurement of Responsibility*. Cambridge, Mass.: Harvard University Press.

Jasinski, F. J., 1959. The dynamics of organizational behavior. *Personnel*, **36**, 60–67.

Jenkins, D. H., & Lippitt, R., 1951. *Interpersonal Perceptions of Teachers, Students, and Parents*. Washington, D. C.: Division of Adult Education Service, National Education Association.

Jennings, Helen H., 1943. *Leadership and Isolation*. New York: Longmans, Green.

Jessor, R., & Readio, J., 1957. The influence of the value of an event upon the expectancy of its occurrence. *Journal of General Psychology*, **56**, 219–228.

Johnson, A. H., 1958. The responses of high school seniors to a set of structured situations concerning teaching as a career. *Journal of Experimental Education*, **26**, 263–314.

Johnson, Miriam M., 1963. Sex role learning in the nuclear family. *Child Development*, **34**, 319–334.

Johnson, Miriam M., & Martin, H. W., 1958. A sociological analysis of the nurse role. *The American Journal of Nursing*, **58**, 373–377.

Jones, E. E., & deCharms, R., 1957. Changes in social perception as a function of the personal relevance of behavior. *Sociometry*, **20**, 75–85.

Jones, E. E., & deCharms, R., 1958. The organizing function of interaction roles in person perception. *Journal of Abnormal and Social Psychology*, **57**, 155–164.

Jones, E. E., Davis, K. E., & Gergen, K. J., 1961. Role playing variations and their informational value for person perception. *Journal of Abnormal and Social Psychology*, **63**, 302–310.

Jones, E. E., & Thibaut, J. W., 1958. Interaction goals as bases of inference in interpersonal perception. In R. Tagiuri & L. Petrullo (Eds.), *Person Perception and Interpersonal Behavior*. Stanford, Calif.: Stanford University Press. Pp. 151–178.

Jones, E. E., Wells, H. H., & Torrey, R., 1958. Some effects of feedback from the experimenter on conformity behavior. *Journal of Abnormal and Social Psychology*, **57**, 207–213.

Jordan, F., 1929. A study of personal and social traits in relation to high-school teaching. *Journal of Educational Sociology*, **3**, 27–43.

Joseph, M. L., 1959. The role of the field staff representative. *Individual and Labor Relations Review*, **12**, 353–370.

Julian, J. W., & Steiner, I. D., 1961. Perceived acceptance as a determinant of conformity behavior. *Journal of Social Psychology*, **55**, 191–198.

Kagan, J., 1956. The child's perception of the parent. *Journal of Abnormal and Social Psychology*, **53**, 257–258.

Kagan, J., Hoskin, B., & Watson, S., 1961. The child's symbolic conceptualization of the parents. *Child Development*, **32**, 625–636.

Kahn, M. W., & Santostefano, S., 1962. The case of clinical psychology: a search for identity. *American Psychologist*, **17**, 185–189.

Kahn, R. L., Wolfe, D. M., Quinn, R. P., Snoeck, J. D., & Rosenthal, R. A., 1964. *Organizational Stress: Studies in Role Conflict and Ambiguity*. New York: Wiley.

Kammerer, T., 1956. La relation entre médecin et inculpé dans l'expertise mentale criminelle. (The relation between doctor and defendant in the evaluation of the criminally insane.) *Evolution Psychiatrique*, **2**, 433–445.

Kammeyer, K., 1964. The feminine role: an analysis of attitude consistency. *Marriage and Family Living*, **76**, 295–305.

Kaplan, H. B., 1960. The concept of institution: a review, evaluation, and suggested research procedure. *Social Forces*, **39**, 176–180.

Kargman, Marie W., 1959. A socio-legal analysis of family role conflict. *Marriage and Family Living*, **21**, 275–278.

Katona, A., 1944. Comment on Brookover: "Social role of teachers." *American Sociological Review*, **9**, 108–109.

Katz, D., & Stotland, E., 1959. A preliminary statement to a theory of attitude structure and change. In S. Koch (Ed.), *Psychology: A Study of a Science, Conceptual and Systematic*, Vol. III. New York: McGraw-Hill.

Katz, E., & Lazarsfeld, P. F., 1955. *Personal Influence*. Glencoe, Ill.: The Free Press.

Katz, F. E., 1964. The school as a complex social organization. *Harvard Educational Review*, **34**, 428–455.

Kavolis, V., 1963. Role theory of artistic interest. *Journal of Social Psychology*, **60**, 31–38.

Kay, Lillian W., 1943. The relation of personal frames of reference to social judgments. *Archives of Psychology*, **40**: 283, 1–53.

Kay, Lillian W., 1944. Social norms as determinants in the interpretation of personal experiences. *Journal of Social Psychology*, **19**, 359–367.

Kay, Lillian W., 1948. Variation in role and group identification. *Journal of Social Psychology*, **27**, 63–78.

Keighin, Mary A., 1948. Thornburn teachers rated on their own terms. *Clearing House*, **23**, 82–83.

Kelley, H. H., 1949. The effects of expectations upon first impressions of persons. *American Psychologist*, **4**, 252.

Kelley, H. H., 1952. Two functions of reference groups. In G. E. Swanson, T. M. Newcomb, & E. L. Hartley (Eds.), *Readings in Social Psychology* (Rev. ed.). New York: Holt. Pp. 410–414.

Kelley, H. H., & Lamb, T. W., 1957. Certainty of judgment and resistance to social influence. *Journal of Abnormal and Social Psychology*, **55**, 137–139.

Kelley, H. H., & Shapiro, M. M., 1954. An experiment on conformity to group-norms where conformity is detrimental to group achievement. *American Sociological Review*, **19**, 667–677.

Kelley, H. H., & Volkart, E. H., 1952. The resistance to change of group-anchored attitudes. *American Sociological Review*, **17**, 453–465.

Kenkel, W. F., 1957. Influence differentiation in family decision making. *Sociology and Social Research*, **42**, 18–25.

Kenkel, W. F., 1961. Dominance, persistence, self-confidence, and spousal roles in decision making. *Journal of Social Psychology*, **54**, 349–358.

Kenkel, W. F., & Hoffman, D. K., 1956. Real and conceived roles in family decision making. *Marriage and Family Living*, **18**, 311–316.

Keniston, E., & Keniston, K., 1964. American anachronism: the image of women and work. *American Scholar*, **33**, 355–375.

Kerckhof, A. C., & Davis, K. E., 1962. Value consensus and need complementarity in mate selection. *American Sociological Review*, **27**, 295–304.

Kidd, J. S., 1958. Social influence phenomena in a task-oriented group situation. *Journal of Abnormal and Social Psychology*, **56**, 13–17.

Kidd, J. S., & Campbell, D. T., 1955. Conformity to groups as a function of group success. *Journal of Abnormal and Social Psychology*, **51**, 390–393.

Killian, L. M., 1952. The significance of multiple group membership in disaster. *American Journal of Sociology*, **57**, 309–314.

Kimball, S. T., 1963. Cultural influences shaping the role of the child. In G. D. Spindler (Ed.), *Education and Culture*. New York: Holt. Pp. 268–282.

Kimbrough, E., Jr., 1958. The role of the banker in a small city. *Social Forces*, **36**, 316–322.

King, H. E., 1962. Anticipatory behavior: temporal matching by normal and psychotic subjects. *Journal of Psychology*, **53**, 425–440.

Kipnis, Dorothy M., 1961. Changes in self concepts in relation to perceptions of others. *Journal of Personality*, **29**, 449–465.

Kirkpatrick, C., 1936. Inconsistencies in marriage roles and marriage conflict. *International Journal of Ethics*, **46**, 444–460.

Kitano, H. L., 1962. Adjustment of problem and non-problem children to specific situations: a study in role theory. *Child Development*, **33**, 229–233.

Klapp, O. E., 1949. The fool as a social type. *American Journal of Sociology*, **55**, 157–162.

Klapp, O. E., 1957. The concept of consensus and its importance. *Sociology and Social Research*, **41**, 336–342.

Klapp, O. E., 1958. Social types: process and structure. *American Sociological Review*, **23**, 674–678.

Klapp, O. E., 1964. Mexican social types. *American Journal of Sociology*, **69**, 404–414.

Kline, Frances F., 1949. Satisfactions and annoyances in teaching. *Journal of Experimental Education*, **18**, 77–89.

Kluckhohn, Florence, 1953. Dominant and variant value orientations. In C. Kluckhohn & H. A. Murray (Eds.), *Personality in Nature, Society and Culture* (2nd ed., rev. & enl.). New York: Knopf. Pp. 342–357.

Kluckhohn, Florence R., & Strodtbeck, F. L., 1961. *Variations in Value Orientations*. Evanston, Ill.: Row, Peterson.

Knoff, W. F., 1961. Role: a concept linking society and personality. *American Journal of Psychiatry*, **117**, 1010–1015.

Knowlton, C. S., 1962. Patron-peon pattern among Spanish Americans of New Mexico. *Social Forces*, **41**, 12–17.

Kob, J., 1958. *Das soziale Berufsbewusstsein des Lehrers der Löheren Schule*. (The Social Consciousness of Teachers in Advanced Education.) Würzburg: Werkbund Verlag.

Kob, J., 1961. Definition of the teacher's role. In A. H. Halsey, Jean Floud, & C. A. Anderson (Eds.), *Education, Economy and Society: A Reader in the Sociology of Education*. New York: The Free Press. Pp. 558–576.

Kochen, M., & Levy, M. J., 1956. The logical nature of an action scheme. *Behavioral Science*, **4**, 265–289.

Koenig, F. W., & King, M. B., 1962. Cognitive simplicity and prejudice. *Social Forces*, **40**, 220–222.

Kogan, K. L., & Jackson, J. K., 1963. Conventional sex-role stereotypes and actual perceptions. *Psychological Reports*, **13**, 27–30.

Kogan, N., & Tagiuri, R., 1958. Interpersonal preference and cognitive organization. *Journal of Abnormal and Social Psychology*, **56**, 113–116.

Kom, R. R., & McCorkle, L. W., 1959. *Criminology and Penology*. New York: Holt.

Komarovsky, Mirra, 1946. Cultural contradictions and sex roles. *American Journal of Sociology*, **52**, 184–189.

Komarovsky, Mirra, 1950. Functional analysis of sex roles. *American Sociological Review*, **15**, 508–516.

Komarovsky, Mirra, 1953. *Women in the Modern World: Their Education and Their Dilemmas*. Boston: Little, Brown.

Koopman, Margaret O., 1946. What one Midwestern community thinks of its teachers. *Educational Research Bulletin*, **25**, 34–41.

Koos, E. L., 1946. *Families in Trouble*. Morningside Heights, N.Y.: King's Crown Press.

Korber, G., 1951. Comments on role conflict and personality. *American Journal of Sociology*, **57**, 48–49.

Koshii, I., 1961. Jiga no shakaiteki keisei to yakuwari shutoku. (Social formation of self-consciousness and role acquisition.) *Soshiorogi*, **9**, 66–81.

Kotlar, Sally L., 1962. Instrumental and expressive marital roles. *Sociology and Social Research*, **46**, 186–194.

Kounin, J., Polansky, N., Biddle, B. J., Coburn, H., & Fenn, A., 1956. Experimental studies of clients' reactions to initial interviews. *Human Relations*, **9**, 265–293.

Kracke, E. A., Jr., 1958. The changing role of the Chinese intellectual: an introductory note. *Comparative Studies of Social History*, **1**, 23–25.

Krasner, L., 1958. Studies of conditioning verbal behavior. *Psychological Bulletin*, **55**, 148–170.

Kriesberg, L., 1952. The retail furrier: concepts of security and success. *American Journal of Sociology*, **57**, 478–485.

Kubička, L., & Kubičkova, Z., 1950. Studie společenshých rolí ve tříde dospivajicich divek. (Study of social roles in a class of adolescent girls.) *Československa Psychiatry*, **56**, 240–249.

Kuhn, M. H., & McPartland, T. S., 1954. An empirical investigation of self-attitudes. *American Sociological Review*, **19**, 68–76.

Kuhn, M. H., 1960. Self-attitudes by age, sex, and professional training. *Sociological Quarterly*, **1**, 39–55.

Kunz, H., 1949. Zür psychologie und psychopathologie der mitmenschlichen rollen. (On the psychology and psychopathology of the role of the neighbor.) *Psyche*, **2**, 551–595.

Lacognata, A. A., 1964. Academic role expectations of extension students. *Adult Education*, **14**, 99–103.

Lagache, D., 1954. La personnalité et les relations avec autrui. (Personality in relations with others.) *Bulletin de Psychologie*, **8**, 124–131.

Lamson, Edna E., 1942. Some college students describe the desirable college teacher. *School and Society*, **56**, 615.

Landreth, Catherine, 1963. Four-year-olds' notions about sex appropriateness of parental care and companionship activities. *Merrill-Palmer Quarterly*, **9**, 175–182.

Landy, D., 1960. Rehabilitation as a sociocultural process. *Journal of Social Issues*, **16**, 3–7.

Landy, D., & Wechsler, H., 1960. Common assumptions, dimensions, and problems of pathway organizations. *Journal of Social Issues*, **16**, 70–78.

Lang, G., 1956. The concepts of status and role in anthropology, their definition and use. *American Catholic Sociological Review*, **17**, 206–217.

Lanter, R., & Spenlé, Anne M., 1952. Le psychodrame et la notion de rôle. (Psychodrama and the concept of role.) *Cahier de Psychiatrie*, **8**, 127–134.

Lasswell, T. E., 1961. The perception of social status. *Sociology and Social Research*, **45**, 170–174.

Laulicht, J., 1955. Role conflict, the pattern variable theory, and scalogram analysis. *Social Forces*, **33**, 250–254.

Lavietes, Ruth, 1962. The teacher's role in the education of the emotionally disturbed child. *American Journal of Orthopsychiatry*, **32**, 854–862.

Lawlor, G. W., 1947. Role therapy. *Sociatry*, **1**, 51–55.

Leary, T., 1956. *Multilevel Measurement of Interpersonal Behavior*. Berkeley, Calif.: Psychological Consultation Service.

Lebovici, S., 1952. Ce que la psychothérapie apporte à la compréhension psychologique des groupes. (The contribution of psychotherapy in the understanding of group psychology.) *Bulletin de Psychologie*, **6**, 101–104.

Lecky, P., 1945. *Self-Consistency: A Theory of Personality*. New York: Island Press.

Lee, Dorothy, 1963. Discrepancies in the teaching of American culture. In G. D. Spindler (Ed.), *Education and Culture*. New York: Holt. Pp. 173–191.

Lee, L. L., 1948. A brief analysis of the role and status of the Negro in the Hawaiian community. *American Sociological Review*, **13**, 419–437.

Lefton, M., 1962. Social class, expectations, and performance of mental patients. *American Journal of Sociology*, **68**, 79–87.

Leiffer, M. H., 1960. *The Role of the District Superintendent in the Methodist Church*. Evanston, Ill.: Bureau of Social and Religious Research.

Leik, R. K., 1963. Instrumentality and emotionality in family interaction. *Sociometry*, **26**, 131–145.

Lennard, H. L., & Bernstein, A., 1960. *The Anatomy of Psychotherapy: Systems of Communication and Expectation*. New York: Columbia University Press.

Lerner, M. J., & Becker, S., 1962. Interpersonal choice as a function of ascribed similarity and definition of the situation. *Human Relations*, **15**, 27–34.

Leveen, L., & Priver, D., 1963. Significance of role playing in the aged person. *Geriatrics*, **18**, 57–63.

Leventhal, H., 1957, Cognitive processes and interpersonal predictions. *Journal of Abnormal and Social Psychology*, **55**, 176–180.

Levinson, D. J., 1959. Role, personality, and social structure in the organizational setting. *Journal of Abnormal and Social Psychology*, **58**, 170–180.

Levinson, D. J., & Gallagher, E. B., 1964. *Patienthood in the Mental Hospital.* Boston: Houghton Mifflin.

Levit, Grace, & Jennings, Helen H., 1953. Learning through role playing. *Adult Leadership*, **2**, 9–16.

Levy, A., 1953. Portraits de meneurs et psychologie du groupe. (Portraits of leaders and group psychology.) *Bulletin de Psychologie*, **7**, 34–51.

Levy, L. H., & Dugan, R. D., 1960. A constant error approach to the study of dimensions of social perception. *Journal of Abnormal and Social Psychology*, **61**, 21–24.

Levy, M. J., Jr., 1949. *The Family Revolution in Modern China.* Cambridge, Mass.: Harvard University Press.

Levy, M. J., Jr., 1952. *The Structure of Society.* Princeton, N.J.: Princeton University Press.

Lewis, D. J., 1959. Stimulus, response, and social role. *Journal of Social Psychology*, **50**, 119–127.

Lewis, O., 1949. Husbands and wives in a Mexican village: a study of role conflict. *American Anthropologist*, **50**, 602–610.

Lichliter, Mary, 1946. Social obligations and restrictions placed on women teachers. *School Review*, **54**, 14–23.

Lichtenberg, P., 1962. Comparative valuation and ideational action. *Journal of Social Psychology*, **56**, 97–105.

Lieberman, S., 1956. The effects of changes in roles on the attitudes of role occupants. *Human Relations*, **9**, 385–402.

Lindesmith, A. R., & Strauss, A. L., 1949. *Social Psychology.* New York: Dryden Press.

Linton, Harriet B., 1955. Dependence on external influence: correlates in perception, attitudes, and judgment. *Journal of Abnormal and Social Psychology*, **51**, 502–507.

Linton, R., 1936. *The Study of Man.* New York: Appleton-Century.

Linton, R., 1938. Culture, society, and the individual. *Journal of Abnormal and Social Psychology*, **33**, 425–436.

Linton, R., 1940. A neglected aspect of social organization. *American Journal of Sociology*, **45**, 870–886.

Linton, R., 1942. Age and sex categories. *American Sociological Review*, **7**, 589–603.

Linton, R., 1945. Foreword. In A. Kardiner, *The Psychological Frontiers of Society.* New York: Columbia University Press. Pp. v–xiii.

Linton, R., 1947. Concepts of role and status. In T. M. Newcomb & E. L. Hartley (Eds.), *Readings in Social Psychology.* New York: Holt. Pp. 367–370. (a)

Linton, R., 1947. *The Cultural Background of Personality.* London: Kegan Paul, Trench, Trubner. (b)

Lippitt, R., Polansky, N., & Rosen, S., 1952. The dynamics of power: a field study of social influence in groups of children. *Human Relations*, **5**, 37–64.

Lippitt, Rosemary, & Hubbell, Anne, 1956. Role playing for personnel and guidance workers: review of the literature with suggestions for application. *Group Psychotherapy*, **9**, 89–114.

Livingood, F. G., 1935. Educational research and statistics estimates of high-school seniors. *School and Society*, **41**, 550–552.

Loeb, M. B., 1963. Social role and sexual identity in adolescent males: a study of culturally provided deprivation. In G. D. Spindler (Ed.), *Education and Culture.* New York: Holt. Pp. 284–300.

Loomis, C. P., 1960. *Social Systems: Essays on Their Persistence and Change.* Princeton, N. J.: Van Nostrand.

Loomis, C. P., & Beegle, J. A., 1948. A typological analysis of social systems. *Sociometry*, **11**, 147–191.

Lowe, C. M., 1961. The self-concept: fact or artifact? *Psychological Bulletin*, **58**, 325–336.

Löwith, K., 1928. *Das Individuum in der Rolle des Mitmenschen.* (The Individual in the Role of Neighbor.) Munich: Drei Masken Verlag.

Lu, Y. C., 1952. Parent-child relationship and marital roles. *American Sociological Review*, **17**, 357–361. (a)

Lu, Y. C., 1952. Marital roles and marriage adjustment. *Sociology and Social Research*, **36**, 364–368. (b)

Lu, Y. C., 1952. Parental role and parent-child relationship. *Marriage and Family Living*, **14**, 294–297. (c)

Lu, Y. C., 1952. Predicting roles in marriage. *American Journal of Sociology*, **58**, 51–55. (d)

Luchins, A. S., & Luchins, Edith H., 1961. Einstellung effect in social learning. *Journal of Social Psychology*, **55**, 59–66.

Luckey, Eleanore B., 1960. Implications for marriage counseling of self-perceptions and spouse perceptions. *Journal of Counseling Psychology*, **7**, 3–9. (a)

Luckey, Eleanore B., 1960. Marital satisfaction and congruent self-spouse concepts. *Social Forces*, **39**, 153–157. (b)

Luckey, Eleanore B., 1961. Perceptual congruence of self and family concepts as related to marital interaction. *Sociometry*, **24**, 234–250.

Lumpkin, Katherine D., 1933. *The Family: A Study of Member Roles*. Chapel Hill: University of North Carolina Press.

Lynn, D. B., 1962. Sex-role and parental identification. *Child Development*, **33**, 556–564.

Lynn, D. B., 1963. Learning masculine and feminine roles. *Marriage and Family Living*, **25**, 163–165.

Lystad, Mary H., & Stone, R. C., 1956. Bureaucratic mass media: a study in role definitions. *Social Forces*, **34**, 356–361.

Maas, H. S., 1958. Use of behavioral sciences in social work education. *Social Work*, **3**, 62–69.

Maccoby, Eleanor E., 1959. Role-taking in childhood and its consequences for social learning. *Child Development*, **30**, 239–252.

Maccoby, Eleanor E., 1961. The taking of adult roles in middle childhood. *Journal of Abnormal and Social Psychology*, **63**, 493–503.

Maccoby, Eleanor E., 1962. Class differences in boys' choices of authority roles. *Sociometry*, **25**, 117–119.

MacCorquodale, K., & Meehl, P. E., 1953. Preliminary suggestions as to a formalization of expectancy theory. *Psychological Review*, **60**, 55–63.

MacDonald, M. E., 1931. Students' opinions as regards desirable and undesirable qualifications and practices of their teachers in teacher-training institutions. *Educational Administration and Supervision*, **17**, 139–146.

Mack, R. W., 1956. Occupational determinateness: a problem and hypotheses in role theory. *Social Forces*, **35**, 20–25.

Mack, R. W., 1957. Occupational ideology and the determinate role. *Social Forces*, **36**, 37–44.

MacRae, D., Jr., 1954. The role of the state legislator in Massachusetts. *American Sociological Review*, **19**, 185–194.

Madigan, F. C., 1962. Role satisfactions and length of life in a closed population. *American Journal of Sociology*, **67**, 640–649.

Maier, N. R. F., & Hoffman, L. R., 1963. Seniority in work groups: a right or an honor? *Journal of Applied Psychology*, **47**, 173–176.

Main, Lucy, 1963. Some current terms in social anthropology. *British Journal of Sociology*, **14**, 20–28.

Maine, H. J. S., 1861. *Ancient Law*. London: Dent. (New York: Dutton, 1917.)

Maisonneuve, J., 1956. Gravitation affective et charactérisation d'autri dans les petits groupes. (Affective attraction and characterization of others in small groups.) *Année Psychologique*, **56**, 397–410.

Makhlakh, E. S., 1962. Igrovaya motivatsiya u pionerskj rabote. (Play motivation in pioneer youth organization work.) *Voprosy Psikhologii*, **3**, 117–126.

Mangus, A. R., 1957. Family impacts on mental health. *Marriage and Family Living*, **19**, 256–262. (a)

Mangus, A. R., 1957. Integration of theory, research, and family counseling practice. *Marriage and Family Living*, **19**, 81–85. (b)

Mangus, A. R., 1957. Role theory and marriage counseling. *Social Forces*, **35**, 200–209. (c)

Mann, J. H., 1956. Experimental evaluations of role playing. *Psychological Bulletin*, **53**, 227–234.

Mann, J. H., 1961. Studies of role performance. *Genetic Psychological Monographs*, **64**, 213–307.

Mann, J. H., & Borgatta, E. F., 1959. Personality and behavior correlates of changes produced by role playing experience. *Psychological Reports*, **5**, 505–526.

Mann, J. H., & Mann, Carola H., 1959. The effect of role-playing experience on role-playing ability. *Sociometry*, **22**, 64–74.

Mann, J. H., & Mann, Carola H., 1960. The relative effectiveness of role playing and task oriented group experience in producing personality and behavior change. *Journal of Social Psychology*, **51**, 313–317.

Mann, R. D., 1959. A review of the relationship between personality and performance in small groups. *Psychological Bulletin*, **56**, 241–270.

Manniche, E., 1963. The head nurse (ward sister). *Sociologiske Meddelelser*, **8**, 61–67.

Manwiller, L. V., 1958. Expectations regarding teachers. *Journal of Experimental Education*, **26**, 315–354.

March, J. G., 1954. Group norms and the active minority. *American Sociological Review*, **19**, 733–741.

Marrow, A. J., & French, J. R. P., Jr., 1945. Changing a stereotype in industry. *Journal of Social Issues*, **1**, 33–37.

Martin, N. H., 1956. Differential decisions in management of an industrial plant. *Journal of Business of the University of Chicago*, **29**, 249–260.

Martire, J. G., 1956. Relationships between the self-concept and differences in the strength and generality of achievement motivation. *Journal of Personality*, **24**, 364–375.

Martire, J. G., & Hornberger, R. H., 1957. Self congruence, by sex and between the sexes, in a "normal" population. *Journal of Clinical Psychology*, **13**, 288–291.

Mason, W. S., Dressel, R. J., & Bain, R. K., 1959. Sex role and the career orientations of beginning teachers. *Harvard Educational Review*, **29**, 370–383.

Mason, W. S., & Gross, N., 1955. Intra-occupational prestige differentiation: the school superintendency. *American Sociological Review*, **20**, 326–331.

Masuoka, Edna C., Masuoka, J., & Kawamura, N., 1962. Role conflicts in the modern Japanese family. *Social Forces*, **41**, 1–6.

Masuoka, J., 1960. Shakai-Kihan to yakuwari-kata ni tsuite no ichi kenkyu. (Conflicting role obligations and role types: with a special reference to race relations.) *Japanese Sociological Review*, **2**, 76–108.

Mathews, D. R., 1959. The folkway of the United States Senate: conformity to group norms and legislative effectiveness. *American Political Science Review*, **53**, 1064–1089.

Mathews, Ravenna, Hardyck, C., & Sarbin, T. R., 1953. Contributions to role-taking theory: V. Self-organization as a factor in the performance of selected cognitive tasks. *Journal of Abnormal and Social Psychology*, **48**, 500–502.

Mathewson, S. B., 1931. *Restriction of Output Among Unorganized Workers*. New York: Viking Press.

Matsui, A. M., 1959. Rôle de la femme dans la nouvelle société japonaise. (The role of women in the new Japanese society.) *Rythmes du Monde*, **33**, 201–210.

Mauksch, H. O., 1963. Becoming a nurse: a selective view. *Annals of the American Academy of Political and Social Science*, **346**, 88–98.

Maxwell, Patricia, Connor, Ruth, & Walters, J., 1961. Family member perception of parent role performance. *Merrill-Palmer Quarterly*, **7**, 31–38.

Mayo, E., 1933. *The Human Problems of an Industrial Civilization*. New York: Macmillan.

Mayo, G. D., & Kinzer, J. R., 1950. A comparison of the "racial" attitudes of white and Negro high school students in 1940 and 1948. *Journal of Psychology*, **29**, 397–405.

Mayo, S. L., 1960. An analysis of the organizational role of the teacher of vocational agriculture. *Rural Sociology*, **25**, 334–345.

McCord, Joan, & McCord, W., 1958. The effects of parental role model on criminality. *Journal of Social Issues*, **14**, 66–75.

McCord, W., Parta, Judith, & McCord, Joan, 1962. Familial genesis of psychoses. *Psychiatry*, **25**, 60–71.

McCormack, Thelma H., 1956. The druggists' dilemma: problems of a marginal occupation. *American Journal of Sociology*, **61**, 308–315.

McCoy, Jacqueline, 1962. Application of the role concept to foster parenthood. *Social Casework*, **43**, 252–256.

McEwen, W. J., 1956. Position conflict and professional orientation in a research organization. *Administrative Science Quarterly*, **1**, 208–225.

McGill, K. H., 1931. The school-teacher stereotype. *Journal of Educational Sociology*, **4**, 642–650.

McGuire, C., 1961. Sex role and community variability in test performances. *Journal of Educational Psychology*, **52**, 61–73.

McKeachie, W. J., 1954. Individual conformity to attitudes of classroom groups. *Journal of Abnormal and Social Psychology*, **49**, 282–289.

McKenna, Sister Helen V., Hofstaetter, P. R., & O'Connor, J. P., 1956. The concepts of the ideal self and of the friend. *Journal of Personality*, **24**, 262–271.

Mead, G. H., 1934. C. W. Morris (Ed.). *Mind, Self and Society from the Standpoint of a Social Behaviorist.* Chicago: University of Chicago Press.

Mead, Margaret, 1948. *Male and Female: A Study of the Sexes in a Changing World.* New York: Wm. Morrow and Publishers.

Mead, Margaret, 1951. *The School in American Culture.* Cambridge, Mass.: Harvard University Press.

Mechanic, D., 1959. Illness and social disability: some problems in analysis. *Pacific Sociological Review*, **2**, 37–41.

Mechanic, D., & Volkart, E. H., 1961. Stress, illness behavior, and the sick role. *American Sociological Review*, **26**, 51–58.

Medinnus, G. R., 1963. Relation between parental prescriptions for child and parent roles. *Journal of Social Psychology*, **60**, 101–106.

Menzel, H., 1957. Public and private conformity under different conditions of acceptance in the group. *Journal of Abnormal and Social Psychology*, **55**, 398–402.

Mercado, Serafin J., Guerrero, R. D. & Gardner, R. W., 1963. Cognitive control in children of Mexico and the U.S. *Journal of Social Psychology*, **59**, 199–208.

Merei, F., 1949. Group leadership and institutionalization. *Human Relations*, **2**, 23–39.

Merrill, M. R., & Jex, F. B., 1964. Role conflict in successful science teachers. *Journal of Educational Research*, **58**, 72–74.

Merton, R. K., 1940. Bureaucratic structure and personality. *Social Forces*, **18**, 560–568.

Merton, R. K., 1949. *Social Theory and Social Structure.* Glencoe, Ill.: The Free Press.

Merton, R. K., 1957. The role-set: problems in sociological theory. *British Journal of Sociology*, **8**, 106–120. (a)

Merton, R. K., 1957. *Social Theory and Social Structure* (Revised Enlarged Edition). Glencoe, Ill.: The Free Press. (b)

Merton, R. K., & Kitt, Alice S., 1950. Contributions to the theory of reference group behavior. In R. K. Merton & P. F. Lazarsfeld (Eds.), *Continuities in Social Research: Studies in the Scope and Method of "The American Soldier."* Glencoe, Ill.: The Free Press.

Merton, R. K., Reader, G. G., & Kendall, Patricia L. (Eds.), 1957. *The Student-Physician.* Cambridge, Mass.: Harvard University Press.

Messinger, S. L., Sampson, H., & Towne, R. D., 1962. Life as theatre: some notes on the dramaturgic approach to social reality. *Sociometry*, **25**, 98–110.

Meyer, A. P., & Hoffer, J., 1963. Preadolescent's adjustment and parental expectations. *Journal of Home Economics*, **55**, 50–52.

Meyer, A. S., 1960. Function of the mediator in collective bargaining. *Industrial and Labor Relations Review*, **13**, 159–165.

Meyers, C. E., 1944. The effect of conflicting authority on the child. *University of Iowa Studies in Child Welfare*, **20**, 31–98.

Middleton, R., 1962. Brother-sister and father-daughter marriage in ancient Egypt. *American Sociological Review*, **27**, 603–611.

Milgram, N., & Goodglass, H., 1961. Role style vs. cognitive maturation in word associations of adults and children. *Journal of Personality*, **29**, 81–93.

Mill, C. R., 1960. Interprofessional awareness of roles. *Journal of Clinical Psychology*, **16**, 411–413.

Miller, D. R., & Swanson, G. E., 1960. *Inner Conflict and Defense.* New York: Holt.

Miller, H., 1955. Role-awareness as an objective of group work in teacher education. *Journal of Teacher Education*, **6**, 128–133.

Miller, R. C., & Fremont, A. S., Jr., 1962. The prediction of administrative role conflict resolutions. *Administrative Science Quarterly*, **7**, 143–160.

Miller, R. R., 1963. Learning objective of beginning psychiatric social workers. *Social Work*, **8**, 44–50.

Mills, T. M., 1962. A sleeper variable in small group research: the experimenter. *Pacific Sociological Review*, **5**, 21–28.

Milton, G. A., 1959. Sex differences in problem solving as a function of role appropriateness of the problem content. *Psychological Reports*, **5**, 705–708.

Mischel, W., 1958. The effect of the commitment situation on the generalization of expectancies. *Journal of Personality*, **26**, 508–516.

Mishler, E. G., 1953. Personality characteristics and the resolution of role conflicts. *Public Opinion Quarterly*, **17**, 115–135.

Mishler, E. G., & Tropp, A., 1956. Status and interaction in a psychiatric hospital. *Human Relations*, **9**, 187–205.

Miyamoto, S. F., & Dornbusch, S. F., 1956. A test of the symbolic interactionist hypothesis of self-perception. *American Journal of Sociology*, **61**, 399–403.

Mizruchi, E. H., & Perrucci, R., 1962. Norm qualities and differential effects of deviant behavior: an exploratory analysis. *American Sociological Review*, **27**, 391–399.

Modigliani, F., & Cohen, K. J., 1963. *The Role of Anticipations and Plans in Economic Behavior and Their Use in Economic Analysis and Forecasting*. Urbana, Ill.: University of Illinois Press.

Mogey, J., & Morris, R., 1960. Causes of change in family role patterns. *The Bulletin of the Research Center on Family Development*, **1**, 1–11.

Moment, D., & Zaleznik, A., 1963. *Role Development and Interpersonal Competence*. Boston: Division of Research, Harvard Business School.

Monk, Mary, & Newcomb, T. M., 1956. Perceived consensus within and among occupational classes. *American Sociological Review*, **21**, 71–79.

Moore, Harriett B., & Levy, S. J., 1951. Artful contrivers: a study of engineers. *Personnel*, **28**, 148–153.

Moore, H. T., 1921. The comparative influence of majority and expert opinion. *American Journal of Psychology*, **32**, 16–20.

Moore, W. E., & Tumin, M. M., 1949. Some social functions of ignorance. *American Sociological Review*, **14**, 787–795.

Moreno, J. L., 1919. *Die Gottheit als Komoediant*. (Godhood as a Comedian.) Vienna: Der Neue Daimon.

Moreno, J. L., 1923. *Das stegreif Theater*. (The Impromptu Theater.) Potsdam: G. Kiepenheuer.

Moreno, J. L., 1934. *Who Shall Survive*? Washington, D.C.: Nervous and Mental Disease Publication. (Rev. ed. New York: Beacon House, 1953.)

Moreno, J. L., 1940. Psychodramatic treatment of psychoses. *Sociometry*, **3**, 115–132.

Moreno, J. L., 1946. *Psychodrama*. New York: Beacon House.

Moreno, J. L., 1947. Contributions of sociometry to research methodology in sociology. *American Sociological Review*, **12**, 287–292.

Moreno, J. L., 1953. *The Sociometry of Subhuman Groups*. Glencoe, Ill.: The Free Press.

Moreno, J. L., (Ed.), 1960. *The Sociometry Reader*. Glencoe, Ill.: The Free Press.

Moreno, J. L., 1961. The role concept, a bridge between psychiatry and sociology. *American Journal of Psychiatry*, **118**, 518–523. (Also appearing as, Le concept du rôle: lien entre la psychiatrie et la sociologie. *Evolution Psychiatrique*, 1962, **27**, 327–337.

Moreno, J. L., 1962. Role theory and the emergence of the self. *Group Psychotherapy*, **15**, 114–117.

Moreno, J. L., 1962. The "united role theory" and the drama. *Group Psychotherapy*, **15**, 253–254.

Moreno, J. L., & Jennings, Helen H., 1945. Sociometric measurement of social configurations. *Sociometry Monographs*, No. 3.

Morgan, L., 1929. Individual and person. *American Journal of Sociology*, **34**, 623–631.

Morris, R. T., 1956. A typology of norms. *American Sociological Review*, **21**, 610–613.

Morse, Nancy C., 1953. *Satisfactions in the White-Collar Job*. Ann Arbor: University of Michigan, Institute for Social Research.

Moscovici, M., 1960. Le changement social en milieu rural et le rôle de la femme. (Social change in the rural milieu and the role of woman.) *Revue Française de Sociologie*, **1**, 314–322.

Moser, A. J., 1961. Marriage role expectations of high school students. *Marriage and Family Living*, **23**, 42–43.

Moss, C. S., & Clark, J. F., 1961. Role satisfaction of psychologists in state hospitals. *American Psychologist*, **16**, 523–528.

Motz, Annabelle B., 1952. The role conception inventory: a tool for research in social psychology. *American Sociological Review*, **17**, 465–471.

Motz, Annabelle B., 1961. The roles of the married woman in science. *Marriage and Family Living*, **23**, 374–376.

Mouton, Jane S., Blake, R. R., & Olmstead, J. A., 1956. The relationship between frequency of yielding and disclosure of personal identity. *Journal of Personality*, **24**, 339–347.

Mower, A. G., Jr., 1961. Role and selection of the chairman of the main committees of the United Nations General Assembly. *Social Science*, **36**, 8–14.

Mowrer, O. H., 1938. Preparatory set (expectancy)—a determinant in motivation and learning. *Psychological Review*, **45**, 62–91.

Müller-Freienfels, R., 1923. *Philosophy der Individualität*. (The Philosophy of Individuality.) Leipzig: Quelle und Meyer.

Müller-Freienfels, R., 1925. *Die Seele des Alltags.* (The Heart of Everyday Life.) Berlin: Wegeveiser Verlag.

Müller-Freienfels, R., 1933. Die Entwicklungsphasen als Psychophysiologische Rollen. (Developmental phases as psycho-physiological roles.) *Vierteljahreshifte der Jugendkunde*, **3**, 73–81.

Murdock, G. P., 1937. Comparative data on the division of labor by sex. *Social Forces*, **15**, 551–553.

Murdock, G. P., 1949., *Social Structure.* New York: Macmillan.

Murdock, G. P., 1954., Sociology and anthropology. In J. Gillin (Ed.), *For a Science of Social Man.* New York: Macmillan. Pp. 14–31.

Murphy, G., 1947. *Personality: A Biosocial Approach to Origins and Structure.* New York: Harper.

Mussen, P. H., & Kagan, J., 1958. Group conformity and perceptions of parents. *Child Development*, **29**, 57–60.

Mussen, P. H., & Rutherford, E., 1963. Parent-child relations and parental personality in relation to young children's sex-role preferences. *Child Development*, **34**, 319–333.

Myrdal, A., & Klein, V., 1956. *Women's Two Roles: Home and World.* London: Routledge.

Nadel, S. F., 1957. *The Theory of Social Structure.* Glencoe, Ill.: The Free Press.

Naegele, K. D., 1956. Clergyman, teachers, and psychiatrists: a study in roles and socialization. *Canadian Journal of Economics and Political Science*, **22**, 46–62.

Nakamura, C. Y., 1958. Conformity and problem solving. *Journal of Abnormal and Social Psychology*, **56**, 315–320.

Nall, F. C., Jr., 1962. Role expectations: a cross-cultural study. *Rural Sociology*, **27**, 28–41.

Nedelsky, Ruth, 1952. The teacher's role in the peer group during middle childhood. *The Elementary School Journal*, **52**, 325–334.

Nehnevajsa, J., 1960. Sociometry: decades of growth. In J. L. Moreno (Ed.), *Sociometry Reader.* Glencoe, Ill.: The Free Press. Pp. 707–753.

Neiman, L. J., 1954. The influence of peer groups upon attitudes towards the feminine role. *Social Problems*, **2**, 104–111.

Neiman, L. J., & Hughes, J. W., 1951. The problem of the concept of role—a re-survey of the literature. *Social Forces*, **30**, 141–149.

Newcomb, T. M., 1942. Community roles in attitude formation. *American Sociological Review*, **7**, 621–630.

Newcomb, T. M., 1943. *Personality and Social Change.* New York: Dryden Press.

Newcomb, T. M., 1947. Autistic hostility and social reality. *Human Relations*, **1**, 69–86.

Newcomb, T. M., 1949. Role behaviors in the study of individual personality and of groups. *Journal of Personality*, **18**, 273–289.

Newcomb, T. M., 1950. *Social Psychology.* New York: Dryden Press.

Newcomb, T. M., 1951. Social psychological theory: integrating individual and social approaches. In J. H. Rohrer & M. Sherif (Eds.), *Social Psychology at the Crossroads.* New York: Harper. Pp. 31–49.

Newcomb, T. M., 1953. An approach to the study of communicative acts. *Psychological Review*, **60**, 393–404.

Newcomb, T. M., 1954. Sociology and psychology. In J. Gillin (Ed.), *For a Science of Social Man.* New York: Macmillan. Pp. 227–256.

Newcomb, T. M., 1956. The prediction of interpersonal attraction. *American Psychologist*, **11**, 575–586.

Newcomb, T. M., 1961. *The Acquaintance Process.* New York: Holt.

Nichols, R. C., 1962. Subtle, obvious, and stereotype measures of masculinity-femininity. *Education and Psychological Measurement*, **22**, 439–448.

Nimnicht, G. P., 1959. How principals perceive their superintendents. *Phi Delta Kappan*, **41**, 65–66.

Nix, H. L., & Bates, F. L., 1962. Occupational role stresses: a structural approach. *Rural Sociology*, **27**, 7–17.

Nottingham, Elizabeth K., 1947. Toward an analysis of the effects of two world wars on the role and status of middle-class women in the English-speaking world. *American Sociological Review*, **12**, 666–675.

Nye, F. I., 1959. Employment status of mothers and marital conflict, permanence, and happiness. *Social Problems*, **6**, 260–267.

Nye, F. I., 1961. Maternal employment and marital interaction: some contingent conditions. *Social Forces*, **40**, 113–119.

Oakes, R. H., & Corsini, R. J., 1961. Social perceptions of one other self. *Journal of Social Psychology*, **53**, 235–242.

Oeser, O. A. (Ed.), 1955. *Teacher, Pupil, and Task*. London: Tavistock.

Oeser, O. A., 1961. Prolegomena to a theory of roles and the measurement of role behavior. *Acta Psychologica*, **19**, 1–24.

Oeser, O. A., & Emery, F. E., 1954. *Social Structure and Personality in a Rural Community*. London: Routledge.

Oeser, O. A., & Harary, F., 1962. A mathematical model for structural role theory. *Human Relations*, **15**, 89–109.

Oeser, O. A., & Harary, F.. 1964. A mathematical model for structural role theory, II. *Human Relations*, **17**, 3–17.

Ofstad, H., 1950. The descriptive definition of the concept "legal norm" proposed by Hans Kelsen. *Theoria*, **16**, 118–151, 211–246.

Ofstad, H., 1951. Objectivity of norms and value-judgments according to recent Scandinavian philosophy. *Philosophy and Phenomenology Research*, **12**, 42–68.

Olds, Victoria, 1962. Role theory and casework: a review of the literature. *Social Casework*, **43**, 3–8.

Olmsted, D. W., 1957. Inter-group similarities of role correlates. *Sociometry*, **20**, 8–20.

Olmsted, D. W., 1961. *Social Groups, Roles, and Leadership: An Introduction to the Concepts*. Lansing: Michigan State University, Board of Trustees.

Olmsted, M. S., 1954. Orientation and role in the small group. *American Sociological Review*, **19**, 741–751.

Olmsted, M. S., 1957. Character and social role. *American Journal of Sociology*, **63**, 49–57.

Oman, M., & Tomasson, R. F., 1952. Disparities in visualizing social norms. *Social Forces*, **30**, 328–333.

Omari, T. P., 1963. Role expectations in the courtship situation in Ghana. *Social Forces*, **42**, 147–156.

Omwake, Katharine T., 1954. The relation between acceptance of self and acceptance of others shown by three personality inventories. *Journal of Consulting Psychology*, **18**, 443–446.

Opler, M. K., 1943. Woman's social status and the forms of marriage. *American Journal of Sociology*, **49**, 125–146.

Ort, R. S., 1950. A study of role-conflicts as related to happiness in marriage. *Journal of Abnormal and Social Psychology*, **45**, 691–699.

Ort, R. S., 1952. A study of role-conflicts as related to class level. *Journal of Abnormal and Social Psychology*, **47**, 425–432.

Orzack, L. H., 1961. Issues underlying role dilemmas of professionals. In A. B. Abramovitz (Ed.), *Emotional Factors in Public Health Nursing: a Casebook for Everyday Practice*. Madison: University of Wisconsin Press.

Osgood, C. E., 1960. Cognitive dynamics in the conduct of human affairs. *Public Opinion Quarterly*, **24**, 341–365.

Osgood, C. E., & Tannenbaum, P. H., 1955. The principle of congruity in the prediction of attitude change. *Psychological Review*, **62**, 42–55.

Ouhashi, M., 1962. Kyôinsô no ishiki kôzô. (Social consciousness of teachers.) *Shisô*, **452**, 50–63.

Overall, Betty, & Aronson, Harriet, 1963. Expectations of psychotherapy in patients of lower socioeconomic class. *American Journal of Orthopsychiatry*, **33**, 421–430.

Owen, Carol, 1962. Feminine roles and social mobility in women's weekly magazines. *Sociology Review*, **10**, 283–296.

Pages, R., 1956. *Rôles et Opérations dans les Groupes*. (Roles and Operations in Groups). Paris: Commissariat Général à la Productivité.

Pages, R., 1957. Psychosociologie des rôles de direction. (The psychosociology of directional roles.) *Hommes Techniques*, **13**, 315–318.

Pallone, N. J., & Grande, P. P., 1964. Public perception or client need: counselor role or image. *The Catholic Educational Review*, **62**, 39–46.

Papanek, H., 1964. Woman field worker in a purdah society. *Human Organization*, **23**, 160–163.

Park, R. E., 1925. The concept of position in sociology. *Publications of the American Sociological Society*, **20**, 1–14.

Park, R. E., 1939. Symbiosis and socialization: a frame of reference for the study of society. *American Journal of Sociology*, **45**, 1–25.

Park, R. E., & Burgess, E. W., 1921. *Introduction to the Science of Sociology*. Chicago: University of Chicago Press.

Parker, C., 1957. Role theory and the treatment of the antisocial acting out disorders. *British Journal of Delinquency*, **4**, 285–300.

Parsons, T., 1937. *The Structure of Social Action.* New York: McGraw-Hill.

Parsons, T., 1942. Age and sex in the social structure of the United States. *American Sociological Review*, **7**, 604–616.

Parsons, T., 1945. La théorie sociologique systématique et ses perspectives. (Systematic sociological theory and its prospects). In G. Gurvitch & W. Moore (Eds.), *Twentieth Century Sociology, A Symposium.* New York: Philosophical Library. Pp. 42–69.

Parsons, T., 1949. *Essays in Sociological Theory: Pure and Applied.* Glencoe, Ill.: The Free Press.

Parsons, T., 1951. Illness and the role of the physician: a sociological perspective. *American Journal of Orthopsychiatry*, **21**, 452–460. (a)

Parsons, T., 1951. *The Social System.* Glencoe, Ill.: The Free Press. (b)

Parsons, T., 1956. Suggestions for a sociological approach to the theory of organizations: I. *Administrative Science Quarterly*, **1**, 63–85.

Parsons, T., 1959. The school class as a social system: some of its functions in American society. *Harvard Educational Review*, **29**, 297–318.

Parsons, T., & Bales, R. F., 1955. *Family, Socialization and Interaction Process.* Glencoe, Ill.: The Free Press.

Parsons, T., & Shils, E. A., 1951. *Toward a General Theory of Action.* Cambridge, Mass.: Harvard University Press.

Patchen, M., 1958. The effect of reference group standards on job satisfactions. *Human Relations*, **11**, 303–314.

Patterson, S. C., 1959. Patterns of interpersonal relations in a state legislative group: the Wisconsin Assembly. *Public Opinion Quarterly*, **23**, 101–109.

Patterson, S. C., 1961. The role of the deviant in the state legislative system: the Wisconsin Assembly. *The Western Political Quarterly*, **14**, 460–472.

Patterson, S. C., 1963. Role of the lobbyist: the case of Oklahoma. *Journal of Politics*, **25**, 72–92.

Pearlin, L. I., 1962. Alienation from work: a study of nursing personnel. *American Sociological Review*, **27**, 314–326.

Pearlin, L. I., 1963. Sources of resistance to change in a mental hospital. *American Journal of Sociology*, **68**, 325–334.

Pearlin, L. I., & Rosenberg, M., 1962. Nurse-patient social distance and the structural context of a mental hospital. *American Sociological Review*, **27**, 56–65.

Peck, R. F., & Galliani, C., 1962. Intelligence, ethnicity and social roles in adolescent society. *Sociometry*, **25**, 64–72.

Pellegrin, R. J., & Bates, F. L., 1959. Congruity and incongruity of status attributes within occupations and work positions. *Social Forces*, **38**, 23–28.

Pepitone, A., & Hayden, R. G., 1955. Some evidence for conflict resolution in impression formation. *Journal of Abnormal and Social Psychology*, **51**, 302–307.

Pepitone, A., & Reichling, G., 1955. Group cohesiveness and the expression of hostility. *Human Relations*, **8**, 327–337.

Perkins, H. V., Jr., 1958. Teachers' and peers' perceptions of children's self-concepts. *Child Development*, **29**, 203–220.

Perlman, Helen H., 1957. *Social Casework: Problem Solving Process.* Chicago: University of Chicago Press.

Perlman, Helen H., 1960. Intake and some role considerations. *Social Casework*, **41**, 171–177.

Perlman, Helen H., 1961. The role concept and social casework: some explorations. I. The "social" in social casework. *Social Service Review*, **35**, 370–381.

Perlman, Helen H., 1962. The role concept and social casework: some explorations. II. What is social diagnosis? *Social Service Review*, **36**, 17–31.

Perlman, Helen H., 1963. Identity problems, role, and casework treatment. *Social Service Review*, **37**, 307–318.

Perry, S. E., & Wynne, L. C., 1959. Role conflict, role redefinition and social change in a clinical research organization. *Social Forces*, **38**, 62–65.

Phillips, B. N., 1955. Community control of teacher behavior. *Journal of Teacher Education*, **6**, 293–300.

Phillips, B. S., 1957. A role theory approach to adjustment in old age. *American Sociological Review*, **22**, 212–217.

Phillips, B. S., 1961. Role change, subjective age, and adjustment: a correlational analysis. *Journal of Gerontology*, **16**, 347–352.

Phillips, E. L., 1951. Attitudes toward self and others: a brief questionnaire report. *Journal of Consulting Psychology*, **15**, 79–81.

Phillips, L., & Rabinovitch, M. S., 1958. Social role and patterns of symptomatic behaviors. *Journal of Abnormal and Social Psychology*, **57**, 181–186.

Piaget, J., 1932. *The Moral Judgment of the Child.* London: Kegan Paul, Trench, & Trubner.

Pierce, A., 1956. On the concepts of role and status. *Sociologus, Zeitschrift für Empirische Soziologie, Sozialpsychologische und Ethnologische Forschung*, **6**, 29–34.

Pine, F., & Levinson, D. J., 1961. A sociopsychological conception of patienthood. *The International Journal of Social Psychiatry*, **7**, 106–122.

Podell, L., 1959. An alternative view of female role conflict. *Human Relations*, **7**, 546–555.

Polansky, N., Lippitt, R., & Redl, F., 1950. An investigation of behavioral contagion in groups. *Human Relations*, **3**, 319–348.

Polansky, N. A., White, R. B., & Miller, S. C., 1957. Determinants of the role-image of the patient in a psychiatric hospital. In M. Greenblatt, D. J. Levinson, & R. H. Williams (Eds.), *The Patient and the Mental Hospital.* Glencoe, Ill.: The Free Press. Pp. 380–401.

Pool, I. S., 1964. The head of the company: conceptions of role and identity. *Behavioral Science*, **9**, 147–155.

Powell, R. M., & La Fave, L., 1958. Some determinants of role-taking accuracy. *Sociology and Social Research*, **42**, 319–326.

Powell, R. M., Zink, D. L., & Miller, J. L., 1956. An experimental study of role taking, group status, and group formation. *Sociology and Social Research*, **40**, 159–165.

Presthus, R. V., 1958. Toward a theory of organizational behavior. *Administrative Science Quarterly*, **3**, 48–72.

Quinney, E. R., 1963. Occupational structure and criminal behavior: prescription violation by retail pharmacists. *Social Problems*, **11**, 179–185.

Quinney, E. R., 1964. Adjustment to occupational role strain: the case of retail pharmacy. *Southwestern Social Science Quarterly*, **44**, 367–376.

Rabban, M., 1950. Sex role identification in young children in two diverse social groups. *Genetic Psychology Monographs*, **42**, 81–158.

Radinsky, E. K., 1950. Parents' role in long time cases. *Child Welfare*, **29**, 8–12.

Radke, M. J., & Trager, H. G., 1950. Children's perceptions of the social roles of Negroes and whites. *Journal of Psychology*, **29**, 3–33.

Raimy, V., 1948. Self-reference in counseling interviews. *Journal of Consulting Psychology*, **12**, 153–163.

Rainwater, L., Coleman, R. P., & Handel, G., 1959. *Workingman's Wife: Her Personality, World and Life Style.* New York: Oceana.

Ramsoy, O., 1963. *Social Groups as Systems and Subsystems.* New York: The Free Press.

Rapaport, R., & Rosow, I., 1957. An approach to family relationships and role performance. *Human Relations*, **10**, 209–221.

Rasmussen, G., & Zander, A., 1954. Group membership and self-evaluation. *Human Relations*, **7**, 239–251.

Raulet, H. M., 1961. The health professional and the fluoridation issue: a case of role conflict. *Journal of Social Issues*, **17**, 45–54.

Raush, H. L., Dittmann, A. T., & Taylor, T. J., 1959. Person, setting, and change in social interaction. *Human Relations*, **12**, 361–378.

Raven, B. H., & Fishbein, M., 1961. Acceptance of punishment and change in belief. *Journal of Abnormal and Social Psychology*, **63**, 411–416.

Raven, B. H., & French, J. R. P., Jr., 1958. Group support, legitimate power, and social influence. *Journal of Personality*, **26**, 400–409.

Raven, B. H., & French, J. R. P., Jr., 1958. Legitimate power, coercive power, and observability in social influence. *Sociometry*, **21**, 83–97.

Record, W., 1956. Community and racial factors in intellectual roles. *Sociology and Social Research*, **41**, 33–38.

Record, W., 1957. Social stratification and intellectual roles in the Negro community. *British Journal of Sociology*, **8**, 235–255.

Redekop, C., & Loomis, C. P., 1960. The development of status-roles in the systemic linkage process. *Journal of Human Relations*, **8**, 276–283.

Redfield, R., & Singer, M., 1954. The cultural role of cities. *Economic and Cultural Change*, **3**, 54–73.

Reeder, L., Donohue, G. A., & Biblarz, A., 1960. Conceptions of self and others. *American Journal of Sociology*, **66**, 153–159.

Reissman, L., 1949. A study of role conceptions in bureaucracy. *Social Forces*, **27**, 305–310.

Renner, K. E., & Maher, B. A., 1962. Effect of construct type on recall. *Journal of Individual Psychology*, **18**, 177–179.

Rettig, S., Jacobson, F. N., & Pasamanick, B., 1958. The status of the professional as perceived by himself, by other professionals, and by lay persons. *Midwest Sociologist*, **20**, 84–89.

Richey, R. W., & Fox, W. H., 1948. How do teachers compare with other community members? *Educational Research Bulletin*, **27**, 238–241, 247–248.

Richter, H. E., 1963. *Eltern, Kind und Neurose: Psychoanalyse der Kindlichen Rolle.* (Adult, Child and Neurosis: Psychoanalysis of the Role of the Child.) Stuttgart: Ernst Klett Verlag.

Riecken, H. W., & Homans, G. C., 1954. Psychological aspects of social structure. In G. Lindzey (Ed.), *Handbook of Social Psychology*. Vol. II. Cambridge, Mass.: Addison-Wesley. Pp. 786–829.

Riesman, D., Potter, R. J., & Watson, Jeanne., 1960. The vanishing host. *Human Organization*, **19**, 17–27.

Riley, Matilda W., Riley, J. W., & Toby, Marcia L., 1952. The measurement of consensus. *Social Forces*, **31**, 97–106.

Robbins, Florence G., 1944. Student reactions to teacher personality traits. *Educational Administration and Supervision*, **30**, 241–246.

Rocheblave-Spenlé, Anne M., 1953. La notion de rôle dans le développement de la personnalité de l'enfant. (The concept of role in the development of the child's personality.) *Cahiers Internationaux de Sociologie*, **14**, 169–178.

Rocheblave-Spenlé, Anne M., 1954. Rôles masculins et rôles féminins dans les états intersexuels. (Masculine and feminine roles in the intersexual state.) *Evolution Psychiatrique*, **11**, 281–312.

Rocheblave-Spenlé, Anne M., 1957. Notes en marge d'une enquête sur les stéréotypes masculins et féminins. (Marginal notes of an investigation of masculine and feminine stereotypes.) *Recherches Sociologiques*, **4**, 19–34.

Rocheblave-Spenlé, Anne M., 1962. *Contribution a l'Etude des Rôles Masculins et Feminins.* (Contributions to the Study of Masculine and Feminine Roles.) Paris: Faculté des Lettres et Sciences Humaines. (a)

Rocheblave-Spenlé, Anne M., 1962. *La Notion de Rôle en Psychologie Sociale: Etude Historico-Critique.* (*The Concept of Role in Social Psychology: An Historical-Critical Study.*) Paris: Presses Universitaires de France. (b)

Rocheblave-Spenlé, Anne M., 1963. La notion de rôle: quelques problèmes conceptuels. (The concept of role: some conceptual problems.) *Revue Française de Sociologie*, **4**, 300–306.

Rodgers, D. A., 1957. Personality correlates of successful role behavior. *Journal of Social Psychology*, **46**, 111–117.

Roethlisberger, F. J., 1941. *Management and Morale*. Cambridge, Mass.: Harvard University Press.

Roethlisberger, F. J., 1945. The foreman: master and victim of double talk. *Harvard Business Review*, **23**, 283–298.

Roethlisberger, F. J., & Dickson, W. J., 1939. *Management and the Worker*. Cambridge, Mass.: Harvard University Press.

Rogers, Dorothy, 1950. Implications of views concerning the "typical" school teacher. *Journal of Educational Sociology*, **23**, 482–487.

Rogers, Dorothy, 1953. A study of the reactions of forty men to teaching in the elementary school. *Journal of Educational Sociology*, **27**, 24–35.

Rommetveit, R., 1954. *Social Norms and Roles*. Minneapolis: University of Minnesota Press.

Rommetveit, R., 1960. *Selectivity, Intuition and Halo Effects in Social Perception*. Oslo: Oslo University Press.

Rose, A. M., 1951. The adequacy of women's expectations for adult roles. *Social Forces*, **30**, 69–77.

Rose, A. M., 1959. Acceptance of adult roles and separation from family. *Marriage and Family Living*, **21**, 120–126.

Rose, A. M., 1962. A systematic summary of symbolic interaction theory. In A. M. Rose (Ed.), *Human Behavior and Social Processes*. Boston: Houghton Mifflin. Pp. 3–19.

Rosen, B. C., 1955. Conflicting group membership: a study of parent-peer group cross-pressures. *American Sociological Review*, **20**, 155–161.

Rosen, H., 1961. Managerial role interaction: a study of three managerial levels. *Journal of Applied Psychology*, **45**, 30–34.

Rosen, H., & Rosen, R. A. H., 1957. Personality variables and role in a union business agent group. *Journal of Applied Psychology*, **41**, 131–136.

Rosenberg, L., 1962. Social status and participation among a group of schizophrenics. *Human Relations*, **15**, 365–377.

Rosenberg, P. P., & Fuller, M., 1957. Dynamic analysis of the student nurse. *Group Psychotherapy*, **10**, 22–37.

Rosenblatt, A., 1962. Application of role concepts to the intake process. *Social Casework*, **43**, 8–14.

Rosencranz, H. A., & Biddle, B. J., 1964. The role approach to teacher competence evaluation. In B. J. Biddle and W. J. Ellena (Eds.), *Contemporary Research on Teacher Effectiveness*. New York: Holt. Pp. 232–263.

Rosengren, W. R., 1961. Social sources of pregnancy as illness or normality. *Social Forces*, **39**, 260–267.

Rosengren, W. R., 1962. Social instability and attitudes towards pregnancy as a social role. *Social Problems*, **9**, 371–377.

Rosengren, W. R., 1962. The sick role during pregnancy: a note on research in progress. *Journal of Health and Human Behavior*, **3**, 213–218.

Rosenthal, R., Persinger, G. W., Kline, Linda V., & Mulay, R. C., 1963. Role of the research assistant in the mediation of experimenter bias. *Journal of Personality*, **31**, 313–335.

Ross, E. A., 1908. *Social Psychology: An Outline and Source Book*. New York: Macmillan.

Royce, J., 1900. *The World and the Individual*. London: Macmillan.

Rutledge, A. L., 1962. Male and female roles in marriage counseling. *Pastoral Psychology*, **13**, 10–16.

Ryans, D. G., 1960. *Characteristics of Teachers, Their Description, Comparison, and Appraisal; a Research Study*. Washington: American Council on Education.

Ryans, D. G., 1961. Inventory estimated teacher characteristics as covariants of observer assessed pupil behavior. *Journal of Educational Psychology*, **52**, 91–97.

Rychlak, J. F., 1958. Task-influence and the stability of generalized expectancies. *Journal of Experimental Psychology*, **55**, 459–462.

Rychlak, J. F., & Eacker, J. N., 1962. The effects of anxiety, delay, and reinforcement on generalized expectancies. *Journal of Personality*, **30**, 123–134.

Rykoff, I., Day, Juliana, & Wynne, L. C., 1959. Maintenance of stereotyped roles in the families of schizophrenics. *Archives of General Psychiatry*, **1**, 93–98.

Sachs, B. M., 1956. "Flexibility" and "rigidity" in the role perception of selected administrators with regard to vocation. *Educational Administration and Supervision*, **42**, 46–53.

Saito, Y., 1959. Yakuwari no Kôzô. (Role structure). *Tôhoku Gakuin Daigaku Ronshû*, **35**, 151–174.

Salzinger, K., 1959. Experimental manipulation of verbal behaviors: a review. *Journal of General Psychology*, **61**, 65–94.

Samelson, F., 1957. Conforming behavior and two conditions of conflict in the cognitive field. *Journal of Abnormal and Social Psychology*, **55**, 181–187.

Samelson, F., 1958. The relation of achievement and affiliation motives to conforming behavior in two conditions of conflict with a majority. In J. W. Atkinson (Ed.), *Motives in Fantasy, Action, and Society*. Princeton, N.J.: Van Nostrand. Pp. 421–433.

Sampson, E. E., 1963. Status congruence and cognition consistency. *Sociometry*, **26**, 146–162.

Sarbin, T. R., 1943. The concept of role taking. *Sociometry*, **6**, 273–285.

Sarbin, T. R., 1950. Contributions to role-taking theory: I. Hypnotic behavior. *Psychological Review*, **57**, 255–270.

Sarbin, T. R., 1952. Contributions to role-taking theory: III. A preface to a psychological analysis of the self. *Psychological Review*, **59**, 11–22.

Sarbin, T. R., 1954. Role theory. In G. Lindzey (Ed.), *Handbook of Social Psychology*, Vol. I. Cambridge, Mass.: Addison-Wesley. Pp. 223–258.

Sarbin, T. R., 1964. Role theoretical interpretation of psychological change. In P. Worchel and D. Byrne (Eds.), *Personality Change*. New York: Wiley. Pp. 176–220.

Sarbin, T. R., & Allen, V. L., 1964. Role enactment, audience feedback, and attitude change. *Sociometry*, **27**, 183–194.

Sarbin, T. R., & Farberow, N. L., 1952. Contributions to role-taking theory: a clinical study of self and role. *Journal of Abnormal and Social Psychology*, **47**, 117–125.

Sarbin, T. R., & Hardyck, C. D., 1955. Conformance in role perception as a personality variable. *Journal of Consulting Psychology*, **19**, 109–111.

Sarbin, T. R., & Jones, D. S., 1955. An experimental analysis of role behavior. *Journal of Abnormal and Social Psychology*, **51**, 236–241.

Sarbin, T. R., & Lim, P. T., 1963. Some evidence in support of the role-taking hypothesis in hypnosis. *International Journal of Clinical and Experimental Hypnosis*, **11**, 98–103.

Sarbin, T. R., & Rosenberg, B. G., 1955. Contributions to role-taking theory: IV. A method for obtaining a qualitative estimate of the self. *Journal of Social Psychology*, **42**, 71–81.

Sargent, S. S., 1951. Conceptions of role and ego in contemporary psychology. In J. H. Rohrer and M. Sherif (Eds.), *Social Psychology at the Crossroads.* New York: Harper. Pp. 355–370.

Sayres, W. C., 1956. Disorientation and status change. *Southwestern Journal of Anthropology*, **12**, 79–86.

Scarborough, O., & Harris, B. M., 1962. Graduate students' perceptions of leadership roles. *Journal of Teacher Education*, **13**, 60–64.

Schachter, S., 1951. Deviation, rejection, and communication. *Journal of Abnormal and Social Psychology*, **46**, 190–207.

Schachter, S., 1959. *The Psychology of Affiliation.* Stanford, Calif.: Stanford University Press.

Schachter, S., Ellertson, N., McBride, Dorothy, & Gregory, Doris, 1951. An experimental study of cohesiveness and productivity. *Human Relations*, **4**, 229–238.

Schachter, S., & Hall, R., 1952. Group-derived restraints and audience persuasion. *Human Relations*, **5**, 397–406.

Schanck, R. L., 1932. A study of a community and its groups and institutions conceived of as behaviors of individuals. *Psychology Monographs*, **43**: 2, 1–133.

Scheler, M. F., 1913. *Wesen und Formen der Sympathie.* (The Nature and Forms of Sympathy.) Bonn: F. Cohen.

Scheler, M. F., 1915. Die Idole der Selbsterkenntnis. (The phantom of self-knowledge.) In M. F. Scheler (Ed.), *Abhandlungen und Aufsütze.* (Essays and Articles.) Leipzig: Weisse Bücher. See also M. F. Scheler (Ed.), *Vom Umsturz der Werte.* (On the Overthrow of Values.) Berne: Francke Verlag, 1955. Pp. 215–292.

Scheler, M. F., 1926. *Die Wissens Formen und die Gesellschaft.* (The Forms of Knowledge and Society.) Leipzig: Der Neve-Geist Verlag.

Schiff, H., 1954. Judgmental response sets in the perception of sociometric status. *Sociometry*, **17**, 207–227.

Schild, E. O., 1962. Foreign student, as stranger, learning the norms of the host-culture. *Journal of Social Issues*, **18**, 41–54.

Schmidt, L. D., 1962. Concepts of the role of secondary school counselors. *Personnel and Guidance Journal*, **40**, 600–605.

Schoenfeld, N., 1942. An experimental study of some problems relating to stereotypes. *Archives of Psychology*, **38**: 270, 1–57.

Schonbar, Rosalea A., 1945. The interaction of observer pairs in judging visual extent and movement: the formation of social norms in "structured" situations. *Archives of Psychology*, **41**: 299, 1–95.

Schroeder, W. W., 1963. Lay expectations of the ministerial role. *Journal for the Scientific Study of Religion*, **2**, 217–227.

Schwarzweller, H. K., 1959. Value orientations in educational and occupational choices. *Rural Sociology*, **24**, 246–256.

Schwarzweller, H. K., 1960. Values and occupational choice. *Social Forces*, **39**, 126–135.

Scodel, A., & Freedman, Maria L., 1956. Additional observations on the social perceptions of authoritarians and nonauthoritarians. *Journal of Abnormal and Social Psychology*, **52**, 92–95.

Scodel, A., & Mussen, P., 1953. Social perception of authoritarians and nonauthoritarians. *Journal of Abnormal and Social Psychology*, **48**, 181–184.

Scofield, N. E., 1960. Some changing roles of women in suburbia: a social anthropological case study. *Transactions of the New York Academy of Science*, **22**, 450–457.

Scott, W. A., 1962. Cognitive complexity and cognitive flexibility. *Sociometry*, **25**, 405–414.

Seaga, E. P. G., 1955. Parent-teacher relationships in a Jamaican village. *Social and Economic Studies*, **4**, 289–302.

Sears, R. R., Maccoby, Eleanor E., & Levin, H., 1957. *Patterns of Child Rearing.* Evanston, Ill.: Row, Peterson.

Secord, P. F., & Backman, C. W., 1961. Personality theory and the problem of stability and change in individual behavior. *Psychological Review*, **68**, 21–32.

Seeman, M., 1953. Role conflict and ambivalence in leadership. *American Sociological Review*, **18**, 373–380.

Seeman, M., 1960. *Social Status and Leadership: the Case of the School Executive*. Columbus: Ohio State University.

Seeman, M., & Evans, J. W., 1962. Apprenticeship and attitude change. *American Journal of Sociology*, **67**, 365–378.

Segal, B. E., 1962. Nurses and patients: time, place, and distance. *Social Problems*, **9**, 257–263.

Seidman, J. M., & Knapp, Leda B., 1953. Teacher likes and dislikes of student behavior and student perceptions of these attitudes. *Journal of Educational Research*, **47**, 143–149.

Service, E. R., 1960. Kinship terminology and evolution. *American Anthropologist*, **62**, 747–763.

Shanner, W. M., 1959. New concepts in norms. In W. M. Shanner (Ed.), *The Positive Values in the American Educational System*. Washington, D. C.: American Council on Education. Pp. 64–74.

Shaw, D. M., & Campbell, E. Q., 1962. Internalization of a normal norm and external supports. *Sociological Quarterly*, **3**, 57–71.

Shelley, H. P., 1960. Status consensus, leadership, and satisfaction with the group. *Journal of Social Psychology*, **51**, 157–164.

Shepherd, C., & Weschler, I. R., 1955. The relation between three interpersonal variables and communication effectiveness: a pilot study. *Sociometry*, **18**, 103–110.

Sherif, M., 1935. A study of some social factors in perception. *Archives of Psychology*, **27**: 187, 1–59.

Sherif, M., 1936. *The Psychology of Social Norms*. New York: Harper.

Sherif, M., 1937. An experimental approach to the study of attitudes. *Sociometry*, **1**, 90–98.

Sherif, M., 1948. *An Outline of Social Psychology*. New York: Harper.

Sherif, M., 1951. A preliminary study of inter-group relations. In J. H. Rohrer and M. Sherif (Eds.), *Social Psychology at the Crossroads*. New York: Harper. Pp. 388–424.

Sherif, M., 1953. The concept of reference groups in human relations. In M. Sherif and M. O. Wilson (Eds.), *Group Relations at the Crossroads*. New York: Harper. Pp. 203–231.

Sherif, M., 1954. Sociocultural influences in small group research. *Sociology and Social Research*, **39**, 1–10.

Sherif, M., & Cantril, H., 1947. *The Psychology of Ego-involvements, Social Attitudes, and Identifications*. New York: Wiley.

Sherif, M., & Sherif, Carolyn W., 1956. *An Outline of Social Psychology* (Rev. ed.). New York: Harper.

Sherif, M., White, B. J., & Harvey, O. J., 1955. Status in experimentally produced groups. *American Journal of Sociology*, **60**, 370–379.

Sherman, B., 1963. Teachers' identifications of childhood authority figures. *School Review*, **71**, 66–78.

Sherwood, C. E., & Walker, W. S., 1960. Role differentiation in real groups. *Sociology and Social Research*, **45**, 14–17.

Sherwood, R., 1958. The Bantu clerk: a study of role expectations. *Journal of Social Psychology*, **47**, 285–316.

Shibutani, T., 1955. Reference groups as perspectives. *American Journal of Sociology*, **60**, 562–569.

Shibutani, T., 1961. *Society and Personality*. Englewood Cliffs, N.J.: Prentice-Hall.

Shils, E. A., 1950. Primary groups in the American Army. In R. K. Merton & P. F. Lazarsfeld (Eds.), *Continuities in Social Research: Studies in the Scope and Method of "The American Soldier."* Glencoe, Ill.: The Free Press. Pp. 16–25.

Showel, M., 1960. Interpersonal knowledge and rated leader potential. *Journal of Abnormal and Social Psychology*, **61**, 87–92.

Shuval, Judith T., 1963. Occupational interests and sex-role congruence. *Human Relations*, **16**, 171–182.

Shuval, Judith T., 1963. Perceived role components of nursing in Israel. *American Sociological Review*, **28**, 37–46.

Shuval, Y. T., 1963. Inyan miktsoi vetafkidey min. (Occupational interest and sex-role congruence.) *Megamot*, **12**, 244–251.

Siegel, Alberta E., & Siegel, S., 1957. Reference groups, membership groups, and attitude change. *Journal of Abnormal and Social Psychology*, **55**, 360–364.

Siegel, L., Coon, H. L., Pepinsky, H. B., & Rubin, S., 1956. Expressed standards of behavior of high school students, teachers and parents. *Personnel and Guidance Journal*, **34**, 261–267.

Silverman, Corinne, 1959. The legislator's view of the legislative process. In J. C. Wahlke and H. Eulau (Eds.), *Legislative Behavior: A Reader in Theory and Research*. Glencoe, Ill.: The Free Press. Pp. 298–303.

Simmel, G., 1920. Zur Philosophie des Schauspielers. (On the philosophy of the actor.) *Logos*, **1**, 339–362.

Simmel, G., 1950. *The Sociology of George Simmel* (K. H. Wolff, tr. & Ed.). Glencoe, Ill.: The Free Press.

Simmel, G., 1953. The social role of the stranger. In E. A. Schuler, D. L. Gibson, Maude L. Fiero, and W. B. Brookover (Eds.), *Outside Readings in Sociology*. New York: Crowell. Pp. 142–147.

Simmel, G., 1955. *Conflict* (K. H. Wolff, tr.) and *The Web of Group-Affiliations* (R. Bendix,tr.). Glencoe, Ill.: The Free Press.

Simmons, L. W., 1945. *The Role of the Aged in Primitive Societies*. New Haven: Yale University Press.

Simmons, O. G., & Freeman, H. E., 1959. Familial expectations and posthospital performance of mental patients. *Human Relations*, **12**, 233–242.

Simpson, R. L., & Simpson, Ida H., 1960. Values, personal influence, and occupational choice. *Social Forces*, **39**, 116–125.

Singer, J. E., Radloff, Lenore S., & Worl, D. M., 1963. Renegades, heretics, and changes in sentiment. *Sociometry*, **26**, 178–189.

Sivertsen, D., 1957. Goal setting, the level of aspiration and social norms. *Nordisk Psykologi*, **9**, 54–60.

Slater, P. E., 1955. Role differentiation in small groups. *American Sociological Review*, **20**, 300–310.

Slater, P. E., 1961. Parental role differentiation. *American Journal of Sociology*, **67**, 296–308.

Slocum, W. L., 1959. Some sociological aspects of occupational choice. *The American Journal of Economics and Sociology*, **18**, 139–148.

Smith, A. A., 1944. What is good college teaching? *Journal of Higher Education*, **15**, 216–218.

Smith, A. J., 1957. Similarity of values and its relation to acceptance and the projection of similarity. *Journal of Psychology*, **43**, 251–260.

Smith, A. J., 1960. The attribution of similarity: the influence of success and failure. *Journal of Abnormal and Social Psychology*, **61**, 419–423.

Smith, E. E., 1957. The effects of clear and unclear role expectations on group productivity and defensiveness. *Journal of Abnormal and Social Psychology*, **55**, 213–217.

Smith, M., 1943. An empirical scale of prestige status of occupations. *American Sociological Review*, **8**, 185–192.

Smith, M., 1945. Social situation, social behavior, social group. *Psychological Review*, **52**, 224–229.

Smith, Patricia C., & Kendall, L. M., 1963. Retranslation of expectancies: an approach to the construction of unambiguous anchors for rating scales. *Journal of Applied Psychology*, **47**, 149–155.

Smith, R. J., 1961. The Japanese rural community: norms, sanctions, and ostracism. *American Anthropologist*, **63**, 522–533.

Smith, Victoria F., 1953. What kind of teachers do parents like? What kind of parents do teachers like? *Understanding the Child*, **22**, 99–103.

Smith, V. I., 1962. Role conflicts in the position of a military education adviser. *Social Forces*, **40**, 176–178.

Solby, B., 1944. The role concept in job adjustment. *Sociometry*, **7**, 222–229.

Soles, S., 1964. Teacher role expectations and the internal organization of secondary schools. *Journal of Educational Research*, **57**, 227–238.

Sommer, R., & Killian, L. M., 1954. Areas of value differences: I. A method for investigation. *Journal of Social Psychology*, **39**, 227–235. (a)

Sommer, R., & Killian, L. M., 1954. Areas of value difference: II. Negro-White relations. *Journal of Social Psychology*, **39**, 237–244. (b)

Sorenson, A. G., Husek, T. R., & Yu, Constance, 1963. Divergent concepts of teacher role: an approach to the measurement of teacher effectiveness. *Journal of Educational Psychology*, **54**, 287–294.

Sorrentino, J. G., 1961. El rol del individuo frente a los desordenes de la conducta. (The role of the individual in the face of behavioral disorders.) *Acta Neuropsychiquiatre*, **7**, 206–207.

South, E. B., 1927. Some psychological aspects of committee work. *Journal of Applied Psychology*, **11**, 348–368.

Southall, A., 1959. An operational theory of role. *Human Relations*, **12**, 17–34.

Spears, H., 1945. What disturbs the beginning teacher. *School Review*, **53**, 458–463.

Spector, A. J., 1956. Expectations, fulfillment, and morale. *Journal of Abnormal and Social Psychology*, **52**, 51–56.

Spencer, T. D., 1964. Sex-role learning in early childhood. *The Journal of Nursery Education*, **19**, 181–187.

Spiegel, J. P., 1954. The social roles of doctor and patient in psychoanalysis and psychotherapy. *Psychiatry*, **17**, 369–376.

Spiegel, J. P., 1957. The resolution of role conflict within the family. *Psychiatry*, **20**, 1–16.

Spindler, G. D., 1963. The role of the school administrator. In G. D. Spindler (Ed.), *Education and Culture*. New York: Holt. Pp. 234–258.

Stagner, R., 1954. Attitude toward authority: an exploratory study. *Journal of Social Psychology*, **40**, 197–210.

Stanton, H., Back, K., & Litwak, E., 1956. Role-playing in survey research. *American Journal of Sociology*, **62**, 172–176.

Steiner, I. D., 1960. Sex differences in the resolution of A-B-X conflicts. *Journal of Personality*, **28**, 118–128.

Steiner, I. D., & Dodge, Joan S., 1956. Interpersonal perception and role structure as determinants of group and individual efficiency. *Human Relations*, **9**, 467–480.

Steiner, I. D., & Dodge, Joan S., 1957. A comparison of two techniques employed in the study of interpersonal perception. *Sociometry*, **20**, 1–7.

Steiner, I. D., & Field, W. L., 1960. Role assignment and interpersonal influence. *Journal of Abnormal and Social Psychology*, **61**, 239–245.

Steiner, I. D., & Peters, S. C., 1958. Conformity and the A-B-X Model. *Journal of Personality*, **26**, 229–242.

Steinmann, Anne, 1961. The vocational roles of older married women. *Journal of Social Psychology*, **54**, 93–101.

Steinmann, Anne, 1963. A study of the concept of the feminine role of 51 middle-class American families. *Genetic Psychology Monographs*, **67**, 275–352.

Steinmetz, M. A., 1964. Role playing in a maternity home: Florence Crittenton Maternity Home Detroit. *Children*, **11**, 61–64.

Stevens, S. R., 1953. Social begavning som funktion av rollforvantan. (Social giftedness as a function of role formation.) *Nordisk Psykologi Sver*, **5**, 203–207.

Stewart, D., & Hoult, T., 1959. A social-psychological theory of the authoritarian personality. *American Journal of Sociology*, **65**, 274–279.

Stiles, L. J. (Ed.), 1957. *The Teacher's Role in American Society*. New York: Harper.

Stock, Dorothy, 1949. An investigation into the interrelations between the self concept and feelings directed toward other persons and groups. *Journal of Consulting Psychology*, **13**, 176–180.

Stock, Dorothy, Whitman, R. M., & Liberman, M. A., 1958. The deviant member in therapy groups. *Human Relations*, **11**, 341–372.

Stogdill, R. M., 1959. *Individual Behavior and Group Achievement*. New York: Oxford University Press.

Stone, S. C., & Shertzer, B., 1963. Militant counselor. *The Personnel and Guidance Journal*, **42**, 342–347.

Stoodley, B., 1957. Normative attitude of Filipino youth compared with German and American youth. *American Sociological Review*, **2**, 553–561.

Story, M. L., 1950. Public attitude is changing toward the teacher's personal freedom. *Nation's Schools*, **45**, 69–70.

Stotland, E., Cottrell, N. B., & Laing, G., 1960. Group interaction and perceived similarity of members. *Journal of Abnormal and Social Psychology*, **61**, 335–340.

Stotland, E., & Cottrell, N. B., 1961. Self-esteem, group interaction, and group influence on performance. *Journal of Personality*, **29**, 273–284.

Stotland, E., Thorley, S., Thomas, E., Cohen, A. R., & Zander, A., 1957. The effects of group expectations and self-esteem upon self-evaluation. *Journal of Abnormal and Social Psychology*, **54**, 55–63.

Stouffer, S. A., 1949. An analysis of conflicting social norms. *American Sociological Review*, **14**, 707–717.

Stouffer, S. A., 1962. Role conflict and sanctioning reference groups. In S. A. Stouffer (Ed.), *Social Research to Test Ideas*. New York: The Free Press. Pp. 39–67.

Stouffer, S. A., Suchman, E. A., DeVinney, L. C., Star, Shirley A., & Williams, R. M., Jr., 1949. *The American Soldier: Adjustment during Army Life*. Princeton, N.J.: Princeton University Press.

Stouffer, S. A., & Toby, J., 1951. Role conflict and personality. *American Journal of Sociology*, **56**, 395–406.

Strauss, A. L., 1956. The learning of roles and of concepts as twin processes. *Journal of Genetic Psychology*, **88**, 211–217.

Strauss, A. L., 1959. *Mirrors and Masks*. Glencoe, Ill.: The Free Press.

Strauss, G., Sayles, L. R., & Sayles, Risha, 1953. Leadership roles in labor unions. *Sociology and Social Research*, **38**, 96–102.

Strickland, L. H., Jones, E. E., & Smith, W. P., 1960. Effects of group support on the evaluation of an antagonist. *Journal of Abnormal and Social Psychology*, **61**, 73–81.

Strodtbeck, F. L., 1951. Husband-wife interaction over revealed differences. *American Sociological Review*, **16**, 468–473.

Strodtbeck, F. L., & Mann, R. D., 1956. Sex role differentiation in jury deliberations. *Sociometry*, **19**, 3–11.

Strong, S. M., 1943. Social types in a minority group—formulation of a method. *American Journal of Sociology*, **48**, 563–573.

Stryker, S., 1957. Role-taking accuracy and adjustment. *Sociometry*, **20**, 286–296.

Stuckert, R. P., 1963. Role perception and marital satisfaction—a configurational approach. *Marriage and Family Living*, **25**, 415–419.

Sullivan, H. S., 1939. A note on formulating the relationship of the individual and the group. *American Journal of Sociology*, **44**, 932–937.

Sullivan, H. S., 1940. *Conceptions of Modern Psychiatry*. New York: Norton.

Sullivan, H. S., 1947. Multidisciplined coordination of interpersonal data. In S. Sargent and Marian W. Smith (Eds.), *Interdisciplinary Conference: Culture and Personality*. New York: Viking Fund.

Sumner, W. G., 1960. *Folkways*. Boston: Ginn.

Super, D. E., 1953. A theory of vocational development. *American Psychologist*, **8**, 185–190.

Sutcliffe, J. P., & Haberman, M., 1956. Factors influencing choice in role conflict situations. *American Sociological Review*, **21**, 695–703.

Sutton-Smith, B., Rosenberg, B. G., & Morgan, E. F., Jr., 1963. Development of sex differences in play choices during preadolescence. *Child Development*, **34**, 119–126.

Swanson, G. E., 1953. A preliminary laboratory study of the acting crowd. *American Sociological Review*, **18**, 522–533.

Swanson, G. E., 1961. Determinants of the individual's defenses against inner conflict: review and reformulation. In J. C. Glidewell (Ed.), *Parental Attitudes and Child Behavior*. Springfield, Ill.: Thomas. Pp. 5–41.

Sylvester, J., 1955. Cognitive rigidity and role reversal. *Tydskrif Vir Maatskaplike Navorsing*, **6**, 25–34.

Taft, R., 1953. The shared frame of reference concept applied to the assimilation of immigrants. *Human Relations*, **6**, 45–55.

Taft, R., 1955. The ability to judge people. *Psychological Bulletin*, **52**, 1–23.

Taft, R., 1957. A psychological model for the study of social assimilation. *Human Relations*, **10**, 141–156.

Taft, R., 1961. A psychological assessment of professional actors and related professions. *Genetic Psychology Monographs*, **63**, 313–383.

Tagiuri, R., 1952. Relational analysis: an extension of sociometric method with emphasis upon social perception. *Sociometry*, **15**, 91–104.

Tagiuri, R., & Kogan, N., 1960. Personal preference and the attribution of influence in small groups. *Journal of Personality*, **28**, 257–265.

Tagiuri, R., & Petrullo, L., 1958. *Person Perception and Interpersonal Behavior*. Stanford, Calif.: Stanford University Press.

Talacchi, S., 1960. Organization size, individual attitudes and behavior: an empirical study. *Administrative Science Quarterly*, **5**, 398–420.

Talbot, E., Miller, S. C., & White, R. B., 1961. Some aspects of self-conceptions and role demands in a therapeutic community. *Journal of Abnormal and Social Psychology*, **63**, 338–345.

Talland, G. A., 1954. The assessment of group opinion by leaders, and the influence on its formation. *Journal of Abnormal and Social Psychology*, **49**, 431–434.

Talland, G. A., 1957. Role and status structure in therapy groups. *Journal of Clinical Psychology*, **13**, 27–33.

Tamura, K., 1961. Kazoku keitai to ishiki tsuite no yakuwari no mondai. (Some role problems in light of family pattern and consciousness.) *Kenkyũ Hyoloku* (Tokyo *Gakugei Daigaku*), **12**, 15–26.

Tasch, Ruth J., 1952. The role of the father in the family. *Journal of Experimental Education*, **20**, 319–361.

Tenbruck, F. H., 1961. Der Deutschen Rezeption der Rollentheorie. (The German acceptance of role theory.) *Kölner Zeitschrift für Soziologie und Sozial-Psychologie*, **13**, 1–40.

Terrien, F. W., 1953. Who thinks what about educators? *American Journal of Sociology*, **59**, 150–158.

Terrien, F. W., 1955. The occupational roles of teachers. *Journal of Educational Sociology*, **29**, 14–20.

Tharp, R. G., 1963. Dimensions of marriage roles. *Marriage and Family Living*, **25**, 389–404.

Theodorson, G. A., 1957. The relationship between leadership and popularity roles in small groups. *American Sociological Review*, **22**, 58–67.

Theodorson, G. A., 1962. The function of hostility in small groups. *Journal of Social Psychology*, **56**, 57–66.

Thibaut, J. W., 1950. An experimental study of the cohesiveness of underprivileged groups. *Human Relations*, **3**, 251–278.

Thibaut, J. W., & Kelley, H. H., 1959. *The Social Psychology of Groups*. New York: Wiley.

Thibaut, J. W., & Strickland, L. H., 1956. Psychological set and social conformity. *Journal of Personality*, **25**, 115–129.

Thomas, E. J., 1957. Effects of facilitative role interdependence on group functioning. *Human Relations*, **10**, 347–366.

Thomas, E. J., 1959. Role conceptions and organizational size. *American Sociological Review*, **24**, 30–37.

Thomas, E. J., Polansky, N., & Kounin, J., 1955. The expected behavior of a potentially helpful person. *Human Relations*, **8**, 165–174.

Thomas, W. I., 1926. The problem of personality in the urban environment. In. E. W. Burgess (Ed.), *The Urban Community*. Chicago: University of Chicago Press. Pp. 38–47.

Thomas, W. I., & Znaniecki, F., 1918. *The Polish Peasant in Europe and America*. Boston: Badger.

Thompson, Clara, 1941. The role of women in this culture. *Psychiatry*, **4**, 1–8.

Thompson, J. D., 1963. Organizations and output transactions. *American Journal of Sociology*, **68**, 309–324.

Thompson, V. A., 1961. *Modern Organization: A General Theory*. New York: Knopf.

Thompson, W. E., 1958. Pre-retirement anticipation and adjustment in retirement. *Journal of Social Issues*, **14**, 35–45.

Tiedeman, S. C., 1942. A study of pupil-teacher relationship. *Journal of Educational Research*, **35**, 657–664.

Toby, J., 1952. Some variables in role conflict analysis. *Social Forces*, **30**, 323–327.

Toby, J., 1953. Universalistic and particularistic factors in role assignment. *American Sociological Review*, **18**, 134–141.

Tolman, E. C., 1948. Cognitive maps in rats and men. *Psychological Review*, **55**, 189–208.

Tolman, E. C., 1951. A psychological model. In T. Parsons and E. A. Shils, *Toward a General Theory of Action*. Cambridge, Mass.: Harvard University Press. Pp. 279–361.

Towle, Charlotte, 1962. Role of supervision in the union of cause and function in social work. *Social Service Review*, **36**, 396–406.

Trabue, M. R., 1953. Judgments by 820 college executives of traits desirable in lower-division college teachers. *Journal of Experimental Education*, **21**, 337–341.

Trendley, Mary B., 1944. The concept of role in social work. *American Sociological Review*, **9**, 665–670.

Trendley, Mary B., 1952. An analysis of the dependency role in American culture. *Social Casework*, **33**, 203–208.

Triandis, N. C., 1960. Cognitive similarity and communication in a dyad. *Human Relations*, **13**, 175–183.

Tuddenham, R. D., 1958. The influence of a distorted group norm upon individual judgment. *Journal of Psychology*, **46**, 227–241.

Tuddenham, R. D., 1959. Correlates of yielding to a distorted group norm. *Journal of Personality*, **27**, 272–284.

Tuddenham, R. D., 1961. The influence upon judgment of the apparent discrepancy between self and others. *Journal of Social Psychology*, **53**, 69–79.

Tuddenham, R. D., MacBride, P., & Zahn, V., 1958. The influence of the sex composition of the group upon yielding to a distorted norm. *Journal of Psychology*, **46**, 243–251.

Tupes, E. C., Carp, A., & Borg, W. R., 1958. Performance in role-playing situations as related to leadership and personality measures. *Sociometry*, **21**, 165–179.

Turk, H., 1961. Instrumental values and the popularity of instrumental leaders. *Social Forces*, **39**, 252–260.

Turk, H., 1963. Norms, persons and sentiments. *Sociometry*, **26**, 163–177.

Turk, H., 1963. Social cohesion through variant values: evidence from medical role relations. *American Sociological Review*, **28**, 28–37.

Turk, H., Hartley, E. L., & Shaw, D. M., 1962. The expectation of social influence. *Journal of Social Psychology*, **58**, 23–29.

Turk, H., & Ingles, Thelma, 1963. *Clinic Nursing: Explorations in Role Innovation*. Philadelphia: Davis.

Turk, H., & Lefcowitz, M. J., 1962. Towards a theory of representation between groups. *Social Forces*, **40**, 337–341.

Turner, R. H., 1952. Moral judgment: a study in roles. *American Sociological Review*, **17**, 70–77.

Turner, R. H., 1954. Self and other in moral judgment. *American Sociological Review*, **19**, 249–259.

Turner, R. H., 1956. Role taking, role standpoint, and reference-group behavior. *American Journal of Sociology*, **61**, 316–328.

Turner, R. H., 1962. Role-taking: process versus conformity. In A. M. Rose (Ed.), *Human Behavior and Social Processes*. Boston: Houghton Mifflin. Pp. 20–40.

Twyman, J. P., & Biddle, B. J., 1963. Role conflict of public school teachers. *Journal of Psychology*, **55**, 183–198.

Ulrich, R., 1952. On the role of teacher. *American Teacher*, **36**, 9–14.

UNESCO, 1962. Images of women in society. *International Social Science Journal*, **14**, 7–174.

Uyeki, E. S., 1962. The service teacher in professional education. *Human Organization*, **21**, 51–55.

Valenti, J. J., 1952. Measuring educational leadership attitudes. *Journal of Applied Psychology*, **36**, 36–43.

Veldman, D. J., Peck, R. F., & McGuire, C., 1961. Measuring the value systems of education professors. *Journal of Educational Psychology*, **52**, 330–334.

Verroort, C., 1959. Positie en rol van de student in de universitaire samenleving. (Position and role of the student in university society.) *Sociologische Gids*, **6**, 242–258.

Vetter, H., 1961. Zur Lage der Frau an den Westdeutschen Hochschulen. (The position of women at the West German universities.) *Köln Zeitschrift für Soziologie und Sozial Psychologie*, **13**, 644–660.

Vetter, L., & Lewis, E. C., 1964. Some correlates of homemaking versus career preference among college home economics students. *Personnel and Guidance Journal*, **42**, 593–598.

Victoroff, D., 1951. Le concept de "rôle" et la notion d'inconscient. (The concept of role and the notion of the unconscious.) *Psyche*, **6**, 630–639.

Videbeck, R., 1958. Dynamic properties of the concept role. *Midwest Sociologist*, **20**, 104–108.

Videbeck, R., 1960. Self-conception and the reactions of others. *Sociometry*, **23**, 351–359.

Videbeck, R., 1964. Norm and status in sociological theory. *Sociological Quarterly*, **5**, 221–230.

Videbeck, R., & Bates, A. P., 1959. An experimental study of conformity to role expectations. *Sociometry*, **22**, 1–11.

Viet, J., 1960. La notion de rôle en politique. (The notion of role in politics.) *Revue Française de Science Politique*, **10**, 309–334.

Vilakazi, A., 1962. Changing concepts of the self and the supernatural in Africa. *Annals of the New York Academy of Science*, **96**, 670–675.

Vinacke, W. E., 1959. Sex roles in a three-person game. *Sociometry*, **22**, 343–360.

Vogel, E., 1961. The go-between in a developing society: the case of the Japanese marriage arranger. *Human Organization*, **20**, 112–120.

Von Wiese, L., 1924. *System der Allgemeinen Soziologie*. (Systematic Sociology.) Munich: Von Drucker und Humbolt. (Also adapted by H. P. Becker, Glencoe, Ill.: The Free Press, 1932.)

de Vos, G., & Wagatsuma, H., 1961. Value attitudes toward role behavior of women in two Japanese villages. *American Anthropologist*, **63**, 1204–1232.

Vroom, V. H., 1960. The effects of attitudes on perception of organizational goals. *Human Relations*, **13**, 229–240.

Wahlke, J. C., Buchanan, W., Eulau, H., & Ferguson, L. C., 1960. American state legislators' role orientations toward pressure groups. *Journal of Politics*, **22**, 203–227.

Wahlke, J. C., Eulau, H., Buchanan, W., & Ferguson, L. C., 1962. *The Legislative System: Explorations in Legislative Behavior*. New York: Wiley.

Walker, E. L., & Heyns, R. W., 1962. *An Anatomy for Conformity*. Englewood Cliffs, N.J.: Prentice-Hall.

Wallace, S., 1951. Problems experienced by 136 new teachers during their induction into service. *The North Central Association Quarterly*, **25**, 291–309.

Wallin, P., 1950. Cultural contradictions and sex roles: a repeat study. *American Sociological Review*, **15**, 288–293.

Walters, J., & Ojemann, R. H., 1952. A study of the components of adolescent attitudes concerning the role of women. *Journal of Social Psychology*, **35**, 101–110.

Ward, D. S., 1958. Conflict between personal and social values: significance for public education. *Educational Research Bulletin*, **37**, 125–131.

Wardwell, W. I., 1952. A marginal professional role: the chiropractor. *Social Forces*, **30**, 339–348.

Wardwell, W. I., 1955. The reduction of strain in a marginal social role. *American Journal of Sociology*, **61**, 16–25.

Wardwell, W. I., 1955. Social integration, bureaucratization, and the professions. *Social Forces*, **33**, 356–359.

Wardwell, W. I., & Wood, A. L., 1956. The extra-professional role of the lawyer. *American Journal of Sociology*, **61**, 304–307.

Warman, R. E., 1960. Differential perceptions of counseling role. *Journal of Counseling Psychology*, **7**, 269–274.

Warren, R. L., 1949. Cultural, personal, and situational roles. *Sociology and Social Research*, **34**, 104–111. (a)

Warren, R. L., 1949. Social disorganization and the interrelationship of cultural roles. *American Sociological Review*, **14**, 83–87. (b)

Washburne, C., 1957. The teacher in the authority system. *Journal of Educational Sociology*, **30**, 390–394.

Waters, R. H., 1947. An experimental test of the dynamic character of expectancy. *American Psychologist*, **2**, 307–308.

Webb, A. B., 1963. Sex-role preferences and adjustment in early adolescents. *Child Development*, **34**, 609–618.

Weil, M., 1962. The career-homemaker role: new orientation for analysis. *Journal of Home Economics*, **54**, 294–296.

Weinberg, S. K., & Arond, H., 1952. The occupational culture of the boxer. *American Journal of Sociology*, **57**, 460–469.

Weinstock, S. A., 1963. Role elements: a link between acculturation and occupational status. *British Journal of Sociology*, **14**, 144–149.

Weisman, Clare, 1963. Social structure as a determinant of the group worker's role. *Social Work*, **8**, 87–94.

Weiss, R. F., 1961. Aspirations and expectations: a dimensional analysis. *Journal of Social Psychology*, **53**, 249–254.

Weiss, R. S., 1956. *Processes of Organization*. Ann Arbor: University of Michigan, Institute for Social Research, Survey Research Center.

Weiss, Viola, & Monroe, R. H., 1959. A framework for understanding family dynamics. *Social Casework*, **40**, 3–9 and 80–87.

Werble, B., 1959. Implications of role theory for casework research. In L. S. Kogan (Ed.), *Social Science Theory and Social Work Research*. New York: National Association of Social Workers. Pp. 28–31.

Wertheimer, Rita R., 1957. Consistency of sociometric status position in male and female high school students. *Journal of Educational Psychology*, **48**, 385–390.

Wheeler, D. K., 1957. Notes on "role differentiation in small decision making groups." *Sociometry* **20**, 145–151.

Wheeler, S., 1961. Socialization in correctional communities. *American Sociological Review*, **26**, 697–712.

Whitlow, C. M., 1935. Attitudes and behavior of high-school students. *American Journal of Sociology*, **40**, 489–494.

Wiener, M., 1958. Certainty of judgment as a variable in conformity behavior. *Journal of Social Psychology*, **48**, 257–263.

Wiener, M., 1959. Some correlates of conformity responses. *Journal of Social Psychology*, **49**, 215–221.

Wiener, M., Carpenter, Janeth T., & Carpenter, B., 1957. Some determinants of conformity behavior. *Journal of Social Psychology*, **45**, 289–297.

Wilensky, H. L., 1956. *Intellectuals in Labor Unions: Organizational Pressures on Professional Roles*. Glencoe, Ill.: The Free Press.

Wilkening, E. A., 1958. Consensus in role definition of county extension agents between the agents and local sponsoring committee members. *Rural Sociology*, **23**, 184–197.

Wilkening, E. A., & Smith, R., 1958. Perception of functions, organizational orientation, and role definition of a group of special extension agents. *Midwest Sociologist*, **21**, 19–28.

Williams, J. J., 1950. The woman physician's dilemma. *Journal of Social Issues*, **6**, 38–44.

Williston, G. C., 1963. Foster-parent role. *Journal of Social Psychology*, **60**, 263–272.

Willower, D. J., 1960. Leadership styles and leaders' perceptions of subordinates. *Journal of Educational Sociology*, **34**, 58–64.

Wilson, A. T. M., Trist, E. L., & Curle, A., 1952. Transitional communities and social reconnection: a study of the civil resettlement of British prisoners of war. In G. E. Swanson, T. M. Newcomb, & E. L. Hartley (Eds.), *Readings in Social Psychology* (Rev. ed.). New York: Holt. Pp. 561–579.

Wilson, B. R., 1959. The pentecostalist minister: role conflicts and status contradictions. *American Journal of Sociology*, **64**, 494–504.

Wilson, B. R., 1962. The teacher's role—a sociological analysis. *British Journal of Sociology*, **13**, 15–32.

Wilson, R. N., 1963. Continuities in the poet's role. In A. W. Gouldner and Helen Gouldner (Eds.), *Modern Sociology*. New York: Harcourt, Brace. Pp. 196–200.

Wilson, R. S., 1960. Personality patterns, source attractiveness, and conformity. *Journal of Personality*, **28**, 186–199.

Winslow, C. N., 1937. A study of the extent of agreement between friends' opinions and their ability to estimate the opinions of each other. *Journal of Social Psychology*, **8**, 433–442.

Wispé, L. G., 1955. A sociometric analysis of conflicting role-expectancies. *American Journal of Sociology*, **61**, 134–137.

Wispé, L. G., 1957. The success attitude: an analysis of the relationship between individual needs and social role expectancies. *Journal of Social Psychology*, **46**, 119–123.

Wispé, L. G., & Lloyd, K. E., 1955. Some situational and psychological determinants of desire for structured interpersonal relations. *Journal of Abnormal and Social Psychology*, **51**, 57–60.

Wispé, L. G., & Thayer, P. W., 1957. Role ambiguity and anxiety in an occupational group. *Journal of Social Psychology*, **46**, 41–48.

Witryol, S. L., 1950. Age trends in children's evaluation of teacher-approved and teacher-disapproved behavior. *Genetic Psychology Monographs*, **41**, 271–326.

Wittermans, T., & Kraus, I., 1964. Structural marginality and social worth. *Sociology and Social Research*, **48**, 348–360.

Wolf, R., 1963. Role of conceptual systems in cognitive functioning at varying levels of age and intelligence. *Journal of Personality*, **31**, 108–123.

Wolfe, D. M., & Snoek, J. D., 1962. A study of tensions and adjustment under role conflict. *Journal of Social Issues*, **18**, 102–121.

Wolfe, S., 1963. Talking with doctors in Urbanville: an exploratory study of Canadian general practitioners. *American Journal of Public Health*, **53**, 631–644.

Wood, J. H., 1963. Expectations, errors, and the team structure of interest rates. *Journal of Politics and Economics*, **71**, 160–171.

Worby, M., 1955. The adolescent's expectations of how the potentially helpful person will act. *Smith College Studies in Social Work*, **26**, 19–59.

Worell, L., 1956. The effect of goal value upon expectancy. *Journal of Abnormal and Social Psychology*, **53**, 48–53.

Wray, D. E., 1949. Marginal men of industry: the foreman. *American Journal of Sociology*, **54**, 258–301.

Wright, Beatrice A., 1960. *Physical Disability*. New York: Harper.

Wrong, D. H., 1961. The oversocialized conception of man in modern sociology. *American Sociological Review*, **26**, 183–193.

Yablonsky, L., 1953. An operational theory of role. *Sociometry*, **16**, 349–354.

Yarrow, Marian R., Campbell, J. D., & Yarrow, L. J., 1958. Acquisition of new norms: a study of racial desegregation. *Journal of Social Issues*, **14**, 8–28.

Young, F. W., 1962. The function of male initiation ceremonies: a cross-cultural test of an alternative hypothesis. *American Journal of Sociology*, **67**, 379–391.

Young, F. W., & Young, R. C., 1962. Occupational role perceptions in rural Mexico. *Rural Sociology*, **27**, 42–52.

Yourglich, Anita, 1955. Study on correlations between college teachers' and students' concepts of "ideal-student" and "ideal-teacher." *Journal of Educational Research*, **49**, 59–64.

Zajonc, R. B., 1952. Aggressive attitudes of the "stranger" as a function of conformity pressures. *Human Relations*, **5**, 205–216.

Zajonc, R. B., 1960. The process of cognitive tuning in communication. *Journal of Abnormal and Social Psychology*, **61**, 159–167.

Zajonc, R. B., & Burnstein, E., 1961. The resolution of cognitive conflict under uncertainty. *Human Relations*, **14**, 113–119.

Zajonc, R. B., & Wahi, N. K., 1961. Conformity and need-achievement under cross-cultural norm conflict. *Human Relations*, **14**, 241–250.

Zaleznik, A., Christensen, C. R., & Roethlisberger, F. J., 1958. *Motivation, Productivity, and Satisfaction of Workers: A Prediction Study*. Boston: Division of Research, Harvard University Graduate School of Business Administration.

Zaleznik, A., & Moment, D., 1964. *The Dynamics of Interpersonal Behavior*. New York: Wiley.

Zander, A., & Cohen, A. R., 1955. Attributed social power of group acceptance: a classroom experimental demonstration. *Journal of Abnormal and Social Psychology*, **51**, 490–492.

Zander, A., Cohen, A. R., & Stotland, E., 1957. *Role Relations in the Mental Health Professions*. Ann Arbor: University of Michigan, Institute for Social Research.

Zelditch, M., Jr., 1955. Role differentiation in the nuclear family: a comparative study. In T. Parsons & R. F. Bales (Eds.), *Family, Socialization and Interaction Process*. Glencoe, Ill.: The Free Press. Pp. 307-352.

Zeleny, L. D., 1951. Status and role among fifth-grade school children. *Sociology and Social Research*, **35**, 425–427.

Zetterberg, H. L., 1957. Compliant actions. *Acta Sociologica*, **2**, 179–210.

Zimmerman, K. A., & Lewton, Elizabeth, 1951. Teacher personality in school relationships. *Educational Leadership*, **8**, 422–428.

Zipf, Sheila G., 1960. Resistance and conformity under reward and punishment. *Journal of Abnormal and Social Psychology*, **61**, 102–109.

Znaniecki, F., 1939. Small groups as products of participating individuals. *American Journal of Sociology*, **44**, 799–811.

Znaniecki, F., 1940. *The Social Role of the Man of Knowledge*. New York: Columbia University Press.

Index of Names

Subject Index